Working With Lotus ® 1-2-3 ®

Release 2.2

Working With Lotus® 1-2-3®

A Comprehensive Manual
Release 2.2

Hossein Bidgoli
California State University, Bakersfield

West Publishing Company
St. Paul   New York   Los Angeles San Francisco

Copy Editor: Sheryl Rose
Composition: green apple graphics
Cover Image: David Bishop

Library of Congress Cataloging-in-Publication Data

Bidgoli, Hossein
        Working with Lotus 1-2-3 a comprehensive manual release 2.2/ Hossein Bidgoli
                p.   cm.
        Includes bibliographical references and index.
        ISBN 0-314-77274-X
1. Lotus 1-2-3 (Computer Program)   2. Business- - Computer programs.
I. Title.
HF5548.4.L678533   1991
650' .0285'5369 - - dc20   90-21172
                                                                CIP
                                                                ∞

To so many fine memories of my brother Mohsen
For his uncompromising belief in the power of education

Contents in Brief

Table of Contents

Preface

There are several books about Lotus on the market. Some of the texts are brief and do not cover the entire Lotus package. Some are detailed and teach Lotus commands but do not tell the reader what to do with them. This book, using Release 2.2, tries to cover the entire Lotus package in an easy-to-understand, step-by-step manner. For Releases 1A, 2, and 2.01 users, we have provided comprehensive coverage in Appendices E and F to highlight the differences between Releases 1A, 2.0/2.01, and 2.2. We also provide the highlights of Releases 3.0 and 3.1 in Appendix G.

All programs and screens shown throughout the book are available from the publisher on four diskettes. Readers of the book can access all programs, assisting both students and computer sophisticates to understand the material presented. Time and frustration can be saved by not having to type these programs from scratch.

Although the text follows a logical sequence, the chapters have been written independently. This means that a reader with no previous background can understand any part of the text with minimum difficulty.

Lengthy topics, such as functions, database operations, and macros, have been divided into logical parts. We present the most important parts first and the least important last. This should make for easy reading and provide not only a textbook, but also an invaluable reference.

In each chapter we present examples highlighting some real-life situations. This should put Lotus into perspective and emphasize the specific command or series of commands being discussed.

Each chapter ends with 15-25 review questions and 5-10 hands-on practice assignments. Review questions reinforce the material covered in the chapter. In order to answer the hands-on practice questions, students must get Lotus started and use the actual package. We provide the answers to selected questions in Appendix I. Readers can use these questions as a self-test on a particular topic.

Appendix A provides brief microcomputer coverage for first-time users, to enhance their understanding of Lotus material.

Appendix B provides basic DOS information. This should benefit inexperienced as well as experienced users.

We discuss technical matters regarding Lotus operations in Appendix C. This presentation should clear up confusion for the first-time user about Lotus installation and utilization.

In Appendix D, we provide guidelines for file transfer to and from Lotus, easing some of the frustration for users who are trying to import or export data.

The text teaches use of commands by example. The command is thus clear to the reader in context, rather than in an abstract discussion. Limitations and strengths of these commands are also discussed.

Comprehensive coverage of database operations, graphics, and Lotus macro commands is extremely important for advanced Lotus users. The text provides excellent coverage of these topics, using many real-life examples.

We have devoted two chapters to the Allways add-in program for generating presentation-quality spreadsheets. This coverage should assist you in generating spreadsheets for business purposes.

Every example and worksheet in the text is fully documented. By looking at the worksheet, the reader should be able to understand the concept underlying a particular command or series of commands.

At the end of several chapters, when appropriate, we have added a list of misconceptions and solutions. In some cases they may not be misconceptions but improper operating procedures or outright mistakes in operation. In any case, these lists should guide readers and provide some tips for avoiding some of the common mistakes and, at the same time, show how to resolve some of these problems.

At the end of the text, we provide a comprehensive command reference list. This should help the reader review the entire Lotus and Allways command structures in a few minutes, aiding a better understanding of Lotus and Allways commands. It is also a refresher when the reader isn't sure about the function of a command.

Versions of this material have been tested by groups including college students (freshmen to graduates), bankers, financial officers, and chief executive officers for profit and nonprofit organizations. Classroom testing provided us with excellent feedback about the suitability of the material for different levels.

Note to Users:

This book has been written for a variety of audiences with different computer backgrounds. We suggest the following guidelines:

1. If this is your first exposure to microcomputers, go directly to Appendix A. Material in this appendix describes the world of microcomputers for you in a nontechnical fashion.
2. If you don't know anything about the disk operating system (DOS), study Appendix A and read Appendix B. The first group of DOS commands in Table B-1 has been organized for the novice. The second group of DOS commands has been selected for advanced DOS users.
3. If you just purchased your Lotus program and are trying to get it started, refer to Appendix C. This material should help you install Lotus on your system.
4. If you are interested in transferring files between Lotus and other programs, such as dBASE and VisiCalc, read Appendix D.
5. To reinforce your understanding of materials presented in the book, we provide answers to selected chapter review questions in Appendix I.
6. First-time Lotus users should read Chapters 1-10 and the beginning of Chapters 11-14, and 21.
7. Advanced Lotus users, after a quick review of Chapters 1-11, should spend more time on Chapters 14 and 16-20. Chapter 21 provides numerous real-life examples of Lotus applications. Advanced Lotus users can develop these applications.
8. Students interested only in Lotus macros should study Chapters 18-21.
9. Students interested in Lotus database capabilities should study Chapters 16-17.
10. For graphics users, Chapter 14 provides a comprehensive coverage of Lotus graphics.
11. For learning spreadsheet publishing, read Chapters 10-11.

We hope you decide to read the entire book. You will see the real power of Lotus when you put all the pieces together.

Acknowledgments

Several colleagues reviewed different versions of this manuscript and made constructive suggestions. Their help and comments are greatly appreciated. The following colleagues reviewed the Release 2.01 Version of the text:

Alfred J. Bird – University of Houston
Donnie Byers – Johnson County Community College
Mike Crews – University of Texas - Pan American
Diane Drozd – College of DuPage
Patricia A. Green – Temple Junior College
Michael P. Harris – Del Mar College
Robert McGlinn – Southern Illinois University
Elizabeth A. Murphy – DePaul University
Beverly Oswalt – University of Central Arkansas
Roy Pipitone – Erie Community College
James E. Stacey – Ithaca College
Robert C. Taylor – Berkshire Community College
Mark Wayne – Chabot College
Louis Wolff – Moorpark College
C. W. Zebrowski – Texas Southmost College

The following colleagues reviewed the Release 2.2 Version of the text:

Mike Crews – University of Texas - Pan American
Jan Coleman – Indiana State University
Joseph C. Otto – California State University Los Angeles
Jan de Lassen – Brigham Young University
Frank A. Lucente – Westmoreland Community College
Roy R. Pipitone – Erie Community College
Barbara T. Grabowski – DePaul University
Beverly Oswalt – University of Central Arkansas

Many different groups assisted me in completing this project. I am grateful to the students who attended my executive seminars and Lotus and MIS classes. They helped me fine-tune the manuscript during its various stages. I would like to thank Andrew Prestage and Kathleen Whelan for assisting me in checking and printing the screens presented in the text.

The help of the women in the reprographics center at California State University, Bakersfield, who typed and prepared the manuscript, is very much appreciated. Jacki Lawson, a true problem-solver, deserves special recognition; her thoroughness and dedication made it easier to complete this project. Denise Simon, Theresa O'Dell, Janine Wilson, Mario Rodriguez, Steve Schonebaum, and Sean Berres, all of West Educational Publishing, were supportive and constructive in their suggestions concerning this project. I am particularly grateful to Denise Simon, my executive editor, for her constructive suggestions and her timely review process. It has always been a joy working with Denise. Last but not least, I want to thank my family for their support and encouragement throughout my education. My two sisters, Azam and Akram, deserve my very special thanks.

About the Author

Dr. Hossein Bidgoli is professor of Management Information Systems at California State University, Bakersfield. He holds a Ph.D. degree in systems science from Portland State University, with a specialization in design and implementation of MIS. His master's degree is in MIS from Colorado State University. Dr. Bidgoli's background includes experience as a systems analyst, an EDP consultant, and a financial analyst. He has been director of the Microcomputer Center at Portland State University and has done computer-related consulting for numerous organizations including Tektronix, Inc. in Oregon.

Dr. Bidgoli, a two-time winner of the MPPP (Meritorious Performance and Professional Promise) award for outstanding performance in teaching, research and university/community service, is the author of fifteen texts and numerous professional papers and articles, presented and published throughout the United States, on the topics of computers and MIS. Dr. Bidgoli has also designed and implemented over twenty executive seminars on all aspects of information systems and decision support systems. These seminars have been well received by several thousands of participants both in Oregon and California.

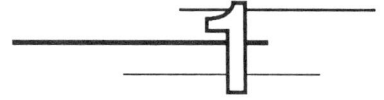

Lotus 1-2-3 at a Glance

1-1 Introduction

This chapter provides you with an overview of Lotus 1-2-3, beginning with a brief history of earlier spreadsheets in order to appreciate what this powerful package can do. We will explain the technical requirements of Lotus and give a brief description of the entire Lotus package. Then we will discuss Lotus as a decision support system tool in detail. This discussion will be reinforced throughout the book. At the end of this chapter, we provide a brief summary of the entire book to give you an idea of what to expect.

1-2 What is a Spreadsheet?

A *spreadsheet* is simply a table or a matrix of rows and columns, very similar to an accounting journal. The intersection of each row and column is called a cell. A *cell* can hold any type of data, including numbers, formulas, texts, and so forth. The major difference between an electronic spreadsheet and an accounting journal is the enhanced flexibility, speed, and accuracy provided by an electronic spreadsheet.

Theoretically, the number of applications that can be handled by an electronic spreadsheet is unlimited. In general terms, any application that can fit into a row and column setting can be handled by a spreadsheet program. This includes such applications as balance sheets, income statements, budgeting analyses, mailing lists, databases, and sales analyses.

The size and sophistication of a spreadsheet depends on the type of program. Some are dedicated spreadsheets such as VisiCalc (they only perform spreadsheet analysis, no graphics or database), while others are integrated packages such as Lotus and Framework that perform many more applications than just spreadsheet analysis. We will discuss these applications in the next section.

1-3 Spreadsheets Prior to Lotus

The spreadsheet era began in 1978 when Robert Frankston, Dan Bricklin, and Dan Fylstra designed and marketed VisiCalc, the most popular microcomputer software prior to Lotus.

VisiCalc was very impressive for its time. The package, designed to perform spreadsheet analysis, included a matrix of 254 rows and 63 columns, many commands, and several built-in functions such as formulas for performing different tasks. However, it had some serious shortcomings. Earlier VisiCalc did not have Boolean operations such as OR, AND, NOT, and IF. These operations are needed in order to use the spreadsheet for decision-making purposes. It could not communicate directly with other software. Furthermore, it performed very limited graphics and database operations.

Some of these limitations were improved in later versions of VisiCalc. Several Boolean operations were introduced. A DIF (Data Interchange Format) utility program developed by Software Arts translated VisiCalc spreadsheets to other programs for graphics, databases, and word processing applications. VisiTrend/VisiPlot and VisiFile could communicate with VisiCalc through the DIF utility. Yet there was still a need for a more sophisticated spreadsheet program.

SuperCalc (by Sorcim Corporation), a CP/M-based program introduced in 1980, was an improvement on VisiCalc. This package also included 254 rows and 63 columns.

Later releases of VisiCalc, ProCalc, and SuperCalc tried to eliminate the shortcomings of the earlier VisiCalc. Integrated packages were introduced that could perform spreadsheet analysis, data management, graphics, word processing, and communication operations. These new packages included Multiplan (by Microsoft Corporation), Context MBA (by Context Management Systems), Framework (by Ashton-Tate), and Lotus 1-2-3 (by Lotus Development Corporation). Some experts believe Lotus is not a true integrated package because it does not have word processing and communication capabilities. This is by no means a serious problem because Lotus files can communicate with several popular word processing programs, as well as with some communication packages.

1-4 Lotus: The Ultimate Spreadsheet

Lotus 1-2-3 Release 1 was introduced in 1982. Within six months it was upgraded to Release 1A and in mid-1985, Release 2 appeared on the market. In 1989, Releases 2.2 and 3.0 were introduced. Release 3.1 was announced in 1990. In this book we cover Release 2.2. At the end of the book we will highlight the differences between all 1-2-3 releases. Lotus Development Corporation has been continuously improving this product. After VisiCalc, Lotus has been one of the best sellers of all time.

Lotus includes three functions in one. Besides spreadsheet analysis, it is able to perform graphics and data management operations.

Lotus Release 2.2 features a spreadsheet of 8,192 rows and 256 columns, which equals 2,097,152 cells. This is the equivalent of approximately 45 feet wide by 200 feet deep. To utilize this capacity, a huge main memory is needed. At the present time there is no microcomputer that can use this spreadsheet without upgrading its memory.

By using a series of commands and built-in functions, Lotus can perform some very impressive operations. Its data management functions are quite effective. Since the database generated by Lotus resides in RAM, the speed of manipulation is impressive (see Chapters 16 and 17).

The Lotus graphics function is also relatively sophisticated. Using spreadsheet data, Lotus can generate bar, pie, stacked-bar, line, and XY graphs. Again, since the data for graphics is provided by the spreadsheet component of Lotus, the speed of calculation and redrawing is very high. As you will see in Chapter 14, doing "What-if" analysis with Lotus graphics is fast and simple.

Release 2.2 added many new functions. By itself, Lotus can serve as a forecasting package (see the discussion of data regression in Chapter 17). Throughout this book you will see these impressive features in action.

1-5 Lotus Technical Requirements

Lotus is written in assembly language (see Appendix A), the closest language to machine language. This has improved the speed of calculation in Lotus as compared to earlier spreadsheet programs. Lotus is available for PC or PC-compatible computers such as the IBM PC, NEC Advanced PC, Wang Professional, AT&T 6300, Zenith Data System, Texas Instruments Professional Computer, etc.

Two 360K double-sided disk drives are needed or a floppy drive and a hard disk. Your computer must also have a minimum of 320K of RAM. With the add-in Allways program you need 512K. A color or monochrome display with Hercules graphics or another graphics adapter is also needed if you want to use the graphics capability. The operating system needed by Lotus is either PC or MS-DOS, version 2 and above (see Appendix B).

1-6 Lotus: The Entire Package

The Lotus package includes the following:

5 1/4" Disks	**3 1/2" Disks**
System disk	System, Help and PrintGraph disk
Help disk	Translate and Sample Files disk
PrintGraph disk	Install and Install Library disk
Translate disk	
Install disk	
Install Library disk	
Sample Files disk	

Release 2.2 also includes the Allways disks in the package.

You will use the System disk most of the time because all Lotus operations except graphics printing are on this disk.

The Help disk includes over 200 on-line help screens of Lotus operations.

The PrintGraph disk allows you to transfer the graphs generated on your monitor to your printer or plotter.

The Install and Install Library disks will help you to tailor Lotus programs to your particular computer system (see Appendix C for more information).

The Translate disk includes a series of programs for file transfer between different software (see Appendix D). The Sample Files disk includes a series of sample programs that you can access.

1-7 Lotus Access System

When your entire package is installed (see Appendix C), you can access any part of Lotus 1-2-3 through the Lotus Access System. All Lotus operations are stored on the System disk except instructions for printing graphics, which is done by the PrintGraph disk. To start the Lotus Access System, put the DOS disk in drive A. At the A> prompt, pull DOS out and put the Lotus System disk in drive A. Type LOTUS and press **Return**. If Lotus is installed on a hard disk, use the DOS CD command to change the directory to the directory that contains 1-2-3, then type LOTUS. Your screen will display the material in Figure 1-1.

FIGURE 1-1 Lotus Access System

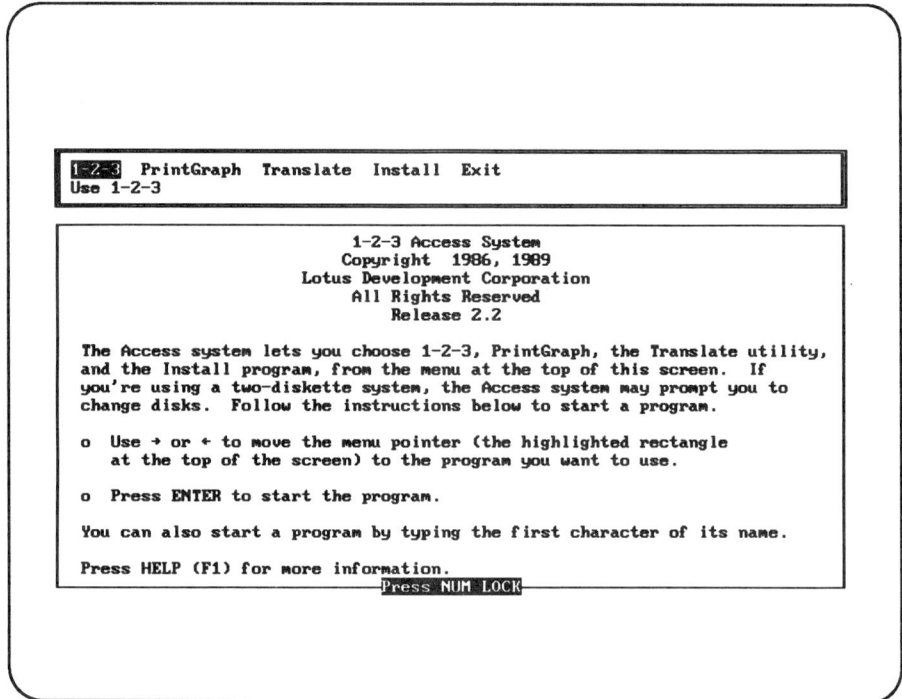

```
┌─────────────────────────────────────────────────────────────┐
│  ┌──────────────────────────────────────────────────────┐   │
│  │ ▋1-2-3▋  PrintGraph  Translate  Install  Exit         │   │
│  │ Use 1-2-3                                              │   │
│  └──────────────────────────────────────────────────────┘   │
│  ┌──────────────────────────────────────────────────────┐   │
│  │              1-2-3 Access System                      │   │
│  │              Copyright  1986, 1989                    │   │
│  │           Lotus Development Corporation               │   │
│  │                All Rights Reserved                    │   │
│  │                  Release 2.2                          │   │
│  │                                                       │   │
│  │  The Access system lets you choose 1-2-3, PrintGraph, │   │
│  │  the Translate utility, and the Install program,      │   │
│  │  from the menu at the top of this screen.  If         │   │
│  │  you're using a two-diskette system, the Access       │   │
│  │  system may prompt you to change disks.  Follow the   │   │
│  │  instructions below to start a program.               │   │
│  │                                                       │   │
│  │  o  Use → or ← to move the menu pointer (the          │   │
│  │     highlighted rectangle at the top of the screen)   │   │
│  │     to the program you want to use.                   │   │
│  │                                                       │   │
│  │  o  Press ENTER to start the program.                 │   │
│  │                                                       │   │
│  │  You can also start a program by typing the first     │   │
│  │  character of its name.                               │   │
│  │                                                       │   │
│  │  Press HELP (F1) for more information.                │   │
│  │                        ▋Press NUM LOCK▋               │   │
│  └──────────────────────────────────────────────────────┘   │
│                                                               │
└─────────────────────────────────────────────────────────────┘
```

You can choose any of the options shown in the figure either by moving the cursor to one of the options and pressing the **Return** key or by typing the first letter of the option name. The last option, Exit, takes you out of the Lotus Access System and puts you back at the DOS A> prompt or to your starting menu on the hard disk.

To get into the main section of Lotus, first put the System disk in drive A. Then you can either go through the Lotus Access System or type 123 at the A> prompt.

When you are in Lotus, you can always access the on-line Help index by pressing the F1 key. The Help index will appear. You have access to more than 200 screens of the Help menu. Figure 1-2 shows an example of the Help index menu.

Point the cursor to any of these options and press the **Return** key. The section on Error Messages, for example, tells you how and when an error might occur and how to resolve the error. To leave the Help menu, just press the **Escape** (ESC) key.

To return to the Lotus Access System, invoke the main menu by pressing the question mark key (the slash key on the IBM keyboard or its equivalent on other keyboards) and then choose the Quit option. This option give you two choices, NO and YES. If you choose YES, you will return to the Lotus Access System.

To access PrintGraph, Translate, or Install, point the cursor to the name of the program and press the **Return** key. The prompt will tell you to insert the proper disk and press the **Return** key.

If you do not want to access 1-2-3 and its companion programs from the Lotus Access System, you can access any of them directly from DOS. To do so, at the A> prompt do the following:

• To access 1-2-3, type 123, assuming the 1-2-3 System disk is in drive A.
• To access PrintGraph, type PGRAPH, assuming the PrintGraph disk is in drive A.

FIGURE 1-2 The Help Index Menu

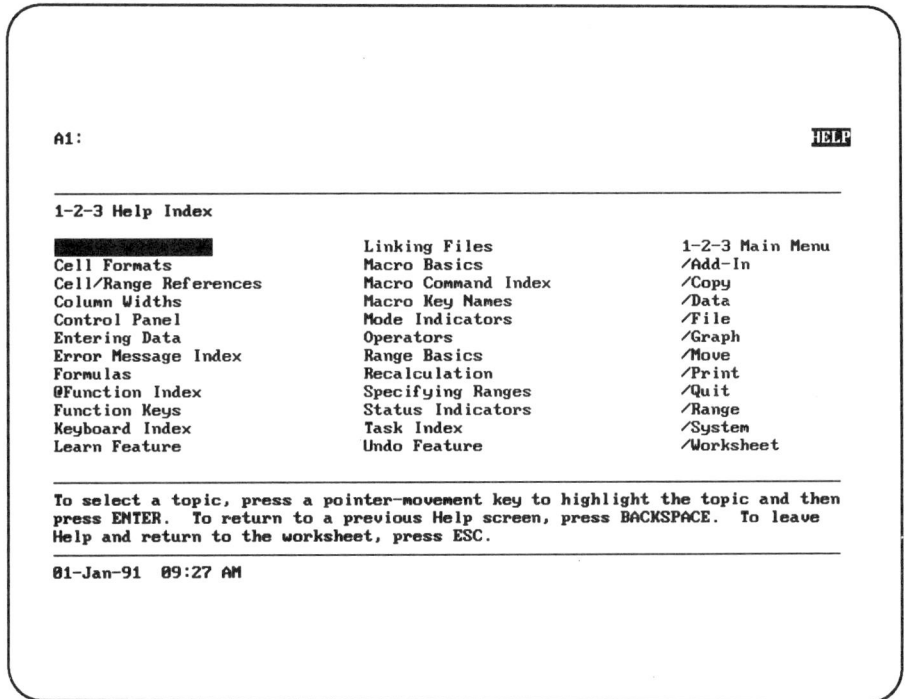

```
A1:                                                                           HELP


  1-2-3 Help Index

  ████████████████          Linking Files              1-2-3 Main Menu
  Cell Formats              Macro Basics               /Add-In
  Cell/Range References     Macro Command Index        /Copy
  Column Widths             Macro Key Names            /Data
  Control Panel             Mode Indicators            /File
  Entering Data             Operators                  /Graph
  Error Message Index       Range Basics               /Move
  Formulas                  Recalculation              /Print
  @Function Index           Specifying Ranges          /Quit
  Function Keys             Status Indicators          /Range
  Keyboard Index            Task Index                 /System
  Learn Feature             Undo Feature               /Worksheet


  To select a topic, press a pointer-movement key to highlight the topic and then
  press ENTER.  To return to a previous Help screen, press BACKSPACE.  To leave
  Help and return to the worksheet, press ESC.

  01-Jan-91  09:27 AM
```

- To access Translate, type TRANS, assuming the Utility disk is in drive A.
- To access Install, type INSTALL, assuming the Utility disk is in drive A.
- To access Access, type LOTUS, assuming the 1-2-3 System disk is in drive A.

1-8 What Can Lotus Do for You?

The number of applications handled by Lotus is practically unlimited. Lotus can be used in any discipline, although its major applications have been in the areas of finance and accounting. In the next sections we will provide you with an overview of some of the more common Lotus applications. Chapter 21 presents specific applications in the areas of finance, accounting, production, forecasting, and so on.

1-9 Lotus as a Decision Support System (DSS) Tool

In the past few years, Lotus has been utilized and evaluated as a *Decision Support System (DSS) tool*. A DSS tool or product is any package that can help a decision maker in making a decision, or making a better decision. It must be able to perform "What-if" analysis, goal-seeking operations, sensitivity analysis, and modeling analysis. As you will see throughout this book, Lotus can perform any of these functions. Some of these capabilities are readily available in the Lotus command structure. Others can be done by developing a series of macros (see Chapters 18 – 21). Let us explain these major functions.

1-10 Using Lotus for What-If Analysis

What-if analysis calculates the effects of a change in one variable over other variables or the entire worksheet. A simple example is a break-even analysis. The break-even point (see Chapter 20) is the number of units generated in which total cost is equal to total revenue. For example, if the fixed cost of an operation is $500, the variable cost of a unit is $10, and the selling price is $15, the break-even point would be 100 units. At this point the company will neither lose nor gain. Above this point, the company will gain; below this point, the company will lose. Lotus can help you discover what will happen to the break-even point if the selling price is increased to $17; or what will happen to the break-even point if the variable costs are decreased by $3.

This feature can be used in a much more complex environment. Think about a budgeting problem. Let us say you have projected the budget of your company for the next five years. Suddenly you notice that the projected income for 1994 will be reduced by 5 percent. What is the impact of this income reduction on the entire budget? Thousands of accurate calculations must be done in order to answer this question. But if the budget is on a Lotus spreadsheet, this amazing program can perform all the recalculations almost instantly with no errors! Just change the old value to the new value and press **Return**.

What-if analysis can be done with graphics as well. Change any data item and press the F10 (Graph) key in READY mode and your graph will be redrawn instantly (see Chapter 14).

As you will see in Chapter 17, Lotus provides you with table-handling procedures; that in itself is a good application of What-if analysis. You can monitor the impact of one or two variables on the entire worksheet, or on a specific range.

1-11 Using Lotus for Goal-Seeking Analysis

Goal-seeking analysis is the reverse of What-if analysis. Here you may ask a question such as, "In order to generate $5,000,000 of total sales, how much should I advertise?" If you build an advertising model (Lotus provides you with the facilities to do this), performing such goal-seeking analysis will be easy.

Goal-seeking can be done by changing one variable or many variables; it depends on the complexity of your model. Remember, using Lotus macros (see Chapters 18–21) you can build fairly complex mathematical models. When the model is built, leave the rest of the calculations to the speed and accuracy of Lotus.

1-12 Using Lotus for Sensitivity Analysis

Sensitivity analysis basically means monitoring the range, elasticity, or variation within a model. Let us say that you are paying $15 per hour to the workers on the assembly line. If the workers ask for more money, how much more can you pay and still make a profit? Sensitivity analysis studies the range of variation for a variable and calculates its effect over the entire system. Again, Lotus will provide you with such a facility.

1-13 Building an Integrated DSS Using Lotus

By combining a powerful spreadsheet, database management, and graphics, Lotus can be used as an integrated DSS package.

The database component can be used for storing data. Basic database operations (see Chapters 16 – 17) can be performed. Data can be organized in different orders, sorted, or searched. This data can be used for modeling analysis. Lotus Release 2.2 has provided you with many different models. Many of the built-in functions, especially the financial functions, can be used directly. The data matrix and data regression commands can be used for building sophisticated forecasting models (see Chapter 17). When the analysis and model building is done, the graphics portion of Lotus provides you with five different graphs. Since all operations (database, spreadsheet, and graphics) are performed within one package, the speed and effectiveness are amazingly high.

1-14 Overview of the Entire Book

Following is a quick overview of the entire book to give you an idea of what to expect.

Chapter 2: Getting Started With Lotus

Walking through worksheets. The first worksheet. Correcting mistakes. Types of data. Types of label prefixes. Arithmetic operations using Lotus. A final example.

Chapter 3: Getting In and Getting Out of Lotus

A view of Lotus as a black box. A brief explanation of the Lotus commands menu. Guidelines for entering, processing, and printing data. Saving and retrieving simple worksheets.

Chapter 4: A Complete Overview of the Lotus Worksheet

An overview of mode indicators, cell and address, control panel, column letter, row number, current position, target position, status indicators, date and time indicators, and so forth.

Chapter 5: Lotus Commands/Part One

A complete review of Copy and Move, Pointing, Range commands and different addressing including relative, absolute, and mixed addressing.

Chapter 6: Lotus Commands/Part Two

A complete review of worksheet, worksheet global and protection facility of Lotus. We also discuss the Undo feature and priority of commands.

Chapter 7: Formats: Dressing Up Your Worksheet

A comprehensive review of format commands for both the worksheet and specific ranges. This includes Fixed, Scientific, Currency, ", ", General, Percent, Date, Text, and Hidden formats.

Chapter 8: File Operations: Interaction between Memory and Disk Files

A comprehensive review of Save, Retrieve, Combine, Xtract, Erase, List, and Directory commands. We also discuss the file linking feature of Lotus.

Chapter 9: Report Generation

A comprehensive review of report generation, including printers and files. A complete coverage of options (Range, Line, Page, Align, etc.).

Chapter 10: Printing with Allways

A review of commonly used commands in Allways, the add-in program for Release 2.2.

Chapter 11: Allways Advanced Features

A discussion of advanced features of Allways. Includes layout design and integration of graphs and worksheets.

Chapter 12: Functions/Part One

A comprehensive review of mathematical functions (@ABS, @INT. etc.), financial functions (@DDB, @FV, etc.), and statistical functions (@STD, @VAR, etc.).

Chapter 13: Functions/Part Two

A comprehensive review of logical functions (@IF, @TRUE, etc.), special functions (@CHOOSE, @CELL, etc.), string functions (@MID, @LOWER, etc.), and date and time functions (@DATE, @TIME, etc.).

Chapter 14: Graphics: Converting Figures into Pictures

A comprehensive review of graphs generated by Lotus (line, bar, XY, stacked-bar, and pie), highlighting specific usage of each graph.

Chapter 15: The PrintGraph Program

A comprehensive discussion of the PrintGraph program for graphics printers and plotters, including a detailed discussion of how to print graphs from files created with the /Graph Save command.

Chapter 16: Database Operations/Part One: Lotus as an Electronic File Cabinet

A comprehensive review of database creation, addition, modification, deletion, searching, and sorting. Searching is broken down into single criteria, double criteria, multiple criteria, and searching with wildcards.

Chapter 17: Database Operations/Part Two: Lotus as a Sophisticated Database

A comprehensive review of advanced database operations, including statistical functions, table handling, frequency distribution, regression analysis, and so on.

Chapter 18: Macros/Part One: Typing Alternatives

A comprehensive review of macro operations. Creation, documentation, and debugging of macros. A table of more than 50 commonly used macros with complete documentation.

Chapter 19: Macros/Part Two: Advanced Commands

A comprehensive review of advanced macro commands. This will include BRANCH, BREAKOFF, GET, BEEP, INDICATE, etc.

Chapter 20: Macros/Part Three: Using Lotus Macros as a Super Programming Language

An overview of the program development life cycle, structured programming, modular programming, etc. More than one dozen simple programs written in macros will be presented.

Chapter 21: Lotus Applications in Specific Disciplines

Several simple worksheets demonstrate specific applications of Lotus in several disciplines, such as accounting, finance, marketing, production/operations, forecasting, economics, budgeting, personnel management, and home use.

Appendix A: You and Your PC: A Friendly Interface

An overview of a complete microcomputer system – keyboard, system unit, monitor, disk drive, floppy disk, hard disk, printer, etc.; a discussion of the types of memories; getting started with PC, etc.

Appendix B: Disk Operating System

A comprehensive discussion of DOS as the starting point for Lotus. An overview of more than 50 important DOS commands; disk file creation; an overview of batch files; and customizing Lotus using DOS.

Appendix C: Installing Lotus

Getting Lotus out of the box! An overview of the Install program, using the Lotus Access System, system configuration, and guidelines for installing the entire system.

Appendix D: File Transfer between Lotus and Other Software

A series of guidelines for file transfer to and from Lotus for a number of popular software packages on the market, including dBASE II, III, and III Plus files, VisiCalc files, and more.

Appendix E: Differences between Release 2/2.01 and Release 1A

Highlights of the differences for 1A users, showing the power of Release 2/2.01.

Appendix F: Differences Between Release 2/2.01 and Release 2.2

Highlights of the differences for 2/2.01 users, showing the power of Release 2.2.

Appendix G: Highlights of Release 3.0/3.1

This appendix highlights the unique features of Release 3.0/3.1.

Appendix H: Lotus International Character Set

This appendix, adopted from the Lotus manual, presents ASCII codes and the extended ASCII codes used by Lotus. This appendix shows the numeric value of different characters used by Lotus.

Appendix I: Answers to the Selected Review Questions

This appendix provides answers to selected questions presented at the end of each chapter to reinforce the reader's understanding of materials presented throughout the text.

SUMMARY

This chapter gave an overview of the functions of a spreadsheet. A quick review shows the power and enhanced features of Lotus compared with other spreadsheets. We also discussed the various applications that Lotus handles. As you will see in the rest of this book, this amazing package is capable of doing many things. Just use your imagination!

REVIEW QUESTIONS

*These questions are answered in Appendix I.

1. How do you compare Lotus and a manual accounting spreadsheet?
2.* Name four spreadsheet packages prior to Lotus.
3. How many versions of Lotus have there been?
4.* What are some of the unique features of Release 2.2 (See Appendix F)?
5. What is Release 3.0/3.1 (see Appendix G)?
6.* What was the most popular spreadsheet prior to Lotus?
7. What are the memory requirements for Lotus Release 2.2?
8. What type of PC can utilize Lotus?
9.* How many disks are included in the Lotus package?
10. What is the most important disk in the entire package? Why?
11. Mention ten specific applications of Lotus.
12. Why is Lotus considered a DSS product?
13. Give an example of What-if analysis using Lotus.
14. What is goal-seeking analysis and how can Lotus perform such a task?
15.* Mention two examples of using Lotus as an integrated DSS package.

HANDS-ON PRACTICE

1. Get Lotus started once only by using the Lotus Access System and once by using 123 and going to the spreadsheet directly. What is the difference?
2. Access the on-line Help menu. What is available there? Go through the menu display of help information on function keys. What is the function of F5? Of F2?
3. Enter the spreadsheet part of 1-2-3. By pressing the slash key invoke the menu. By selecting Q (quit) exit the menu.

4. By consulting computer magazines, investigate some of the practical applications of 1-2-3. What other packages are considered to be close competitors of 1-2-3? What are their advantages/disadvantages compared with 1-2-3? Discuss.

MISCONCEPTIONS AND SOLUTIONS

M – Lotus provides a very large spreadsheet, 8,192 rows by 256 columns. At the present time there is no way to use this entire facility with a typical PC because of the memory requirements.

S – To utilize most of this facility, some computers can be upgraded to a bigger memory, up to four megabytes. This can be done with either Intel Above Board or AST Rampage Board.

M – The processing power of Lotus 1-1-3 is relatively higher than that of other spreadsheets. Even so, this speed will not be high enough to deal with very large spreadsheets.

S – Install a coprocessor chip. This will immensely increase the speed of calculation. It will be very helpful when your worksheet includes a lot of mathematical calculations, sorts, table handling, etc.

Getting Started with Lotus

2-1 Introduction

In this chapter you will learn the fundamentals of Lotus 1-2-3. After studying the chapter, you should be able to build some simple worksheets, walk through your worksheet, correct your errors, and differentiate types of data (numeric, labels, and formulas). We will also discuss priority rules for arithmetic operations using Lotus 1-2-3. The chapter concludes with several of 1-2-3's most important commands.

2-2 What Is a Worksheet?

A *worksheet*, or *spreadsheet*, is simply a matrix or a table consisting of rows and columns. Lotus features a worksheet of 8,192 rows and 256 columns. Rows are numbered from 1 to 8,192 and columns are indicated by the letters A to IV. The intersection of a row and a column is called a *cell* and is uniquely identified by a column letter and a row number. A cell is 9 characters long by default (see section on label prefixes below). It can be much wider depending on your needs. Figure 2-1 illustrates an empty Lotus worksheet with a table of 20 rows and 8 columns.

2-3 Walking Through Your Worksheet

After the Lotus system disk has been installed (see Appendix C for detailed explanations of how to install Lotus 1-2-3), put MS-DOS or PC-DOS in drive A and turn on the computer. At the "A" prompt, insert the Lotus system disk in drive A and type Lotus. From the five options presented to you, choose option 1-2-3, the spreadsheet part of Lotus. (For detailed explanations on how to boot your system, see Appendices A and B.) If your Lotus program is stored on the hard disk, this procedure may be slightly different.

The cursor is at column A, row 1, or cell A1. You are now able to move around the entire worksheet as follows:

→ (Right arrow)	Moves the cursor one cell to the right.
← (Left arrow)	Moves the cursor one cell to the left.
↑ (Up arrow)	Moves the cursor up one cell.
↓ (Down arrow)	Moves the cursor down one cell.
PgUp	Moves the cursor up one screen.

FIGURE 2-1 A Sample Worksheet

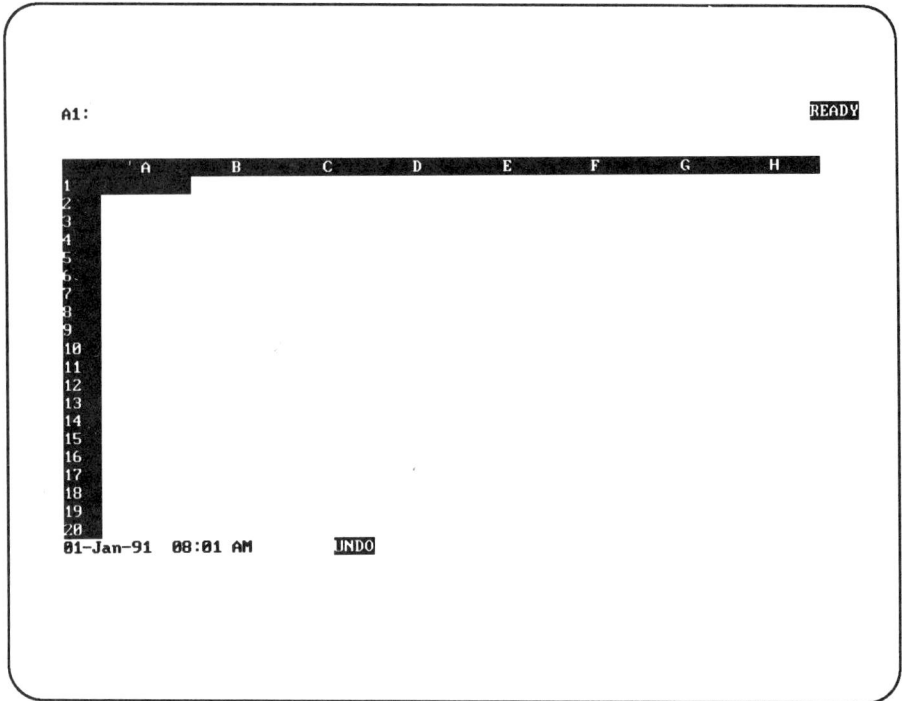

PgDn	Moves the cursor down one screen.
Goto	Will take you to any location in the worksheet. To activate Goto, press function key F5 and the system will request a position. Type the address of the desired cell, press the **Return** key, and there you go!
Home	Will take you to the cell in the upper left corner of the worksheet (e.g., A1).
End	Used in combination with arrow keys.
End & Home	Moves the cursor to the bottom right cell of your active worksheet.
End & Up arrow	Moves the cursor up to the last cell above the current position (occupied or empty).
End & Down arrow	Moves the cursor down to the last empty cell or last occupied cell below the current position.
End & Right arrow	Moves the cursor to the last right cell of the worksheet to the right of the current position.
End & Left arrow	Moves the cursor to the last left cell of the worksheet to the left of the current position.

2-4 Your First Worksheet

You can enter data items in your worksheet by typing the data item and pressing the **Return** key or typing the data and pressing one of the arrow keys. The second method is

FIGURE 2-2 Sample Worksheet with Some Data Items

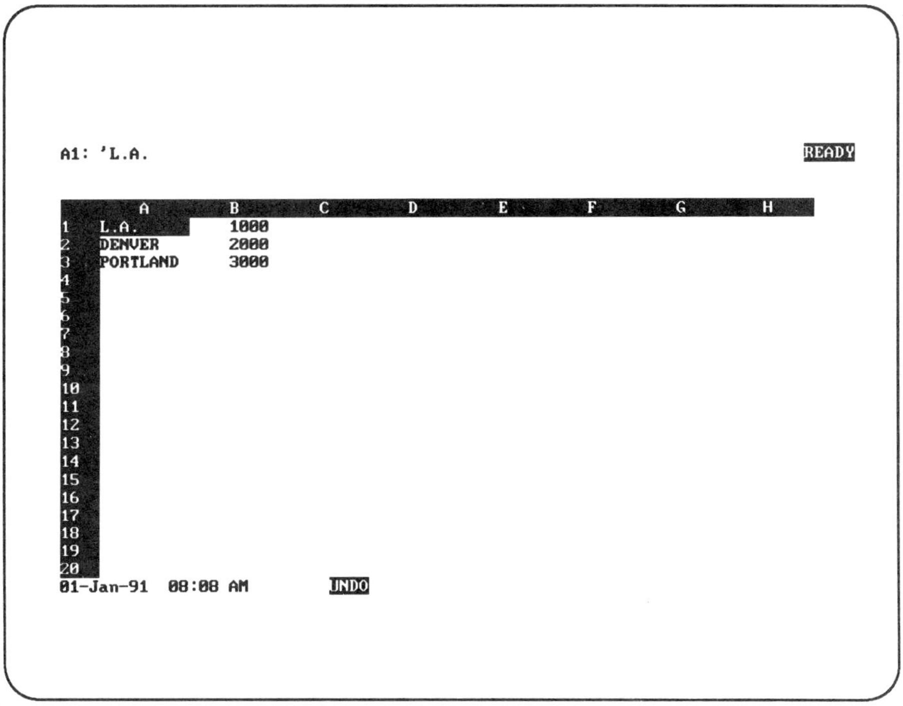

```
A1: 'L.A.                                                              READY

         A          B          C       D       E       F       G       H
    1  L.A.       1000
    2  DENVER     2000
    3  PORTLAND   3000
    4
    5
    6
    7
    8
    9
   10
   11
   12
   13
   14
   15
   16
   17
   18
   19
   20
 01-Jan-91  08:08 AM        UNDO
```

faster than the first one. Let's create a worksheet. Enter the data shown in Figure 2-2 as follows:

1. Move the cursor to cell A1 and type L.A.
2. Move the cursor to cell B1 and type 1000.
3. Move the cursor to cell A2 and type DENVER.
4. Move the cursor to cell B2 and type 2000.
5. Move the cursor to cell A3 and type PORTLAND.
6. Move the cursor to cell B3 and type 3000.

As you see, you can enter the data by typing the data item and moving the cursor or by typing the data, pressing the **Return** key and then moving the cursor to the next cell. The first option is faster but the second will work just as well.

As the worksheet illustrates, L.A. is in row 1, column A. 1000 is in row 1, column B. DENVER is in row 2, column A, and so on.

A new entry will replace an old entry. For example, if you move the cursor to cell A3, type ORLANDO, and press the **Return** key, the new content of cell A3 will be OR-LANDO. Try this on your worksheet.

2-5 How To Correct Your Mistakes

If you make a mistake, do not panic. There are three ways to correct an error. The first method is to replace the content of the cell by reentering the data item. This may not be efficient, especially if the content of a cell is a long series of characters.

The second method, the preferred alternative, is to edit the content of the cell that contains the mistake(s). This is how you do it:

1. Move the cursor to the cell that contains the error.
2. Press function key F2 (**Edit** key). Now the cursor is at the end of the last character in that cell in the control panel. (Control panel is the top part of the screen.)
3. Using the **Left** or **Right arrow** key, move to where the mistake is and type the correct character(s). The new character will be inserted to the left of the cursor position.
4. Delete the unwanted character(s) by highlighting and pressing the **Del** key.

Let us assume that in Figure 2-2 you have mistakenly typed PORTLAND as PORTLLAND, and you wish to correct the spelling.

1. Move the cursor to cell A3.
2. Press F2.
3. Use the **Left arrow** key to move the cursor to one of the Ls.
4. Press **Del** and then press the **Return** key.

The third method is erasing (/**RE Return**). This method will be introduced later.
Other keys are extremely helpful when you are editing data. These are as follows:

Backspace	Erases the character to the left of the cursor.
Insert (**Ins**)	Toggles the **Ins** key on and off. Inserts text by moving existing characters to the right and inserting the new character if the key is off. Replaces the previous character with the new one if the key is on.
Escape (**Esc**)	When editing or replacing a cell entry, pressing **Esc** before you press **Return** results in keeping the old entry. Pressing **Esc** when entering data into a blank cell cancels the data entry for that cell. Think of pressing **Esc** as a way of changing your mind about your current data entry.

2-6 Types of Data

Throughout your Lotus program you will see three types of data:

• numbers
• formulas
• labels

Numbers (values) are any data items starting with the digits 0 through 9, -, $, (, . Numbers can be up to 240 characters long but cannot include spaces or commas. Numbers can have up to 15 decimal places. Very small and very large numbers are presented in scientific notation.

For those of you who have forgotten scientific notation, the following are some examples:

Regular Numbers		Scientific Notation Equivalent	
5000	=	5E+03	$5 * 10^3$
2500000	=	25E+05	$25 * 10^5$
.0000006	=	6E-07	$6 * 10^{-7}$
.00007	=	7E-05	$7 * 10^{-5}$

Formulas must begin with the digits 0 through 9, ., +, -, (, @, #, or $, and can be up to 240 characters long. For example, +A7+A8 is a valid Lotus formula. Formulas cannot contain spaces. If the first part of the formula is a cell address, the formula must start with a plus sign (+) or a minus sign (-).

Data items that are neither formulas nor numbers are considered *labels*. Labels can be up to 240 characters long. They either begin with a prefix (see the next section) or start with characters that are not included in the starting position of numbers or formulas. However, labels can be made up of numeric digits, i.e., phone numbers, street addresses, etc., as long as this data will not be used in any arithmetic operations. To enter numeric data as a label, precede it with a label prefix (see the next section). Long labels occupy the next right cell(s). If the next right cell is already occupied, Lotus will truncate the label on the screen but not in memory.

2-7 Types of Label Prefixes

Labels may begin with four different prefixes indicating whether they are left-justified, right-justified, centered, or repeated. By default, Lotus will left-justify a label. Following are the types of prefixes:

' (apostrophe)	Left-justified.
" (double quotation)	Right-justified.
^ (caret)	Centered (this character is the uppercase of key 6, i.e., press the **Shift** key and then key 6).
\ (backslash)	Repeat the same character until the length of the cell is filled out.

We have used two words that may not be familiar to you. *Default* means the computer performs a task automatically without input from the user. For example, the length of a cell in Lotus is nine characters by default. You can override this rule any time you wish (this will be explained later). *Justified* refers to the order in which the computer fills out a cell. Right-justified means the characters will occupy the cell from right to left. If you type COBOL in cell A1 as a right-justified data item, Lotus will display three spaces, then COBOL, and leave the rightmost space in the cell empty.

Remember, prefixes are only used for labels. Numbers are always right-justified and don't need a prefix. Figure 2-3 illustrates different prefixes.

2 8 Arithmetic Operations in Lotus

Like any other programming language or software tool, Lotus follows a series of rules to perform arithmetic operations. These priority rules are as follows:

1. Expressions inside parentheses have the highest priority.
2. Exponentiation (raising to power) has the next highest priority.
3. Multiplication and division have the third highest priority.
4. Addition and subtraction have the fourth highest priority.
5. When there are two or more operators with the same priority, Lotus proceeds from left to right.

Table 2-1 illustrates the order of operations of 1-2-3 tasks, from the highest priority to the lowest. We will talk about these operations in future chapters.

FIGURE 2-3 *Examples of Different Types of Prefixes*

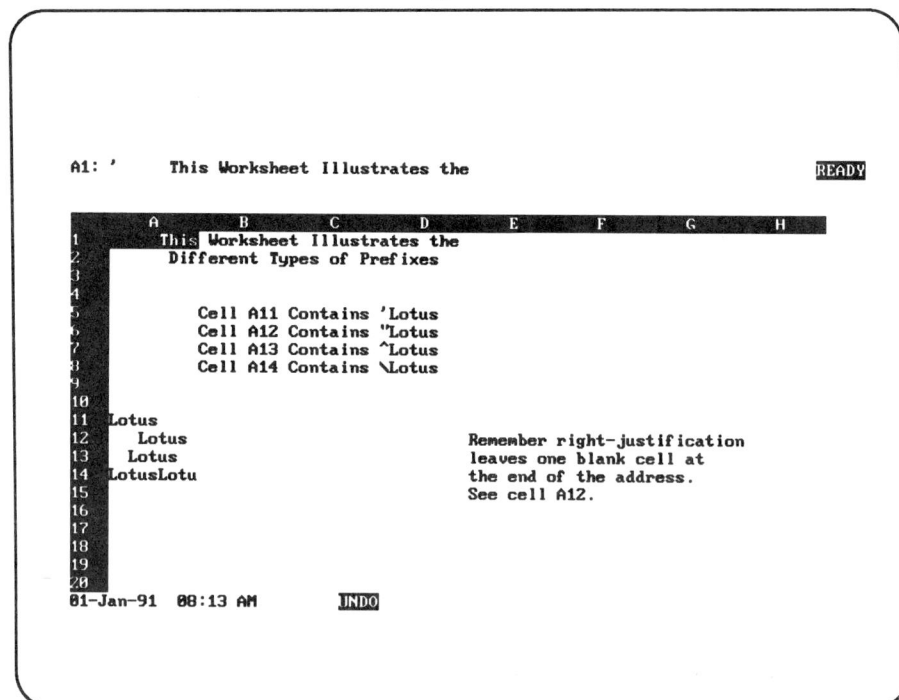

```
A1: '      This Worksheet Illustrates the                              READY

            A         B         C         D       E       F       G       H
    1    This Worksheet Illustrates the
    2       Different Types of Prefixes
    3
    4
    5       Cell A11 Contains 'Lotus
    6       Cell A12 Contains "Lotus
    7       Cell A13 Contains ^Lotus
    8       Cell A14 Contains \Lotus
    9
   10
   11  Lotus
   12      Lotus                     Remember right-justification
   13    Lotus                       leaves one blank cell at
   14  LotusLotu                     the end of the address.
   15                                See cell A12.
   16
   17
   18
   19
   20
    01-Jan-91  08:13 AM        UNDO
```

TABLE 2-1 *ORDER OF OPERATIONS*

Operator	Meaning	Precedence No.
^	Exponentiation	7
-	Negative	6
*	Multiplication	5
/	Division	5
+	Addition	4
-	Subtraction	4
=	Equal	3
<	Less than	3
<=	Less than or equal to	3
>	Greater than	3
>=	Greater than or equal to	3
<>	Not equal to	3
#NOT#	Logical not	2
#AND#	Logical and	1
#OR#	Logical or	1

The following examples should make this clear. First, Lotus uses * (asterisk) for multiplication, ^ (caret) for exponentiation, and / (slash) for division. If A=5, B=10, C=2, calculate the following:

FIGURE 2-4 *Arithmetic Operations Using Lotus*

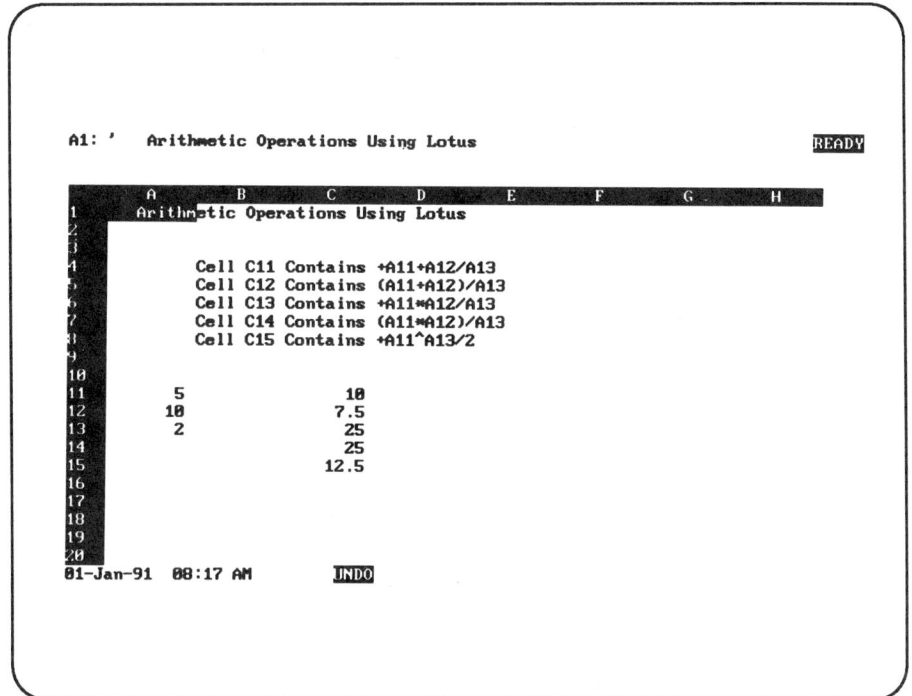

1. A+B/C   = 10
2. (A+B)/C = 7.5
3. A*B/C   = 25
4. (A*B)/C = 25
5. A^C/2   = 12.50

Figure 2-4 illustrates these examples.

2-9 A More Comprehensive Example

Now that you have learned how to walk through your worksheet and perform simple tasks, let us construct a simple worksheet. Figure 2-5 illustrates three salespersons who have sold four products for Always Smile Merchant. You have been asked to calculate the total sales for each product, for each salesperson, and finally for the business.

In cells B10, C10, D10 and E10 we entered PROD 1, PROD 2, PROD 3, and PROD 4. Cells A11, A12, and A13 contain the three salespersons' names. Cells B11 through E13 contain the total sales for each salesperson for different products. As we discussed earlier, you can enter a data item, move the cursor to the next cell and continue until all your data has been entered.

In this particular example, we have added the cells by using the plus sign. Total sales generated by Sue are found by entering +B11+C11+D11+E11 in cell H11.

Jack's total sales are in cell H12;
we entered +B12+C12+D12+E12.

FIGURE 2-5 Sales Analysis Using Lotus

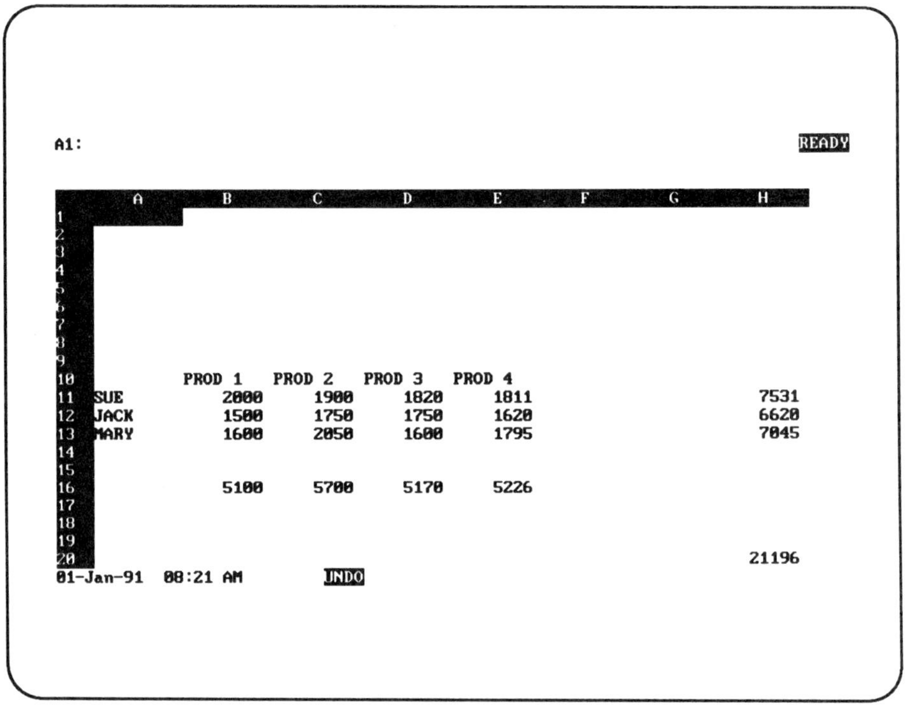

```
A1:                                                              READY

        A        B         C         D         E      F     G      H
1
2
3
4
5
6
7
8
9
10              PROD 1    PROD 2    PROD 3    PROD 4
11      SUE     2000      1900      1820      1811                7531
12      JACK    1500      1750      1750      1620                6620
13      MARY    1600      2050      1600      1795                7045
14
15
16              5100      5700      5170      5226
17
18
19
20                                                               21196
01-Jan-91  08:21 AM            UNDO
```

In cell H13, Mary's total sales are stored;
we entered +B13+C13+D13+E13.
In cell B16 we entered +B11+B12+B13;
in cell C16 we entered +C11+C12+C13;
in cell D16 we entered +D11+D12+D13;
and finally, in cell E16 we entered +E11+E12+E13.

Cells B16, C16, D16, and E16 contain the total sales for four products. What did we enter in cell H20? As you will see in future chapters, there is a much easier way to accomplish this task.

2-10 Entering Formulas

As you saw in the last example, we entered the formula for addition in different cells by typing. This process is straightforward. However, you must remember to start a formula with a plus sign, +.

There is another way to enter formulas, called *pointing* . Let us say that in the next worksheet (Figure 2-6) we would like to add cells A1, B1, C1, and D1 and store the result in cell G1 by pointing. Do the following:

1. Move the cursor to G1 and enter a + sign.
2. Move the cursor to cell A1 (you will see A1 in the control panel), then add another + sign.
3. Move the cursor to cell B1, then add another + sign.
4. Move the cursor to cell C1, then add another + sign.
5. Move the cursor to cell D1.

FIGURE 2-6 *Adding the Contents of Four Different Cells by Pointing*

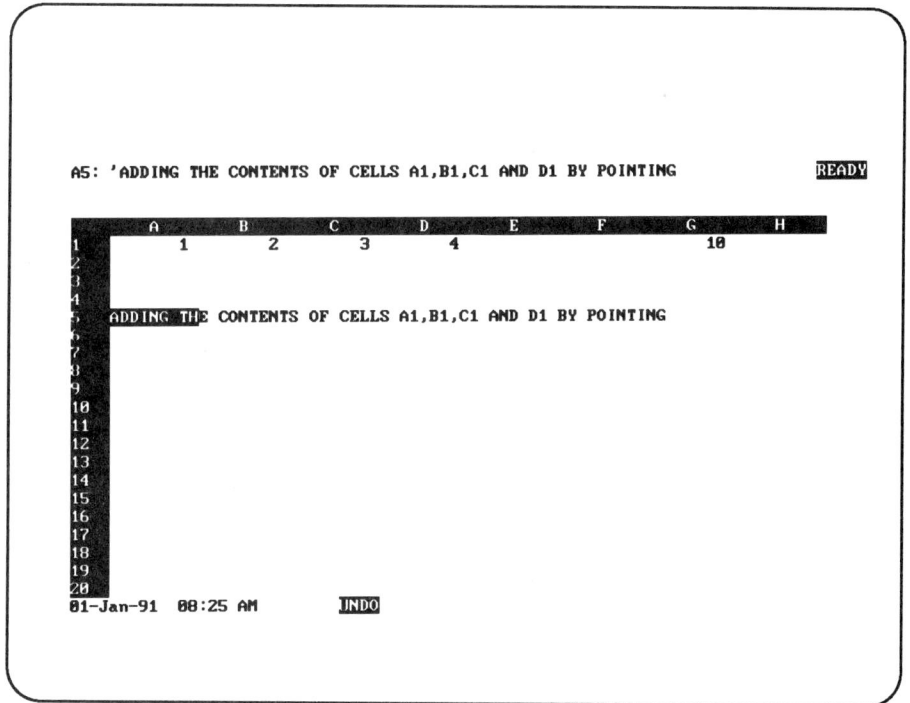

```
A5: 'ADDING THE CONTENTS OF CELLS A1,B1,C1 AND D1 BY POINTING        READY

         A         B         C         D       E       F       G         H
1        1         2         3         4                       10
2
3
4
5    ADDING THE CONTENTS OF CELLS A1,B1,C1 AND D1 BY POINTING
6
7
8
9
10
11
12
13
14
15
16
17
18
19
20
01-Jan-91   08:25 AM        UNDO
```

Now you are done adding; just press the **Return** key. You will see that the result, 10, is stored in cell G1.

When you design a formula, remember to always use the cell address instead of the cell value (A1 vs. 1 or B1 vs. 2 in this example). The reason for this is that you can change the contents of the cells and the result would be automatically recalculated. If you use values instead of cell addresses, you have to change the formula whenever you change the values.

Pointing can be very helpful if you are dealing with long, complicated formulas. You can transfer the content of a cell to another one by just starting with a plus sign in the destination cell, moving the cursor to the target cell and pressing **Return**. Pointing is more accurate since we humans are prone to make transpositions and typographical errors.

2-11 Lotus 1-2-3 Survival Commands

So far we have not talked about any of the 1-2-3 commands. Here you will learn a few of the most important 1-2-3 commands. To invoke 1-2-3's command menu press the /(slash) key. At this point Figure 2-7 will be displayed. A full discussion of these commands will be presented later. For now, try to memorize the following:

1. To erase a particular cell, move the cursor to the cell, press **/RE** (Range Erase), **Return**.
2. To erase the entire worksheet press **/WEY** (Worksheet Erase Yes).
3. To save a file on your default drive press **/FS Filename Return** (File Save—File name). A file name can be any name up to 8 characters long.
4. To retrieve an old file from your default drive press **/FR Filename** (File Retrieve). If you are saving to or retrieving from a drive other than your default drive you must identify the drive name and/or the directory along with the file name.

FIGURE 2-7 *Lotus 1-2-3 Main Menu*

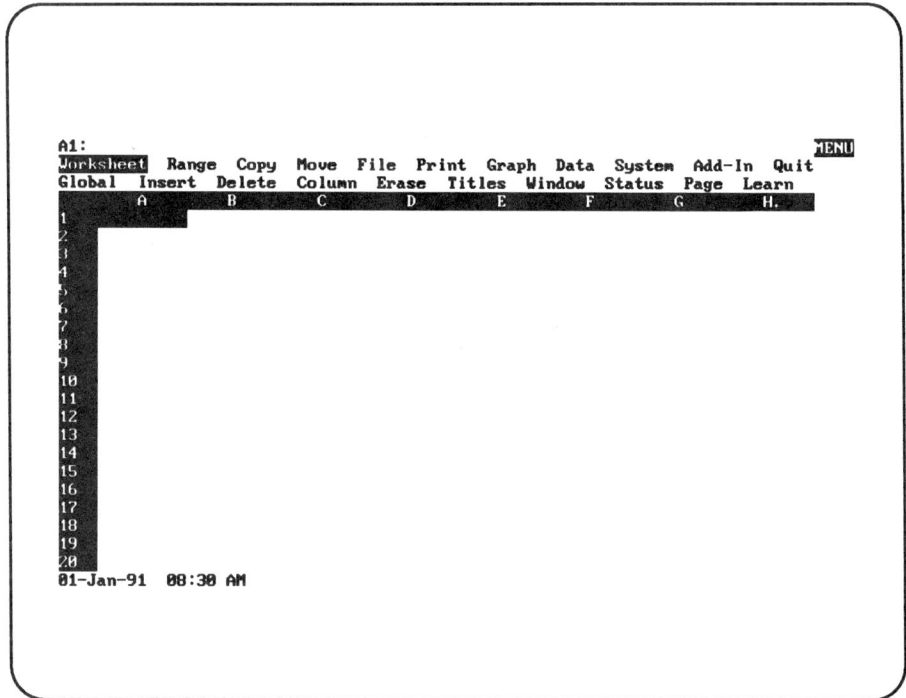

5. To exit 1-2-3, press **/QYE** (Quit Yes Exit).
6. In many cases, 1-2-3 will allow you to reverse your last action. This can be done by pressing Alt-F4 (UNDO).

SUMMARY

In this chapter you learned the basics of Lotus: how to build simple worksheets, enter data items in the worksheet, and edit a cell. We also discussed data types and the arithmetic operations. The chapter concluded with six of the most important 1-2-3 commands.

REVIEW QUESTIONS

* These questions are answered in Appendix I.
1. How do you start your Lotus worksheet?
2.* What is the A prompt? Do we have any other prompts?
3. What is the simplest way to correct errors in your worksheet?
4.* What is the role of the **Home** key?
5. How do you move the cursor to the last row of the worksheet?
6. Which function key performs the editing task?
7.* What is the role of the **Esc** key?
8. How many types of data does 1-2-3 have?
9. How do you make a data item right-justified?
10.* How do you center a data item?

11. In performing arithmetic operations, which expression has the highest priority?

12.* How do you override the priority of operations?

HANDS-ON PRACTICE

1. Get Lotus started and do the following arithmetic operations in cells A1, A2, A3, and A4:

   2 +2/2

   (2+2)/2

   2*2/2

   2^2/2

   Check your answers manually. See if Lotus is correct!

2. Erase your worksheet and calculate the average of the following four test scores:

   100

    95

    85

    80

3. Design a worksheet with ten salespersons in cells A1 through A10. For each salesperson, input a four-digit sales data in column C. In cell H1 calculate the average sales for these ten individuals.

4. Jack's Social Security number is 524-13-1439. Is this numeric data or nonnumeric?

5. Enter 555 in cell A10 as nonnumeric data. How does it look? Is it right- or left-justified?

6. The area of a triangle is calculated by B*H/2 where B is the base and H is the height. Enter a value for the base in cell A1 and a value for the height in cell A2. Now enter the formula for the area in cell A3. Enter different values for the base and the height and see how quickly Lotus calculates the area.

7. Erase your worksheet and do the following:

   a. Move down one screen.

   b. Move to the right by three screens (*hint*: Use the **Tab** key).

   c. Move to the last cell of the worksheet.

   d. Move back to cell A1.

8. Mary receives a base salary of $360 a week and three different commissions of 5%, 7%, and 10% on Persian rugs, color TVs and general appliances, respectively. Last week she sold $12,000, $5,000, and $10,000 worth of these three items, respectively. Calculate her total pay.

MISCONCEPTIONS AND SOLUTIONS

M – When you perform editing you can move back and forth by using left or right arrows. This may be time-consuming for long labels.

S – Use the **Home** key to move to the beginning of the label and use the **End** key to move to the end of the label. Also, pressing the TAB key moves the cursor 5 positions to the right and SHIFT-TAB moves the cursor 5 positions to the left.

M – Nonnumeric data that starts with numbers, e.g., 29 Avenue, will be considered numeric data. You can always watch the mode indicator at the top right corner of the screen. This will tell you what type of data you are entering. The mode indicator for numbers is VALUE, for labels, LABEL.

S – Enter such data with one of the label prefixes, e.g., ', ", or ^.

M – Cell addresses, e.g., A5, A69, will be considered nonnumeric data by Lotus.

S – These values must be preceded by a plus sign, e.g., +A9, or any other numeric characters, -, (or $.

M – Entering long formulas may be time-consuming; also, accuracy may be jeopardized.

S – Use the pointing technique to enter long formulas.

M – Sometimes your arrow keys do not move.

S – Press the **Esc** key to return to READY mode. If the arrow keys still do not work, check if the **Num Lock** key is on. If this is the case, press the **Num Lock** key again.

M – You are entering a formula and at the end you press the **Return** key. Lotus gives you a beep and you cannot get out of EDIT mode.

S – Check your parentheses to make sure that every left parenthesis is matched with a right one.

Getting In and Getting Out of Lotus

3-1 Introduction

In this chapter, we explain the entire cycle of entering and exiting from Lotus, methods of data entry, how to perform mathematical operations, and how to print reports from the worksheet. We will also teach you how to save your worksheet on disk and how to recall data from disk to your computer's memory.

3-2 Lotus as a Black Box

Throughout this book we view Lotus as a black box. This means you will send some information to Lotus, it will perform some calculations, and the result will be given to you either in printed form or on a screen. In order to use this black box you should be able to answer the following three questions:

1. How do I send data or information to Lotus?
2. How does Lotus perform calculations?
3. How do I receive output from Lotus?

Sending data to Lotus, as you have already seen, is very easy. You have two options. You can enter data directly by typing it, moving to the next cell, and continuing this process until all data has been entered. If your data is a formula, you can enter it directly or by pointing.

What happens if you make a mistake? No problem. You can correct your mistake either by reentering the data or by editing the content of a cell. We discussed these options in Chapter 2.

How does Lotus perform calculations? Lotus performs calculations in many ways; we will discuss these methods throughout this text. For now, remember that most basic calculations in Lotus, or any other programming language, are done by performing arithmetic operations. As you saw in Chapter 2, Lotus can do addition, subtraction, multiplication, division, and exponentiation. In Chapters 12 and 13 you will learn Lotus functions (predefined formulas) that can perform mathematical and logical (comparison) operations. You can translate any mathematical formula into Lotus and it will give you the result. We will talk about all this later.

How do you receive output from Lotus? You have seen the output of your Lotus program on the monitor but how do you generate a paper report from the data on the screen? There are two methods for generating reports or hard copies. The simplest way, using an IBM PC or compatible keyboard, is to press the **Shift** key (the thick arrow key) and the **PrtSc** (print screen) key at the same time. (On enhanced keyboards, you only need to press the **PrtSc** key.) What is displayed on the monitor will be sent to the printer.

Lotus has provided a more convenient method for generating a report. This method uses the Print command. All Lotus operations are done through a series of commands. Before we go any further, consider this example of the entire input/process/output cycle, or the black box approach.

Here are some students in our Lotus class. You have been asked to generate a worksheet with their names and grades and the average grade of this group:

Craig Johnson   95
Mary Freeman   98
Debbie Freeman   90
Reid Stuart   92
Debbie Campbell   70
Jack Jones   65

Figure 3-1 is the worksheet generated for this task. Data was entered as usual. Then we entered the formula (C1+C2+C3+C4+C5+C6) /6 in cell E15.

3-3 Lotus Command Menu

To activate the Lotus command menu, press the slash key (the question mark key). You will be given the screen shown in Figure 3-2. A complete command map of Lotus is presented at the end of the book.

Any of these menu items can be selected. Either type the first letter of each command, or point to the command, moving the right or left arrow to the item and pressing the **Return** key. (For a complete discussion of a Lotus worksheet, see Chapter 4.)

You will see three lines at the top of the worksheet. These three lines are called the *control panel*. The first line shows the present position of the cursor. In this case the cursor is in A1 and cell A1 is empty.

The second line highlights the Lotus main menu:

Worksheet Range Copy Move File Print Graph Data System Add-In Quit

The third line highlights options available under the selected menu item. For example, in Figure 3-2 the options available under Worksheet are:

Global Insert Delete Column Erase Titles Window Status Page Learn

These options will be explained in detail later.

3-4 Lotus as a Black Box: The Second Look

All you need to do to utilize Lotus as a sophisticated calculator is enter data and ask Lotus to perform calculations. No matter how simple or how complicated your application is, it always includes three distinct components: input, process, and output. The diagram shows this process:

FIGURE 3-1 Students' Average in Lotus Class

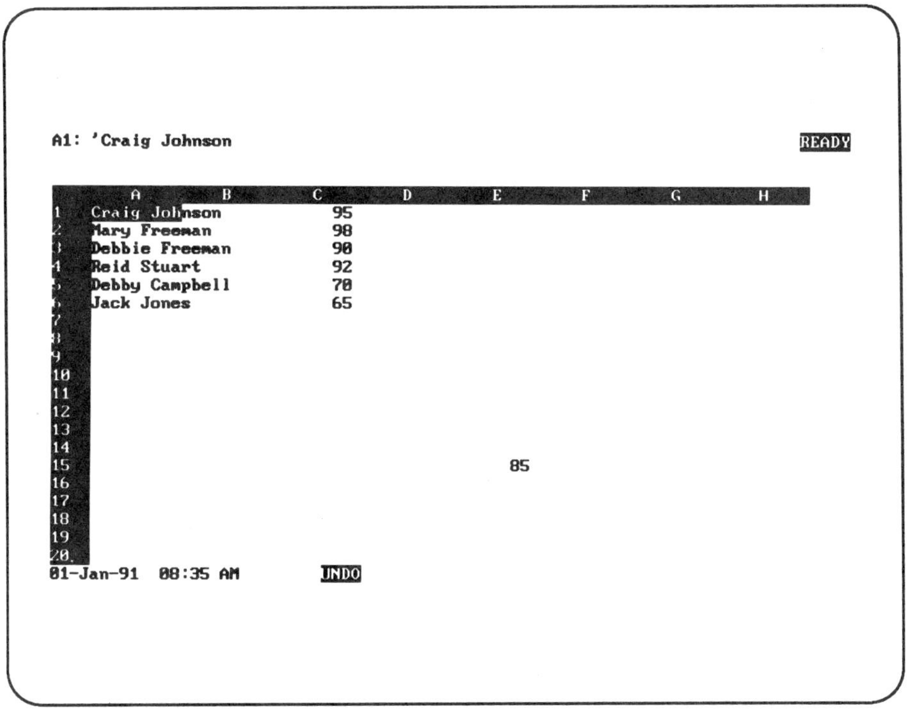

```
A1: 'Craig Johnson                                                      READY

        A         B          C        D        E        F        G        H
1  Craig Johnson            95
2  Mary Freeman             98
3  Debbie Freeman           90
4  Reid Stuart              92
5  Debby Campbell           70
6  Jack Jones               65
7
8
9
10
11
12
13
14
15                                            85
16
17
18
19
20
01-Jan-91  08:35 AM            UNDO
```

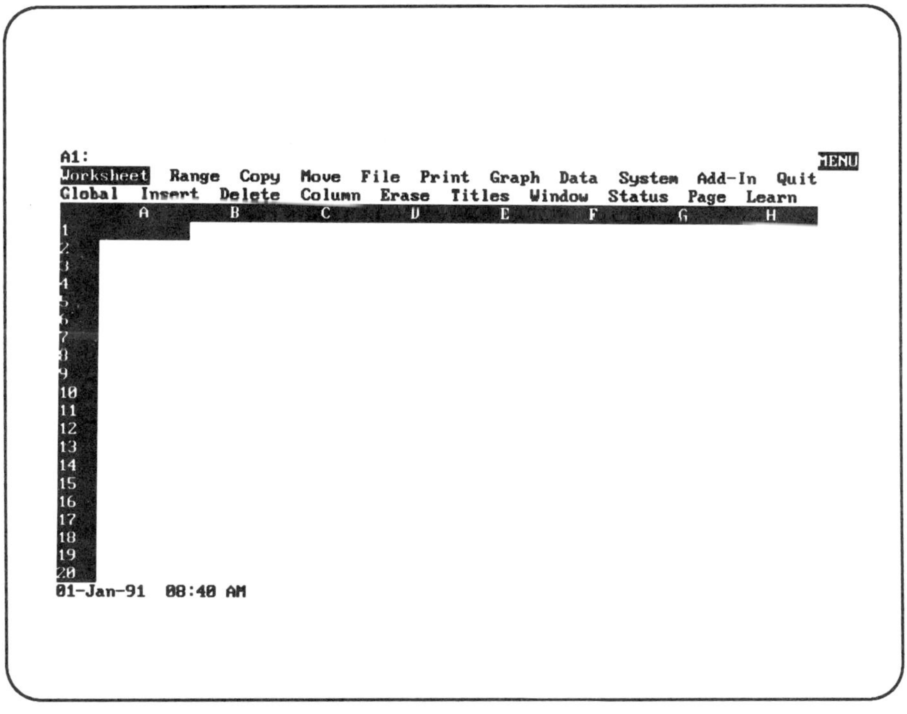

```
A1:                                                                     MENU
Worksheet  Range  Copy  Move  File  Print  Graph  Data  System  Add-In  Quit
Global  Insert  Delete  Column  Erase  Titles  Window  Status  Page  Learn
        A         B          C        D        E        F        G        H
1
2
3
4
5
6
7
8
9
10
11
12
13
14
15
16
17
18
19
20
01-Jan-91  08:40 AM
```

FIGURE 3-2 Lotus Command Menu

Input ➡️➡️➡️➡️➡️➡️	Process ➡️➡️➡️➡️➡️➡️	Output
Typing the data directly	+, -, *, / (arithmetic operators)	Print
Entering formulas by pointing	Functions	Format (to dress up the output)
	Macros	Graph (to generate graphs)
	Lotus commands	

After performing the input/process/output cycle, how do you save your work for future reference? And how do you recall your previous work? We will answer these questions in the next section.

3-5 Creating a Worksheet

Let us assume that the following students have taken three tests in our Lotus class:

	Test #1	Test #2	Test #3
Craig	90	78	75
Mary	92	95	80
Debbie	80	85	96
Reid	95	75	94
Debby	70	85	76
Jack	65	75	85

You have been asked to do the following:

1. Create a worksheet for the class.
2. Add an additional column for the average score of each student.
3. Add an additional row for the average of each test.
4. Generate a hard copy of this worksheet.
5. Save your worksheet for future reference.

Figure 3-3 shows this worksheet. Entering data and calculating averages should not pose any problem. For example, Craig's average was calculated by the formula (B3+C3+D3) /3. Mary's average was calculated by (B4+C4+D4) /3. The first test average was calculated by (B3+B4+B5+B6+B7+B8) /6 and so on. Please remember to use parentheses here, otherwise you will receive a wrong answer. See section on priority of operations in Chapter 2.

As we mentioned earlier, you have available two options to generate a hard copy. The first option is to press the **Shift** key and the **PrtSc** (using a standard keyboard; using an enhanced keyboard, press **PrtSc** alone) key at the same time.

The second option is to use the Print command. As you saw in Figure 3-2, one of the selections available in the main Lotus menu is Print. If you choose Print, two choices will be given to you: Printer or File (see Figure 3-4). This means that you can either send the worksheet to the printer directly or send the worksheet to a file for future printing. If you choose either of these options you will be given the screen shown in Figure 3-5.

We will explain these options in detail in Chapter 9. For now, just choose Range, which refers to the part of the worksheet you want to print. Specify the desired area by typing the upper left and lower right corners. For example, A1..F12 means everything from cell A1 to cell F12, inclusive (the entire rectangle). Choose Go. Your worksheet will be printed. The Quit option gets you out of the Print menu.

FIGURE 3-3 *A More Comprehensive Students' Average Problem*

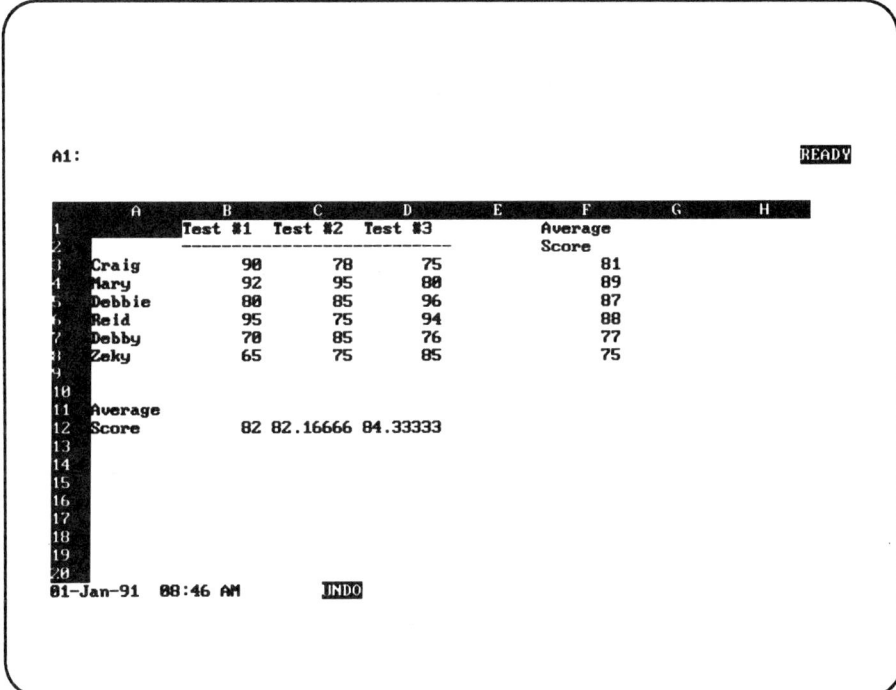

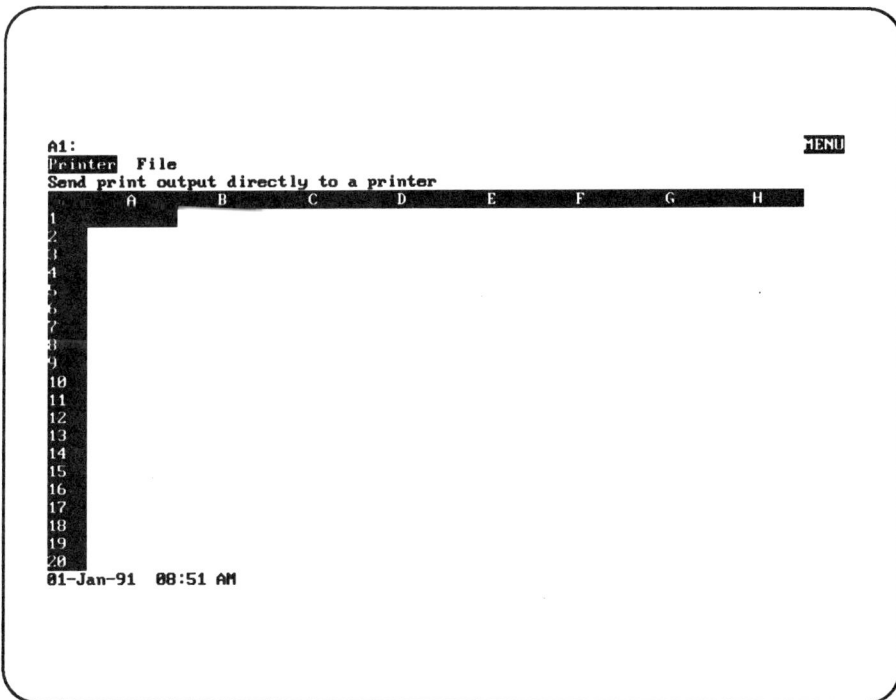

```
A1:                                                                    READY

          A         B        C         D       E        F        G        H
                  Test #1  Test #2  Test #3          Average
1
2                 -----------------------------      Score
3    Craig         90       78        75             81
4    Mary          92       95        80             89
5    Debbie        80       85        96             87
6    Reid          95       75        94             88
7    Debby         70       85        76             77
8    Zeky          65       75        85             75
9
10
11   Average
12   Score         82   82.16666  84.33333
13
14
15
16
17
18
19
20
01-Jan-91   08:46 AM            UNDO
```

```
A1:                                                                    MENU
Printer  File
Send print output directly to a printer
          A            B      C        D       E        F        G        H
1
2
3
4
5
6
7
8
9
10
11
12
13
14
15
16
17
18
19
20
01-Jan-91   08:51 AM
```

FIGURE 3-4 *Options Available under Print Command*

How do you save your worksheet for future reference? First you must have a formatted disk. (To format a disk, see Appendix B.) Put your formatted disk in your default drive and choose the File option from the main menu. You will be given the screen shown in Figure 3-6.

Choose the Save option from this submenu. You will be given the default directory. Save your worksheet using a unique file name of up to eight characters. (For more information on File commands, see Chapter 8.) If you do not want to save to the default directory, you must identify the desired directory.

You may have access to a hard disk. If this is the case, you can save your worksheet on it. When you save your worksheet on a floppy or a hard disk, you have made a permanent copy of it. This worksheet will remain until it is erased.

How do you recall a previously saved worksheet? Look at the choices given to you under the File command. Retrieve is among them. When you choose the Retrieve option, you will be given the names of all the files in your directory. Either by typing the name of a file (and pressing **Return**) or by pointing to it (and pressing **Return**), you will be able to bring a file (a worksheet) back from disk to memory.

Remember, when you bring a file to memory (to the screen), this file will replace the current worksheet in the memory. In other words, the file on the screen will be lost. If you don't want to lose this worksheet, you must save it first and retrieve the other file. When you bring a file from disk to memory, the original file will stay on the disk. Only a copy of it will be transfered to the memory (screen).

3-6 Exiting from Lotus

When your worksheet has been saved and you are finished working with Lotus, you should exit from the program to maintain control over the contents and provide some security for the system.

To exit from Lotus, choose the Quit option from the main menu. Lotus will give you the options of No or Yes. If you choose Yes, Quit will put you back to either the DOS A> prompt or the Lotus Access System. If your worksheet is blank, by choosing Yes, you will immediately exit Lotus. If there is data in your worksheet, after choosing Yes, Lotus give you a warning:

WORKSHEET CHANGES NOT SAVED! End 1-2-3 anyway?

You can either change your mind or exit Lotus anyway.

By typing Lotus at the beginning of the session at the A> prompt, you enter the Lotus Access System. By typing 123 at the A> prompt, you go directly to the spreadsheet section of Lotus.

SUMMARY

This chapter explained the cycle of input, process, and output, and methods of data entry. Using arithmetic operators, you can ask Lotus to perform any mathematical operation.

To receive hard copy from Lotus, use the Print command or press both the **Shift** and **PrtSc** keys.

Commands for printing, saving, and retrieving a worksheet were introduced. These commands will be explained in detail in later chapters.

FIGURE 3-5 Options Available under either Print Printer or Print File Command

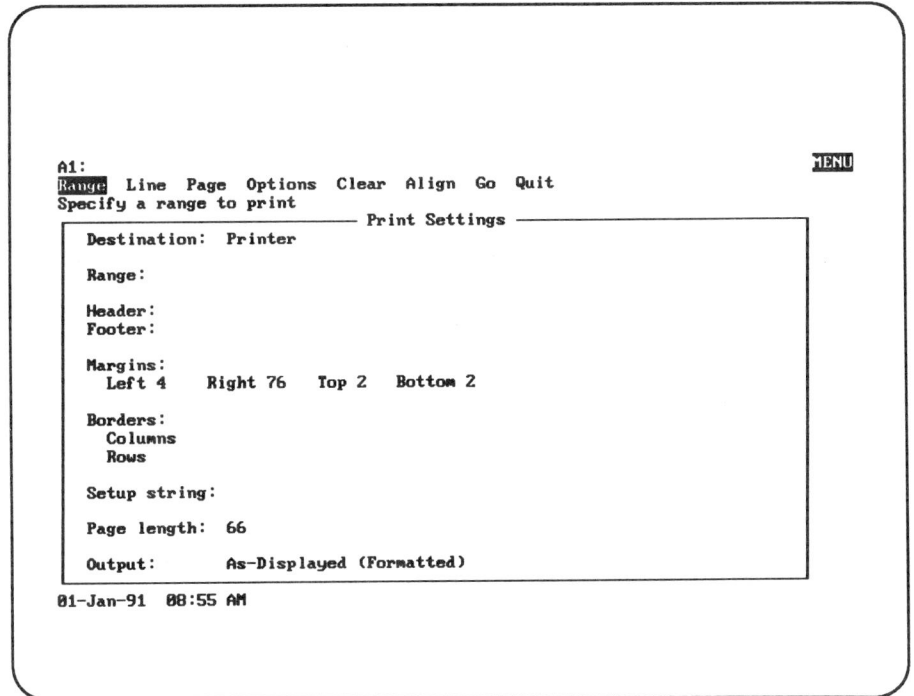

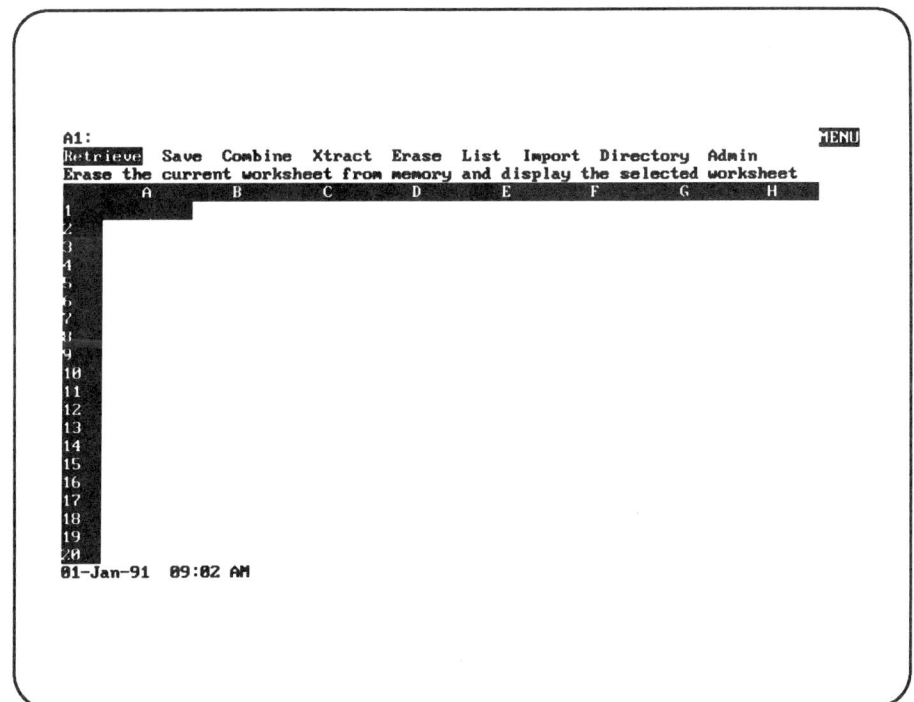

```
A1:                                                              MENU
Range  Line  Page  Options  Clear  Align  Go  Quit
Specify a range to print
                          ———— Print Settings ————
   Destination:  Printer

   Range:

   Header:
   Footer:

   Margins:
     Left 4      Right 76    Top 2    Bottom 2

   Borders:
     Columns
     Rows

   Setup string:

   Page length:  66

   Output:       As-Displayed (Formatted)

01-Jan-91  08:55 AM
```

```
A1:                                                              MENU
Retrieve  Save  Combine  Xtract  Erase  List  Import  Directory  Admin
Erase the current worksheet from memory and display the selected worksheet
        A         B         C         D         E       F        G        H
1
2
3
4
5
6
7
8
9
10
11
12
13
14
15
16
17
18
19
20
01-Jan-91  09:02 AM
```

FIGURE 3-6 Options Available under File Command

REVIEW QUESTIONS

* These questions are answered in Appendix I.
 1.* How do you start Lotus?
 2. How do you start the Lotus Access System?
 3. How do you enter numbers into a worksheet?
 4.* Is entering numbers different from entering labels?
 5. Generate a worksheet with 10, 20, and 30 in cells A1, A2, and A3. Add them up and store the result in cell H10 by pointing.
 6.* How do you activate the Lotus command menu?
 7. How many options are available in the Lotus main menu?
 8. What is the control panel?
 9. What is the third line in the control panel?
10.* How do you generate a hard copy of your worksheet?
11. How do you save your worksheet?
12.* How do you format a blank disk?
13. How do you recall a previous worksheet?
14.* How do you exit from Lotus?
15. When you recall a file from disk to memory, do you still have the file on disk or is the file destroyed?

HANDS-ON PRACTICE

1. Design a worksheet with your first name in cell A1, your last name in cell A2, and your Social Security number in cell A3. Generate a hard copy of this worksheet first by using **Shift** and **PrtSc** and then by using the Print command.
2. Save the worksheet in Question 1 under "First." Exit from the Lotus worksheet. Turn the computer off.
3. Get Lotus started again and retrieve worksheet "First." In cell A4 enter your age, in cell A5 enter your street address. Save this worksheet under "Second."
4. When you enter a long label such as the street address, what will happen? Will your data occupy more than one cell or will it be truncated? Try this.

COMPREHENSIVE LAB ASSIGNMENT

Design the following worksheet for the students in your Lotus class.

	A	B	C	D	E	F	G	H
	Name	Major	Sex	Standing	Age	Test 1	Test 2	Test 3
1	Name	Major	Sex	Standing	Age	Test 1	Test 2	Test 3
2	Brown	MIS	M	JR	20	90	85	75
3	Jones	CS	M	JR	25	95	70	60
4	Smith	ACC	F	SO	19	85	90	90
5	Rudd	MKT	F	SO	20	99	85	100
6	Gerlads	MIS	F	SR	23	100	85	80
7	Moseley	CS	F	SR	28	80	90	100
8	Erb	CS	M	FR	18	80	90	100
9	Thomson	MIS	F	GD	35	95	80	80
10	Sapp	MGT	M	GD	45	98	90	65
11	Lopez	FIN	M	JR	22	95	92	95

1. Using the right label prefix, line up all the headings.
2. Save this worksheet under CHAPT3.
3. Using the Print command, print this worksheet.

A Complete Overview of the Lotus Worksheet

4-1 Introduction

In this chapter we will discuss a Lotus worksheet, areas of a worksheet, the control panel as the starting point of your worksheet, and indicators such as mode, status, time and date. We will explain function keys and special keys. The information provided in this chapter should help you manage your Lotus worksheet more effectively.

4-2 What Is a Worksheet?

As discussed earlier, a Lotus worksheet is a matrix of 8,192 rows and 256 columns. The rows are numbered from 1 to 8,192 and the columns are labeled from A to IV (e.g., A–Z, AA–AZ, etc.).

The intersection of a row and a column is a cell. A cell can hold values, variables, formulas, and so forth. If you look at Figure 4-1, you will see several specific locations on that worksheet. Let us explain these locations.

4-3 Control Panel

The first three lines from the top are called the *control panel*. The first line usually gives you four types of information.

The first item on the first line is the cell address. This is the present position of the cursor. In our case, cell D16 is the present cell. This position can be changed by using one of the arrows in READY mode.

The second item gives the format of the present cell. In our case it is C4, meaning currency with four decimal places (discussed in Chapter 7).

The third item is the column width of the present cell. In this case it is 20 characters (discussed in Chapter 6).

The fourth item is the content of the present cell. This can be labels, numbers, formulas, etc. In our case it is 500000.

The second line of the control panel provides you with the main menu.

The third line of the control panel lists either options available to the menu that can be chosen by the cursor, or the menu selected by the present position of the cursor.

FIGURE 4-1 A Sample Worksheet

```
D16: (C4) [W20] 500000                                              MENU
Worksheet  Range  Copy  Move  File  Print  Graph  Data  System  Add-In  Quit
Global  Insert  Delete  Column  Erase  Titles  Window  Status  Page  Learn
          A          B          C          D          E
1            THIS IS AN EXAMPLE OF AN UNFORMATTED INCOME STATEMENT
2
3                                        1989       1990
4
5   Sales                                500000     650000
6       Cost of Goods Sold              -225000    -310000
7   Gross Profit                         275000     340000
8       Expenses                        -200000    -230000
9   Net Income                            75000     110000
10
11
12           THIS IS AN EXAMPLE OF THE CURRENCY FORMAT
13
14                                        1989       1990
15
16  Sales                          $500,000.0000    $650,000
17      Cost of Goods Sold        ($225,000.0000)  ($310,000)
18  Gross Profit                   $275,000.0000    $340,000
19      Expenses                  ($200,000.0000)  ($230,000)
20  Net Income                      $75,000.0000    $110,000
01-Jan-91  08:00 AM                                      CAPS
```

4-4 Indicators

In the upper right corner of Figure 4-1, at the lower right, and at the lower left you will see information called *indicators*. There are four types of indicators.

Mode Indicators

This indicator appears at the upper right corner of the worksheet. There are eleven types of mode indicators, as follows:

WAIT   Lotus is executing or processing a command. Wait until this indicator goes off before performing any task. For example, you may have to wait while Lotus recalculates a balance sheet after changing one of the figures.

VALUE   The user is entering a number or a formula; for example, +A1+A2 or 655.

READY   Lotus is ready to accept the next command or the next action. For example, in this mode you can enter data into the worksheet, call the menu, and so on.

POINT   The cell pointer is pointing to a cell or a range. For example, if you copy the contents of cell A1 to B1..B10 and you are at the From or To choices of the copy command, the indicator mode shows POINT (discussed in Chapter 5).

MENU   The Lotus menu is being displayed. For example, when you press the / key (the question mark key) in order to invoke the main menu, the indicator shows MENU (as shown in Figure 4-1).

LABEL   Indicates that the user is entering a label. This means any nonnumeric data. For example, if you type I AM BUSY, you will see LABEL as the indicator.

HELP   Indicates that the user has invoked the HELP facility. To see this, press F1.

FIND This indicator is displayed when the /Data Query Find operation is in progress (see Chapter 16).

FILES This indicator appears whenever a File menu is invoked; for example, /File Save or /File Retrieve, etc. (see Chapter 8).

ERROR This indicator appears whenever an error occurs. For example, if you try to save a file in drive B and it does not have any disk, you will receive the ERROR indicator. To clear the error indicator, press either **Return** or **Escape**.

EDIT This indicator appears when you perform any kind of editing. To see this, press F2.

Status Indicators

Status indicators appear at the lower right corner of the worksheet. There are twelve of these indicators, as follows:

SST This indicator, which means single step (in earlier releases of Lotus, before 2.2), appears when a macro is being executed one step at a time. As we discuss in Chapter 18, you can execute a Lotus macro one step at a time for debugging purposes.

STEP When this indicator appears, it means the SINGLE STEP mode has been turned on. To turn STEP on, press Alt and F2 at the same time. To leave STEP mode, press Alt and F2 again.

SCROLL Shows that the **Scroll Lock** key is on. If you move the cursor down, the worksheet will scroll.

OVR This indicator appears if the **Insert** key is on. This is used when you perform some editing task.

NUM Indicates that the **Num Lock** key is on. When this key is on, the arrow keys serve as a numeric pad (a ten-key machine) and cannot be used for moving the cursor around the worksheet.

END Indicates that the **End** key is on. This is used in combination with any of the arrow keys.

CMD Appears during the execution of a macro. As soon as the macro execution is over, this indicator will disappear.

CIRC This indicator appears if a cell is referring to itself. For example, if you type +A11 in cell A11, you will see CIRC. This will only happen if the recalculation order is natural. (For different types of recalculation, see Chapter 6.) A circular reference may or may not be an error. In the majority of cases a circular reference can be resolved by recalculating a worksheet several times. To do that use the /Worksheet Global Recalculation Iteration command. For the number of iterations type 5. The default is 1. Every time you press F9 your worksheet will be calculated once. If 5 won't do it, change the number to a bigger one. However, if an error has caused CIRC to appear, you have to find the error and correct it. Use /Worksheet Status to find the location of the error and then correct it. We will talk about worksheet commands in detail in Chapter 6.

CAPS Indicates that the **Caps Lock** key is on. To turn it off, press the key again. You see CAPS in Figure 4-1.

CALC Indicates that the worksheet needs to be recalculated. If you press F9 this indicator will disappear.

RO Indicates that the current file is a read-only file. The file can only be saved with a different name. This feature applies to a network or multiuser environment.

UNDO Indicates that the UNDO feature is on. This means you can reverse (cancel) the last action by pressing Alt-F4.

Date and Time Indicators

This indicator appears at the lower left corner of the screen. You can change this format by using /Worksheet Global Default Other or suppress the indicator with /Worksheet Global Default Other Clock None.

File and Clock Indicator

By invoking the /Worksheet Global Default Other Clock Filename Quit command, you can display the name of the current file in place of the date and time. Figure 4-2 shows our worksheet with its name displayed. This means this file is saved on the disk under this name.

4-5 Function Keys

Lotus utilizes the IBM-type keyboard function keys very effectively. These keys make it much easier for you to perform different tasks. Some of these keys are used individually, such as F1 through F10; some of them are used in conjunction with other keys, such as F2 - **Alt** for STEP. Following are descriptions of these keys.

F1 (Help)   Accesses the Lotus on-line help facility.

F2 (Edit)   Shifts Lotus into EDIT mode. The contents of the current cell will be displayed in the control panel and the cursor will be positioned at the end of the cell's content. Now you can perform any editing. When you are done, press the **Return** key.

F3 (Name)   Displays all the range names in POINT mode. If you press this key a second time, you will receive a full screen listing of all the range names. This is helpful if you would like to know all the range names before issuing another name (discussed in Chapter 5).

F4 (Abs)   In POINT mode, changes an address from absolute, to mixed, to relative. The cycle can continue (discussed in Chapter 5).

FIGURE 4-2 *A Sample Worksheet with File Name Displayed*

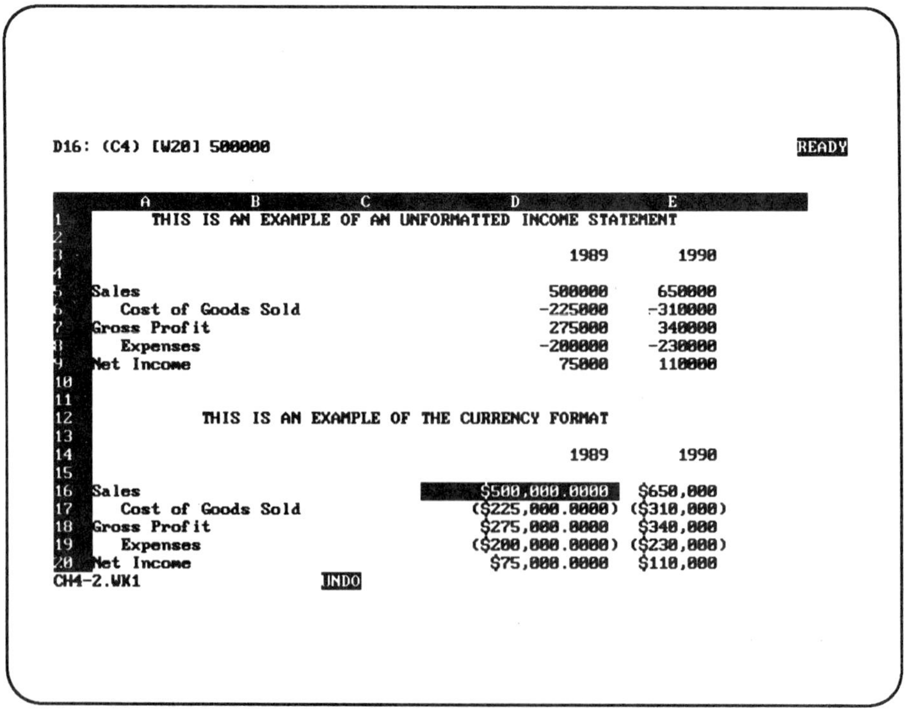

F5 (Goto) Gives you the opportunity to move to any location in the worksheet.

F6 (Window) Moves the cursor between two split screens (discussed in Chapter 6).

F7 (Query) Performs the most recent /Data Query operation (discussed in Chapter 16).

F8 (Table) Operates the last /Data Table command, e.g., recalculates the present table (discussed in Chapter 17).

F9 (Calc) Recalculates the worksheet. All formulas will be calculated into their most recent values (discussed in Chapter 6).

F10 (Graph) In READY mode, redraws the most recent graph. This is very handy for what-if analysis performed on a graph by changing different variables (discussed in Chapter 14).

Alt - F1 (Compose) In conjunction with other keys, used to generate international characters. For example, try Alt - F1 - ((left parenthesis).

Alt - F2 (Step) Switches Lotus into SINGLE STEP mode for debugging a macro.

Alt-F3 (Run) Runs a macro. Macros will be discussed in Chapters 18–21.

Alt-F4 (Undo) Reverses the last action.

Alt-F5 (Learn) Allows you to save up to 512 keystrokes in a cell or to repeat a series of commands. To turn this recording feature off, press **Alt-5** once again.

Alt-7 (Appl) Starts and LDE (Lotus Development Environment) application assigned to this key.

Alt-F8 (App2) Starts an LDE application assigned to this key.

Alt-F9 (App3) Starts an LDE application assigned to this key.

Alt-F10 (add-in) Accesses LDE applications.

4-6 Special Keys

Besides function keys, some other very useful keys are:

Backspace Erases a character or a range.

Backtab (←) In READY mode, moves the cursor one screen to the left. In EDIT mode, moves the cursor five positions to the left. To do this press SHIFT-TAB together.

Tab (→) In READY mode, moves the cursor one screen to the right. If the **Shift** and **Tab** keys are pressed together, they move the cursor one screen to the left. In EDIT mode, moves the cursor five positions to the right.

Break Cancels the current operation. (To activate this key, hold down the **Ctrl** key while pressing the **Break** key.)

Delete (Del) In EDIT mode, erases the current character.

Escape Cancels the current operation, e.g., gets you out of the Lotus menu, erases a line, etc.

Alt (Macro) In conjunction with a macro name, it will invoke a particular macro.

Period (.) When you try to enter a range, it anchors the cursor if it is unanchored for pointing (discussed in Chapter 5).

Return It finalizes the operation: entering data, issuing a command, and so on.

SUMMARY

This chapter gave an overview of a worksheet, explaining the control panel, indicators, function keys, and special keys. The information in this chapter can help you utilize the Lotus worksheet more effectively.

Review Questions

*These questions are answered in Appendix I.

1. What is a control panel?
2. How many lines are usually included in the control panel?
3. What information is presented in the second line of a control panel?
4. What is a mode indicator?
5. How do you create a POINT mode indicator?
6. How and why might the indicator display ERROR?
7.* What is the most commonly used mode indicator?
8. When the mode indicator shows VALUE, what does it mean?
9. What is a status indicator?
10.* How do you create STEP as your status indicator?
11. When the **Num Lock** key is on, can you use the arrow keys for cursor movements?
12.* When can you see CMD as the status indicator?
13. How is CIRC generated? How do you find the location on the worksheet of a CIRC cell?
14. How many function keys are there?
15. What is the function of F9?
16. What is the function of F10?
17. What does the **Escape** key do?
18. Start your Lotus worksheet and generate as many mode indicators as you can.
19. Generate as many status indicators as you can.
20. Can you suppress date and time indicators from the bottom of your worksheet? If yes, how?
21. Try as many function keys as you can. At this point, some of them may not work. Why is this?

Hands-On Practice

1. Get Lotus started. Type your name in cell A1. Now, without putting any disk in drive A, try to save this worksheet under "W1." What will you see in the mode indicator?
2. Enter 55 in cell A5. Check the mode indicator. You must see VALUE. Is this correct? In cell A6, type Lotus. You must see LABEL in the mode indicator. Is this correct?
3. In cell A10, type +A10. Your status indicator must show CIRC. Do you see why?
4. Press the **End** key, then press the **Down arrow**. Check your status indicator.
5. Press the **Num Lock** key. Now try to use the arrow keys. They will not show the arrow movement. Why? Now you have a ten-key machine!
6. Press the **F1** key and check the mode indicator. What do you see?
7. Press the **Scroll Lock** key. Check your status indicator. Now, using the **Down arrow** key, try to move the cursor down. Do you see what is happening? You always see new cells; the old ones are scrolled out of the screen.
8. Create a worksheet similar to Figure 4-3. Enter data of your choice and generate comparable results. Generate a hard copy of this worksheet.

Comprehensive Lab Assignment

Retrieve CHAPT3 and perform the following:

FIGURE 4-3 A Sample Worksheet

```
A1:                                                                READY

          A                    B                   C
1                         NORTHWEST TEXTILE
2                      PROFIT AND LOSS STATEMENT
3                         FOR THE YEAR ENDED
4                         DECEMBER 31, 1990
5
6  GROSS SALES. . . . . . . . . . . . . . .        $982,400.00
7  DEDUCT RETURNED SALES AND ALLOWANCES . . . . .    $13,260.00
8                                                  ---------------
9  NET SALES. . . . . . . . . . . . . . . .         $969,140.00
10                                                 ---------------
11 DEDUCT COST OF GOODS SOLD. . . . . . . . . .     $615,460.00
12                                                 ---------------
13 GROSS PROFIT ON SALES. . . . . . . . . . . .     $353,680.00
14                                                 ---------------
15 DEDUCT EXPENSES. . . . . . . . . . . . . .       $278,240.00
16                                                 ---------------
17 NET PROFIT . . . . . . . . . . . . . . .          $75,440.00
18                                                 ===============
19
20
01-Jan-91  09:26 AM              UNDO
```

1. Save the worksheet under the name EX1.
2. What is the mode indicator while you are saving the worksheet?
3. Erase EX1 by using the /File Erase command.
4. Save the worksheet under CHAPT4.

Lotus Commands/
Part One

5-1 Introduction

In this chapter we will review commands related to range operations. A range can be any rectangular block within your worksheet, varying from a cell to the entire worksheet. We will also discuss relative, absolute, and mixed addressing.

5-2 What Is a Range?

A *range* is a rectangular block within a worksheet. This can be a cell, a row, part of a row, a column, part of a column, or the entire worksheet.

A range in Lotus is presented by two opposite corners, from upper left to lower right. To show a range, we type the first corner, two periods, and then the second corner. For example, A1..B5 means the rectangle of column A to column B and row 1 to row 5. This is a matrix of two columns and five rows. Range A1..H20 is a matrix of eight columns and twenty rows. Following are some more examples of a range:

A1..A1	a cell
A1..A8192	a column
A1..A50	part of a column
A1..IV1	a row
A1..H1	part of a row
A1..H30	a block (8 columns by 30 rows)
A1..IV8192	the entire worksheet

5-3 /Copy Command

The /Copy command enables you to copy a portion of a worksheet to another section of the same worksheet. The origin and the destination cells do not need to be symmetrical. This means that you can copy one cell to another cell, one cell to many cells, or many cells to many cells.

To use this command, choose the Copy command from the main menu. Lotus will ask for the range to copy FROM (showing you the present cell). Type the address of the original cell (the cell you want to copy), then press the **Return** key. If you want to make a copy of the cell in which the cursor is residing, just press the **Return** key. Lotus will ask for the range to copy TO (the destination cell). Type the destination range and then press the **Return** key. You can also point to the original and/or destination cells, as discussed in Section 5-5.

Figure 5-1 illustrates an example of the /COPY command. In this example we entered the word LOTUS in cell A4 and chose Copy from the main menu. In response to FROM (original cell) we typed A4; in response to To (destination cell) we typed A8..H20, then pressed the **Return** key.

Since this command is very important, we will summarize the steps involved:

1. From the main menu choose Copy.
2. Type the range that you would like to copy from.
3. Press the **Return** key.
4. Type the range that you would like to copy to.
5. Press the **Return** key.

When you are more comfortable with pointing, you will find this process to be much easier. For now this should do it just fine!

5-4 /Move Command

With the /Move command, you can move a portion of a worksheet to another section of the same worksheet. All you need to do is issue the Move command from the main menu. Lotus then prompts you for the FROM range. Type in the cell or range of cells that you

FIGURE 5-1 *An Example of the /Copy Command*

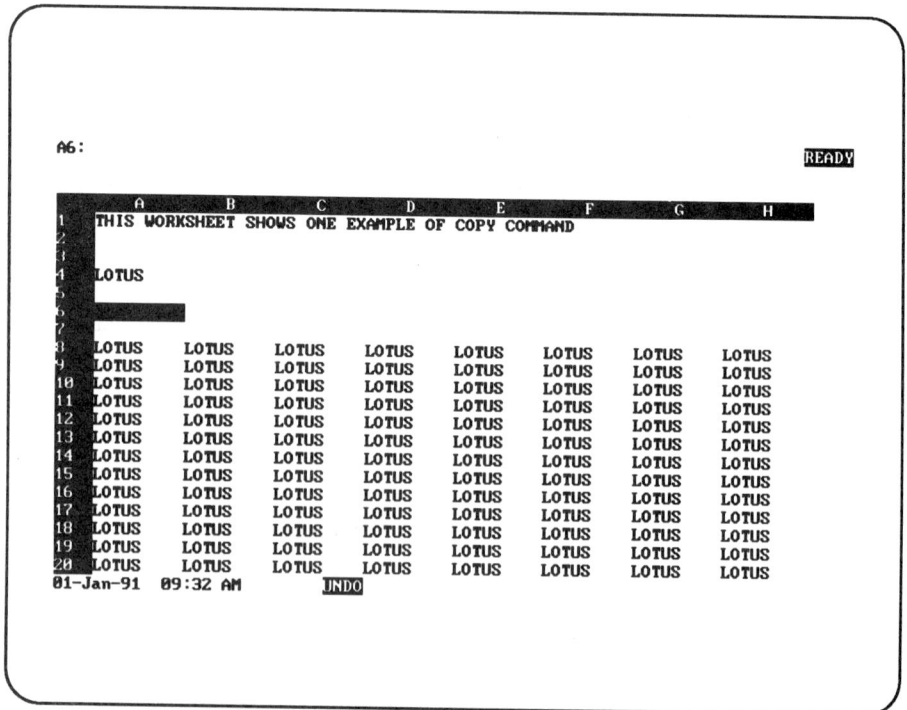

want to move and press the **Return** key. Now Lotus asks for the destination range. Type in the destination range, or point to it, and press the **Return** key. Figure 5-2 illustrates a sample worksheet before we used /Move. We generated Figure 5-3 by typing /Move A1..G1 (press **Return**) A15 (press **Return**). This process moved row 1 to row 15.

5-5 Pointing

To define a range in a worksheet, you have three options. The first option is to type the address of a range, for example, A1..A5. The second option is to use the /Range Name command and give a name to the range and then use this name instead of typing the coordinates of the range. The third option is to use *pointing*. To use the pointing technique, the mode indicator must be in POINT. The easiest way to get into POINT mode is to press F5 (the **Goto** key). At this time, press the **period** key . (>key). You have now anchored the first corner of the range. You can move the cursor in any direction until you have specified the range. When the desired range is established, press the **Return** key.

The **Esc** key removes the anchor from a range or breaks the pointing process. **Backspace**, **Home**, and **End** can also be used with pointing.

Let us show an example. By using the pointing technique we want to copy the word TRY from cell A1 to range A10 . . H20. Do the following steps:

1. In a blank screen type TRY in cell A1.
2. From the main menu select C.
3. Press **Return**.
4. Move the cursor to cell A10. At this point the mode indicator displays POINT.
5. Press the **period** key. Now you have anchored cell A10.
6. Move the cursor to cell H10, then down to H20. At this point range A10 . . H20 is highlighted.
7. Press **Return**.

5-6 /Range Erase

This command can be used for erasing a specified portion of a worksheet. (Remember, it cannot erase a protected area of a worksheet. The protection facility of Lotus will be discussed in Chapter 6). To erase a single cell, move the cursor to that particular cell, type /Range Erase and then press the **Return** key. In Figure 5-4 we have generated two identical portions of a worksheet. A portion of the second worksheet was later erased by using /Range Erase B14..C18 (press **Return**).

5-7 /Range Label

As we discussed in Chapter 2, Lotus enters numbers by default as right-justified and labels by default as left-justified. The arrangement for labels can be changed either by including a label prefix (as in Figure 2-3), or by using /Range Label, Left, Right, or Center. These commands change the label prefix of a cell that contains labels (nonnumeric data). They do not have any effect on numbers. Figure 5-5 illustrates an example. In this example we first entered Lotus in cells A3, A4, and A5. Then we issued /Range Label Left for cell A3, /Range Label Right for cell A4, and /Range Label Center for cell A5.

FIGURE 5-2 A Sample Worksheet before the /Move Command

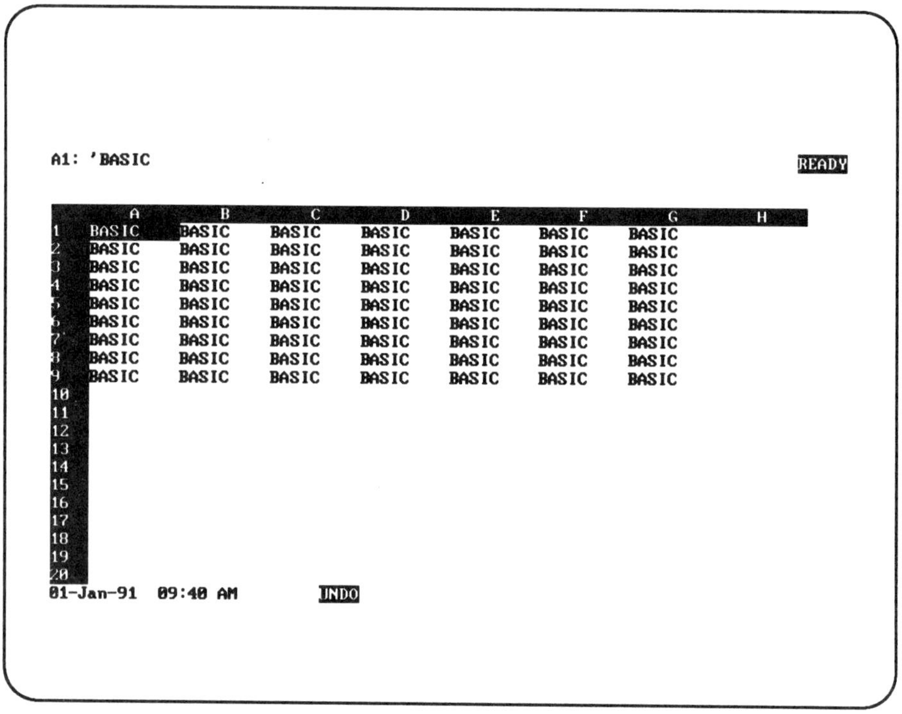

```
A1: 'BASIC                                                              READY

        A          B          C          D          E          F          G          H
1    BASIC      BASIC      BASIC      BASIC      BASIC      BASIC      BASIC
2    BASIC      BASIC      BASIC      BASIC      BASIC      BASIC      BASIC
3    BASIC      BASIC      BASIC      BASIC      BASIC      BASIC      BASIC
4    BASIC      BASIC      BASIC      BASIC      BASIC      BASIC      BASIC
5    BASIC      BASIC      BASIC      BASIC      BASIC      BASIC      BASIC
6    BASIC      BASIC      BASIC      BASIC      BASIC      BASIC      BASIC
7    BASIC      BASIC      BASIC      BASIC      BASIC      BASIC      BASIC
8    BASIC      BASIC      BASIC      BASIC      BASIC      BASIC      BASIC
9    BASIC      BASIC      BASIC      BASIC      BASIC      BASIC      BASIC
10
11
12
13
14
15
16
17
18
19
20
01-Jan-91  09:40 AM        UNDO
```

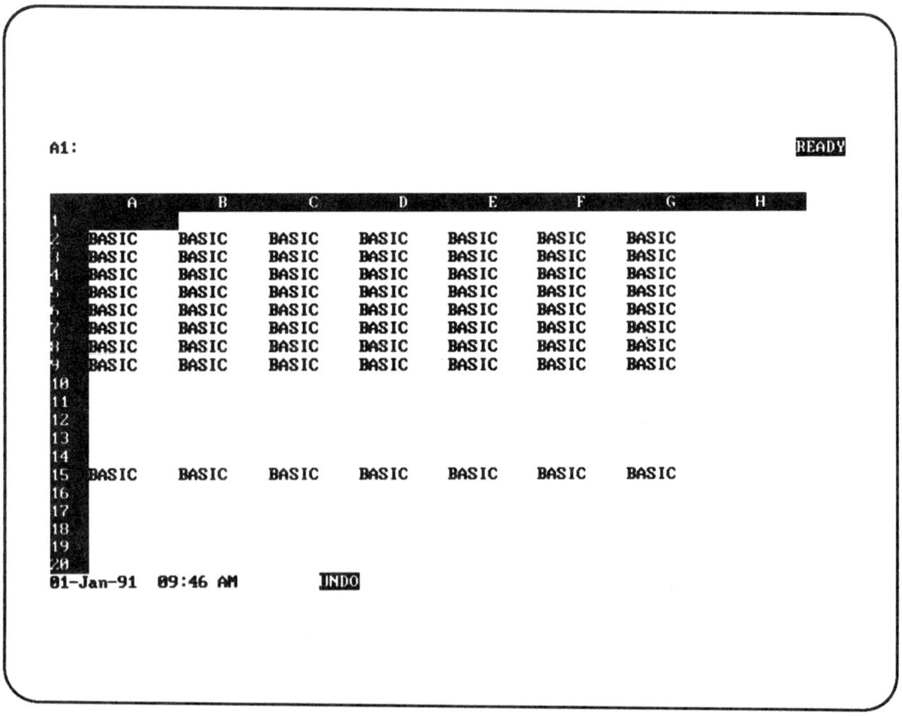

```
A1:                                                                    READY

        A          B          C          D          E          F          G          H
1
2    BASIC      BASIC      BASIC      BASIC      BASIC      BASIC      BASIC
3    BASIC      BASIC      BASIC      BASIC      BASIC      BASIC      BASIC
4    BASIC      BASIC      BASIC      BASIC      BASIC      BASIC      BASIC
5    BASIC      BASIC      BASIC      BASIC      BASIC      BASIC      BASIC
6    BASIC      BASIC      BASIC      BASIC      BASIC      BASIC      BASIC
7    BASIC      BASIC      BASIC      BASIC      BASIC      BASIC      BASIC
8    BASIC      BASIC      BASIC      BASIC      BASIC      BASIC      BASIC
9    BASIC      BASIC      BASIC      BASIC      BASIC      BASIC      BASIC
10
11
12
13
14
15   BASIC      BASIC      BASIC      BASIC      BASIC      BASIC      BASIC
16
17
18
19
20
01-Jan-91  09:46 AM        UNDO
```

FIGURE 5-3 A Sample Worksheet after the /Move Command

FIGURE 5-4 Example of /Range Erase Command

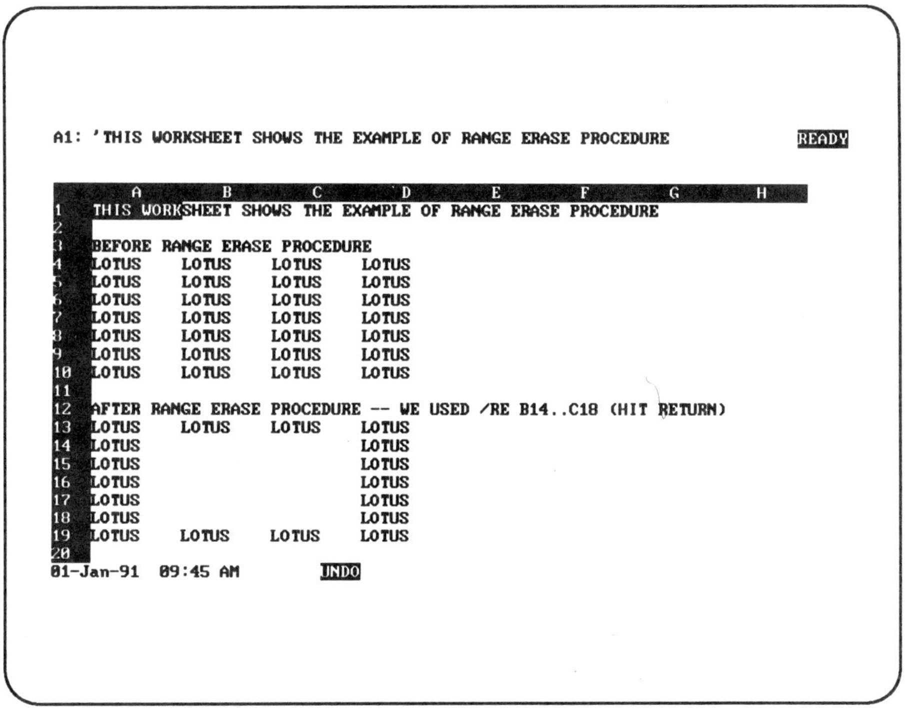

```
A1: 'THIS WORKSHEET SHOWS THE EXAMPLE OF RANGE ERASE PROCEDURE            READY

        A        B        C        D        E        F        G        H
1   THIS WORKSHEET SHOWS THE EXAMPLE OF RANGE ERASE PROCEDURE
2
3   BEFORE RANGE ERASE PROCEDURE
4   LOTUS    LOTUS    LOTUS    LOTUS
5   LOTUS    LOTUS    LOTUS    LOTUS
6   LOTUS    LOTUS    LOTUS    LOTUS
7   LOTUS    LOTUS    LOTUS    LOTUS
8   LOTUS    LOTUS    LOTUS    LOTUS
9   LOTUS    LOTUS    LOTUS    LOTUS
10  LOTUS    LOTUS    LOTUS    LOTUS
11
12  AFTER RANGE ERASE PROCEDURE -- WE USED /RE B14..C18 (HIT RETURN)
13  LOTUS    LOTUS    LOTUS    LOTUS
14  LOTUS                      LOTUS
15  LOTUS                      LOTUS
16  LOTUS                      LOTUS
17  LOTUS                      LOTUS
18  LOTUS                      LOTUS
19  LOTUS    LOTUS    LOTUS    LOTUS
20
01-Jan-91  09:45 AM          UNDO
```

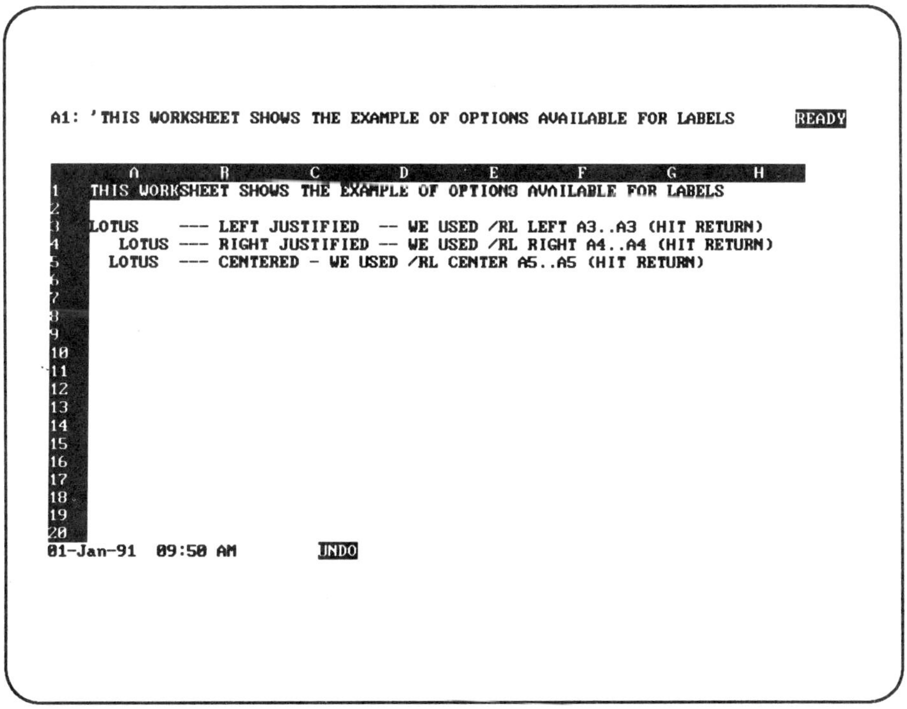

```
A1: 'THIS WORKSHEET SHOWS THE EXAMPLE OF OPTIONS AVAILABLE FOR LABELS      READY

        A        B        C        D        E        F        G        H
1   THIS WORKSHEET SHOWS THE EXAMPLE OF OPTIONS AVAILABLE FOR LABELS
2
3   LOTUS    --- LEFT JUSTIFIED  -- WE USED /RL LEFT A3..A3 (HIT RETURN)
4       LOTUS --- RIGHT JUSTIFIED -- WE USED /RL RIGHT A4..A4 (HIT RETURN)
5     LOTUS  --- CENTERED - WE USED /RL CENTER A5..A5 (HIT RETURN)
6
7
8
9
10
11
12
13
14
15
16
17
18
19
20
01-Jan-91  09:50 AM          UNDO
```

FIGURE 5-5 Example of /Range Label Command

5-8 /Range Name

To perform any Lotus operations in a certain range, two options are available. Let us say you are trying to add the contents of cells A1, A2, A3, and A4. You can refer to these four cells as A1..A4 or you can give this range a name; then from this point you may refer to the range by using its name. To name a range you must use the /Range Name Create command. A range name can have up to 14 characters. Try to use meaningful names and avoid names such as A14 or G23. These names are misleading because you do not know if they are cell addresses or range names.

You can use /Range Name Labels to name an adjacent cell. With this option you can use Right, Down, Left, and Up. To make this more clear, in a blank worksheet in cell D3, E3, F3, and G3 type Sam, Tom, Joe, and Sue. To assign these names to cells D4, E4, F4, and G4, respectively, do the following:

1. Position the cursor in cell which contains Sam (e.g. D3).
2. Invoke /Range Name Labels Down.
3. Specify D3. .G3 as the label range.
4. Press **Return**.

Now each name has been assigned to the cell right below it. You could select Up in order to assign these names to cells immediately above them, e.g., to cells D2, E2, F2, and G2.

To delete a range name use /Range Name Delete. This will erase a specific range name. To erase all the range names in your worksheet, you must use /Range Name Reset. What happens if you duplicate a range name? Lotus assigns the most recent range to the specific range name.

To get an alphabetical listing of all the range names and their addresses, use /Range Name Table. This command will give you the names of all the ranges in your current worksheet in alphabetical order. Remember to position the cursor in a blank area of the worksheet so the table does not overwrite good data. To issue this command all you need is the upper left corner cell of the table, which will show all range names. From this point on you will get the listing of all the range names.

When you try to use a new range name, if you are not sure which names have been utilized, press F3 in POINT mode. This will give all the range names that are already in your worksheet. Remember, whenever you save a worksheet the range names will also be saved.

Using range names can be much easier than using range addresses. For example, if you are designing a balance sheet your total assets would be the sum of current assets and fixed assets. All you need to use is the @SUM function. Type in the following formula: @SUM (current asset, fixed asset). (All Lotus functions will be discussed in Chapters 12 and 13.)

5-9 /Range Justify

This command treats a continuous column of text as a line. You can use it to break a long title or heading into several shorter ones. The shorter titles will be lined up in one or several columns; it is up to you how many columns will be occupied. All you need to do is type your title and use the /Range Justify command. Remember, if there is data underneath the line that you are justifying, that data will also be justified and moved down. Therefore, your data won't be destroyed. Figure 5-6 is a sample worksheet before justification. We choose /RJA1 . . A1 Return. The result is presented in Figure 5-7.

FIGURE 5-6 A Sample Worksheet

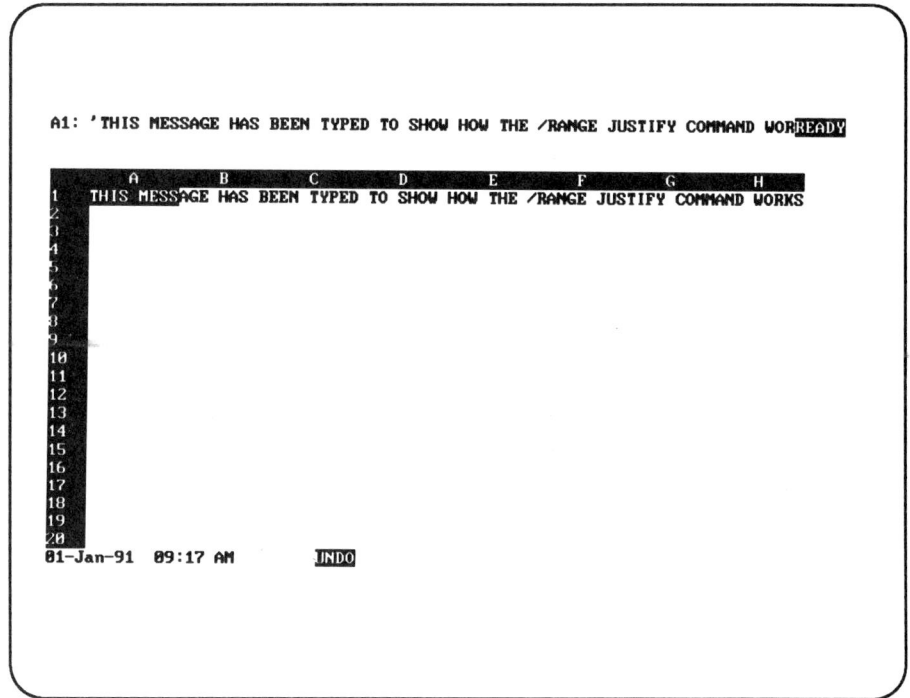

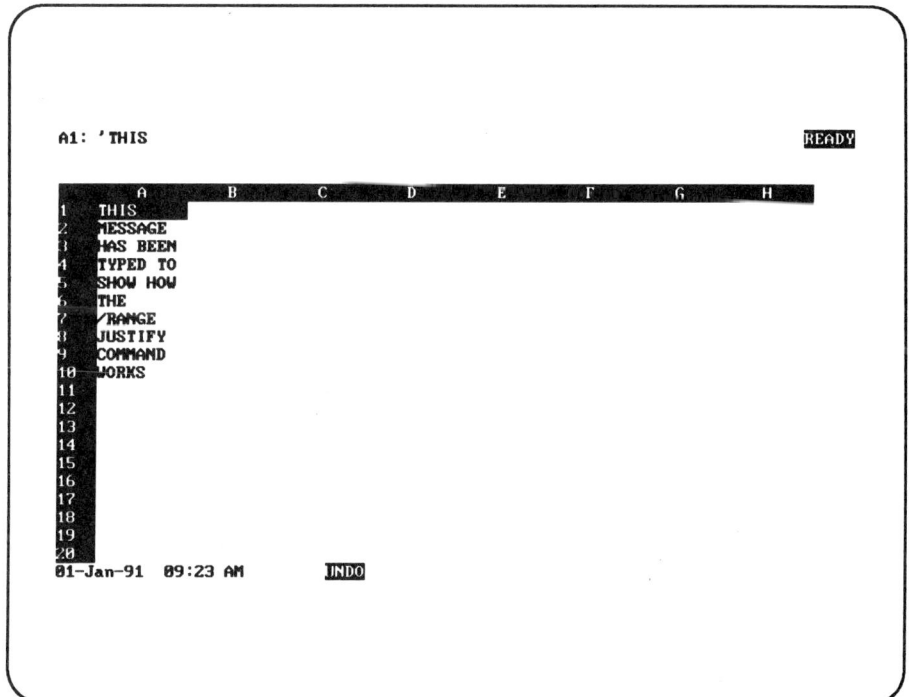

FIGURE 5-7 The Sample Worksheet Has Been Justified

5-10 /Range Transpose

This command exchanges the rows and columns of a given range; rows become columns and columns become rows. For example, a two-by-three table (two rows and three columns) becomes a three-by-two table (three rows and two columns). All you need to do is use the /Range Transpose command. Lotus will ask you for the original range. Specify the range and press the **Return** key. Now Lotus asks you the range for the transposed table. Specify only the upper left corner cell of the range and press the **Return** key. Be careful. If you direct the transposed table to a part of the worksheet that is already occupied, you will lose that portion of data. Figure 5-8 illustrates an example of this command.

5-11 /Range Value

This command converts formulas in a given range to their numeric values. Let us assume cells A1 and A2 contain values 5 and 10. Cell A3 contains +A1+A2. If you want to copy the exact value of this formula and not the formula itself, you must use the /Range Value command first to translate the formula to its numerical value, then do the copying.

To see how this command works, get Lotus started. Type 1 in cell A1 and 2 in cell B1. Move to cell D1 and add the first two cells by typing +A1+B1. You will see 3 in cell D1. With the /Copy command, copy cell D1 to cell D5 and in D5 you will see a zero. Why? As you will learn in the next section, Lotus transfers the relative address of a cell, so in cell D5 you will see +A5+B5, because we are in row 5. Since A5 and B5 are empty, they have the value of zero, therefore the final result is zero.

Go back to cell D1 and use the /Range Value command, then copy to cell D10 (or any other cell). You will now see 3, not 0, in D10.

5-12 Relative Addressing

Lotus maintains the address of a particular cell and compares it to the origin of the worksheet. For example, in relation to a formula in cell E10, cell G4 is two columns to the right and six rows above cell E10. To make this clear, look at Figure 5-9. In cell B11 we have the formula +B9+B8+B7+B6. If we copy this formula to cell C11, Lotus is smart enough to recognize that in this cell you have to add +C9+C8+C7+C6. If you copy the same formula to cells D11 and E11, in cell D11 you will see +D9+D8+D7+D6 and in cell E11 you will see +E9+E8+E7+E6. This is called *relative addressing*, a powerful feature. It will make the task of copying a more efficient operation. Let us say you have sales data related to 100 different businesses in the first 100 columns of a worksheet. To calculate the sum of each column, all you need to do is to type a formula for one column and then copy the same formula to the other 99 columns.

5-13 Absolute Addressing

There are many times when you must refer to an exact location or an exact value. Sometimes you may want to use some predefined numbers or ratios. In these cases you have to use *absolute addresses*. For example, in relation to a formula in cell E10, cell G4 is G4, when used as an absolute address.

To make this distinction clear, look at Figure 5-10. Five divisions of XYZ Company sold different amounts of a particular product. Your task is to calculate the percentage of

FIGURE 5-8 *Example of /Range Transpose Command*

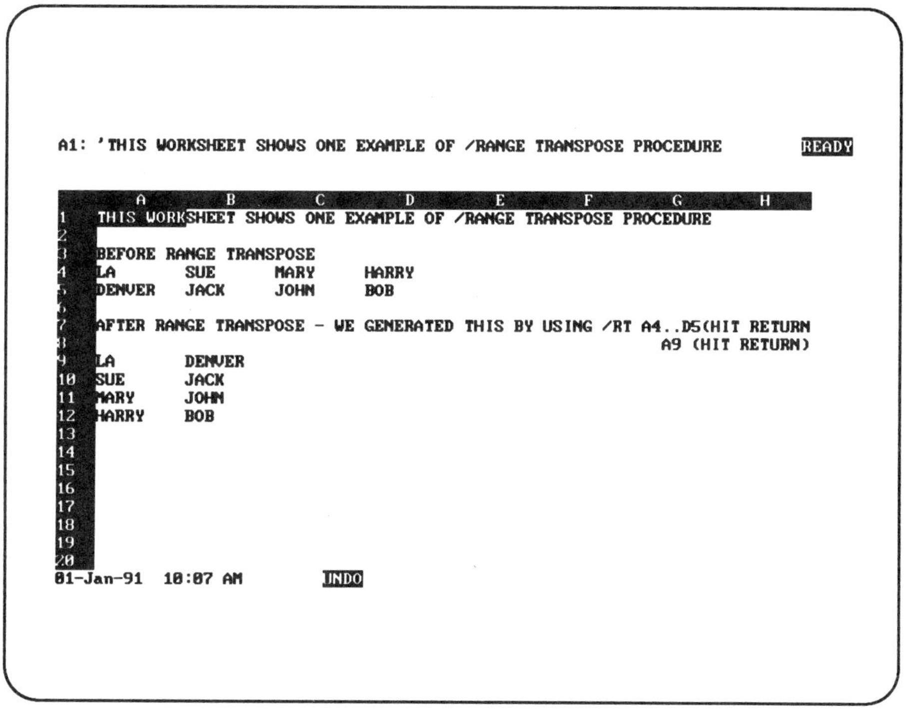

```
A1: 'THIS WORKSHEET SHOWS ONE EXAMPLE OF /RANGE TRANSPOSE PROCEDURE      READY

        A        B        C        D        E        F        G        H
1    THIS WORKSHEET SHOWS ONE EXAMPLE OF /RANGE TRANSPOSE PROCEDURE
2
3    BEFORE RANGE TRANSPOSE
4    LA       SUE      MARY     HARRY
5    DENVER   JACK     JOHN     BOB
6
7    AFTER RANGE TRANSPOSE - WE GENERATED THIS BY USING /RT A4..D5(HIT RETURN
8                                                       A9 (HIT RETURN)
9    LA       DENVER
10   SUE      JACK
11   MARY     JOHN
12   HARRY    BOB
13
14
15
16
17
18
19
20
01-Jan-91  10:07 AM          UNDO
```

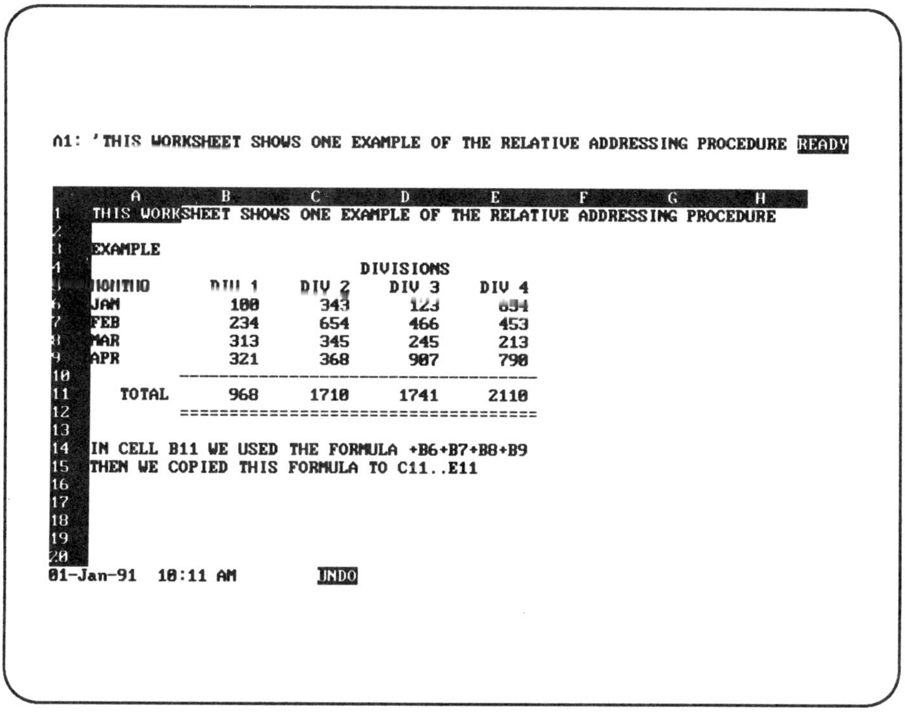

```
A1: 'THIS WORKSHEET SHOWS ONE EXAMPLE OF THE RELATIVE ADDRESSING PROCEDURE READY

        A        B        C        D        E        F        G        H
1    THIS WORKSHEET SHOWS ONE EXAMPLE OF THE RELATIVE ADDRESSING PROCEDURE
2
3    EXAMPLE
4                                  DIVISIONS
5    MONTH     DIV 1    DIV 2    DIV 3    DIV 4
6    JAN        100      343      123      654
7    FEB        234      654      466      453
8    MAR        313      345      245      213
9    APR        321      368      907      790
10             ------------------------------------
11    TOTAL     968     1710     1741     2110
12             ====================================
13
14   IN CELL B11 WE USED THE FORMULA +B6+B7+B8+B9
15   THEN WE COPIED THIS FORMULA TO C11..E11
16
17
18
19
20
01-Jan-91  10:11 AM          UNDO
```

FIGURE 5-9 *An Example of Relative Addressing*

FIGURE 5-10 An Example of Absolute Addressing

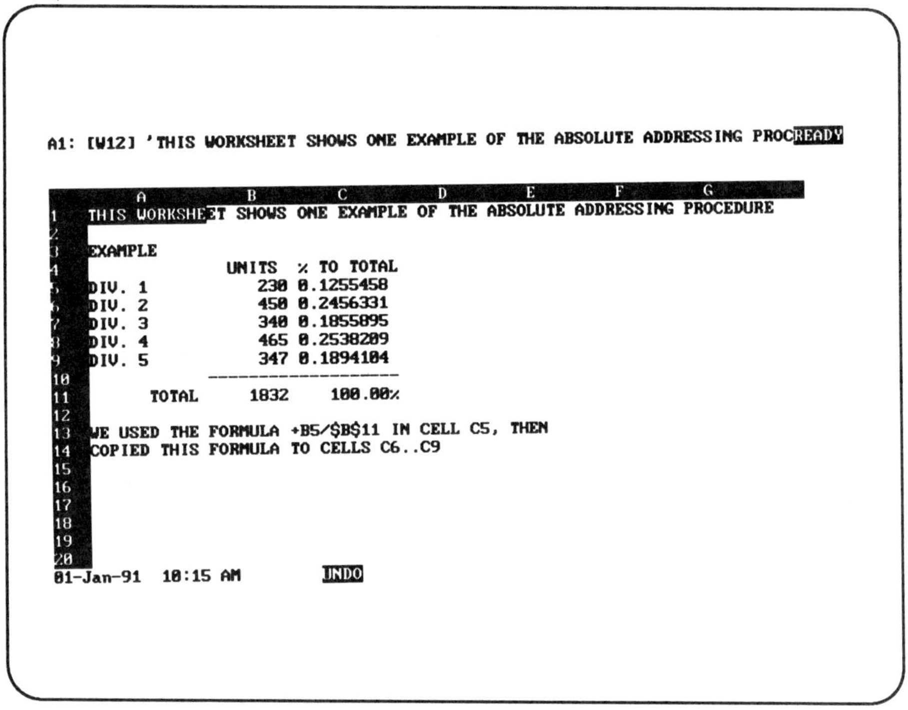

```
A1: [W12] 'THIS WORKSHEET SHOWS ONE EXAMPLE OF THE ABSOLUTE ADDRESSING PROC READY

          A           B        C        D        E        F        G
1    THIS WORKSHEET SHOWS ONE EXAMPLE OF THE ABSOLUTE ADDRESSING PROCEDURE
2
3    EXAMPLE
4                  UNITS   % TO TOTAL
5    DIV. 1          230   0.1255458
6    DIV. 2          450   0.2456331
7    DIV. 3          340   0.1855895
8    DIV. 4          465   0.2538209
9    DIV. 5          347   0.1894104
10                  -------------------
11       TOTAL      1832    100.00%
12
13   WE USED THE FORMULA +B5/$B$11 IN CELL C5, THEN
14   COPIED THIS FORMULA TO CELLS C6..C9
15
16
17
18
19
20
01-Jan-91  10:15 AM          UNDO
```

total sales for each division. In cell C5, type the formula +B5/B11. If you copy this formula to range C6..C9, you will get an error. In cell C6 you will see B6/B12. Cell B12 is empty, therefore it contains zero. The reason is that in every case the division unit must be divided by the total units currently in cell B11. Relative addressing will not work here. You have to make cell B11 absolute, meaning always fixed.

To make a cell absolute, put a dollar sign ($) in front of the row number and one in front of the column letter. You can either type ($) or use F4, the **Abs** function key. This key can change and show you four variations of relative, absolute, and mixed addressing. For example, if your cell address is A10 and in POINT mode you press F4 four times you will see $A$10, A$10, $A10, and finally A10. Remember, to use this key you must be in POINT mode. The simplest way to enter POINT mode is to press the F5 function key (**Goto** key).

Cell $B$11 is absolute. To make a range name absolute, precede it with a dollar sign, e.g., $ASSET.

In Figure 5-10, first we typed (+B5/$B$11) in Cell C5, then copied this formula to range C6..C9.

5-14 Mixed Addressing

In some cases you want to have both relative and absolute addressing. You can have either the row or the column fixed and the other absolute. For example, $A10 means that the column remains the same but the row changes; B$10 means that the row is fixed but the column changes. Figure 5-11 illustrates two examples of mixed addressing.

FIGURE 5-11 An Example of Mixed Addressing

```
A1: (G) [W9] 'THIS WORKSHEET SHOWS TWO EXAMPLES OF MIXED ADDRESSING          READY

        A         B         C         D         E         F         G         H
1   THIS WORKSHEET SHOWS TWO EXAMPLES OF MIXED ADDRESSING
2
3   EXAMPLE #1
4                         DISCOUNTED PRICE AT X%
5   PRICE           0.05      0.15      0.25      0.35      0.45      0.55      0.65
6           12      11.4      10.2         9       7.8       6.6       5.4       4.2
7           30      28.5      25.5      22.5      19.5      16.5      13.5      10.5
8
9   WE USED THE FORMULA +$A$6*(1-B$5) IN CELL B6,THEN COPIED THIS FORMULA TO
10  CELLS C6..H6.WE USED FORMULA +$A$7*(1-B$5) IN CELL B7 THEN COPIED TO
11  CELLS C7..H7.
12  EXAMPLE #2                     PRICES
13  DISCOUNT VALUE               60       100
14                  0.05         57        95
15                  0.15         51        85
16                  0.25         45        75
17                  0.35         39        65
18
19  WE USED THE FORMULA +$C$13*(1-$B14) IN CELL C14, +$D$13*(1-$B14) IN
20  CELL D14, THEN COPIED THE FORMULA TO CELLS C15..D17.
01-Jan-91  10:19 AM          UNDO
```

The first example in Figure 5-11 shows the discounted prices under different discount rates for two products whose original prices were $12 and $30.

The second example in this figure shows the same thing with a different format. Can you tell what is different?

5-15 /Range Search

The /Range Search command allows you to search a range of cells in order to find a particular string and replace it with another string. The size of the search string and the replacement string do not need to be identical. You can search in formulas, in labels, or in both. You can search only for a particular string, or you can search and then replace it with another string.

Figure 5-12 is a sample worksheet. In column A we typed BASIC and in column C we typed 100. In column D we typed +C1*2 and copied it down through row 20. Let us say you want to replace BASIC with COBOL and the +C1*2 formula with C1*3. This is how you would do it:

1. /Range, Search, A1..A20, **Return**, BASIC, **Return**, Labels, Replace, COBOL, **Return**, ALL.
2. /Range, Search, D1..D20, **Return**, 2, **Return**, Formulas, Replace, 3, **Return**, ALL.

The final worksheet is presented in Figure 5-13. Do you know why the content of cell D20 is 0? The reason is that +C20*2 was changed to C30*3 (both 2s were replaced by 3). Since C30 is an empty cell, this is why you received 0 in that cell.

FIGURE 5-12 A Sample Worksheet

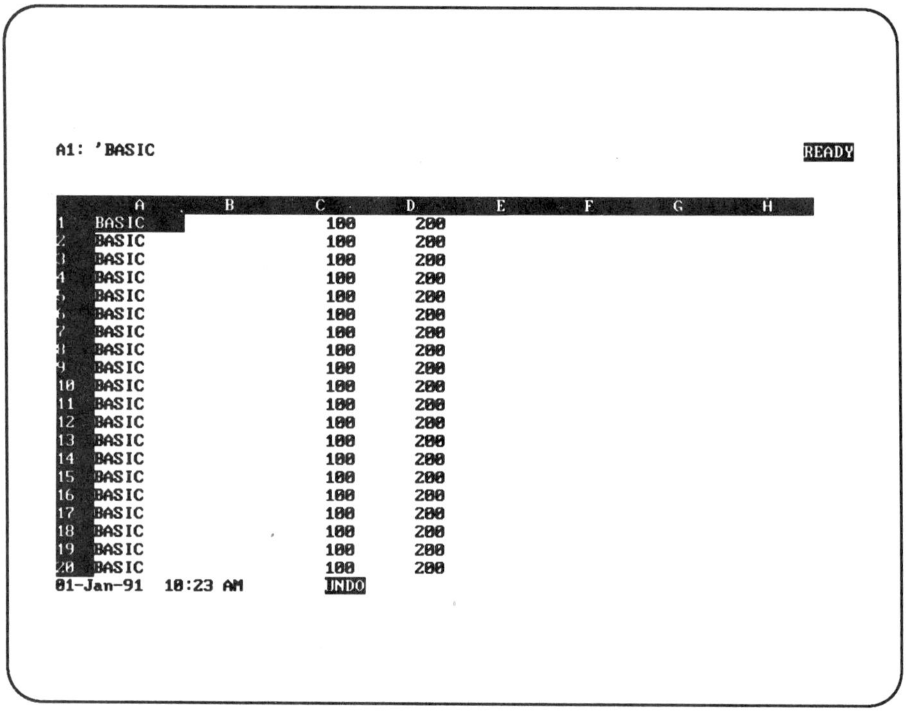

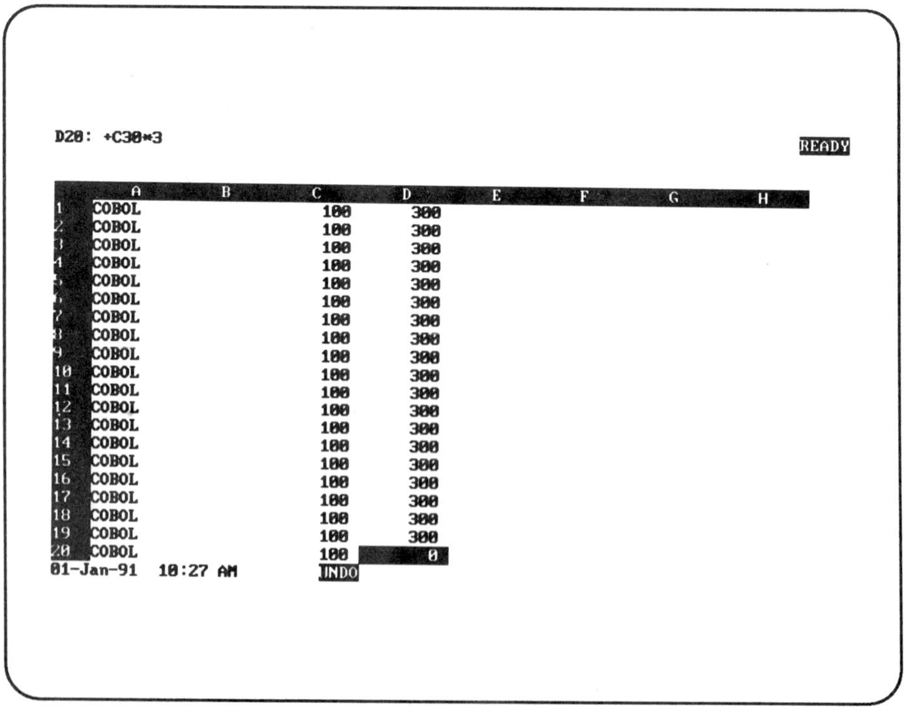

FIGURE 5-13 The Sample Worksheet after Search and Replace Operations

The search feature can be particularly helpful if you want to replace a variable in a series of complex formulas. The search and replace feature can be useful when there are several cells in a worksheet that needs to be modified to reflect a new value, but you are unsure about their specific location.

SUMMARY

In this chapter we explained a series of commands helpful for manipulating a portion of your worksheet, or a range. You can erase, name, transpose, and search a range. Relative, absolute, and mixed addressing are features that let you manipulate references to cells and ranges.

Review Questions

* These questions are answered in Appendix I.
1. What is a range?
2.* Can a range and a worksheet be the same?
3. Can you copy one cell to 20 cells? If yes, how?
4. What are the advantages of the pointing technique?
5. What is the function of /Range Label Center?
6. How do you erase a range?
7. How do you name a range?
8.* How do you know a range name has not been used already?
9. How do you erase all range names?
10. How many characters can be used as a range name?
11. What are some applications of the /Range Justify command?
12. What is the application of the /Range Value command?
13. What are some uses of the /Range Transpose command?
14. What is relative addressing?
15. Why can relative addressing be dangerous?
16. What is mixed addressing?
17.* How do you make a range name absolute?
18. Can a cell have both absolute and relative addresses at the same time?
19. What are some of the applications of /Range Search?

HANDS-ON PRACTICE

1. Type COBOL in cell A1, then center it using /Range Label Center.
2. Type 10, 20, 30, and 40 in cells A1 to A4. Using the appropriate command, give this range a valid name.
3. Using /Range Transpose, first generate a five-by-three table, then make it a three-by-five.
4. Enter 10, 20, and 30 in cells A1 to A3. Add them up and store the result in cell G1. Copy this cell to cell H1. Use /Range Value first and do the copying again. What is the difference?
5. Complete the worksheet in Figure 5-14.
6. Do the exercise shown in Figure 5-15.

FIGURE 5-14 *A Sample Worksheet*

```
A1: 'EXERCISE TO UNDERSTAND ABSOLUTE VALUES                          READY

      A        B        C        D        E        F        G        H
 1  EXERCISE TO UNDERSTAND ABSOLUTE VALUES
 2  =======================================
 3
 4        PERCENT TO BE USED FOR COLUMN D          12.0%
 5
 6
 7                  AMOUNT   FIXED %  % TOTAL
 8                  ------------------------------
 9                  120,000                           Fill out columns
10                   23,456                           D and E by using
11                   32,000                           absolute addresses
12                   45,000                           in the formulas as
13                   49,125                           you see fit.
14                   34,560                           Include the totals
15                  250,000                           and formats to
16                  ------------------------------    make it look nice.
17        TOTALS
18                  ============================
19
20
01-Jan-91  10:31 AM            UNDO
```

```
A7: [W7] 1986                                                       READY

      A        B        C        D        E        F        G        H
 1            ALPHA-TEK ACCOUNTS RECEIVABLE SUMMARY
 2                      (Range-Label Exercise)
 3
 4            BEGINNING    END      TOTAL
 5   YEAR     BALANCE    BALANCE    PAID    INTEREST
 6
 7   1986      60,000     55,000    5,717      717
 8   1987      88,000     85,000    3,430      430
 9   1988     324,500    300,000   28,015    3,515
10   1989     125,750    115,000   12,292    1,542
11   1990      18,000     14,000    4,574      574
12
13        Use /Range Name Create to give a
14        name to the data in the "TOTAL PAID"
15        column.  Also perform /Range Name Label
16        to label cells B8, B9, B10, B11, B12 with
17        the years that are labels.
18        Then see results using /Range Name Table.
19
20
01-Jan-91  11:50 PM            UNDO                          NUM
```

FIGURE 5-15 *A Sample Worksheet*

COMPREHENSIVE LAB ASSIGNMENT

Retrieve CHAPT4 and perform the following:
1. Move all graduate students to the top of the worksheet.
2. Move the entire worksheet down four rows.
3. Enter a title for the entire worksheet as follows:
   This worksheet illustrates the performance of a group of students in the Lotus class.
4. Using /Range Justify, justify this title into two lines.
5. Save the final worksheet under CHAPT5.

MISCONCEPTIONS AND SOLUTIONS

M – If you have a series of range names in a worksheet and delete a portion of that worksheet by using /Worksheet Delete or /Range Erase, your range becomes undefined, even though the names are still intact.

S – First check the addresses and listing of all your range names by using F3 in POINT mode. Then issue the command to erase.

M – The /Move command does not transfer cell addresses in the same way that the /Copy command does. /Copy transfers relative addresses of cells. Absolute cell addresses will be transferred as absolute with /Copy but not with /Move. For example, in cells A1 and B1 type numbers 1 and 2 respectively, then use the formula $A$1+$B$1 in cell C1. Transfer this entire row to row 10 by using /Copy. You will see in cell C10 the same formula as in cell C1. If you move the original row to row 10, you will see $A$10+$B$10 in cell C10.

S – Don't try to transfer absolute addresses with the /Move command.

M – /Range Name Table will give you a listing of all the range names. This command may overwrite a part of your worksheet.

S – Before invoking this command, find an empty location in your worksheet. Then invoke the command.

M – You cannot use /Range Justify if any cells in a particular range are protected.

S – First use /Worksheet Global Protection Disable to turn off the protection facility, then use /Range Justify.

M – Using /Range Transpose, if a particular range contains formulas with relative addresses, Lotus won't adjust relative addresses to refer to the same cells.

S – Use /Move instead.

M – In the middle of your spreadsheet you see the error message ILLEGAL CELL OR RANGE ADDRESS.

S – Check your range specification to see if this is what you wanted to do. You may have typed an undefined range.

Lotus Commands/ Part Two

6-1 Introduction

In this chapter we will explain /Worksheet commands. /Worksheet commands have been divided into two groups. The first group controls the entire worksheet. These are called /Worksheet Global commands. For example, /Worksheet Global Column-Width is used to set the column width for the entire worksheet. The second group controls only part of a worksheet. For example, /Worksheet Column Set-Width allows you to set the column width for one column of the current worksheet.

6-2 Worksheet Global Commands

If you choose the /Worksheet Global command from the main menu, you will see the following menu:

Format Label-Prefix Column-Width Recalculation Protection Default Zero

In this chapter we will explain these options. See Figure 6-1.

6-3 /Worksheet Global Label-Prefix

If you choose /Worksheet Global Label-Prefix from the main menu, you will be presented with the following three choices:

Left Right Center

As we discussed in Chapter 2, either enter a label prefix manually or use these commands for inserting left, right, or center justification. Remember that by default numbers are right-justified and labels are left-justified.

You should always issue the command and then type data into the worksheet. The command has no effect on data already entered in the worksheet.

6-4 /Worksheet Global Column-Width

This command enables you to set the column width for the entire worksheet. By default, the size of the column is nine characters. In many cases this default setting must be

FIGURE 6-1 *Options under the /Worksheet Global Command*

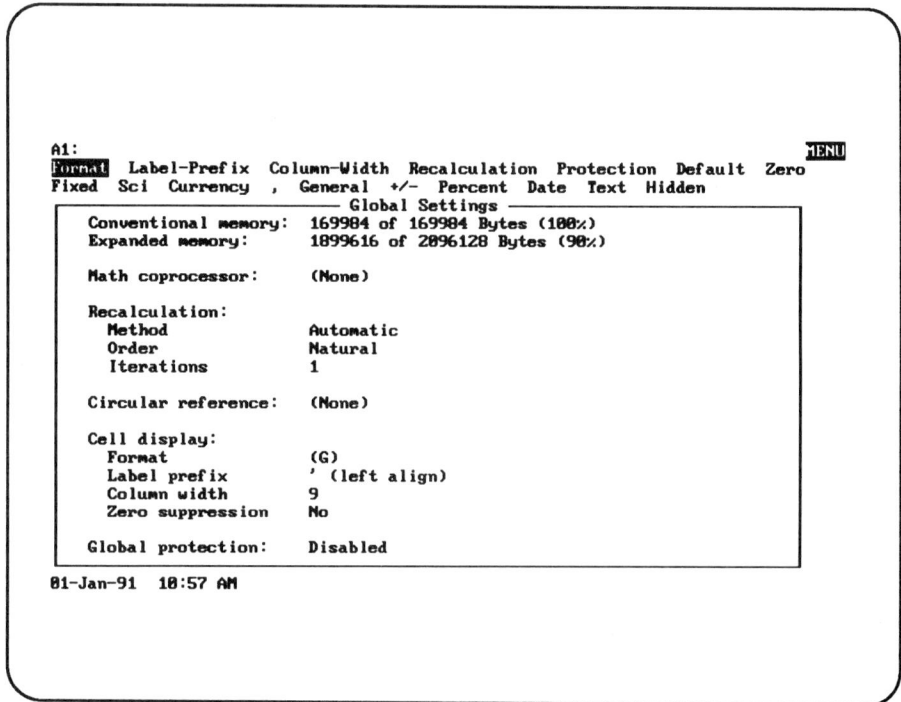

```
A1:                                                                    MENU
Format  Label-Prefix  Column-Width  Recalculation  Protection  Default  Zero
Fixed  Sci  Currency  ,  General  +/-  Percent  Date  Text  Hidden
─────────────────────── Global Settings ───────────────────
      Conventional memory:    169984 of 169984 Bytes (100%)
      Expanded memory:        1899616 of 2096128 Bytes (90%)

      Math coprocessor:       (None)

      Recalculation:
        Method                Automatic
        Order                 Natural
        Iterations            1

      Circular reference:     (None)

      Cell display:
        Format                (G)
        Label prefix          '  (left align)
        Column width          9
        Zero suppression      No

      Global protection:      Disabled

  01-Jan-91  10:57 AM
```

changed. For long names or labels you must extend the column width; for short labels or numbers you may want to reduce this default setting. For example, for a Sex field you need a column width of one character, e.g., M or F. The column width can be changed to any number between 1 and 240, inclusive. Figure 6-2 shows the default setting.

Figure 6-3 shows the column width extended to 12 characters. To select this option, type /Worksheet Global Column-Width, then type any number between 1 to 240 inclusive and press **Return**.

6-5 /Worksheet Global Recalculation

If you choose Worksheet Global Recalculation from the main menu, you will be given the following menu:

Natural Columnwise Rowwise Automatic Manual Iteration

In the *Natural* option, Lotus will first recalculate all values that have an impact on a particular formula. For example, if a formula in cell A10 depends on cell H35, Lotus first recalculates cell H35 and then goes to cell A10.

In the *Columnwise* option, all columns will be recalculated first, from A to B to C, etc., from top to bottom.

In the *Rowwise* option, all rows will be recalculated first, from 1 to 2, to 3, etc., from left to right.

In *Automatic*, Lotus recalculates the entire worksheet whenever you change any value. This is the default setting. However, you should remember that Release 2.2 uses the

FIGURE 6-2 Default Column-Width Setting

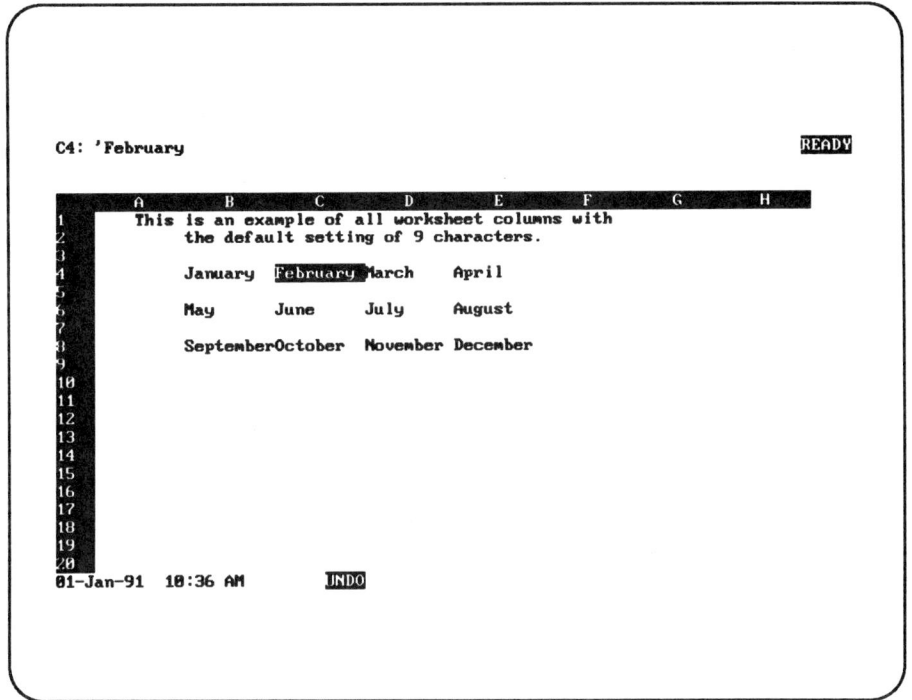

```
C4: 'February                                                          READY

        A       B        C        D        E        F        G       H
1           This is an example of all worksheet columns with
2           the default setting of 9 characters.
3
4           January  February March    April
5
6           May      June     July     August
7
8           SeptemberOctober  November December
9
10
11
12
13
14
15
16
17
18
19
20
01-Jan-91  10:36 AM            UNDO
```

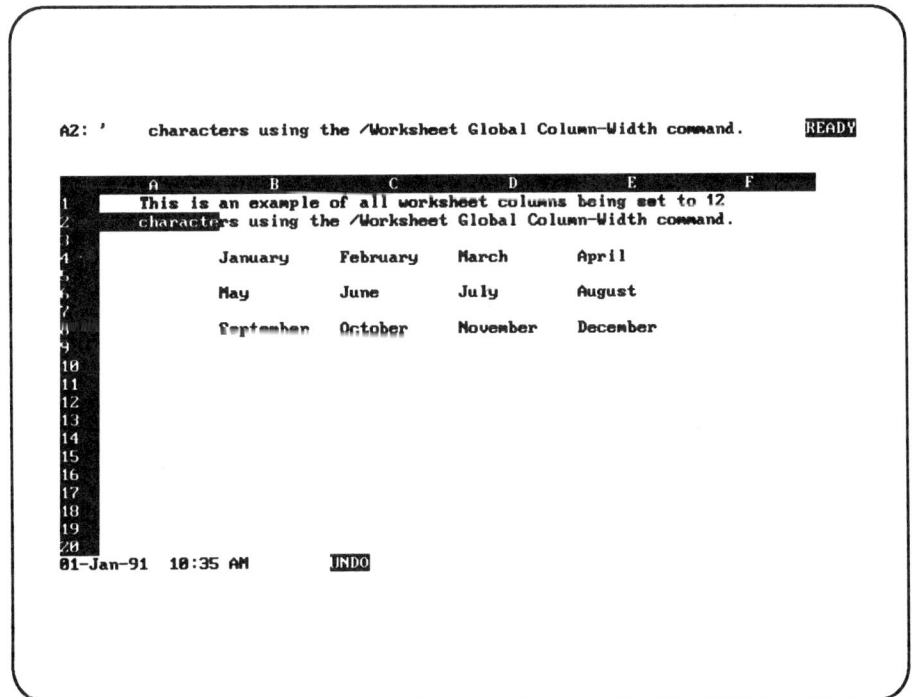

```
A2: '    characters using the /Worksheet Global Column-Width command.    READY

        A        B        C        D        E        F
1           This is an example of all worksheet columns being set to 12
2           characters using the /Worksheet Global Column-Width command.
3
4           January      February     March        April
5
6           May          June         July         August
7
8           September    October      November     December
9
10
11
12
13
14
15
16
17
18
19
20
01-Jan-91  10:35 AM            UNDO
```

FIGURE 6-3 Column-Width Extended to 12 Characters

optimal recalculation. This means it only recalculates those cells that are affected by the change.

In the *Manual* option, Lotus recalculates the entire worksheet whenever you press F9. This is a very useful option if you are dealing with a large worksheet and you do not want to spend a lot of time recalculating the worksheet for a minor change. It is also useful when you are making many changes but you don't need to see intermediate results. Enter all your changes, then press F9.

In the *Iteration* option, Lotus uses an iteration number between 1 and 50 for Columnwise, Rowwise, and Natural options or whenever there is a circular reference (a cell referring to itself). When the iteration number is reached, the calculation will stop.

6-6 /Worksheet Global Protection

This command works in conjunction with /Range Protect and /Range Unprotect to protect a worksheet or a portion of a worksheet from unwanted changes. When you issue this command (/WGP) you will be given two choices: Enable or Disable. With the Enable facility on, only unprotected areas can be accessed and modified. Remember, the / Worksheet Erase command can always erase your protected or unprotected worksheet.

To make this discussion more clear, we will walk through an example.

From the main menu choose WGP. You will be given two options: Enable or Disable. Choose the Enable option. As soon as you choose this option you will see the PR sign on the control panel. This means that your worksheet is now protected.

6-7 /Range Protect and /Range Unprotect

You can protect a portion of your worksheet from being deleted by using the /Range Protect command. This means that you will not be able to erase this portion accidentally. To use this command, first you must use /Worksheet Global Protection Enable in order to turn on the protection facility. Now you can remove the protection from any range in the worksheet with the /Range Unprotect command, enter data into the range, and then protect it using the /Range Protect command. If a range is protected and you try to erase its contents, you will get an error message.

To verify this, try to enter a data item anywhere in the worksheet. For example, type check and press the **Return** key. You will hear a beep and "protected cell" appears at the bottom of the screen. This means that you cannot enter anything in this worksheet.

To cancel this facility, again choose WGP from the main menu. This time choose the Disable option. When you do this, the PR sign will disappear.

You may be interested in protecting a portion of the worksheet, but you want a range such as A1..H10 to be unprotected. To do this follow the following steps:

1. Choose WGP from the main menu.
2. Choose the Enable option. Now the entire worksheet is protected.
3. Choose Range Unprotect from the main menu.
4. Type A1..H10 to be unprotected.
5. Press **Return**.

Now you can enter data only in range A1..H10. The rest of the worksheet is protected.

Again, to remove the protection from the entire worksheet, choose /WGP and then choose Disable.

6-8 /Range Input

This command can be used to limit user input to a particular unprotected portion of the worksheet; thus, it can be very helpful during data-entry routines. If you use the command /Range Input and specify a range, you can move the cursor only to the unprotected cells in the range.

To see how the /Range Input command works, get Lotus started. Use /Worksheet Global Protection Enable in order to protect the entire worksheet. At this point, you cannot enter any data into this worksheet; all of it is protected.

Use the /Range Unprotect command to remove protection from range A1..A10. You can now enter data into this range with no problem. Now use the /Range Input command and define A1..A5 as your input range. At this point you can only move back and forth between A1 and A5, inclusive. There is no way to get out of this area. Using this technique, you can limit beginning users to a specified portion of your worksheet so that they cannot mistakenly erase or damage your worksheet.

Several keys can be used with /Range Input. These include **Backspace, Edit, End, Escape, Help, Home, Return, Down, Left, Right,** and **Up. End** will move the cursor to the end of the Input range. **Home** will move the cursor to the beginning of the Input range, and so on. To terminate the /Range Input command, press **Escape** or **Return** without typing any data.

6-9 /Worksheet Global Default

When you choose Worksheet Global Default from the main menu, you will be presented with the following menu (see Figure 6-4):

Printer Directory Status Update Other Autoexec Quit

The *Printer* option will give all the settings for the printer, as follows:

• Interface describes the connection between Lotus and your printer (parallel or serial).
• AutoLF tells you whether your printer automatically issues a line feed after a carriage return.
• Left sets the left margin; default is 4.
• Right sets the right margin; default is 76.
• Top sets the top margin; default is 2.
• Bottom sets the bottom margin; default is 2.
• Pg-Length sets page length; default is 66.
• Wait allows you to pause.
• Setup specifies a string of control characters; default is a blank (see Chapter 9).
• Name tells you which printer to use; default is the first printer.
• Quit gets you out of the Printer menu.

The Directory option tells you the current directory.

The Status option gives you the present default settings of your system, for example, left margin, right margin, and so forth. This is a helpful command to use periodically in order to find out the default settings of your system. (See Figure 6-5.)

The Update option enables you to save current settings in the configuration file (123.CNF file). If you change the default drive from B to A or C, you must use /Worksheet Global Default Update in order to save these new settings. If you do not do this, the next

FIGURE 6-4 Options under /Worksheet Global Default

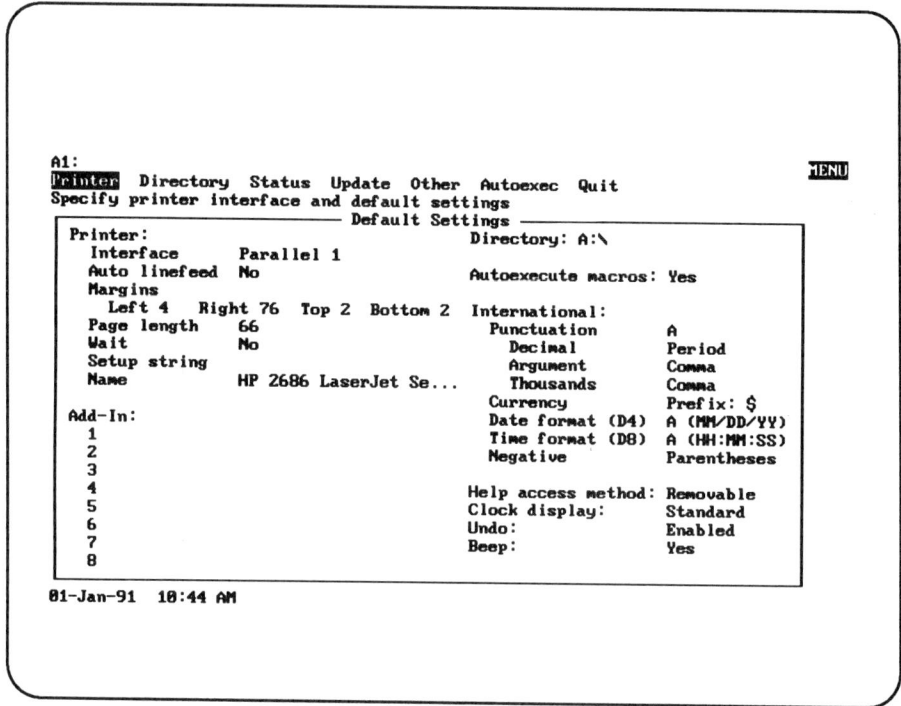

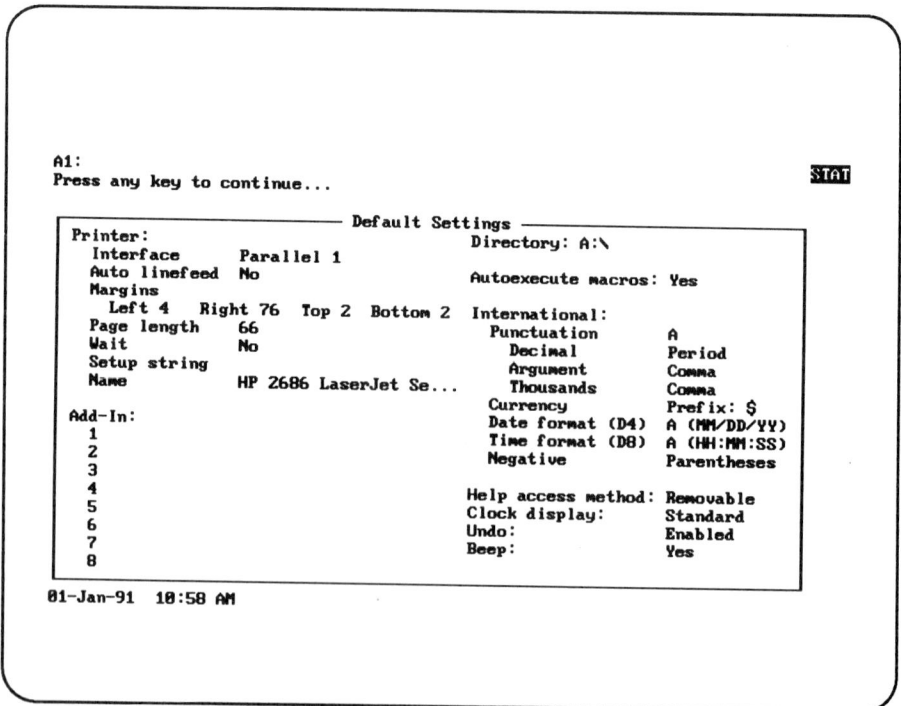

```
A1:                                                                    MENU
Printer  Directory  Status  Update  Other  Autoexec  Quit
Specify printer interface and default settings
                           ─── Default Settings ───
 Printer:                                  Directory: A:\
  Interface      Parallel 1
  Auto linefeed  No                        Autoexecute macros: Yes
  Margins
   Left 4   Right 76   Top 2  Bottom 2  International:
  Page length    66                          Punctuation      A
  Wait           No                            Decimal        Period
  Setup string                                 Argument       Comma
  Name           HP 2686 LaserJet Se...        Thousands      Comma
                                             Currency       Prefix: $
 Add-In:                                     Date format (D4)  A (MM/DD/YY)
  1                                          Time format (D8)  A (HH:MM:SS)
  2                                          Negative       Parentheses
  3
  4                                        Help access method: Removable
  5                                        Clock display:     Standard
  6                                        Undo:              Enabled
  7                                        Beep:              Yes
  8
 01-Jan-91  10:44 AM
```

```
A1:                                                                    STAT
Press any key to continue...
                           ─── Default Settings ───
 Printer:                                  Directory: A:\
  Interface      Parallel 1
  Auto linefeed  No                        Autoexecute macros: Yes
  Margins
   Left 4   Right 76   Top 2  Bottom 2  International:
  Page length    66                          Punctuation      A
  Wait           No                            Decimal        Period
  Setup string                                 Argument       Comma
  Name           HP 2686 LaserJet Se...        Thousands      Comma
                                             Currency       Prefix: $
 Add-In:                                     Date format (D4)  A (MM/DD/YY)
  1                                          Time format (D8)  A (HH:MM:SS)
  2                                          Negative       Parentheses
  3
  4                                        Help access method: Removable
  5                                        Clock display:     Standard
  6                                        Undo:              Enabled
  7                                        Beep:              Yes
  8
 01-Jan-91  10:58 AM
```

FIGURE 6-5 Options under /Worksheet Global Default Status time you access your worksheet, your current directory will be B. If you do not want to save this new change, you must use /Worksheet Global Default Quit to leave the menu.

The Other option will give the following choices:

• International—Under this option you get Punctuation, Currency, Date, Time and Quit. Punctuation describes the characters used by Lotus for thousands separators, argument separators, etc. Currency tells you the sign used for currency, e.g., $. Date specifies different date options (discussed in Chapter 7). Time will give you four different time formats (discussed in Chapter 7). Quit will put you back into the previous menu.

• Help—This option is used for accessing the Help facility. You have two choices: Instant and Removable. If you choose the Instant option, Lotus provides you with Help when you press F1. If you choose the Removable option, Lotus closes the Help facility whenever you leave. To make this change permanent, you have to use the Update command.

• Clock—This option gives you the format for the date and time presented in the lower left portion of your screen. There are three options: Standard, International, and None. The Standard option is the default setting. If you choose the International option, you must use the international settings for date (D4) and time (D9), as discussed in Chapter 7. If you choose None, the date and time will not be displayed on the screen. This is nice if you do not want to see these items all the time.

• Undo—Turns the UNDO feature on or off.

• Beep—Determines if the computer bell will sound when an error occurs.

• Add-In—Specifies add-ins to be loaded automatically whenever you start 1-2-3.

6-10 /Worksheet Global Zero

This command gives you the option of displaying or suppressing zeros in the worksheet. If you invoke /Worksheet Global Zero, you will be given No and Yes options. Choosing Yes will suppress the display of zero. Refer to the worksheet presented in Figure 6-6. As you see in this figure, there is a zero in cell D9. In Figure 6-7 we have used the /WGZY command. As you see, the zero has been suppressed. You can also use /WGZ Label and specify a label such as NA (not available or not applicable), None, Zero, etc. In this case one of these labels will be displayed in place of the zero.

6-11 /Worksheet Insert

This command allows you to insert either a row or a column into your worksheet. This command can be very helpful during database operations, discussed in Chapter 16. To activate this command, type /Worksheet Insert. Lotus gives you the options of Column or Row. Choose either Row or Column, then press the **Return** key. Lotus will ask for the cell address of the row or the column. For row or column insertion all you need is the address of one cell. For example, D1..D1 will insert a blank in column D if the option chosen was Column. A1..A1 will insert a blank in Row 1 if the option chosen was Row.

Figure 6-8 is a sample worksheet in which we will insert a row and a column. For row insertion we typed /WIR A5..A5 **Return**. For column insertion we types /WIC C1..C1 **Return**. As you see in Figure 6-9, column C is empty and the other columns have been shifted one column to the right. Also row 5 is empty and the other rows have been shifted one row down.

FIGURE 6-6 *A Sample Worksheet for Zero Suppression*

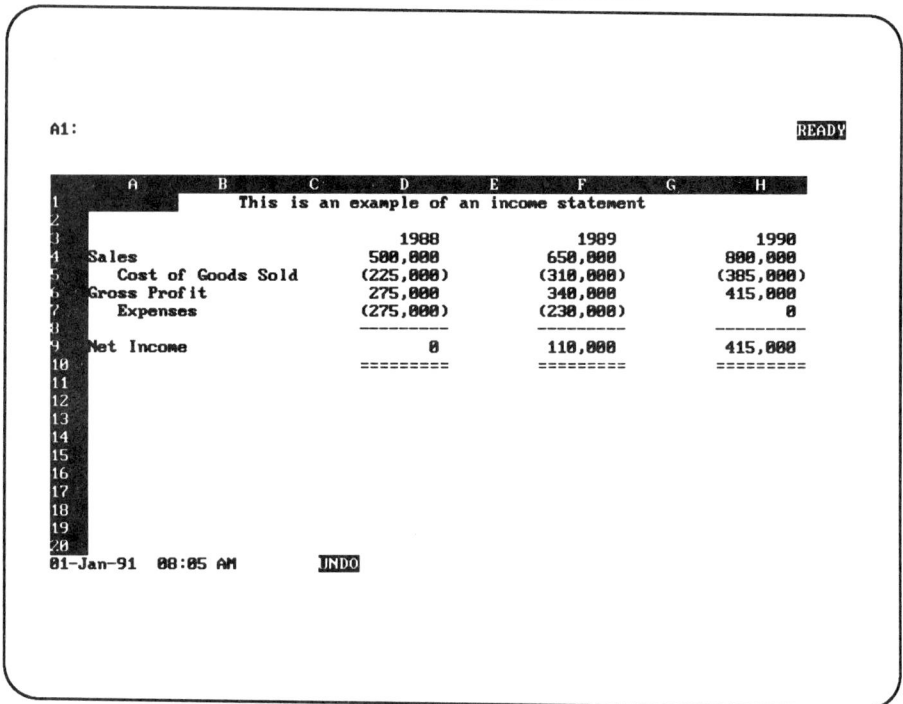

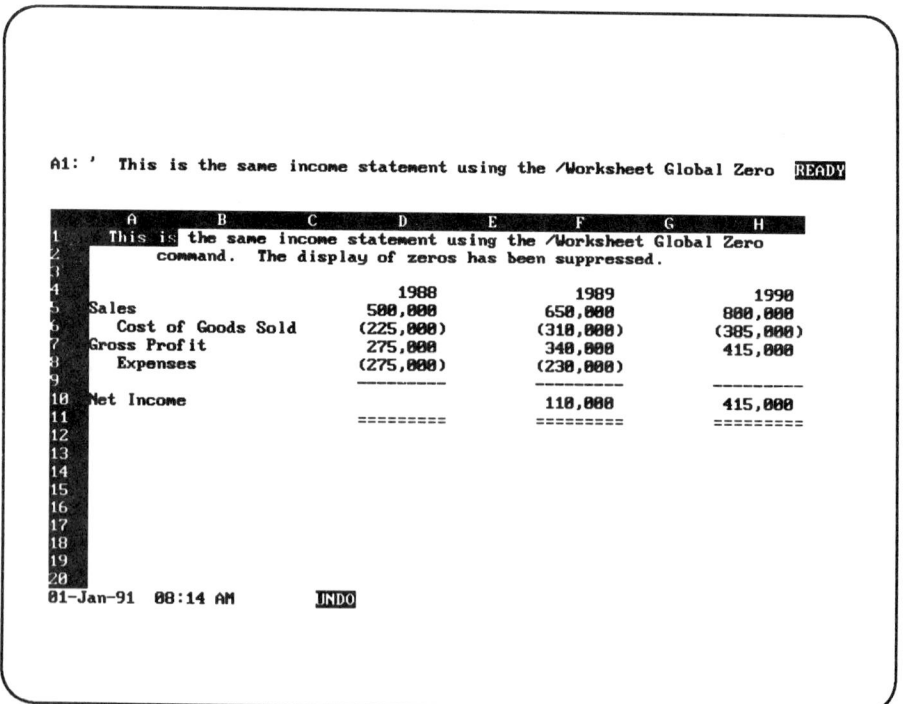

```
A1:                                                                    READY

          A        B        C        D        E        F        G        H
 1                    This is an example of an income statement
 2
 3                                      1988              1989              1990
 4    Sales                          500,000           650,000           800,000
 5        Cost of Goods Sold        (225,000)         (310,000)         (385,000)
 6    Gross Profit                   275,000           340,000           415,000
 7        Expenses                  (275,000)         (230,000)                0
 8                                 ----------        ----------        ----------
 9    Net Income                           0           110,000           415,000
10                                 =========         =========         =========
11
12
13
14
15
16
17
18
19
20
01-Jan-91  08:05 AM              UNDO
```

```
A1: '   This is the same income statement using the /Worksheet Global Zero   READY

          A        B        C        D        E        F        G        H
 1           This is the same income statement using the /Worksheet Global Zero
 2              command.  The display of zeros has been suppressed.
 3
 4                                      1988              1989              1990
 5    Sales                          500,000           650,000           800,000
 6        Cost of Goods Sold        (225,000)         (310,000)         (385,000)
 7    Gross Profit                   275,000           340,000           415,000
 8        Expenses                  (275,000)         (230,000)
 9                                 ----------        ----------        ----------
10    Net Income                                       110,000           415,000
11                                 =========         =========         =========
12
13
14
15
16
17
18
19
20
01-Jan-91  08:14 AM              UNDO
```

FIGURE 6-7 *Sample Worksheet Using /Worksheet Global Zone*

FIGURE 6-8 A Sample Worksheet for Row and Column Insertion

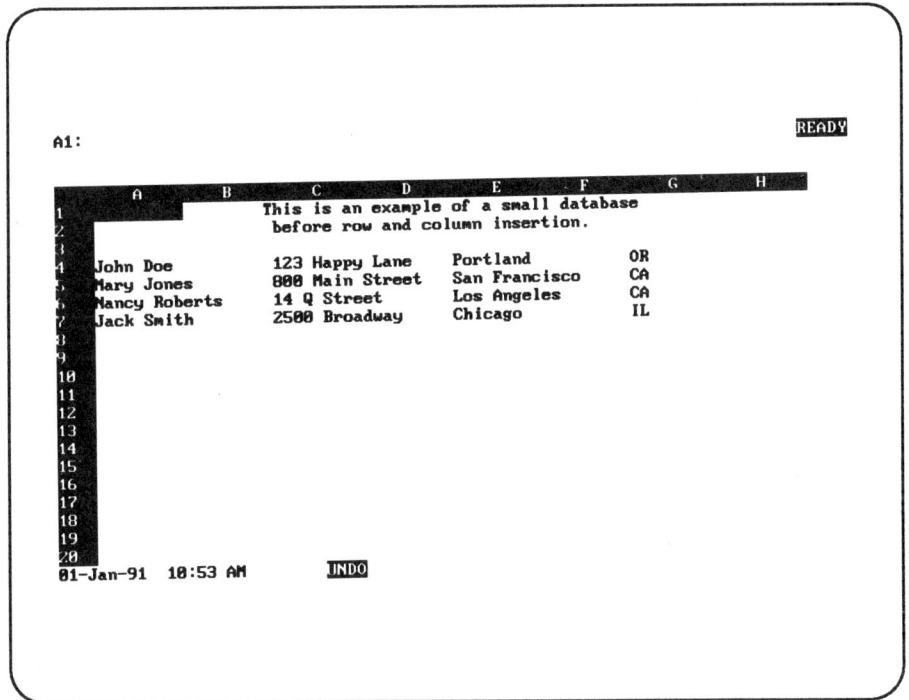

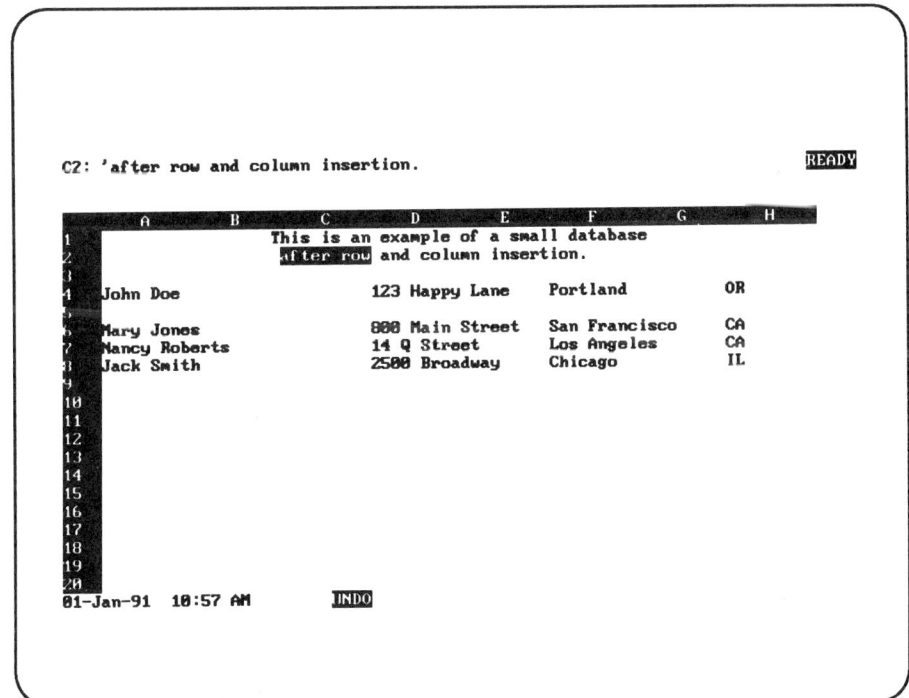

FIGURE 6-9 A Worksheet with One Row and One Column Inserted

6-12 /Worksheet Delete

This command allows you to delete rows or columns. When you invoke /WD you will be given two options: Row and Column. When you delete a row or column with this command, the deleted area will be closed up.

In Figure 6-10, we deleted the empty row and the empty column. The row was deleted with /WDR A5..A5 (Return). The column was deleted with /WDC C1..C1 (Return). The result is presented in Figure 6-10.

6-13 /Worksheet Column

If you type Worksheet Column from the main menu, you will be given the following options:

Set-Width   Reset-Width   Hide   Display   Column-Range

Set-Width allows you to change the width of a column. The default setting is 9 characters. You can extend the size of a column from 1 to 240 characters, inclusive. Reset-Width allows you to return the column width to its default setting.

The Hide option allows you to hide a portion of the worksheet without erasing anything. This command is useful in report generation. You may hide data that you do not want to print and redisplay it after printing.

The Display option redisplays the hidden columns, which will be marked by asterisks next to the column letters.

If you are interested in setting the width of several consecutive columns you either have to use /Worksheet Column several times or use the /Worksheet Column Column-Range command. The second option is a much more efficient method of doing this. Let us say you would like to reset the width of columns A through E to 12. Follow these steps:

1. /Worksheet, Column, Column-Range, Set-Width, A1 .. E1, **Return**
2. 12, **Return**

To reset these columns back to their normal settings:

3. /WCC, Reset-Width, A1 .. E1, **Return**

6-14 /Worksheet Erase

This command allows you to erase the entire worksheet. If you invoke /Worksheet Erase, you will be given two options: Yes and No. The Yes option erases the worksheet. Be careful. Make sure that this is what you want to do. If you haven't saved it, the erased worksheet is gone for good.

6-15 /Worksheet Titles

The /Worksheet Titles command freezes rows or columns along the top or left side of the screen. This enables you to see either the top portion, the side portion, or both portions of your worksheet as you move around it. If you use /Worksheet Titles, you will be given the following options:

Both   Horizontal   Vertical   Clear

FIGURE 6-10 A Sample Worksheet after an Empty Row and an Empty Column Have Been Deleted

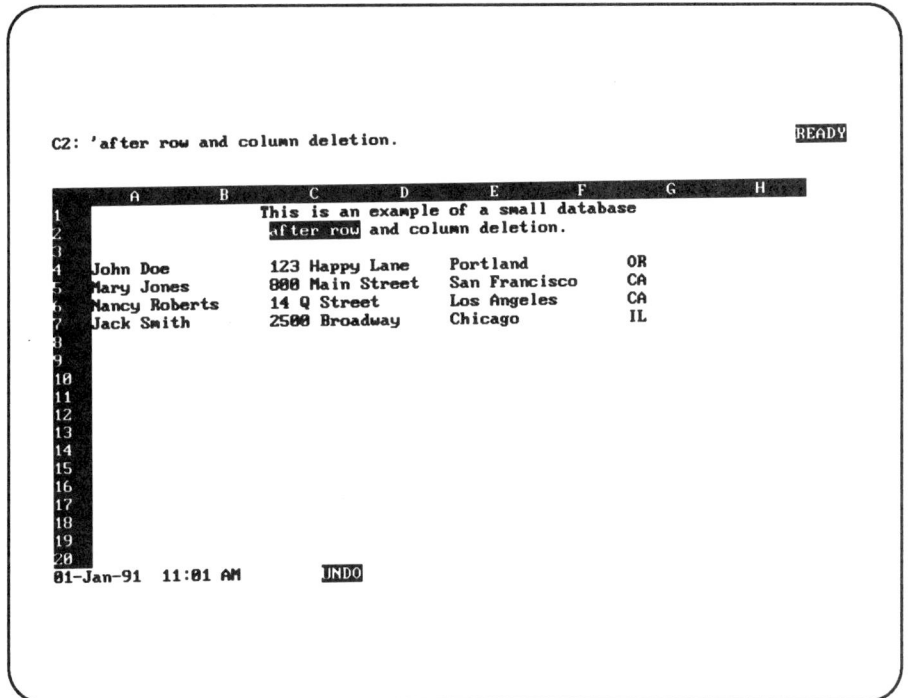

- Both freezes the rows above and the columns to the left of the cursor.
- Horizontal freezes the rows above the cursor. This means you can move around the cursor vertically in the worksheet, but the row or rows above the cursor are fixed.
- Vertical freezes the columns to the left of the cursor. This means you can move around the cursor horizontally in the worksheet but the column or columns to the left of the cursor are fixed.
- Clear unfreezes the worksheet.

To see this command in use, type in the worksheet presented in Figure 6-11. Dc the following:

1. Move the cursor to cell A5.
2. Select /WTH.

At this point lines 1 through 4 of this worksheet are frozen. You can move the cursor vertically to any cell and these four lines will be untouched.

By using /WTC (Clear) let us clear the frozen title. Now we would like to freeze this worksheet vertically. Do the following:

1. Move the cursor to column B.
2. Select /WTV.

At this point if you move the cursor horizontally to any cell, column A will remain untouched.

To freeze both vertically and horizontally, all the data must be to the left and above the cursor position.

FIGURE 6-11 A Sample Worksheet for the /Worksheet Titles Command

```
A1: (G)                                                              READY

       A          B         C         D        E         F        G         H
1                           This is an example of a simple budget
2
3                           January  February March    April    May      June
4                           -------- -------- -------- -------- -------- --------
5      Rent                    500      500      500      500      550      550
6      Electricity              62       79       58       47       49       44
7      Water                    12       10     10.5       13    14.25       17
8      Telephone                25       32       36       28       17       31
9      Food                    150      135      147      152      146      129
10
11
12
13
14
15
16
17
18
19
20
01-Jan-91   11:03 AM          UNDO
```

6-16 /Worksheet Window

Using /Worksheet Window allows you to split the screen to view two versions of a worksheet, formatted and unformatted, at the same time. When you invoke /Worksheet Window you will be given the following choices:

Horizontal   Vertical   Sync   Unsync   Clear

• The Horizontal option creates a split screen with two horizontal windows. To produce such a worksheet, move the cursor to a particular row (row 2 or any row below this), then type /WWH. If you invoke this command in row 1 you will hear a beep. This means you cannot split the screen in row 1.
• The Vertical option creates a split screen with two vertical windows. To produce such a worksheet, move the cursor to a particular column (column B or any column to the right of column B), then type /WWV.
• The Sync option allows two windows to move harmoniously. This means that data scrolls across the screen in the same direction.
• The Unsync option allows independent movement in either window.
• The Clear option removes the second window from your worksheet.

To move the cursor between the two windows, press F6. The default for scrolling is Sync. Figures 6-12 and 6-13 show examples of this command.

6-17 /Worksheet Status

This command provides you with information about available memory, recalculation

FIGURE 6-12 An Example of /Worksheet Window Vertical

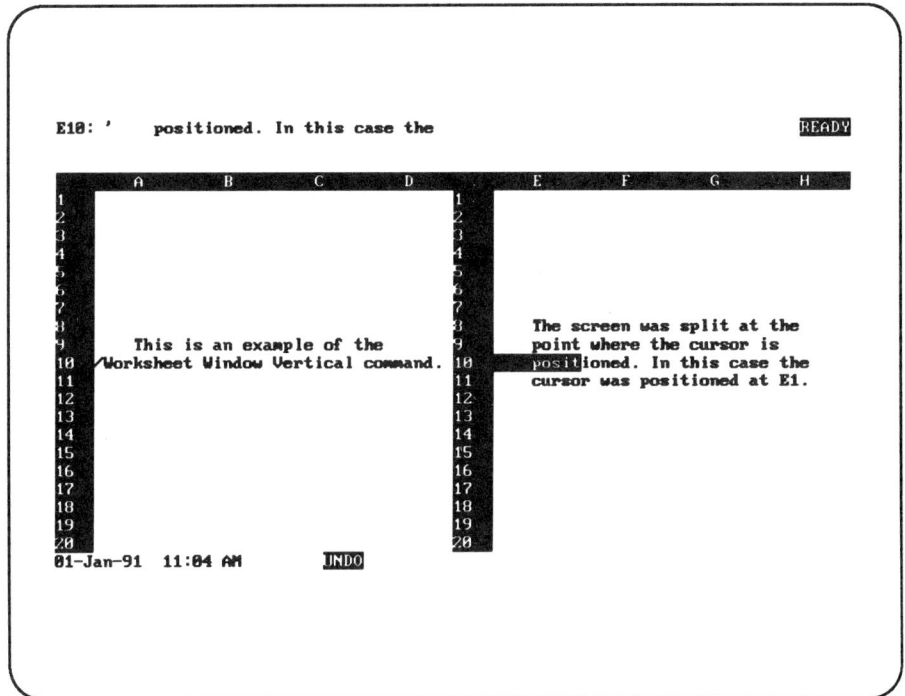

method, current format, label prefix, column width, zero suppression, and global protection. This can be very helpful when you want to erase some unwanted data, speed up the processing time by changing the recalculation method, get a view of the current settings, and so on.

Figure 6-14 shows the worksheet status of the system used in this text. To generate this figure we first chose /Worksheet, then Status. As you see, this figure reveals a lot of information. It tells us the recalculation method, the format, and so on.

6-18 /Worksheet Page

This command inserts a page break into the worksheet, useful when writing reports. When you print a worksheet, a new page will start at the page break. To use this command, move the cursor to the row below the one where you would like to have a page break, then issue the /Worksheet Page command. The location of the break will be given by ::, which must be positioned in column A. Figure 6-15 shows an example of this command. The page break is in cell A15. The page break option can be removed using /Range Erase, /Worksheet Delete Column, etc.

6-19 Using the Undo Feature

The UNDO feature enables you to reverse the most recent change made to the worksheet. When you get 1-2-3 started the UNDO feature is enabled. The status indicator at the bottom of the screen displays UNDO. To invoke the UNDO feature press Alt-F4. You can

FIGURE 6-13 *An Example of /Worksheet Window Horizontal*

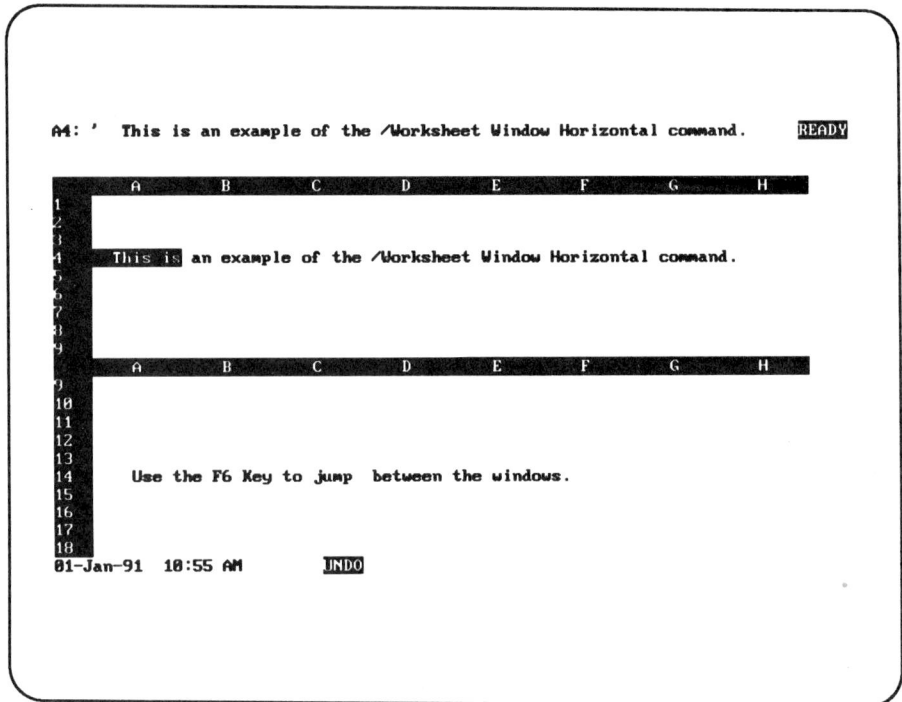

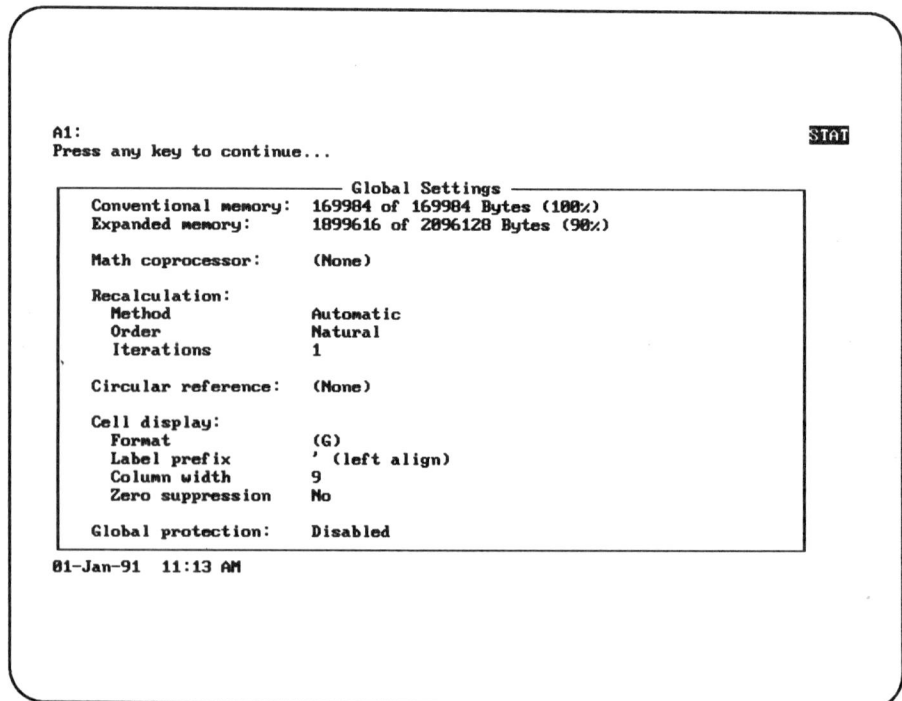

FIGURE 6-14 *Output of the /Worksheet Status Command*

FIGURE 6-15 An Example of /Worksheet Page Command

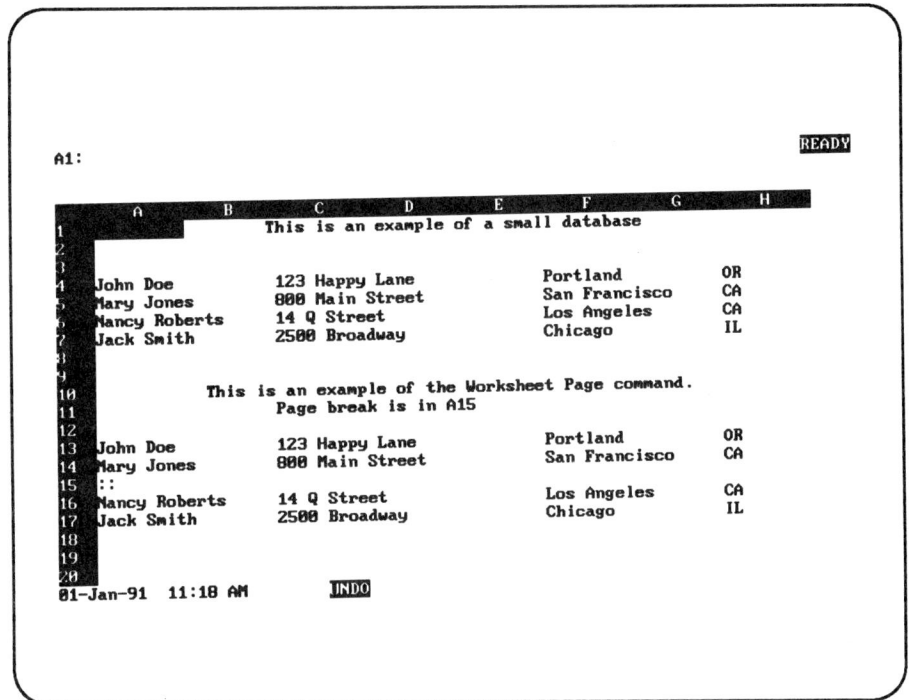

```
A1:                                                                READY

      A       B       C        D        E        F       G        H
              This is an example of a small database
1
2
3
4  John Doe          123 Happy Lane           Portland          OR
5  Mary Jones        800 Main Street          San Francisco     CA
6  Nancy Roberts     14 Q Street              Los Angeles       CA
7  Jack Smith        2500 Broadway            Chicago           IL
8
9
10            This is an example of the Worksheet Page command.
11                   Page break is in A15
12
13  John Doe          123 Happy Lane          Portland          OR
14  Mary Jones        800 Main Street         San Francisco     CA
15  ::
16  Nancy Roberts     14 Q Street             Los Angeles       CA
17  Jack Smith        2500 Broadway           Chicago           IL
18
19
20
01-Jan-91  11:18 AM            UNDO
```

disable the UNDO feature by using /Worksheet Global Default Other UNDO Disable. To make this change permanent you must use /Worksheet Global Default Update.

Remember that the UNDO feature reverses only the last change made to the worksheet. Understanding the last change can be a tricky matter. The last change includes a cycle from one READY mode to the next READY mode. Let us give a couple of examples to make this feature more understandable.

In a blank screen (the mode is READY) type CHECK. While you are typing this data the mode indicator displays LABEL. As soon as you press the **Return** key the mode indicator is changed back to READY. This is one cycle. Now, if you press Alt-F4 the worksheet will return to a blank worksheet. (The word CHECK is erased.)

In some cases the cycle may include several commands. For example, you may press /Graph, Type, Pie, A, C1..C3, **Return**, View, Esc, Quit. At this point you are back in READY mode. This is one cycle. By pressing the UNDO key you are reversing all these commands.

Depending on the complexity of the operations the UNDO feature consumes various amounts of memory. Whenever there is not enough memory to save the current status in the UNDO buffer before the change, 1-2-3 will pause and present you with the following message:

YOU WILL NOT BE ABLE TO UNDO THIS ACTION..DO YOU WISH TO PROCEED?

Answer YES to disable the UNDO feature temporarily and complete the command. If this is the case you will not be able to undo this command; however, UNDO is reenable as soon as the command is completed. If you select NO, you are cancelling the command in progress. This will return you to READY mode.

If you press the UNDO key, you can change your mind and press the UNDO key again in order to undo the UNDO! In this manner, 1-2-3 allows you to use the UNDO key like a toggle switch.

6-20 Priority of Commands

Remember that /Range commands take precedence over /Worksheet Global commands. For example, a cell formatted by /Range Format cannot be overwritten by /Worksheet Global Format. Also, /Worksheet commands take precedence over /Worksheet Global commands. For example, if you set the width of column A by /Worksheet Column, this cannot be overwritten by /Worksheet Global Column-Width.

SUMMARY

In this chapter, we discussed /Worksheet commands. These commands have been divided into two groups. /Global commands affect the entire worksheet; for example, setting column widths. The second group controls a portion of the worksheet; for example, inserting a row or a column. These commands and the /Range commands will be important as we learn how to work with Lotus. Practice them and learn to understand them.

REVIEW QUESTIONS

* These questions are answered in Appendix I.
1. What is the difference between the /Worksheet commands and the /Worksheet Global commands?
2. What does global mean?
3.* What is the default value for column-width in your worksheet?
4. How many recalculation methods are available in Lotus?
5.* What are some specific applications of manual recalculation?
6. What is the default value for the recalculation method?
7.* When you use /Worksheet Global Label-Prefix, should the data be entered first, before issuing the command?
8. How do you activate /Worksheet Global Protection?
9. If a worksheet is protected, can you erase it?
10. What is the purpose of /Worksheet Global Zero?
11. What is the difference between /Worksheet Delete and /Range Erase?
12. How many options are available under the /Worksheet Column command?
13. What are some applications of the /Worksheet Titles command?
14. How many ways can /Worksheet Window be utilized?
15. How do you move the cursor between two split screens?
16. What are some applications of /Worksheet Window?
17.* What does /Worksheet Page do? Is there any specific column for page break or can it be placed anywhere?

HANDS-ON PRACTICE

1. Sometimes the date and time displayed in the lower left corner of the screen is disturbing. What is the command to suppress time and date?
2. Create a worksheet with your first name in cell A1 and copy your name into cells A1..H20.
3. In the worksheet created in Question 2, move rows 1 and 2 to rows 50 and 51.
4. Repeat the process in Question 3 using pointing instead of typing the range coordinates.
5. Extend all the columns width in the worksheet to a width of 30.
6. Split the worksheet in Question 2 first vertically and then horizontally.
7. Using /Worksheet Erase, erase the above worksheet.
8. Generate a worksheet with row 1 and column A frozen.
9. Enter your last name in cell A1. Then by using the pointing technique copy your name in range A1..H10.
10. Generate a protected worksheet. Then use /Range Unprotect on cell H10. Now enter your last name in cell H10.
11. Invoke /Worksheet Global Default and see the status of your system.
12. Enter the number 10 in cells A1 and A2. In cell A3 enter formula +A1-A2. Naturally you will see zero in this cell. Suppress the zero in the worksheet. Replace the zero with label Not Available.
13. In the above worksheet, first hide Column A, then reveal it.
14. Design the following worksheet:

A	B	C ...
1	Financial Data	
2 Branch A		
3 Branch B		
4 Branch C		
.		
.		
.		

Using /Worksheet Titles, freeze both horizontal and vertical titles. Now, to verify your work, move the cursor to the right, then downward. Both titles must be untouched. Is this correct?

15. Either type the worksheet presented in Figure 6-16 or load it from the disk. Do the following:
   a. Using the /Copy command calculate and complete the TOTAL column.
   b. Freeze the worksheet both horizontally and vertically. By moving to the right and then downward, verify your work.

COMPREHENSIVE LAB ASSIGNMENT

Retrieve CHAPT5 and perform the following:

1. Adjust the length of each column in order to display data more clearly. For example, the length of the sex column should be only 3; major should be 5, etc.

FIGURE 6-16 A Sample Worksheet

```
                                        ON-LINE MARKETING
                                        SALES RESULTS - 1990

EMP.NO. NAME           DATE/HIRED  BRTHDATE    RANK REGION  1ST QTR   2ND QTR   3RD QTR   4TH QTR    TOTAL
   1001 Lyman,Emerson  20-Nov-61  24-June-24  JR   NE      $34,500   $24,450   $40,500   $41,350
   1002 Nesbit,LeRoy   26-Jun-79  16-Jun-55   MGR  SE      $32,100   $26,850   $21,850   $16,400
   1003 Healy,Harold   24-Sep-78  13-Sep-56   JR   MW      $16,300   $31,000   $32,450   $29,500
   1004 Lloyd,June     13-Aug-82  30-Sep-61   JR   SW      $47,500   $19,950   $24,700   $16,700
   1005 Stubbs,Sharron 18-Nov-80  06-Apr-54   JR   SW      $18,900   $23,500   $23,700   $34,800
   1006 Maag,Lisa      11-Jul-66  31-May-61   JR   MOU     $23,570   $34,650   $39,670   $25,050
   1007 Harris,Phil    18-Nov-67  25-Dec-47   NE   SW      $32,150   $21,350   $31,500   $18,600
   1008 Lynn,Grant     19-Ju;-76  29-Aug-52   MGR  NE      $39,210   $48,100   $34,780   $21,200
   1009 Reynolds,Donald14-Aug-74  11-Aug-51   JR   SW      $24,400   $15,650   $23,950   $45,850
   1010 Leavitt,Leo    28-Feb-68  07-Mar-42   JR   PAC     $24,300   $41,000   $21,000   $23,000
   1011 Farley,Cheryl  27-May-83  21-Oct-59   SR   MW      $21,000   $17,500   $28,600   $39,050
   1012 Wade,Elaine    02-Apr-71  26-Feb-47   SUP  SW      $26,550   $39,600   $24,700   $21,500
   1013 Thomas,Kenny   11-Mar-64  03-Sep-31   SR   SE      $39,950   $19,100   $21,350   $23,800
   1014 Hurst,Connie   14-Aug-75  25-Apr-49   MGR  PAC     $15,000   $16,350   $22,780   $32,200
   1015 Park,Clara     15-May-69  22-Nov-44   SR   MOU     $45,100   $32,200   $35,800   $27,150
   1016 Ritchie,Marc   30-Nov-72  04-Sept-44  SR   MOU     $27,000   $23,700   $24,600   $49,600
   1017 Tanner,Amy     21-Jul-77  29-Oct-51   SR   NE      $21,000   $23,550   $19,250   $45,600
   1018 Larse,Max      21-Dec-79  02-Nov-58   JR   SW      $19,500   $15,400   $41,300   $16,600
   1019 Turner,Wayne   07-Dec-65  17-Jun-34   JR   NE      $38,950   $21,200   $41,800   $23,750
   1020 Rodney,Luella  29-Mar-62  19-May-33   SR   SW      $43,000   $24,550   $27,350   $15,900
   1021 Dixon,Linda    15-Dec-69  29-Aug-41   SR   MOU     $27,000   $43,750   $18,350   $30,100
   1022 Payne,Shirley  10-Oct-71  15-May-45   SR   SE      $23,450   $49,200   $15,700   $35,000
   1023 Price,Kevin    21-Sep-82  01-Feb-53   MGR  MOU     $15,400   $45,300   $49,450   $32,400
   1024 Harson,Craig   03-Feb-60  20-Jan-29   JR   ME      $29,500   $27,850   $21,500   $44,600
   1025 Clark,Gus      04-Oct-63  20-Jan-30   SUP  SE      $43,400   $26,300   $38,600   $17,000
   1026 Adams,Robert   01-Jan-80  02-Nov-60   JR   SW      $15,500   $21,750   $30,440   $25,150
   1027 Whitehead,Aaron26-Jul-76  01-Sep-49   JR   MW      $21,560   $24,500   $26,900   $42,900
   1028 Pace,Alfred    12-Oct-71  11-Apr-37   SR   SW      $35,600   $21,600   $32,300   $27,100
   1029 Bowen,Glen     10-Mar-73  12-Oct-38   SR   SE      $21,500   $30,250   $16,200   $27,300
   1030 Cox,Nathan     19-Mar-73  24-Jul-47   JR   MOU     $17,000   $38,000   $43,900   $23,900
   1031 Madsen,Linda   24-Oct-66  04-Oct-39   SUP  SE      $24,500   $39,400   $23,900   $52,500
   1032 Seamons,Jackie 22-May-72  24-Jan-47   MGR  SW      $34,500   $43,200   $35,950   $24,650
   1033 Shelley,Scott  08-Feb-61  13-Jun-32   JR   PAC     $44,400   $35,800   $34,770   $27,500
   1034 Carlile,Kay    17-Apr-82  18-May-52   JR   MOU     $37,800   $22,100   $29,250   $30,650
   1035 Marks,Merlin   04-Jan-71  27-Sep-50   SR   SE      $41,000   $23,770   $25,400   $34,800
   1036 Nelson,Henry   05-Dec-77  03-Dec-48   JR   SW      $19,550   $26,850   $26,950   $16,600
   1037 Slater,Derek   02-Sep-76  04-Apr-49   JR   MW      $23,450   $34,650   $44,850   $43,650
   1038 McCurdy,Steven 18-Oct-81  29-Aug-53   MGR  MW      $16,300   $43,500   $31,600   $24,100
   1039 Savage,Brian   13-Jan-78  22-Dec-44   JR   PAC     $35,670   $27,100   $43,410   $24,100
   1040 Wilde,Stuart   15-Oct-70  23-Dec-44   JR   SW      $30,100   $26,800   $21,950   $42,300
   1041 Vincent,Bret   25-Jun-75  27-Jun-52   JR   NE      $23,450   $41,200   $41,600   $19,350
   1042 Marshall,Clyde 23-Mar-73  21-May-42   JR   SW      $30,000   $24,750   $44,000   $39,910
   1043 Sperry,Bruce   23-Mar-76  16-Jul-43   SR   NE      $23,450   $44,650   $23,650   $40,100
   1044 Miller,Paula   04-Jan-65  18-Jul-36   SR   SE      $26,700   $16,350   $16,300   $46,000
```

2. Using /Worksheet Titles freeze both horizontal and vertical titles.
3. Generate an input data entry over the three test scores (this means the cursor must be able to move around only in this area).
4. Return input data entry to normal.
5. Save the final worksheet under CHAPT6.

MISCONCEPTIONS AND SOLUTIONS

M – If you enter a new data item in very large worksheets, Lotus immediately recalculates the entire worksheet. If you keep entering different values, this may slow down the process.

S – You can use /Worksheet Global Recalculation Manual. This turns the automatic recalculation off. Enter all your numbers, then press F9 (CALC).

M – If you try to erase a portion of a row or a column of a worksheet, don't use /Worksheet Delete Row or /Worksheet Delete Column. This command erases the entire row or the entire column.

S – Use /Range Erase to erase a portion of a worksheet.

Formats: Dressing Up Your Worksheet

7-1 Introduction

In this chapter we will discuss the different formatting options available in Lotus. We will present examples to demonstrate a specific application for each option and briefly discuss format limitation. (The /Range Justify command, also used for formatting, was discussed in Chapter 5.)

7-2 Why Formats?

In the business world a good report is one that is presented in a format that aids comprehension. Lotus provides a number of formatting options, so a variety of reports can be generated easily.

To access the /Format command in Lotus there are two options, /Worksheet Global Format or /Range Format. /Worksheet Global Format is used when the entire worksheet needs to be formatted; /Range Format is used if only a specific portion is to be formatted. Remember that /RF takes precedence over the /WGF. Also, the Reset option is not available in /WGF. Figure 7-1 shows all the options available under the Format command:

Fixed   Scientific   Currency   ,   General   +   Percent   Date   Text   Hidden   Reset

The Reset option is used to change the existing setting to the global default setting.

7-3 General Option

The General option is the default format command. You may check the worksheet status to verify this. In this format the insignificant zeros to the right of a decimal place are eliminated. Very large and very small numbers are presented in scientific notation. Labels (nonnumeric data) are left-justified. You can change this setting manually by inserting one of the prefixes, by using /Worksheet Global Label-Prefix, or by using /Range Label. Figure 7-2 illustrates the formatted portion of the worksheet generated by /Range Format General A17..E20 **Return.**

7-4 Fixed Option

The Fixed option format does not display commas or dollar signs in the formatted

FIGURE 7-1 *Different Format Options Available in Lotus*

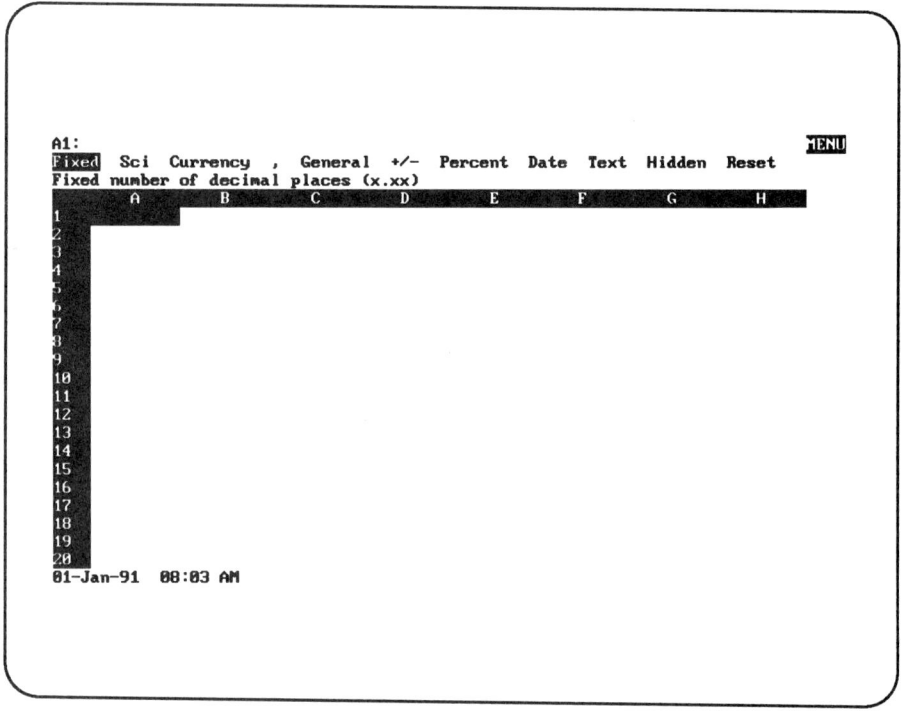

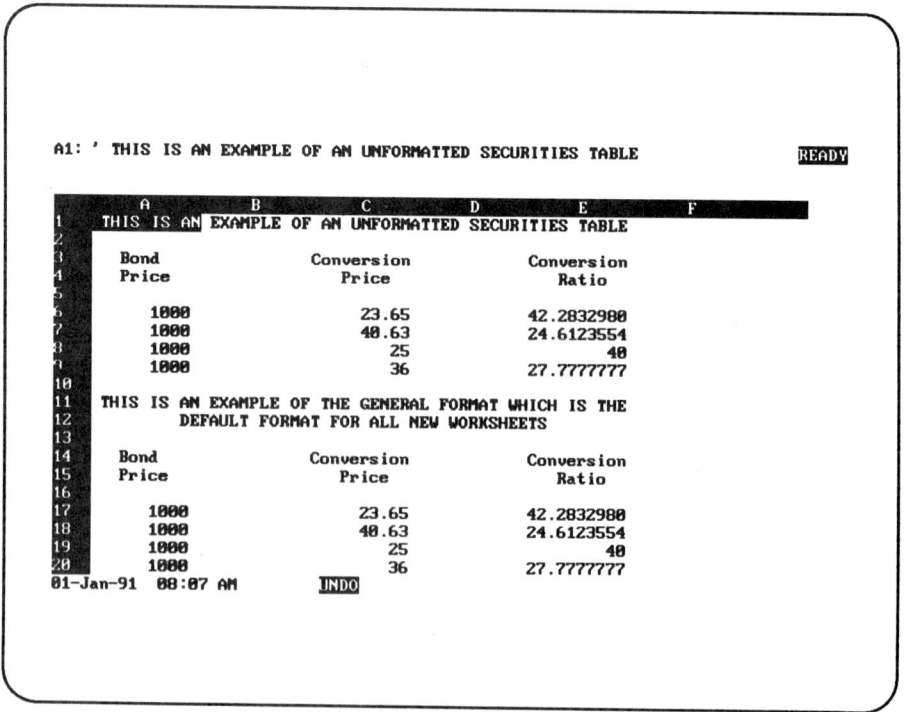

FIGURE 7-2 *Example of General Options*

worksheet. Numbers can include up to 15 decimal places. If you specify fewer decimal places, the number will be rounded up. For example, if you specify three decimal positions, 6.7786 would be displayed as 6.779. This option is suitable for printing checks or financial statements, such as an income statement or balance sheet. Figure 7-3 compares a formatted and unformatted worksheet.

The formatted portion of Figure 7-3 was generated by /Range Format Fixed 2 (decimal places) **Return** A17..E20 **Return**.

7-5 Scientific Option

The Scientific option is used for very large or very small numbers. You may specify up to 15 decimal places. Figure 7-4 illustrates the format generated by /Range Format Scientific 2 (decimal places) **Return** E15..E18 **Return**.

7-6 Currency Option

In the Currency option, the dollar sign ($) will appear immediately to the left of the numbers. A comma will separate every third digit. Negative numbers will appear in parentheses. The placement of the decimal is determined as in the other options. If the specified column width does not include enough space, a series of asterisks will be displayed (of course, this is true for all the options). Figure 7-5 illustrates this option. The formatted portion was generated by /Range Format Currency 0 (zero decimal places) **Return** D16..F20 **Return**.

7-7 Comma Option

The Comma option is very similar to Currency; the only difference is that the dollar sign is suppressed. This option is suitable for nonfinancial reports. Figure 7-6 illustrates this option. The formatted portion of this figure was generated by /Range Format , (comma) 0 (zero decimal places) **Return** D16..F20 **Return**.

7-8 +/- Options

In the +/- format, a positive number will be presented by the plus sign (+), a negative number by the minus sign (-), and zero by a period. This option is considered a limited graphics option, making the job of comparing different numbers an easy task. Figure 7-7 illustrates this option. In this example, we have used the +/- option to present an activity chart known as a Gantt chart. The formatted portion of this worksheet was generated by /Range Format +/- D16..D20 **Return**.

7-9 Percent Option

The Percent option presents numbers as a percentage of 100, for example, .05 = 5%. This option can be very useful when comparing a portion of data to the total: for example, the portion of total cost of production belonging to raw materials. Figure 7-8 illustrates this

FIGURE 7-3 Example of Fixed Option

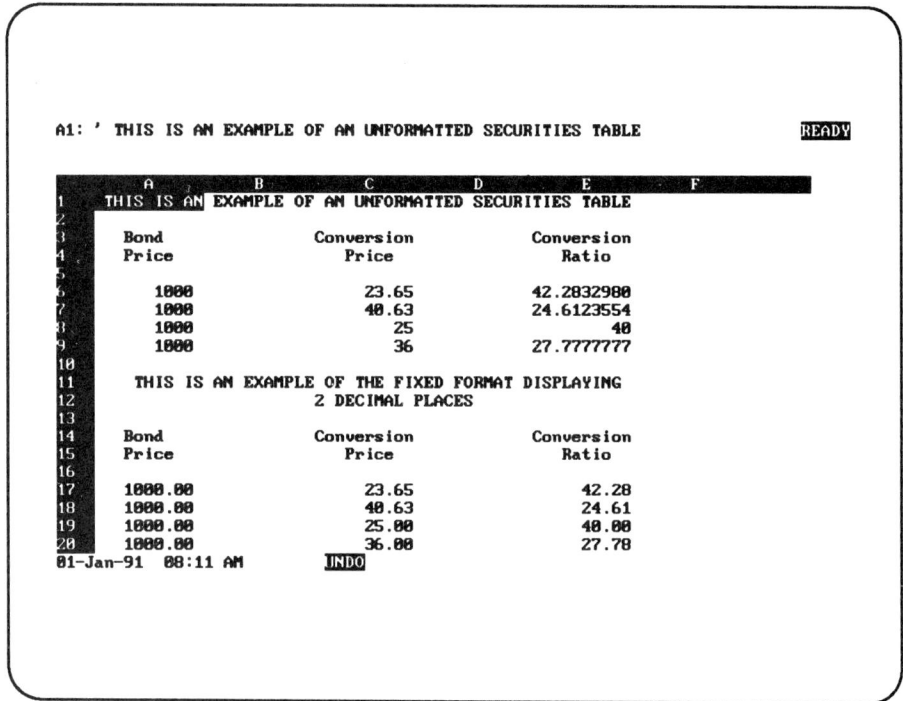

```
A1: ' THIS IS AN EXAMPLE OF AN UNFORMATTED SECURITIES TABLE          READY

        A            B            C            D            E        F
1   THIS IS AN EXAMPLE OF AN UNFORMATTED SECURITIES TABLE
2
3       Bond                  Conversion              Conversion
4       Price                 Price                   Ratio
5
6       1000                  23.65                   42.2832980
7       1000                  40.63                   24.6123554
8       1000                  25                      40
9       1000                  36                      27.7777777
10
11      THIS IS AN EXAMPLE OF THE FIXED FORMAT DISPLAYING
12                   2 DECIMAL PLACES
13
14      Bond                  Conversion              Conversion
15      Price                 Price                   Ratio
16
17      1000.00               23.65                   42.28
18      1000.00               40.63                   24.61
19      1000.00               25.00                   40.00
20      1000.00               36.00                   27.78
01-Jan-91  08:11 AM          UNDO
```

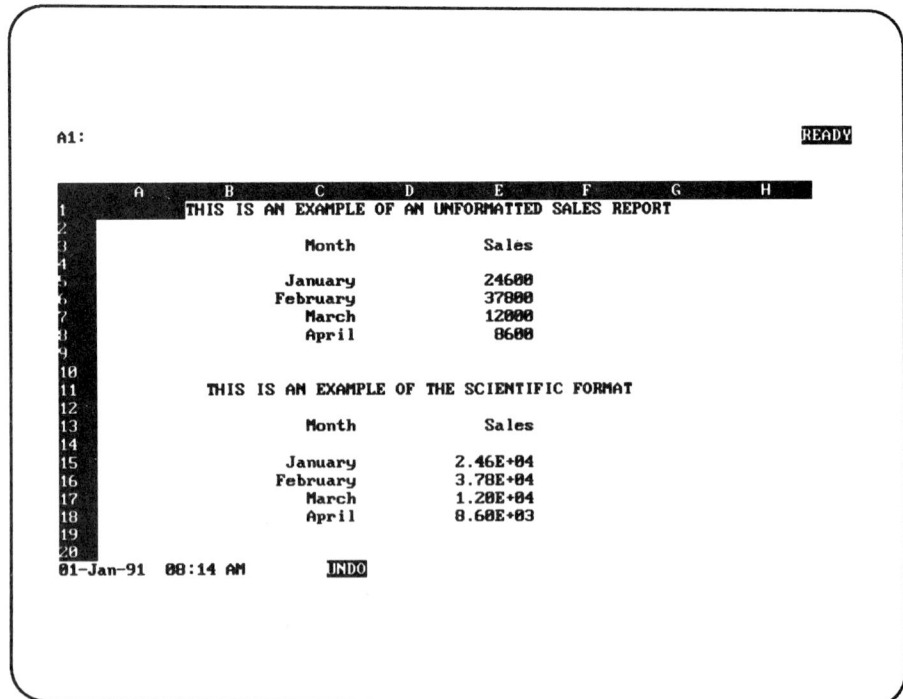

```
A1:                                                                  READY

        A            B            C            D            E        F        G        H
1                  THIS IS AN EXAMPLE OF AN UNFORMATTED SALES REPORT
2
3                  Month                 Sales
4
5                  January               24600
6                  February              37800
7                  March                 12000
8                  April                 8600
9
10
11                 THIS IS AN EXAMPLE OF THE SCIENTIFIC FORMAT
12
13                 Month                 Sales
14
15                 January               2.46E+04
16                 February              3.78E+04
17                 March                 1.20E+04
18                 April                 8.60E+03
19
20
01-Jan-91  08:14 AM          UNDO
```

FIGURE 7-4 Example of Scientific Option

FIGURE 7-5 Example of Currency Option

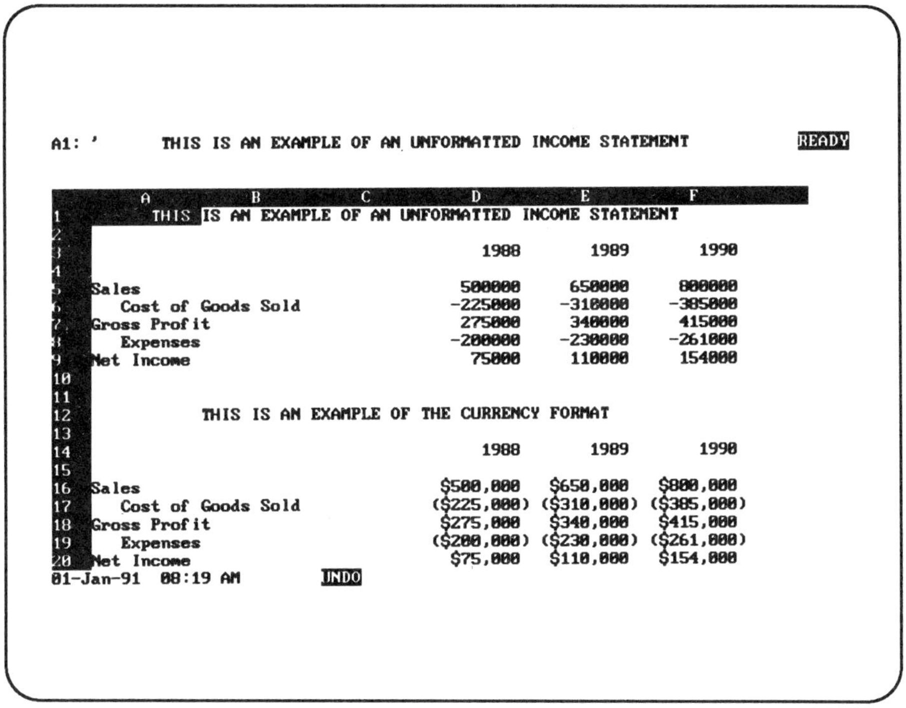

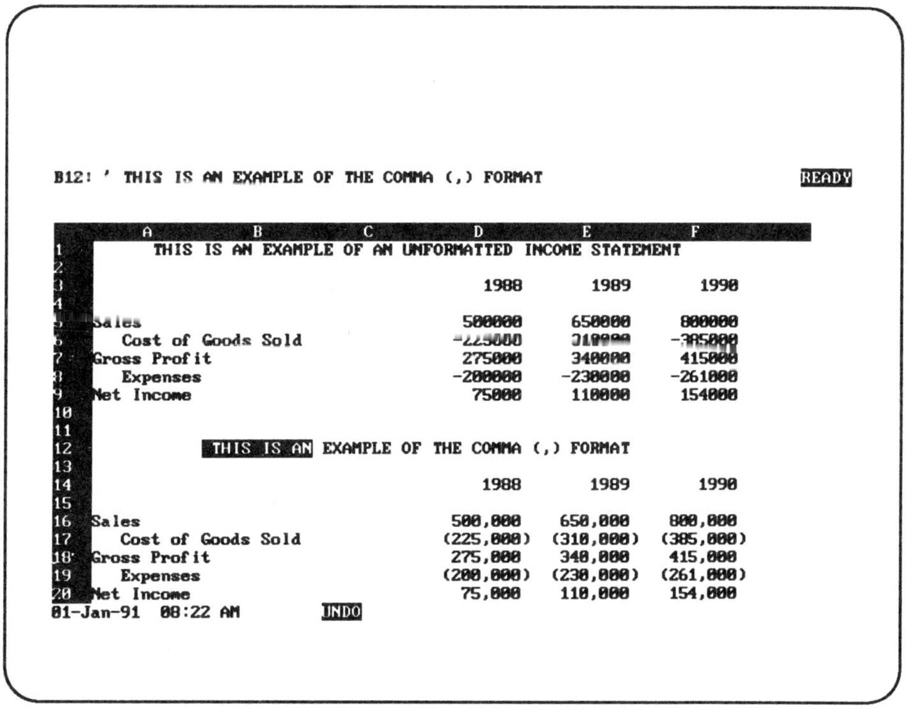

FIGURE 7-6 Example of Comma (,) Option

FIGURE 7-7   Example of +/- Options

```
A12: '   THIS IS AN EXAMPLE OF THE +/- FORMAT FOR RANGE D16..D20          READY

        A       B       C       D       E       F      . G       H
 1      THIS IS AN EXAMPLE OF AN UNFORMATTED GANTT ACTIVITY SCHEDULE
 2
 3                              Expected Time
 4              Activity        (in weeks)      Variance
 5                 A                 7           1.784
 6                 B                 4           0.439
 7                 C                 0           0.261
 8                 D                -5           1.593
 9                 E                -2           0.107
10
11
12      THIS IS AN EXAMPLE OF THE +/- FORMAT FOR RANGE D16..D20
13
14                              Expected Time
15              Activity        (in weeks)      Variance
16                 A            +++++++          1.784
17                 B            ++++             0.439
18                 C            .                0.261
19                 D            ------           1.593
20                 E            --               0.107
01-Jan-91   08:26 AM          UNDO
```

```
E10:                                                                     READY

        A       B       C       D       E       F       G       H
 1      THIS IS AN EXAMPLE OF AN UNFORMATTED VERTICAL ANALYSIS OF ASSETS
 2
 3                                      1990                    1989
 4      Current Assets                 90000    0.404   70000    0.328
 5      Property, Plant & Equipment   117000    0.526  122000    0.57
 6      Intangible Assets               9950    0.045   14500    0.068
 7      Other Assets                    5600    0.025    7200    0.034
 8                                   --------          --------
 9      TOTAL ASSETS                  222550    1       213700    1
10
11
12              THIS IS AN EXAMPLE OF THE PERCENT FORMAT
13
14                                      1990                    1989
15      Current Assets                 90000   40.4%   70000   32.8%
16      Property, Plant & Equipment   117000   52.6%  122000   57.0%
17      Intangible Assets               9950    4.5%   14500    6.8%
18      Other Assets                    5600    2.5%    7200    3.4%
19                                   --------  ------ --------  -------
20      TOTAL ASSETS                  222550  100.0%  213700  100.0%
01-Jan-91   08:27 AM          UNDO
```

FIGURE 7-8   Example of Percent Option

option. The formatted portion of this illustration was generated by /Range Format Percent 1 **Return** F15..F20 **Return** and /Range Format Percent 1 **Return** H15..H20 **Return**.

7-10 Date Options

Lotus allows five different formats for dates. The beginning date in the Lotus calendar is December 31, 1899 and the last date in the calendar is December 31, 2099. December 31, 1899 is defined by Lotus as zero; January 1, 1900 equals 1; and December 31, 2099 equals 73050. Figure 7-9 shows the five different date options. We generated the formatted portion of this worksheet using the following commands:

/Range Format D1 E16..F16 **Return**
/Range Format D2 E17..F17 **Return**
/Range Format D3 E18..F18 **Return**
/Range Format D4 E19..F19 **Return**
/Range Format D5 E20..F20 **Return**

See Chapter 13 for various Date functions.

7-11 Time Options

Lotus has four different time options. In time formats fractional parts of serial numbers represent time (.000 = midnight, .5000 = noon, 20/24 = 8:00 P.M., and so on) as parts of a 24-hour period. You can use the @TIME and @NOW functions to generate these numbers. Figure 7-10 illustrates different time options. The formatted portion of the worksheet was generated using the following commands:

/Range Format Date Time 1 C16..E16 **Return**
/Range Format Date Time 2 C17..E17 **Return**
/Range Format Date Time 3 C18..E18 **Return**
/Range Format Date Time 4 C19..E19 **Return**

7-12 Text Option

The content of each cell will be displayed as text using the Text option. For example, if cell A30 contains +H1*P1 (hours multiplied by pay rate), this formula will be displayed using the Text format. The Text option can be helpful in debugging lengthy formulas. Also, the Text format is useful for documentation purposes. Figure 7-11 illustrates this option. We have generated the formatted worksheet by using /Range Format Text H6..H19 **Return** (on the right window).

7-13 Hidden Option

The Hidden option is useful for hiding a portion of the worksheet or the entire worksheet. This format can generate reports that do not need to display a portion of the worksheet. (Remember that the hidden portion is still a part of your worksheet and is included in any calculations.) This format also provides security by hiding some portions of a worksheet

FIGURE 7-9 *Example of Date Options*

```
A1: '          THIS IS AN EXAMPLE OF AN UNFORMATTED INVESTMENT RECORD        READY

      A         B         C         D         E         F         G
 1      THIS IS AN EXAMPLE OF AN UNFORMATTED INVESTMENT RECORD
 2
 3   Investment               Cost    Purchase Date  Sale Date  Sold For
 4
 5   ABC Manufacturing        5600        30758        31578      8300
 6   Precision Industries     3200        30367        30791      7300
 7   Hometown Distributors    8600        30868        31442     10400
 8   Moneymakers, Inc.        4500        31333        31555      5900
 9   Creative Enterprises     7200        30576        31200      9800
10
11      THIS IS AN EXAMPLE OF THE DATE FORMAT: Row 16 = D1, Row 17 = D2,
12           Row 18 = D3, Row 19 = D4, and Row 20 = D5
13
14   Investment               Cost    Purchase Date  Sale Date  Sold For
15
16   ABC Manufacturing        5600      17-Mar-84    15-Jun-86    8300
17   Precision Industries     3200        20-Feb       19-Apr     7300
18   Hometown Distributors    8600        Jul-84       Jan-86    10400
19   Moneymakers, Inc.        4500      10/13/85     05/23/86     5900
20   Creative Enterprises     7200        09/17        06/02      9800
01-Jan-91  08:33 AM          UNDO
```

```
G6: 8.06                                                                  READY

      A         B         C         D         E         F         G
 1            THIS IS AN EXAMPLE OF AN UNFORMATTED TIME SHEET
 2
 3      NAME          CHECK-IN            CHECK-OUT          HOURS WORKED
 4
 5   J. Taylor     0.333333333         0.222222222              9.3
 6   B. Smith      0.330555555         0.166666666             8.06
 7   D. West       0.583333333         0.255555555             4.13
 8   L. Jackson       0.4375           0.145833333               5
 9
10
11      THIS IS AN EXAMPLE OF THE TIME FORMAT: Row 16 = T1, Row 17 = T2,
12             Row 18 = T3, and Row 19 = T4
13
14      NAME          CHECK-IN            CHECK-OUT          HOURS WORKED
15
16   J. Taylor     08:00:00 AM         05:20:00 PM              9.3
17   B. Smith        07:56 AM           04:00 PM               8.06
18   D. West        14:00:00           18:00:00                4.13
19   L. Jackson       10:30              15:30                   5
20
01-Jan-91  08:37 AM          UNDO
```

FIGURE 7-10 *Example of Time Options*

FIGURE 7-11 Example of Text Format

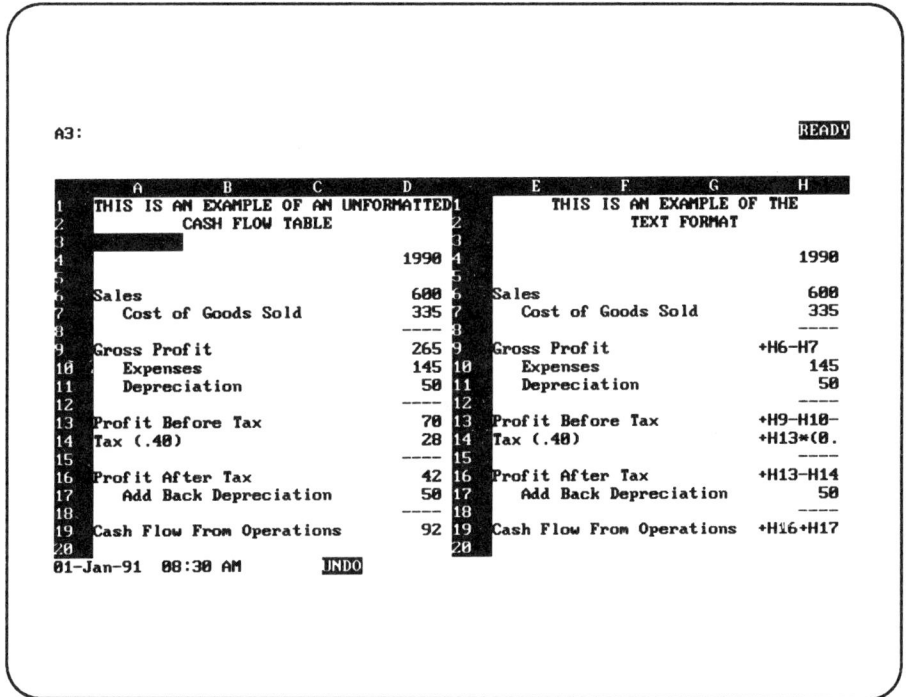

```
A3:                                                                    READY

      A       B       C       D           E       F       G       H
1  THIS IS AN EXAMPLE OF AN UNFORMATTED 1     THIS IS AN EXAMPLE OF THE
2          CASH FLOW TABLE              2              TEXT FORMAT
3                                       3
4                              1990     4                            1990
5                                       5
6  Sales                        600     6  Sales                      600
7      Cost of Goods Sold       335     7      Cost of Goods Sold     335
8                              ----     8                            ----
9  Gross Profit                 265     9  Gross Profit           +H6-H7
10     Expenses                 145     10     Expenses               145
11     Depreciation              50     11     Depreciation            50
12                             ----     12                           ----
13 Profit Before Tax            70      13 Profit Before Tax      +H9-H10-
14 Tax (.40)                    28      14 Tax (.40)              +H13*(0.
15                             ----     15                           ----
16 Profit After Tax             42      16 Profit After Tax      +H13-H14
17     Add Back Depreciation    50      17     Add Back Depreciation   50
18                             ----     18                           ----
19 Cash Flow From Operations    92      19 Cash Flow From Operations +H16+H17
20                                      20
01-Jan-91  08:30 AM        UNDO
```

from unauthorized users. To reveal the hidden portion, move the cursor to any other format option and press the **Return** key. Figure 7-12 illustrates this option. We have generated the hidden range by using /Range Format Hidden D14..D20 **Return**.

7-14 Override Option

As we mentioned earlier, the /Format command can be accessed either by /Worksheet Global Format or /Range Format. /Range Format always has priority over /Worksheet Global Format. This means that the portion of the worksheet formatted by /Range Format is not affected by /Worksheet Global Format.

Figure 7-13 illustrates this case. Column D in the upper worksheet was formatted by /Range Format Currency 0 (zero) **Return** D5..D9 **Return**. Then the entire worksheet was formatted by /Worksheet Global Format, (comma) 0 (zero) **Return**. As you see, column D is untouched. This is helpful for generating worksheets that use different formats for different tasks.

7-15 Miscellaneous Formatting Features

If you want to display your negative numbers with a leading minus sign instead of parentheses, choose /Worksheet, Global, Default, Other, International, Negative, Sign. To return back to parenthetical negative number display, use /Worksheet, Global, Default, Other, International, Negative, Parentheses.

FIGURE 7-12 Example of Hidden Format

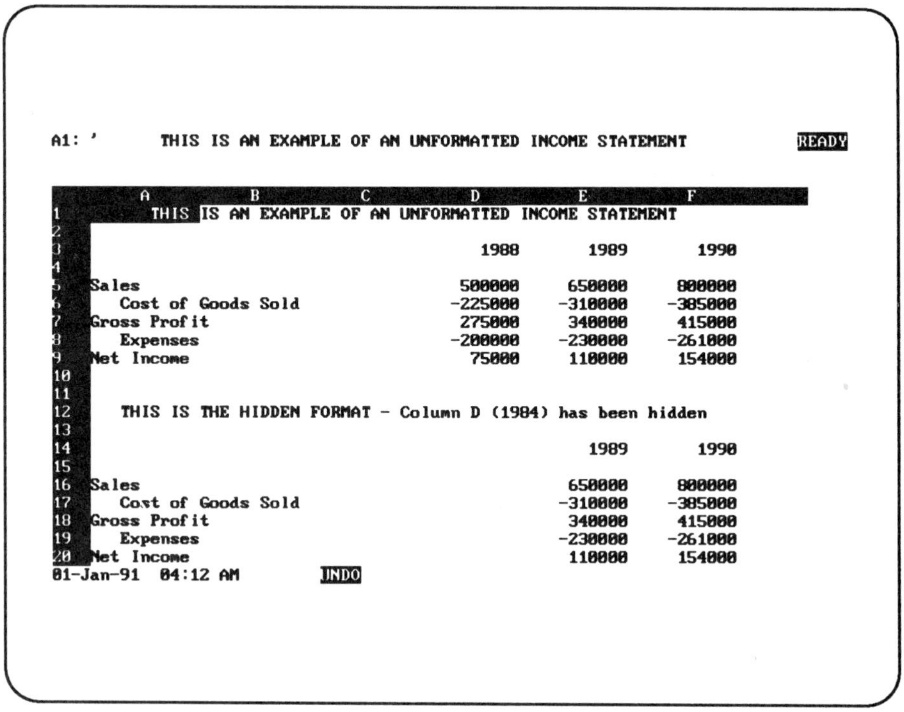

```
A1: '      THIS IS AN EXAMPLE OF AN UNFORMATTED INCOME STATEMENT          READY

        A        B       C        D         E         F
1          THIS IS AN EXAMPLE OF AN UNFORMATTED INCOME STATEMENT
2
3                                1988      1989      1990
4
5  Sales                        500000    650000    800000
6     Cost of Goods Sold       -225000   -310000   -385000
7  Gross Profit                 275000    340000    415000
8     Expenses                 -200000   -230000   -261000
9  Net Income                    75000    110000    154000
10
11
12    THIS IS THE HIDDEN FORMAT - Column D (1984) has been hidden
13
14                                         1989      1990
15
16 Sales                                 650000    800000
17    Cost of Goods Sold                -310000   -385000
18 Gross Profit                          340000    415000
19    Expenses                          -230000   -261000
20 Net Income                            110000    154000
01-Jan-91  04:12 AM        UNDO
```

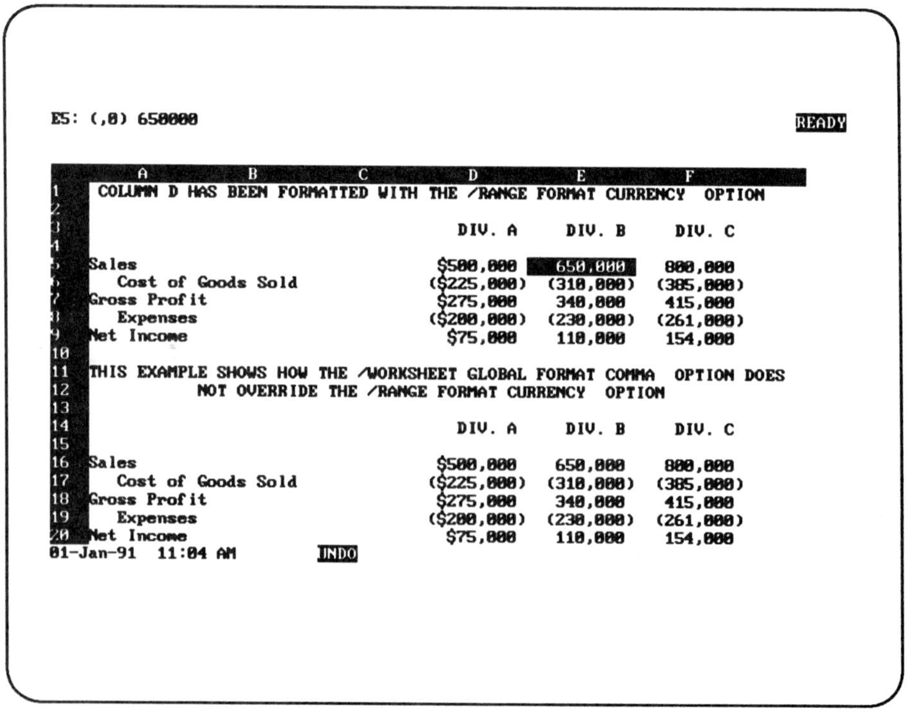

```
E5: (,0) 650000                                               READY

        A        B       C        D         E         F
1  COLUMN D HAS BEEN FORMATTED WITH THE /RANGE FORMAT CURRENCY  OPTION
2
3                              DIV. A    DIV. B    DIV. C
4
5  Sales                      $500,000   650,000   800,000
6     Cost of Goods Sold     ($225,000) (310,000) (385,000)
7  Gross Profit               $275,000   340,000   415,000
8     Expenses               ($200,000) (230,000) (261,000)
9  Net Income                  $75,000   110,000   154,000
10
11 THIS EXAMPLE SHOWS HOW THE /WORKSHEET GLOBAL FORMAT COMMA  OPTION DOES
12          NOT OVERRIDE THE /RANGE FORMAT CURRENCY  OPTION
13
14                              DIV. A    DIV. B    DIV. C
15
16 Sales                      $500,000   650,000   800,000
17    Cost of Goods Sold     ($225,000) (310,000) (385,000)
18 Gross Profit               $275,000   340,000   415,000
19    Expenses               ($200,000) (230,000) (261,000)
20 Net Income                  $75,000   110,000   154,000
01-Jan-91  11:04 AM        UNDO
```

FIGURE 7-13 Example of Override Option

You can also change the currency sign from $ (dollar sign) to other currency signs such as the Japanese yen, British pound, and so on. To create any special symbol you must press the compose key (Alt-F1) then the compose sequence (see Appendix H). For example, to create the British pound sterling symbol you must first press Alt-F1, then L=, then **Return**. To create the Japanese yen symbol press Alt-F1, then Y=, then **Return**. Let us walk through an example. In Figure 7-14 we have formatted the worksheet with /Range, Format, Currency, 2, **Return**, A1..A6, **Return**. The column width is 12.

To change the dollar sign to the Japanese yen do the following: /Worksheet, Global, Default, Other, International, Currency. At this point the $ (dollar sign) is displayed on the control panel. Press the Backspace key to erase the $. Now press Alt-F1 (the compose key), then type Y= (compose sequence). Now you see the Japanese yen displayed. Press **Return** and select **Prefix, Quit, Quit**. Your worksheet should be similar to Figure 7-15.

7-16 A Complete Example

To put the whole thing together we have created a final worksheet that uses the seventeen Format options generated by Lotus to serve as a quick reference. Figure 7-16 demonstrates these options.

SUMMARY

The Format options should help you generate eye-pleasing and useful reports. As we discussed earlier, Lotus Release 2.2 is capable of generating 17 format options (including all the Date and Time options).

Even with all these options there are still some limitations and we do not see any way around them. Numeric data is always right-justified and nonnumeric data is always left-justified. There is no provision for centering numbers. Large and small numbers are not lined up from the left margin. If a number is larger than the specified column size, a series of asterisks will be displayed until you widen the column. We believe these are minor limitations. The available options are adequate for most operations.

REVIEW QUESTIONS

* These questions are answered in Appendix I.
1. Why is formatting necessary?
2.* How many format options are available?
3.* What is the difference between the Currency option and the Comma option?
4. How many Date options are available? What is the application of each?
5. How many Time options are available? What is the application of each?
6.* What is an application of the Text format?
7. What are some applications of the Hidden format?
8. What is the difference between /Worksheet Global Format and /Range Format?
9. What are the beginning and ending dates in the Lotus calendar?
10.* Can you do arithmetic operations with dates and times (e.g., can you subtract two dates or two times from each other)?

FIGURE 7-14 *A Sample Worksheet Formatted with the Dollar Sign*

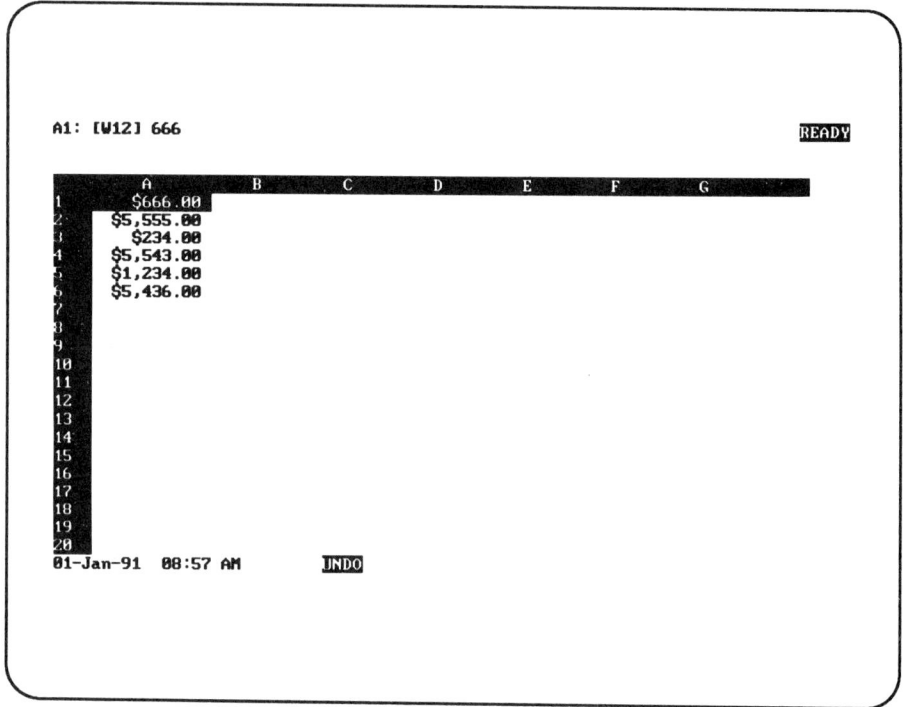

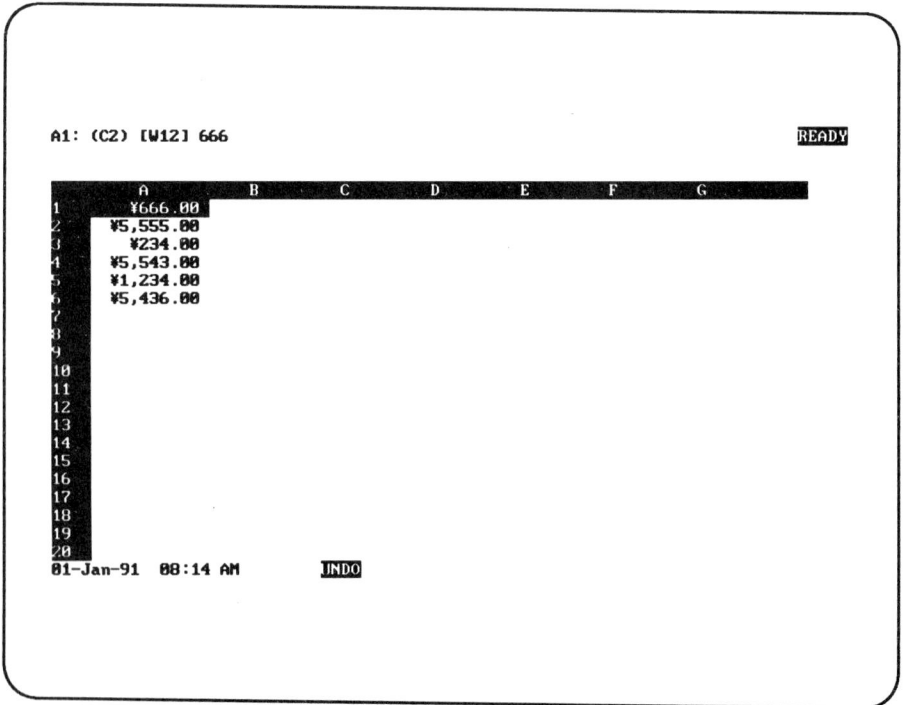

```
A1: [W12] 666                                              READY

         A           B       C       D       E       F       G
1      $666.00
2    $5,555.00
3      $234.00
4    $5,543.00
5    $1,234.00
6    $5,436.00
7
8
9
10
11
12
13
14
15
16
17
18
19
20
01-Jan-91   08:57 AM          UNDO
```

```
A1: (C2) [W12] 666                                         READY

         A           B       C       D       E       F       G
1      ¥666.00
2    ¥5,555.00
3      ¥234.00
4    ¥5,543.00
5    ¥1,234.00
6    ¥5,436.00
7
8
9
10
11
12
13
14
15
16
17
18
19
20
01-Jan-91   08:14 AM          UNDO
```

FIGURE 7-15 *Formatted with the Japanese Yen Sign*

FIGURE 7-16 *A Complete Example of All Format Options*

```
E18: (T) [W12] +C7*C8                                           READY

        A          B         C        D         E        F        G
   FORMAT OPTION        UNFORMATED        FORMATTED
1
2
3  GENERAL               25000              25000
4  FIXED                 25000           25000.00
5  SCIENTIFIC            25000           2.50E+04
6  CURRENCY              25000            $25,000
7                        25000             25,000
8  +/-                       6            ++++++
9  D1                    31621          28-Jul-86
10 D2                    31621             28-Jul
11 D3                    31621             Jul-86
12 D4                    31621           07/28/86
13 D5                    31621              07/28
14 T1                 0.448263        10:45:30 AM
15 T2                 0.448263           10:45 AM
16 T3                 0.448263           10:45:30
17 T4                 0.448263              10:45
18 TEXT                150000            +C7*C8
19 HIDDEN                25000
20
01-Jan-91  08:53 AM            UNDO
```

HANDS-ON PRACTICE

1. Design a worksheet with 5, 66, 777, 8888, and 99999 in cells A1 to A5. Now do the following:

    • Format this worksheet using the Comma option with three decimals.
    • Format this worksheet using the Fixed option with two decimals.
    • Format this worksheet using the Scientific option with two decimals.
    • Format this worksheet using the Currency option with two decimals.

    In some of these cases, you may see a series of asterisks. Why? This means your cell is not wide enough to hold your formatted number. You have to extend the cell width. Do you know how?

2. In cell A1 using D3 (Date Option 3), enter 32152 (e.g., January, 1988). Now generate the next 11 months by using the /Copy command. *Hint:* In cell A2 enter +A1+30.

3. In cells H1 and H2 enter 500 and 1000. In cell H3 enter +H1+H2. Naturally you will see 1500. Which format option will give you the formula +H1+H2 in cell H3, not its numeric value?

4. Enter 2, 22, 222, 2222 and 22222 in cells A1 to A5. Copy these numbers in cells F1 to F5. Now split the screen vertically in column D. Format the first screen using the Currency option. Format the second screen using the Comma option. Do you see the difference?

5. Type numbers 2, -5, 0, 7, -3 and 10 in cells A1 through A6 respectively. Format these cells using the +/- option. What are the applications of this type of format?

COMPREHENSIVE LAB ASSIGNMENT

Retrieve CHAPT6 and perform the following:
1. Using the /Format Fixed Option, add two decimals to each test score.
2. Hide the first test score.
3. Reveal the hidden test score.
4. Save this worksheet under CHAPT7.

MISCONCEPTION AND SOLUTION

M – You invoke a particular Format command and press the **Return** key. The particular cell may give you a solid line of asterisks.

S – The cell is not wide enough. Use /WCS, /WGC, or /WCC (Column-Range) to widen the cell width.

File Operations: Interaction Between Memory and Disk Files

8-1 Introduction

File operations enable you to save a worksheet file on disk, retrieve a file, incorporate parts of a file in your current worksheet, erase a file on disk, and import an ASCII file (discussed in Appendix D) from other programs to your worksheet. We will discuss these features in this chapter. Appendix D gives a comprehensive presentation of file transfer between Lotus and other programs. The chapter concludes with a discussion on File linking, a power feature for consolidating worksheets.

8-2 An Overview of File Operations

When you choose the File option from the main menu, you will be given the following choices:

Retrieve   Save   Combine   Xtract   Erase   List   Import   Directory   Admin

In the following pages we will explain these commands using several examples.

8-3 /File Save and Retrieve

The Save option enables you to save a Lotus file on a disk to make it permanent. A file can be saved under any valid file name (valid names are discussed in the next section). Remember that your disk must be formatted first (see Appendix B on formatting a disk).

To save a new file, simply choose the /File Save option and enter a name. However, if you are working with an old file that has already been saved at least once and you try to save it again, Lotus will give you three options:

Cancel   Replace   Backup

If you choose the Cancel option, nothing will be saved and you return to READY mode. Your old file will stay on the disk, untouched. If you choose the Replace option, the current worksheet will replace the old version on the disk, regardless of any difference in size.

The Backup option saves the previous file with the .BAK extension and saves the new file under the same file name with the .WK1 extension. At this time you have both files on the disk. You must remember that the backup file is one version older than the new file. In other words, your most recent changes will not be saved on the backup file. However, these changes are saved on the file itself. This is a nice feature to have. For example, if you are not happy with the changes you made to your worksheet, you can retrieve your backup file, which is your original file before any changes were made to it.

To retrieve a file from a disk, choose the Retrieve option, then press the **Return** key. Lotus will give you a listing of all your worksheet files. Either type the name of the file or move the cursor to a particular file and press the **Return** key.

8-4 Lotus File Specifications

Lotus file specifications are very similar to those for DOS files (discussed in Appendix B). Lotus accepts any valid file name up to eight characters in length. Digits zero through 9 and the underscore are accepted as part of a file name. Spaces are not allowed. The following are some examples of valid and invalid Lotus file names:

PAYROLL	Valid
PAY-ROLL	Valid
ROLL55	Valid
PARTNUMBER	Lotus cuts it to eight characters, then accepts it
PAY ROLL	Invalid (a space is not accepted)

Lotus generates and manipulates five types of files. These include Worksheet (WK1), Backup (BAK), Graph (PIC), Print (PRN), and Add-In (ADN). Non-Lotus files are identified under Others (non-Lotus type ASCII files, discussed in Appendix D). For example, when you save a worksheet, Lotus automatically attaches the extension WK1 to it. When you save a file, you can type your own extension. However, this file will not be retrieved automatically by Lotus nor will it appear on your menu. To retrieve such a file, type the name with the extension. Any Lotus file created in version 1A, 2, and 2.01 can be retrieved when using version 2.2 but the opposite is not true. Version 2.2 files must be translated prior to retrieval when using earlier versions.

Two wild card characters are accepted by Lotus: the question mark (?) and the asterisk (*). The question mark, used for one character only, means any character in a particular position. For example, B:\PAYROLL?.WK1 will give you all the files whose first seven characters are payroll and which are worksheet files. The asterisk, used for one or more characters, means any character in the file name or extension. For example, B:*.WK1 will give you all the worksheet files (all files with the extension WK1). The *.WK? will give you a listing of all WK1, WKS, WKQ and WKE files.

Lotus always starts its root directory with the drive name and a backslash (B:\). Within the root directory you can establish a subdirectory. (For more information on directories and subdirectories, see Appendix B.)

You can make your Lotus file self-booting. If you save your worksheet under AUTO123, Lotus will automatically load this file as soon as you start the spreadsheet.

To erase a permanent file, use the /File Erase command. But remember that if you erase a file, it is gone for good. You can use wild card characters to erase Lotus files in order to expedite the process, but this maximizes the danger of losing a file.

You can have one current file and many permanent files at any time. The current file is your current worksheet and permanent files are the files saved on your disk. If you retrieve another file, the current worksheet will be erased. If you do not want to lose this worksheet, you must save it before retrieving another file.

Lotus also allows you to save a file with a password. To do this, follow these steps:

1. Create or load a file.
2. Choose File Save from the main menu.
3. Type your desired file name.
4. press the space bar.
5. Type P (for password).
6. Press the **Return** key.
7. Type the desired password. Your password can be any of the LICS (Lotus International Character Set) characters, up to 15 characters. Do not use spaces. (See Appendix H for Lotus LICS).
8. Press the **Return** key.
9. Type the password again to verify it and press the **Return** key.

If you change your mind, you can always change or delete the password. To delete a password but save the file itself, first retrieve the file with the present password. When you are ready to save it again (/File Save), you will be given the following message: B: \Myfile.WK1 [PASSWORD PROTECTED] (Myfile.WK1 is your file name). Press the backspace to erase [PASSWORD PROTECTED], then press the **Return** key. Now your file will be saved under the desired name, in this case Myfile. To change a password, first delete the password as we just did, press the space bar, and type P followed by the **Return** key.

If you forget the password, you cannot retrieve the file. The password must be typed exactly as you created it every time you retrieve the file. Uppercase characters are considered to be different from lowercase characters.

8-5 /File Combine

The Combine option gives you three choices:

Copy   Add   Subtract

The Copy option enables you to copy an entire file or a portion of a file to the current worksheet. Be careful to remember the present position of the cursor; Copy can overwrite the current worksheet. This option gives you two choices:

Entire-File   Named/Specified-Range

Either the entire file or a specific range can be copied. Lotus will ask you for the name of the file, the range name, or range coordinates. Copy will not change the current worksheet *if* the cursor is in an empty location of the current worksheet.

The Add option enables you to add a file or a portion of a file to the current worksheet. Again, the position of the cursor is important. When you choose Add you will be given two choices:

Entire-File   Named/Specified-Range

You can choose either of these. The difference between Add and Copy is that Add adds the contents of the incoming file or range to the current worksheet. For example, if the cursor is at cell A1 and cell A1 contains 5 and if cell A1 from the incoming file contains 15, the final value of cell A1 in the current worksheet will be 20.

The Subtract option gives you the opportunity to subtract an entire file or a portion of a file from the current worksheet. Remember the present position of the cursor. In each of these three options the incoming data will be entered in the worksheet from the present position of the cursor to the right and down.

Remember, when you use the Add option, if an incoming file overlays a cell containing a label or a formula, Lotus discards the incoming value and retains the label or formula in the current worksheet. For example, if cell A1 in the current worksheet contains the label "COBOL", the incoming data will not have any effect on it. To see how this powerful command works, study the following examples.

Figure 8-1 is an example of an income statement for Division A of a company. Figure 8-2 shows the income statement for Division B.

Figure 8-3 was generated by using the Copy option. The income statement for Division B was copied at the bottom of Division A's income statement. This was done by using / File, Combine, Copy, Entire-file, Ch8-2 (the file name for Figure 8-2), and **Return**. Remember, the cursor must be in an empty area of the worksheet. In this example, the cursor was placed at cell A12.

Figure 8-4 is the consolidated income statement of Division A and Division B, using the Add option. Figures from Division B were added to those from Division A. Figure 8-4 was generated by choosing /File, Combine, Add, Named/Specified-Range, D5..D9, **Return**, Ch8-2, and **Return**.

The cursor must be positioned at the top left corner of the range for which you want to add the incoming data. In this case, the cursor was placed at cell D5.

Figure 8-5 shows the Subtract option. Figures for Division A were subtracted from the figures of Division B. In this example, the cursor was placed at cell D5. This figure was generated by using /File, Combine, Subtract, Named/Specified-Range, D5..D9, **Return**, Ch8-1 (the file name for Figure 8-1), and **Return**.

FIGURE 8-1   An Example of an Income Statement for Division A

```
A1: ' THIS IS AN EXAMPLE OF AN INCOME STATEMENT FOR DIVISION A          READY

        A           B           C           D           E           F
 1   THIS IS AN EXAMPLE OF AN INCOME STATEMENT FOR DIVISION A
 2
 3                                        1990
 4
 5   SALES                              $500,000
 6      COST OF GOODS SOLD             ($225,000)
 7   GROSS PROFIT                       $275,000
 8      EXPENSES                       ($200,000)
 9   NET INCOME                          $75,000
10
11
12
13
14
15
16
17
18
19
20
01-Jan-91  08:34 AM          UNDO
```

FIGURE 8-2 *An Example of an Income Statement for Division B*

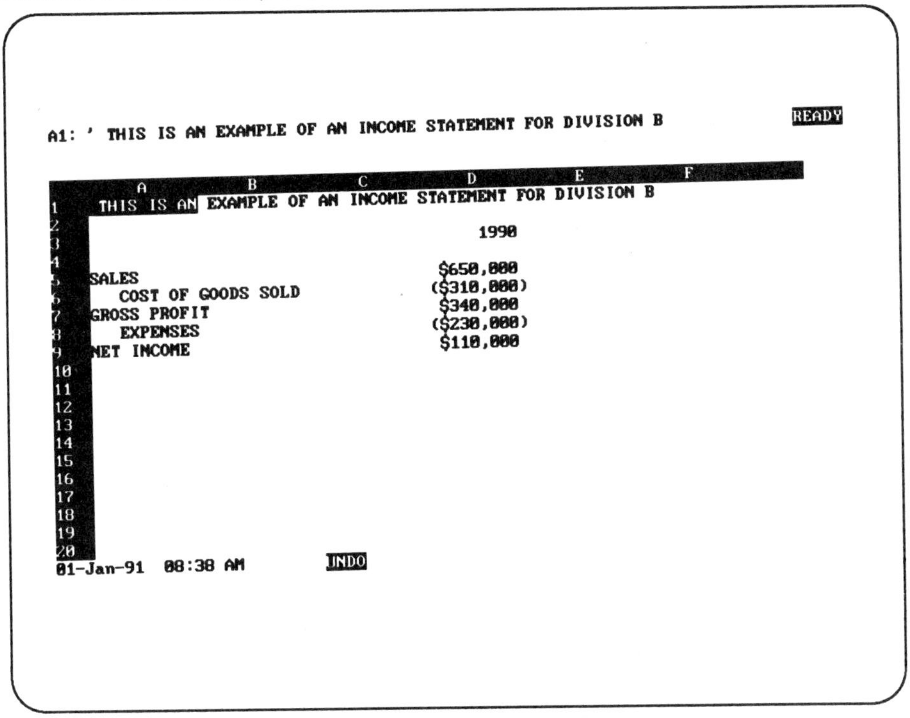

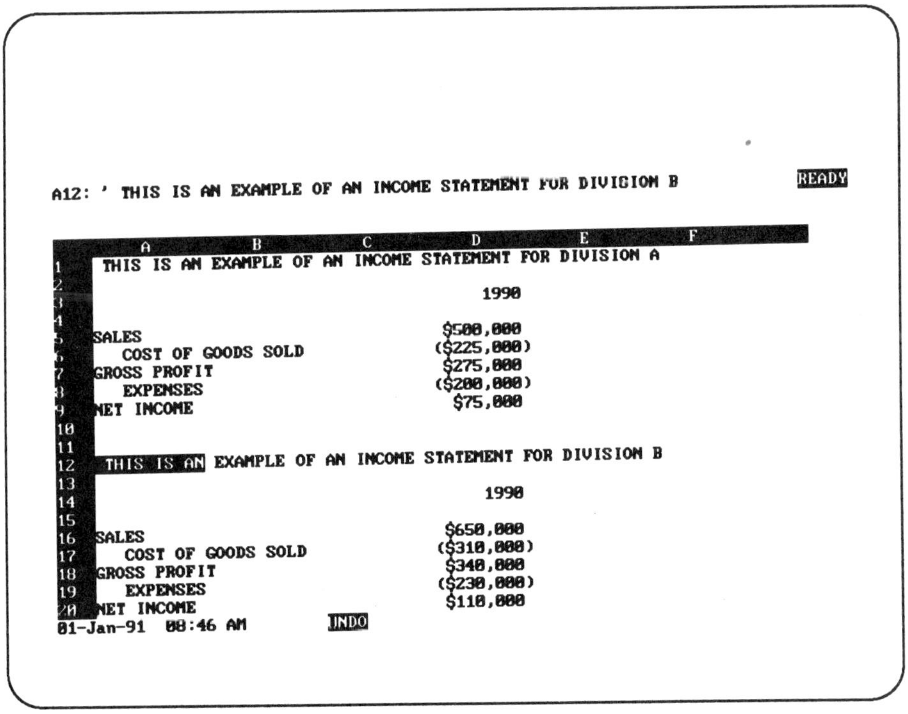

FIGURE 8-3 *An Example of the Copy Option*

FIGURE 8-4 *Example of the Add Option*

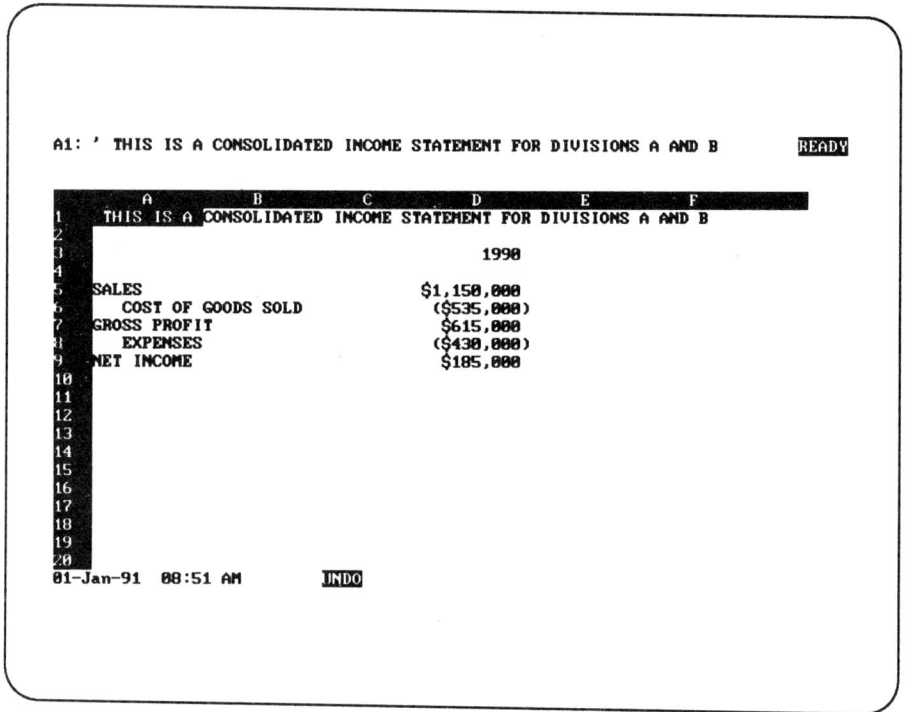

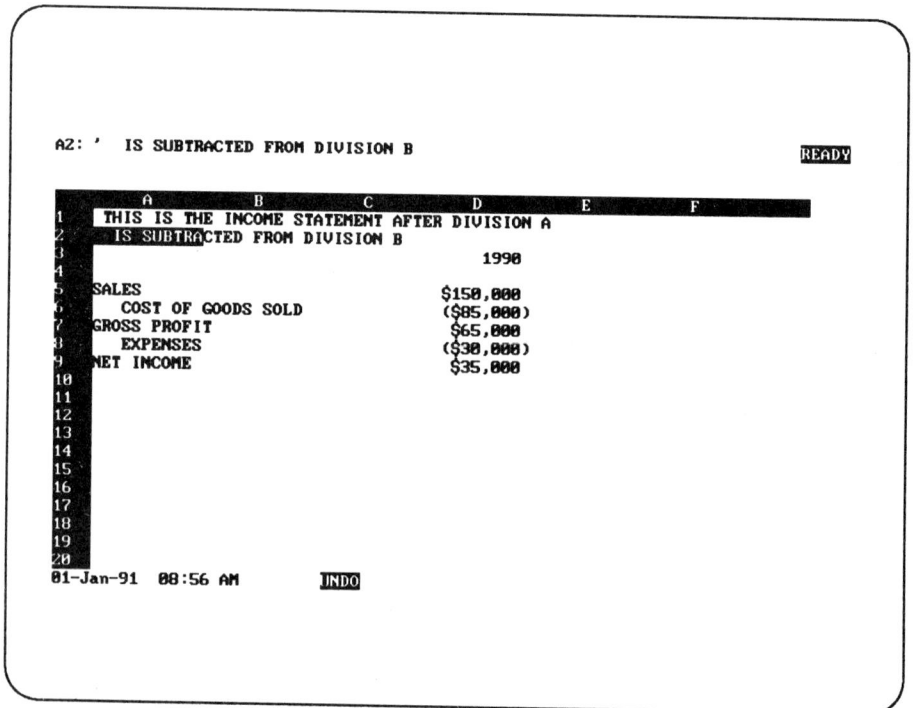

```
A1: ' THIS IS A CONSOLIDATED INCOME STATEMENT FOR DIVISIONS A AND B        READY
          A          B          C          D          E          F
 1    THIS IS A CONSOLIDATED INCOME STATEMENT FOR DIVISIONS A AND B
 2
 3                                       1990
 4
 5   SALES                            $1,150,000
 6      COST OF GOODS SOLD             ($535,000)
 7   GROSS PROFIT                       $615,000
 8      EXPENSES                       ($430,000)
 9   NET INCOME                         $185,000
10
11
12
13
14
15
16
17
18
19
20
01-Jan-91  08:51 AM            UNDO
```

```
A2: '  IS SUBTRACTED FROM DIVISION B                                        READY
          A          B          C          D          E          F
 1    THIS IS THE INCOME STATEMENT AFTER DIVISION A
 2    IS SUBTRACTED FROM DIVISION B
 3                                       1990
 4
 5   SALES                              $150,000
 6      COST OF GOODS SOLD              ($85,000)
 7   GROSS PROFIT                        $65,000
 8      EXPENSES                        ($30,000)
 9   NET INCOME                          $35,000
10
11
12
13
14
15
16
17
18
19
20
01-Jan-91  08:56 AM            UNDO
```

FIGURE 8-5 *Example of the Subtract Option*

8-6 /File Xtract

This option extracts and saves a portion of the current worksheet in a file on disk. Unlike Combine, Xtract does not change information in the current worksheet. Two options are given under Xtract: Formulas and Values. With the Formulas option, Lotus saves the worksheet with any formulas from the current worksheet to the extracted file. For example, if cells A1 and A2 contain 5 and 10 and cell A3 contains their sum, e.g., +A1+A2, then the Formulas option saves this worksheet and the formula.

With the Values option, Lotus saves the worksheet with only calculated values for formulas. In the above example, 15 will be extracted and saved with the worksheet, not +A1+A2. This means that you will not know how the value was obtained.

Figure 8-6 is an income statement for three divisions of a company. In Figure 8-7 we have extracted Division A from Figure 8-6 with the Formulas option. We used /File, Xtract, Formulas, Ch8-7 (the file name for Figure 8-7), **Return**, A3..D9, and **Return**.

In Figure 8-8 we have extracted Division A from Figure 8-6 with the Values option. We used /File, Xtract, Values, Ch8-8 (the file name for Figure 8-8), **Return**, A3..D9, and **Return**.

As you can see, with the Formulas option, the original formulas are transferred exactly, while with the Values option, only the values are transferred, not the formulas. Remember, to see the formulas in any worksheet you must choose the Text option from the Format command.

Now, if you go to Figure 8-8 and try the Format Text option in cell D5, you will see the value 275000.

If you go to Figure 8-7 and try the Format Text option in cell D5, you will see the formula +D3-D4, because this was transferred by /File Xtract Formulas.

8-7 /File List

With the /File List command you can get the listing of your entire directory. Your Lotus directory will include five types of files: WK1, PIC, PRN, and Others and Linked. You can choose any of these options and Lotus will give you a complete listing of files within any group.

8-8 /File Erase

The Erase option allows the deletion of files WK1, PIC, PRN, and Others. (Others includes all the files in your directory, both Lotus and non-Lotus files.)

8-9 /File Directory

The Directory option will tell you the current directory of your system. Usually your directory is in drive B (in a floppy system), but it can be changed. To find the status of your directory, you can also use the /Worksheet Global Default Directory command. This will display the current directory. If you have access to a hard disk, type /File Directory A:\ to access files on a floppy disk and then place the floppy disk in drive A; for example, if you have a hard disk and you are trying to use the disks provided with this book, you have to first issue /File Directory A:\, then put one of the disks in drive A.

FIGURE 8-6 *Example of an Income Statement for Three Divisions of a Company*

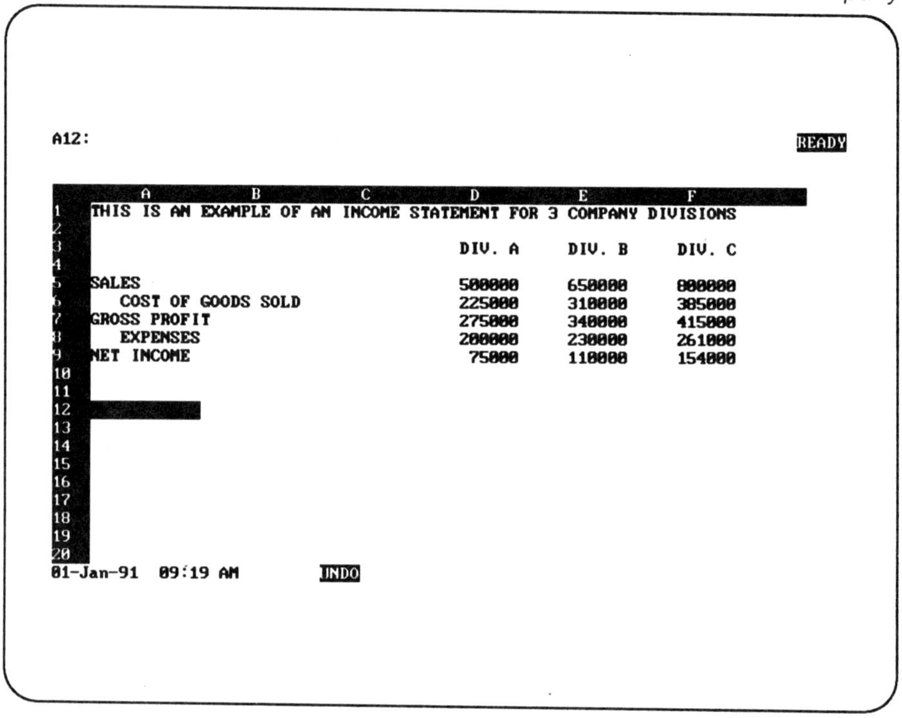

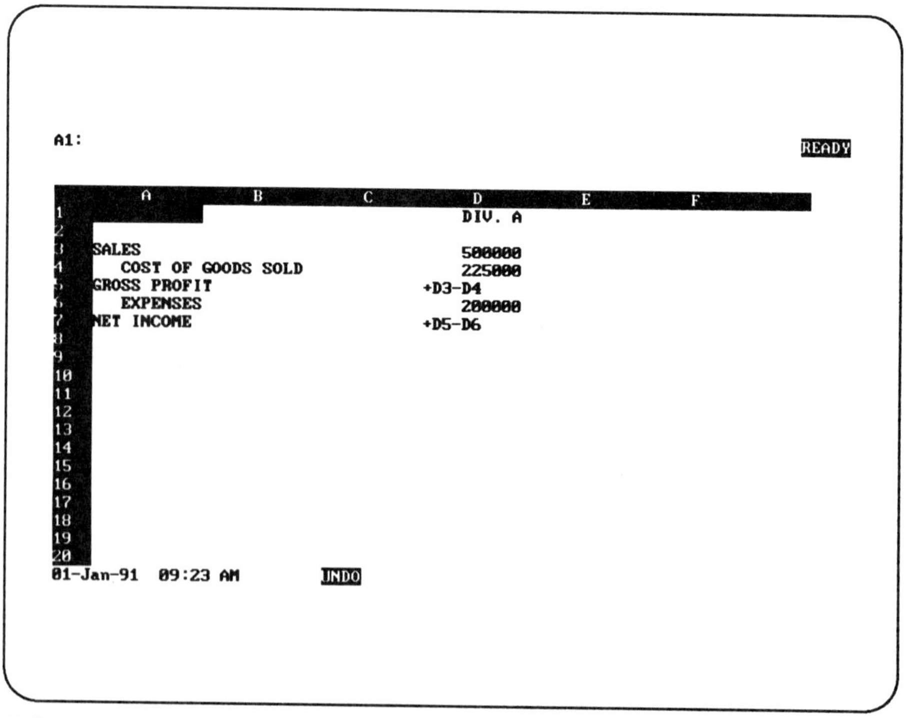

```
A12:                                                                    READY

           A          B          C          D          E          F
 1  THIS IS AN EXAMPLE OF AN INCOME STATEMENT FOR 3 COMPANY DIVISIONS
 2
 3                                          DIV. A     DIV. B     DIV. C
 4
 5  SALES                                   500000     650000     800000
 6      COST OF GOODS SOLD                  225000     310000     385000
 7  GROSS PROFIT                           275000     340000     415000
 8      EXPENSES                            200000     230000     261000
 9  NET INCOME                              75000     110000     154000
10
11
12
13
14
15
16
17
18
19
20
01-Jan-91  09:19 AM          UNDO
```

```
A1:                                                                     READY

           A          B          C          D          E          F
 1                                          DIV. A
 2
 3  SALES                                   500000
 4      COST OF GOODS SOLD                  225000
 5  GROSS PROFIT                           +D3-D4
 6      EXPENSES                            200000
 7  NET INCOME                             +D5-D6
 8
 9
10
11
12
13
14
15
16
17
18
19
20
01-Jan-91  09:23 AM          UNDO
```

FIGURE 8-7 *Example of the Xtract Option with Formulas*

FIGURE 8-8 Example of the Xtract Option with Values

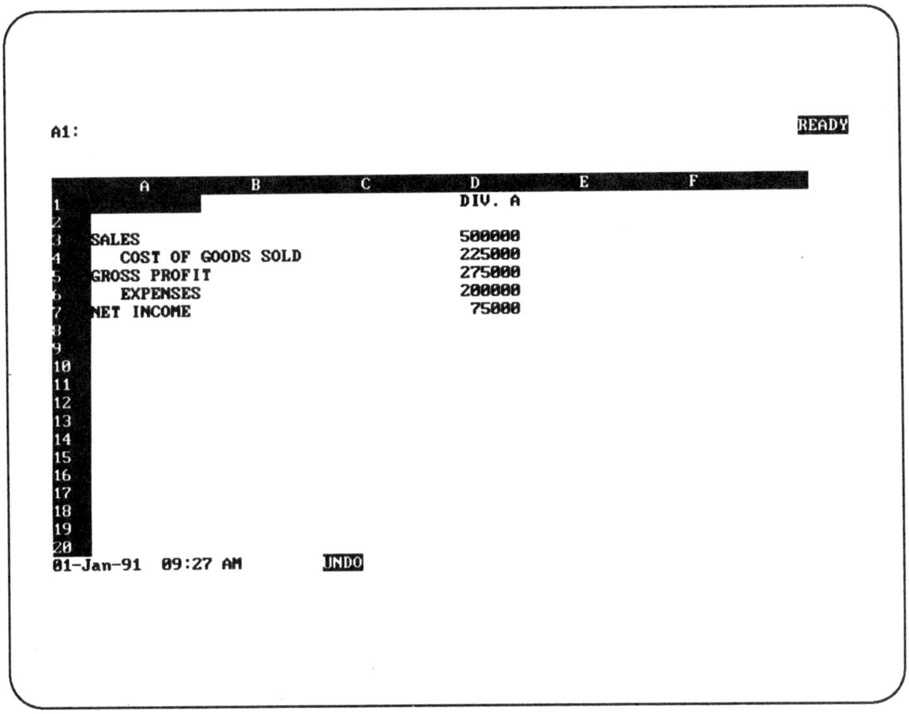

```
A1:                                                                    READY


          A           B          C          D          E          F
   1                                      DIV. A
   2
   3  SALES                               500000
   4      COST OF GOODS SOLD              225000
   5  GROSS PROFIT                        275000
   6      EXPENSES                        200000
   7  NET INCOME                           75000
   8
   9
  10
  11
  12
  13
  14
  15
  16
  17
  18
  19
  20
  01-Jan-91   09:27 AM        UNDO
```

8-10 /File Import

The /File Import command allows you to enter ASCII files into your worksheet. ASCII (American Standard Code for Information Interchange) is a data format generated and accepted by many applications software packages.

An ASCII file, or simply a "print image" file, is a file in standard keyboard characters. To verify whether a file is ASCII or not is very simple. At the A> prompt in DOS, type TYPE filename.extension. If a file is listed in standard keyboard characters, it is an ASCII file; otherwise it is not. For example, Lotus files generated by the /Print File command (files with the PRN extension) are ASCII files. VisiCalc generates all its files in ASCII, as do Wordstar, dBASE II and III, and BASICA.

When you invoke the /File Import command, Lotus gives you two options: Text and Numbers. you can select either one; then you will be prompted with the file name. Type the file name (and the extension if it is not .PRN) and press **Return**. Your file will be entered in the worksheet at the present position of the cursor—left to right and top to bottom.

8-11 Linking Files

One of the improvements in Release 2.2 over earlier releases of 1-2-3 is that you can link files together. This simply means that a worksheet can refer to cells in other worksheets. File linking enables you to build large worksheets that are too large to fit into the memory of your computer all at once. Theoretically this means you can expand your memory indefinitely. To do this you must use the following format:

+<<file name>>cell reference

To make this more clear let us walk through a simply example. Let us say you have typed 5 in cell A1, file S1 and 10 in cell A2, file S2. The S1 and S2 files are saved on your default drive. In your third file (S3) you would like to refer to these two cells in S1 and S2. In file S3, cells B1 and B2 (or any other cells) you will type:

(in cell B1) + <<S1.WK1>>A1
(in cell B2) + <<S2.WK1>>A2

As soon as you type these formulas, you will see 5 in cell B1 and 10 in cell B2. In the above formulas you did not need to type WK1 as the file extension. However, if your file extension is any other extension besides WK1, you must type it. You must also provide the drive identifier and/or the specific directory and path if the files are not in your default drive and/or directory.

The file that provides data is called the source file. The file that receives the data is called the target file. If you make any changes to the source file you must first save it under its present name by using the /File Save Replace command. As soon as you retrieve the target file it will be updated automatically. Remember the importance of hierarchical order. If you first retrieve the target file before updating the source file you will receive erroneous results.

If you are using the file linking feature in a network, to update the target file you must use /File Admin Link-Refresh. The /File List Linked command displays a listing of all the source files referred to by linking formulas in the current worksheet. /File Admin Table Linked creates a table in the worksheet that lists linked files for a specified directory.

/File Admin Reservation allows you to get and release a file's reservation, or lock it. This command is used when you share worksheet files on a network and want to save files or allow other people to save files. /File Admin Table creates a table of information about files on disk. This can be on worksheet, print, graph, other, or linked files. When you invoke this command, you must specify the beginning of the range for the file listing. The listing will be displayed in four columns. The first column is the file name, the second column is the date, the third column is the time, and the fourth column is the file size. To see the actual date and time you must format the second and third columns with date and time, respectively.

While working with linked files, remember the following rules:

1. The target worksheet can refer to a single cell in the source file or to a range of cells. For example, in cell C1 in the target file you can type:

    +<<S1>>A1

    or

    +<<S1>>A1..A10

    However, 1-2-3 will change the formula to +<<S1>>A1, since it only uses the cell in the upper left corner of the range as the source cell.
2. You can use range names instead of the cell addresses. For example, you give the name asset to range B2..D2, if in the source file, S1, in the target file you can type:

    +<<S1>>Asset

    However, 1-2-3 only uses the cell in the upper left corner of the range as the source cell.
3. You can use absolute or mixed addresses as well as relative addresses.

8-12 File Linking: A Comprehensive Example

The National Computer Consulting Firm has two divisions: Western and Eastern. The Western division includes California, Oregon, and Washington. The Eastern division includes Virginia, New York, and Massachusetts. Figure 8-9 illustrates an organization chart for this firm. For simplicity we have included only two items in the worksheet for each state: revenues and expenses before taxes. Using the file linking feature of 1-2-3, we would like to generate two subconsolidated statements for the Western and Eastern divisions, in addition to a consolidated statement for the firm as the whole. The worksheets for California, Oregon, Washington, Western Division, Virginia, New York, Massachusetts, Eastern Division, and total company data are saved in the default drive under CH8-10 to CH8-18 (for easy access).

In the Western, Eastern, and total company worksheets we have created an extra column formatted with the Text option to show you the actual formulas in each cell (see Figures 8-10 through 8-18). To update these worksheets you must start from the lowest level. Enter the new data and save the worksheet under the same name (/FS Replace option). Then when you retrieve the higher level worksheets, they will be automatically updated.

SUMMARY

Using the file operations provided by Lotus, you can save a worksheet, combine several worksheets together, erase an unwanted worksheet, and so forth. Lotus provides a series of choices within the /File command. You can add a password to a file for security purposes, extract a portion of a file and send it to another worksheet, and so on. Appendix D discusses file transfer between Lotus and other programs. The chapter concluded with a discussion on file linking.

REVIEW QUESTIONS

* These questions are answered in Appendix I.
  1. How many choices are provided by the File option?
  2. What is a Lotus file?
  3.* How many types of files can be generated by Lotus?
  4. How many current and permanent worksheets can you have at one time?
  5. How do you generate a password for a disk file?
  6.* What are the requirements for a password?
  7. How many options do you have under /File Combine?
  8.* What is the difference between /File Combine Add and /File Combine Copy?
  9. Why is the present position of the cursor so important in the /File Combine command?
  10.* Is it possible for you to lose your current worksheet when you use /File Combine options? If yes, how?
  11. What is the difference between /File Combine Copy and /File Xtract?
  12. What are some of the uses of /File Xtract?
  13. What is the purpose of /File Directory?
  14.* How can wild card characters be used with the /File Erase option?
  15. Can you change your directory? If yes, how?

FIGURE 8-9 *An Organizational Chart for the National Computer Consulting Firm*

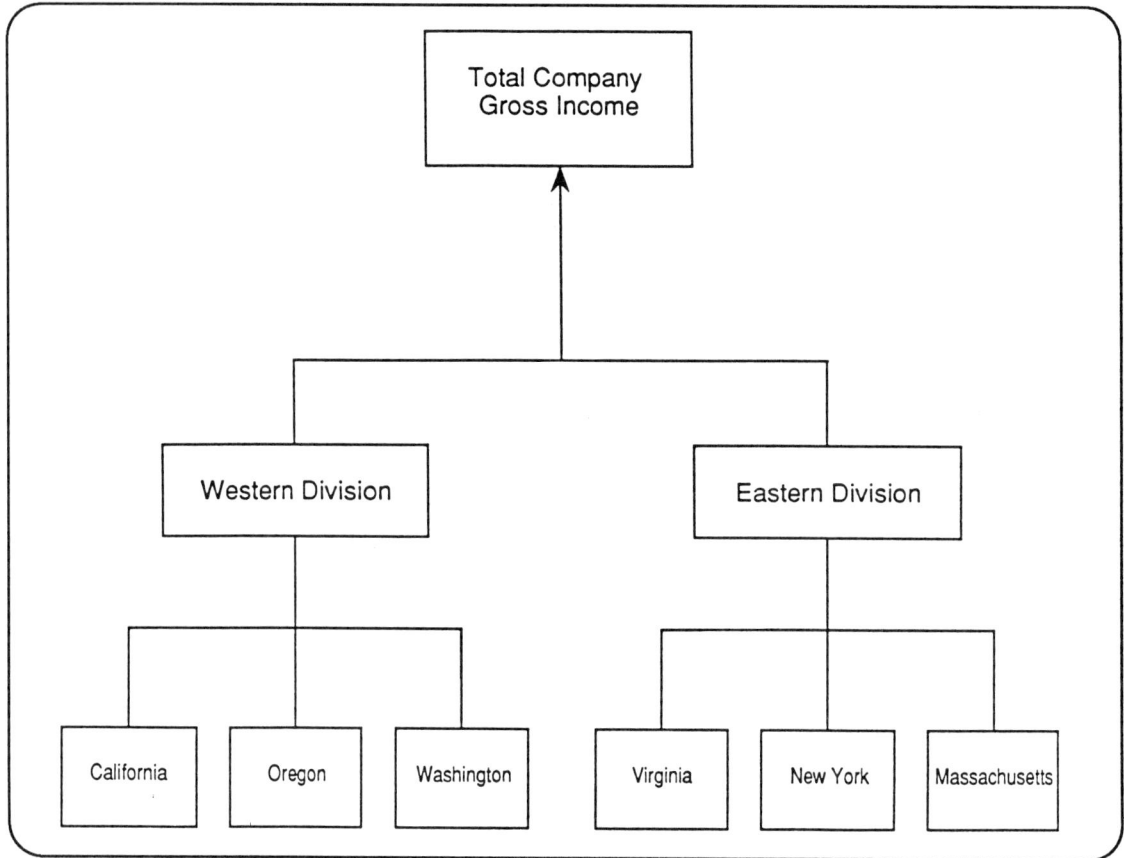

16. Can the /File Combine Add or /File Combine Copy commands generate the same final result? If yes, under what circumstances?

HANDS-ON PRACTICE

1. Store 10, 20, 30, and 40 in cells A1, A2, A3, and A4. Save this worksheet under W1. Now retrieve this file using the /File Combine Add, /File Combine Copy, and /File Combine Subtract commands. What command should you use in order to generate a worksheet with zeros in cells A1, A2, A3, and A4?
2. Generate three worksheets with five values in column A for the first one, five values in column B for the second one, and five values in column C for the third one. Now, using the /File Combine command, generate a worksheet that includes three columns with values from worksheets 1, 2, and 3.
3. Using the /File Xtract command, copy column A of the above worksheet to another file called W5.
4. Store values 5, 10, and 15 in cells A1, A2, and A3, respectively. Store the sum of these values in cell A10 (+A1+A2+A3). Using the /File Xtract command, save this

FIGURE 8-10   Worksheet for California

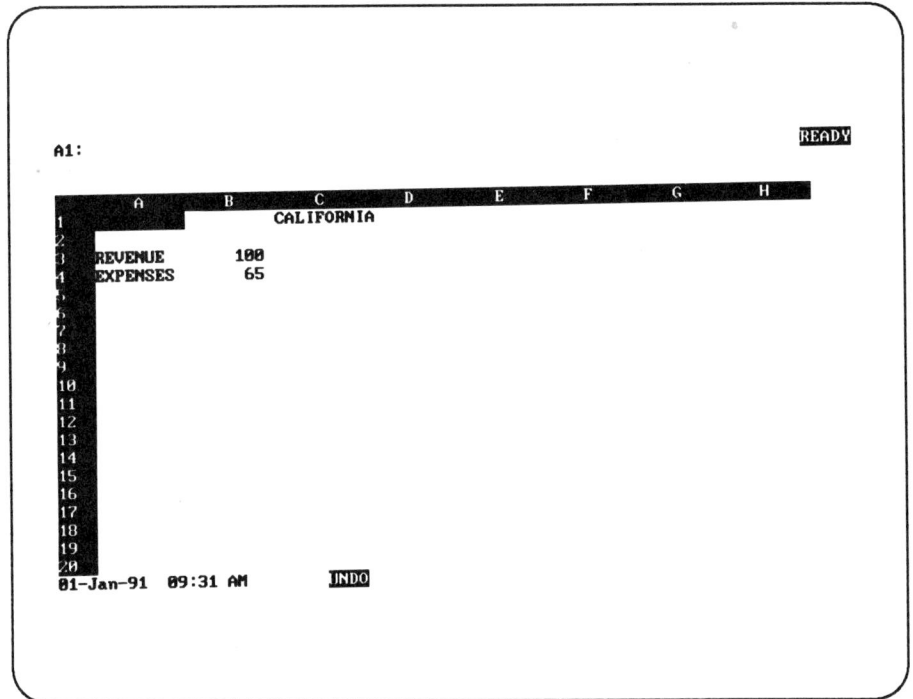

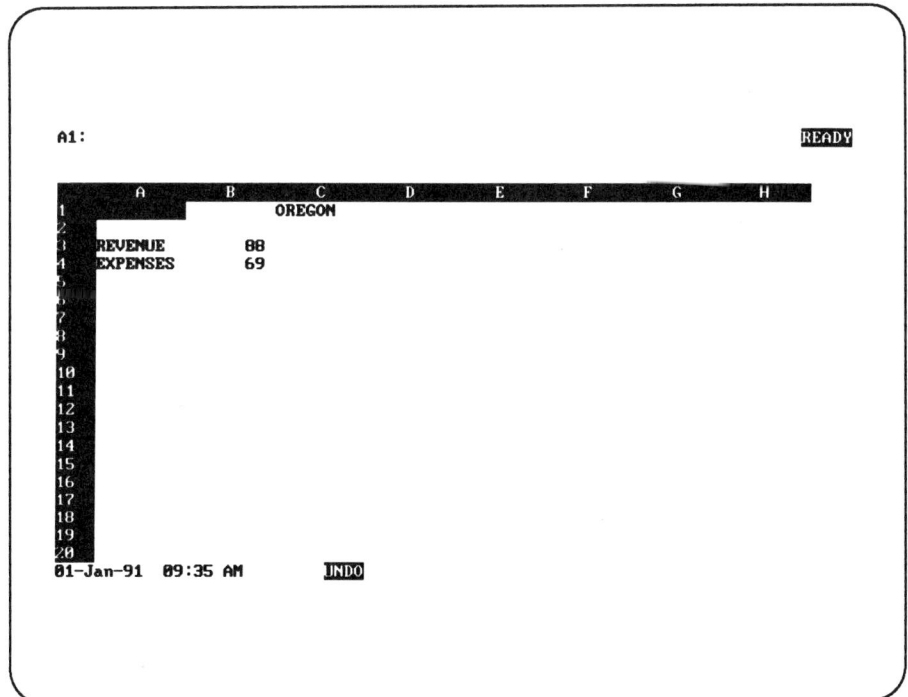

FIGURE 8-11   Worksheet for Oregon

FIGURE 8-12 Worksheet for Washington

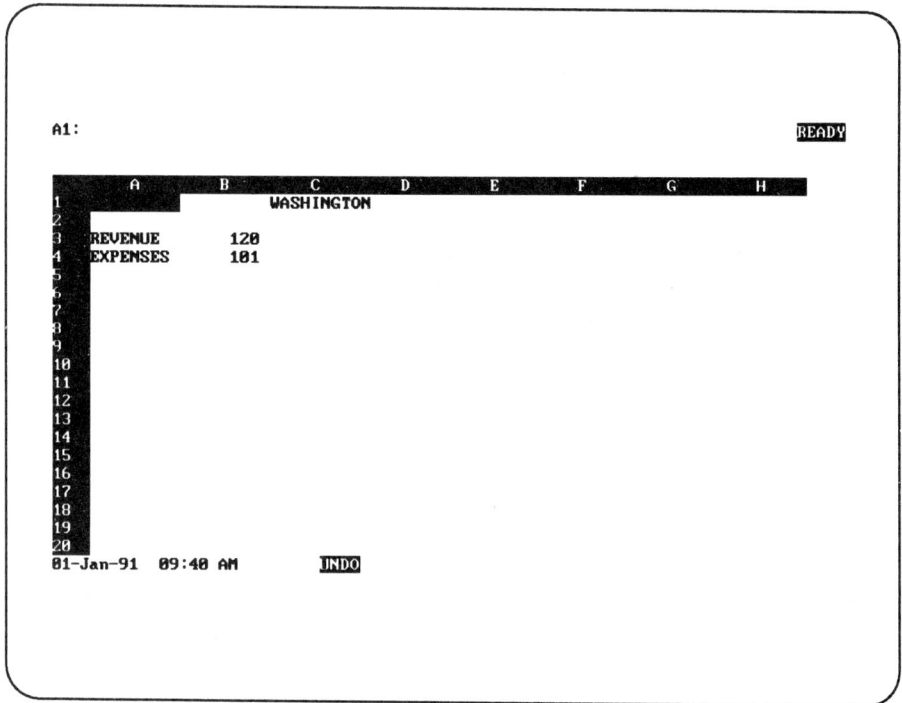

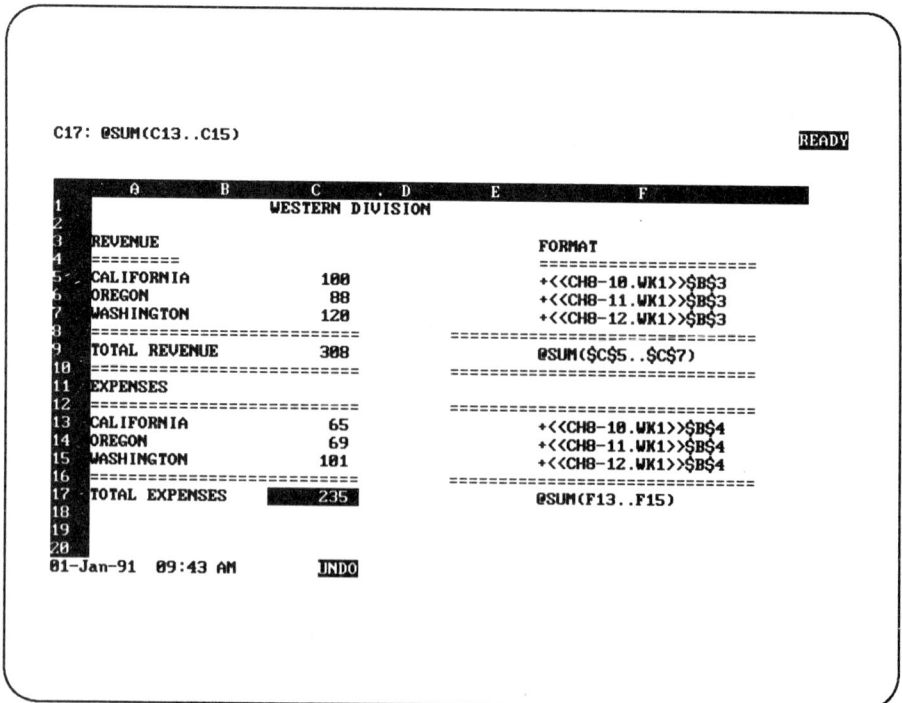

FIGURE 8-13 Worksheet for Western Division

FIGURE 8-14 Worksheet for Virginia

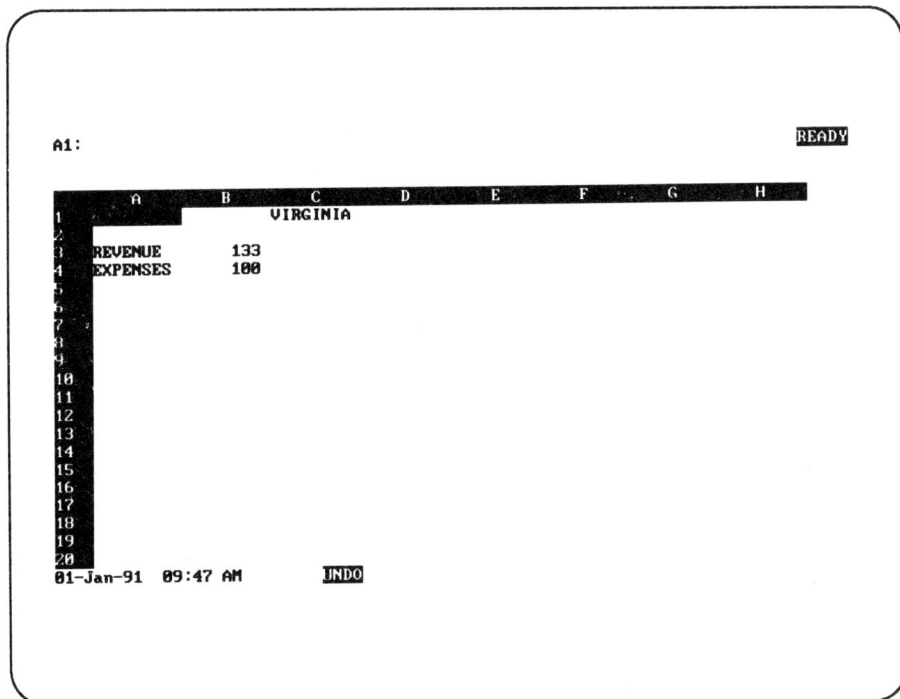

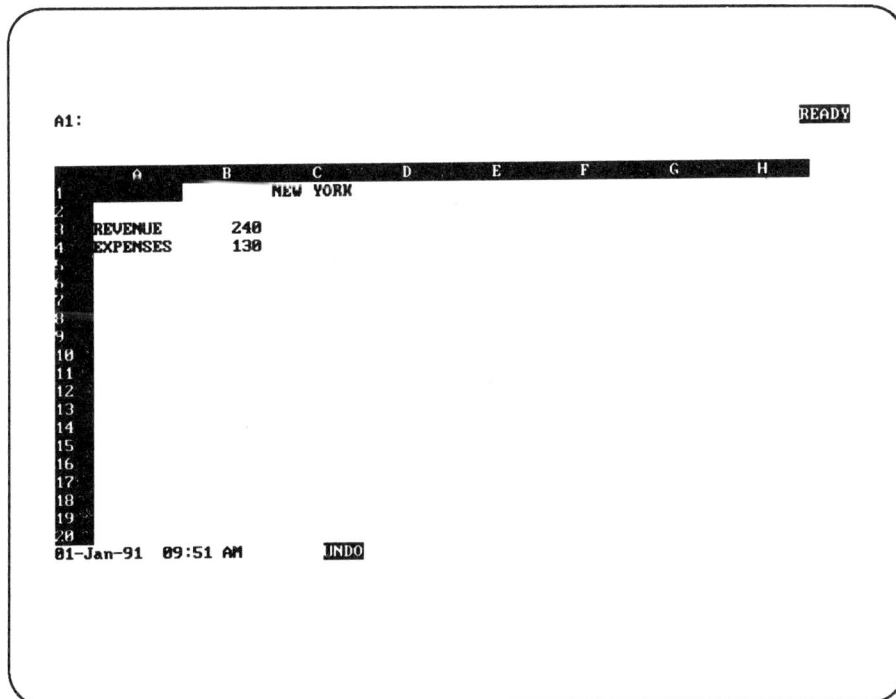

```
A1:                                                                    READY

        A         B         C         D         E         F         G         H
 1                        VIRGINIA
 2
 3   REVENUE        133
 4   EXPENSES       100
 5
 6
 7
 8
 9
10
11
12
13
14
15
16
17
18
19
20
01-Jan-91  09:47 AM              UNDO
```

```
A1:                                                                    READY

        A         B         C         D         E         F         G         H
 1                        NEW YORK
 2
 3   REVENUE        240
 4   EXPENSES       130
 5
 6
 7
 8
 9
10
11
12
13
14
15
16
17
18
19
20
01-Jan-91  09:51 AM              UNDO
```

FIGURE 8-15 Worksheet for New York

FIGURE 8-16 Worksheet for Massachusetts

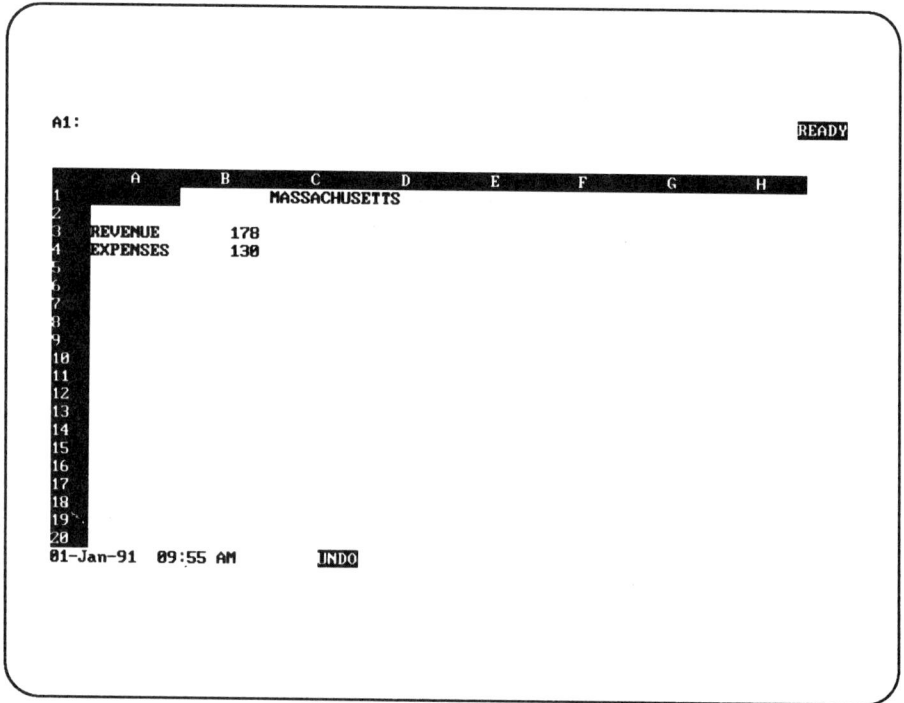

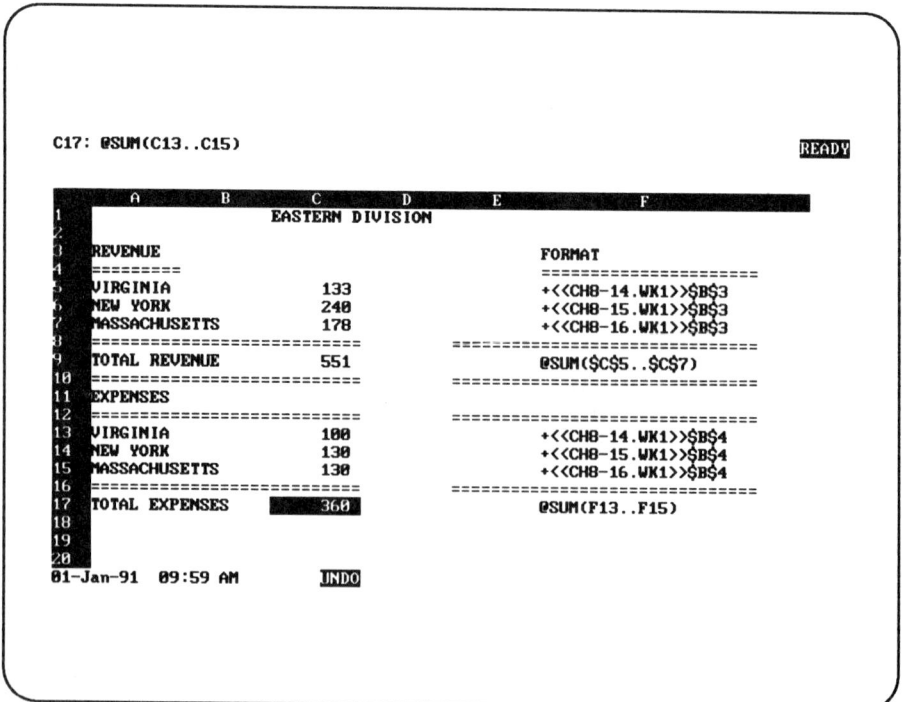

```
A1:                                                              READY

        A          B          C          D      E      F      G      H
 1                        MASSACHUSETTS
 2
 3  REVENUE           178
 4  EXPENSES          130
 5
 6
 7
 8
 9
10
11
12
13
14
15
16
17
18
19
20
01-Jan-91  09:55 AM            UNDO
```

```
C17: @SUM(C13..C15)                                             READY

        A          B          C          D      E           F
 1                        EASTERN DIVISION
 2
 3  REVENUE                                    FORMAT
 4  ========                                   =======================
 5  VIRGINIA              133                  +<<CH8-14.WK1>>$B$3
 6  NEW YORK              240                  +<<CH8-15.WK1>>$B$3
 7  MASSACHUSETTS         178                  +<<CH8-16.WK1>>$B$3
 8  ============================              ===============================
 9  TOTAL REVENUE         551                  @SUM($C$5..$C$7)
10  ============================              ===============================
11  EXPENSES
12  ============================              ===============================
13  VIRGINIA              100                  +<<CH8-14.WK1>>$B$4
14  NEW YORK              130                  +<<CH8-15.WK1>>$B$4
15  MASSACHUSETTS         130                  +<<CH8-16.WK1>>$B$4
16  ============================              ===============================
17  TOTAL EXPENSES        360                  @SUM(F13..F15)
18
19
20
01-Jan-91  09:59 AM            UNDO
```

FIGURE 8-17 Worksheet for Eastern Division

FIGURE 8-18 Worksheet for the Entire Company

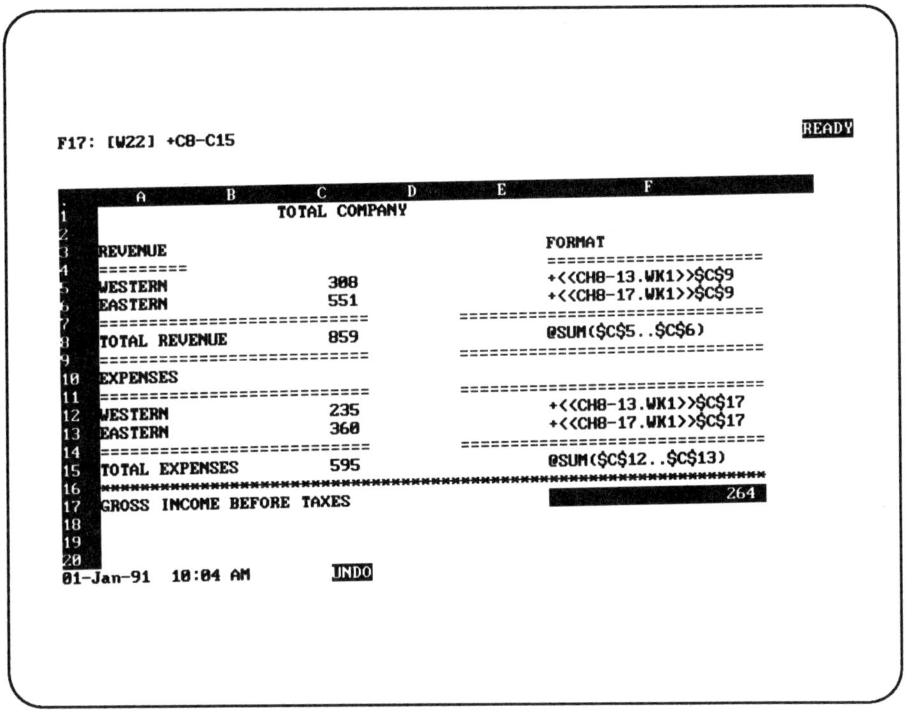

worksheet once with the Values option in a file called Value. Use the Formulas option and save this worksheet in a file called Formula. What is the difference between files Value and Formula?

5. Generate the following worksheet for Branch A of Tasty Pizza Company:

Column A	Column B
Quarter 1	10,000
Quarter 2	15,000
Quarter 3	12,500
Quarter 4	11,500

Save this file with the password "Secret."

6. Retrieve this file and change the password to "not-secret." Is this a valid name?

7. The following data comes from Branch B of Tasty Pizza Company:

Column C	Column D
Quarter 1	8,000
Quarter 2	11,200
Quarter 3	10,000
Quarter 4	10,500

   • Add Branches A and B together using /File Combine Add.
   • Subtract Branch A from Branch B using /File Combine Subtract.
   • Save Branch B data under BranchB.

8. Erase the worksheet and copy Branch A data in range A1..B4. Now copy Branch B data underneath Branch A with one empty line between.

9. Extract Quarter 1 and Quarter 2 data for Branch A and save it in a file called "Half."

10. Retrieve Branch B data, add the four quarters, and store the result in cell D10. Now extract this total once with the option Formulas and once with the option Values. What is the difference?

11. Using /File List, generate a listing of all your worksheet files in drive B or C.

12. Using the diagram presented in Figure 8-9 add a new item under the heading "new expenses for R&D" as follows:

California	52
Oregon	42
Washington	47
Virginia	70
New York	64
Massachusetts	71

   By using the file linking feature generate a consolidated financial statement for the Western and Easter divisions as well as for the company as a whole.

13. Invoke the /File Admin Table Worksheet command. Then, by using Date and Time formats convert these dates and times to standard DOS format.

COMPREHENSIVE LAB ASSIGNMENT

Retrieve CHAPT7 and perform the following:

1. Using /File Xtract, extract the name and major of all the students into a file called NAME.

2. Save the worksheet under CHAPT8.

3. Save this file once again with a password. This time use SECRET as the password and IMPORTANT as the file name.

4. Retrieve IMPORTANT and change the password to SECRET1.

MISCONCEPTIONS AND SOLUTIONS

M – When you save a file with a password, if you forget the password, you will never be able to retrieve that file.

S – Use a password that has a special meaning for you.

M – One of the options in the Lotus main menu is Quit. When you choose this option, you will leave Lotus and your work will not be saved.

S – Save your worksheet first; Lotus will not save your worksheet automatically.

M – FILE NOT FOUND is a common unfriendly error message.

S – The particular file is not on the disk, or you spelled the name wrong, or you have a wrong disk in the drive. Type the right file name and possibly the drive identifier. If it still doesn't work, there should not be such a file.

M – You try to save or retrieve a file, but the mode indicator says DISK DRIVE NOT READY.

S – Check if there is a disk in your default drive, or if the door is closed.

Report Generation

9-1 Introduction

In this chapter we discuss the /Print command, one that enables you to generate reports. Using this command and its subcommands, you can print directly to a printer or to a file for future printing. You have flexibility in determining the look of your report by specifying such aspects as margins and lengths. This command also assists you in generating reports that can be utilized later by other software such as databases, word processors, other spreadsheets, and so on (for more information see Appendix D). For presentation-quality reports, see the discussion of Allways in the next two chapters.

9-2 Printing to a File or a Printer

As mentioned earlier, a report can be printed directly to a printer or to a file. Since the commands are the same for both printer and file, we will only refer to the printer as the print device.

When you try to print to a file, you must define the file name, following the rules discussed in Chapter 8. The file generated by the /Print command will use PRN as an extension, as opposed to WK1 (for worksheet) or PIC (for graphic files).

Files generated by /Print File can later be printed in DOS. At the A> prompt type TYPE filename.PRN. This file can be brought to the worksheet by the /File Import command; however, the file will lose its column and row structures. The reason for this transformation is that filename.PRN is an ASCII file (see Appendix D).

Whether printing to a printer or to a file, you have complete control over a file's size and format. This means that you can choose a specific range or ranges.

9-3 Overview of the /Print Command

When you invoke the /Print command, you will be given two options: Printer and File. Both have the following further options (see Figure 9-1):

Range Line Page Options Clear Align Go Quit

Range allows you to print either a specific portion of the worksheet or the entire worksheet. As usual, you can specify the range address or use pointing.

Line inserts a line or skips a line. If the printer is at the bottom of the report, this command will advance the printer to the next page.

FIGURE 9-1 *Options under /Print Printer or /Print File Command*

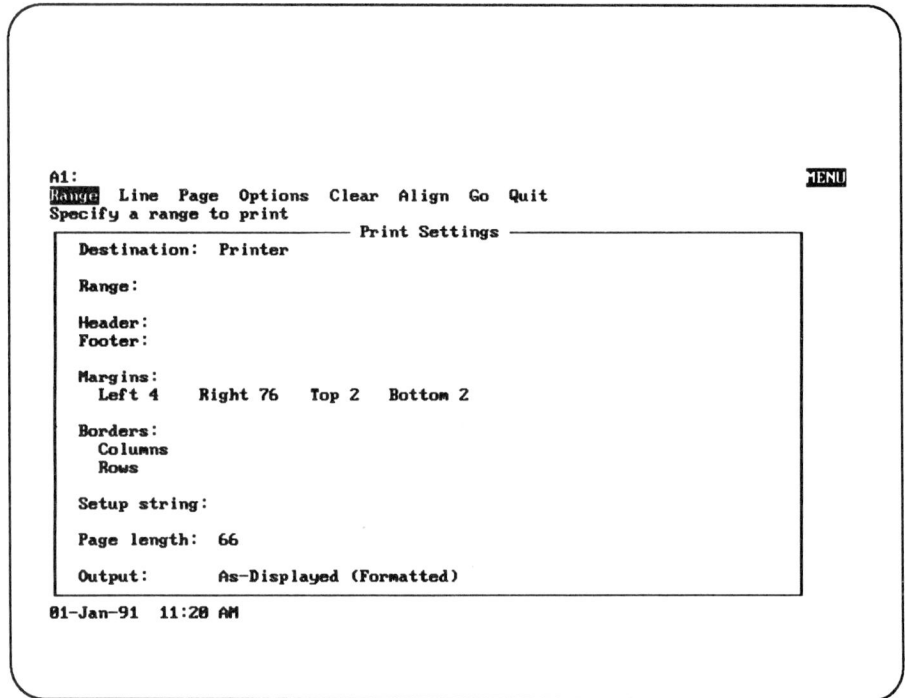

```
A1:                                                                    MENU
Range  Line  Page  Options  Clear  Align  Go  Quit
Specify a range to print
─────────────────────────── Print Settings ───────────────────────
   Destination:  Printer

   Range:

   Header:
   Footer:

   Margins:
      Left 4     Right 76    Top 2    Bottom 2

   Borders:
      Columns
      Rows

   Setup string:

   Page length:  66

   Output:       As-Displayed (Formatted)

01-Jan-91  11:20 AM
```

Page skips a page or advances a page. If there is a footer, it will be printed at the bottom of the page.

Options includes several interesting choices:

    Header Footer Margins Borders Setup Pg-Length Other Quit

Header prints a line of text up to 240 characters below the top margin.

Footer prints a line of text up to 240 characters above the bottom margin.

You can include the contents of a worksheet cell in a header or footer. Instead of typing the header or footer text, type \(backslash) followed by the address of the cell that contains the label. For example, if a title is in cell B10, type \B10 as your header or footer.

Margins allows you to define Left, Right, Top, and Bottom margins.

Borders prints designated column or row headings on every page. This can be either above or to the left of the specified range you are printing. With this option you can choose rows or columns. The areas you have identified as borders are not supposed to be included in your print range. If they are, you will get duplicate information.

Setup specifies the style and font size for a printer. The setup string, up to 39 characters, comes from a printer control code (you should consult your printer manual for specifics). It must begin with a backslash (\) and a three- or four-digit code. For example, \015 on an Epson FX80 prints compressed output.

Pg-Length defines the number of lines of text to be printed. This can be any number between 1 and 100.

Other options include several powerful commands:

    As-Displayed Cell-Formulas Formatted Unformatted

As-Displayed prints the report as it appears on the monitor.

Cell-Formulas prints the contents of each occupied cell in the specified print range, one cell per line.

Formatted restores the format settings for headers, footers, and page breaks.

Unformatted prints a specified range without headers, footers, and page breaks. This option can be very helpful when printing to a file. This will generate a so-called plain ASCII file.

The *Clear* command in the main menu provides you with the following options:

    All   Range   Borders   Format

All cancels print range, borders, footers, and headers. Everything is returned to the default settings.

Range cancels the present print range.

Borders clears the present borders.

Format restores page length, margins, and setup settings to their default settings.

Align tells the printer that the user has positioned the paper at the top of a new page. This command should be used before printing a worksheet. If you do not use this command, there may be gaps in the middle of the report.

Go in the main menu executes the Print command.

Quit, as usual, gets you out of the Print menu.

9-4 Default Settings

In most cases, the printer's default settings should satisfy your needs (to see the entire default settings, use /Worksheet Global Default Printer). The default settings include the following:

Page Length	66 lines
Left Margin	4 characters from the left side of the paper
Right Margin	76 characters from the left side of the paper
Top Margin	2 lines from the top of the page
Bottom Margin	2 lines from the bottom of the page

As you have seen in the main menu of the /Print command, any of these settings can be changed, either temporarily or permanently. For temporary changes issue the command /Print Printer Options. Under Options you have:

    Header   Footer   Margins   Borders   Setup   Pg-Length   Other   Quit

For permanent changes first issue the command /Worksheet Global Default Printer. Change whatever you want, then choose /Worksheet Global Default Update.

9-5 Controlling Your Printer More Effectively

Several commands that we have already discussed can be used individually or collectively to enhance the effectiveness of your printer by reducing manual intervention and generating more readable output. You will see the enhanced features more clearly when you design a macro (discussed in Chapters 18–21) for printing and /or when you print to a file rather than to the printer.

/Print Printer Line skips a line. If you would like to skip a page, choose /Print Printer Page. After printing a report, select /Print Printer Align. This command will skip the printer to the beginning of a new page.

As we discussed in Chapter 6, /Worksheet Page gives a page break. This command will start a new page no matter how much of the present page is empty. When you use / Worksheet Page, you must check to see how many lines you have specified in /Print Printer Options Pg-Length. /Worksheet Page may not override this command *if* the number of lines specified by /Print Printer Options Pg-Length is less than the number of lines covered by /Worksheet Page.

9-6 Special Characters

Three special characters can be utilized for entering page numbers and the current date and for specifying the position of the header or footer, as follows:

\# (number sign)   Enter a page number starting at 1.

@ (at sign)   Enter system date in international format (month/day/year).

¦ (split vertical bar)   Separate portions of the header or footer, either left, center, or right-justified. We show examples of this at the end of the chapter. Text by itself will be left-justified. Preceded by one split vertical bar it will be centered; preceded by two split vertical bars (¦¦), it will be right-justified.

9-7 Planning Your Printed Report More Accurately

A standard page is 66 lines; standard means 11 inches, or six lines per inch. By default, Lotus leaves two lines blank between the text and the header or footer. If your printed line is longer than the right margin, Lotus will wrap around to the next line. To avoid this, use compressed type in your setup string. Of the 66 lines, only 56 lines are available for the text.

Lines 1–2	Top margin
Line 3	Header, if any
Lines 4–5	Blank by default
Lines 6–61 (56 lines)	Your text
Line 64	Footer, if any
Lines 65–66	Bottom margin

Different printers have different setup options. To stop a printing session use the **Ctrl** and **Break** keys together. This may not stop the printer immediately, but it will stop as soon as its buffer is empty.

9-8 Printing Reports with Different Options

To show you how the /Print command works, we developed several examples. Figure 9-2 is a balance sheet worksheet for four quarters of Ocean City Tourist Attraction.

In Figure 9-3, we printed three worksheets in one report using the default option. This report was generated by using /Print, Printer, Range, A1..E52, **Return**, Align, Go. As you see, even the default setting will give you a readable report.

In Figure 9-4, we generated a page of a report with Header and Footer options. This report was generated by /Print, Printer, Range, A1..E52, **Return**, Options, Header ¦¦ , @ , **Return**, Footer ¦ , Page #, **Return**, Pg-Length 66, Return, Margins Right 78, **Return**, Margins Top 4, **Return**, Margins Bottom 4, **Return**, Quit, Align, Go.

FIGURE 9-2 Ocean City Tourist Attraction Balance Sheet in Worksheet Form

```
A1: [W32] '                    OCEAN CITY TOURIST ATTRACTION              READY

              A            B        C        D        E
1                    OCEAN CITY TOURIST ATTRACTION
2               (1989-90  Figures in thousands of dollars)
3          -----------------------------------------------
4                       Spring   Summer    Fall   Winter
5          -----------------------------------------------
6  Current Assets
7     Cash            $36,249  $42,495  $58,761  $72,300
8     Accounts Receivable 26,700  23,821   22,545   22,768
9     Inventory         8,000    7,625    9,825    8,475
10                    -------  -------  -------  -------
11 Total Current Assets 70,949  73,941   90,331  103,543
12
13 Fixed Assets
14    Property, Plant and Equipment
15       Land           49,121   48,700   45,600   40,410
16       Building       82,212   82,212   79,100   78,275
17       Leasehold Improvements 22,400 18,586 17,900 20,145
18       Equipment       8,364    8,544    9,106    9,364
19    Gross P, P and E 162,097  157,962  151,706  148,194
20    Accumulated Depreciation (48,814) (37,600) (36,945) (29,725)
01-Jan-91  04:17 AM        UNDO
```

```
A21: [W32]                                                              READY

              A            B        C        D        E
21                    -------  -------  -------  -------
22    Net P, P and E   113,283  120,362  114,761  118,469
23
24    Other Assets        545      489      513      606
25
26 Total Fixed Assets  113,828  120,851  115,274  119,075
27
28 Total Assets       $184,777 $194,792 $205,685 $222,618
29                     ======= ======= ======= =======
30
31 ::
32 Current Liabilities
33    Accounts Payable  34,522   37,819   33,245   31,009
34    Notes Payable     10,000   11,321    7,369    8,655
35    Income Tax Payable 4,500    4,789    5,802    6,134
36                    -------  -------  -------  -------
37 Total Current Liabilities 49,022 53,929 46,416 45,798
38
39 Noncurrent Liabilities
40    Long Term Debt    52,242   48,700   46,345   40,300
01-Jan-91  11:28 AM        UNDO
```

FIGURE 9-2 (Continued)

FIGURE 9-2 (Continued)

```
A41: [W32]                                                          READY

                          A                    B       C       D       E
41                                          -------- ------- ------- -------
42  Total Liabilities                       101,264 102,629  92,761  86,098
43
44  Stockholders' Equity
45      Common Stock                          2,555   2,644   2,750   2,936
46      Retained Earnings                    80,958  89,519 110,094 133,584
47                                          -------- ------- ------- -------
48  Total Stockholders' Equity              83,513  92,163 112,844 136,528
49
50  Total Liabilities and Equity         $184,777 $194,792 $205,605 $222,618
51                                          ======== ======= ======= =======
52
53
54
55
56
57
58
59
60
01-Jan-91  11:32 AM            UNDO
```

In Figure 9-5, we generated two pages of a report using a page break. We used the Borders Rows command under Options to show headings on both pages. This report was generated by /Print, Printer, Range A6..E52, **Return**, Options, Borders, Rows, A1..E5, **Return**, Quit, Align, Go.

In Figure 9-6, we used the Borders Columns command showing winter figures with column headings. In this case, Borders Columns was A6..A52 and Print Range was E3..E52. The report was generated by /Print, Printer, Range E3..E52, **Return**, Options, Borders, Columns A3..A52, **Return**, Quit, Align, Go.

In Figure 9-7, we used the Compressed option to print the spring quarter. The setup character on the HP Laser Jet IIP is \027 &l7.27c\027(SOP16.66H). The report was generated by /Print, Printer, Range A3..B52, **Return**, Options, Setup \027 &l7.27c\027(SOP16.66H), **Return**, Quit, Align, Go.

In Figure 9-8 we displayed the spring quarter without enhancements. We used /Print, Printer, Range B3..B52, **Return**, Options, Other, As-Displayed, Quit, Align, Go.

In Figure 9-9 we displayed the spring quarter using cell formulas. We used /Print, Printer, Range B3..B52, **Return**, Options, Other, Cell-Formulas, Quit, Align, Go.

SUMMARY

Using the /Print command and its subcommands, you can generate reports. You can print to a printer or to a file for future printing. Margins, headers, and footers can be specified. Depending on the type of printer you use, you can specify strings. This means you can

FIGURE 9-3 *Ocean City Tourist Attraction Balance Sheet*

```
                     OCEAN CITY TOURIST ATTRACTION
               (1989-90  Figures in thousands of dollars)
    --------------------------------------------------------------------
                                   Spring    Summer    Fall     Winter
    --------------------------------------------------------------------
    Current Assets
      Cash                        $36,249   $42,495  $58,761   $72,300
      Accounts Receivable          26,700    23,821   22,545    22,768
      Inventory                     8,000     7,625    9,025     8,475
                                   -------   -------  -------   -------
    Total Current Assets           70,949    73,941   90,331   103,543

    Fixed Assets
      Property, Plant and Equipment
        Land                       49,121    48,700   45,600    40,410
        Building                   82,212    82,212   79,100    78,275
        Leasehold Improvements     22,400    18,506   17,900    20,145
        Equipment                   8,364     8,544    9,106     9,364
      Gross P, P and E            162,097   157,962  151,706   148,194
      Accumulated Depreciation    (48,814)  (37,600) (36,945)  (29,725)
                                   -------   -------  -------   -------
      Net P, P and E              113,283   120,362  114,761   118,469

      Other Assets                    545       489      513       606

    Total Fixed Assets            113,828   120,851  115,274   119,075

    Total Assets                 $184,777  $194,792 $205,605  $222,618
                                   =======   =======  =======   =======
    Current Liabilities
      Accounts Payable             34,522    37,819   33,245    31,009
      Notes Payable                10,000    11,321    7,369     8,655
      Income Tax Payable            4,500     4,789    5,802     6,134
                                   -------   -------  -------   -------
    Total Current Liabilities      49,022    53,929   46,416    45,798

    Noncurrent Liabilities
      Long Term Debt               52,242    48,700   46,345    40,300
                                   -------   -------  -------   -------
    Total Liabilities            101,264   102,629   92,761    86,098

    Stockholders' Equity
      Common Stock                  2,555     2,644    2,750     2,936
      Retained Earnings            80,958    89,519  110,094   133,584
                                   -------   -------  -------   -------
    Total Stockholders' Equity     83,513    92,163  112,844   136,520

    Total Liabilities and Equity $184,777  $194,792 $205,605  $222,618
                                   =======   =======  =======   =======
```

FIGURE 9-4 *Ocean City Tourist Attraction: A Fancier Report!*

```
                                                          01-Jan-91
                    OCEAN CITY TOURIST ATTRACTION
                 (1989-90  Figures in thousands of dollars)
-----------------------------------------------------------------
                             Spring   Summer    Fall   Winter
-----------------------------------------------------------------

Current Assets
  Cash                      $36,249  $42,495  $58,761  $72,300
  Accounts Receivable        26,700   23,821   22,545   22,768
  Inventory                   8,000    7,625    9,025    8,475
                            -------  -------  -------  -------
Total Current Assets         70,949   73,941   90,331  103,543

Fixed Assets
  Property, Plant and Equipment
    Land                     49,121   48,700   45,600   40,410
    Building                 82,212   82,212   79,100   78,275
    Leasehold Improvements   22,400   18,506   17,900   20,145
    Equipment                 8,364    8,544    9,106    9,364
  Gross P, P and E          162,097  157,962  151,706  148,194
  Accumulated Depreciation  (48,814) (37,600) (36,945) (29,725)
                            -------  -------  -------  -------
  Net P, P and E            113,283  120,362  114,761  118,469

  Other Assets                  545      489      513      606

Total Fixed Assets          113,828  120,851  115,274  119,075

Total Assets               $184,777 $194,792 $205,605 $222,618
                            =======  =======  =======  =======


Current Liabilities
  Accounts Payable           34,522   37,819   33,245   31,009
  Notes Payable              10,000   11,321    7,369    8,655
  Income Tax Payable          4,500    4,789    5,802    6,134
                            -------  -------  -------  -------
Total Current Liabilities    49,022   53,929   46,416   45,798

Noncurrent Liabilities
  Long Term Debt             52,242   48,700   46,345   40,300
                            -------  -------  -------  -------
Total Liabilities           101,264  102,629   92,761   86,098

Stockholders' Equity
  Common Stock                2,555    2,644    2,750    2,936
  Retained Earnings          80,958   89,519  110,094  133,584
                            -------  -------  -------  -------
Total Stockholders' Equity   83,513   92,163  112,844  136,520

Total Liabilities and Equity $184,777 $194,792 $205,605 $222,618
                            =======  =======  =======  =======

                              Page 1
```

FIGURE 9-5 Ocean City Tourist Attraction: With Borders, Rows and Page Break

```
                  OCEAN CITY TOURIST ATTRACTION
            (1989-90  Figures in thousands of dollars)
         -----------------------------------------------------
                          Spring   Summer    Fall   Winter
         -----------------------------------------------------
Current Assets
   Cash                  $36,249  $42,495  $58,761  $72,300
   Accounts Receivable    26,700   23,821   22,545   22,768
   Inventory               8,000    7,625    9,025    8,475
                         -------  -------  -------  -------
Total Current Assets      70,949   73,941   90,331  103,543

Fixed Assets
   Property, Plant and Equipment
      Land                49,121   48,700   45,600   40,410
      Building            82,212   82,212   79,100   78,275
      Leasehold Improvements 22,400 18,506  17,900   20,145
      Equipment            8,364    8,544    9,106    9,364
   Gross P, P and E      162,097  157,962  151,706  148,194
   Accumulated Depreciation (48,814) (37,600) (36,945) (29,725)
                         -------  -------  -------  -------
   Net P, P and E        113,283  120,362  114,761  118,469

   Other Assets             545      489      513      606

Total Fixed Assets       113,828  120,851  115,274  119,075

Total Assets            $184,777 $194,792 $205,605 $222,618
                         =======  =======  =======  =======
```

```
                  OCEAN CITY TOURIST ATTRACTION
            (1989-90  Figures in thousands of dollars)
         -----------------------------------------------------
                          Spring   Summer    Fall   Winter
         -----------------------------------------------------
Current Liabilities
   Accounts Payable       34,522   37,819   33,245   31,009
   Notes Payable          10,000   11,321    7,369    8,655
   Income Tax Payable      4,500    4,789    5,802    6,134
                         -------  -------  -------  -------
Total Current Liabilities 49,022   53,929   46,416   45,798

Noncurrent Liabilities
   Long Term Debt         52,242   48,700   46,345   40,300
                         -------  -------  -------  -------
Total Liabilities        101,264  102,629   92,761   86,098

Stockholders' Equity
   Common Stock            2,555    2,644    2,750    2,936
   Retained Earnings      80,958   89,519  110,094  133,584
                         -------  -------  -------  -------
Total Stockholders' Equity 83,513  92,163  112,844  136,520

Total Liabilities and Equity $184,777 $194,792 $205,605 $222,618
                         =======  =======  =======  =======
```

FIGURE 9-5 (Continued)

FIGURE 9-6 *Ocean City Tourist Attraction: With Borders Columns*

```
-------------------------------------------
                                    Winter
-------------------------------------------
Current Assets
   Cash                             $72,300
   Accounts Receivable              22,768
   Inventory                         8,475
                                    -------
Total Current Assets                103,543

Fixed Assets
   Property, Plant and Equipment
      Land                           40,410
      Building                       78,275
      Leasehold Improvements         20,145
      Equipment                       9,364
   Gross P, P and E                 148,194
   Accumulated Depreciation         (29,725)
                                    -------
   Net P, P and E                   118,469

   Other Assets                         606

Total Fixed Assets                  119,075

Total Assets                       $222,618
                                   =======


Current Liabilities
   Accounts Payable                  31,009
   Notes Payable                      8,655
   Income Tax Payable                 6,134
                                    -------
Total Current Liabilities            45,798

Noncurrent Liabilities
   Long Term Debt                    40,300
                                    -------
Total Liabilities                    86,098

Stockholders' Equity
   Common Stock                       2,936
   Retained Earnings                133,584
                                    -------
Total Stockholders' Equity          136,520

Total Liabilities and Equity       $222,618
                                   =======
```

FIGURE 9-7 Spring Quarter of Ocean City Tourist Attraction, Compressed

```
-----------------------------------------
                                 Spring
-----------------------------------------

Current Assets                          Current Liabilities
   Cash                     $36,249        Accounts Payable            34,522
   Accounts Receivable       26,700        Notes Payable               10,000
   Inventory                  8,000        Income Tax Payable           4,500
                            -------                                   -------
Total Current Assets         70,949     Total Current Liabilities     49,022

Fixed Assets                            Noncurrent Liabilities
   Property, Plant and Equipment           Long Term Debt              52,242
      Land                   49,121                                   -------
      Building               82,212     Total Liabilities            101,264
      Leasehold Improvements 22,400
      Equipment               8,364     Stockholders' Equity
   Gross P, P and E         162,097        Common Stock                 2,555
   Accumulated Depreciation (48,814)       Retained Earnings           80,958
                            -------                                   -------
   Net P, P and E           113,283     Total Stockholders' Equity     83,513

   Other Assets                545     Total Liabilities and Equity $184,777
                                                                     =======
Total Fixed Assets          113,828

Total Assets               $184,777
                            =======
```

FIGURE 9-8 Spring Quarater of Ocean City Tourist Attraction As Is

```
        ---------
         Spring                    $184,777
        ---------                  =======

         $36,249
          26,700
           8,000                     34,522
        -------                      10,000
          70,949                      4,500
                                   -------
                                     49,022

          49,121
          82,212                     52,242
          22,400                  -------
           8,364                    101,264
         162,097
         (48,814)
        -------                       2,555
         113,283                     80,958
                                   -------
             545                     83,513

         113,828                   $184,777
                                   =======
```

```
B3:  \-
B4:  ^Spring                  B26:  (,0)  +B22+B24
B5:  \-                       B28:  (C0)  +B11+B26
B7:  (C0)  36249              B29:  "=======
B8:  (,0)  26700              B33:  (,0)  34522
B9:  (,0)  8000               B34:  (,0)  10000
B10: "-------                 B35:  (,0)  4500
B11: (,0)  @SUM(B7..B10)      B36:  "-------
B15: (,0)  49121              B37:  (,0)  @SUM(B33..B35)
B16: (,0)  82212              B40:  (,0)  52242
B17: (,0)  22400              B41:  "-------
B18: (,0)  8364               B42:  (,0)  +B37+B40
B19: (,0)  @SUM(B15..B18)     B45:  (,0)  2555
B20: (,0)  -48814             B46:  (,0)  80958
B21: "-------                 B47:  "-------
B22: (,0)  +B19+B20           B48:  (,0)  +B45+B46
B24: 545                      B50:  (C0)  +B42+B48
                              B51:  "=======
```

FIGURE 9-9 Spring Quarter of Ocean City Tourist Attraction: Cell-Formulas print with different type sets, in compressed types, and so forth. The /Print command also gives you the Cell-Formulas option, which lets you print the "guts" of your worksheet in order to debug it or make further modifications.

REVIEW QUESTIONS

* These questions are answered in Appendix I.
1. What is the difference between printing to a file and printing to a printer?
2.* If you print to a file, how do you print the content of this file in DOS?
3. What are some of the advantages of printing to a file over printing to a printer?
4. What are the printer default settings?
5. What is the maximum and the minimum page length?
6.* Which character is used to display the current date?
7. What is the role of the Borders command?
8. How many ways can you split 58 lines of text into two pages?
9.* Does /Worksheet Page always override Pg-Length?
10.* What are some uses of the Cell-Formulas option?
11. When do you use the Align option?
12. How do you advance the printer to the top of a new page?
13. What is the file extension of a file generated by /Print File?
14.* How many of the 66 lines of a page (by default) are available to you for writing text (excluding top and bottom margins)?
15. How do you change default settings temporarily?
16.* How do you change default settings permanently?
17. When and why do you use the Clear option?

HANDS-ON PRACTICE

1. Generate a ten-row by five-column worksheet. Print this worksheet as follows:
   - Using the **Shift** and **PrtSc** keys or just **PrtSc** in enhanced keyboards.
   - Using /Print Printer with default settings.
   - Using /Print Printer with top and bottom margins of eight.
   - Using the Cell-Formulas option.
   - Using the Compressed option.
2. Load Figure 6-16 (Chapter 6) into your computer. Print this worksheet as follows:
   - Using /Print Printer with default settings.
   - Using the Cell-Formulas option.
   - Using the Compressed option.

COMPREHENSIVE LAB ASSIGNMENT

Retrieve CHAPT8 and perform the following:
1. Print the file using the Shift and PrtSc keys.
2. Print the existing file into an ASCII file called CHAPT9 (remember that the extension of this file will be PRN).

3. Using the /PP command, print this with default settings.
4. Print the existing file with the given left and right margins.
5. Using the appropriate commands, generate a page number and today's date on the printed file.
6. Using the appropriate commands, generate a compressed output.
7. Print the file using Cell-Formulas.
8. Save the existing file under CHAPT9.
9. Using /File Import, retrieve CHAPT9.PRN.

MISCONCEPTIONS AND SOLUTIONS

M – You try to use the /Print Printer command and receive an error message, PRINTER ERROR.

S – Check your printer. It may be loosely connected, not connected at all, out of paper, or turned off!

M – You are trying to print on single sheet but you cannot.

S – Invoke /Worksheet, Global, Default, Printer, Wait, Yes. This will make the printer pause after printing each sheet.

Printing with Allways

10-1 Introduction

In this chapter we review the Allways Add-In program. We introduce the process of getting Allways started and how to get in and out of Allways. Next we explain important keys, modes, and status indicators and highlight the relationship between 1-2-3 and Allways. We review the Allways command menu and several formatting features. Our discussion will be accompanied by several examples. More advanced features of Allways will be presented in Chapter 11. A complete Allways command map is presented at the end of the book.

10-2 What Is Allways?

Allways is a spreadsheet publishing add-in program. It is included in 1-2-3's Release 2.2 package or can be purchased separately. Allways is used for formatting and printing the output generated by Lotus 1-2-3. Using Allways you should be able to generate presentation-quality output. Allways works in a what-you-see-is-what-you-get (WYSIWYG) mode. In other words, what you see on the screen is exactly what you'll get on your printout. Allways enables you to boldface, underline, double-underline, draw lines, draw boxes, and most important of all, integrate graphs in the same printout with your worksheet data. With Allways you can use up to eight fonts with any printer. (A font is a typeface in a particular point size, for example, Triumvirate 24 point. A point is a unit of measurement that determines the height of a character.)

To use Allways all you need is an IDM or IBM-compatible personal computer, Release 2.0 or above of Lotus 1-2-3, a hard disk, and 512K of RAM. To see the power of Allways, take a look at Figures 10-1 and 10-2. The first figure was generated by 1-2-3's print command and the second by using Allways. To create Figure 10-2, we got Allways started and did the following:

1. /Format, Font, Triumvirate 20 point, Enter, A1..B1, Enter
2. Format, Shade, Dark, A2..B2, Enter
3. Format, Font, Times 14 point, Enter, B4..E4, Enter
4. Format, Font, Triumvirate 14 point, Enter, A6..A6, Enter
5. Format, Font, Triumvirate 14 point, Enter, A12..A12, Enter
6. Format, Lines, Outline, B6..E19, Enter

In this chapter we will teach you how to use all these fancy features to produce great-looking reports.

FIGURE 10-1 A Report Printed by 1-2-3's Print Command

```
                    OCEAN CITY TOURIST ATTRACTION
              (1989-90   Figures in thousands of dollars)
       ---------------------------------------------------------
                          Spring    Summer    Fall    Winter
       ---------------------------------------------------------
       Current Assets
          Cash            $36,249   $42,495  $58,761  $72,300
          Accounts Receivable 26,700  23,821   22,545   22,768
                          -------   -------  -------  -------
       Total Current Assets 62,949   66,316   81,306   95,068

       Fixed Assets
          Property,  and Plant
             Land          49,121    48,700   45,600   40,410
             Building      82,212    82,212   79,100   78,275
          Gross P,  and P 131,333   130,912  124,700  118,685
          Accumulated Depreciation (48,814) (37,600) (36,945) (29,725)
                          -------   -------  -------  -------
          Net P,  and P    82,519    93,312   87,755   88,960
```

10-3 Getting Allways Started

After installing Allways (see Appendix C for installation information), follow these steps:

1. Get 1-2-3 started.
2. From the main menu select **Add-In**.

OCEAN CITY TOURIST ATTRACTION

(1989–90 Figures in thousands of dollars)

	Spring	Summer	Fall	Winter
Current Assets				
Cash	$36,249	$42,495	$58,761	$72,300
Accounts Receivable	26,700	23,821	22,545	22,768
Total Current Assets	62,949	66,316	81,306	95,068
Fixed Assets				
Property, and Plant				
Land	49,121	48,700	45,600	40,410
Building	82,212	82,212	79,100	78,275
Gross P, and P	131,333	130,912	124,700	118,685
Accumulated Depreciation	(48,814)	(37,600)	(36,945)	(29,725)
Net P, and P	82,519	93,312	87,755	88,960

FIGURE 10-2 A Report Generated by Allways

3. From this menu select **Attach**.
4. From the Attach menu select **ALLWAYS.ADN** and press the **Return** key. You will be prompted with:

No-Key 7 8 9 10

It is up to you to select your desired choice. For example, if you select 10, later you can invoke Allways by pressing Alt-F10. This is what we did.

If you select No-Key, you will not be able to invoke Allways by pressing Alt and one of the function keys. In this case you must activate Always by using /Add-In Invoke.

5. Press Q (for Quit) to exit this menu. This will take you back to 1-2-3's Ready mode.

Remember that Alt-F10 is used initially to set up to display the Add-In menu. This is the same as selecting Add-In from the main menu of 1-2-3.

To exit Allways press the **Esc** key (when the mode indicator displays Allways). This will put you back in 1-2-3's Ready mode. You can also exit Allways by selecting Quit from the Allways menu or press the same function key that put you into Allways in the first place. In our case Alt-F10 allowed us to exit Allways.

Since Allways occupies a considerable amount of RAM memory, when you no longer need the program you can detach it from memory by selecting Detach from the /Add-In menu.

You can also automate the attaching processes by using /Worksheet Global Default Other Add-In Set. you can have up to 8 Add-Ins attached to Lotus at a time. Select 1, then specify ALLWAYS.ADN as your add-in to attach automatically. To finalize this you must also use the /Worksheet Global Default Update command to save the new Add-In settings.

10-4 Allways Two Modes

Allways operates in two different modes: graphics and text. In graphics mode you will be able to see all the formatting, drawing, and graphs on the screen just as they will appear in the final printed output. To use the graphics mode of Allways you must have a graphics monitor and a display card capable of displaying graphics images. In text mode you will not be able to see the formats on the screen. However, when you print the document all the formatting features will be there on your printed output. You can switch between the two modes by using the F6 function key. Figure 10-3 illustrates a sample worksheet in text mode. Figure 10-4 illustrates a sample worksheet in graphics mode. Remember, we have not added any formatting features to this figure yet.

10-5 Your First Official Meeting with Allways

Attach Allways and press / (the slash key) to get into the Allways main menu. Like 1-2-3, Allways includes three distinct areas which you should become familiar with: the worksheet area, the control panel, and the status line. Figure 10-5 illustrates a sample worksheet. Depending on the type of font you select, the worksheet on your computer may be displayed slightly differently.

When the Allways menu is activated, as usual the control panel includes three lines. The first line includes the type of font used and the format of the cell, e.g., boldface, underline, or shading. The second line displays the Allways main menu. If the Allways

FIGURE 10-3 A Sample Worksheet in Text Mode

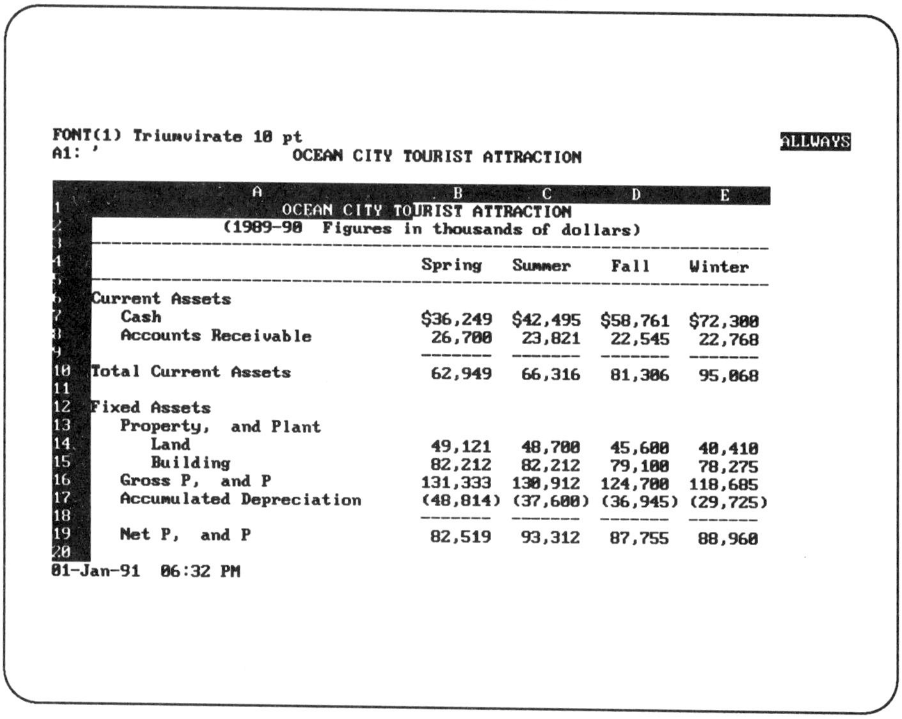

FIGURE 10-4 A Sample Worksheet in Graphics Mode

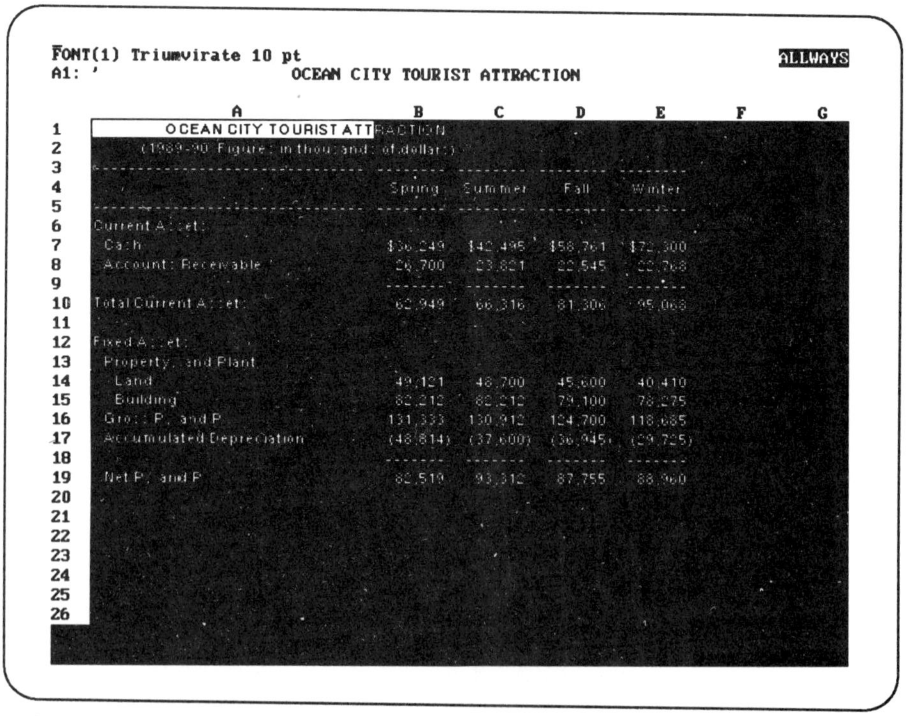

FIGURE 10-5 *A Sample Worksheet with the Allways Main Menu Displayed*

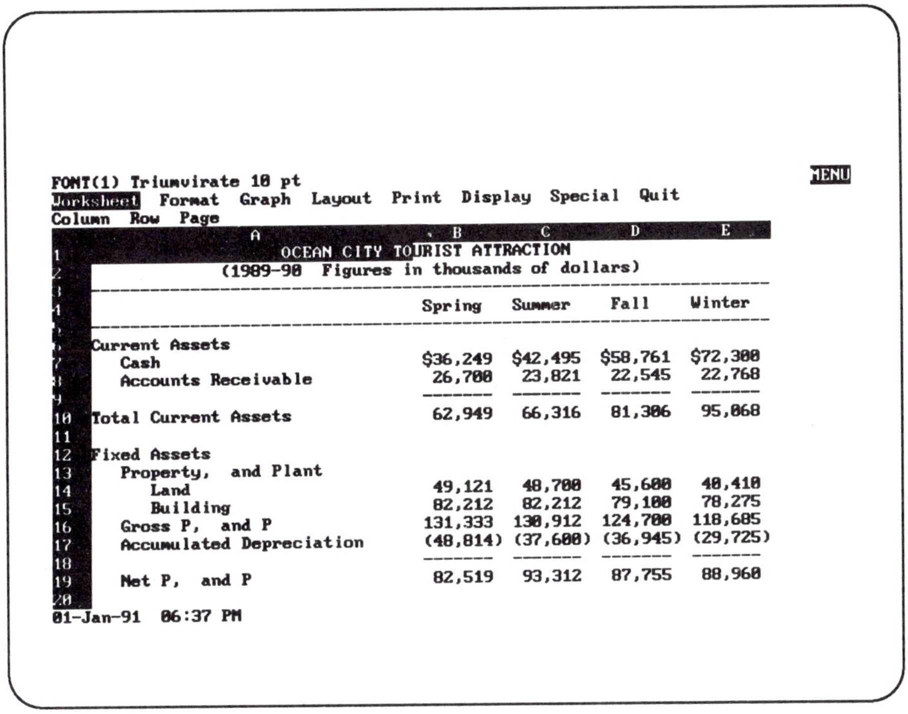

```
FONT(1) Triumvirate 10 pt                                          MENU
Worksheet  Format  Graph  Layout  Print  Display  Special  Quit
Column  Row  Page
                 A           B          C         D        E
 1              OCEAN CITY TOURIST ATTRACTION
 2          (1989-90  Figures in thousands of dollars)
 3      -------------------------------------------------------
 4                        Spring   Summer    Fall    Winter
 5      -------------------------------------------------------
 6   Current Assets
 7      Cash                $36,249  $42,495  $58,761  $72,300
 8      Accounts Receivable  26,700   23,821   22,545   22,768
 9                          -------  -------  -------  -------
10   Total Current Assets    62,949   66,316   81,306   95,068
11
12   Fixed Assets
13      Property,  and Plant
14        Land               49,121   48,700   45,600   40,410
15        Building           82,212   82,212   79,100   78,275
16      Gross P,  and P     131,333  130,912  124,700  118,685
17      Accumulated Depreciation (48,814) (37,600) (36,945) (29,725)
18                          -------  -------  -------  -------
19      Net P,  and P        82,519   93,312   87,755   88,960
20
01-Jan-91  06:37 PM
```

menu is not displayed, you will see two lines in the control panel. The first line tells you about the type of font used and the second line tells you the present position (cell reference) of the cursor. At the upper right corner of the control panel you will see the mode indicators. Table 10-1 displays all the mode indicators. The status line, at the bottom of the screen, displays valuable information such as CAPS, END, or SCROLL. Also at the bottom of the screen are all the status indicators. Table 10-2 displays all the status indicators.

TABLE 10-1 ALLWAYS MODE INDICATORS

Mode Indicator	Meaning
ALLWAYS	Similar to Ready mode in 1-2-3. Allways is ready to accept any command.
ERROR	An error has occurred. Press Esc or Enter to clear the message, then correct the error.
FILES	Allways is requesting a file name.
HELP	Allways' on-line help is displayed. You receive on-line help by pressing the F1 function key.
MENU	The Allways menu is displayed.
POINT	Allways is requesting the user to indicate a range for the desired operation.
WAIT	Allways is performing a task, Wait until the task is finished.
WARN	Allways is displaying a warning message.

TABLE 10-2 ALLWAYS STATUS INDICATORS

Status Indicator	Meaning
ANC	The user has attached the cell pointer to highlight a range before a command is selected.
CALC	Formulas in the worksheet need to be recalculated. You must return to 1-2-3 and press the F9 recalculation key.
CAPS	The Caps Lock feature has been activated.
CIRC	The worksheet includes a formula that refers to itself.
END	The End key has been activated.
NUM	The Num Lock key has been activated.
SCROLL	The Scroll Lock key has been activated.

10-6 How 1-2-3 and Allways Work Together

The 1-2-3 and Allways programs work in harmony. This means that as long as Allways is attached, saving and retrieving your files is automatic. All the formatting done to your worksheet become part of your worksheet file. However, these formatting features are stored in another file with the ALL extension. The next time you retrieve a spreadsheet that has been dressed up with Allways, Lotus will "remember" to format the spreadsheet using settings from the appropriate corresponding ALL file.

Whatever changes done to the worksheet in 1-2-3 will be reflected in Allways. For example, if you erase a cell or change its format from currency to fixed, these changes are automatic and be reflected in Allways.

To maintain your formatting features make sure that the Allways is attached. Also make sure to save your work in 1-2-3 by using the /File Save command. If you forget to save your worksheet, all your changes will be lost.

10-7 Formatting Features of Allways

Remember that any formatting you perform in 1-2-3 will carry over to Allways. For example, a cell formatted as comma option with four decimal places will be displayed as such in Allways. However, the changes that you make through Allways will not modify your worksheet. All the formatting done through Allways will be saved in a file with the same name as the original file using the extension ALL. For example, file FIRST will be saved as FIRST.WK1 (in 1-2-3) and FIRST. ALL (in Allways).

Allways allows you to adjust column widths and row heights more finely than in 1-2-3. For example, a column width can be set to 8.2 or 14.57 characters. Column width and row height adjustments can be done by using the /Worksheet Column command. We will talk about worksheet commands in detail in the next chapter. In Allways one character width is equal to the width of a number such as 1, 2, or 9 formatted in Font 1.

Using Allways, row heights are set to Auto. This means that Allways adjusts the height of a row automatically. This is done in order to accommodate the largest font in a given row. Row heights are measured in points. By using /Worksheet Row Set-Height you can change the automatic feature to your own format.

10-8 Allways' Important Keys

In addition to the arrow movement keys used in 1-2-3, Allways includes two sets of its own keys: function keys and accelerator keys. Tables 10-3 and 10-4 summarize these keys. When you use the accelerator keys, remember that these keys will not prompt for a range, so you must select a cell or a range prior to using an accelerator key. Also remember when using accelerator keys that each press of the key puts you in the next option;. For example, if you press Alt-U, the first time your cell will be single-underlined, the second press will enable double underlining, and the third press will disable the underline feature for the particular cell or range of cells that you are dealing with.

TABLE 10-3 ALLWAYS FUNCTION KEYS

Name	Description
F1 (Help)	Displays on-line help.
F3 (Name)	In Point mode, displays a menu of named ranges in a particular worksheet.
F4 (Reduce)	In Allways mode, reduces the display. You can reduce the worksheet to 60% of its normal size by continuous pressing.
F5 (GoTo)	In Allways mode, moves the cell pointer to any location.
F6 (Display)	In Always mode, switches between graphics and text mode.
F10 (Graph)	In Allways mode, displays the graph. If you press it again you will see hatched boxes that indicate the position of the graph.
Alt-F4 (Enlarge)	In Allways mode, enlarges the display up to 140%.

TABLE 10-4 ALLWAYS ACCELERATOR KEYS

Name	Function
Alt-B	Boldface: Set/Clear
Alt-G	Grid Lines: On/Off
Alt-L	Lines: Outline/All/None
Alt-S	Shading: Light/Dark/Solid/None
Alt-U	Underline: Single/Double/None
Alt-1	Set Font 1
Alt-2	Set Font 2
Alt-3	Set Font 3
Alt-4	Set Font 4
Alt-5	Set Font %
Alt-6	Set Font 6
Alt-7	Set Font 7
Alt-8	Set Font 8

10-9 A Quick Review of the Allways Command Menu

The main menu of Allways includes eight options as follows:

Worksheet	Sets column widths, row heights, and page breaks.
Format	Changes the format of a cell or a range. This includes boldfacing, underlining, shading and drawing lines.
Graph	Changes graph settings. Adds or removes graphs to and from the worksheet.
Layout	Controls the appearance of the printed page such as size, margins, headers and footers.
Print	Prints the worksheet and specifies print settings.
Display	Changes the display mode;. Enlarges and reduces the worksheet display.
Special	Justifies tables, copies, moves, and imports formats from one worksheet to another worksheet.
Quit	Returns to 1-2-3.

We will talk about these commands in detail later.

10-10 Defining a Range in Allways

Defining a range in Allways is similar to the process in 1-2-3. You can use any of the following options:

• Type the range address, e.g., A1. .A10.
• Use a range name, e.g., asset or liability.
• Highlight the range.

To format a range you can either issue the command first and then specify the range, or vice versa. Each method has its own application. For example, defining the range first, then issuing the command would be helpful if a given range requires several formatting features. To specify a range before issuing the command follow the following steps:

1. Put the cursor in the upper left corner of the range.
2. Press . (the period key). This will anchor the cell pointer.
3. Highlight the range by using the cursor control keys.
4. DO NOT PRESS ENTER.
5. Issue your desired command, e.g., /Format Shade.

Moving the cursor to another area or pressing the Esc key will deselect the selected range.

10-11 /Format Lines Command

The /Format Lines command lets you generate horizontal and vertical lines, draw boxes around cells, and create outlines around ranges. Each cell on your worksheet can have a line along any of its four edges. When you invoke the /Format Lines command the following options will be presented:

Outline   Left   Right   Top   Bottom   All   Clear

The *Outline* option draws an outline around a range.
The *Left* option draws a line at the left side of each cell in a range.
The *Right* option draws a line at the right side of each cell in a range.
The *Top* option draws a line at the top of each cell in a range.
The *Bottom* option draws a line at the bottom of each cell in a range.

The *All* option draws a box around each cell in a range.

The *Clear* option removes all the lines (you must specify the desired range).

You can choose any of these options and then specify the range. To understand this, consider Figures 10-6 and 10-7. The sample worksheet in Rigure 10-6 has had outlines, lines, and boxes added in Figure 10-7. These were created with the following keystrokes:

1. Get Allways started.
2. /Format, Lines, Outline, C2. .D2, **Return**
3. /Format, Lines, Bottom, A4. .F4, **Return**
4. /Format, Lines, All, A6. .E13, **Return**
5. /Print, Range, Set, A1. .F13, **Return**, Go

If you change your mind, selecting /Format Lines Clear will allow you to remove the lines from your worksheet.

10-12 Format Shade Command

The /Format Shade command allows you to use three types of shading: light, dark, and solid black. Shades are used to emphasize the data on the worksheet. If you invoke the /Format shade command you see:

Light   Dark   Solid   Clear

Look at Figure 10-7. We would like to put the title in dark shading, the first column in light, and the last column solid. Do the following:

FIGURE 10-6 A Sample Worksheet

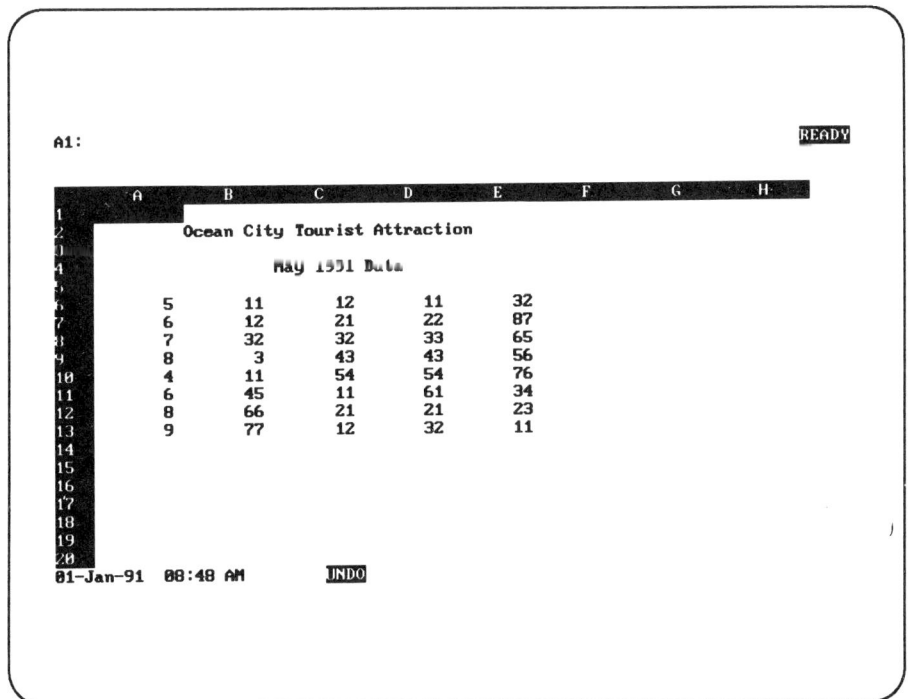

FIGURE 10-7 *An Example of a Worksheet with Outlines, Lines and Boxes*

	Ocean City Tourist Attraction			
	May 1991 Data			
5	11	12	11	32
6	12	21	22	87
7	32	32	33	65
8	3	43	43	56
4	11	54	54	76
6	45	11	61	34
8	66	21	21	23
9	77	12	32	11

1. Get Allways started and load Figure 10-7
2. /Format, Shade, Dark, C2. .D2, **Return**
3. /Format, Shade, Light, A5. .A13, **Return**
4. /Format, Shade,Solid, E5. .E13, **Return**
5. /Print, Range, Set, A1. .F13, **Return**, Go

Figure 10-8 shows the results.

10-13 /Format Underline Command

The /Format Underline command allows you to do two types of underlining: single and double. Single underlining applies only to the data contained in the cell that you specified and appears only if there is data in the cell. Double underlining results in a double bar at the base of the cell. It extends across the entire cell width regardless of whether that cell has data in it or not. We used the sample worksheet in Figure 10-6 to create Figure 10-9 as follows:

1. /Format, Underline, Single, A5. .E6, **Return**
2. /Format, Underline, Double, A13. .E13, **Return**
3. /Print, Range, Set, A1. .F13, **Return**, Go

10-14 /Print Command

The /Print command allows you to control the printing process. When you invoke the /Print command from the Allways main menu the following options will be displayed:

FIGURE 10-8 *Example of Dark, Light, and Solid Shading*

Ocean City Tourist Attraction				
May 1991 Data				
5	11	12	11	
6	12	21	22	
7	32	32	33	
8	3	43	43	
4	11	54	54	
6	45	11	61	
8	66	21	21	
9	77	12	32	

Ocean City Tourist Attraction

May 1991 Data

5	11	12	11	32
6	12	21	22	87
7	32	32	33	65
8	3	43	43	56
4	11	54	54	76
6	45	11	61	34
8	66	21	21	23
9	77	12	32	11

FIGURE 10- 9 *An Example of Single and Double Underlining*

Go   File   Range   Configuration   Settings   Quit

Here is a brief description of each option:

Go	Prints the specified range
File	Sends the output to a file on your disk
Range	Specifies or clears the print range
Configuration	Specifies the printer, interface, and printer options
Settings	Gives the following options:

Begin   End   First   Copies   Wait   Reset   Quit

The Begin option starts printing on page 1 and ends printing on page 9,999. The End option allows you to specify a number from 1 and 9,999. The First option allows you to specify the page numbers for the first page. The Copies option allows you to request between 1 and 9,999 copies. The Wait option waits for paper before printing each page. The Reset option restores the default print settings. The Quit option exits the Print menu.

You can print wide worksheets by using /Print Configuration Orientation, then select Landscape mode to print your worksheet sideways. The default is Portrait mode. Also, wide worksheets can be printed in Compressed option, which allows more characters to be printed on an 80-column page.

10-15 /Print File Command

The /Print File command allows you to save your Allways output in an encoded file on the disk. This file will have .ENC as its extension. This feature can be useful if you would like to print a number of files at once.

To print the encoded file, you must end the 1-2-3 session and use the DOS COPY command with the /B switch. For example, if you wan to print EXAMPLE.ENC using the LPT1 interface port, at the DOS prompt you must type:

COPY EXAMPLE.ENC/B LPT1 (Enter)

10-16 Creating Thick Horizontal and Vertical Lines

To highlight certain portions of a worksheet, you can draw thick lines in any location. Figure 10-10 shows an example. To add thick lines, as shown in Figure 10-11: For the horizontal line, /Format, Shade, Solid, B3. .E3, **Return**, /Worksheet, Row, Set-Height, 6 (or any number you like), **Return**. For the vertical line, /Format, Shade, Solid, E5. .E17, **Return**, /Worksheet, Column, Set-Width, 2 (or any number you like), **Return**. To print this worksheet type: /Print, Range, Set, A1. .E18, **Return**, Go.

10-17 Creating a Shadow Box

Shadow boxes can be useful to highlight a certain portion of a worksheet. Figure 10-12 shows a sample worksheet; Figure 10-13 was created from it as follows:

1. /Format, Lines, Outline, B3..E18, **Return**. This will draw a box around the specified range.

FIGURE 10-10 A Sample Worksheet

```
A1: [W32]                                                        READY

                        A                  B       C       D     E
1
2                        OCEAN CITY TOURIST ATTRACTION
3
4                                   Spring   Summer   Fall
5
6       Current Assets
7         Cash                      $36,249  $42,495 $58,761
8         Accounts Receivable        26,700   23,821  22,545
9                                   -------  ------- -------
10      Total Current Assets         62,949   66,316  81,306
11
12      Fixed Assets
13        Property,  and Plant
14          Land                     49,121   48,700  45,600
15          Building                 82,212   82,212  79,100
16        Gross P,  and P           131,333  130,912 124,700
17        Accumulated Depreciation  (48,814) (37,600)(36,945)
18                                   -------  ------- -------
19        Net P,  and P              82,519   93,312  87,755
20
01-Jan-91  09:11 AM        UNDO
```

```
                 OCEAN CITY TOURIST ATTRACTION
                                  Spring   Summer    Fall


      Current Assets
        Cash                      $36,249  $42,495  $58,761
        Accounts Receivable        26,700   23,821   22,545
                                  -------  -------  -------
      Total Current Assets         62,949   66,316   81,306

      Fixed Assets
        Property,  and Plant
          Land                     49,121   48,700   45,600
          Building                 82,212   82,212   79,100
        Gross P,  and P           131,333  130,912  124,700
        Accumulated Depreciation  (48,814) (37,600) (36,945)
                                  -------  -------  -------
```

FIGURE 10-11 A Sample Worksheet with Thick Horizontal and Vertical Lines

FIGURE 10-12 *A Sample Worksheet*

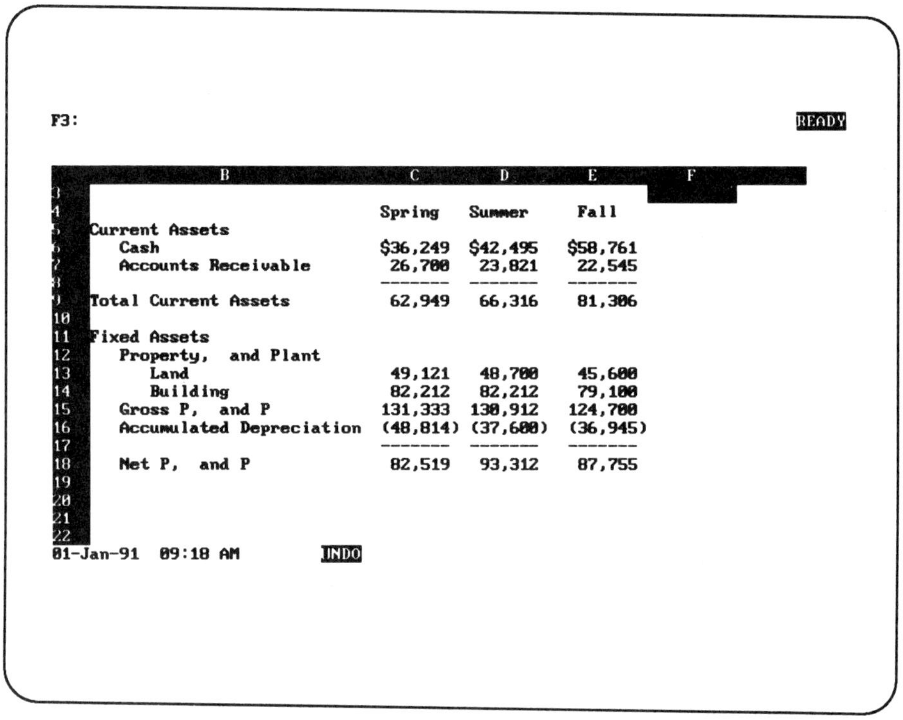

```
F3:                                                                    READY

                  B                    C        D        E          F

                                    Spring   Summer     Fall
Current Assets
   Cash                             $36,249  $42,495  $58,761
   Accounts Receivable               26,700   23,821   22,545
                                    --------  -------  -------
Total Current Assets                 62,949   66,316   81,306

Fixed Assets
   Property,  and Plant
      Land                           49,121   48,700   45,600
      Building                       82,212   82,212   79,100
   Gross P,  and P                  131,333  130,912  124,700
   Accumulated Depreciation         (48,814) (37,600) (36,945)
                                    --------  -------  -------
   Net P,  and P                     82,519   93,312   87,755



01-Jan-91   09:18 AM          UNDO
```

	Spring	Summer	Fall
Current Assets			
Cash	$36,249	$42,495	$58,761
Accounts Receivable	26,700	23,821	22,545
	--------	--------	--------
Total Current Assets	62,949	66,316	81,306
Fixed Assets			
Property, and Plant			
Land	49,121	48,700	45,600
Building	82,212	82,212	79,100
Gross P, and P	131,333	130,912	124,700
Accumulated Depreciation	(48,814)	(37,600)	(36,945)
	--------	--------	--------
Net P, and P	82,519	93,312	87,755

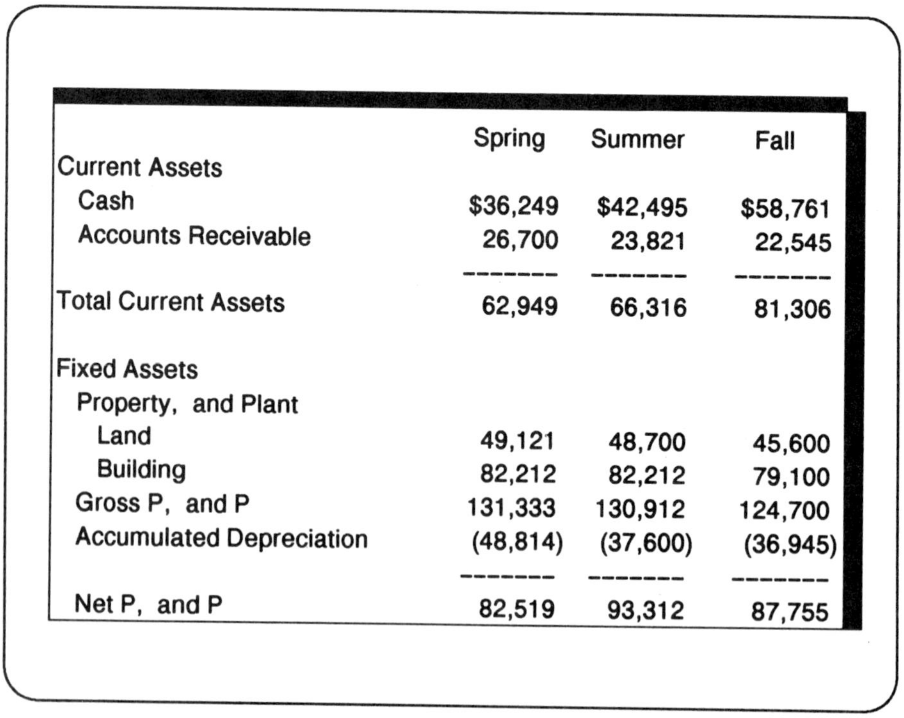

FIGURE 10-13 *A Shadow Box*

2. /Format, Shade, Solid, B2. .E2, **Return**. This will draw a solid shade in row 2 of the worksheet.
3. /Worksheet, Row, Set-Height, 5, **Return**. This will convert the shade into a thick horizontal line.
4. /Format, Shade, Solid, F3. .F18, **Return**. This will draw a solid shade in column F.
5. Move the cursor to column F, then invoke /Worksheet, Column, Set-Width, 1, **Return**. This will convert the shade into a thick vertical line.

10-18 The Undo Feature and Allways

The Undo feature does not work with Allways. If you do not have a large amount of RAM memory, you should turn off the Undo feature before attaching Allways. To turn off the Undo feature, select Worksheet Global Default Other Undo Disable from the 1-2-3 main menu.

SUMMARY

This chapter reviewed Allways, the add-in program for 1-2-3 Release 2.2. Allways can assist you in producing presentation-quality output. We described the process of getting in and getting out. Important keys in the Allways environment were highlighted. The relationship between Allways and 1-2-3 was discussed. Several formatting features such as underlining, shading, and outlining were introduced. We provided a quick review of the Allways command menu. In the next chapter we will discuss more advanced features of Allways.

REVIEW QUESTIONS

* These questions are answered in Appendix I.
1. What is Allways? What are its unique advantages for printing worksheets?
2.* What does WYSIWYG mean?
3. How do you get Allways started? What key can be assigned to Allways as the start-up key?
4. Can you make the Allways start-up an automatic process? If yes, how?
5. If you assign no key to Allways, how do you get it started?
6. What are the three distinct areas of an Allways worksheet?
7.* How many different ways can you exit Allways?
8. How many mode indicators does Allways have? Give two examples.
9. What are status indicators? Give two examples.
10. Can you save a file from the Allways menu? If no, then how can you save your work?
11. How are Allways files identified?
12.* What are Allways' two modes? How do you switch between the two?
13. What are Allways' keys? Give three examples.
14. What are Allways' accelerator keys? Give three examples.
15. How many options are there in Allways' main menu? Briefly explain them.
16. How do you define a range in Allways?
17. What are the options under /Format Lines? What is the difference between the Outline option and the All option?

18.   What are the options under /Format Shade?

19.* How many underlining features are supported by Allways?

20.   What are the options under the /Print command?

21.   What are the options under /Print Settings?

22.* What are the applications of the /Print File command?

23.   Does the Undo feature work with Allways?

HANDS-ON PRACTICE

1. Get Allways started. By pressing function key F1 invoke the On-line Help. What type of Help is available?

2. By pressing function key F6 switch between graphics and text modes. What is the difference between these two modes?

3. What is displayed on the control panel of the Allways menu? Where are node indicators displayed? Status indicators? What are the applications of function keys in the Allways environment? What are the applications of accelerator keys?

4. Using Figure 10-14, do the following:

    a) Draw an outline around the title of the worksheet.

    b) Using /Format Lines left draw a line on the first column.

    c) Using /Format Lines Right draw a line on the last column.

    d) Using /Format Lines Top draw a line on the top of the first row.

    e) Using /Format Lines Bottom draw a line on the bottom of the last row.

    At this point your worksheet should be similar to the worksheet displayed in Figure 10-15.

FIGURE 10-14 A Sample Worksheet

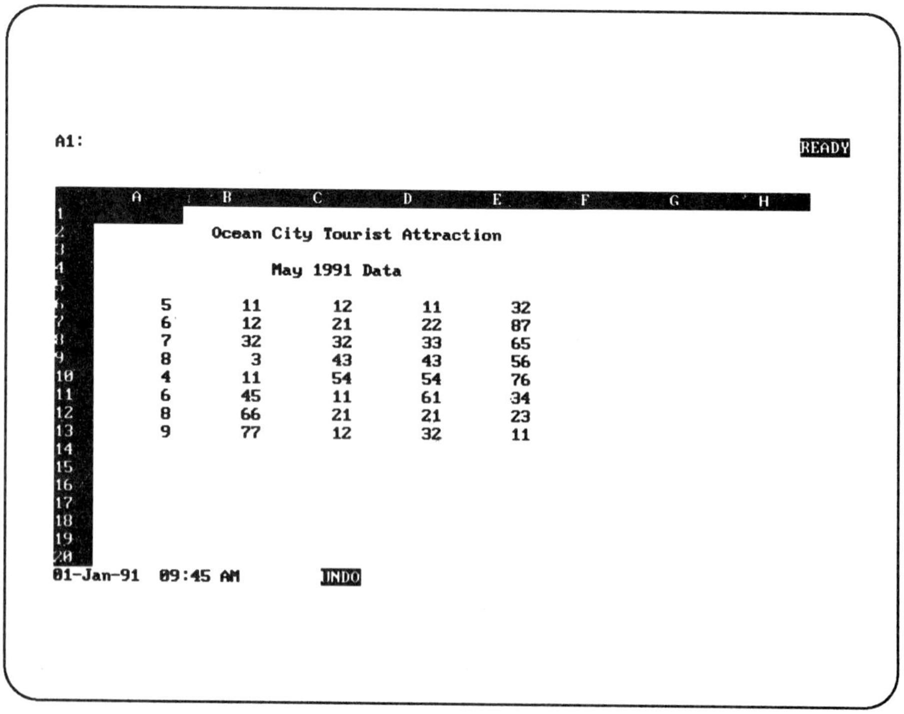

FIGURE 10-15 A Formatted Worksheet

		Ocean City Tourist Attraction		
		May 1991 Data		
5	11	12	11	32
6	12	21	22	87
7	32	32	33	65
8	3	43	43	56
4	11	54	54	76
6	45	11	61	34
8	66	21	21	23
9	77	12	32	11

5. Using Figure 10-14 draw a line around each cell in the worksheet (Hint: Use/Format Lines All.) Do the following:
   a) Using /Format Shade draw a dark shade for the worksheet title.
   b) Draw a dark shade for the last row.
   c) Using /Format Underline, draw a double underline for the first row.
   d) Print the final work.
6. Using Figure 10-14 do the following:
   a) Create a thick horizontal and vertical line for this worksheet.
   b) Create a shadow box for this worksheet.
   c) Print the worksheet.

COMPREHENSIVE LAB ASSIGNMENT

Retrieve CHAPT9 and perform the following:

1. Using /Format Shade draw a dark shade for the worksheet.
2. Create a shadow box for this worksheet.
3. Save the worksheet under CHAPT10.
4. Print the worksheet.

MISCONCEPTIONS AND SOLUTIONS

M – You are pressing / (slash) key and an unfamiliar menu is presented.

S – Most likely Allways is active. In such a case / brings up the Allways menu, not 1-2-3's menu.

M – You have performed several formatting features, but they are not present in your worksheet.

S – Probably you forgot to save your worksheet. Allways does not save the formatting features automatically. You must exit Allways and use 1-2-3's File Save command to save your worksheet before you terminate the session. Or you may have detached Allways before saving your work.

M – You have made changes to your worksheet during the Allways session, but the changes are not reflected in your worksheet.

S – Changes made to your worksheet are saved on a different worksheet with the same name and the ALL extension. Changes made in 1-2-3 are transferred to Allways. The Allways /Special Justify command is the only command that alters the contents of cells in a 1-2-3 worksheet.

M – You are performing several formatting features in a range. Issuing the command, then specifying the range may be a time-consuming process.

S – Define the range first, then apply all the formatting commands to this range. In this way you save a lot of time.

M – You have specified a print range in 1-2-3 but the actual printout from Allways is different from what you have specified.

S – Print ranges do not transfer form 1-2-3 to Allways.

Allways Advanced Features

11-1 Introduction

In this chapter we introduce more advanced features of Allways. We review the Allways font capabilities for producing worksheets with different typefaces, the /Layout commands for further dressing up a worksheet, and the /Graph command for integrating worksheets and graphs. Next we examine /Display Colors and /Format Color for controlling the color of your display and printout and /Display Zoom for reducing or enlarging the worksheet on the display monitor. We will review the /Worksheet and / Special commands for various formatting tasks. The chapter concludes with a discussion on macros and their relationship to Allways.

11-2 What Are Allways Fonts?

A font is a typeface of a particular size. The size is usually measured by its height in points. A point is approximately 1/72 of an inch. Thus, a 20-point Triumvirate font, for example, is approximately .27 inch high.

Allways lets you combine up to eight fonts in a given output. Figure 11-1 illustrates the font set available to you. This figure was generated by /Format Font. In addition to the choices in the font set you can also use soft fonts. These fonts can be printed either by downloading the fonts to your printer or by using the printer's graphics mode. Figure 11-2 illustrates a sample worksheet of different typefaces in different point sizes.

11-3 /Format Font Command: An Overview

If you invoke the /Format Font command you will see the following options (see Figure 11-1):

  Use   Replace   Default   Library   Quit

The Use option applies the highlighted font to a specified range. The Replace option replaces the highlighted font in the current font set. When you select this option another menu will be presented (see Figure 11-3). The Default option saves the current font set as the default or replaces the current font set with the default set. The Library option retrieves, saves, or erases a font set library file on the disk. The font sets saved in library files have the extension AFS.

FIGURE 11-1 *The Allways Font Set*

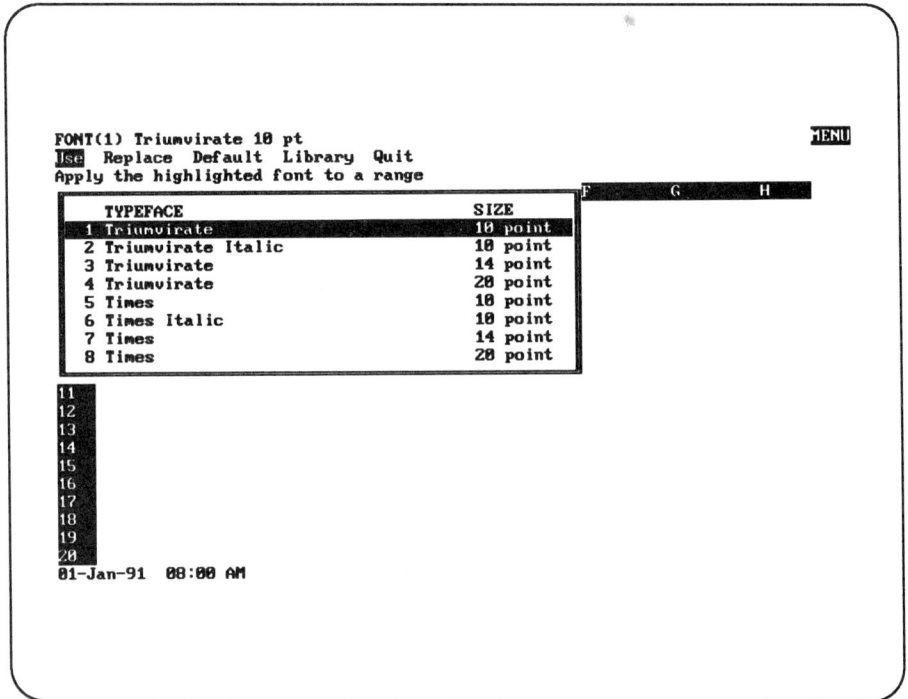

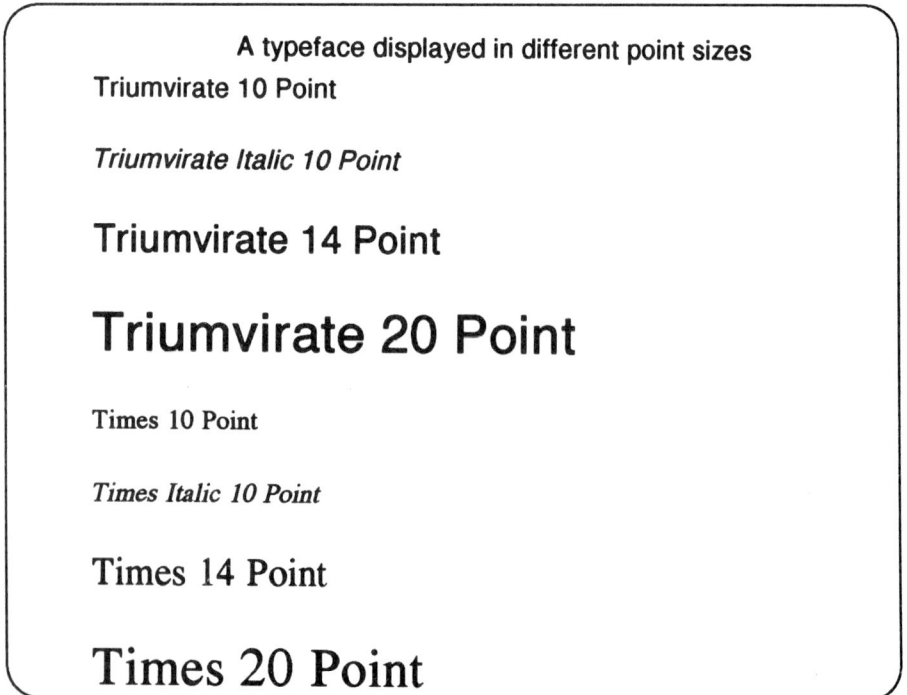

```
FONT(1) Triumvirate 10 pt                                          MENU
Use  Replace  Default  Library  Quit
Apply the highlighted font to a range
                                                  F      G        H
        TYPEFACE                       SIZE
      1 Triumvirate                    10 point
      2 Triumvirate Italic             10 point
      3 Triumvirate                    14 point
      4 Triumvirate                    20 point
      5 Times                          10 point
      6 Times Italic                   10 point
      7 Times                          14 point
      8 Times                          20 point

   11
   12
   13
   14
   15
   16
   17
   18
   19
   20
   01-Jan-91  08:00 AM
```

A typeface displayed in different point sizes

Triumvirate 10 Point

Triumvirate Italic 10 Point

Triumvirate 14 Point

Triumvirate 20 Point

Times 10 Point

Times Italic 10 Point

Times 14 Point

Times 20 Point

FIGURE 11-2 *A Sample Worksheet with Typeface in Different Point Sizes*

FGURE 11-3 Allways' Additional Typefaces

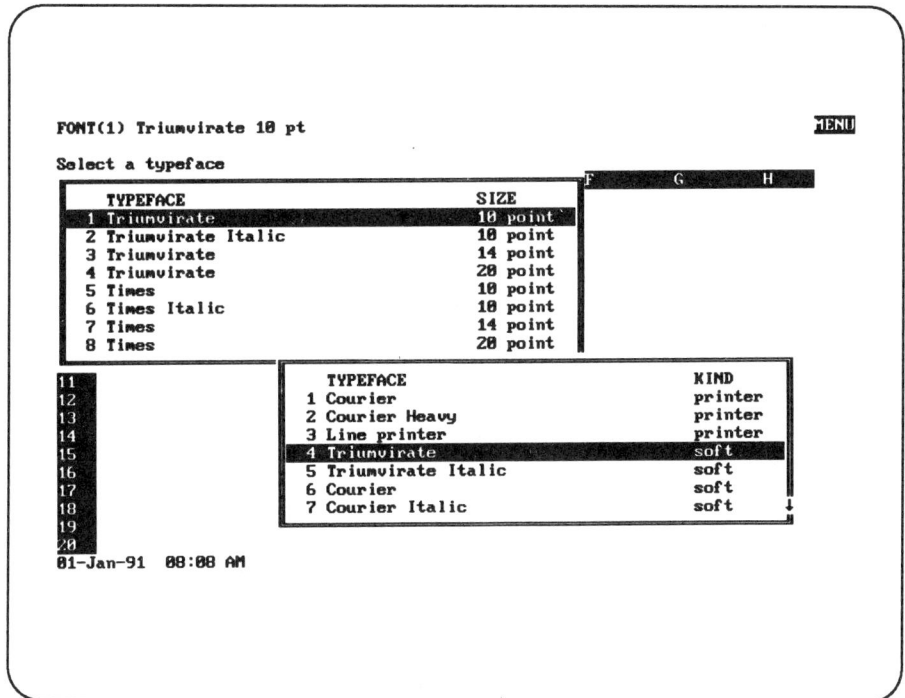

11-4 /Layout Command

The layout command allows you to control the overall appearance of your printed page. Using this command you can:

• Print a header at the top or a footer at the bottom of every page (/Layout Titles).
• Print grid lines (dotted lines) between each row and column (/Layout Options Grid).
• Include a repeating border on each page (/Layout Borders). The border can be on the top, left, or bottom of the page.
• Change the thickness of lines created (/Layout Options Line-Weight).
• Save commonly used layouts for future use with other worksheets (/Layout Library).

Figure 11-4 is a sample worksheet. Figure 11-5 was created from it as follows:

1. /Layout, Options, Line-Weight, Heavy, Esc, Esc, Format, Lines, Outline, A2. .B3, **Return**.
2. /Layout, Options, Grid, Yes. If you press **Esc**, **Esc**, you will see a worksheet similar to Figure 11-5.

11-5 Adding Headers and Footers

Using the Layout menu you will be able to add headers and/or footers to your worksheets. Using Figure 11-4 we created a new worksheet with headers and footers displayed in Figure 11-6. This figure was created as follows:

FIGURE 11-4 A Sample Worksheet

```
A1: [W32]                                                        READY

                         A                    B      C      D      E
 1
 2
 3                   OCEAN CITY TOURIST ATTRACTION
 4
 5   Current Assets
 6      Cash                          $36,249 $42,495 $58,761 $72,300
 7      Accounts Receivable            26,700  23,821  22,545  22,768
 8                                     ------- ------- ------- -------
 9   Total Current Assets              62,949  66,316  81,306  95,068
10
11   Fixed Assets
12      Property,  and Plant
13         Land                        49,121  48,700  45,600  40,410
14         Building                    82,212  82,212  79,100  78,275
15      Gross P,  and P               131,333 130,912 124,700 118,685
16      Accumulated Depreciation      (48,814)(37,600)(36,945)(29,725)
17                                     ------- ------- ------- -------
18      Net P,  and P                  82,519  93,312  87,755  88,960
19
20
01-Jan-91  08:15 AM          UNDO
```

OCEAN CITY TOURIST ATTRACTION			
Current Assets			
Cash	$36,249	$42,495	$58,761	$72,300
Accounts Receivable	26,700	23,821	22,545	22,768
	-------	-------	-------	-------
Total Current Assets	62,949	66,316	81,306	95,068
Fixed Assets			
Property, and Plant			
Land	49,121	48,700	45,600	40,410
Building	82,212	82,212	79,100	78,275
Gross P, and P	131,333	130,912	124,700	118,685
Accumulated Depreciation	(48,814)	(37,600)	(36,945)	(29,725)
	-------	-------	-------	-------
Net P, and P	82,519	93,312	87,755	88,960

FIGURE 11-5 A Worksheet with Heavy Outlines and Grids

FIGURE 11-6 A Worksheet with Header and Footer

A SAMPLE BALANCE SHEET

OCEAN CITY TOURIST ATTRACTION

Current Assets				
Cash	$36,249	$42,495	$58,761	$72,300
Accounts Receivable	26,700	23,821	22,545	22,768
	-------	-------	-------	-------
Total Current Assets	62,949	66,316	81,306	95,068
Fixed Assets				
Property, and Plant				
Land	49,121	48,700	45,600	40,410
Building	82,212	82,212	79,100	78,275
Gross P, and P	131,333	130,912	124,700	118,685
Accumulated Depreciation	(48,814)	(37,600)	(36,945)	(29,725)
	-------	-------	-------	-------
Net P, and P	82,519	93,312	87,755	88,960

BALANCE SHEET FOR   01–Jan–91

1. Layout, Titles, Header. Allways responds with Enter Up to 240 Characters. We typed A SAMPLE BALANCE SHEET, Enter.
2. /Footer. Allways responds Enter Up to 240 Characters. We typed BALANCE SHEET FOR ‖@, Return. The ‖ (two broken lines) and @ (the "at" symbol) enters the DOS date at the lower right corner of your printed report.
3. Press **Quit** to return to the /Layout menu.
4. Press **Quit** again to return to the worksheet. If you print this worksheet you will see a figure similar to Figure 11-6.

11-6 /Graph Command: An Overview

The /Graph command allows you to include graphs in the worksheet. Using this feature you can:

• Change the size of text in a graph
• Add white space around the graph
• Place a graph alongside your data

Using Allways you can print the worksheet and graphs together. You can have up to 20 graphs in the worksheet, and you can position them any way you like. To export a graph from 1-2-3 to Allways, first save the graph in 1-2-3 by using the /Graph Save command. This will generate a file with the extension PIC. (See Chapter 14 for a detailed discussion of 1-2-3 graphs.) When you choose Graph from the Allways main menu you will see the following options:

Add   Remove   Goto   Settings   Font-Directory   Quit

Add	Adds a graph to the current worksheet
Remove	Removes a graph from the current worksheet
Goto	Moves the cell pointer to a graph
Settings	Changes the fonts, colors, margins, range or PIC file for a graph
Font-Directory	Sets the directory that contains the graph font files
Quit	Returns to Allways mode

11-7 Inserting Graphs into the Worksheet

You must first select the range that indicates the position of the graph. Allways automatically sizes the graph to fit within the selected range. When the graph is exported to your worksheet you can view the graph in text or graphics mode. The /Display Graphs command displays your graph. You can also press F10 to view your graph. In text mode, graphs are represented as a series of "G" characters. In graphics mode you will see the actual graph. Let us walk through a simple example. We want to export the graph presented in Figure 11-7 to the worksheet presented in Figure 11-8. Remember, the graph in Figure 11-7 is saved as CH11-7.PIC. Do the following:

1. Get Allways started
2. /Graph, Add, CH11-7.PIC, **Return**, B19. .D30, **Return**, Quit

At this point, if you are in text mode, you will see a series of Gs. Press F6 to switch to graphics mode and you will see a figure similar to Figure 11-9. Remember, when you specify your PIC file you must specify the drive and/or directory (if the graphic file is not in your default drive and/or directory).

11-8 Integrating Two Graphs into the Worksheet

We want to export the graph presented in Figure 11-10 into our worksheet in Figure 11-9. Do the following:

1. Get Allways started.
2. Load Figure 11-9 by using /File, Retrieve, CH11-9 (in 1-2-3).
3. Remove the previous graph from the worksheet by /Graph, Remove, CH11-7.PIC, **Return**. Now you can add the two graphs in more appropriate places.
4. Add, CH11-7.PIC, **Return**, A20. .B30, **Return**.
5. Add, CH11-10.PIC, **Return**, C20. .F30, **Return**, Quit. If you print this worksheet you should see something similar to Figure 11-11.

11-9 /Graph Settings PIC-File

The /Graphs Settings PIC-File allows you to replace a graph in the worksheet with a different graph by specifying the name of the new graph (PIC-File). This process saves you a few steps by not forcing you to use the /Graph Remove command before adding the new graph to the worksheets.

FIGURE 11-7 A Sample Graph

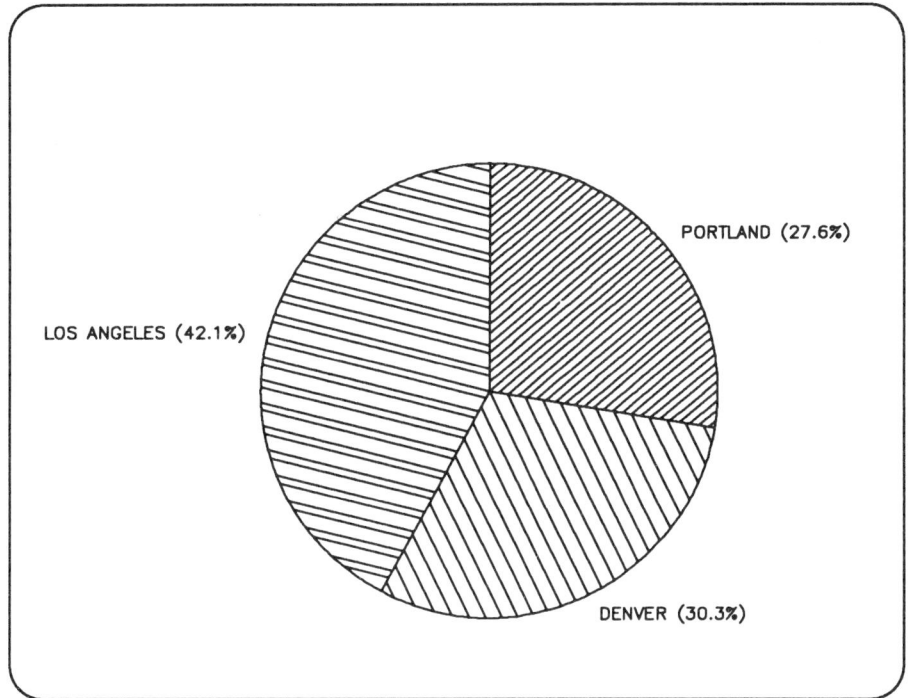

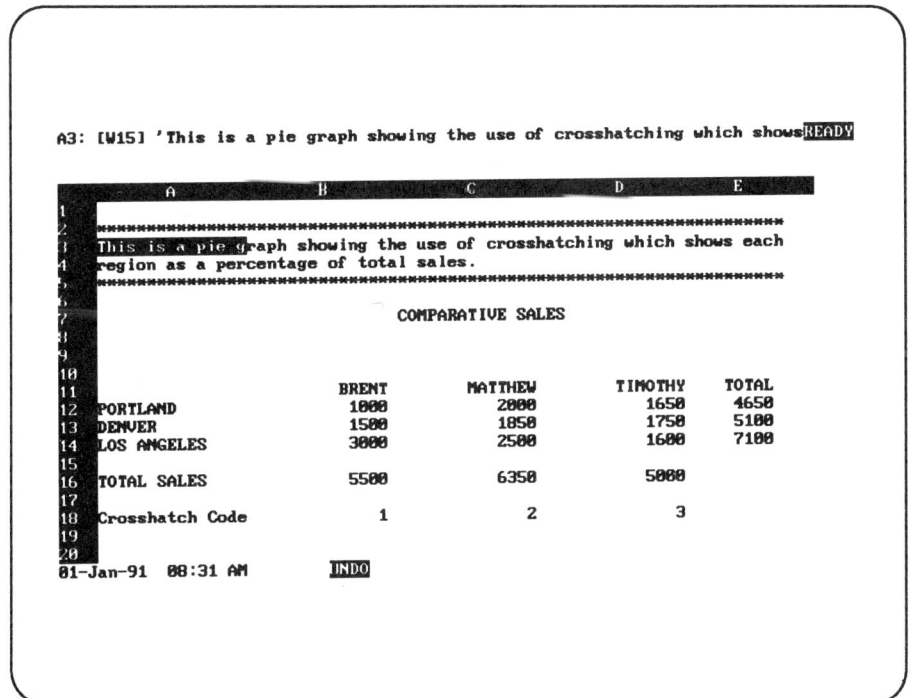

Figure 11-8 A Sample Worksheet

FIGURE 11-9 A Worksheet and Graph Integrated

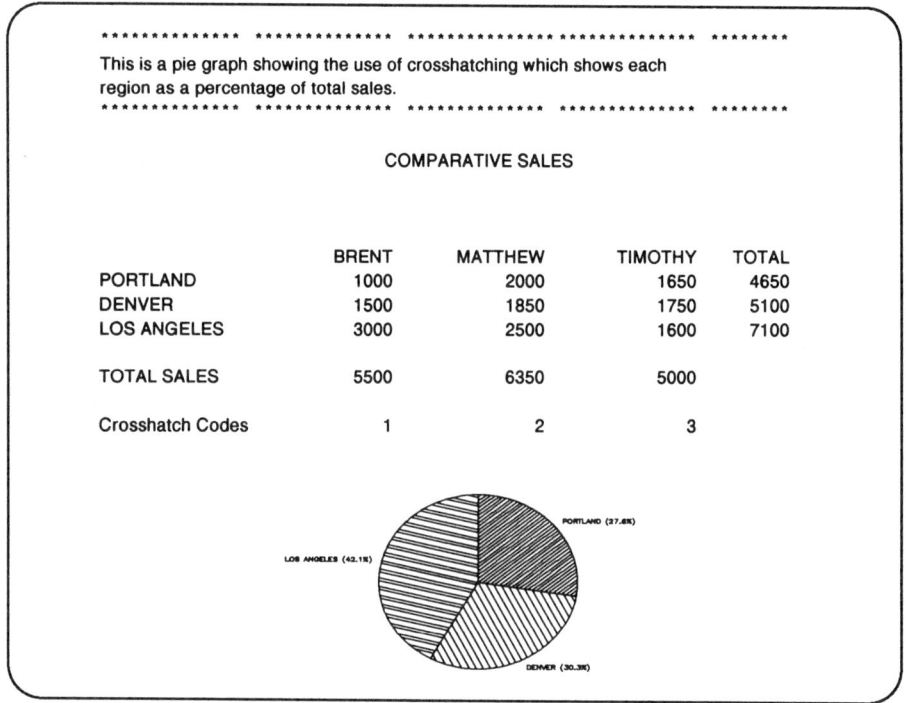

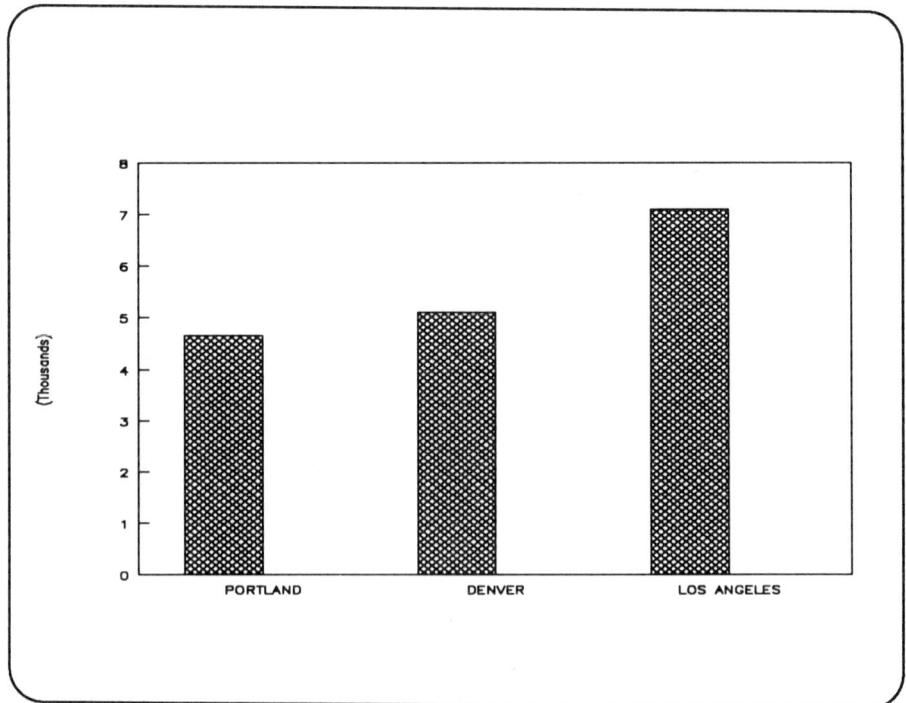

************** ************** ***************** ************** *******

This is a pie graph showing the use of crosshatching which shows each
region as a percentage of total sales.

************** ************** ***************** ************** *******

COMPARATIVE SALES

	BRENT	MATTHEW	TIMOTHY	TOTAL
PORTLAND	1000	2000	1650	4650
DENVER	1500	1850	1750	5100
LOS ANGELES	3000	2500	1600	7100
TOTAL SALES	5500	6350	5000	
Crosshatch Codes	1	2	3	

FIGURE 11-10 A Sample Graph

FGURE 11-11 Two Graphs Integrated with the Worksheet

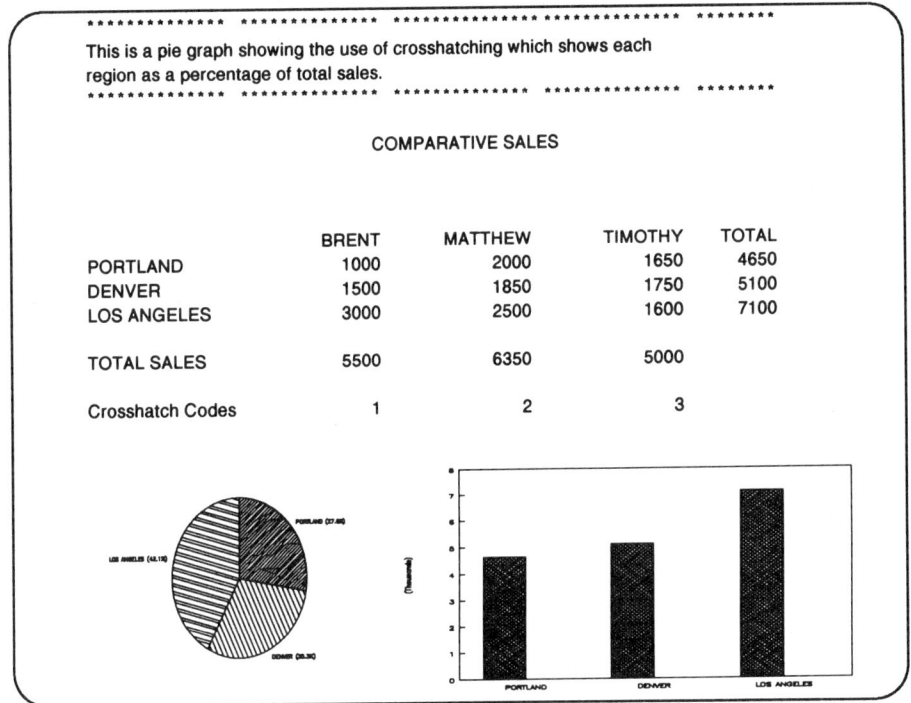

11-10 /Graph Settings Scale

The /Graph Settings Scale option allows you to adjust the size of the text on your graphs by scaling the fonts. You can specify a scale factor between .5 and 3 for either of the graph fonts. The default scale factor is 1. This scale produces graphs identical to the graph produced by the PrintGraph program(see Chapters 14 and 15). A scale factor of 2 would produce graphs twice as large.

11-11 /Display Colors

If you have a color monitor and a color display card, you can use /Display Colors to change the colors that Allways uses. When you invoke /Display Colors the following menu will be presented:

Background   Foreground   Cell-Pointer   Quit

The Background option allows you to select the background screen color from eight choices. The Foreground option allows you to select the foreground screen color; you have four choices here. The Cell-Pointer option selects the color of the cell pointer—six choices. The Quit option puts you back in the Display menu.

11-12 /Format Color

The /Format Color command allows you to print text and numbers in different colors on printers that support this feature. When you invoke /Format Color you will see the following options:

1   Black
2   Red
3   Green
4   Blue
5   Cyan
6   Magenta
7   White
8   Red-on-negs

The eighth option (Red-on-negs) allows Allways to print the number in red if it is negative, or in black otherwise.

11-13 /Display Zoom

The /Display Zoom command allows you to select from a number of different worksheet font size attributes when you are working in graphics mode. When you invoke /Display Zoom the following options will be displayed:

Tiny   Small   Normal   Large   Huge

The Tiny option reduces cells to 60% of their normal size. The Small option reduces cells to 84% of their normal size. The Normal option displays cells at their normal size. The Large option enlarges cells to 120% of their normal size. The Huge option enlarges cells to 140% of their normal size. Remember, enlarging or reducing has no effect on your printouts; it only affects the presentation of the worksheet on the screen. To see the enlarged or reduced worksheet you must be in graphics mode.

Enlarging the display is useful if you are working with very small fonts. Reducing the display is useful if you are working with very large fonts.

11-14 /Worksheet Commands

If you invoke the /Worksheet command from the Allways main menu you will see the following options:

Column   Row   Page

The Column option gives you two alternatives: Set-Width and Reset-Width. When you choose the Set-Width option, you can specify any number between 0 and 240 with up to two decimals. You can either type the number or use the left and right arrow to visually adjust the column-width.

The Row option allows you to set the height of a row. The default row height is 13 points. You can specify any number between 0 and 255. /Worksheet Row Auto is used to automatically adjust row heights to accommodate the largest font in a row. If you want to adjust the height of one row, move the cell pointer to that row and invoke /Worksheet Row Auto. To adjust the height of a series of consecutive rows, move the cell pointer to the first or last row in the range and press the period key. This will anchor the cursor at the beginning of the range. Highlight the desired range and invoke /Worksheet Row Auto.

The /Worksheet Page command allows you to manually insert row and column page breaks. If you do not invoke this feature, Allways automatically breaks up the range into page-sized segments. A dashed line will appear within the print range wherever Allways has determined that a page break is necessary. Allways breaks a page in two ways:

• A column page break occurs when the range specified exceeds the paper width.

• A row page break occurs when the range specified exceeds the paper length.

For printing worksheets that are too long or too wide Allways proceeds vertically, as does 1-2-3: top to bottom, then left to right. This means it prints the length of the worksheet page by page then it proceeds with the width. To use the page break feature, all you have to do is to invoke /Worksheet Page, then select Row, Column, or Delete. After this selection you must specify the first column or the first row of the range. Figure 11-12 illustrates a sample worksheet. Figure 11-13 illustrates a vertical and a horizontal page break. This is how the page breaks were created. For the column page break we chose / Worksheet, Page, Column, D4, **Return**, Quit; for the row page break we typed /Worksheet, Page, Row, All, **Return**, Quit.

Some of the common applications of /Worksheet commands are:

• Add solid black shading to a row (/Format Shade), then make the row height very short (/Worksheet Row). This will produce the effect of a thick horizontal line. Using the same feature and /Worksheet Column command, will produce the effect of a thick vertical line.

• By using the /Worksheet Page command you can break large worksheets into your customized pages of different sizes.

11-15 The /Special Commands

If you invoke /Special from the Allways main menu you will see the following options:

   Copy   Move   Justify   Import

FIGURE 11-12 A Sample Worksheet

```
A1: [W32] '                    OCEAN CITY TOURIST ATTRACTION              READY


               A              B       C       D       E
                      OCEAN CITY TOURIST ATTRACTION
1                (1989-90  Figures in thousands of dollars)
2     ++++++++++++++++++++++++++++++++++++++++++++++++++++++++++++++
3                            Spring  Summer   Fall   Winter
4     ++++++++++++++++++++++++++++++++++++++++++++++++++++++++++++++
5   Current Assets
6     Cash                   $36,249 $42,495 $58,761 $72,300
7     Accounts Receivable     26,700  23,821  22,545  22,768
8                            _____ _____ _____ _____
9
10  Total Current Assets       62,949  66,316  81,306  95,068
11
12  Fixed Assets
13    Property,  and Plant
14      Land                   49,121  48,700  45,600  40,410
15      Building               82,212  82,212  79,100  78,275
16    Gross P, and P          131,333 130,912 124,700 118,685
17    Accumulated Depreciation (48,814)(37,600)(36,945)(29,725)
18                            _____ _____ _____ _____
19    Net P, and P             82,519  93,312  87,755  88,960
20
01-Jan-91  11:00 AM      UNDO
```

FIGURE 11-13 A Sample Worksheet with a Vertical and Horizontal Page Break

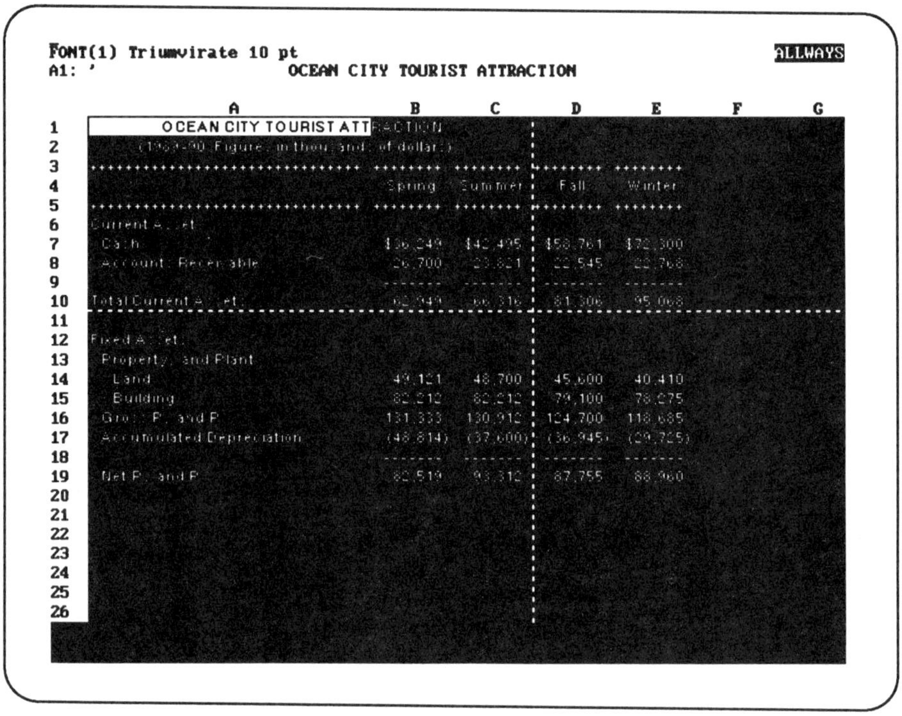

The Copy option allows you to copy the format of a cell or a range to another cell or range. Remember, this command only copies the format of the cell, not the data. Also, you cannot copy graphs with /Special Copy. The /Copy command can save ;you a lot of time if you are dealing with identical worksheets, tables or ranges. You can format one of these worksheets, tables, or ranges, then copy it to another worksheet, table, or range. The format attributes of a cell include the font, boldface, color, lines, underlining, and shading modes.

The Move command allows you to move the format of a cell or range to another cell or range. When you use the Move command the formats of the original cell or range is set to default. The destination cell or range adopts the format of the original cell or range. This command is useful if you import the format of a different worksheet and the cell locations do not quite match. By using /Special Move you can correct this problem.

The Justify command allows you to justify text in accordance with the fonts and column widths you have selected in Allways. Justification in Allways will affect the appearance of the worksheet in 1-2-3. The /Special Justify command works only on labels. It does not affect values. Unlike /Range Justify in 1-2-3, Allways will justify a range containing a blank row.

The Import command is used to import the format of an existing worksheet to a new worksheet. Remember that all the formats in the receiving worksheet will be replaced by the incoming worksHEet. This command can save you a lot o time when you work with identical worksheets. You can format one of them, then import this worksheet to all the new ones.

11-16 Allways and Macros

You can design simple macros (discussed in Chapters 18 through 21) to invoke Allways and perform certain tasks. There are a few exceptions:

1. You must invoke a macro from 1-2-3. You cannot invoke a macro from Allways because Allways uses the Alt key as part of its accelerator key.
2. Macro commands such as {GET}, {GETNUMBER}, {GETLABEL}, and {LOOK} will not work in Allways.
3. Advanced macro commands that control screen output such as INDICATE, PANELOFF, and PANELON will not work in Allways graphics mode, but will work in text mode.

The following simple macro will activate Allways from the 1-2-3 worksheet:

/AIALLWAYS~~

SUMMARY

In this chapter some of the advanced features of Allways were introduced. We reviewed Allways fonts and layout commands. The process of integrating graphs into your worksheet using Allways was discussed. Displaying color on the monitor and/or printout was examined. We provided an overview of /Worksheet and /Special commands. The chapter concluded with a brief discussion of 1-2-3 macros and their relationship with Allways.

REVIEW QUESTIONS

* These questions are answered in Appendix I.
1. What is a font? How many fonts are supported by Allways?
2. What is a font library? Can you transfer a font from one worksheet to another? If yes, how?
3. What are the applications of /Layout commands? How do you change the thickness of a line?
4. How do you add a header to a worksheet? A footer? How many characters are allowed in the footer or the header?
5.* How do you include the DOS date as a part of the header or footer?
6. What is the application of Goto in /Graph?
7.* How do you remove a graph from a worksheet?
8. How many graphs can be included in a worksheet?
9.* How is a graph displayed in text mode?
10. What are the applications of /Graph Settings PIC-File?
11. What are the applications of /Graph Settings Scale?
12.* How many colors are supported by Allways? What does /Display Colors do?
13. What are the applications of /Display Zoom? Does this command have any effect on the printout?
14. What are the applications of the /Worksheet command?
15. How does Allways perform a page break? What are the differences between 1-2-3 column and row commands and their counterparts in Allways?
16. Using Worksheet command, how do you draw a thick line?

17. What are the applications of /Special commands? What is the difference between the Allways /Copy command and the 1-2-3 /Copy command?

18. What are the differences between the Allways /Justify command and the 1-2-3 / Justify command?

19. What are macros? Are 1-2-3 macros compatible with Allways? What are the exceptions?

HANDS-ON PRACTICE

1. Load the worksheet presented in Figure 11-12 and do the following:
   a) Change the title to Triumvirate 20 point.
   b) Change the last row to Times 20 point.
   c) Change the first row to Triumvirate 10 point.
   d) Print the final result.

2. Load Figure 11-12 and print grid lines in the worksheet. Add a footer as "Sample Footer" and a header as "Sample Header" to this worksheet. Include the DOS date as part of your header.

3. Load the worksheet in Figure 11-12 and do the following:
   a) Import the graph presented in Figure 11-10 to this worksheet.
   b) Remove this graph and replace it with the graph in Figure 11-7.
   c) Using the Settings option change the font on this graph to a font of your choice.
   d) Print the final work.

COMPREHENSIVE LAB ASSIGNMENT

Retrieve CHAPT10 and do the following:
1. Change the title to 20 point Triumvirate.
2. Add a Header as sample and a footer as Sample1 to the worksheet.
3. Print the worksheet.
4. Save the worksheet under CHAPT11.

MISCONCEPTIONS AND SOLUTIONS

M – Changing fonts through the Allways menu can be a time consuming process.

S – By using the accelerator keys (Alt-1 to Alt-8) you can save a lot of time.

M – Creating a set of fonts from worksheet to worksheet can be time consuming.

S – Save these fonts in a font library.

M – Specifying the width of columns in Allways by typing numbers may be misleading.

S – Use right and left arrows to define the width of a column as finely as required or desired.

M – Repeating the same format from cell to cell can be time consuming.

S – Use /Special Copy to easily duplicate formatting from a cell to any other cell(s).

M – You have imported a graph to your worksheet but all you see is a series of Gs.

S – Probably you are in text mode. By pressing F6 change the Allways mode from text to graphics. At this point you should be able to see your graph.

M – You have specified headers, footers, borders, and margins in 1-2-3, but they do not show up in Allways.

S – These features must be re-specified in Allways.

M – There are certain cells that you do not want to include as part of your printed output.

S – Use /Format Colors White for the specified cells. If you want to suppress entire rows, use /Format Colors White on the specified rows and then set the height of these rows to 0 by using /Worksheet Row Set-Height.

Functions/Part One

12-1 Introduction

In this chapter we will explain the general format of mathematical, financial, and statistical functions. Numerous examples will accompany our discussion. Chapter 13 continues the discussion by covering string, date and time, and special functions. Database statistical functions will be the subject of Chapter 17.

12-2 What Is a Lotus Function?

A Lotus *function* is a built-in formula for the calculation of a specific task. Lotus has eight function groups. Each has been designed to perform a unique task. For example, you have learned how to add the contents of cells A1, A2, A3 and A4 by adding +A1+A2+A3+A4. Instead of doing this, you could simply type @SUM(A1..A4). Now you can see how easy it is to perform the task using a function.

Every function follows this format:

@FUNCTION(argument1,argument2,...)

A function must begin with the at sign (@). Next comes the name of the function and one or a series of arguments in parentheses. The *argument* is the information Lotus needs in order to perform a task. Consider the function @SUM(X1,X2,X3). The function name is SUM and the arguments are X1, X2, and X3. Some functions, however, do not need any arguments.

12-3 Argument Types

Lotus accepts three types of arguments:

1. Numeric values. In the function @ABS(y), y is a value; @ABS(-5) = 5.
2. Range values. In the function @SUM(A1..A9), A1..A9 is the range address. In the function @SUM(Asset), Asset is a range name.
3. String (non-numeric) values. In the function @UPPER("rose") = ROSE, rose is the string value. Remember, strings must be enclosed in double quotation marks.

Numeric values can have one of the following forms:

actual value   @ABS(-5)
cell address   @ABS(A11)

cell range name	@SUM(asset)
formula	@ABS((-20/4)/5)
function	@INT(@ABS(A11)+@SQRT(64))
combination	@INT(@SUM(A1..A10)+asset+2500)

Range values can have one of the following forms:

range name	@SUM(DIVISION1)
range address	@SUM(A1..A10)
combination	@SUM(DIVISION1,A1..A9,DIVISION9)

And finally, string values can have one of the following forms:

cell address	@LOWER(A1)
cell name	@LOWER(STREET) (remember street is a cell name)
actual value	@LOWER("I AM A STUDENT")
formula	@LENGTH("TITLE"&"SUB-TITLE")

When you are working with functions you must keep in mind the exact type of argument accepted by each function. For example, @SUM("TITLE") will cause an error because the @SUM function requires a numeric value or a range value, not a string value.

Seven functions do not require any arguments. These include @ERR, @FALSE, @NA, @NOW, @PI, @RAND, and @TRUE. We will talk about these in Chapter 13.

The functions @CELL, @N, and @S require single-cell values as arguments. However, you must enter these values as a range, for example @N(A1..A1), or a cell address preceded by an exclamation mark, as in @N(!A1). We will discuss these in Chapter 13.

12-4 Mathematical Functions

Lotus offers 17 mathematical functions. All except @PI require arguments. The arguments can be values, cell addresses, range names, formulas, or other functions. Arguments for sine, cosine, and tangent must be expressed in radians. (To convert degrees to radians, multiply the number of degrees by @PI/180.)

The trigonometric functions arc sine, arc cosine, and arc tangent return all angles in radians. (To convert radians to degrees, multiply the number of radians by 180/@PI.)

12-4-1   @ABS(A)

This function's argument must be numeric. The function calculates the absolute and always returns the positive value of the argument. Examples:

```
@ABS(5)  = 5
@ABS(0)  = 0
@ABS(-5) = 5
@ABS("Happy Birthday")  = ERR — invalid argument
```

This function is useful for calculation of the root of a quadratic equation. In such cases only the positive root is needed.

12-4-2   @ACOS(A)

The function calculates the arc cosine of an angle and returns the angle, in radians, whose cosine is A. Argument A must be between -1 and +1. Examples:

@ACOS(.25)	= 1.318116 (radians)
@ACOS(-0.5)	= 2.094395 (radians)
@ACOS(1)*180/@PI	= 0 (degrees)
@ACOS(.75)*180/@PI	= 41.40962 (degrees)
@ACOS(9.5)	= ERR — invalid argument

12-4-3 @ASIN(A)

Argument A must be between -1 and +1. The function calculates the arc sine of an angle and returns the angle, in radians, whose sine is A. Examples:

@ASIN(0.25)	= 0.252680 (radians)
@ASIN(-0.5)	= -0.52359 (radians)
@ASIN(.5)*180/@PI	= 30 (degrees)
@ASIN(1)*180/@PI	= 90 (degrees)
@ASIN(9.5)	= ERR — invalid argument

12-4-4 @ATAN(A)

This function's argument can take any value. It calculates the two-quadrant arc tangent of an angle and returns the angle, in radians, whose tangent is A. Examples:

@ATAN(90)	= 1.559685 (radians)
@ATAN(-45)	= -1.54857 (radians)
@ATAN(1)*180/@PI	= 45 (degrees)

12-4-5 @ATAN2(A,B)

The arguments can take any numeric value. The function calculates the four-quadrant arc tangent of an angle and returns the angle, in radians, whose tangent is B/A. If both A and B are zero, the result is ERR. Examples:

@ATAN2(4,590)	= 1.564016
@ATAN2(-30, -60)	= -2.03444
@ATAN2(0, 0)	= ERR

12-4-6 @COS(A)

This function calculates the cosine of angle A, which must be measured in radians. The result is always between -1 and 1. Examples:

@COS(90*@PI/180)	= 3.4E-19
@COS(60*@PI/180)	= 0.5

12-4-7 @EXP(A)

This function calculates the result of *e* (2.7182) to the *A*th power. The upper limit for A is 709; beyond this the result is too large to be stored by Lotus. Examples:

@EXP(0)	= 1
@EXP(1)	= 2.718281
@EXP(-2)	= 0.135335
@EXP(2)	= 7.389056
@EXP(1000)	= ERR — too large

12-4-8   @INT(A)

This function returns the integer portion of the argument, but it does not round the number. If you would like to round a number, either use the @ROUND function or simply add .50 to the argument of the @INT(A) function. Examples:

```
@INT(5.5645)     = 5
@INT(-6.45698)   = -6
@INT(9.9)        = 9
@INT(9.9+.50)    = 10
```

12-4-9   @LN(A)

Argument A must be greater than zero. The function calculates the natural logarithm of A. Examples:

```
@LN(58)   = 4.060443
@LN(1)    = 0
@LN(-5)   = ERR — invalid argument
```

12-4-10   @LOG(A)

Argument A must be greater than zero. The function calculates the logarithm (base 10) of A. Examples:

```
@LOG(25)   = 1.397940
@LOG(1)    = 0
@LOG(-5)   = ERR — invalid argument
```

12-4-11   @MOD(A,B)

Argument A can be any number; argument B can be any number except zero. The function calculates the remainder of A/B. The sign returned by this function will always be the same as the sign of A. Examples:

```
@MOD(13,7)    = 6
@MOD(11,3)    = 2
@MOD(-14,2)   = 0
@MOD(-15,4)   = -3
@MOD(15,-4)   = 3
@MOD(7,0)     = ERR — invalid argument
```

12-4-12   @PI

This function returns 3.141592 or PI, the ratio of the circumference of a circle to its diameter (2*PI*R/(2*R) = PI, where R is the radius of a circle).

12-4-13   @RAND

This function generates a random number between zero and one. You can use it to generate a random number between any range of numbers as follows:

@INT(@RAND*(U-L+1)+L)

where U is the upper bound, L is the lower bound. For example, if you are interested in a random number between 1000 and 100, your formula would be:

@INT(@RAND*(901)+100).

This formula will return an integer between 100 and 1000.

12-4-14 @ROUND(A,n)

Argument n must be a value between -15 and +15. The function rounds argument A to n places. This function can round on either side of the decimal point. Examples:

```
@ROUND(2.435678,3)  = 2.436
@ROUND(5.567564,3)  = 5.568
@ROUND(145.267,-1)  = 150
@ROUND(145.267,-2)  = 100
@ROUND(145.267,-3)  = 0
```

12-4-15 @SIN(A)

This function returns the sine of angle A. The angle must be measured in radians. Examples:

```
@SIN(45*@PI/180)  = 0.707106
@SIN(60*@PI/180)  = 0.866025
```

12-4-16 @SQRT(A)

Argument A must be a positive number. The function returns the positive square root of A. Examples:

```
@SQRT(16)  = 4
@SQRT(25)  = 5
@SQRT(56)  = 7.483314
@SQRT(-4)  = ERR — invalid argument
```

12-4-17 @TAN(A)

Argument A must be measured in radians. The function returns the tangent of angle A. Examples:

```
@TAN(45*@PI/180)   = 1
@TAN(90*@PI/180)   = 2.9E+18
@TAN(180*@PI/180)  = -3.4E-19
```

12-5 Financial Functions

Lotus has 11 financial functions. They can be utilized for cash flow analysis, investment analysis, loan installment, and three methods of depreciation analysis. Before you use these functions, you should remember that term and interest rate must be expressed for the same time frame (for monthly payment, the yearly interest rate must be divided by 12 and the term must be multiplied by 12). The interest rate can be entered either as a percentage (10%) or as a decimal (.10). Lotus assumes ordinary annuity. This means that a payment is made at the end of each period and the annuity due is made at the beginning of each period.

12-5-1 @FV(payment,interest rate,term)

This function calculates the future value of a series of equal payments with a given interest rate over a period of time. The @FV function uses the following formula:

$$FV = \text{Payment} * \frac{(1 + \text{interest})^{n-1}}{\text{interest}} \quad \text{where n = number of periods}$$

Figure 12-1 shows the future value of an IRA plan over 20 years with a $2,000 payment and an interest rate of 9 percent. This function can be very helpful for calculating the future value of an investment.

12-5-2 @PV(payment,interest rate,term)

This function calculates the present value of an investment. The payments must be equal. The function uses the following formula:

$$PV = \text{Payment} * \frac{(1 - (1 + \text{interest})^{-n})}{\text{interest}} \quad \text{where } n = \text{term}$$

This function can be used for discounting a series of future income payments to today's value. Let us say somebody will pay you $5,000 for the next five years. How much can you sell this portfolio for today? Figure 12-2 shows an example of this function.

12-5-3 @IRR(estimate,range)

This function calculates the internal rate of return (IRR) of a series of cash inflows and outflows. Estimate can be any figure between zero and one. Range is the entire cash inflow and outflow of a particular investment. This function can be very helpful for investment analysis. Let us assume you have an investment portfolio that includes a series of cash outflows (initial cost, labor, raw materials, etc.) and a series of cash inflows (the income that may be generated by the investment). Let us assume that you have no money to invest in this project. You go to a bank for a loan. At what interest rate can you afford to implement the project? It depends on the internal rate of return. If the IRR is 12 percent and the bank is willing to lend you money at a rate less than 12 percent, you can proceed. At an interest rate of 12 percent you will neither lose nor gain and at a rate more than 12 percent you will lose. Figure 12-3 illustrates an example of this function.

12-5-4 @NPV(interest rate,range)

This function calculates the present value of a series of future cash flows discounted at a fixed interest rate, assuming that each cash flow occurs at the end of each period. This function uses the following formula:

$$\sum \frac{Vi}{(1 + \text{interest})^i} \quad \text{where } Vi \ldots \quad Vm \quad = \text{series of cash flows}$$

$$m \quad = \text{number of cash flows}$$

$$i \quad = \text{number of iterations (1 to m)}$$

The cash inflows or outflows do not need to be equal. This function is very helpful for calculating today's worth of an investment that may generate different future cash inflows and outflows. Figure 12-4 illustrates an example of this function.

12-5-5 @PMT(principal,interest rate,term)

This function calculates the amount of the periodic payment on a loan, using the following formula:

$$PMT = \text{principal} * \frac{\text{interest rate}}{1 - (\text{interest rate} + 1)^{-n}} \quad \text{where } n = \text{term}$$

FIGURE 12-1 Future Value of an IRA Investment

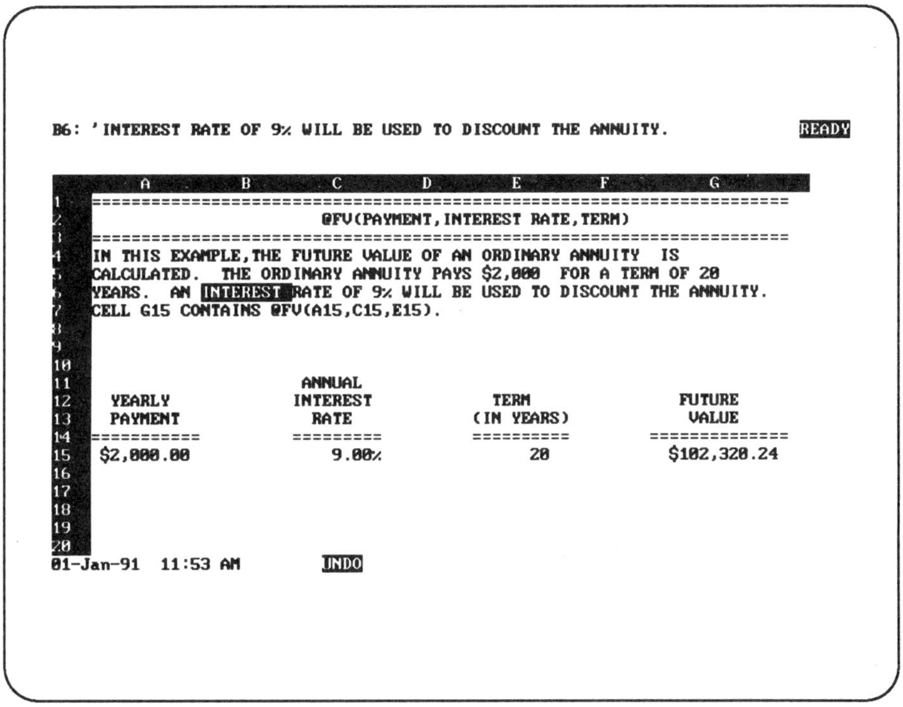

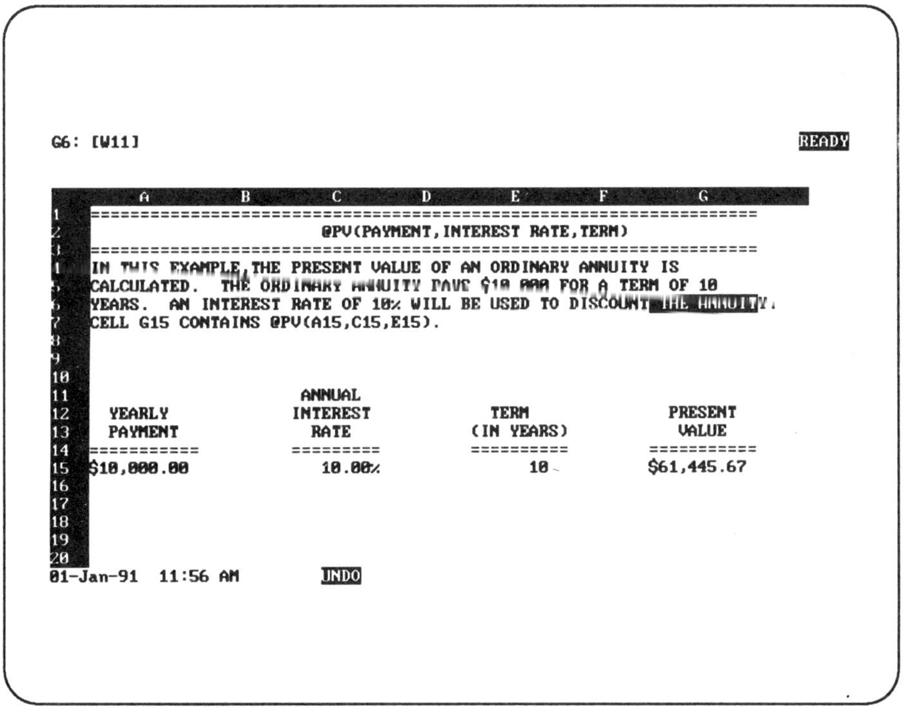

```
B6: 'INTEREST RATE OF 9% WILL BE USED TO DISCOUNT THE ANNUITY.              READY

         A          B          C          D          E          F          G
 1  =============================================================================
 2                        @FV(PAYMENT,INTEREST RATE,TERM)
 3  =============================================================================
 4  IN THIS EXAMPLE,THE FUTURE VALUE OF AN ORDINARY ANNUITY  IS
 5  CALCULATED.  THE ORDINARY ANNUITY PAYS $2,000  FOR A TERM OF 20
 6  YEARS.  AN INTEREST RATE OF 9% WILL BE USED TO DISCOUNT THE ANNUITY.
 7  CELL G15 CONTAINS @FV(A15,C15,E15).
 8
 9
10
11                         ANNUAL
12      YEARLY            INTEREST            TERM                FUTURE
13      PAYMENT             RATE            (IN YEARS)            VALUE
14    ==========         =========         ==========        ===============
15    $2,000.00            9.00%               20             $102,320.24
16
17
18
19
20
01-Jan-91  11:53 AM          UNDO
```

```
G6: [W11]                                                                   READY

         A          B          C          D          E          F          G
 1  =============================================================================
 2                        @PV(PAYMENT,INTEREST RATE,TERM)
 3  =============================================================================
 4  IN THIS EXAMPLE,THE PRESENT VALUE OF AN ORDINARY ANNUITY IS
 5  CALCULATED.  THE ORDINARY ANNUITY PAYS $10,000 FOR A TERM OF 10
 6  YEARS.  AN INTEREST RATE OF 10% WILL BE USED TO DISCOUNT THE ANNUITY.
 7  CELL G15 CONTAINS @PV(A15,C15,E15).
 8
 9
10
11                         ANNUAL
12      YEARLY            INTEREST            TERM                PRESENT
13      PAYMENT             RATE            (IN YEARS)            VALUE
14    ==========         =========         ==========        ===========
15    $10,000.00          10.00%              10              $61,445.67
16
17
18
19
20
01-Jan-91  11:56 AM          UNDO
```

FIGURE 12-2 Present Value of an Ordinary Annuity

FIGURE 12-3 Internal Rate of Return Analysis

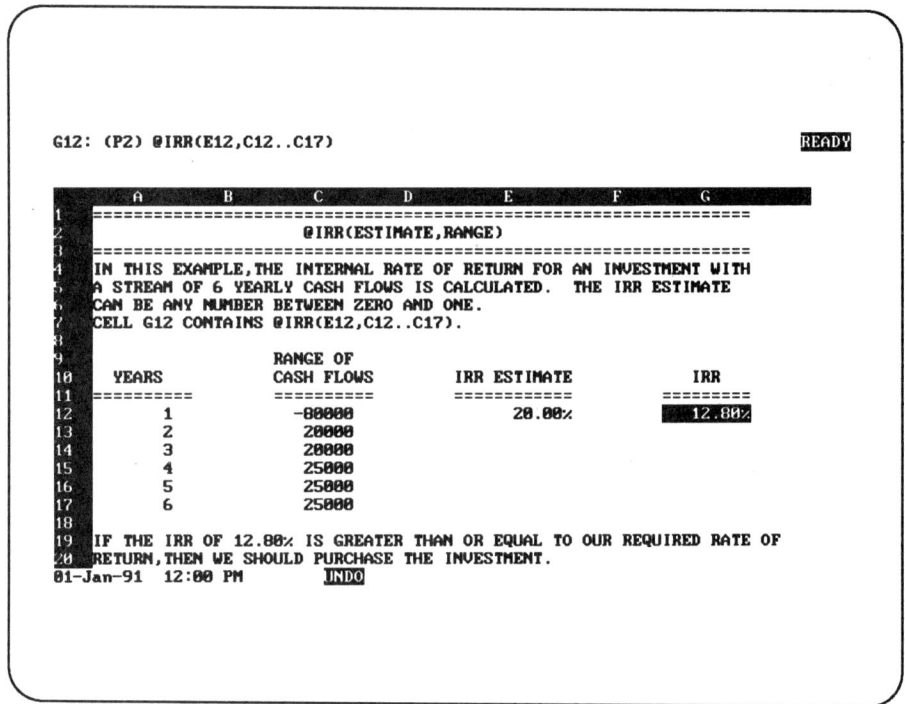

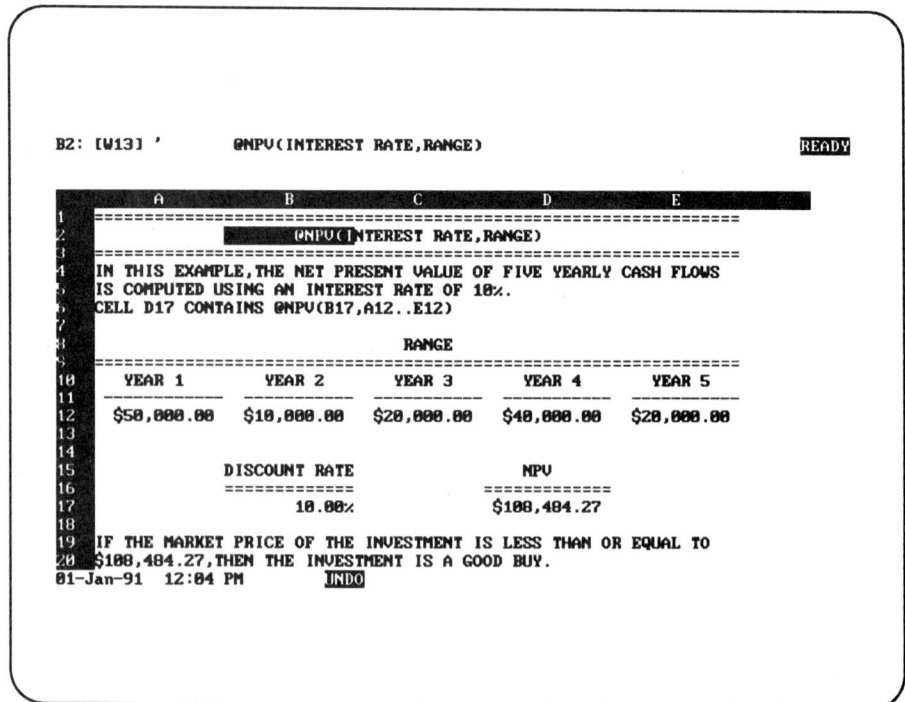

```
G12: (P2) @IRR(E12,C12..C17)                                        READY

          A        B        C          D           E          F          G
    1 ===================================================================
    2                       @IRR(ESTIMATE,RANGE)
    3 ===================================================================
    4 IN THIS EXAMPLE,THE INTERNAL RATE OF RETURN FOR AN INVESTMENT WITH
    5 A STREAM OF 6 YEARLY CASH FLOWS IS CALCULATED.  THE IRR ESTIMATE
    6 CAN BE ANY NUMBER BETWEEN ZERO AND ONE.
    7 CELL G12 CONTAINS @IRR(E12,C12..C17).
    8
    9                       RANGE OF
   10    YEARS             CASH FLOWS       IRR ESTIMATE           IRR
   11 ==========           ==========       ============       ==========
   12       1               -80000             20.00%             12.80%
   13       2                20000
   14       3                20000
   15       4                25000
   16       5                25000
   17       6                25000
   18
   19 IF THE IRR OF 12.80% IS GREATER THAN OR EQUAL TO OUR REQUIRED RATE OF
   20 RETURN,THEN WE SHOULD PURCHASE THE INVESTMENT.
   01-Jan-91  12:00 PM           UNDO
```

```
B2: [W13] '       @NPV(INTEREST RATE,RANGE)                          READY

          A           B           C           D           E
    1 ===================================================================
    2               @NPV(INTEREST RATE,RANGE)
    3 ===================================================================
    4 IN THIS EXAMPLE,THE NET PRESENT VALUE OF FIVE YEARLY CASH FLOWS
    5 IS COMPUTED USING AN INTEREST RATE OF 10%.
    6 CELL D17 CONTAINS @NPV(B17,A12..E12)
    7
    8                               RANGE
    9 ===================================================================
   10    YEAR 1      YEAR 2      YEAR 3      YEAR 4      YEAR 5
   11 ------------ ------------ ------------ ------------ ------------
   12 $50,000.00   $10,000.00   $20,000.00   $40,000.00   $20,000.00
   13
   14
   15              DISCOUNT RATE               NPV
   16              ============            ============
   17                 10.00%                $108,484.27
   18
   19 IF THE MARKET PRICE OF THE INVESTMENT IS LESS THAN OR EQUAL TO
   20 $108,484.27,THEN THE INVESTMENT IS A GOOD BUY.
   01-Jan-91  12:04 PM           UNDO
```

FIGURE 12-4 Net Present Value Analysis

This function is very helpful for determining the payments for a new car, house, boat, and so forth. Figure 12-5 illustrates an example of this function.

12-5-6 @CTERM(interest rate,future value,present value)

This function calculates the number of compounding periods an investment reaches from a given present value to a given future value with a given fixed interest rate. Lotus utilizes the following formula in this function:

$$\frac{Ln \text{ (future value/present value)}}{Ln \text{ (1 + interest rate)}} \quad \text{where Ln = natural logarithm}$$

This function can be very helpful for future planning, let us say for your children's college expenses. It tells you how many years it will take to accumulate a certain amount of money. Figure 12-6 shows an example of this function.

12-5-7 @TERM(payment,interest rate,future value)

This function calculates the number of payment periods necessary to accumulate a given future value. All payments must be equal. The function uses the following formula:

$$\frac{Ln \text{ (1 + (Future value * interest/payment))}}{Ln \text{ (1 + interest)}} \quad \text{where Ln = natural logarithm}$$

To calculate the term of an annuity that is due, the following formula should be used:

@TERM(payment, interest rate, future value/(1+ interest))

Figure 12-7 illustrates an example of this function.

12-5-8 @RATE(future value,present value,term)

This function calculates the interest rate necessary for a present value to reach a future value over the number of compounding periods, using the following formula:

$$\left(\frac{Future \ value}{present \ value} \right)^{\frac{1}{n}} \quad -1 \quad \text{where n = term}$$

Figure 12-8 illustrates an example of this function.

12-5-9 @SLN(cost,salvage value,life)

This function calculates the straight-line depreciation of a piece of equipment for one period, assuming the same amount of depreciation for every period. The function uses the following formula:

$$\frac{(Cost - Salvage \ Value)}{useful \ life \ of \ the \ asset}$$

Figure 12-9 illustrates an example of this function.

12-5-10 @SYD(cost,salvage value,life,period)

This function calculates the sum-of-the-years'-digits depreciation for a selected period using the following formula:

FIGURE 12-5 *Payment Analysis of a Particular Loan*

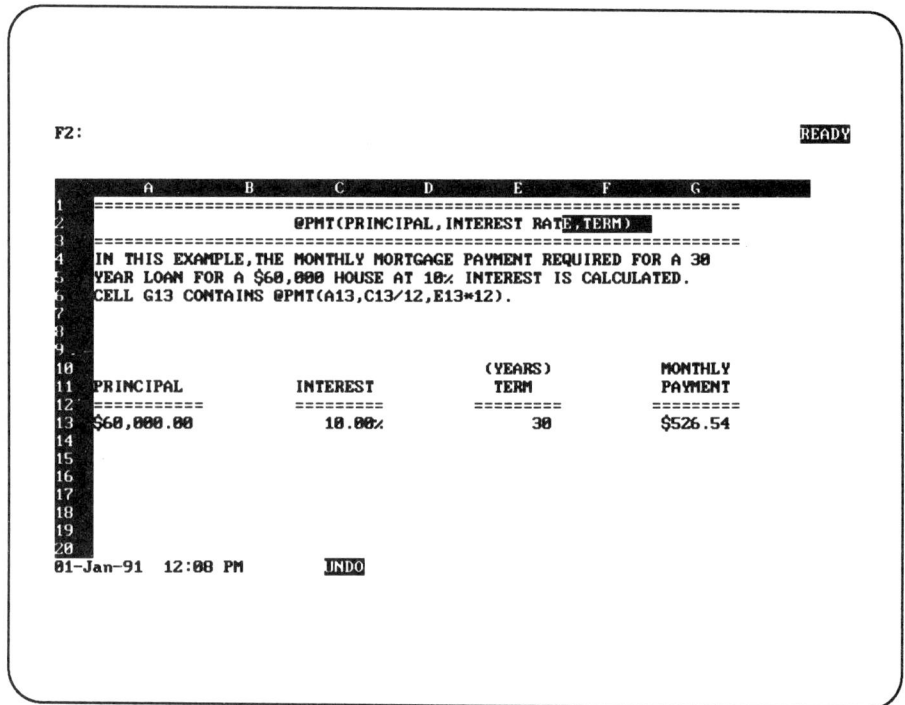

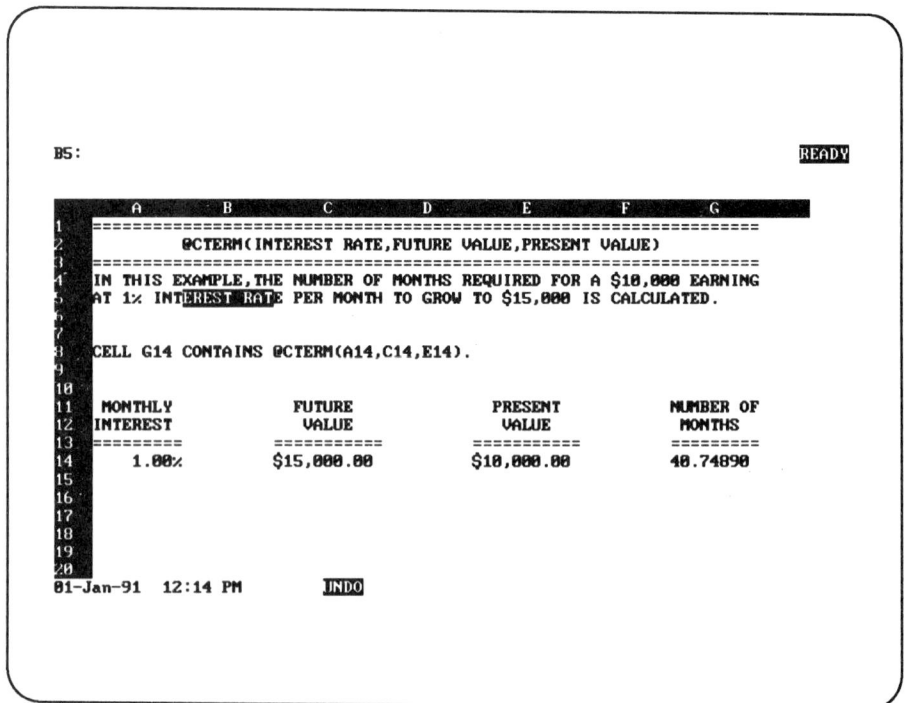

```
F2:                                                                    READY

        A         B         C         D         E         F         G
1  ==================================================================
2                  @PMT(PRINCIPAL,INTEREST RATE,TERM)
3  ==================================================================
4  IN THIS EXAMPLE,THE MONTHLY MORTGAGE PAYMENT REQUIRED FOR A 30
5  YEAR LOAN FOR A $60,000 HOUSE AT 10% INTEREST IS CALCULATED.
6  CELL G13 CONTAINS @PMT(A13,C13/12,E13*12).
7
8
9
10                                      (YEARS)           MONTHLY
11 PRINCIPAL          INTEREST           TERM             PAYMENT
12 ==========         ========          ========         ========
13 $60,000.00          10.00%              30             $526.54
14
15
16
17
18
19
20
01-Jan-91   12:08 PM          UNDO
```

FIGURE 12-6 *Number of Compounding Periods Analysis*

```
B5:                                                                    READY

        A         B         C         D         E         F         G
1  ==================================================================
2             @CTERM(INTEREST RATE,FUTURE VALUE,PRESENT VALUE)
3  ==================================================================
4  IN THIS EXAMPLE,THE NUMBER OF MONTHS REQUIRED FOR A $10,000 EARNING
5  AT 1% INTEREST RATE PER MONTH TO GROW TO $15,000 IS CALCULATED.
6
7
8  CELL G14 CONTAINS @CTERM(A14,C14,E14).
9
10
11 MONTHLY            FUTURE             PRESENT          NUMBER OF
12 INTEREST           VALUE              VALUE            MONTHS
13 ========          ==========         ==========       ========
14   1.00%           $15,000.00         $10,000.00        40.74890
15
16
17
18
19
20
01-Jan-91   12:14 PM          UNDO
```

FIGURE 12-6 *Number of Compounding Periods Analysis*

FIGURE 12-7 *Number of Payment Periods Analysis*

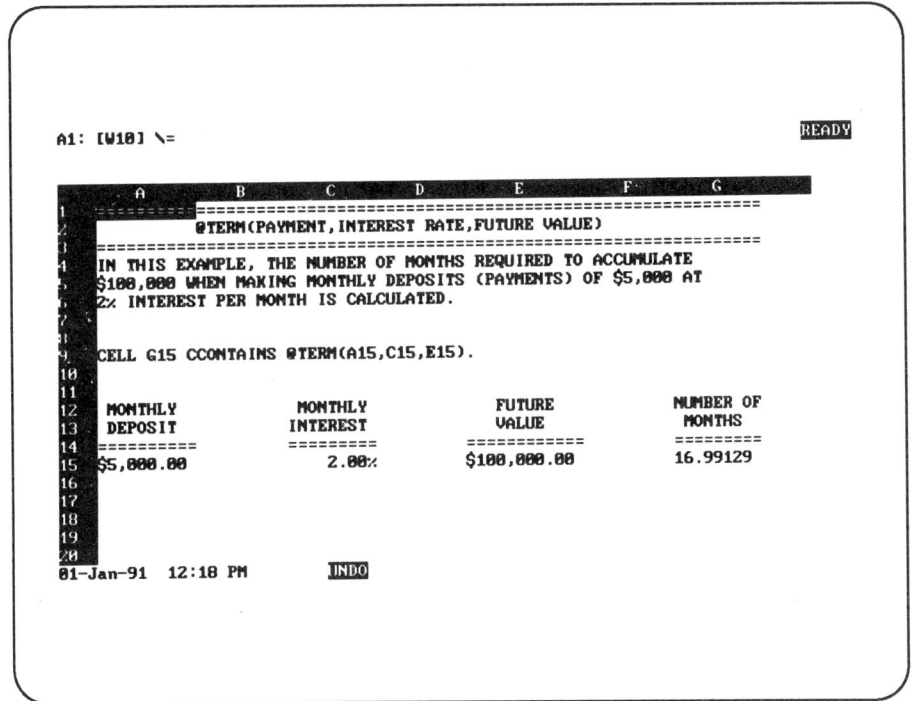

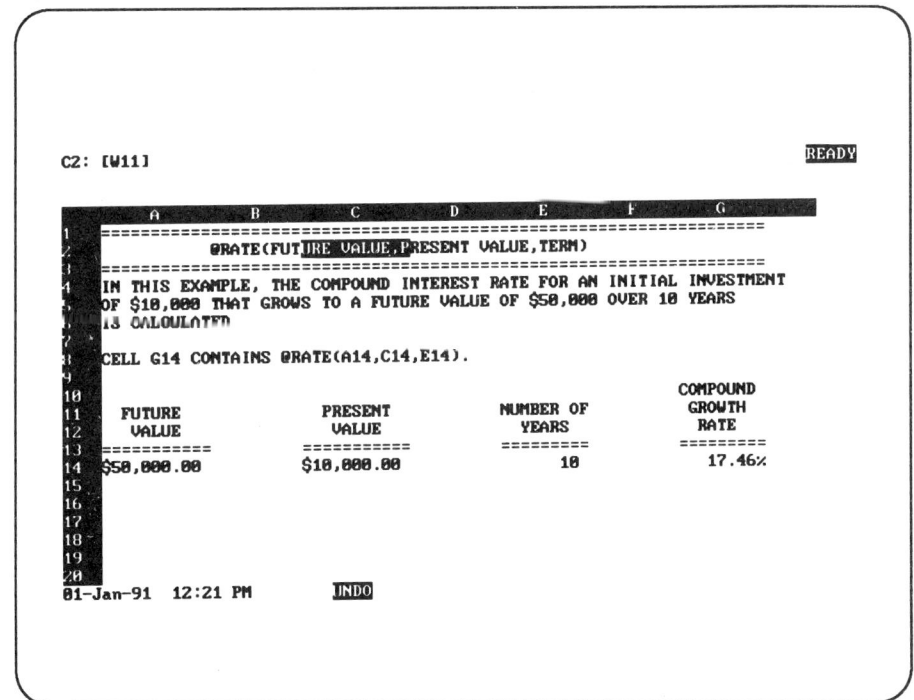

```
A1: [W10] \=                                                          READY

        A         B          C         D         E          F      G
1   ==========================================================================
2               @TERM(PAYMENT,INTEREST RATE,FUTURE VALUE)
3   ==========================================================================
4   IN THIS EXAMPLE, THE NUMBER OF MONTHS REQUIRED TO ACCUMULATE
5   $100,000 WHEN MAKING MONTHLY DEPOSITS (PAYMENTS) OF $5,000 AT
6   2% INTEREST PER MONTH IS CALCULATED.
7
8
9   CELL G15 CCONTAINS @TERM(A15,C15,E15).
10
11
12  MONTHLY            MONTHLY            FUTURE            NUMBER OF
13  DEPOSIT            INTEREST           VALUE             MONTHS
14  =========          =========          ============      =========
15  $5,000.00           2.00%             $100,000.00       16.99129
16
17
18
19
20
01-Jan-91  12:18 PM          UNDO
```

```
C2: [W11]                                                            READY

        A         B          C         D         E          F      G
1   ==========================================================================
2               @RATE(FUTURE VALUE,PRESENT VALUE,TERM)
3   ==========================================================================
4   IN THIS EXAMPLE, THE COMPOUND INTEREST RATE FOR AN INITIAL INVESTMENT
5   OF $10,000 THAT GROWS TO A FUTURE VALUE OF $50,000 OVER 10 YEARS
6   IS CALCULATED
7
8   CELL G14 CONTAINS @RATE(A14,C14,E14).
9
10                                                        COMPOUND
11  FUTURE             PRESENT            NUMBER OF        GROWTH
12  VALUE              VALUE              YEARS            RATE
13  =========          =========          =========        =========
14  $50,000.00         $10,000.00            10            17.46%
15
16
17
18
19
20
01-Jan-91  12:21 PM          UNDO
```

FIGURE 12-8 *Interest Rate Analysis*

FIGURE 12-9 Straight-line Depreciation

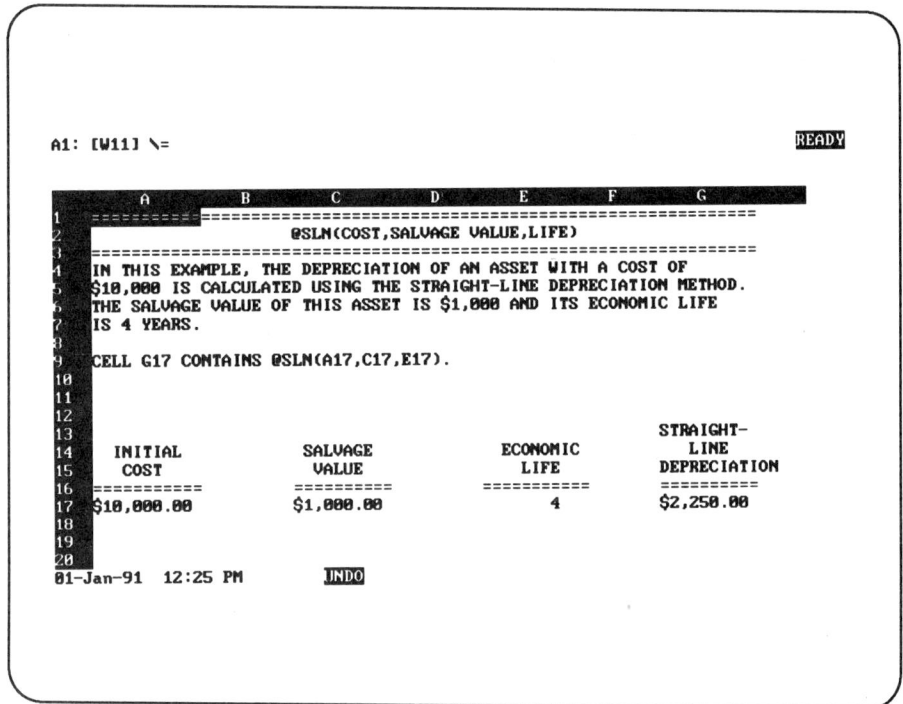

```
A1: [W11] \=                                                          READY

        A         B         C         D         E         F         G
1  ==========  ==================================================================
2                          @SLN(COST,SALVAGE VALUE,LIFE)
3  ==================================================================
4  IN THIS EXAMPLE, THE DEPRECIATION OF AN ASSET WITH A COST OF
5  $10,000 IS CALCULATED USING THE STRAIGHT-LINE DEPRECIATION METHOD.
6  THE SALVAGE VALUE OF THIS ASSET IS $1,000 AND ITS ECONOMIC LIFE
7  IS 4 YEARS.
8
9  CELL G17 CONTAINS @SLN(A17,C17,E17).
10
11
12                                                              STRAIGHT-
13                                                                LINE
14      INITIAL            SALVAGE          ECONOMIC          DEPRECIATION
15       COST               VALUE             LIFE
16   ==========         ==========       ==========          ==========
17  $10,000.00          $1,000.00              4             $2,250.00
18
19
20
01-Jan-91  12:25 PM              UNDO
```

$$\frac{(\text{Cost - Salvage Value}) * (\text{Useful life} - P + 1)}{(n * (n + 1)/2)}$$

where n = useful life of the equipment

     P = period for which depreciation is being computed

This method accelerates the rate of depreciation; therefore, more depreciation expenses occur in earlier periods than in later ones. Since the maintenance costs are minimal in the first few years, this method will balance out the total cost of a piece of equipment. In later years there are fewer depreciation costs and more maintenance costs. Figure 12-10 illustrates an example of this function.

12-5-11 @DDB(cost,salvage value,life,period)

This function calculates the depreciation for a selected period of time, using the double-declining-balance method. Depreciation stops when the book value of the equipment reaches the salvage value. At any given period, the book value is equal to the total cost minus total depreciation over all prior periods. This function uses the following formula:

$$\frac{(\text{Book value in that period} * 2)}{(\text{life of the equipment})}$$

Figure 12-11 illustrates an example of this function.

FIGURE 12-10 Sum-of-the-Years'-Digits Depreciation

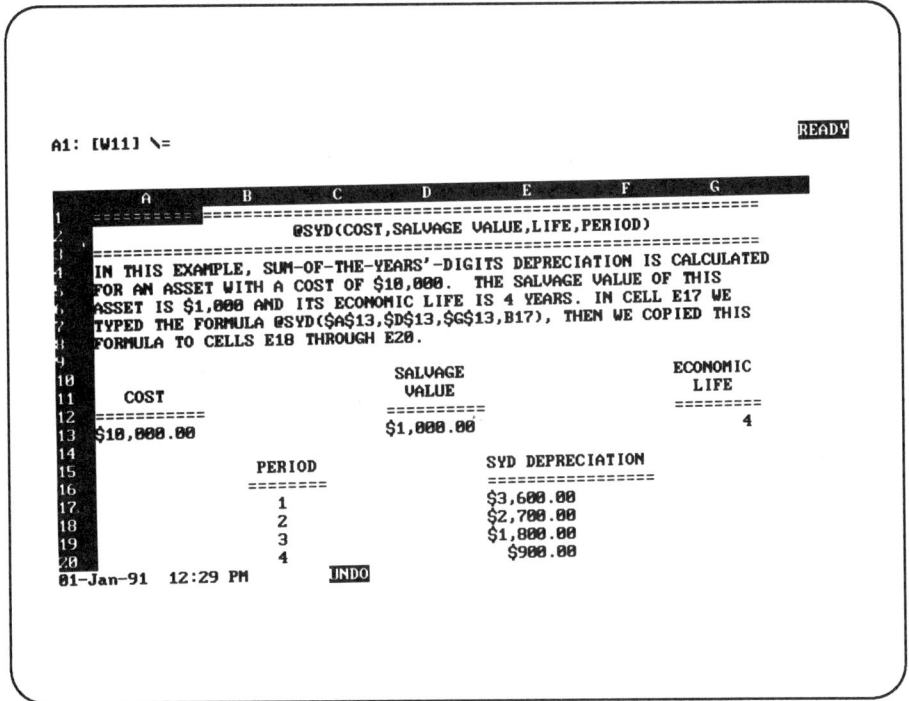

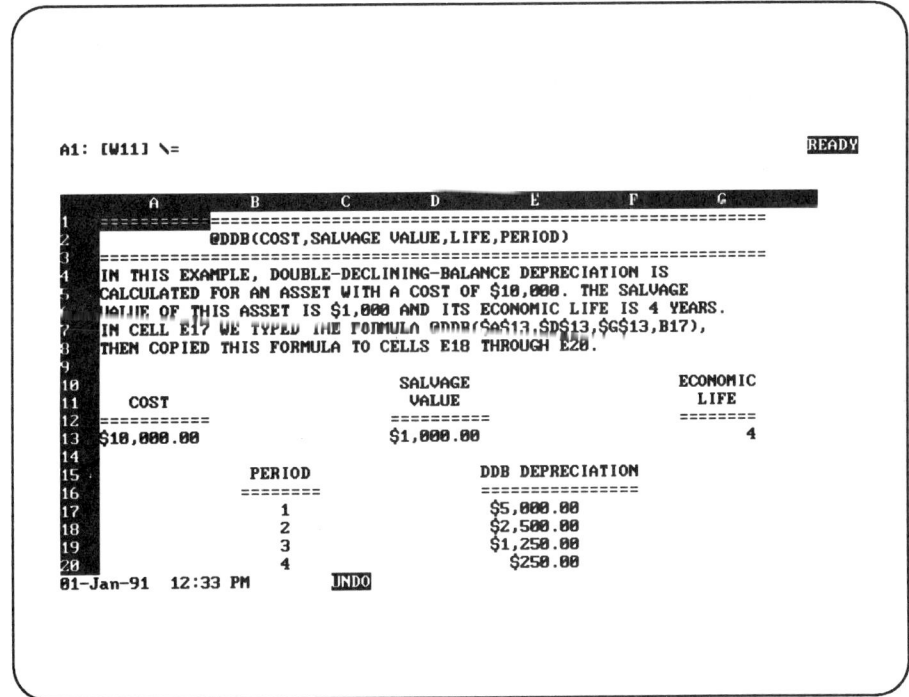

FIGURE 12-11 Double-Declining-Balance Depreciation

12-6 Statistical Functions

Lotus offers seven statistical functions. All except the @COUNT function accept both numeric and range values for arguments. The @COUNT function accepts numeric as well as string values. In these functions arguments can be a single address or group addresses. For example, @SUM (A1..A9, B5, ASSET) is valid.

Lotus considers a blank cell used as an argument in the list as the value zero.

12-6-1   @AVG(range)

This function calculates the average of all values included in the list or range. Examples: @AVG (A1..A15) or @AVG(Asset).

If you do not want to use the @AVG function you can use its equivalent, which is @SUM(range)/@COUNT(range).

12-6-2   @COUNT(range)

This function counts the number of occupied (nonblank) cells in the range. For example, if cells A1, A2, and A5 are occupied, @COUNT(A1..A5) = 3. If range includes only blank cells, the result is zero; for example, if cells A1 through A5 are all empty, @COUNT(A1..A5) = 0. However, if you use @COUNT(A10), even if A10 is empty, you still receive 1.

12-6-3   @MAX(range)

This function returns the maximum value in the range.

12-6-4   @MIN(range)

This function returns the minimum value in the range.

12-6-5   @STD(range)

This function calculates the standard deviation of the values included in the range. The standard deviation is the square root of the variance, a measure of deviation around the mean. If you deal with two populations, let us say two sales regions, and their mean (average) is equal, the one with smaller standard deviation is considered to be a more harmonic population. Lotus uses the following formula for standard deviation calculations:

$$\sqrt{\frac{(\Sigma \text{Value i - average})^2}{n}}$$

where n = number of items in the range
value i = the ith item in the range

12-6-6   @SUM(range)

This function calculates the sum of all values in the range.

12-6-7   @VAR(range)

This function computes the variance of the values included in the range. Lotus uses the following formula in this function:

$$\sum \frac{(\text{Value i - average})^2}{n}$$

where Value i = the ith item in the range
n = number of items in the range

The formulas for variance and standard deviation are for a population (the entire group). To calculate the variance and standard deviation of the sample (random sample), use the following formulas:

Variance   = @COUNT(range)/(@COUNT(range)-1) * @VAR (range)
Standard Deviation = @SQRT(@COUNT(range)/(@COUNT(range)-1))*
                    @STD(range)

Figure 12-12 illustrates an example of these seven statistical functions.

SUMMARY

In this chapter we reviewed three groups of Lotus functions: mathematical, financial, and statistical. These functions can be very helpful for a variety of applications in different fields. In the next chapter we will talk about more advanced functions offered by Lotus.

REVIEW QUESTIONS

* These questions are answered in Appendix I.
1.   What is a Lotus function?
2.* What is the major task performed by a Lotus function?
3.   How many groups of functions are offered by Lotus?
4.   What is a function argument?

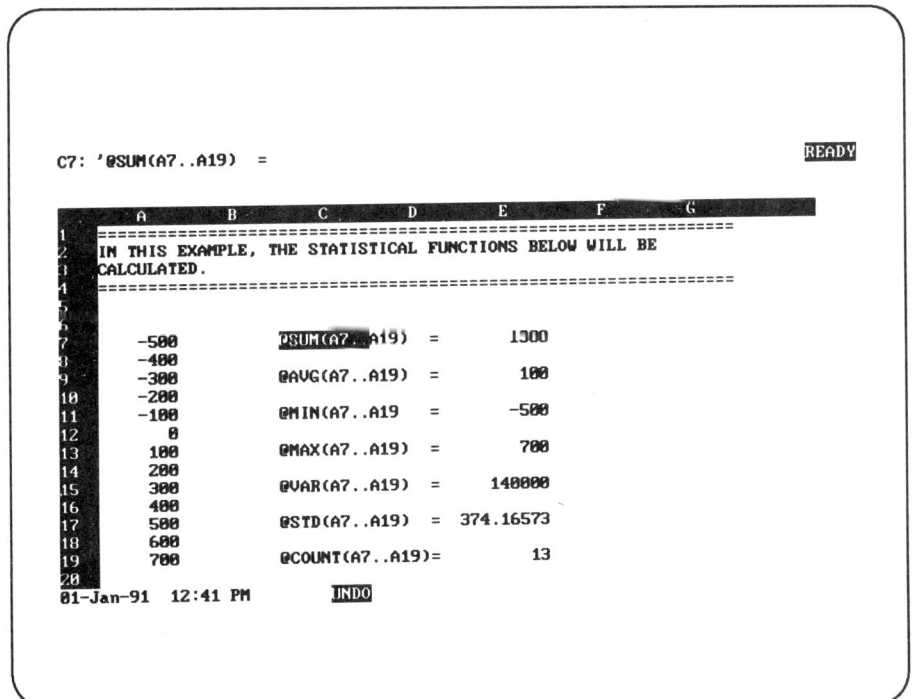

FIGURE 12-12 Statistical Functions

5. How many types of arguments are accepted by Lotus?

6.* What is an invalid argument?

7. Do all Lotus functions require arguments?

8.* What is one use of the @ABS function?

9. What are some of the uses of the @INT function?

10.* Can you do rounding with the @INT function?

11. What does the @MOD function do?

12. The @RAND function has many business applications. Name three of these applications.

13.* If you do not want to use the @SQRT function, for example, @SQRT(B10), what is its equivalent?

14.* What are some of the applications of the @FV and @PV functions?

15. In general, is a higher or lower @IRR more desirable for any project?

16.* What is the difference between the @PV and @NPV functions?

17. If you are trying to buy a house, which function in this chapter can help you the most? Why?

18. What is the difference between the @CTERM and @TERM function?

19. What depreciation method assumes an accelerated rate in the first few years of its life?

20. How many statistical functions are offered by Lotus?

21. One statistical function allows for a string argument. Which one?

22. What is the difference between variance and standard deviation of a population and a random sample?

HANDS-ON PRACTICE

1. Using the @RAND function, generate five random numbers between 100 and 200.

2. What is the IRR of a project with the following cash flows:
   -500,000, -300,000, -50,000, 32,000, 200,000, 700,000

3. What is the NPV of the above project with the calculated IRR from Question 2?

4. Let us say the IRR of a project is 15 percent. What is the NPV of this project with a 15 percent interest rate?

5. Perform the seven statistical functions on the following data:
   10, 15, 20, 90, 60, 70, 85, 5, 85

6. What is the future value of a pension plan over 30 years with a $1,500 payment, if the interest rate is 8.25 percent?

7. What is the NPV of a portfolio with the following cash flows (interest rate is 10 percent):
   -25,000, -22,000, 1,000, 20,000, 36,000, 40,000

8. If you buy a car for $30,000, with no down payment and a fixed interest rate of 9.25 percent, how much is your payment in a five-year agreement?

9. Using the straight-line method, how much is the yearly depreciation of a piece of equipment with an original price of $10,000, a salvage value of $2,000, and six years' economic life?

10. How much is the depreciation for the next six periods using sum-of-the-years'-digits depreciation?

11. Using the double-declining-balance method, how much is the depreciation for the next six periods?

12. Load Figure 12-13 from the disk. Complete it and print it.

FIGURE 12-13 A Sample Worksheet

```
                        ACME SALES PERSONNEL
                        ====================
                                                TOTAL      1990
      DPT   SALESPERSON       1889      1990     SALES     %TOTAL
      ==============================================================

      111  Jim Thomas      $435,200   $490,250    $925,450
      113  Don Smith       $234,525   $375,255    $609,780
      106  Bill Green      $175,675   $225,500    $401,175
      112  Sharon Moon     $345,525   $385,750    $731,275
      109  Jack Traves     $672,900   $825,345  $1,498,245
      118  John Bowin      $575,000   $585,255  $1,160,255
      114  Bob Wood        $670,100   $627,450  $1,297,550
      117  Rich Asborne    $450,000   $465,275    $915,275
      124  Shelli Hansen   $375,255   $325,225    $700,480
      121  Lisa Myers      $401,250   $398,700    $799,950
      126  Gary June       $275,750   $325,725    $601,475
      104  Linda Smith     $297,655   $310,755    $608,410
      116  Pam Greene      $372,500   $375,210    $747,710
      129  Ann Thompson    $497,500   $150,000    $647,500
                         ----------- ----------- -----------

      TOTAL

                         =========== =========== ===========

      NO OF SALES STAFF
      STD.DEVIATION
      VARIANCE
      MAXIMUM VALUE
      MINIMUM VALUE

      NOTE: Use pointer and cell formula to do departmental totals as you
            are not familiar with any Database tools yet.

      10X   DPT-10 TOTAL
      20X   DPT-11 TOTAL
      12X   DPT-12 TOTAL
                         ----------- ----------- ----------- --------
      VERIFY TOTAL           $0          $0          $0
                         =========== =========== =========== ========
```

COMPREHENSIVE LAB ASSIGNMENT

Retrieve CHAPT11 and perform the following:
1. Add an additional column to the worksheet (column I); give the title Total to the column.
2. Using the @SUM function, calculate the total score of each student and store the result in this column.
3. Generate another column (column J); give the title Statistics to this column.
4. Generate the seven statistical functions for the total scores of all the students.
5. Save this worksheet under CHAPT12.

MISCONCEPTIONS AND SOLUTIONS

M – Usually the interest rate in a mortgage problem is stated as yearly and the payment is monthly. Using yearly interest rate and monthly payment will cause mistakes in payment calculation.

S – Divide the yearly interest rate by 12 and multiply the number of years by 12. This adjustment will calculate the correct payment.

M – You are entering a function. When you try to enter the function by pressing the **Return** key, Lotus gives you a beep.

S – Check the syntax of any @ functions that you have used to make sure you have typed the name and the syntax of the function correctly.

Functions/Part Two

13-1 Introduction

In this chapter we will explain logical, string, date and time, and special functions with numerous examples. Database statistical functions will be discussed in Chapter 17.

13-2 Logical Functions

Lotus offers nine logical functions that generate values based on the results of conditional statements. When you use logical functions, remember that a blank cell has the value of zero. If you use a range name that represents a multiple cell range, Lotus examines the cell in the upper left corner.

13-2-1 @FALSE

This function returns the logical value zero. For example, if you type @FALSE in cell A1, you will get zero.

13-2-2 @IF(condition,A,B)

The condition must be a numeric value or one that results in a numeric value. The function returns the value A if the condition is true or the value B if the condition is false. Examples:

@IF(3<0,"T","F")	T
@IF(3>0,"T","F")	T
@IF(3<5,10,-50)	10
@IF((10+5)/2<10,"T","F")	T

There are numerous practical applications for the @IF function. You may use it to check a customer's credit limit. If the credit is negative, send the customer a message. If the credit is positive, send the customer a different message. In an inventory management situation you may use the @IF function to check the inventory on hand. If the inventory on hand is below 500 units, order; otherwise, do not order new inventory.

The @IF function with logical #NOT#, #AND#, and #OR# operators adds a strong decision-making facility to your 1-2-3 program. Consider Figure 13-1. In the AND operation all the conditions must be correct. In the OR operation only one of the conditions must be correct. In the NOT operation the opposite must be true. In row 4, the student is accepted because he has met both conditions, e.g., his GMAT is greater than 600 and his GPA is also greater than 3.3. In row 6, the student is accepted because her GMAT score

FIGURE 13-1 The @IF Function with NOT, AND, and OR

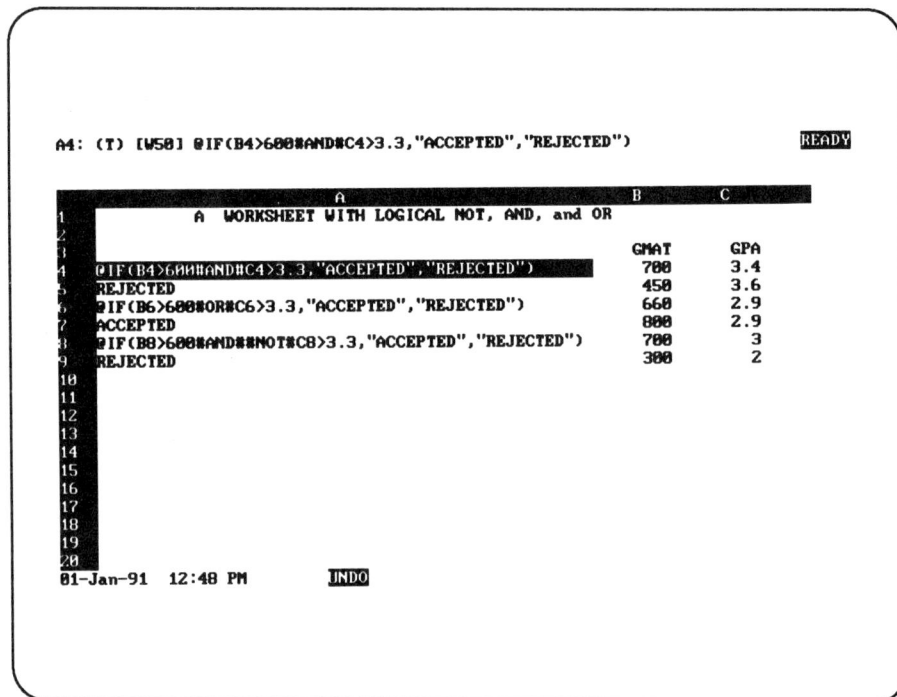

is greater than 600 and the GPA condition does not matter. In row 9, the student is rejected because both conditions must be true and in this case they are not true. We have used the Text format in every other cell, in order to show the actual formulas.

Figure 13-2 illustrates another example of the @IF function. Northwest Lumber Company pays commission to its employees as follows:

Under $15,000 total sales, no commission
From $15,000 to $20,000 total sales, $800 commission
Over $20,000 total sales, $800 + 15% of all the sales over $20,000

This example illustrates a "nested" @IF function.

In the last cell we used the Text format to show the actual format of the cell entry.

13-2-3 @ISAAF

This function checks the status of an add-in function. It returns 1 (true) for a defined add-in @function or 0 (false) for any other entry. For example, if you think you have an add-in function in cell A200 you can check for it with @ISAAF("A200"). If the function returns 1, the function is available, otherwise it is not. @ISAAF will also return 0 if the function is a built-in function.

13-2-4 @ISAPP

This function checks whether a particular program has been installed or attached with the add-in, or 0 (false) for any other entry. For example, to see if Allways is attached you can type @ISAPP ("Allways"). A 1 will be returned if Allways is attached and 0 if not. Remember to press F9 key in order to see the most recent update of your worksheet.

FIGURE 13-2 An Example of the Nested @IF Function

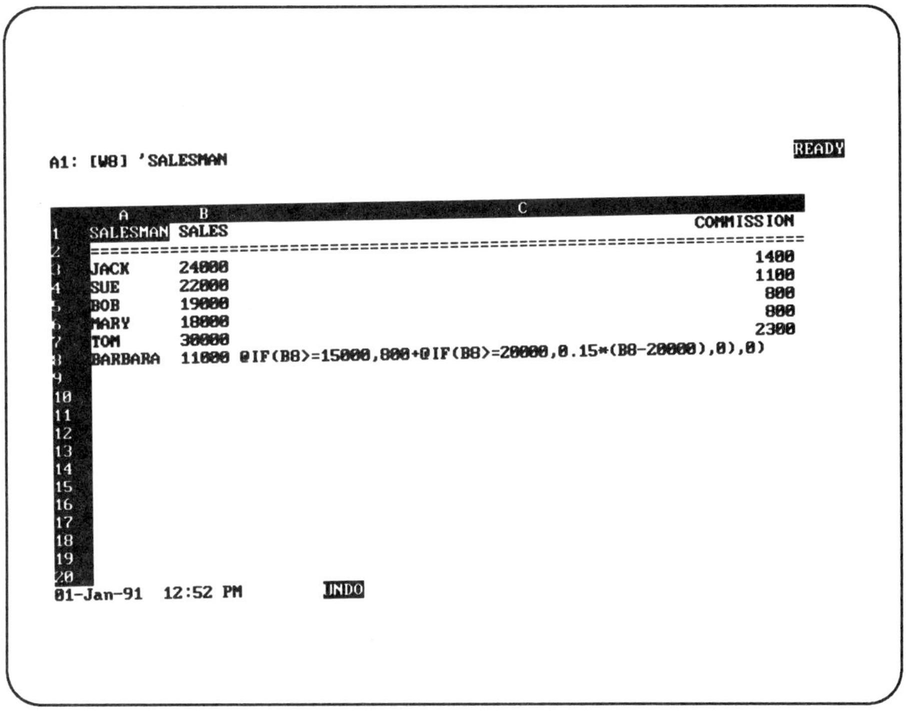

13-2-5 @ISERR(A)

This function examines cell A to see if it contains the value ERR. The function will return one if cell A contains the value ERR; otherwise it returns zero. Examples:

    @ISERR(5/0)   = 1
    @ISERR(2/2)   = 0

In the first example the value 1 is returned because 5/0 is invalid.

13-2-6 @ISNA(A)

This function tests A to see if it contains the value NA (not available). The function returns one if A contains the value NA; otherwise, it returns zero. Let us say in cell A15 we have stored function @NA, @ISNA(A15) = 1, and @ISNA(A16) = 0. Cell A16 can contain anything except @NA. This function is used to show a particular number is not available to calculate a formula, therefore it shows NA in the current cell and in all other cells that depend on a particular formula. This is useful for building worksheets when they need values that are not yet defined.

13-2-7 @ISNUMBER(A)

This function tests cell A to see if it contains a numeric value. The function returns one if cell A contains a number or a calculation (formula) resulting in a numeric value; otherwise it returns zero. Examples:

    @ISNUMBER(5)   = 1
    @ISNUMBER("7") = 0

$$@ISNUMBER(68/8+@SQRT(16)) \quad = \quad 1$$
$$@ISNUMBER("PORTLAND") \qquad = \quad 0$$

13-2-8   @ISSTRING(A)

This function is similar to @ISNUMBER(A), but it tests for a string. It returns one if A is a string, otherwise it returns zero. Examples:

$$@ISSTRING(7) \qquad = \quad 0$$
$$@ISSTRING("LOTUS") \quad = \quad 1$$

13-2-9   @TRUE

This function returns the logical value one. Let us assume cell A10 contains the string "BASIC". Then @IF(A10="BASIC",@TRUE,@FALSE) = 1, so TRUE or 1 are the same.

13-3 String Functions

Lotus offers 19 string functions that are extremely helpful for nonnumeric manipulations. If a string is used as an argument, it must be enclosed in a pair of quotation marks. The characters of strings enclosed in quotation marks are numbered starting from zero. For example, string "DISK" is numbered from zero to 3.

13-3-1   @CHAR(A)

Argument A can be any numeric value between 0 and 255. The function returns the ASCII/LICS character corresponding to the number A (see Appendix H). For values outside this range, you get ERR. If your argument is a decimal, Lotus will convert it to an integer. Examples:

$$@CHAR(77) \qquad = \quad M$$
$$@CHAR(100) \quad = \quad d$$
$$@CHAR(81.5) \quad = \quad Q$$
$$@CHAR(280) \quad = \quad ERR$$

(ASCII, American Standard Code for Information Interchange, is a data presentation code accepted by a majority of computer manufacturers. LICS, Lotus International Character Set, includes numbers 0 to 255 for all the codes and characters accepted by Lotus.)

13-3-2   @CODE(string)

This function returns the ASCII/LICS code number for the first character in the string (argument). If the argument is not a string, you will get ERR. Examples:

$$@CODE("TEST") \qquad = \quad 84$$
$$@CODE("T") \qquad = \quad 84$$
$$@CODE("PASCAL") \quad = \quad 80$$
$$@CODE("JONES") \quad = \quad 74$$
$$@CODE(65) \qquad = \quad ERR$$

13-3-3   @CLEAN(string)

Strings imported with the /File Import command, especially if they are imported by modem from a different site, may contain nonprintable characters or noise (ASCII codes below 32). This function eliminates the nonprintable characters from the strings. The argument of this function must be a string value or a cell address that contains a string value. The cell address cannot be a range.

13-3-4 @EXACT(String1,String2)

This function compares two strings to see if they are identical. If they are, the function returns one, otherwise it returns zero. Remember, uppercase and lowercase characters are different. Both arguments must be strings, otherwise you get ERR. Examples:

```
@EXACT("TRYOUT","TRYOUT")    = 1
@EXACT("TRYOUT","TRYUT")     = 0
@EXACT("555","555")          = 1
@EXACT("555",555)            = ERR
```

13-3-5 @FIND(Search String,String,Start Number)

This function searches for a string starting from a specified position. It returns the exact position of the first occurrence of the desired string. If the search fails, you get ERR. The starting number must be either zero or positive. If the starting number is not an integer, Lotus considers only the integer part. Examples:

```
@FIND("LOTUS","LOTUS IS POWERFUL",0) = 0
@FIND("LOTUS","ONE OF THE BEST SPREADSHEETS IS LOTUS",10) = 32
@FIND("HAPPY","WE HAVE LEARNED SO MUCH ALREADY",0) = ERR
@FIND("M", "I HAD A GOOD MONTH IN MEXICO",15.6) = 22
```

13-3-6 @LEFT(String,m)

This function returns the first m characters in the string. Examples:

```
@LEFT("COBOL",3) = COB
@LEFT("HAPPINESS IS HERE",5) = HAPPI
```

13-3-7 @LFNGTH(String)

This function returns the number of characters included in the string. Examples:

```
@LENGTH("LESSON")                = 6
@LENGTH("YESTERDAY WAS SUNNY")   = 19
@LENGTH("")                      = 0
@LENGTH(555)                     = ERR
```

13-3-8 @LOWER(String)

This function converts all the letters in the string to lowercase. Examples:

```
@LOWER("Portland")    = portland
@LOWER("PORTLAND")    = portland
```

13-3-9 @MID(String,Start Number,m)

This function extracts m characters from a string after skipping the start number characters. Examples:

```
@MID("JACKSON",2,5)   = CKSON
```

@MID("I AM GOING HOME NOW",6,60) = OING HOME NOW
@MID("LOTUS DOES GRAPHICS",0,5)   = LOTUS

13-3-10 @N(RANGE)

This function returns the value of the upper left corner of a particular range as a number. For example, if values 100, 200, 300, and 400 are stored in cells A1, A2, A3, and A4, then @N(A2..A4) will return 200.

13-3-11 @PROPER(String)

This function puts a string into proper order by converting the first letter of each word to a capital letter and the rest to lowercase letters. Examples:

@PROPER("SUSAN BROWN") = Susan Brown
@PROPER("Susan BROWN") = Susan Brown

13-3-12 @REPEAT(String,m)

This function repeats a particular string m times. Examples:

@REPEAT("HB",2)   = HBHB
@REPEAT("BH",1)   = BH
@REPEAT("I AM HAPPY",2) = I AM HAPPY I AM HAPPY
@REPEAT("=",80) prints 80 equal signs—good application for dressing up your worksheet.

13-3-13 @REPLACE(Original String, Start Number,m, New String)

This function removes m characters in an original string beginning at the start number and then inserts a new string in the same position in the original string. Examples:

@REPLACE("ATTENTION",1,3,"XXXXX")   = AXXXXXNTION
@REPLACE("ATTENTION",1,-1,11XXXXX) = ERR

In the first example, position zero is at A, position one is at T, so TTE will be removed and five Xs will be inserted. The second example is invalid. Why?

13-3-14 @RIGHT(String,m)

The function returns the last m characters in a particular string, m must be >= 1. Examples:

@RIGHT("FORTRAN",3)   = RAN
@RIGHT("DATABASE",1) = E

A practical application would be in a database. Let us say all the addresses of your employees are typed in column A. To extract all the ZIP codes, type @RIGHT(A1,5). You can then copy this formula all the way down.

13-3-15 @S(Range)

This function returns the value in the upper left corner cell of the range as a string value (if the cell contains a value). For example, if cells A1, A2, A3, and A4 contain strings SUE, JACKSON, BOB, and JACK, the following can be seen:

@S(!A1)   = SUE
@S(A2..A3) = JACKSON
@S(A1..A4) = SUE

13-3-16 @STRING(Y,m)

In this function, m specifies the number of decimal places from 0 to 15. M must be >= 0. The function converts a number Y to a string with m places to the right of the decimal point. In order to convert a string to its numeric equivalent, use @VALUE. Examples:

```
@STRING(125.8735,3)  =  125.874
@STRING(125.87,0)    =  126
@STRING(125.87,-1)   =  ERR
```

13-3-17 @TRIM(String)

This function eliminates excess space characters from a particular string. Examples:

@TRIM("IT   HAS   BEEN   A   LONG   DAY") = IT HAS BEEN A LONG DAY

@TRIM("THIS   IS   A   TEST")   = THIS IS A TEST

13-3-18 @UPPER(String)

This function converts all the letters in a string to uppercase. Examples:

```
@UPPER("First Computer")  =  FIRST COMPUTER
@UPPER("happy")           =  HAPPY
```

13-3-19 @VALUE(String)

This function converts a string to a numeric value. Examples:

```
@VALUE("12 4/3")     =  13.3333333333
@VALUE("1.567E+5")   =  156700
@VALUE("15.55")      =  15.55
@VALUE("-10/-2*2")   =  ERR
```

13-4 Date and Time Functions

Lotus offers 11 date and time functions. These functions generate or use numbers to represent dates and times, so that you can use them in calculations. Before you use these functions, remember the following:

1. Any date between January 1, 1900 and December 31, 2099 inclusive is valid and has an equivalent integer serial number.
2. The first serial number is 1, the last is 73050.
3. January 1, 1900 is equivalent to 1 and December 31, 2099 is equivalent to 73050.
4. Each hour of the day has a serial number as well, e.g., midnight = 0, noon = .50, etc.
5. The following functions generate serial numbers: @DATE, @DATEVALUE, @NOW, @TIME, and @TIMEVALUE
6. The following functions use serial numbers: @DAY, @MONTH, @YEAR, @HOUR, @MINUTE, and @SECOND

13-4-1 @DATE(Year,Month,Day)

This function returns the serial number corresponding to a certain year, month, or day. Remember, since there was no February 29, 1900 (we did not have leap year then), Lotus assigns a date number to this particular day. This does not invalidate any of your calculations, unless you use any dates between January 1 and March, 1, 1900. (Remember, D1 through D5 are five date options provided by Lotus, discussed in Chapter 7.) Examples:

@DATE(90,7,1)	=	33055	Equivalent in	D1	=	01-Jul-90
@DATE(86,12,1)	=	31747	"	"	D2	=	01-DEC
@DATE(87,6,1)	=	31929	"	"	D3	=	Jun-87
@DATE(87,10,1)	=	32051	"	"	D4	=	10/01/87
@DATE(91,10,1)	=	33512	"	"	D5	=	10/01

13-4-2   @DATEVALUE(Date String)

This function, similar to @DATE, returns the serial number of a date written as a string. The difference is that @DATEVALUE uses a single string value as its argument. The date string must be in one of the five date formats discussed in Chapter 7. Examples:

@DATEVALUE("01-JUL-91")	=	33420
@DATEVALUE("01-DEC-80")	=	29556
@DATEVALUE("JUN-87")	=	31929
@DATEVALUE("10/01/87")	=	32051
@DATEVALUE("02-JUN-86")	=	31565

13-4-3   @DAY(Date Number)

This function returns the day of the month (1 through 31) of the argument. Examples:

@DAY(@DATE(91,9,1))	=	1
@DAY(31700)	=	15

13-4-4   @MONTH(Date Number)

This function returns a month (1 through 12) of the year in the string. Examples:

@MONTH(@DATE(91,9,1))	=	9
@MONTH(31625)	=	8

13-4-5   @YEAR(Date Number)

This function returns any year between 0 to 199 of the argument. Examples:

@YEAR(@DATEVALUE("1-SEP-91"))	=	91
@YEAR(33000)	=	90

13-4-6   @NOW

This function returns the current date and time. Example:

We typed @NOW on our Lotus worksheet. The function returned 29221.02, indicating January 1, 1980 at 12:28 A.M. The integer part is the date and the decimal portion is the time. Other examples:

@INT(@NOW)	=	29221
@YEAR(29221)	=	80
@MONTH(29221)	=	1
@DAY(29221)	=	1
@TODAY	=	29221

One good application of the @NOW function is to generate the serial number for the DATE function. Assume that during the log-on time you have entered the correct date and time. Now, you can convert this serial number to any of the five Date formats.

To generate the time portion, you should do the following:

@NOW-@INT(@NOW), then use any of the four TIME formats.

Another interesting test would be to find out the number of days lived: @INT(@NOW)-@DATE(yy,mm,dd)+1. For example, if you were born on March 25, 1972, the number of days you lived is:

@INT(@NOW)-@DATE(72,03,25)=6856 (today's date is January 1, 1991).

13-4-7   @TIME(Hour,Minute,Second)

In this function hour must be between 0 and 23, minute must be between 0 and 59 and second must be between 0 and 59. The function returns a serial number between 0 and 1 for hour, minute, and second. The serial number is a fraction of a day. (Remember T1 through T4 are hour time options provided by Lotus, discussed in Chapter 7.) Examples:

```
@TIME(10,52,40) = 0.453240 is equal to 10:52:40 A.M.    T1
@TIME(2,10,59)  = 0.090960 "    "    " 02:10 A.M.         T2
@TIME(22,50,50) = 0.951967 "    "    " 22:50:50           T3
@TIME(23,45,10) = 0.989699 "    "    " 23:45              T4
@TIME(30,30,30) = ERR
```

13-4-8   @TIMEVALUE(Time String)

This function returns a serial time number for the string. It is similar to @TIME except that the argument here is only one string. The time string must be in one of the four accepted Lotus time formats (discussed in Chapter 7) and must be enclosed in double quotes. Examples:

```
@TIMEVALUE("12:30:45")  = 0.5213541667
@TIMEVALUE("12:30")     = 0.5208333333
```

13-4-9   @HOUR(Time Number)

This function extracts and returns the hour from a time number. The returned value is between 0 and 23; 0 refers to midnight and 23 to 11:00 P.M. Examples:

```
@HOUR(0.1876736111) = 4
@HOUR(31774.5)      = 12
```

13-4-10   @MINUTE(Time Number)

This function extracts and returns the minutes from a time number. The returned value is between 0 and 59. Examples:

```
@MINUTE(0.1567) = 45
@MINUTE(12)     = 0
```

13-4-11   @SECOND(Time Number)

This function extracts and returns the seconds from a time number. The returned value is between 0 and 59. Examples:

$$@SECOND(0.639) \qquad = 10$$
$$@SECOND(@TIME(10,10,10)) \quad = 10$$

13-5 Special Functions

Lotus offers 11 special functions, most of which are used to search for a value in a table.

13-5-1 @@(Cell Address)

The argument of this function can be a cell address written as a label, a range name, or a string formula whose value is a cell address or cell name. This function returns the content of the cell referenced by the cell address. Let us say cell A10 contains label H20 and cell H20 contains 200. Then @@(A10) returns 200.

This function is useful when several formulas each have the same argument and the argument must be changed from time to time during the execution of an application.

In Figure 13-3, the @FV, @PV, and @PMT functions all use one of the five interest rates. As the screen shows they are all using .08 percent interest. To change to 8.5 percent all you have to do is to change label G3 to G4. Otherwise you have to edit all the individual functions. By using the @@ function you save a lot of time. To show the exact formula we have used the Text format in cell A5. In Cell A3 we typed the @FV(2000, @@(E3),30) and in Cell A4 we typed the @PV (10000, @@ (E3), 5).

13-5-2 @CELL(Attribute,Range)

This function returns the attribute of a cell or range from the attribute table (see Table 13-1). The attribute must be enclosed in double quotation marks; uppercase or lowercase does not matter. If you use a single cell as range, you must express it as a range (A1..A1 or !A1). If the range includes more than one cell, Lotus uses the upper left corner of the given range. To update cell attributes, you must press F9, the **Calc** function key. Figure 13-4 illustrates the following examples of this function:

$$@CELL("row",A10..A10) \qquad = 10$$
$$@CELL("ADDRESS",A3..A3) \quad = \$A\$3$$
$$@CELL("CONTENTS",!A7) \quad = HELLO$$
$$@CELL("FORMAT",!A10) \qquad = G$$
$$@CELL("PREFIX",!A5) \qquad = "$$
$$@CELL("WIDTH",!A10) \qquad = 9$$
$$@CELL("TYPE",!A3) \qquad = V$$

13-5-3 @CELLPOINTER(Attribute)

This function returns attribute information about the current cell. It is very useful for testing the content of a cell; for example, finding out if a cell holds a value or is blank. Examples:

@CELLPOINTER("width") = 9 (by default each column width is 9 characters in length)

If the current row is row 30, then

$$@CELLPOINTER("ROW") = 30$$

FIGURE 13-3 An Example of the @@ Function

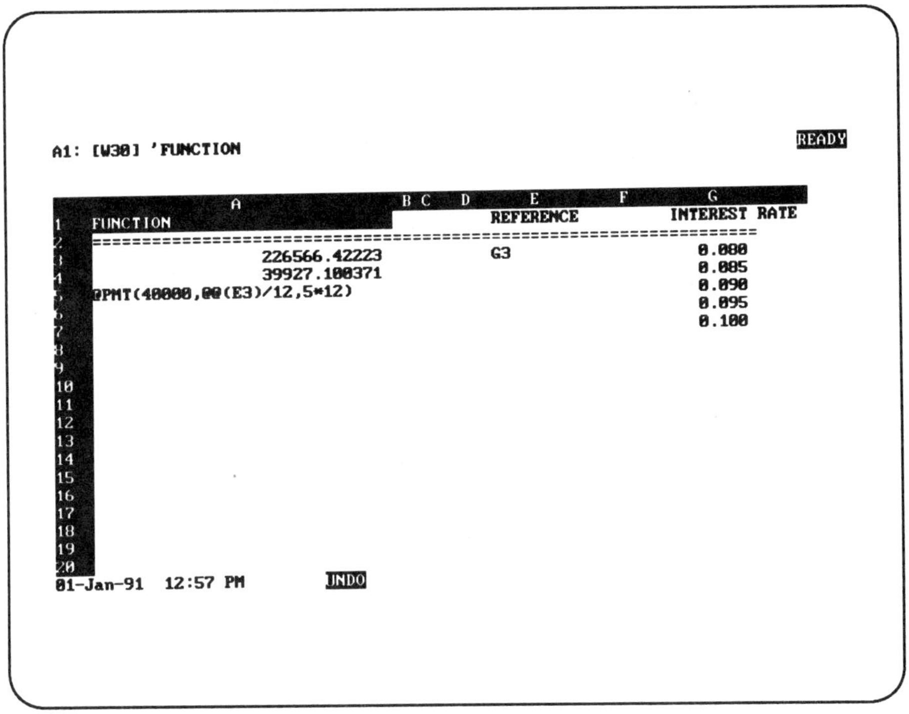

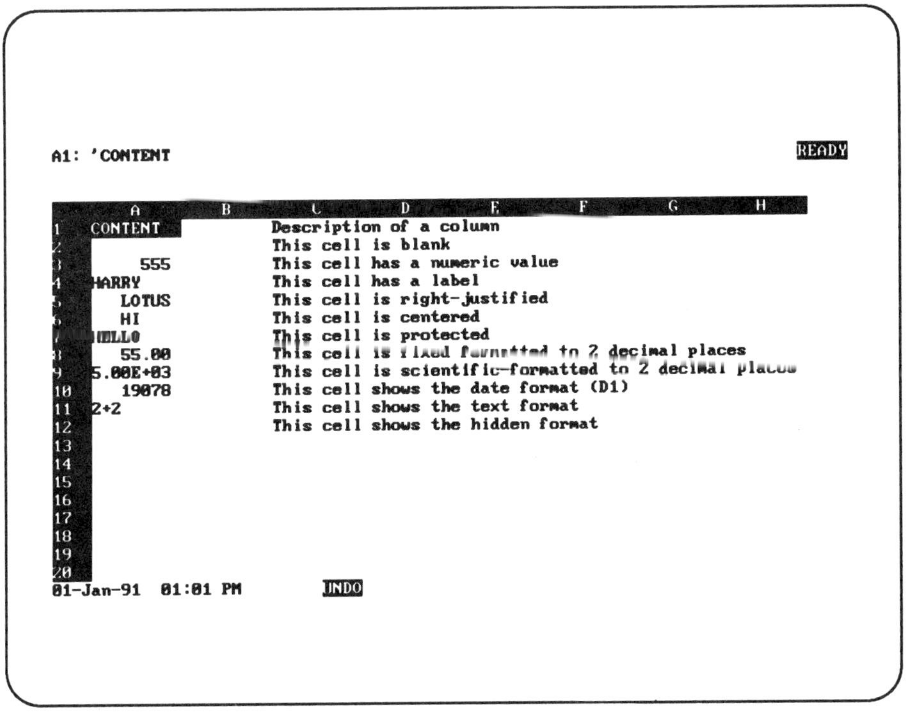

```
A1: [W30] 'FUNCTION                                              READY

          A                    B C  D      E       F        G
1  FUNCTION                                REFERENCE      INTEREST RATE
2  ================================================================
3              226566.42223               G3              0.080
4              39927.100371                               0.085
5  @PMT(40000,@@(E3)/12,5*12)                             0.090
6                                                         0.095
7                                                         0.100
8
9
10
11
12
13
14
15
16
17
18
19
20
01-Jan-91  12:57 PM        UNDO
```

```
A1: 'CONTENT                                                     READY

        A        B       C        D        E        F      G      H
1  CONTENT              Description of a column
2                       This cell is blank
3        555            This cell has a numeric value
4  HARRY                This cell has a label
5      LOTUS            This cell is right-justified
6       HI              This cell is centered
7  HELLO                This cell is protected
8      55.00            This cell is fixed formatted to 2 decimal places
9  5.00E+03             This cell is scientific-formatted to 2 decimal places
10     19078            This cell shows the date format (D1)
11 2+2                  This cell shows the text format
12                      This cell shows the hidden format
13
14
15
16
17
18
19
20
01-Jan-91  01:01 PM        UNDO
```

FIGURE 13-4 Sample Worksheet for the @CELL Function

TABLE 13-1 ATTRIBUTE TABLE FOR THE @CELL FUNCTION

ATTRIBUTE	THE CALCULATED RESULT
"ADDRESS"	Returns the current cell address, e.g., A10
"COL"	Returns the current column number (1 to 256)
"CONTENTS"	Returns the content of the current cell
"FORMAT"	Returns the current numeric formula of a given address:
	F0 to F15 for fixed, 0 to 15 decimal places
	S0 to S15 for scientific, 0 to 15 decimal places
	C0 to C15 for currency, 0 to 15 decimal places
	G for general
	P0 to P15 for percent
	D1 to D5 for date 1 to date 5 and D6 to D9 for Time 1 to Time 4
	format (see Chapter 7)
	T for Text
	A blank if the content of the cell is an empty string, e.g., ""
"PREFIX"	Returns the current label prefix:
	' (apostrophe) for left-justified
	" for right-justified
	∧ for centered
"PROTECT"	Returns the protection status:
	1 if it is protected
	0 if it is not protected
"ROW"	Returns the current row number (1 to 8192)
"TYPE"	Returns the data type in a cell:
	b for blank
	v for numeric value or formula
	l for label or string
"WIDTH"	Returns the current column width (1 to 240)

13-5-4   @CHOOSE(Y,V0,V1,V2...Vn)

This function uses the numeric value of Y to return an item from the list V0 to Vn. The first value in the list is 0; therefore if Y = 2, @CHOOSE will select the third item. You can have up to 240 numeric or string values in the list. Examples:

@CHOOSE(3,10,17,25,29,35,38,41)	= 29
@CHOOSE(0,10,17,25,29,35,38,41)	= 10
@CHOOSE(3,"TONY","SAM","JOE","STEVE")	= STEVE

13-5-5   @COLS(Range)

This function returns the number of columns in a specific range. Examples:

@COLS(A1..C1)	= 3
@COLS(A1..H20)	= 8

13-5-6   @ERR

This function returns the numerical value ERR. This cannot be substituted with the label ERR, e.g., "ERR".

13-5-7 @HLOOKUP(Y,Range,Row Number)

This function performs a horizontal table search beginning with row zero and comparing the value of Y to each cell in the top row of a specified range. As soon as it finds a number larger than Y, it stops and backs up one cell. It moves down the specified row number and returns the content of the appropriate cell. If there is an exact match to Y, the search stops at that cell without backtracking. Then it moves down the specified row number and returns the content of the appropriate cell. If Y (the search value) is smaller than the first value, the function returns ERR. If Y is larger than all the values, the search stops at the last cell in the top row of the range without backtracking. Then it moves down the specified row number and returns the content of the appropriate cell. Remember, the top row of the table used by @HLOOKUP must be sorted in ascending order; this is row 0. Figure 13-5 illustrates this function. Examples:

@HLOOKUP(475,B4..H9,2) = 12
@HLOOKUP(850,B4..H9,3) = 15
@HLOOKUP(450,B4..H9,5) = 20
@HLOOKUP(375,B4..H9,1) = 18
@HLOOKUP(150,B4..H9,3) = ERR

13-5-8 @INDEX(Range, Column Number, Row Number)

This function returns the content of the cell located at the intersection of the column and row number in a specified range. The first row and column numbers are 0. If the argument is out of range (the row or column number is larger than the table), you get an ERR. We have used the data in Figure 13-5 for this function for the following examples:

@INDEX(A4..H9,0,0)   = 0
@INDEX(A4..H9,1,2)   = 13
@INDEX(A4..H9,5,5)   = 16
@INDEX(A4..H9,5,15) = ERR

13-5-9 @NA

This function returns the numeric value NA whenever a particular number is not available in order to complete a formula. The function can be helpful for alerting the user. For example, if cell A10 contains 100, then @IF(A10/2>25,@NA,"I AM BUSY") = NA

13-5-10 @ROWS(Range)

This function returns the number of rows in a given range. If we use data from Figure 13-5, we will see the following:

@ROWS(A3..D9) = 7
@ROWS(A6..E4) = 3
@ROWS(A6..H20) = 15

13-5-11 @VLOOKUP(Y, Range, Column Number)

This function, similar to @HLOOKUP, performs a vertical search.

The function compares the value of Y to each cell in the first column of a specified range. As soon as it finds a number larger than Y in a cell, it backs up one cell. @VLOOKUP moves across the specified column number and returns the content of the

FIGURE 13-5 Horizontal Table Search with the @HLOOKUP Function

```
A1:                                                                    READY

        A        B        C        D        E        F        G        H
1              OIL EXPLORATION DATA FOR EVER-DRY PETROLEUM
2                              CREW SIZE
3       ----------------------------------------------------------------
4              250      300      350      450      550      650      750
5    REGION 1   10       18       18       13       13       15       18
6    REGION 2   13       17       17       12       18       18       17
7    REGION 3   11       14       15       11       15       17       15
8    REGION 4   15       13       15       19       16       17       16
9    REGION 5   18       12       14       20       16       16       13
10
11
12
13   EXAMPLES OF @HLOOKUP :
14
15   @HLOOKUP(475,B4..H9,2) =          12
16   @HLOOKUP(850,B4..H9,3) =          15
17   @HLOOKUP(450,B4..H9,5) =          20
18   @HLOOKUP(375,B4..H9,1) =          18
19   @HLOOKUP(150,B4..H9,3) =         ERR
20
01-Jan-91  01:04 PM          UNDO
```

appropriate cell. If there is an exact match to Y, the search stops at the cell (no backup will take place), then moves across the specified column number and returns the content of the appropriate cell. If the search value is smaller than the first value in the search column, the function returns ERR. If Y is larger than all the values, the search stops at the last cell in the first column of the range, then moves across the specified column number and returns the content of the appropriate cell. Remember, the first column in the table is column 0 and the values in the first column (e.g., the index column) must be in ascending order. (See Figure 13-6.)

You can also give a name to the table and use it in conjunction with either @HLOOKUP or @VLOOKUP. In Figure 13-6, by using /RNC we gave the name TABLE to range A4. .G10. This makes your lookup operations more meaningful. The following examples are illustrated in Figure 13-6.

@VLOOKUP(26500,A4..G10,2) = 3000
@VLOOKUP(45000,A4..G10,3) = 7100
@VLOOKUP(37300,A4..G10,4) = 5200
@VLOOKUP(41000,A4..G10,5) = 6300
@VLOOKUP(47000,A4..G10,6) = 7400
@VLOOKUP(19000,A4..G10,1) = ERR
@VLOOKUP(50000,A4..G10,7) = ERR

SUMMARY

In this chapter we explained the logical, string, date and time, and special functions. These functions perform numerous operations, mostly for advanced users. As you will see in Chapters 19 and 20, many of these functions can be used effectively with macros.

FIGURE 13-6 Vertical Table Search with the @VLOOKUP Function

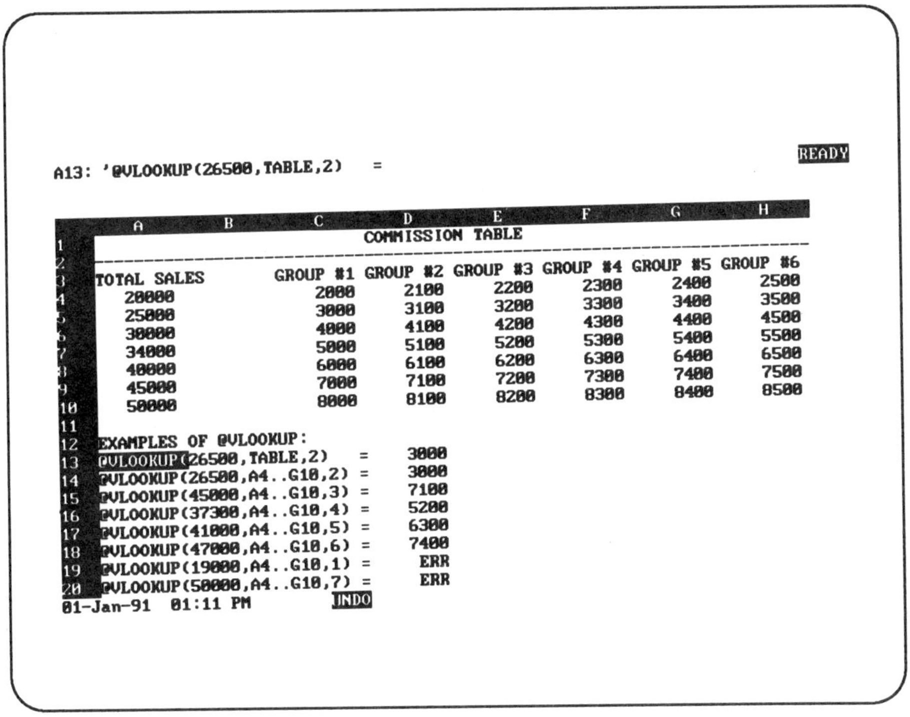

REVIEW QUESTIONS

* These questions are answered in Appendix I.

1. What is the main purpose of logical functions?
2.* What are some of the uses of @ISNUMBER?
3.* What does @CHAR do?
4. What are some of the uses of @EXACT?
5. What are some of the uses of @FIND?
6. What are some of the uses of @LENGTH?
7. What is the main purpose of the @DATE functions?
8.* What is the difference between @DATE and@DATEVALUE?
9. What are some of the uses of @CELL?
10. If the argument of @CELL is "FORMAT", what does this function return?
11. If the argument of @CELL is "PREFIX", what does this function return?
12. What may be returned by @CELLPOINTER?
13.* What is the difference between @HLOOKUP and @VLOOKUP?
14. What is the difference between @INDEX and @HLOOKUP?
15.* What are some of the practical applications of @HLOOKUP and @VLOOKUP?

HANDS-ON PRACTICE

1. What is the answer to @EXACT("VisiCalc", "Lotus")
2. What is the answer to @LEFT("Database",1)?
3. What is the answer to @LENGTH("Database")?
4. What is the answer to @REPEAT("Lotus",3)?

5. Using Figure 13-5, what are the answers to the following functions:
@HLOOKUP(250,B4..H9,3) =
@HLOOKUP(275,B4..H9,3) =
@HLOOKUP(575,B4..H9,5) =

6. Using Figure 13-6, what are the answers to the following functions:
@VLOOKUP(2000,A4..G10,3) =
@VLOOKUP(60000,A4..G10,2) =
@VLOOKUP(47000,A4..G10,5) =

7. Figure 13-7 is a sample tax table. Using this table, calculate the amount of tax for individuals who are making:
$20,000 and belong to Group #3
$34,600 and belong to Group #2
$56,000 and belong to Group #6

8. Figure 13-8 uses the @CHOOSE function. Enter different product codes in cell A16 and different total sales in C16. The @CHOOSE function in cell A18 will calculate different commissions for you. Under what condition will you receive an error?

9. Using @CHOOSE and @MOD, design a worksheet that generates the days of the week. Hint:

Saturday   = 1
Sunday   = 2
Monday   = 3
Tuesday   = 4
Wednesday = 5
Thursday   = 6
Friday   = 7

A1:   READY

	A	B	C	D	E	F	G	H
1				TAX TABLE				
3	TOTAL SALES		GROUP #1	GROUP #2	GROUP #3	GROUP #4	GROUP #5	GROUP #6
4	20000		2000	2100	2200	2300	2400	2500
5	25000		3000	3100	3200	3300	3400	3500
6	30000		4000	4100	4200	4300	4400	4500
7	34000		5000	5100	5200	5300	5400	5500
8	40000		6000	6100	6200	6300	6400	6500
9	45000		7000	7100	7200	7300	7400	7500
10	50000		8000	8100	8200	8300	8400	8500
12	EXAMPLES OF @VLOOKUP:							
13	@VLOOKUP(26500,TABLE,2) =			3000				
14	@VLOOKUP(26500,A4..G10,2) =			3000				
15	@VLOOKUP(45000,A4..G10,3) =			7100				
16	@VLOOKUP(37300,A4..G10,4) =			5200				
17	@VLOOKUP(41000,A4..G10,5) =			6300				
18	@VLOOKUP(47000,A4..G10,6) =			7400				
19	@VLOOKUP(19000,A4..G10,1) =			ERR				
20	@VLOOKUP(50000,A4..G10,7) =			ERR				

01-Jan-91   01:21 PM   UNDO

FIGURE 13-7 A Sample Tax Table

FIGURE 13-8 A Sample Worksheet

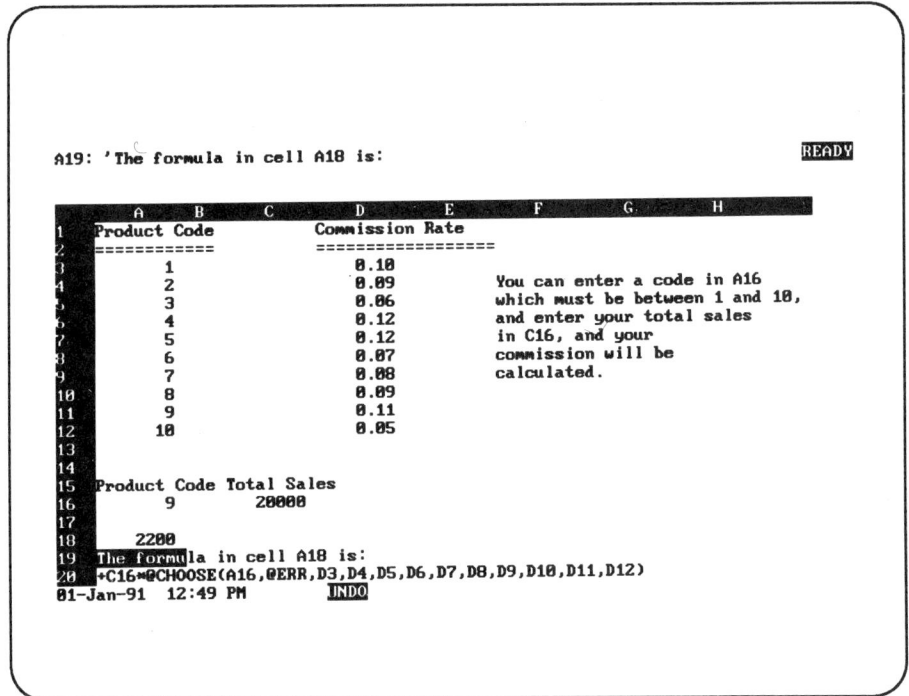

```
A19: 'The formula in cell A18 is:                                    READY

      A    B    C        D         E        F        G        H
 1 Product Code          Commission Rate
 2 ============          ==================
 3        1               0.10
 4        2               0.09      You can enter a code in A16
 5        3               0.06      which must be between 1 and 10,
 6        4               0.12      and enter your total sales
 7        5               0.12      in C16, and your
 8        6               0.07      commission will be
 9        7               0.08      calculated.
10        8               0.09
11        9               0.11
12       10               0.05
13
14
15 Product Code Total Sales
16        9          20000
17
18     2200
19 The formula in cell A18 is:
20 +C16*@CHOOSE(A16,@ERR,D3,D4,D5,D6,D7,D8,D9,D10,D11,D12)
01-Jan-91  12:49 PM          UNDO
```

You should be able to enter any date in cell A1 and your worksheet must tell you which day of the week it is.

10. Using a nested @IF function calculate the commission for different sales amounts as follows:

Sales less than $15,000 $200 base
  "   between $15,001 and $20,000 $200 base + 7% over $15,000
  "   between $20,001 and $25,000 $200 + 7% as above + 11% over $20,000
  "   over $25,000   As above + 13% over $25,000

You should be able to enter any sales amount and your worksheet should tell you the amount of commission.

11. In cell A1 type @TIME(12,17,15). By using @HOUR, @MINUTE, and @SECOND extract the hour, minute, and second components of this time.

Graphics: Converting Figures into Pictures

14-1 Introduction

In this chapter, we will study the types of graphs generated by Lotus, which include pie charts, bar, line, stacked-bar, and XY graphs. Specific applications of each graph will illustrate its use. In Chapter 15 we will discuss how to print your graph on a graphic printer and/or plotter.

14-2 Why Graphics?

In today's competitive world, business executives and decision makers need to obtain information in the most effective and efficient way. Graphs achieve these goals by condensing massive amounts of data into simple, understandable form.

Lotus generates five different types of graphs:

1. Line graphs show changes in data over time. These graphs are suitable for time series analysis, in which one variable is time and the others could be such items as total sales, total cost, total advertising budget. Using line graphs, you can easily depict budget trends, total sales trends, administrative cost trends, and so forth.

2. Bar graphs emphasize differences between data items. For example, a bar graph can compare the total sales of five products of a particular company, the oil production from five oil wells, or the student population of six state universities.

3. XY graphs show relationships between two sets of data. This might be amount of sales and advertising budget, or years of education and yearly income.

4. Pie charts compare parts to the whole. For example, you can compare advertising expenses to total sales expenses.

5. Stacked-bar graphs compare different sets of data by arranging them on top of each other. This helps to visualize the meaning of the data.

There are many graphics packages on the market. Some may offer more variety and more sophistication compared to Lotus graphics. However, since Lotus graphs are based on the data available in the spreadsheet, they can be drawn fast and what-if analysis can be performed quickly. You can change data items, press F10 in READY mode, and the entire graph will be redrawn immediately.

14-3 Overview of Lotus Graphics

To set up a graph, first invoke Graph from the main menu. The following options will be presented (see Figure 14-1):

Type   X A B C D E F   Reset   View   Save   Options   Name   Group   Quit

Type indicates the graphs generated by Lotus: line, bar, XY, stacked-bar, and pie chart.

The X range is used for labeling the X-Axis and is also used in the pie chart and the XY graph.

A, B, C, D, E, F indicates six different data ranges, allowing you to plot up to six ranges at the same time in all graphs except the pie chart.

Reset is used if you want to change the graph parameters. This means that all the previous data ranges, settings, and so forth will be erased.

View is used to display the graph on the screen if your computer has graphics capabilities.

Save is used to save a graph to be printed with the PrintGraph program.

Options gives you choices for dressing up your graph.

Name is used to name graph settings. Remember that a single worksheet can generate many different graphs with different names.

Group allows you to select several graph ranges at once.

Finally, Quit is used to get back to the worksheet.

To create and display a graph, follow this procedure:

1. Enter your data.
2. Select /Graph.
3. Select Type.

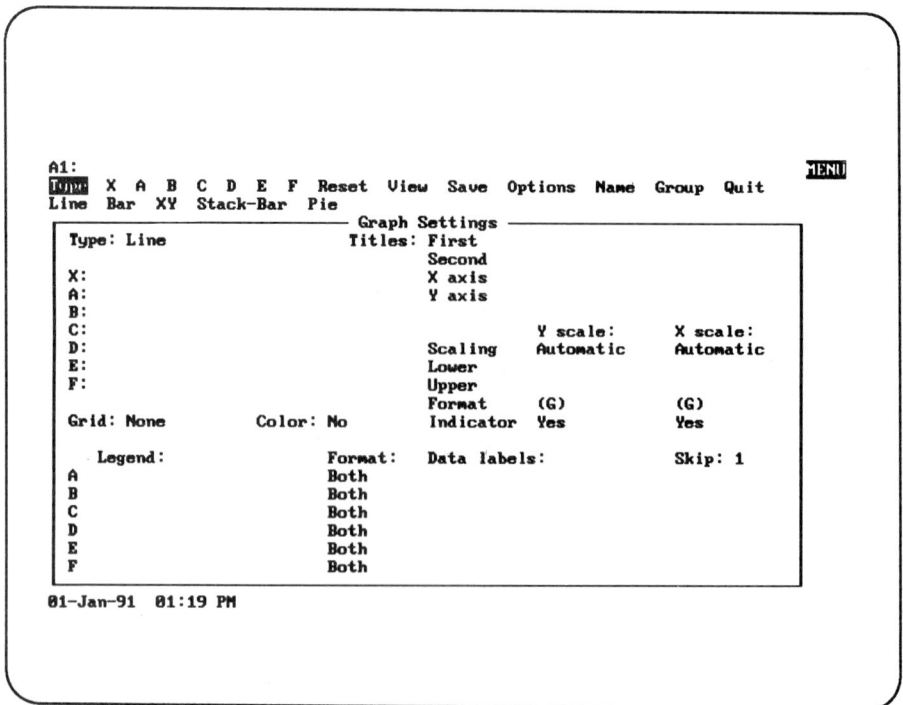

FIGURE 14-1 The Graph Menu

4. Select a graph type: line, bar, XY, stacked-bar, or pie chart.
5. Select one or more data ranges (X and/or A through F).
6. Specify the data for each range either by pointing or by typing the address.
7. Select View to display the graph type.
8. Press any key to return to the worksheet and the graph main menu.

14-4 Creating a Simple Pie Chart

Sunset Travel Agency has the following three expenses as part of its operating costs. Enter the expenses into a worksheet.

	A	B	C
4	Utilities		1850
5	Rent		1250
6	Supplies		700

Now plot these expenses using a pie chart.

Figure 14-2 shows this graph. It was generated with the commands /Graph, Type, Pie, X (A4..A6), **Return**, A (C4..C6), **Return**, View.

14-5 Saving the Graph Parameters

Once the graph is created, you may give it a name for later reference. In order to save a graph parameter, type /Graph Name Create. You can save a graph parameter under any name having up to 14 characters. After the graph is saved, you can change the parameters and save it under another name if you want. Don't forget to save (/File Save) the worksheet as well, because if you forget to save your worksheet, your graph will be lost. In addition, if you forget to name your graph (/Graph Name Create) and save only your worksheet, your graph will be lost.

To make a graph active (bring it back to memory), use /Graph Name Use. You can have only one graph active at one time. However, a worksheet can generate as many graphs as you want.

14-6 Deleting a Graph

To delete a graph, use /Graph Name Delete. Lotus will display all graph names for the current worksheet. You can either type the name to be deleted or move the cursor to the name and press the **Return** key. The graph is deleted. If you want to delete all the graphs under the current worksheet, use /Graph Name Reset. Be careful. When you issue this command all the graphs under the current worksheet will be gone and there is no way to retrieve them.

14-7 Saving a Graph for Printing

The Lotus spreadsheet program is not capable of printing your graph. To print your graph, first you must save it using /Graph Save. Lotus creates a graphic file on your disk with PIC as the extension. Now you can exit the 1-2-3 worksheet and load the PrintGraph disk for

FIGURE 14-2 A Simple Pie Chart

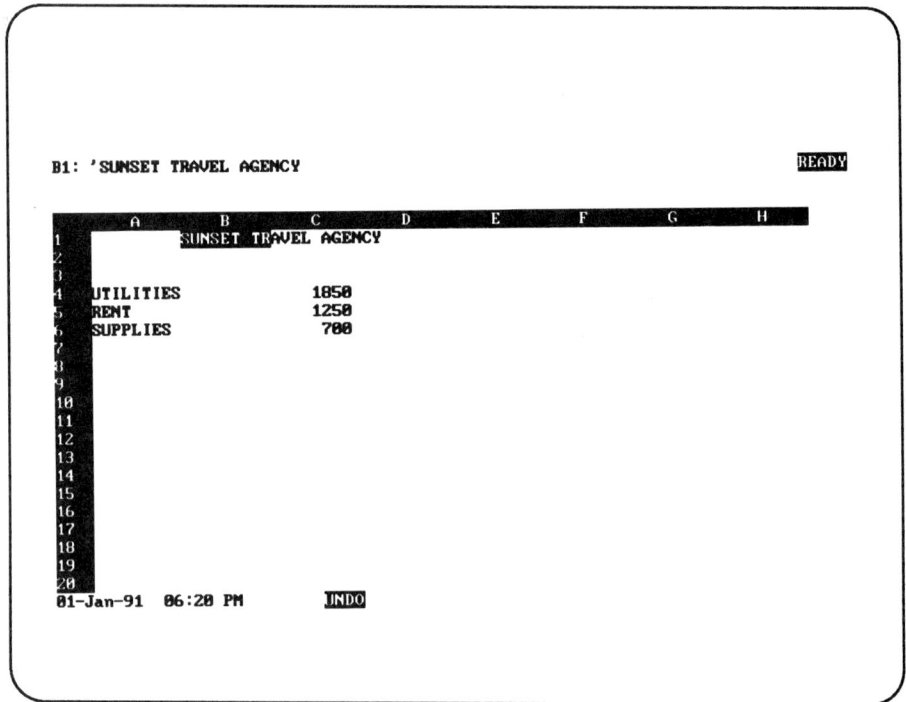

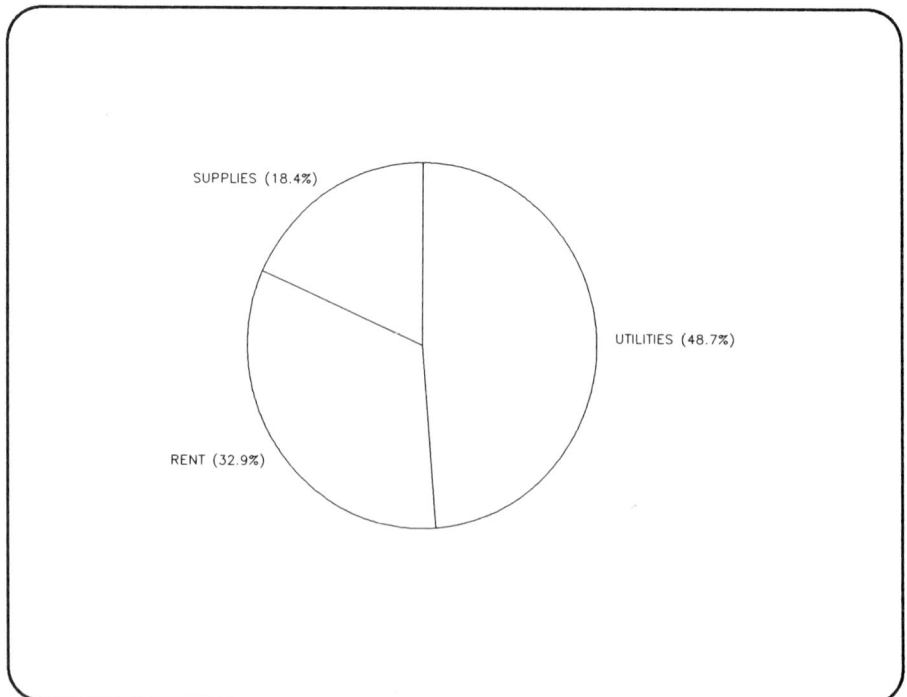

B1: 'SUNSET TRAVEL AGENCY   READY

```
            A         B         C         D      E      F      G      H
1                    SUNSET TRAVEL AGENCY
2
3
4  UTILITIES                  1050
5  RENT                       1250
6  SUPPLIES                    700
7
8
9
10
11
12
13
14
15
16
17
18
19
20
01-Jan-91  06:20 PM          UNDO
```

SUPPLIES (18.4%)

UTILITIES (48.7%)

RENT (32.9%)

FIGURE 14-2 (Continued)

printing your graph. When the graph is saved in a graphic file you can access it only from the PrintGraph program. Chapter 15 shows how to print your graphs using PrintGraph. You can also use Allways to print your graphs without going through the PrintGraph program.

14-8 Pie Chart – A Second Look

As we mentioned earlier, pie charts are very useful for comparing some data to the whole. To activate the pie chart from the main menu, first select /Graph. Then from the Type menu choose Pie. To draw a pie chart, you need one data range. After you specify your data range, choose View and the graph will appear.

Figure 14-3 shows a pie chart of a simple regional analysis. Sales for each region are compared with total sales. This graph was generated by using /Graph, Type, Pie, X (A11..A13), **Return**, A (E11..E13), **Return**, View.

Figure 14-4 uses the same data for a sales performance analysis. This time the performance of each salesperson is compared with total sales. This graph was generated with /Graph, Type, Pie, X (B10..D10), **Return**, A (B15..D15), **Return**, View.

Generating a Pie Chart Using Crosshatches

Lotus can generate eight different crosshatches, which make data comparison an easy task. Each crosshatch has its own shape, and with color graphics, each crosshatch has a unique color. (We will discuss color later in this chapter.) Figure 14-5 illustrates these crosshatches. This figure was generated by using the commands /Graph, Type, Pie, X (B2..I2), **Return**, A (B3..I3), **Return**, B (B6..I6), **Return**, View.

To generate a crosshatch, you have to define a separate data range outside your original data range. The location of this new data range is not important. However, you must call this data range the B range. This means you must choose the B range then specify the address of the data in your worksheet. In this data range you can enter any number between 0 to 7 inclusive. Codes 0 or 7 indicate an unshaded wedge.

Regional Analysis Using Crosshatches

In Figure 14-6 we show another example of the pie chart with crosshatches. This figure performs regional analysis on the data shown in this worksheet. This figure was generated with /Graph, Type, Pie, X (A12..A14), **Return**, A (E12..E14), **Return**, B (B18..D18), **Return**, View.

Exploding a Pie Chart

Sometimes you may be interested in highlighting or "exploding" a portion or portions of a pie chart. Lotus provides you with a facility to perform this task. You can explode one or all portions of your pie chart. To do so, add 100 to the codes of your crosshatches. In Figure 14-7 we added 100 to cell B18. Now this cell contains 101.

This will explode that particular section of the pie with its original crosshatch. This figure was generated with /Graph, Type, Pie, X (A12..A14), **Return**, A (E12..E14), **Return**, B (B18..D18), **Return**, View.

Figure 14-8 illustrates a pie chart with all its components exploded. This figure was generated by using /Graph, Type, Pie, X (A12..A14), Return, A (E12..E14), **Return**, B (B18..D18), **Return**, View.

FIGURE 14-3 Regional Analysis Using a Pie Chart

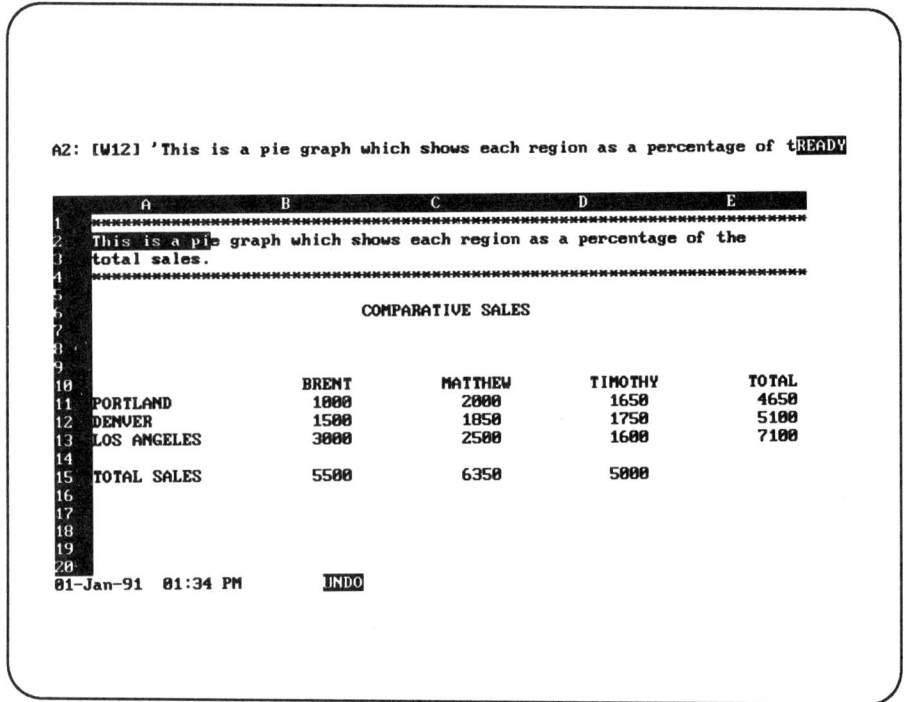

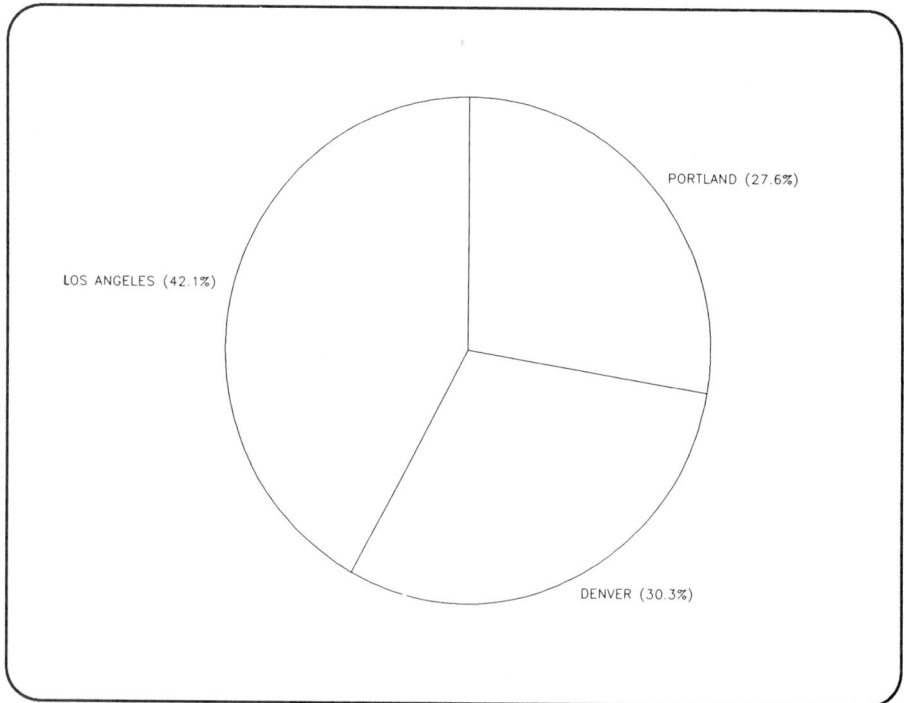

```
A2: [W12] 'This is a pie graph which shows each region as a percentage of t READY

        A              B              C              D              E
1  *********************************************************************
2  This is a pie graph which shows each region as a percentage of the
3  total sales.
4  *********************************************************************
5
6                        COMPARATIVE SALES
7
8
9
10                      BRENT        MATTHEW        TIMOTHY        TOTAL
11 PORTLAND             1000          2000           1650          4650
12 DENVER               1500          1850           1750          5100
13 LOS ANGELES          3000          2500           1600          7100
14
15 TOTAL SALES          5500          6350           5000
16
17
18
19
20
01-Jan-91  01:34 PM        UNDO
```

FIGURE 14-3 (Continued)

FIGURE 14-4 Sales Performance Analysis Using a Pie Chart

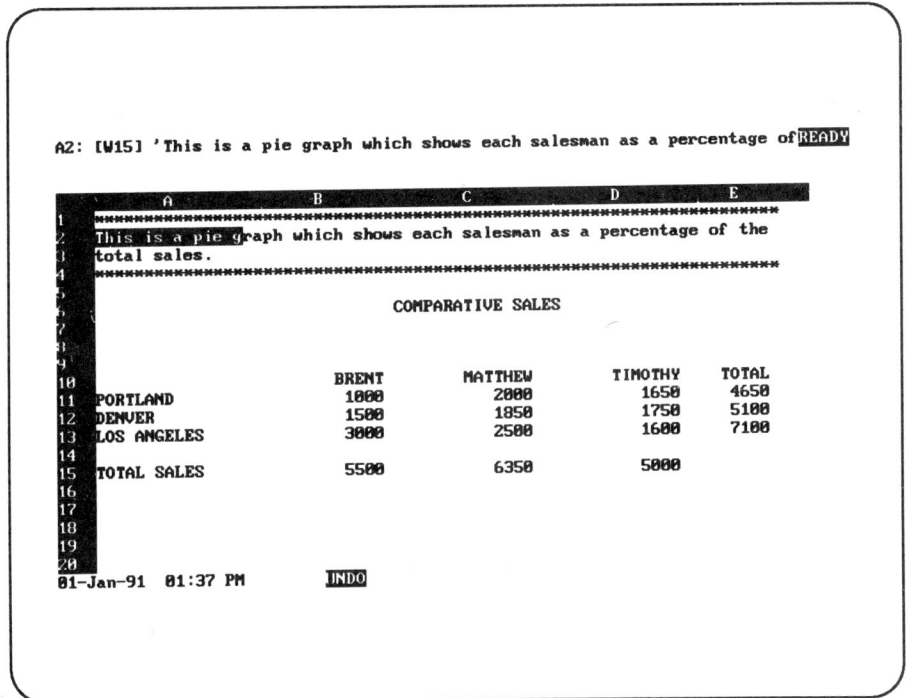

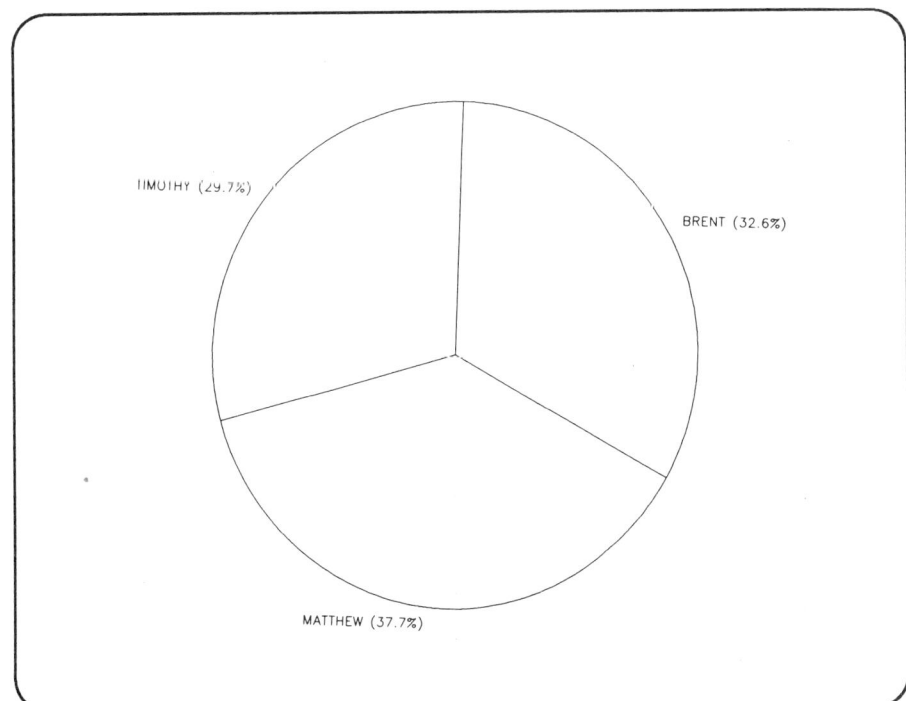

```
A2: [W15] 'This is a pie graph which shows each salesman as a percentage of READY

              A              B              C              D              E
1  *********************************************************************************
2  This is a pie graph which shows each salesman as a percentage of the
3  total sales.
4  *********************************************************************************
5
6                          COMPARATIVE SALES
7
8
9                         BRENT         MATTHEW       TIMOTHY       TOTAL
10                         1000          2000          1650          4650
11 PORTLAND                1500          1850          1750          5100
12 DENVER                  3000          2500          1600          7100
13 LOS ANGELES
14
15 TOTAL SALES             5500          6350          5000
16
17
18
19
20
01-Jan-91  01:37 PM          UNDO
```

FIGURE 14-4 (Continued)

FIGURE 14-5 Crosshatch Options

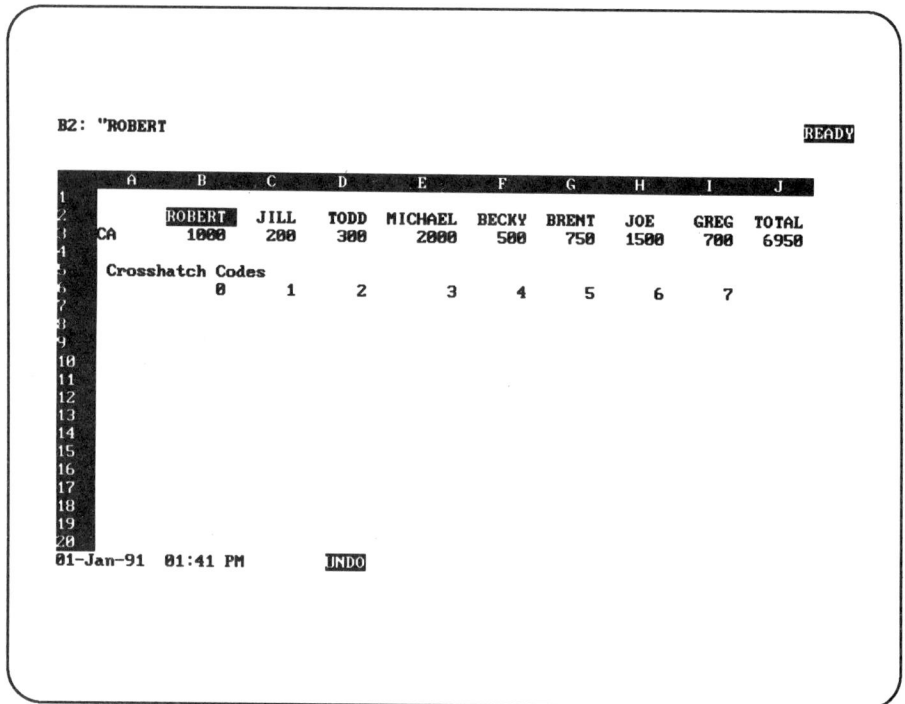

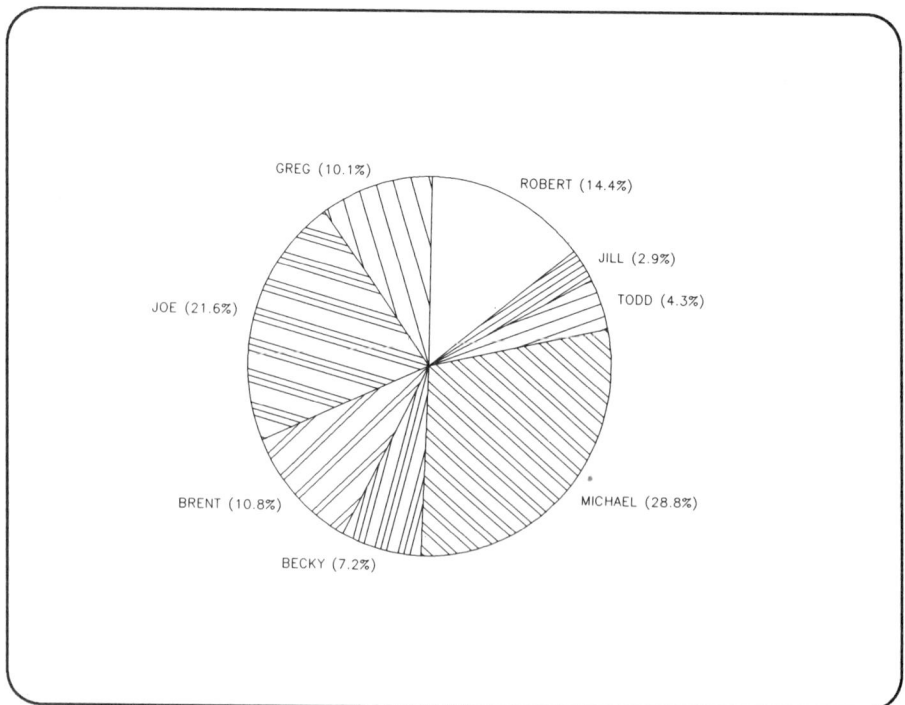

```
B2: "ROBERT                                                      READY

      A     B      C      D       E       F       G      H       I      J
1
2           ROBERT  JILL   TODD  MICHAEL  BECKY   BRENT   JOE    GREG   TOTAL
3   CA       1000   200    300    2000     500    750    1500    700   6950
4
5   Crosshatch Codes
6            0      1      2        3       4      5       6      7
7
8
9
10
11
12
13
14
15
16
17
18
19
20
01-Jan-91  01:41 PM           UNDO
```

FIGURE 14-5 (Continued)

FIGURE 14-6   *Regional Analysis Using Crosshatches*

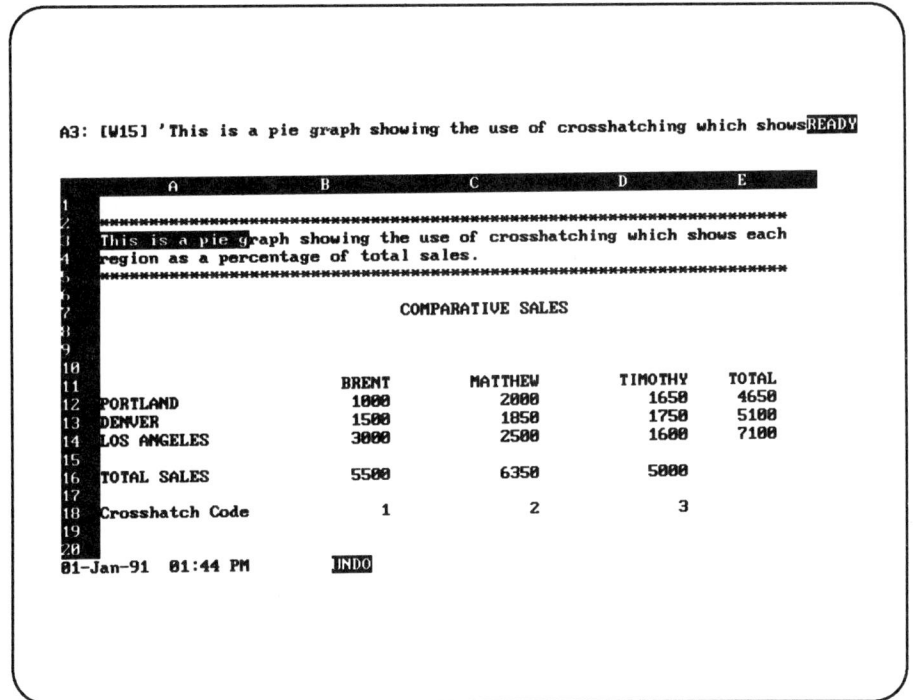

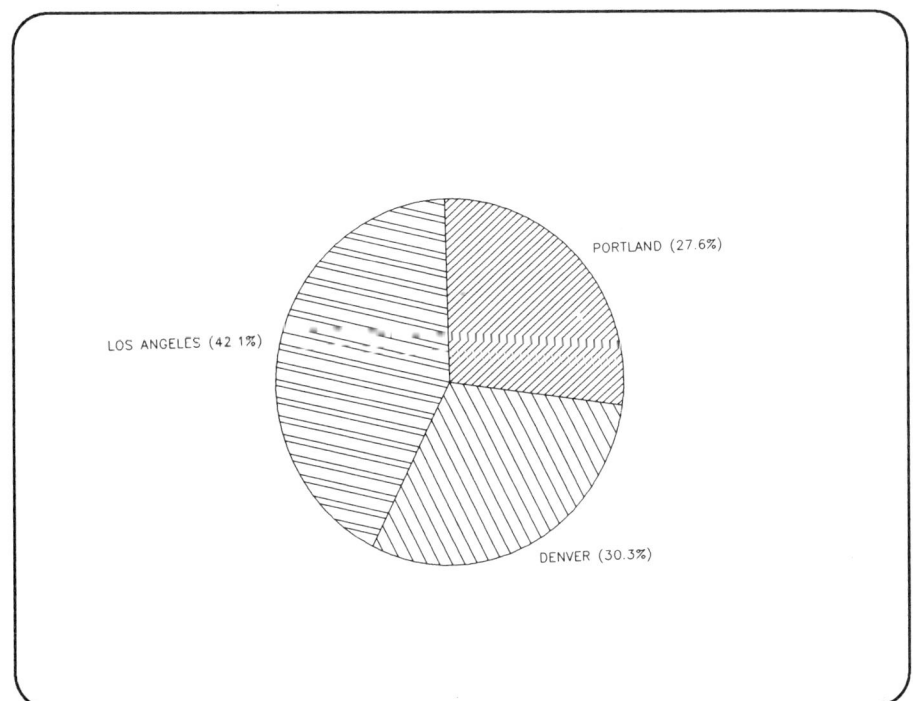

```
A3: [W15] 'This is a pie graph showing the use of crosshatching which shows READY

         A              B              C              D          E
1
2  *********************************************************************
3  This is a pie graph showing the use of crosshatching which shows each
4  region as a percentage of total sales.
5  *********************************************************************
6
7                     COMPARATIVE SALES
8
9
10
11                    BRENT        MATTHEW       TIMOTHY    TOTAL
12 PORTLAND           1000         2000          1650       4650
13 DENVER             1500         1850          1750       5100
14 LOS ANGELES        3000         2500          1600       7100
15
16 TOTAL SALES        5500         6350          5000
17
18 Crosshatch Code       1            2             3
19
20
01-Jan-91  01:44 PM      UNDO
```

FIGURE 14-6   *(Continued)*

FIGURE 14-7 _Exploding One Section of a Pie Chart_

A2: [W15] 'This is an exploded pie graph showing region as a percentage of `READY`

	A	B	C	D	E
1	***				
2	`This is an expl`oded pie graph showing region as a percentage of total				
3	sales. To explode a portion, 100 is added to the crosshatch code.				
4	***				
5					
6					
7		COMPARATIVE SALES			
8					
9					
10					
11		BRENT	MATTHEW	TIMOTHY	TOTAL
12	PORTLAND	1000	2000	1650	4650
13	DENVER	1500	1850	1750	5100
14	LOS ANGELES	3000	2500	1600	7100
15					
16	TOTAL SALES	5500	6350	5000	
17					
18	Crosshatch Code	101	2	3	
19					
20					

01-Jan-91 01:45 PM   `UNDO`

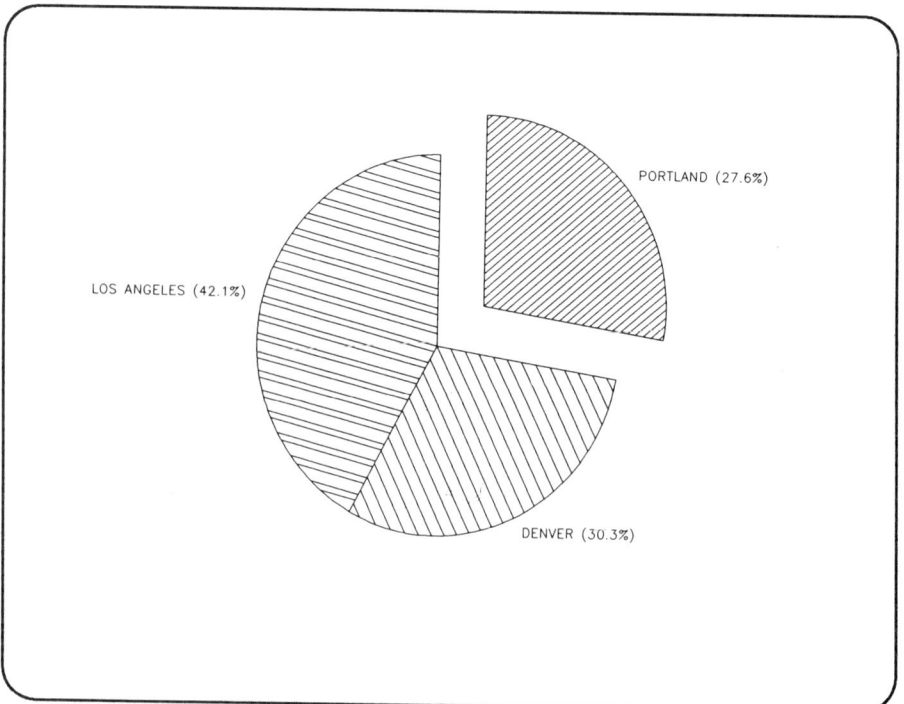

FIGURE 14-7 _(Continued)_

FIGURE 14-8 Explosion of the Entire Pie Chart

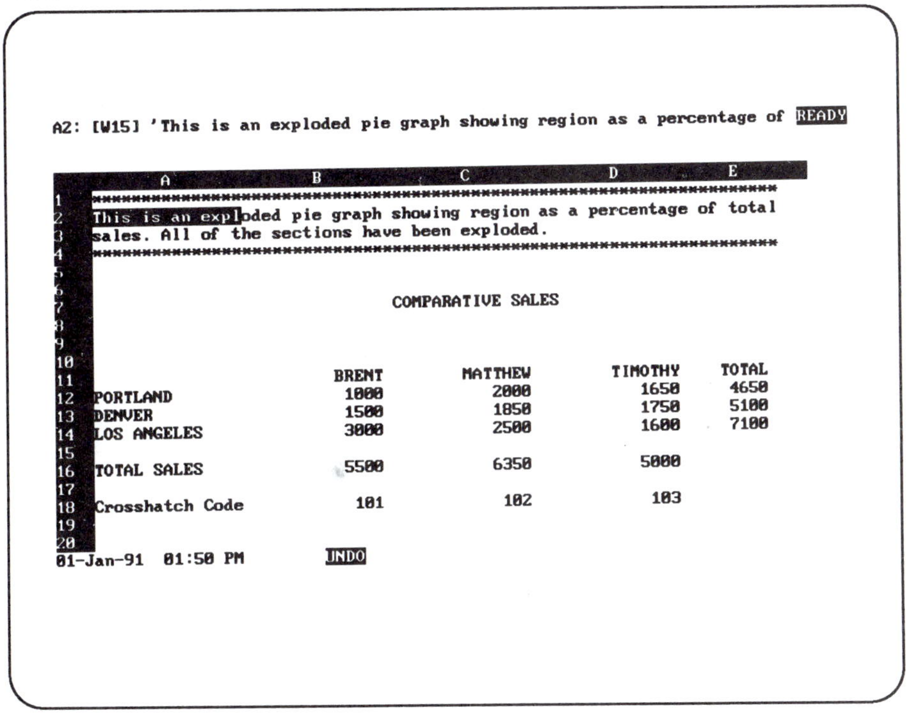

```
A2: [W15] 'This is an exploded pie graph showing region as a percentage of  READY

            A              B              C              D              E
************************************************************************
This is an exploded pie graph showing region as a percentage of total
sales. All of the sections have been exploded.
************************************************************************

                              COMPARATIVE SALES


                         BRENT        MATTHEW      TIMOTHY       TOTAL
PORTLAND                  1000         2000         1650         4650
DENVER                    1500         1850         1750         5100
LOS ANGELES               3000         2500         1600         7100

TOTAL SALES               5500         6350         5000

Crosshatch Code            101          102          103


01-Jan-91   01:50 PM       UNDO
```

PORTLAND (27.6%)

LOS ANGELES (42.1%)

DENVER (30.3%)

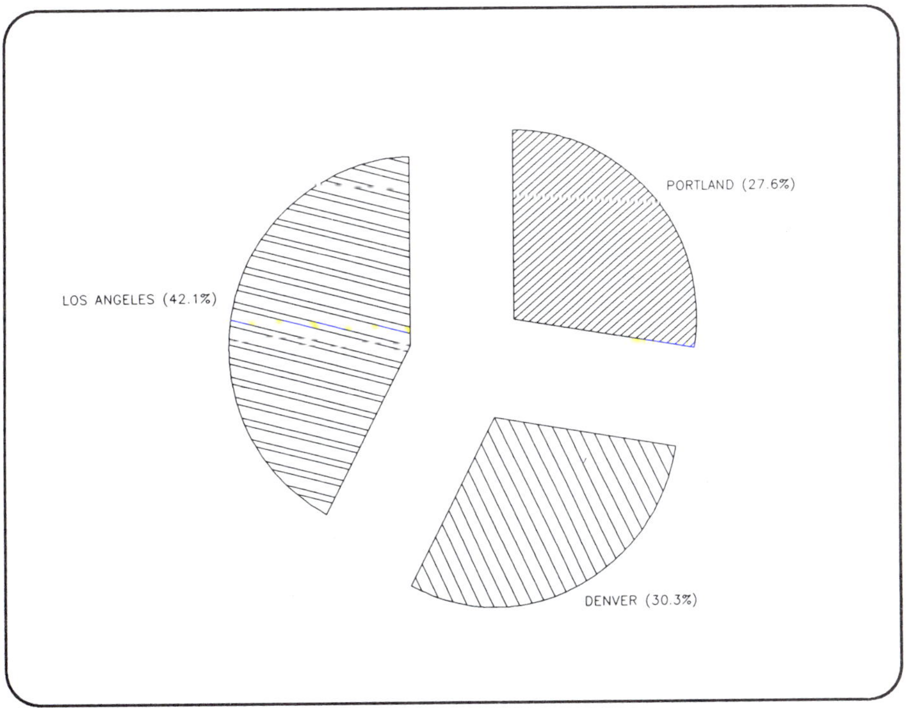

FIGURE 14-8 (Continued)

14-9 Bar Graphs

Bar graphs are useful for comparing differences between data items. Lotus allows you to choose up to six data ranges for bar graph presentation. Figure 14-9 is a bar graph showing the performance of three salespersons in three regions. This graph was generated as follows:

/Graph, Type, Bar, X (B10..D10), **Return**, A (B11..D11), **Return**, B (B12..D12), **Return**, C (B13..D13), **Return**, Options, Titles, First, COMPARATIVE SALES, **Return**, Titles, Second, FOR THE HAPPY TRAVELER, **Return**, Titles, X-Axis, SALESMEN, **Return**, Titles, Y-Axis, SALES, **Return**, Legend, A (\A11), **Return**, Legend, B (\A12), **Return**, Legend, C (\A13), **Return**, Quit, View.

As usual, the Graph option was chosen from the main menu. The type chosen was Bar. The X data range can be whatever labels you are interested in showing on the X-Axis. In Figure 14-9, we have chosen the names of three salesmen. The A range shows the performance of Brent, Matthew, and Timothy in Portland. The B and C ranges show the performances of these three salespersons in Denver and Los Angeles respectively. You can include up to six such data ranges.

Lotus gives you the option of choosing a title and a subtitle for the graph. Choose Options, then Titles, then First. This is the heading, so we entered COMPARATIVE SALES. To enter this heading, either type it or use a backslash (\) followed by a cell address or a range name containing the heading. In this case, \C6 will do it. The Second option is for the subtitle, which is FOR THE HAPPY TRAVELER.

Now you choose the X-Axis. We put SALESMEN on the X-Axis and SALES for the Y-Axis. To make the presentation clearer, you can choose up to six legends. We chose Legend A for PORTLAND, B for DENVER, and C for LOS ANGELES. These items can be either typed or entered with a back slash followed by the cell reference or range name.

Figure 14-10 is a slightly different version of Figure 14-9. In this figure we display the performance of each region. This figure was generated as follows:

/Graph, Type, Bar, X (A11..A13), **Return**, A (B11..B13), **Return**, B (C11..C13), **Return**, C (D11..D13), **Return**, Options, Titles, First, COMPARATIVE SALES, **Return**, Titles, Second, FOR THE HAPPY TRAVELER, **Return**, Titles, X-Axis, REGION, **Return**, Titles, Y-Axis, SALES, **Return**, Legend, A(\B10), **Return**, Legend, B(\C10), **Return**, Legend, C(\D10), **Return**, Quit, View.

Setting Scale Limits

So far, the graphs we have discussed have been plotted using automatic scaling. This means that Lotus always automatically fits your data in the X and Y axes; for example, your first data item appears first and the last data item appears last. However, there may be cases where you are interested in highlighting a portion of the graph or in changing the automatic scaling. If you issue the command /Graph Options Scale, the following menu will be illustrated:

Y-Scale   X-Scale   Skip

Choose Y-Scale and the following menu will be illustrated:

Automatic   Manual   Lower   Upper   Format   Indicator   Quit

If you choose Manual, you will be given all the other choices. The Format option is the same as /Range Format or /Worksheet Global Format. This means you can format your number(s) in the X or Y axis.

FIGURE 14-9 Bar Graph for Sales Performance Analysis

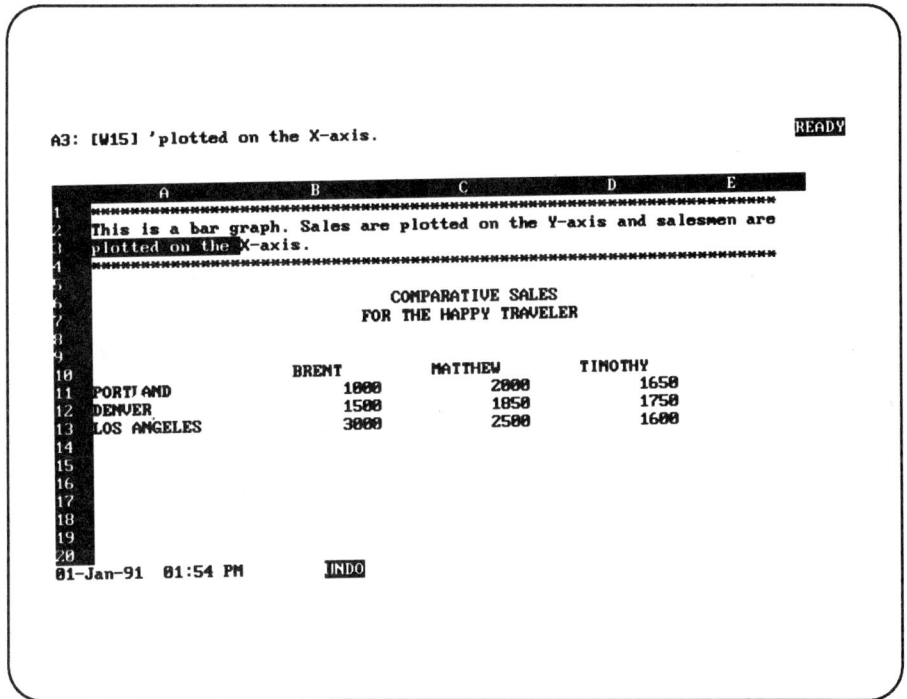

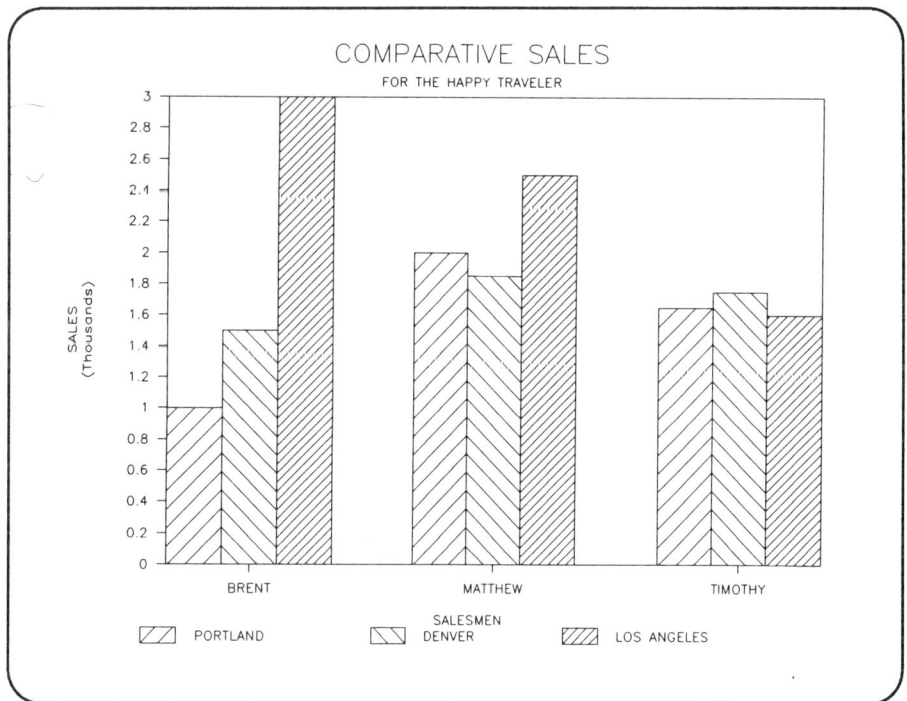

```
A3: [W15] 'plotted on the X-axis.                                    READY

        A              B              C              D        E
1   *************************************************************************
2   This is a bar graph. Sales are plotted on the Y-axis and salesmen are
3   plotted on the X-axis.
4   *************************************************************************
5
6                        COMPARATIVE SALES
7                        FOR THE HAPPY TRAVELER
8
9
10                 BRENT          MATTHEW        TIMOTHY
11  PORTLAND        1000           2000           1650
12  DENVER          1500           1850           1750
13  LOS ANGELES     3000           2500           1600
14
15
16
17
18
19
20
01-Jan-91  01:54 PM       UNDO
```

COMPARATIVE SALES
FOR THE HAPPY TRAVELER

FIGURE 14-9 (Continued)

FIGURE 14-10   Bar Graph for Regional Analysis

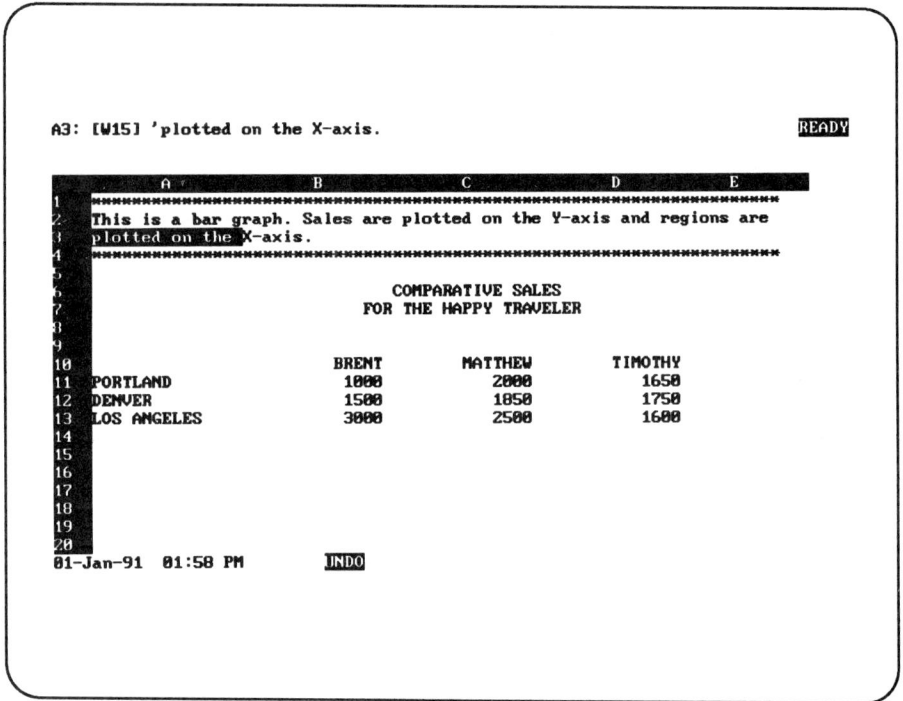

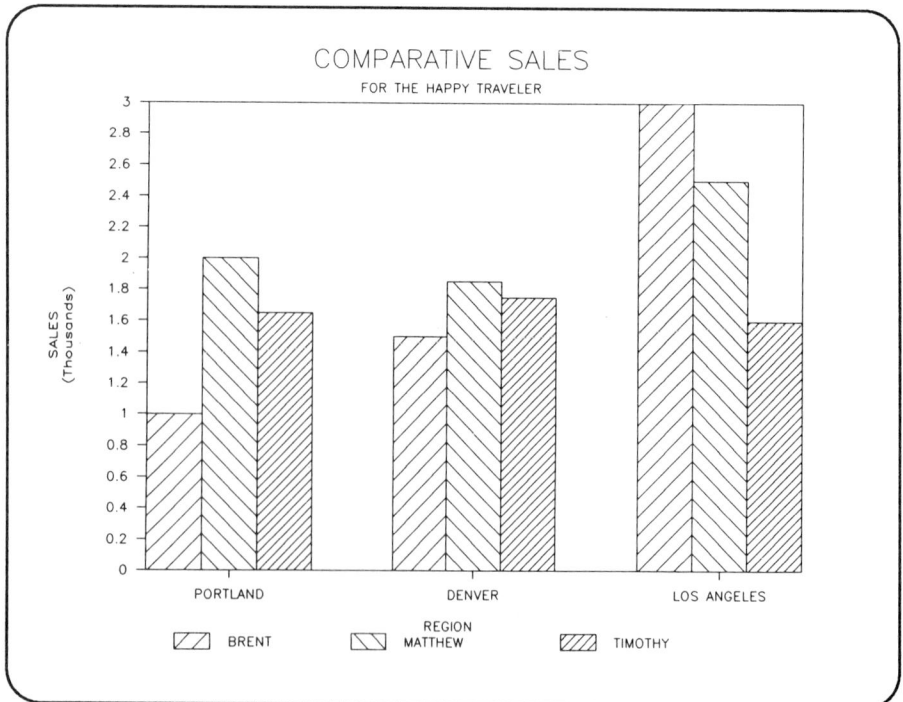

A3: [W15] 'plotted on the X-axis.   READY

	A	B	C	D	E
1	**				
2	This is a bar graph. Sales are plotted on the Y-axis and regions are				
3	plotted on the X-axis.				
4	**				
5					
6		COMPARATIVE SALES			
7		FOR THE HAPPY TRAVELER			
8					
9					
10		BRENT	MATTHEW	TIMOTHY	
11	PORTLAND	1000	2000	1650	
12	DENVER	1500	1850	1750	
13	LOS ANGELES	3000	2500	1600	
14					
15					
16					
17					
18					
19					
20					

01-Jan-91 01:58 PM   UNDO

FIGURE 14-10   (Continued)

Figure 14-11 shows an example of a manual scale. This figure was generated as follows:

/Graph, Type, Bar, X (B11..D11), **Return**, A (B12..D12), **Return**, B (B13..D13), **Return**, C (B14..D14), **Return**, Options, Legend, A (\A12), **Return**, Legend, B (\A13), **Return**, Legend, C (\A14), **Return**, Titles, First, COMPARATIVE SALES, **Return**, Titles, Second, FOR THE HAPPY TRAVELER, **Return**, Titles, X-Axis, SALESMEN, **Return**, Titles, Y-Axis, SALES, **Return**, Scale, Y-Scale, Manual, Lower (-1,000), **Return**, Upper (4,000), **Return**, Quit, Quit, View.

The Indicator option allows you to suppress the scale indicator, or, more simply put, Lotus rescales the axis in order to fit the data. If your scale is too low and there are large differences between your data ranges you may see only a portion of your data. Figure 14-12 illustrates this case. This graph was generated as follows:

/Graph, Type, Bar, X (B11..D11), **Return**, A (B12..D12), **Return**, B (B13..D13), **Return**, C (B14..D14), **Return**, Options, Legend, A (\A12), **Return**, Legend, B (\A13), **Return**, Legend, C (\A14), **Return**, Titles, First, COMPARATIVE SALES, **Return**, Titles, Second, FOR THE HAPPY TRAVELER, **Return**, Titles, X-Axis, SALESMEN, **Return**, Titles, Y-Axis, SALES, **Return**, Scale, Y-Scale, Manual, Lower (-1000), **Return**, Upper (2000), **Return**, Quit, Quit, View.

14-10 Line Graphs

Line graphs are very useful when you want to observe the performance of one variable over a period of time; for instance, a company's total advertising budget for the years 1986 to 1990. The Format option is used to draw lines or symbols in line or XY graphs. When the Options Format is chosen, the following menu will be presented:

Graph A B C D E F Quit

The Graph option sets the format for all ranges, while options A–F are used to set the format for a particular range. Lines, Symbols, Both, and Neither are choices under the Graph option. Lines will draw lines between data points; Symbols will draw symbols at data points; Both will draw both lines and symbols; and Neither will display data labels only.

Horizontal and vertical grid lines can be used to make graphs easier to read. These lines can be drawn by using the Grid option from the Options menu. A choice of horizontal grid lines, vertical grid lines, or both are available for the flexible presentation of line graphs.

The Data Labels option from the Options menu is used to specify a label corresponding to the data range. Up to six data ranges can be labeled. These labels can be aligned in five convenient ways relative to data points: center, left, above, right, or below.

Figure 14-13 is an example of a line graph. This figure shows the total sales for Alpha-Talk Company from 1986 to 1990. The graph was generated as follows:

/Graph, Type, Line, X (C11..C15), **Return**, A (F11..F15), **Return**, Options, Titles, First, ALPHA-TALK COMPANY, **Return**, Titles, X-Axis, YEAR, **Return**, Titles, Y-Axis, TOTAL SALES, **Return**, Format, Graph, Lines, Quit, Quit, View.

Line Graph with Lines and Symbols

Figure 14-14 displays the same data as Figure 14-13 except that we have chosen both lines and symbols. This graph was generated as follows:

/Graph, Type, Line, X (C11..C15), **Return**, A (F11..F15), **Return**, Options, Titles,

FIGURE 14-11 Manual Scaling of Sales Performance Analysis

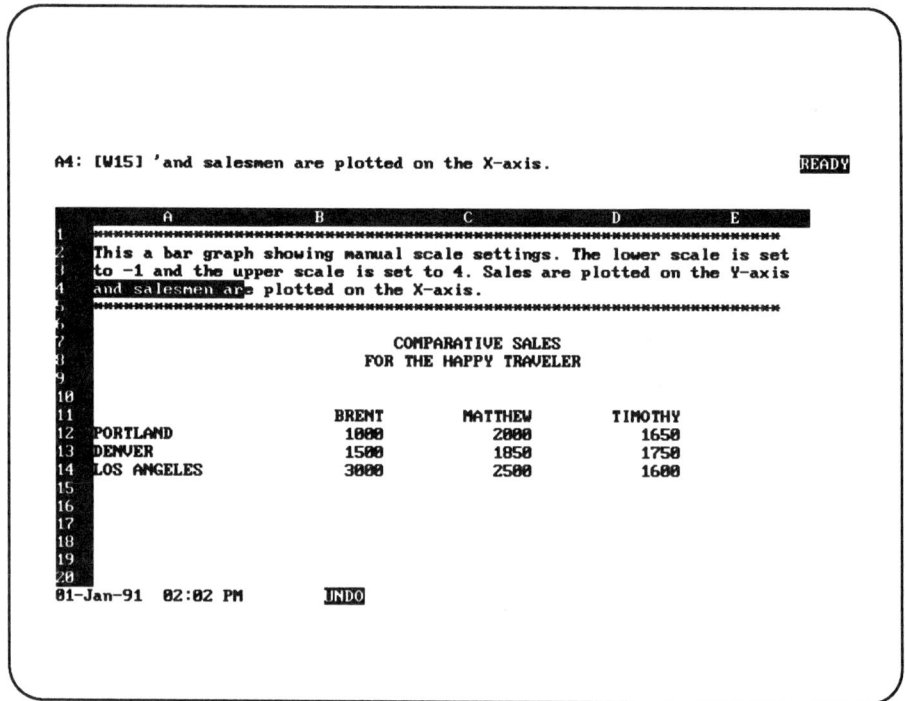

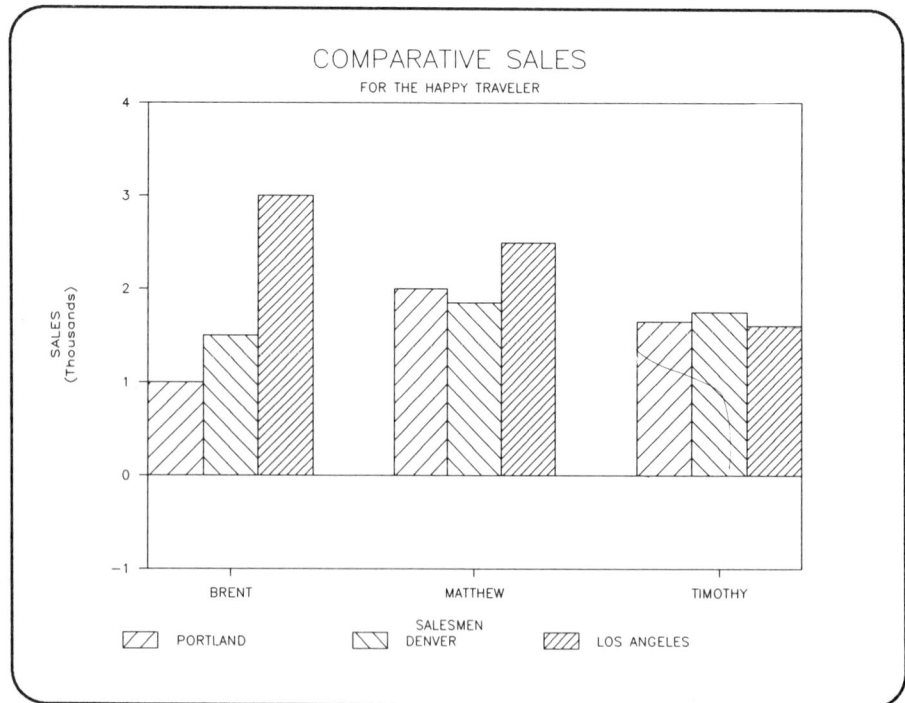

```
A4: [W15] 'and salesmen are plotted on the X-axis.                    READY

           A            B            C            D            E
1  ****************************************************************
2  This a bar graph showing manual scale settings. The lower scale is set
3  to -1 and the upper scale is set to 4. Sales are plotted on the Y-axis
4  and salesmen are plotted on the X-axis.
5  ****************************************************************
6
7                          COMPARATIVE SALES
8                        FOR THE HAPPY TRAVELER
9
10
11                      BRENT        MATTHEW      TIMOTHY
12 PORTLAND             1000         2000         1650
13 DENVER               1500         1850         1750
14 LOS ANGELES          3000         2500         1600
15
16
17
18
19
20
01-Jan-91  02:02 PM           UNDO
```

FIGURE 14-11 (Continued)

FIGURE 14-12 Manual Scaling of Sales Performance

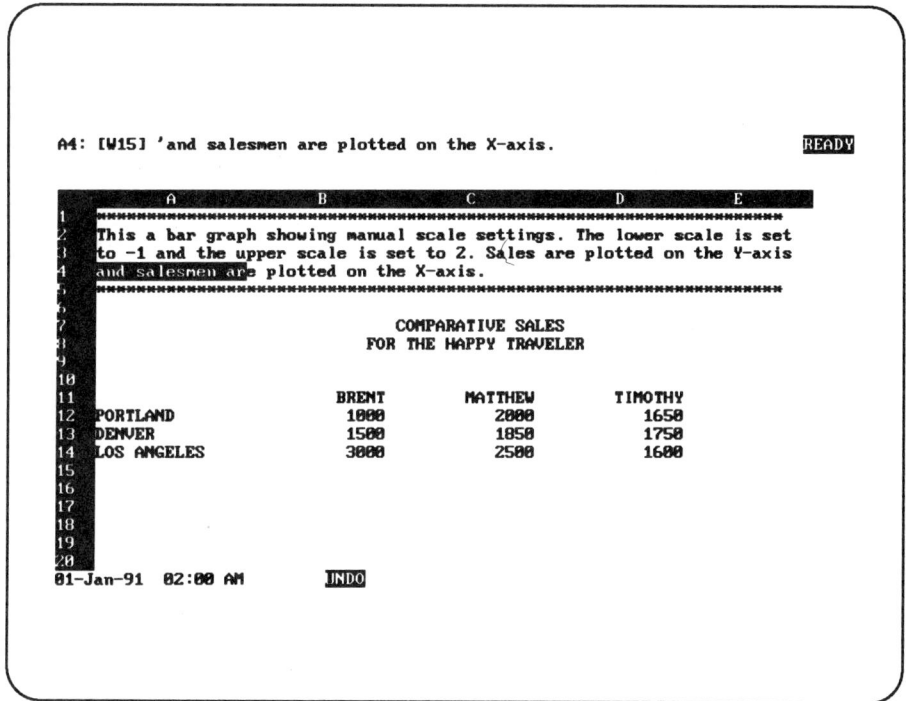

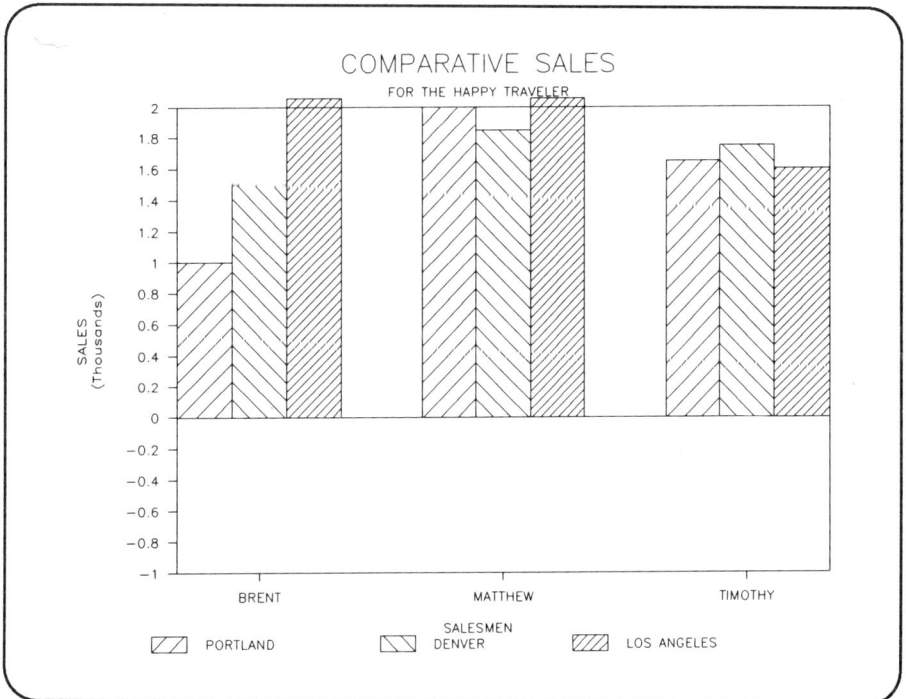

FIGURE 14-12 (Continued)

FIGURE 14-13 Line Graph with Lines Only

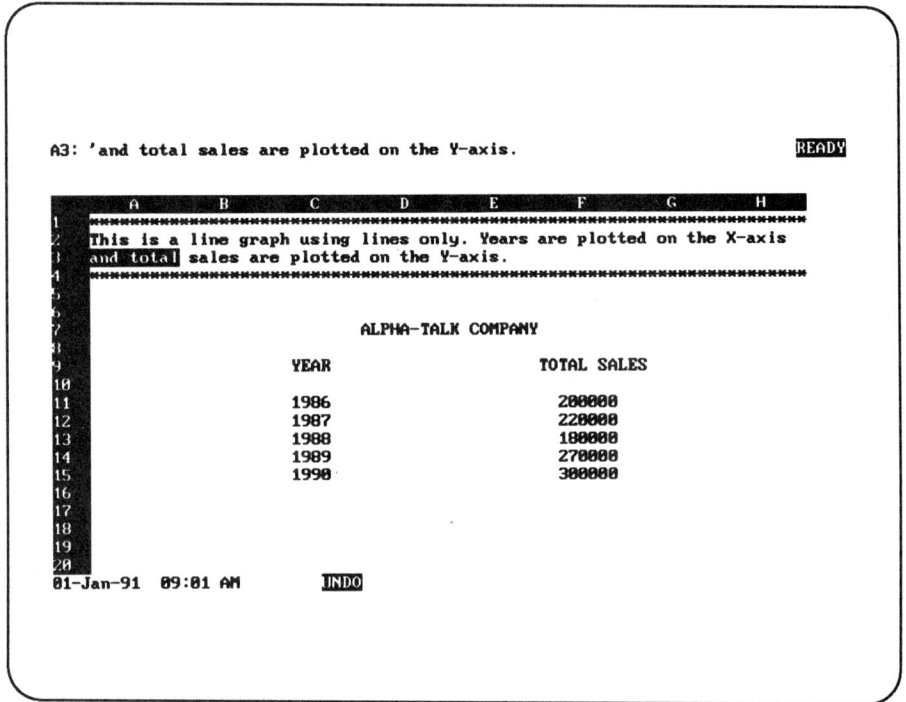

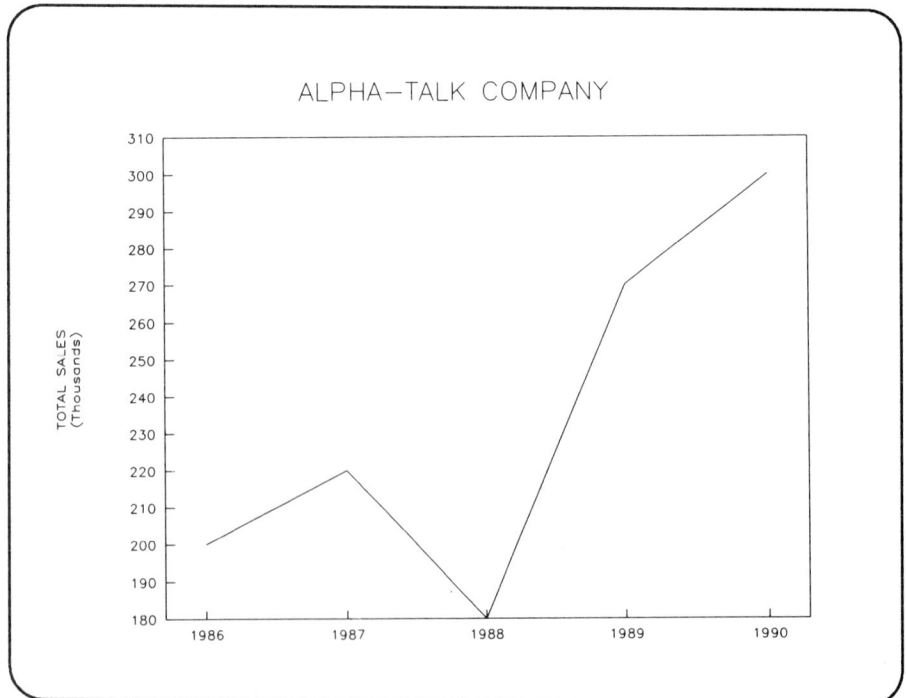

A3: 'and total sales are plotted on the Y-axis.   READY

```
      A       B       C       D       E       F       G       H
**********************************************************************
This is a line graph using lines only. Years are plotted on the X-axis
and total sales are plotted on the Y-axis.
**********************************************************************

                        ALPHA-TALK COMPANY

                 YEAR                    TOTAL SALES

                 1986                      200000
                 1987                      220000
                 1988                      180000
                 1989                      270000
                 1990                      300000
```

01-Jan-91 09:01 AM   UNDO

FIGURE 14-13 (Continued)

FIGURE 14-14 Line Graph with Lines and Symbols

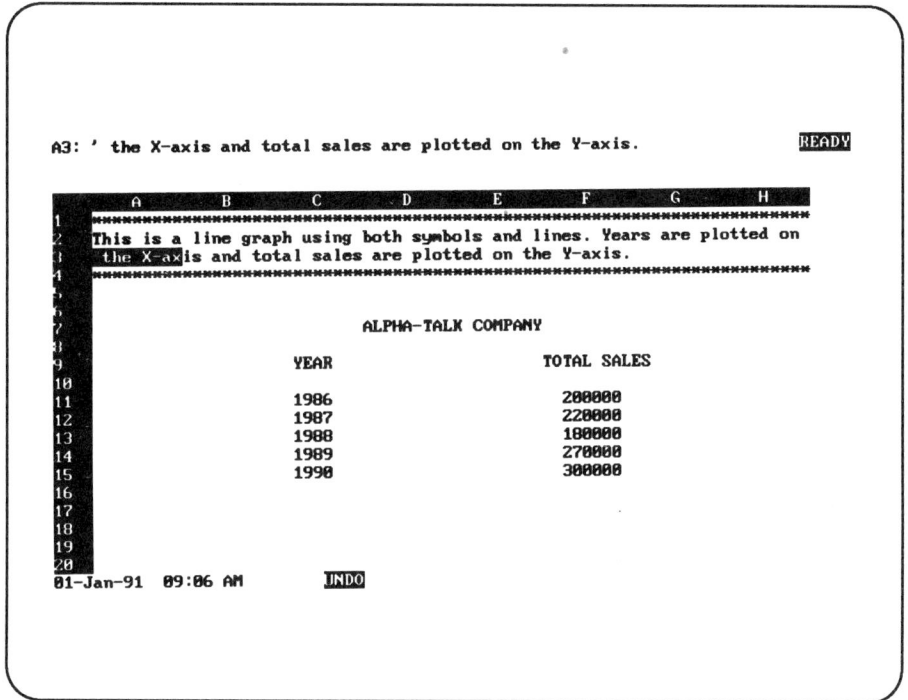

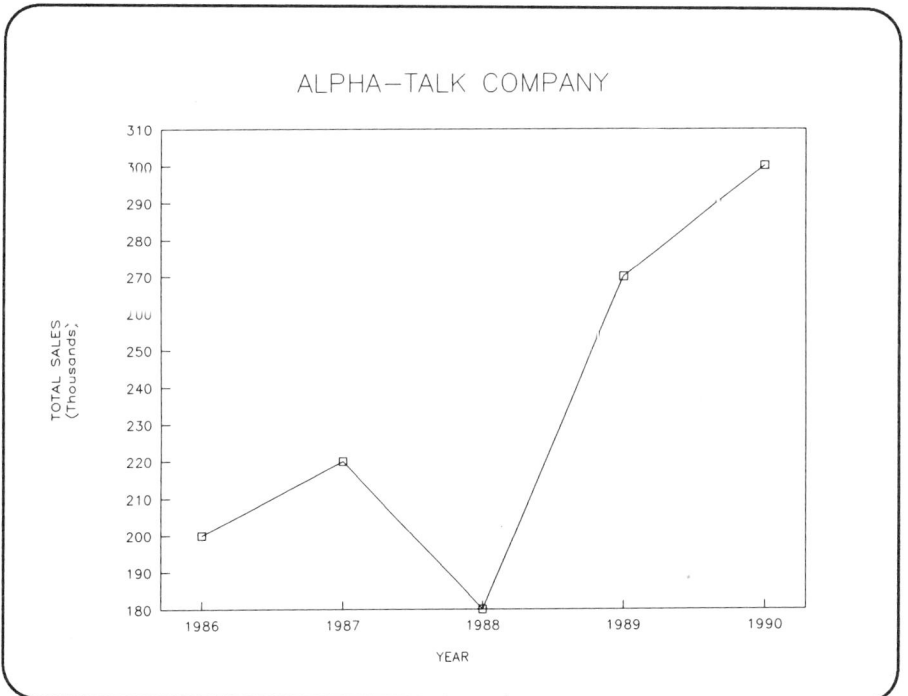

FIGURE 14-14 (Continued)

First, ALPHA-TALK COMPANY, **Return**, Titles, X-Axis, YEAR, **Return**, Titles, Y-Axis, TOTAL SALES, **Return**, Format, Graph, Both, Quit, Quit, View.

Line Graph with Lines, Symbols, and Grids

Figure 14-15 plots the same data as Figures 14-13 and 14-14 but uses a vertical grid. This figure was generated as follows:

/Graph, Type, Line, X (C12..C16), **Return**, A (F12..F16), **Return**, Options, Titles, First, ALPHA-TALK COMPANY, **Return**, Titles, X-Axis, YEAR, **Return**, Titles, Y-Axis, TOTAL SALES, **Return**, Grid, Vertical, Format, Graph, Both, Quit, Quit, View.

Figure 14-16 shows the same data, this time on a horizontal grid. This figure was generated as follows:

/Graph, Type, Line, X (C12..C16), **Return**, A (F12..F16), **Return**, Options, Titles, First, ALPHA-TALK COMPANY, **Return**, Titles, X-Axis, YEAR, **Return**, Titles, Y-Axis, TOTAL SALES, **Return**, Grid, Horizontal, Format, Graph, Both, Quit, Quit, View.

Figure 14-17 displays the same data once again. This time, we are using both vertical and horizontal grids. This figure was generated as follows:

/Graph, Type, Line, X (C12..C16), **Return**, A (F12..F16), **Return**, Options, Titles, First, ALPHA-TALK COMPANY, **Return**, Titles, X-Axis, YEAR, **Return**, Titles, Y-Axis, TOTAL SALES, **Return**, Grid, Both, Format, Graph, Both, Quit, Quit, View.

Figure 14-18 displays the same graph, this time using no lines, only symbols. This graph was generated as follows:

/Graph, Type, Line, X (C12..C16), **Return**, A (F12..F16), **Return**, Options, Titles, First, ALPHA-TALK COMPANY, **Return**, Titles, X-Axis, YEAR, **Return**, Titles, Y-Axis, TOTAL SALES, **Return**, Grid, Both, Format, Graph, Symbols, Quit, Quit, View.

Figure 14-19 displays the same data. This time, however, neither lines nor grids are used, just symbols. This figure was generated as follows:

/Graph, Type, Line, X (C11..C15), **Return**, A (F11..F15), **Return**, Options, Titles, First, ALPHA-TALK COMPANY, **Return**, Titles, X-Axis, YEAR, **Return**, Titles, Y-Axis, TOTAL SALES, **Return**, Format, Graph, Symbols, Quit, Quit, View.

Figure 14-20 displays a line graph that plots an advertising budget for twelve periods, using symbols. This figure was generated as follows:

/Graph, Type, Line, X (A7..A18), **Return**, A (B7..B18), **Return**, Options, Format, Graph, Both, Quit, Titles, First, SUNSHINE TRAVEL, **Return**, Titles, X-Axis, YEAR, **Return**, Titles, Y-Axis, PERCENTAGE OF ADVERTISING BUDGET, **Return**, Quit, View.

Figure 14-21 displays the same data as Figure 14-20, however, this time we have used the Skip option. This option lets you skip every *n*th label on the X axis. The graph was generated as follows:

/Graph, Type, Line, X (A7..A18), **Return**, A (B7..B18), **Return**, Options, Scale, Skip, 2, **Return**, Titles, First, SUNSHINE TRAVEL, **Return**, Titles, X-Axis, YEAR, **Return**, Titles, Y-Axis, PERCENTAGE OF ADVERTISING BUDGET, **Return**, Format, Graph, Both, Quit, Quit, View.

Figure 14-22 compares the total sales of two divisions using a line graph with two lines and different symbols. This figure was generated as follows:

/Graph, Type, Line, X (A4..A13), **Return**, A (C4..C13), **Return**, B (E4..E13), **Return**, Options, Legend, A (DIVISION #1), **Return**, Legend, B (DIVISION #2), **Return**, Format, Graph, Both, Quit, Titles, X-Axis, YEAR, **Return**, Titles, Y-Axis, TOTAL SALES, **Return**, Quit, View.

Line Graph with Lines, Symbols, and Data Labels

Figure 14-23 plots the same data as Figure 14-20, but this time data labels are used. This

FIGURE 14-15 *Line Graph with Both Lines and Symbols and a Vertical Grid*

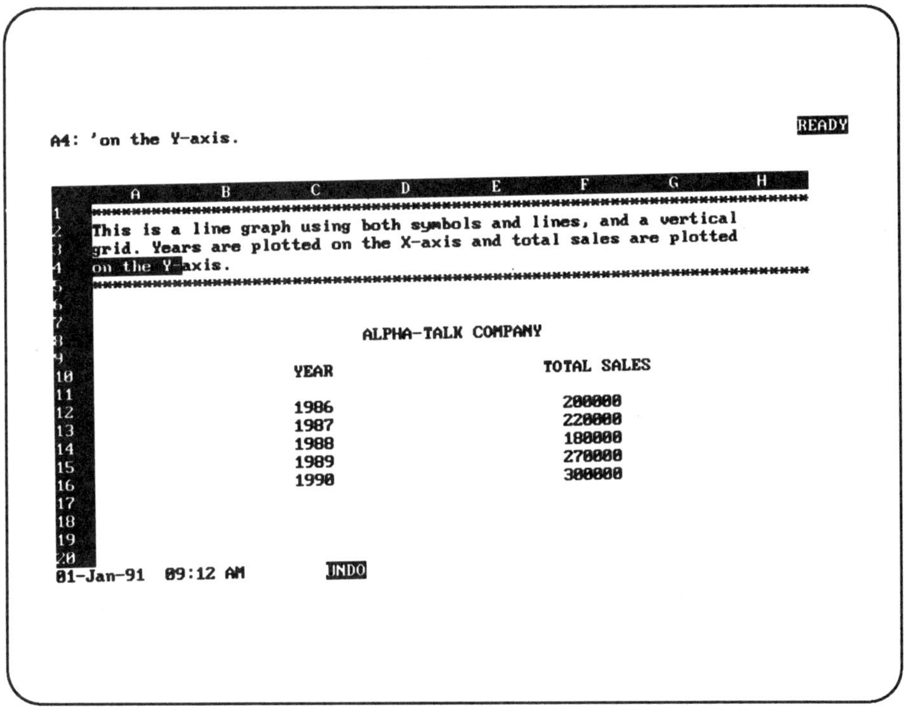

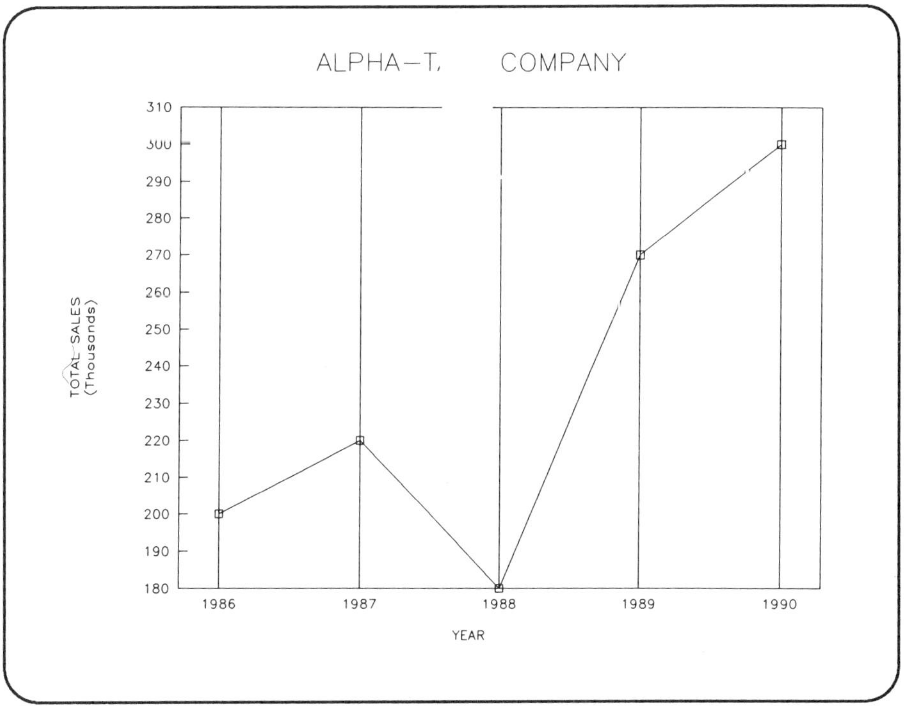

FIGURE 14-15 *(Continued)*

FIGURE 14-16 Line Graph with Both Lines and Symbols and a Horizontal Grid

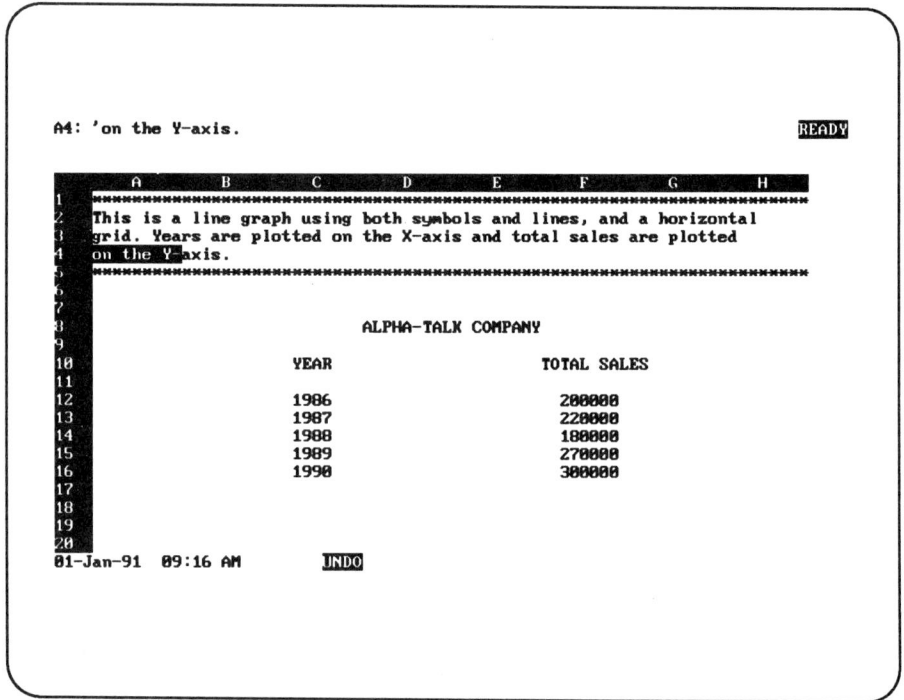

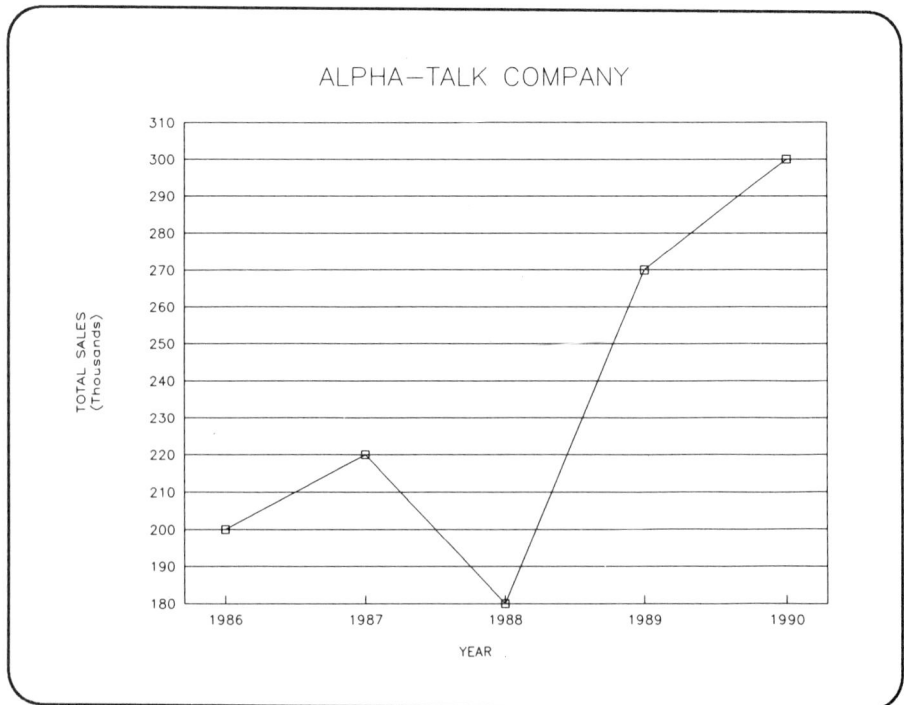

A4: 'on the Y-axis.   READY

```
        A      B      C      D      E      F      G      H
1  ***********************************************************************
2  This is a line graph using both symbols and lines, and a horizontal
3  grid. Years are plotted on the X-axis and total sales are plotted
4  on the Y-axis.
5  ***********************************************************************
6
7
8                        ALPHA-TALK COMPANY
9
10              YEAR                    TOTAL SALES
11
12              1986                      200000
13              1987                      220000
14              1988                      180000
15              1989                      270000
16              1990                      300000
17
18
19
20
01-Jan-91   09:16 AM          UNDO
```

ALPHA-TALK COMPANY

FIGURE 14-16 (Continued)

FIGURE 14-17 Line Graph with Lines, Symbols, Vertical, and Horizontal Grids

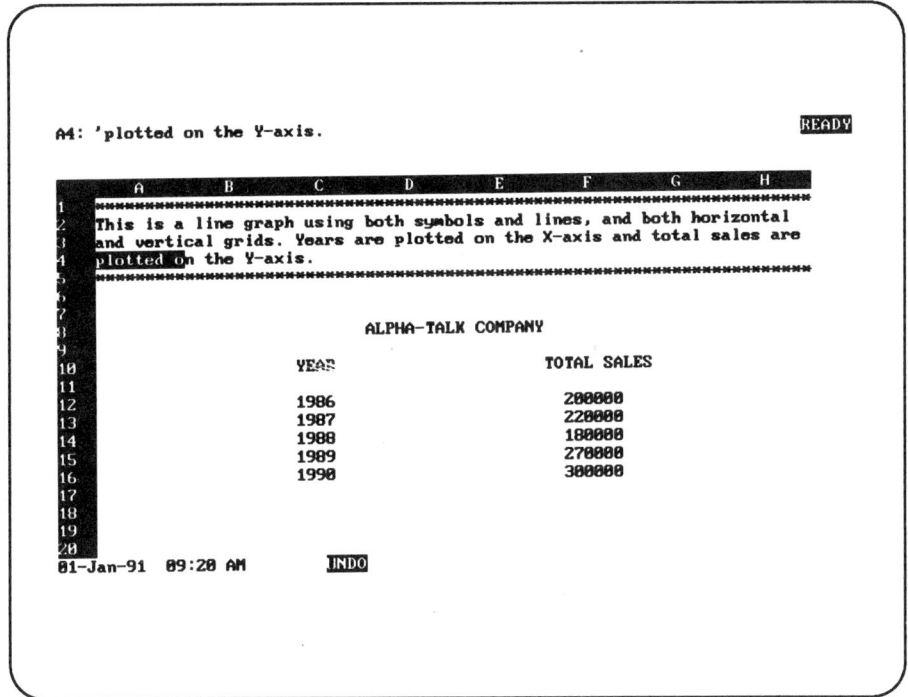

```
A4: 'plotted on the Y-axis.                                          READY

        A        B       C        D        E       F        G       H
1
2   This is a line graph using both symbols and lines, and both horizontal
3   and vertical grids. Years are plotted on the X-axis and total sales are
4   plotted on the Y-axis.
5
6
7
8                          ALPHA-TALK COMPANY
9
10             YEAR                         TOTAL SALES
11
12             1986                           200000
13             1987                           220000
14             1988                           180000
15             1989                           270000
16             1990                           300000
17
18
19
20
01-Jan-91   09:20 AM        UNDO
```

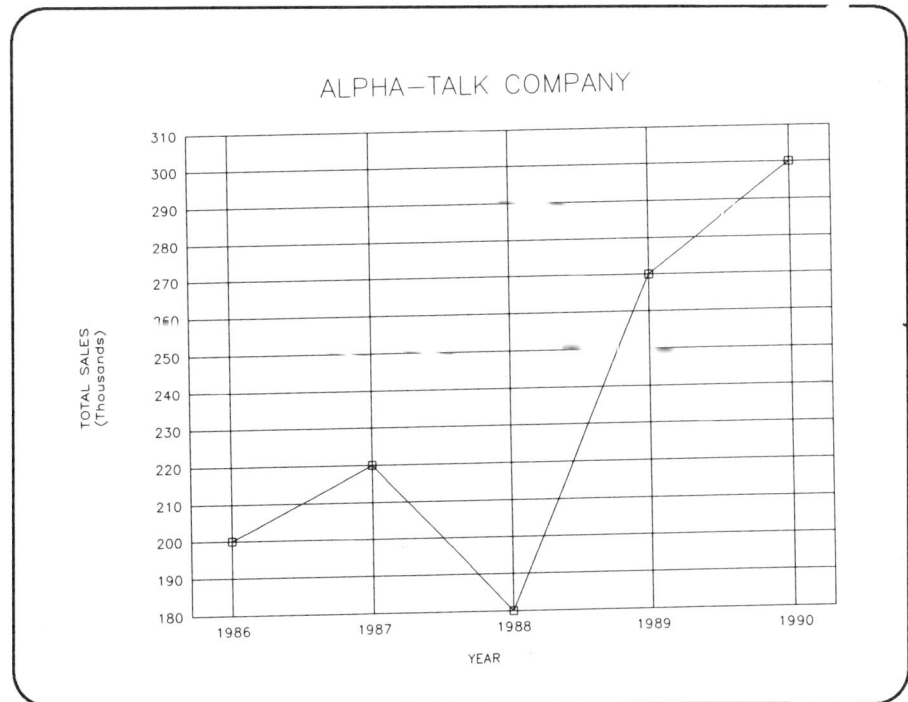

FIGURE 14-17 (Continued)

FIGURE 14-18 Line Graph with Symbols and Vertical and Horizontal Grids

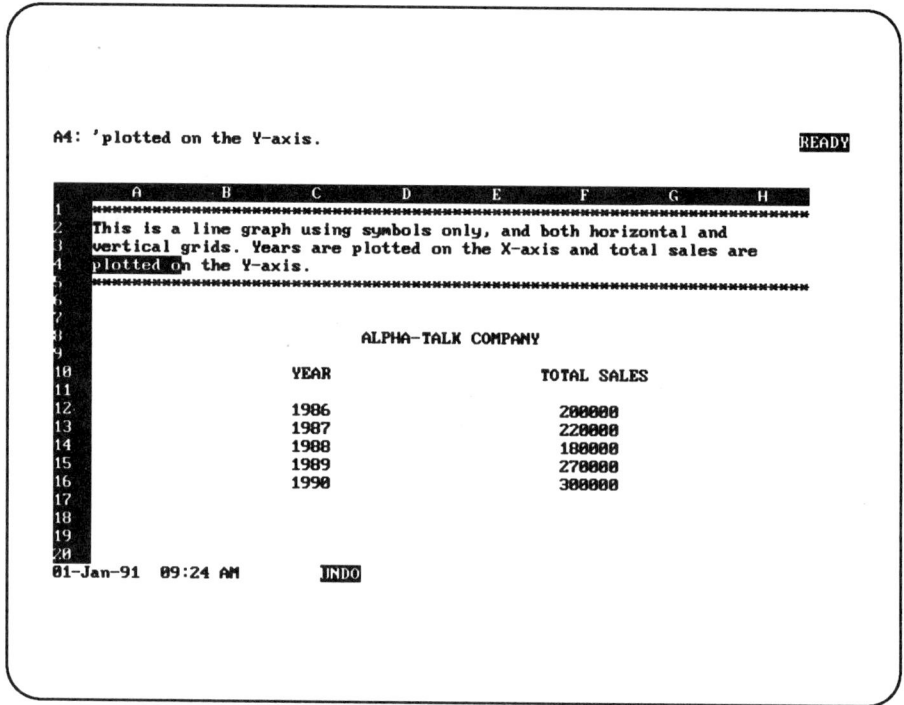

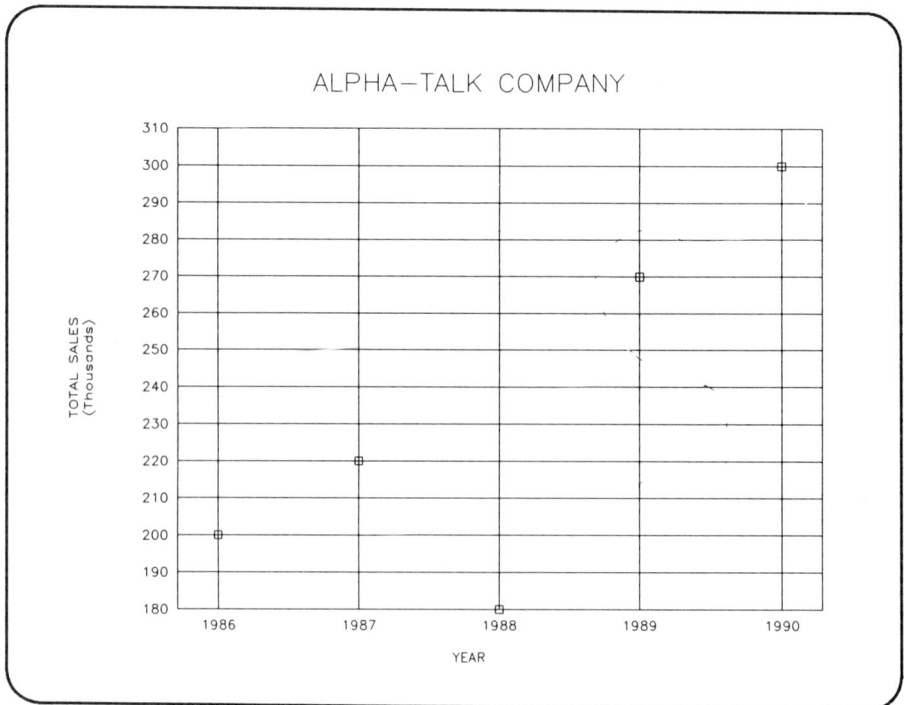

```
A4: 'plotted on the Y-axis.                                          READY

          A       B       C       D       E       F       G       H
1  ***********************************************************************
2  This is a line graph using symbols only, and both horizontal and
3  vertical grids. Years are plotted on the X-axis and total sales are
4  plotted on the Y-axis.
5  ***********************************************************************
6
7
8                            ALPHA-TALK COMPANY
9
10              YEAR                      TOTAL SALES
11
12              1986                        200000
13              1987                        220000
14              1988                        180000
15              1989                        270000
16              1990                        300000
17
18
19
20
01-Jan-91  09:24 AM         UNDO
```

FIGURE 14-18 (Continued)

FIGURE 14-19 Line Graph with Symbols Only

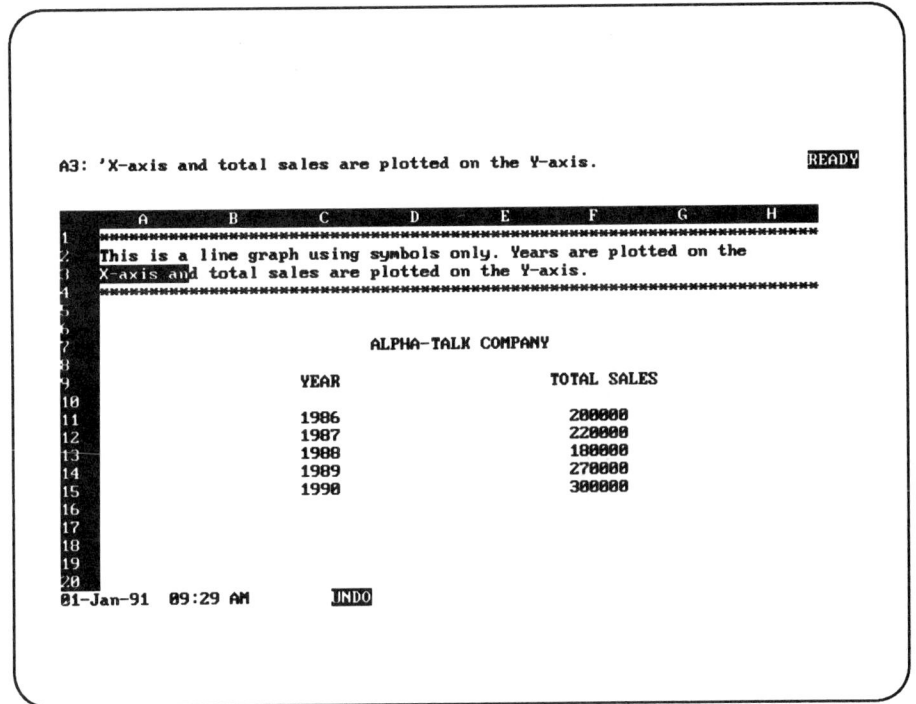

A3: 'X-axis and total sales are plotted on the Y-axis.   READY

```
        A        B        C        D        E        F        G        H
1  **********************************************************************
2  This is a line graph using symbols only. Years are plotted on the
3  X-axis and total sales are plotted on the Y-axis.
4  **********************************************************************
5
6
7                           ALPHA-TALK COMPANY
8
9            YEAR                        TOTAL SALES
10
11           1986                          200000
12           1987                          220000
13           1988                          180000
14           1989                          270000
15           1990                          300000
16
17
18
19
20
01-Jan-91  09:29 AM           UNDO
```

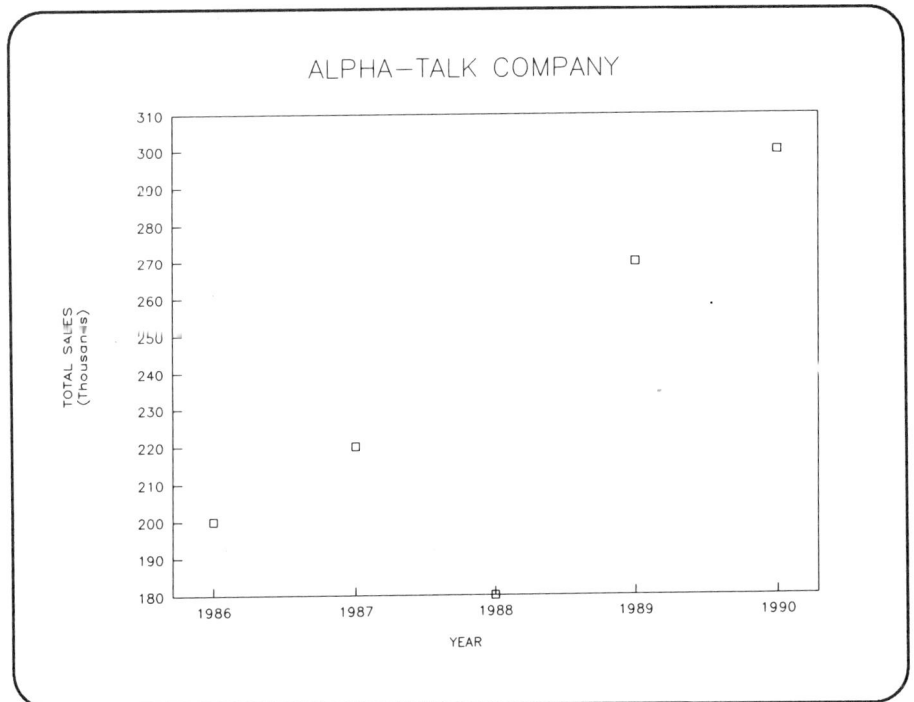

FIGURE 14-19 (Continued)

FIGURE 14-20 Line Graph of Advertising Budget without Skip Option

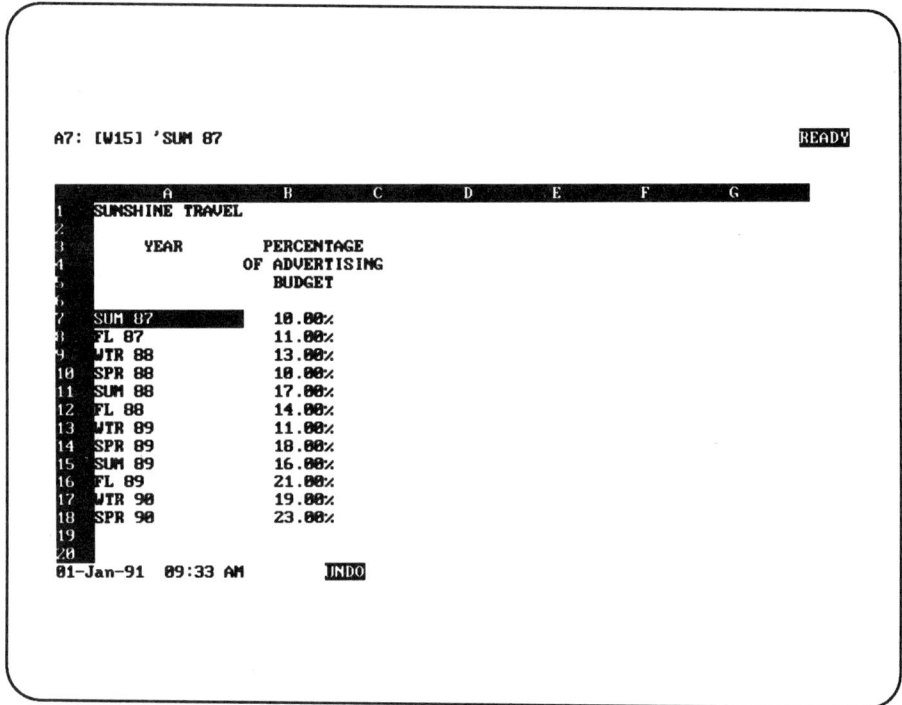

```
A7: [W15] 'SUM 87                                                    READY

        A              B          C          D          E         F         G
1 SUNSHINE TRAVEL
2
3        YEAR       PERCENTAGE
4                   OF ADVERTISING
5                   BUDGET
6
7 SUM 87            10.00%
8 FL 87             11.00%
9 WTR 88            13.00%
10 SPR 88           10.00%
11 SUM 88           17.00%
12 FL 88            14.00%
13 WTR 89           11.00%
14 SPR 89           18.00%
15 SUM 89           16.00%
16 FL 89            21.00%
17 WTR 90           19.00%
18 SPR 90           23.00%
19
20
01-Jan-91  09:33 AM           UNDO
```

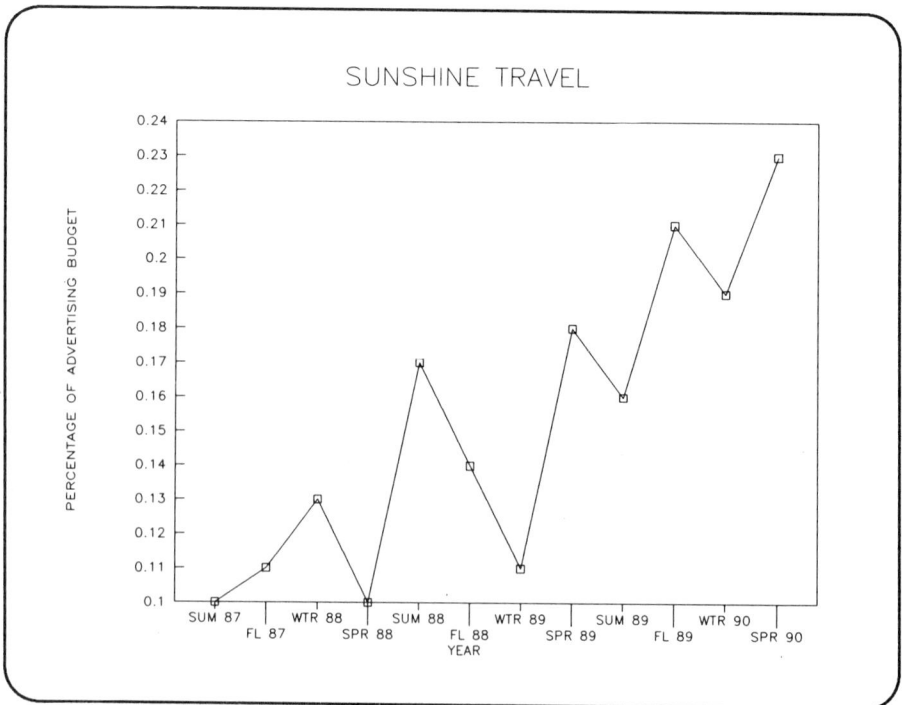

FIGURE 14-20 (Continued)

FIGURE 14-21 Line Graph of Advertising Budget with Skip Option

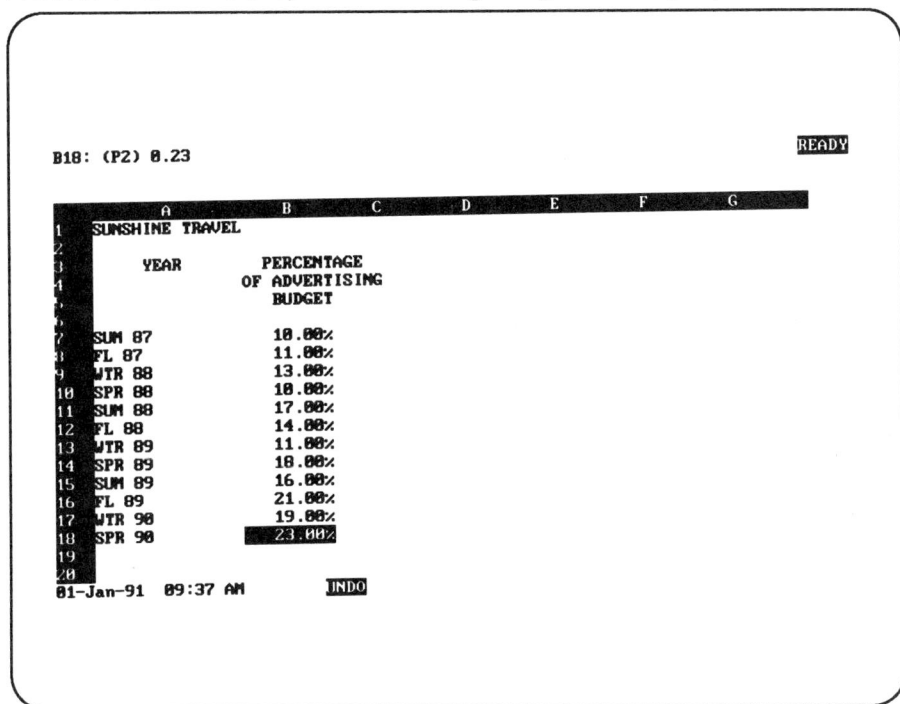

```
B18: (P2) 0.23                                                    READY

              A            B            C        D        E        F        G
 1  SUNSHINE TRAVEL
 2
 3           YEAR       PERCENTAGE
 4                     OF ADVERTISING
 5                        BUDGET
 6
 7  SUM 87               10.00%
 8  FL 87                11.00%
 9  WTR 88               13.00%
10  SPR 88               10.00%
11  SUM 88               17.00%
12  FL 88                14.00%
13  WTR 89               11.00%
14  SPR 89               18.00%
15  SUM 89               16.00%
16  FL 89                21.00%
17  WTR 90               19.00%
18  SPR 90               23.00%
19
20
01-Jan-91  09:37 AM        UNDO
```

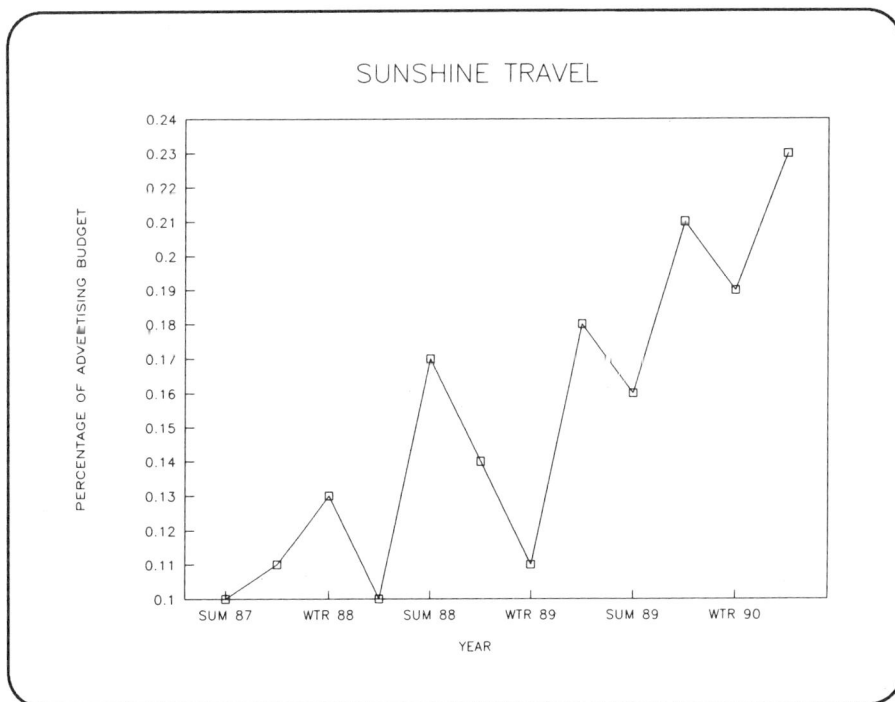

FIGURE 14-21 (Continued)

FIGURE 14-22 Comparative Sales Analysis of Two Divisions

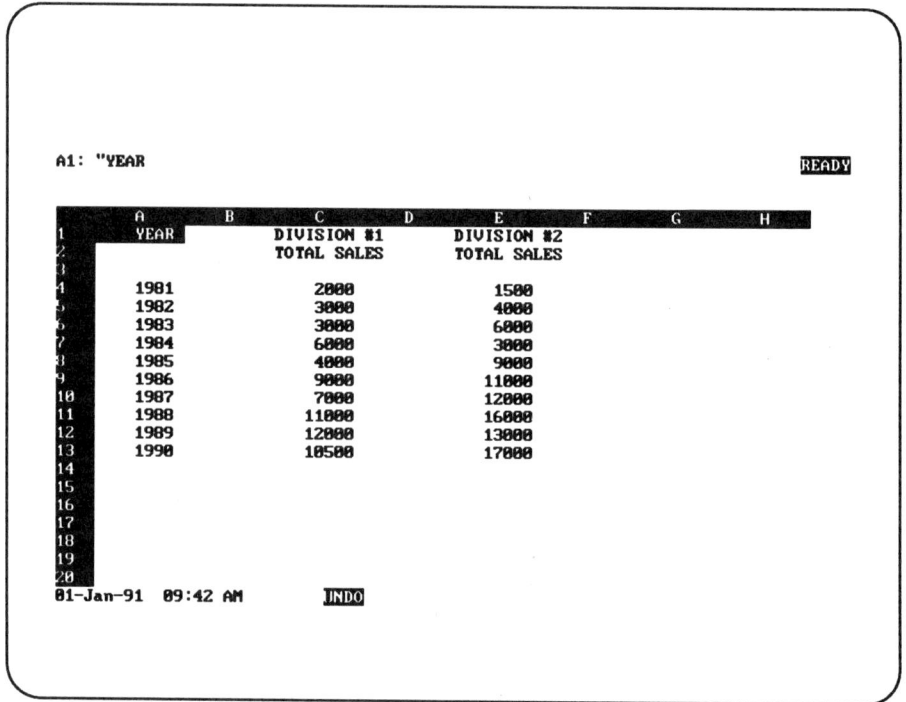

A1: "YEAR   READY

	A	B	C	D	E	F	G	H
1	YEAR		DIVISION #1		DIVISION #2			
2			TOTAL SALES		TOTAL SALES			
3								
4	1981		2000		1500			
5	1982		3000		4000			
6	1983		3000		6000			
7	1984		6000		3000			
8	1985		4000		9000			
9	1986		9000		11000			
10	1987		7000		12000			
11	1988		11000		16000			
12	1989		12000		13000			
13	1990		10500		17000			

01-Jan-91 09:42 AM   UNDO

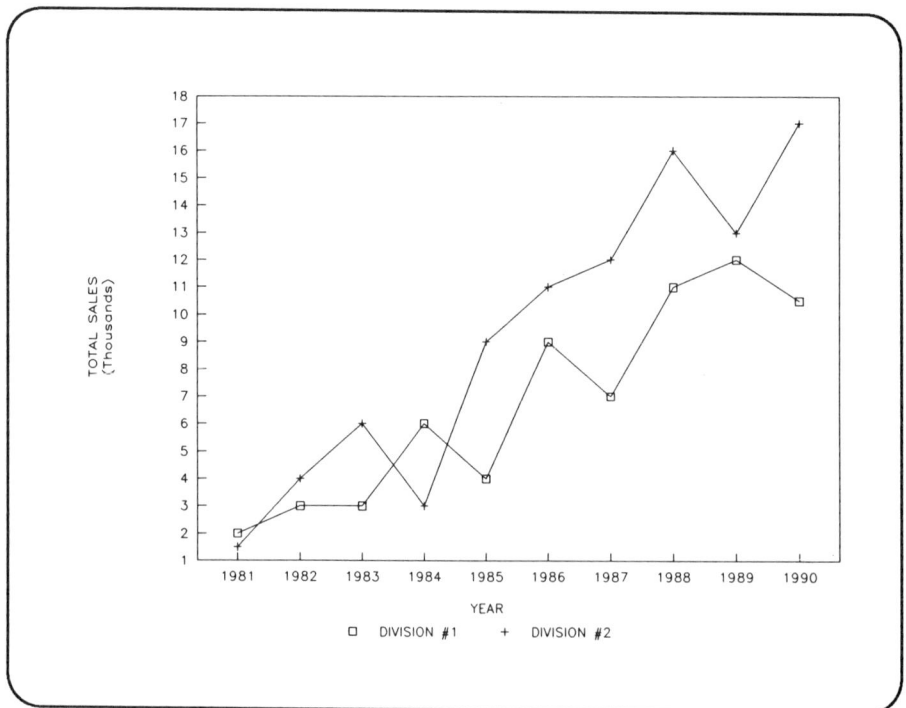

FIGURE 14-22 (Continued)

FIGURE 14-23 *Total Budget for Advertising Using Data Labels*

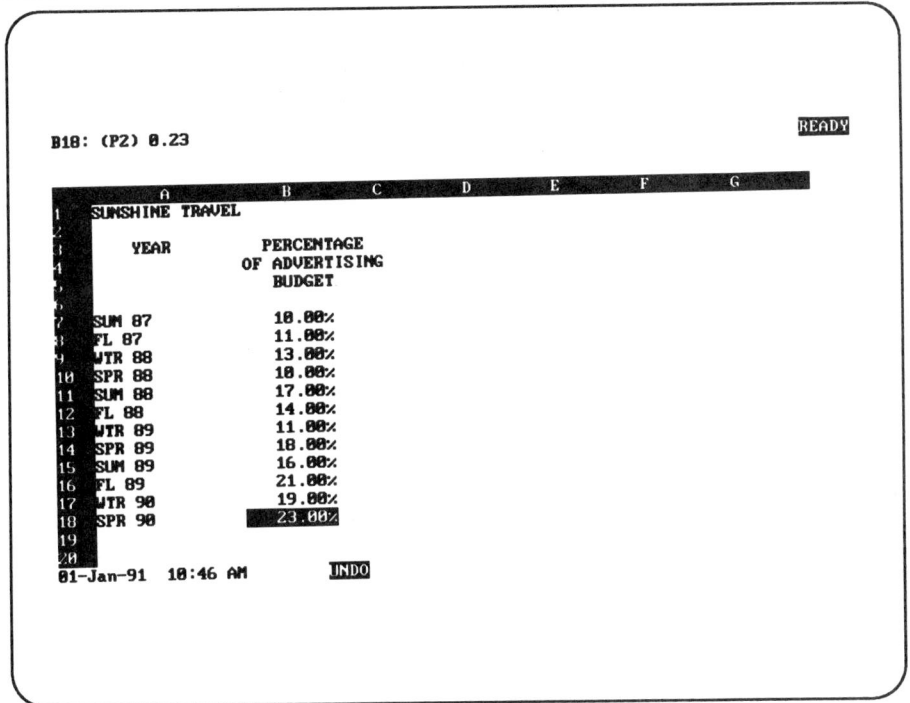

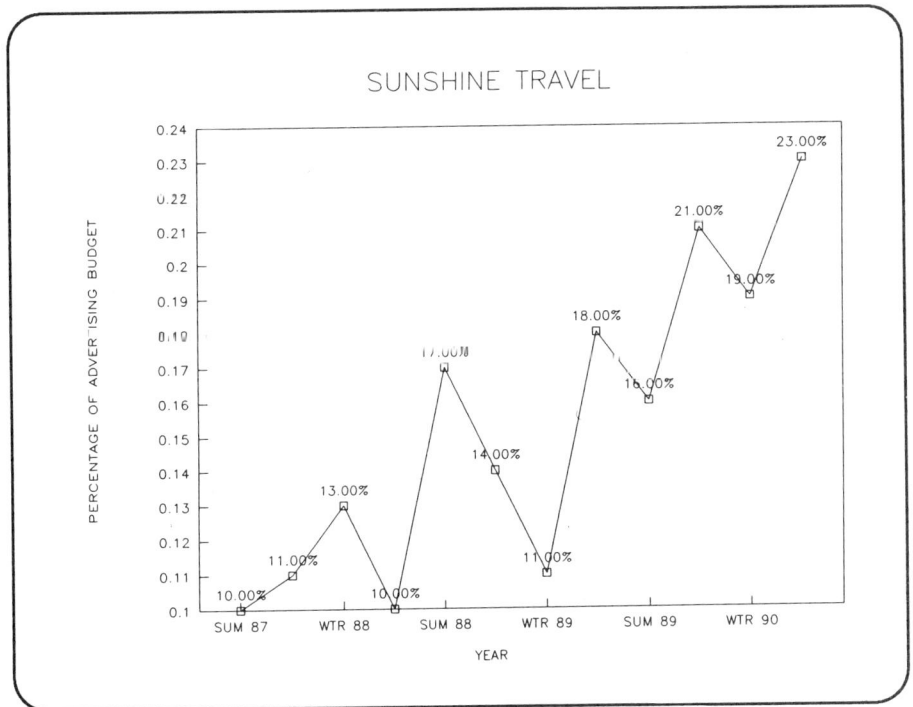

FIGURE 14-23 (Continued)

graph was generated as follows:

/Graph, Type, Line, X (A7..A18), **Return**, A (B7..B18), **Return**, Options, Format, Graph, Both, Quit, Titles, First, SUNSHINE TRAVEL, **Return**, Titles, X-Axis, YEAR, **Return**, Titles, Y-Axis, PERCENTAGE OF ADVERTISING BUDGET, **Return**, Data-Labels, A (B7..B18), **Return**, Above, Quit, Scale, Skip, 2, **Return**, Quit, View.

14-11 Stacked-Bar Graphs

In a stacked-bar graph, Lotus displays the corresponding value from each data range stacked on the top of the preceding data item in each bar. You can build a stacked-bar graph with six corresponding data items on the top of each other. Shadings or colors represent each data item. When you define your data ranges, A corresponds to the lowest and F corresponds to the highest. As usual, the X range is used for data labels on the X-Axis.

Figure 14-24 illustrates an example of the stacked-bar graph. The performance of each salesperson in the three regions is displayed with the regions stacked on top of each other. The first bar shows Brent's performance in Portland (the bottom portion), Denver (the middle), and Los Angeles (the top). This graph is generated as follows:

/Graph, Type, Stacked-Bar, X (B11..D11), **Return**, A (B12..D12), **Return**, B (B13..D13), **Return**, C (B14..D14), **Return**, Options, Legend, A (\A12), **Return**, Legend, B (\A13), **Return**, Legend, C (\A14), **Return**, Titles, First, COMPARATIVE SALES, **Return**, Titles, X-Axis, SALESMEN, **Return**, Titles, Y-Axis, SALES, **Return**, Quit, View.

Figure 14-25 is a different version of Figure 14-24. The performance of each salesperson in the same region is compared with the performances of the other salespeople. The first bar from the left shows Brent's performance (the bottom portion) compared with Matthew and Timothy in Portland. This graph is generated as follows:

/Graph, Type, Stacked-Bar, X (A12..A14), **Return**, A (B12..B14), **Return**, B (C12..C14), **Return**, C (D12..D14), **Return**, Options, Legend, A (\B11), **Return**, Legend, B (\C11), **Return**, Legend, C (\D11), **Return**, Titles, First, COMPARATIVE SALES, **Return**, Titles, X-Axis, REGION, **Return**, Titles, Y-Axis, SALES, **Return**, Quit, View.

Figure 14-26 is another example of a stacked-bar graph. Here we have used manual scaling. This figure was generated as follows:

/Graph, Type, Stacked-Bar, X (B11..D11), **Return**, A (B12..D12), **Return**, B (B13..D13), **Return**, C (B14..D14), **Return**, Options, Legend, A (\A12), **Return**, Legend, B (\A13), **Return**, Legend, C (\A14), **Return**, Titles, First, COMPARATIVE SALES, **Return**, Titles, X-Axis, SALESMEN, **Return**, Titles, Y-Axis, SALES, **Return**, Scale, Y-Scale, Manual, Lower (-1000), **Return**, Upper (4000), **Return**, Quit, Quit, View.

14-12 XY Graph

In an XY graph, Lotus pairs each value from the X data range with the corresponding data from each of the A-F ranges to plot the graph. You can generate up to six data ranges in a XY graph. Lotus uses different symbols to show each distinct range. Figure 14-27 is one example of an XY graph. Total sales are shown on the Y-Axis and advertising on the X-Axis. Remember, in an XY graph, one of your data ranges must be the X range. In a line graph there is no restriction in choosing a data range. This is the major difference between a line graph and an XY graph. Also in an XY graph you must have at least two data ranges to plot a graph such as X and A, X and B and so on. In a line graph, one set of data is enough to plot on a graph. We have used both lines and symbols. This was generated as follows:

FIGURE 14-24 Comparative Sales in Three Regions using Stacked-Bar

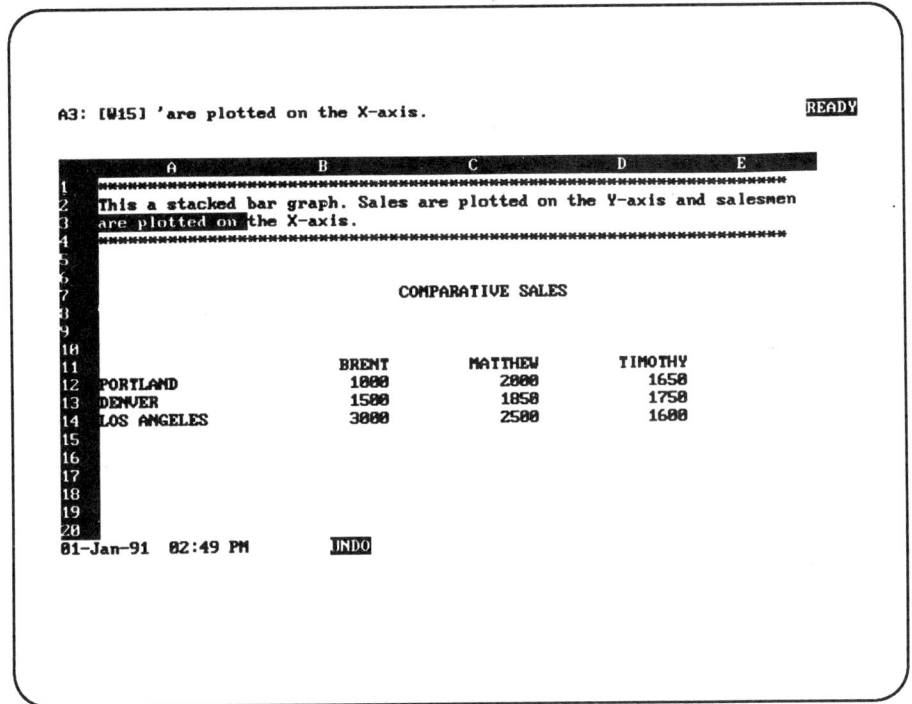

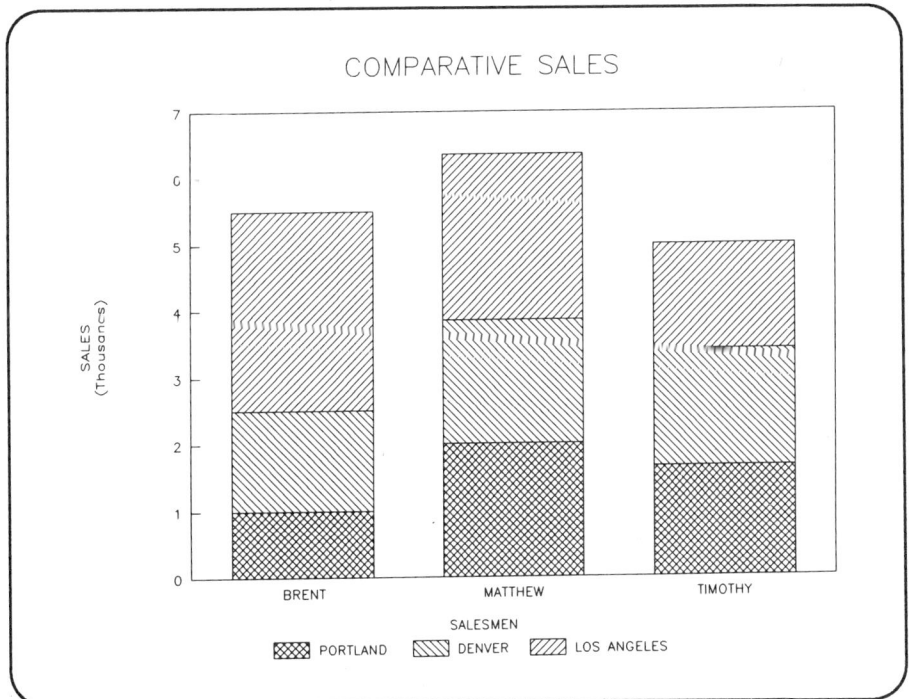

```
A3: [W15] 'are plotted on the X-axis.                                    READY

          A              B              C              D              E
     ***********************************************************************
1    This a stacked bar graph. Sales are plotted on the Y-axis and salesmen
2    are plotted on the X-axis.
3
4    ***********************************************************************
5
6
7                             COMPARATIVE SALES
8
9
10
11                        BRENT          MATTHEW        TIMOTHY
12   PORTLAND             1000           2000           1650
13   DENVER               1500           1850           1750
14   LOS ANGELES          3000           2500           1600
15
16
17
18
19
20
01-Jan-91  02:49 PM          UNDO
```

FIGURE 14-24 (Continued)

FIGURE 14-25 *Comparative Sales for Three Salesmen in Three Regions, using Stacked-Bar*

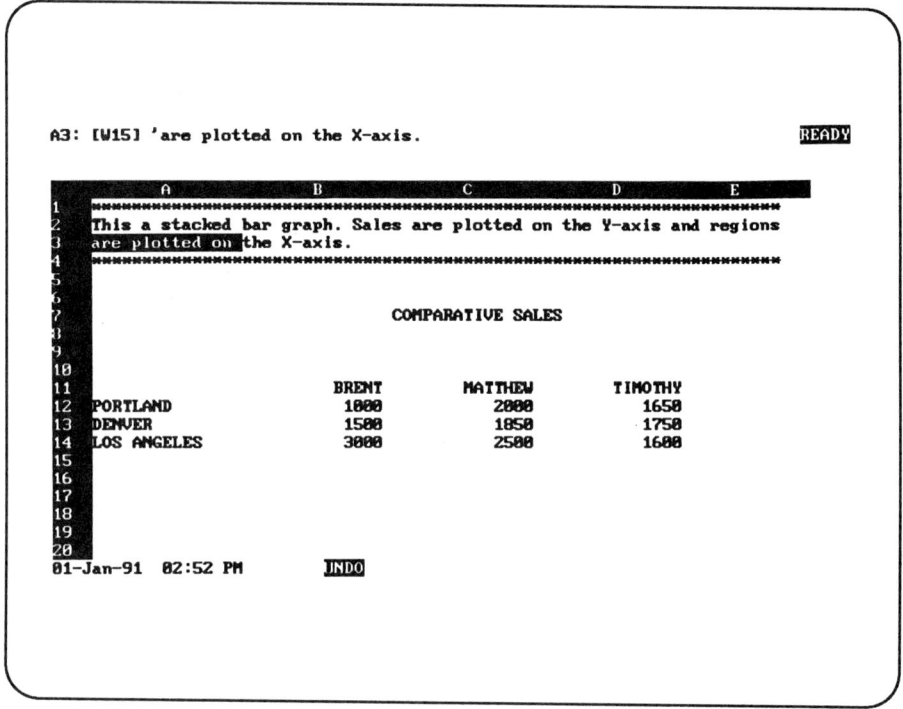

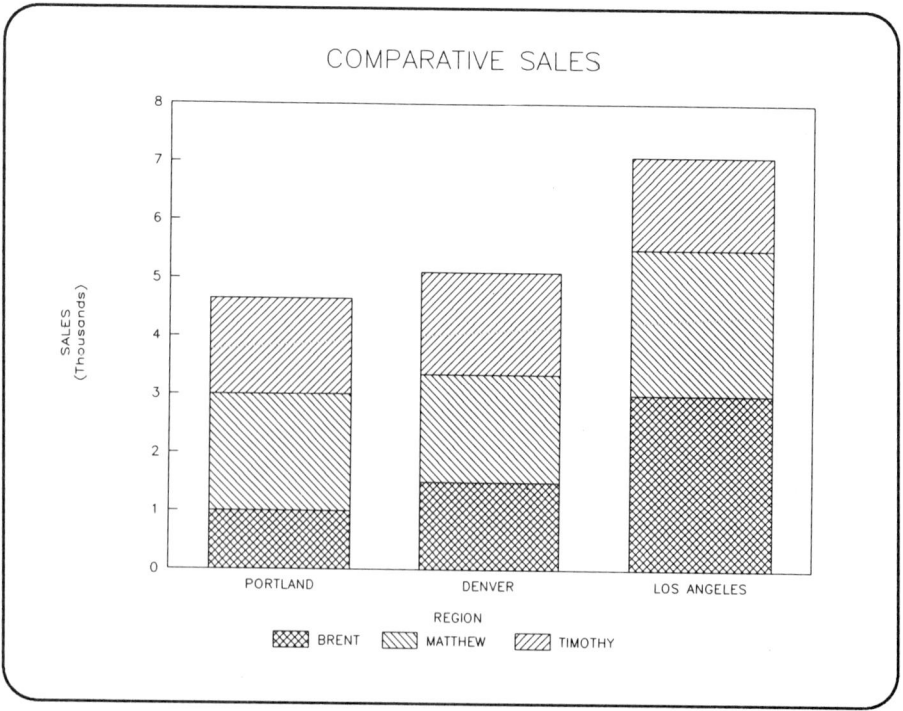

```
A3: [W15] 'are plotted on the X-axis.                              READY

        A              B            C            D            E
1  ****************************************************************
2  This a stacked bar graph. Sales are plotted on the Y-axis and regions
3  are plotted on the X-axis.
4  ****************************************************************
5
6
7                         COMPARATIVE SALES
8
9
10
11                     BRENT        MATTHEW      TIMOTHY
12 PORTLAND            1000         2000         1650
13 DENVER              1500         1050         1750
14 LOS ANGELES         3000         2500         1600
15
16
17
18
19
20
01-Jan-91  02:52 PM       UNDO
```

FIGURE 14-25 *(Continued)*

FIGURE 14-26   *Sales Analysis Using Stacked-Bar with Manual Scaling*

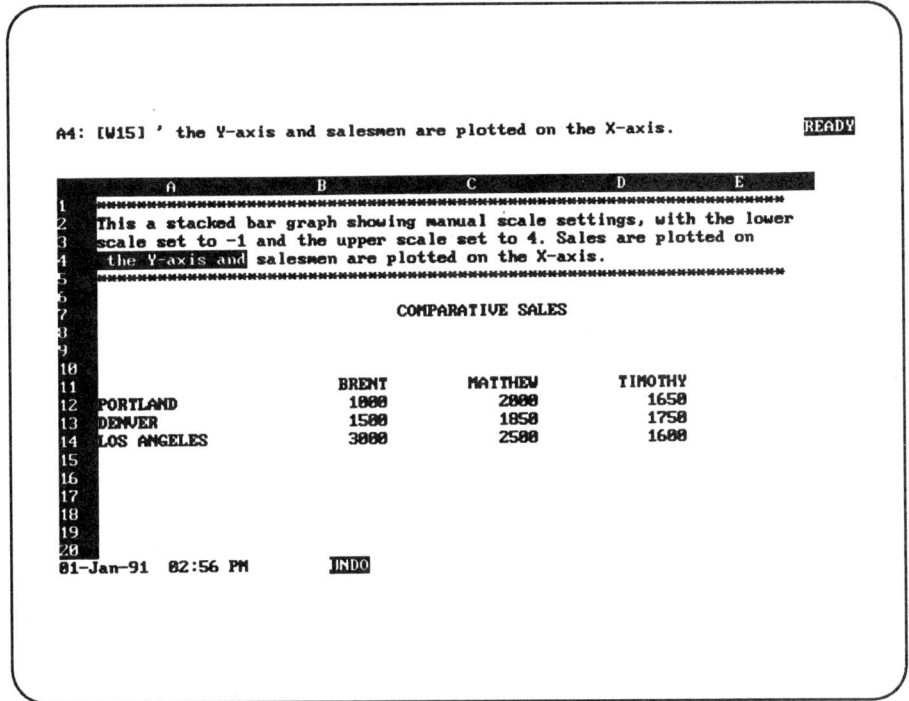

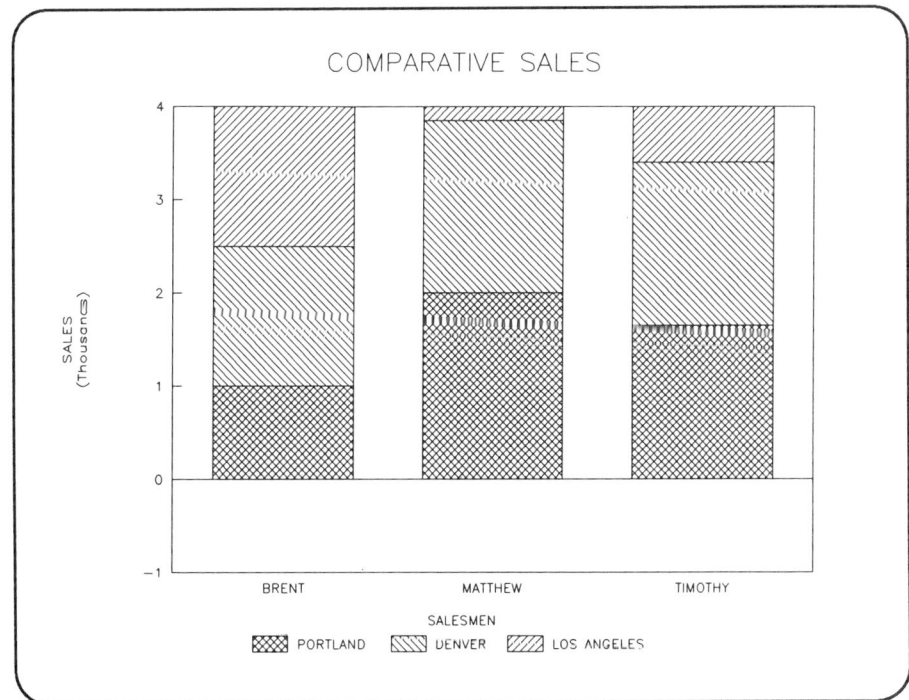

A4: [W15] ' the Y-axis and salesmen are plotted on the X-axis.   READY

	A	B	C	D	E
1					
2	This a stacked bar graph showing manual scale settings, with the lower				
3	scale set to -1 and the upper scale set to 4. Sales are plotted on				
4	the Y-axis and salesmen are plotted on the X-axis.				

COMPARATIVE SALES

	BRENT	MATTHEW	TIMOTHY
PORTLAND	1000	2000	1650
DENVER	1500	1850	1750
LOS ANGELES	3000	2500	1600

01-Jan-91 02:56 PM   UNDO

FIGURE 14-26   (Continued)

FIGURE 14-27 XY Graph for Total Sales and Advertising

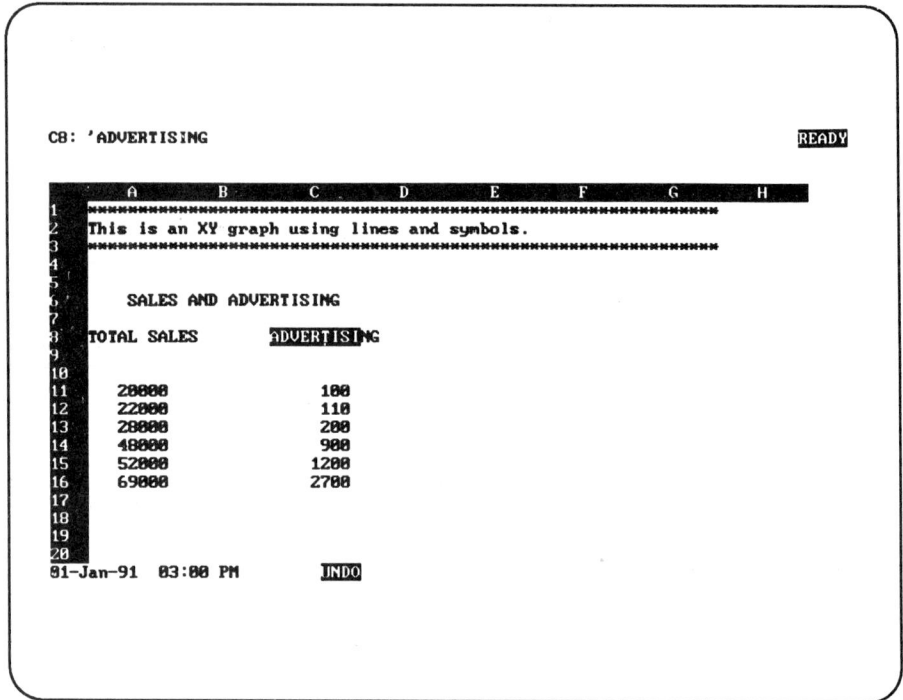

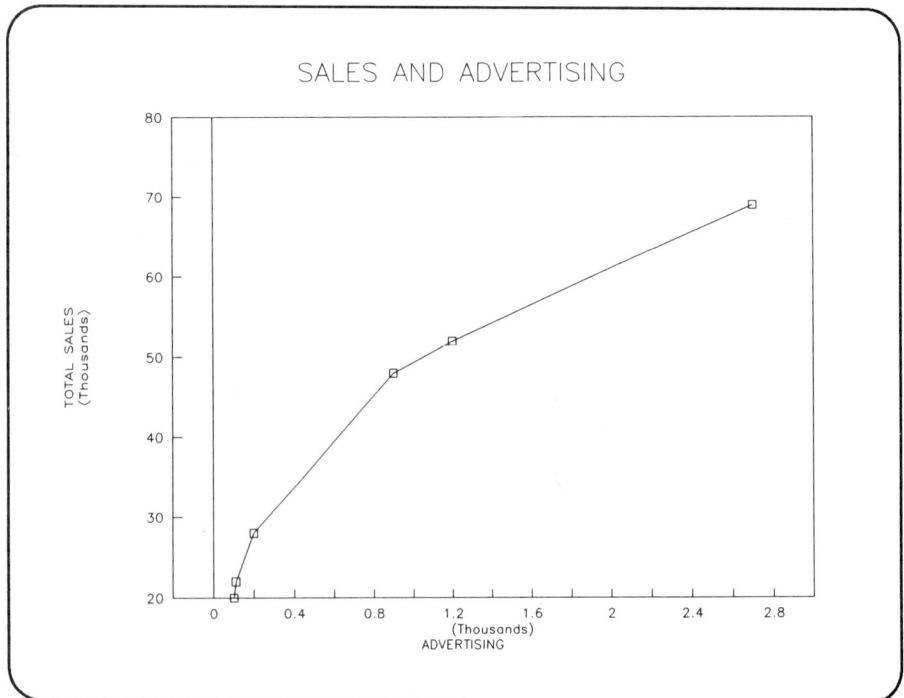

```
C8: 'ADVERTISING                                              READY

        A        B        C        D        E        F        G        H
1  *************************************************************************
2  This is an XY graph using lines and symbols.
3  *************************************************************************
4
5
6        SALES AND ADVERTISING
7
8  TOTAL SALES        ADVERTISING
9
10
11      20000               100
12      22000               110
13      28000               200
14      48000               900
15      52000              1200
16      69000              2700
17
18
19
20
01-Jan-91  03:00 PM        UNDO
```

FIGURE 14-27 (Continued)

/Graph, Type, XY, X (C11..C16), **Return**, A (A11..A16), **Return**, Options, Titles, First, SALES AND ADVERTISING, **Return**, Titles, X-Axis, ADVERTISING, **Return**, Titles, Y-Axis, TOTAL SALES, **Return**, Format, Graph, Both, Quit, Quit, View.

14-13 /Graph Group Command

Using the /Graph Group command you can specify all graph data ranges (X and A–F) at once, when the X and A–F data ranges are in consecutive columns or rows of a worksheet. When you invoke /Graph Group, 1-2-3 asks you to specify the group range. This group range will be divided columnwise or rowwise.

1-2-3 Uses the first column or row of the group range as the X data range and subsequent columns or rows as the A–F data ranges. If you have more than seven rows or columns, 1-2-3 ignores the excessive data. Figure 14-28 has been created by using the /Graph Group command as follows:

/Graph, Group, B11..D14, Rowwise, Type, Bar, Options, Titles, First, COMPARA-TIVE SALES, **Return**, Titles, Second, FOR THE HAPPY TRAVELER, **Return**, Titles, X-Axis, **Return**, REGION, Return, Titles, Y-Axis, **Return**, SALES, **Return**, Legend, A(\B10), **Return**, Legend, B (\C10), **Return**, Legend, C(\D10), **Return**, Quit, View

The /Graph Name Table command provides a listing of all the named graphs in the worksheet. It occupies three columns including graph name, type, and the first title. Remember to direct the output of this command to an empty area of the worksheet, otherwise the output may overwrite some of your existing data.

To take full advantage of the /Group command you must make sure that the data in your worksheet is set up in the proper format. This means that you should not include any blank rows or columns in the data range and that the data should be arranged in the order you want it graphed.

You can also use the /Group command with data labels and legends or when you reset graph settings. To choose data labels in a group, invoke /Graph Options Data-Labels Group and then specify the range that includes the data labels. After selecting the range you must select either columnwise or rowwise. When you select one of these options, as usual you will be prompted by the following menu:

Center   Left   Above   Right   Below

Legends can also be selected by using the /Group command. To do so select /Graph Options Legend Range, then specify the desired range.

14-14 Miscellaneous

We have not talked about the color option yet. If you have access to color graphics, you will be able to create pleasant looking graphs in different colors both on screen and in print. The /Graph Options Color command provides this facility. This command displays data range bars, graph lines, and symbols in different colors only if your monitor is capable of displaying color graphics.

/Graph Options B&W displays data ranges in contrasting monochrome crosshatches. You should use /Graph Options B&W *only* if you have previously selected /Graph Options Color and want to return to a monochrome display.

Graphics: Converting Figures into Pictures   229

FIGURE 14-28 A Sample Worksheet

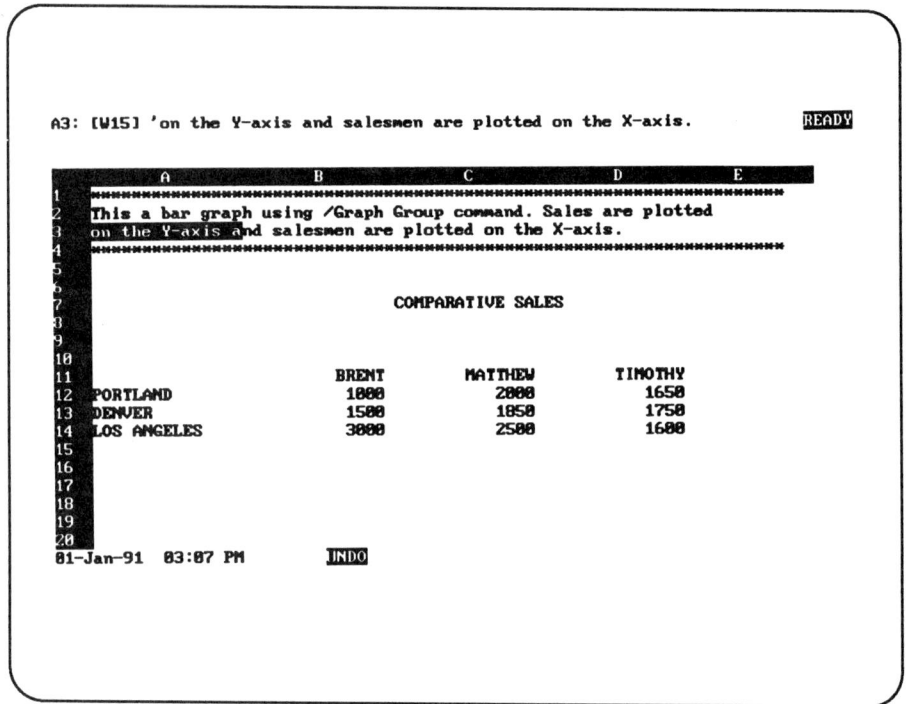

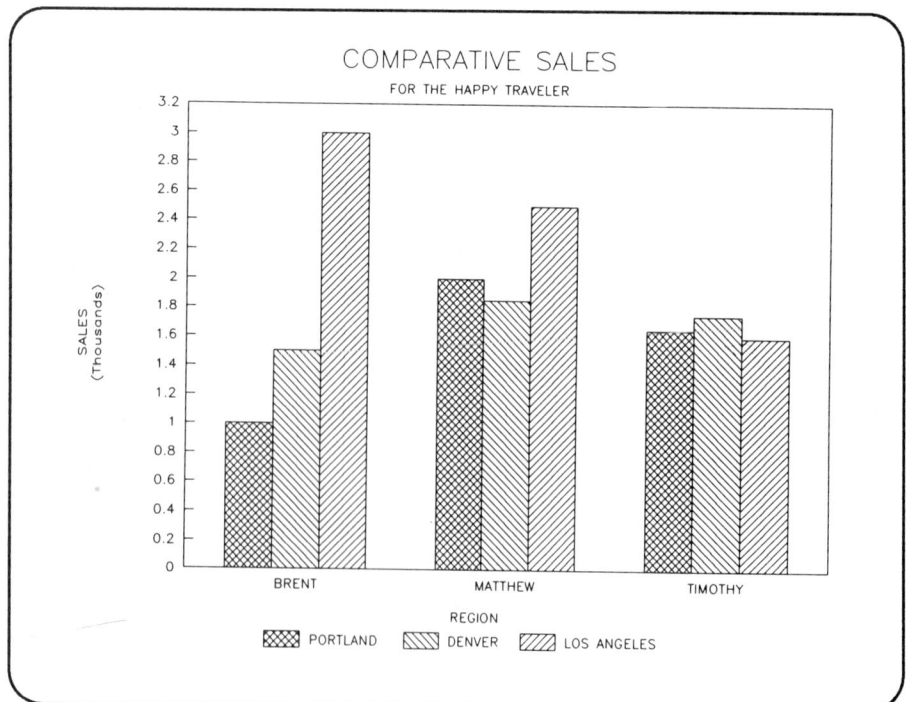

```
A3: [W15] 'on the Y-axis and salesmen are plotted on the X-axis.        READY

        A            B            C            D            E
1  ===============================================================
2  This a bar graph using /Graph Group command. Sales are plotted
3  on the Y-axis and salesmen are plotted on the X-axis.
4  ===============================================================
5
6
7                    COMPARATIVE SALES
8
9
10
11                   BRENT       MATTHEW      TIMOTHY
12 PORTLAND          1000        2000         1650
13 DENVER            1500        1850         1750
14 LOS ANGELES       3000        2500         1600
15
16
17
18
19
20
01-Jan-91  03:07 PM        UNDO
```

COMPARATIVE SALES
FOR THE HAPPY TRAVELER

FIGURE 14-28 (Continued)

If you have a color monitor, you can view your graph in color by selecting /Graph Options Color. Remember, if you can view (but not print) your graphs in color, restore the B&W (black and white) setting by choosing /Graph Options B&W before you save your graphs. Otherwise, each data range in the graph will be printed in all black.

14-15 A Comprehensive Model

To wrap up this chapter we have presented a comprehensive model for Happy Traveler Merchant. A portion of an income statement is presented in Figure 14-29. The following eight graphs (presented in Figures 14-30-1 through 14-30-8) will be illustrated:

1. A pie chart with crosshatches for total expense (in five groups).
2. A stacked-bar graph for six months of five expenses. The X-Axis shows months and the Y-Axis shows total expense.
3. A bar graph with multiple ranges; on the X-Axis different months, on the Y-Axis the total of different expenses.
4. An XY graph with symbols and data labels. This graph displays total revenue vs. total expense.
5. A line graph of five different expenses over time using different symbols.
6. A simple bar chart for total monthly expenses.
7. An exploded pie chart for total revenue of six different months.
8. A line graph like the one in Figure 14-30-5, but with horizontal and vertical grids.

I8: [W7] 'crosshatches READY

	A	B	C	D	E	F	G	H	I
1									
2				HAPPY TRAVELER MERCHANT					
3									
4		JAN	FEB	MAR	APR	MAY	JUNE	TOTAL	
5									
6	SALES	$2,000	$2,100	$1,900	$1,750	$2,200	$2,500	$12,450	
7									Code for
8	EXPENSES								crosshatches
9	Raw Mat.	600	650	590	550	600	700	3690	1
10	Labor	300	275	310	280	310	375	1850	2
11	Rent	150	175	140	120	150	200	935	3
12	Electric	75	100	95	100	145	165	680	4
13	Advert.	50	65	70	75	100	150	510	5
14									
15	Total Exp.	1175	1265	1205	1125	1305	1590	7665	
16									
17	Total Pro.	$825	$835	$695	$625	$895	$910	$4,785	
18									
19	Code for								
20	exploded Pie chart			101	102	103	104	105	106

01-Jan-91 03:11 PM UNDO

FIGURE 14-29 A Partial Income Statement for Happy Traveler Merchant

FIGURE 14-30-1 Happy Traveler Merchant in Action

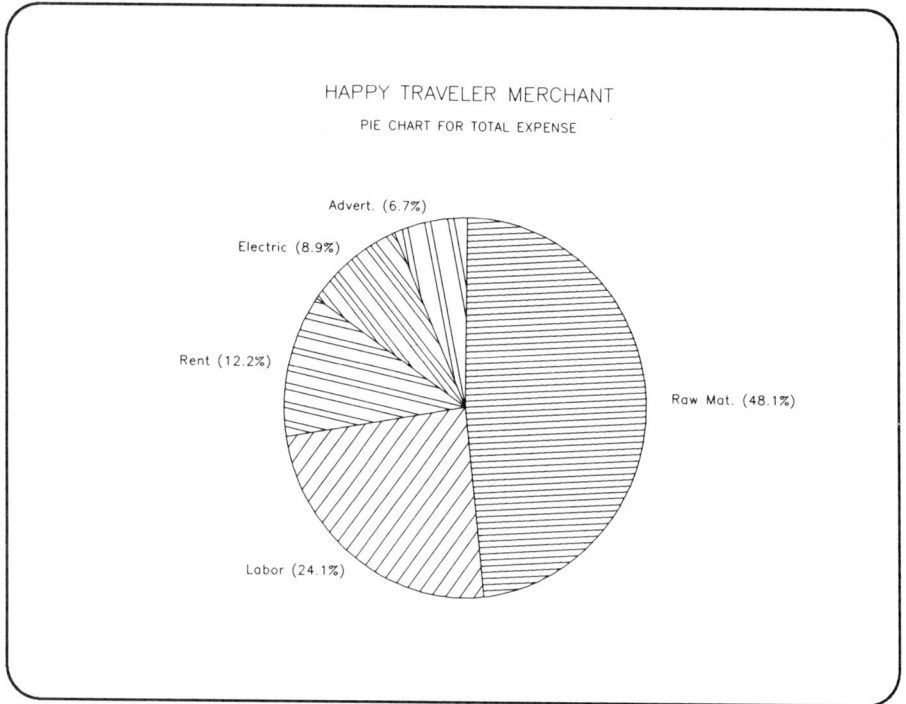

```
/Graph Type Pie
    X   A9. .A13      Return
    A   H9. .H13      Return
    B   I9. .I13      Return
    Options Titles First  "HAPPY TRAVELER MERCHANT" Return
            Titles Second  "PIE CHART FOR TOTAL EXPENSE" Return
            Quit

    View
```

FIGURE 14-30-1 (Continued)

FIGURE 14-30-2

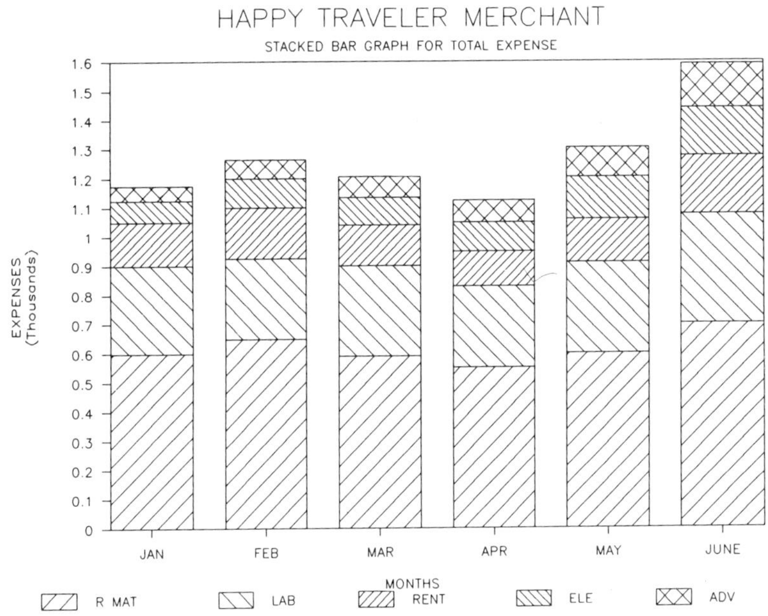

HAPPY TRAVELER MERCHANT
STACKED BAR GRAPH FOR TOTAL EXPENSE

EXPENSES (Thousands)

MONTHS

R MAT   LAB   RENT   ELE   ADV

/Graph Type Stacked-Bar
  X   B4. .G4 Return
  A   B9. .G9 Return
  B   B10. .G10 Return
  C   B11. .G11 Return
  D   B12. .G12 Return
  E   B13. .G13 Return

  Options Legend A   "R MAT" Return
          Legend B   "LAB" Return
          Legend C   "RENT" Return
          Legend D   "ELE" Return
          Legend E   "ADV" Return
          Titles First   "HAPPY TRAVELER MERCHANG" Return
          Titles Second   "STACKED BAR GRAPH FOR TOTAL EXPENSE"
                    Return
          Titles X-axis   "MONTHS" Return
          Titles Y-axis"EXPENSES" Return
    Quit

  View

FIGURE 14-30-2 (Continued)

FIGURE 14-30-3

HAPPY TRAVELER MERCHANT
BAR GRAPH FOR TOTAL EXPENSE

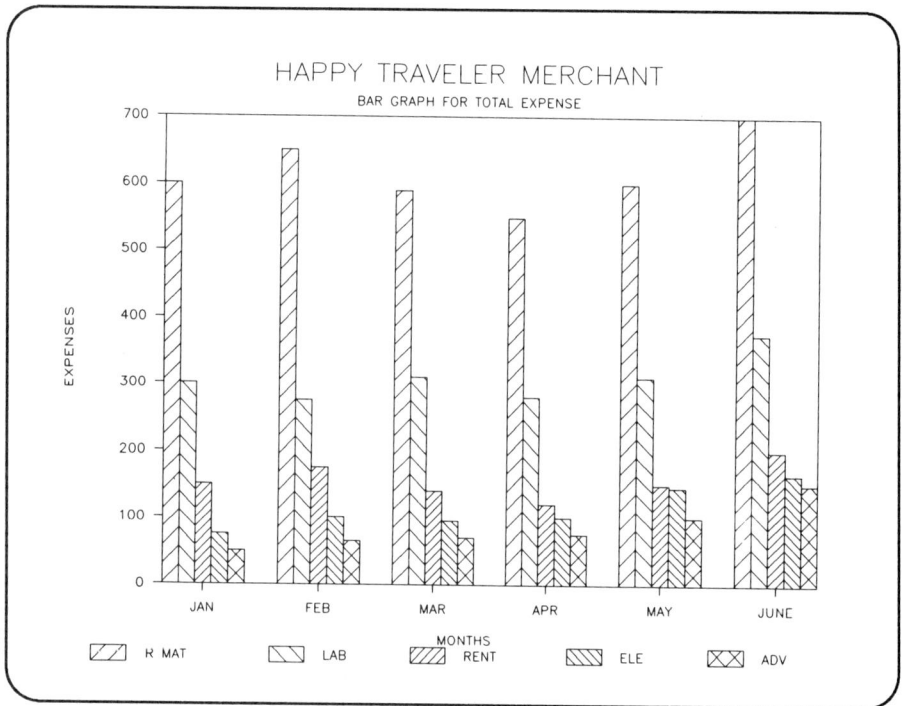

```
/Graph Type Bar
   X   B4. .G4 Return
   A   B9. .G9 Return
   B   B10. .G10   Return
   C   B11. .G11   Return
   D   B12. .G12   Return
   E   B13. .G13   Return

Options Legend A     "R MAT"  Return
        Legend B     "LAB"  Return
        Legend C     "RENT"  Return
        Legend D     "ELE"  Return
        Legend E     "ADV"  Return
        Titles First  "HAPPY TRAVELER MERCHANT"  Return
        Titles Second    "BAR GRAPH FOR TOTAL EXPENSE"  Return
        Titles X-axis    "MONTHS"  Return
        Ttitles Y-axis    "EXPENSES"  Return
     Quit

   View
```

FIGURE 14-30-3 (Continued)

FIGURE 14-30-4

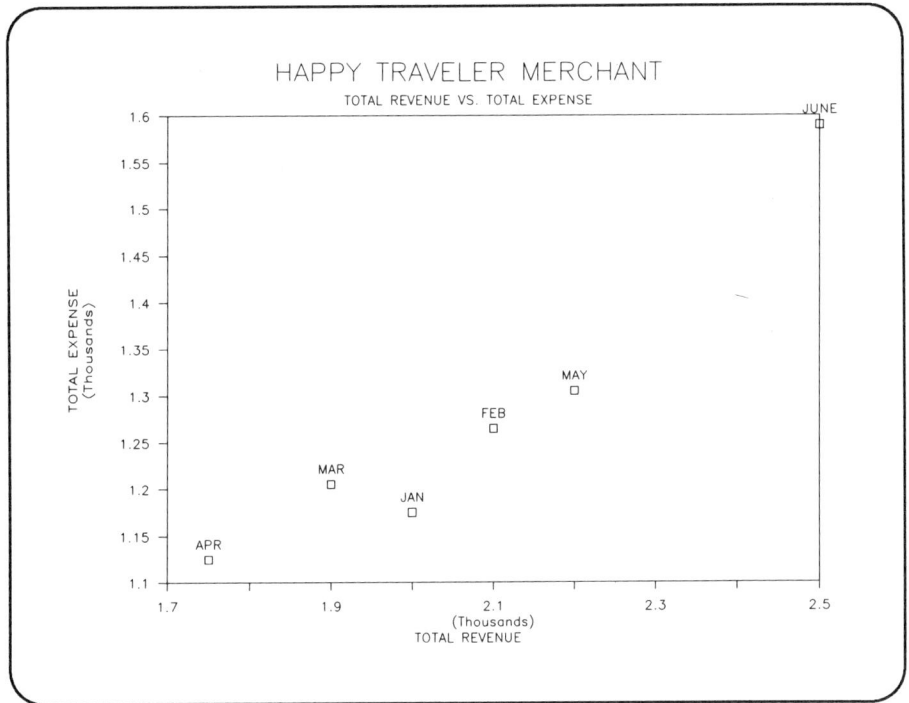

HAPPY TRAVELER MERCHANT
TOTAL REVENUE VS. TOTAL EXPENSE

/Graph Type XY

X   B6. .G6 Return
A   B15. .G15 Return

Options Format A Symbols
              Quit
        Titles First "HAPPY TRAVELER MERCHANT" Return
        Titles Second "TOTAL REVENUE VS. TOTAL EXPENSE"
                Return
        Titles X-axis "TOTAL REVENUE" Return
        Titles Y-aaxis "TOTAL REXPENSE" Return
        Data labels A B4. .G4 Return Above
                    Quit
        Quit

View

FIGURE 30-4 (Continued)

FIGURE 14-30-5

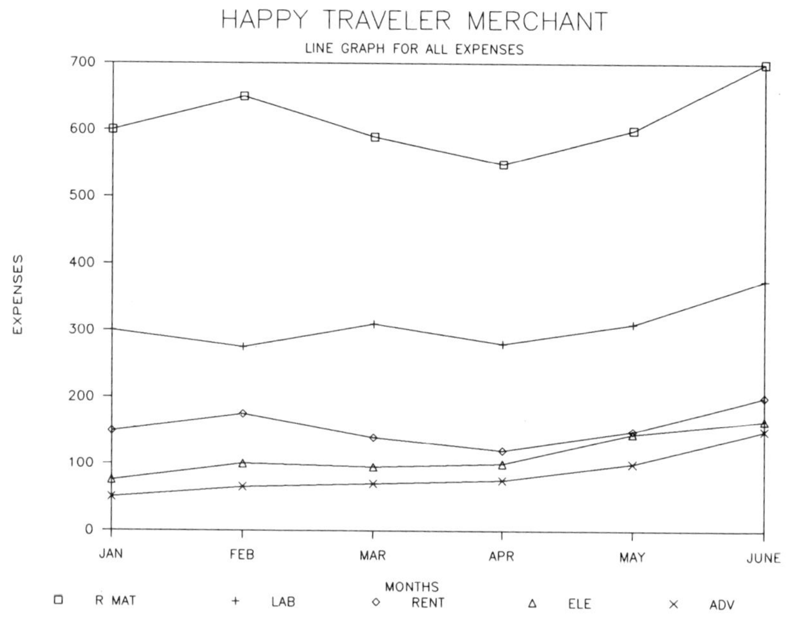

FIGURE 14-30-5 (Continued)

FIGURE 14-30-5

HAPPY TRAVELER MERCHANT
LINE GRAPH FOR ALL EXPENSES

EXPENSES

700

600

500

400

300

200

100

0

JAN   FEB   MAR   APR   MAY   JUNE

MONTHS

□ R MAT   + LAB   ◇ RENT   △ ELE   × ADV

/Graph Type Line
    X   B4. .G4 Return
    A   B9. .G9 Return
    B   B10. .G10 Return
    C   B11. .G11 Return
    D   B12. .G12 Return
    E   B13. .G13 Return

Options Legend A   "R MAT" Return
        Legend B   "LAB" Return
        Legend C   "RENT" Return
        Legend D   "ELE" Return
        Legend E   "ADV" Return
        Titles First   "HAPPY TRAVELER MERCHANT" Return
        Titles Second   "LINE GRAPH FOR ALL EXPENSES" Return
        Titles X-axis   "MONTHS" Return
        Titles Y-axis "EXPENSES" Return
        Quit

    View

FIGURE 14-30-5 (Continued)

FIGURE 14-30-6

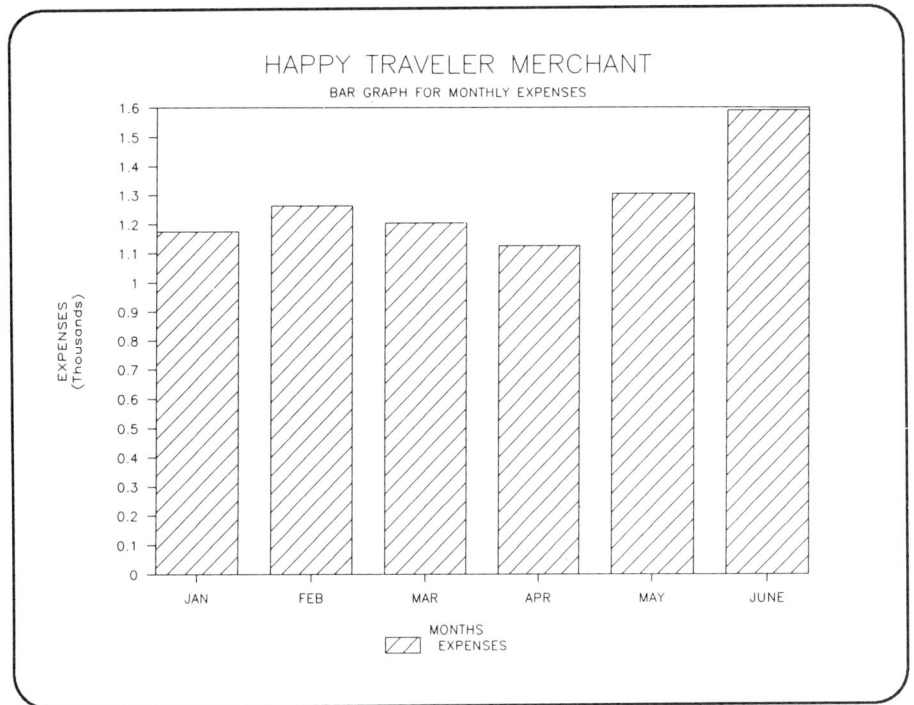

FIGURE 14-30-6 (Continued)

FIGURE 14-30-7

HAPPY TRAVELER MERCHANT

AN EXPLODED PIE CHART FOR MONTHLY REV.

JUNE (20.1%)   JAN (16.1%)

FEB (16.9%)

MAY (17.7%)

MAR (15.3%)

APR (14.1%)

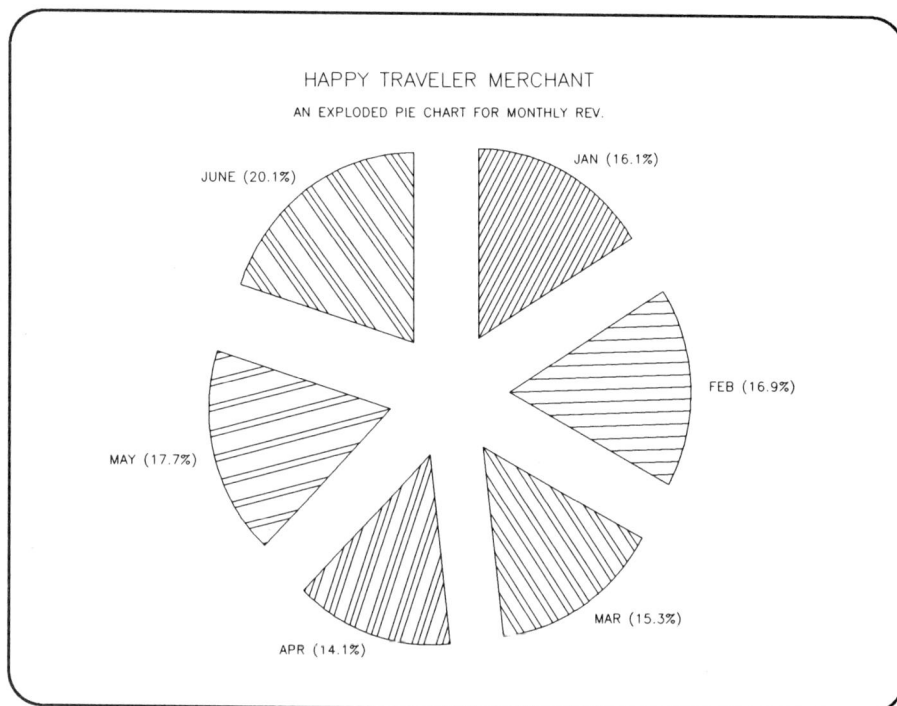

/Graph Type Pie
   X   B4. .G4   Return
   A   B6. .G6   Return
   B   D20. .I20   Return
   Options Titles   First   "HAPPY TRAVELER MERCHANT" Return
          Titles   Second "AN EXPLODED PIE CHART FOR MONTHLY
                              REV." Return

        Quit

   View

FIGURE 14-30-7 *(Continued)*

FIGURE 14-30-8

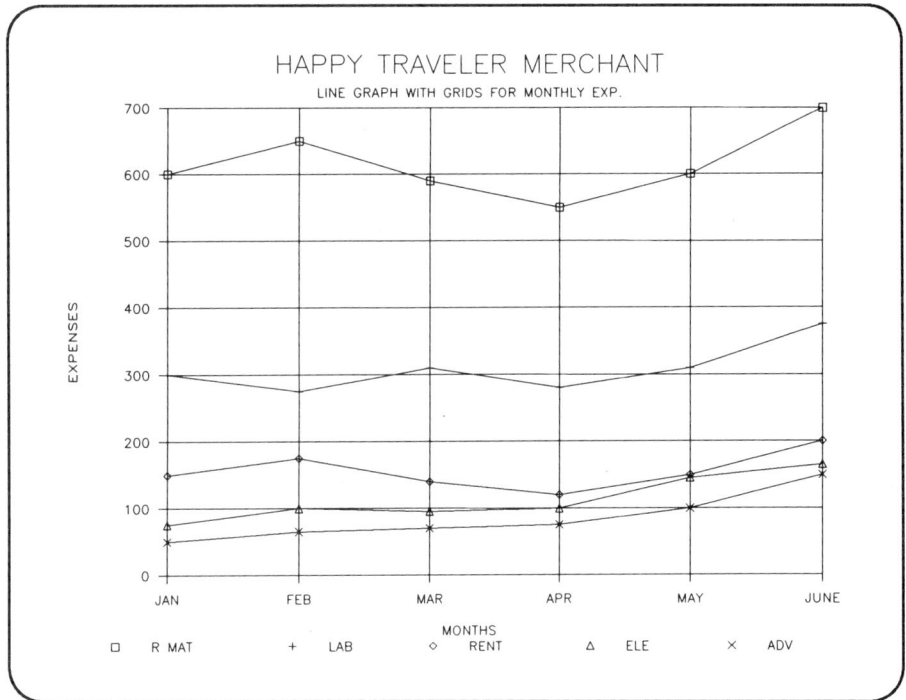

FIGURE 14-30-8 (Continued)

/Graph Type Line
```
   X   B4. .G4      Return
   A   B9. .G9      Return
   B   B10. .G10    Return
   C   B11. .G11    Return
   D   B12. .G12    Return
   E   B13. .G13    Return
```

```
   Options    Legend A        "R MAT"  Return
              Legend B        "LAB"  Return
              Legend C        "RENT"  Return
              Legend D        "ELE"  Return
              Legend E        "ADV"  Return
              Titles   First  "HAPPY TRAVELER MERCHANT"  Return
              Titles   Second "LINE GRAPH WITH GRIDS FOR MONTHLY
                                 EXP."  Return
              Titles   X-axis "MONTHS"  Return
              Titles   Y-axis "EXPENSES"  Return
              Grid     Both
          Quit
   View
```

SUMMARY

Lotus can generate five different graphs: pie charts, bar graphs, stacked-bar graphs, XY graphs, and line graphs. As you can see from the examples, Lotus has a very impressive graphics operation. The last section of this chapter presented a comprehensive model of the variety of information that can be illustrated in Lotus graphics.

REVIEW QUESTIONS

* These questions are answered in Appendix I.
1.   How many types of graphs can be generated by Lotus?
2.   What is the unique application of each type?
3.* What are some of the limitations of Lotus graphics?
4.* What is the difference between XY graphs and line graphs?
5.   How many data ranges can be used in Lotus graphics?
6.* What are the specific uses of the X range?
7.   How do you save a graph for printing?
8.* Can your graph and your worksheet be saved under the same name?
9.* Can you retrieve a graphic file (e.g., PIC) from a system disk?
10.   How do you delete a graph?
11.* How many different graphs can be generated by a worksheet?
12.   What are the choices available under Options in the graph menu?
13.* How many types of grids can you have?
14.   How many symbols are available for line graphs?
15.   What are data labels? What are their applications?
16.* What is the Scale option?
17.   Why do you use the Scale option?
18.* What are the uses of legends?
19.   How many different legends can you have?
20.   What is the function of the reset command in the graph menu?

HANDS-ON PRACTICE

1. Using the worksheet presented in Figure 14-31, do the following:
   a) Create a pie chart showing the breakdown of all the expenses (see Figure 14-30-1).
   b) Generate a stacked-bar graph to display different expenses for each month (see Figure 14-30-2).
   c) Generate a bar graph for each month of all the expenses (see Figure 14-30-3).
   d) Plot an XY graph for revenue versus total expense (see Figure 14-30-4).
   e) Using a line graph, plot each expense for the past six months (see Figure 14-30-5).
   f) Using a bar graph, plot all expenses for each month (see Figure 14-30-6).
   g) Plot an exploded pie chart for six different months for all the revenue (see Figure 14-30-7).
   h) Plot a line graph with horizontal and vertical grids for all the expenses for the past six months (see Figure 14-30-8).
2. Using the worksheet presented in Figure 14-32, plot an XY graph.

FIGURE 14-31 A Sample Worksheet

```
D10: [W7] 295                                                    READY

     A        B       C        D       E       F      G      H       I
1                           NORTHWEST TEXTILE
2
3                  JAN     FEB    MAR     APR     MAY    JUNE   TOTAL
4
5  SALES        $1,600  $1,950  $2,000  $2,500  $2,600  $2,800  $13,450
6  ===============================================================Code for
7  EXPENSES                                                       crosshatches
8  Raw Mat.      550     700     800     850     875     900     4675     1
9  Labor         250     350     295     400     420     450     2165     2
10 Rent          100     150     140     220     230     200     1040     3
11 Electric       75      85      95     175     140     165      735     4
12 Advert.        50      65      70     100     100     150      535     5
13
14 Total Exp.   1025    1350    1400    1745    1765    1865     9150
15 ===============================================================
16 Total Pro.   $575    $600    $600    $755    $835    $935    $4,300
17
18 Code for
19 exploded Pie chart       101     102     103     104     105     106
20 01-Jan-91  08:09 AM       UNDO
```

```
A1: [W12]                                                        READY

     A        B       C        D       E       F      G
1              XY-GRAPH DATA
2              ==================
3
4  INDIVIDUAL    AGE    WEIGHT
5  AA            35      175
6  AB            70      168
7  AC            26      220
8  AD            54      140
9  AE            40      195
10 AF            33      183
11 AG            28      225
12 AH            22      201
13
14 NOTE: Remember to sort one data set
15       before ploting XY graph.
16
17
18
19
20 01-Jan-91  09:12 AM       UNDO
```

FIGURE 14-32 A Sample Worksheet

COMPREHENSIVE LAB ASSIGNMENT

Retrieve CHAPT12 and perform the following:

1. Generate a line graph of the total scores of all the students. Name the graph G1, save it under G1, and save the worksheet under CHAPT14.
2. Generate a bar graph for three tests. This graph should compare the total scores of three tests. Name this graph G2 and save it under G2. Save the worksheet under CHAPT14.
3. Generate a stacked-bar for three test scores for six selected students. Name this graph G3, save it under G3, and save the worksheet under CHAPT14.
4. Generate a pie chart comparing the total scores of each test. Name the graph G4, save it under G4, and save the worksheet under CHAPT14.
5. Generate a cross-hatch pie chart.
6. Explode the pie chart.
7. Generate a final line graph from the total scores of each student with heading and subheading (any title); label both X and axes.
8. Name this graph G5, and save the final worksheet under CHAPT14.

MISCONCEPTIONS AND SOLUTIONS

M – When you invoke /Graph Name Delete, Lotus immediately erases the present graph settings and automatically returns you to the graph options menu. There is no confirmation step.

S – Before you use /GND, make sure this is what you want to do.

M – /GNR erases all the named graphs for a particular worksheet. If you issue this command there is no confirmation step.

S – Before issuing this command make sure this is what you want to do.

M – Sometimes no matter what you do, your graph does not show on the screen.

S – Check Graph, Options, Format, Graph, Neither. You may have accidentally formatted your graph to display neither lines nor symbols!

The PrintGraph Program

15-1 Introduction

In this chapter, we will explain how graphs generated on the screen can be transferred to graphic printers or plotters and how to generate hard copies of the graphs we studied in Chapter 14. We give an overview of the PrintGraph menu, discussing how to start it and how to exit from it. We explain ways you can control the look of your graph by specifying size, angle, typeface style, and so on. If you have access to a color printer or plotter, you will learn how to generate beautiful color graphics using 1-2-3 and the PrintGraph programs. You can further enhance the quality of your graphs by using the Allways add-in program discussed in Chapters 10 and 11.

15-2 What Is the PrintGraph Program?

As you have seen so far, Lotus operations are stored on the 1-2-3 System disk. The only function not stored on the System disk is the PrintGraph program, which is stored on a separate disk. The reason for storing this program on a separate disk is to keep 1-2-3 at a manageable size. This program enables you to generate hard copies from graphs on your monitor. Using PrintGraph is possible only if you have access to a plotter or if your printer is capable of printing graphics as well as text.

To use the PrintGraph program, first save your graph with the /Graph Save command. Then exit from 1-2-3 and enter PrintGraph.

15-3 Starting PrintGraph

You can get PrintGraph started either from DOS or from the Lotus Access System. To load PrintGraph from DOS, at the A> prompt, put the PrintGraph disk in drive A, type PGRAPH, and press the **Return** key. If you are using a driver other than the default 1-2-3 set, you must type PGRAPH and the driver set, e.g., PGRAPH Name.

To load PrintGraph from the Lotus Access System, move the cursor to PrintGraph, press the **Return** key, and follow the prompt. To exit from the PrintGraph program, choose the Exit option from the PrintGraph main menu. This will return you either to the Lotus Access System or to the DOS A> prompt.

15-4 Overview of the PrintGraph Main Menu

When you get the PrintGraph program started, you will see the main menu, as shown in Figure 15-1. This menu gives you six options as follows:

Image-Select   Settings   Go   Align   Page   Exit

You can use Left and Right arrows to move around the menu and press the **Return** key to select an option.

The Image-Select option allows you to choose one or more graphs to be printed. When you get the listing of your graph directory, move the cursor to the desired graph and press the space bar. Your graph will be marked by a # sign. This means the graph is a candidate for printing. To remove the # sign, press the space bar again and the # sign will disappear. Later, if you want to print another graph, first remove the # sign from the present graph and choose your next candidate. If you don't remove the #, you will always print the first graph. Figure 15-2 shows the graph menu and the candidate for printing. This menu also tells you the date when a graph was generated, the time, and the size of the graph in bytes.

At this time, you can display your graph on the monitor (if you have graphics capability) by pressing F10.

The Settings option monitors the settings for the PrintGraph program. This includes size, fonts, color, and so forth.

Go starts the printing.

Align tells PrintGraph if the paper is positioned at the top of the page.

Page advances the paper to the top of the next page.

Exit gets you out of the PrintGraph program. You will return to DOS or to the Lotus Access System.

When you choose a graph from your graph directory for printing, remember that you cannot make changes to any of the graph parameters in the PrintGraph program. If you want to make any changes, you must exit from PrintGraph, get into 1-2-3, retrieve your worksheet file, make the changes on the file, and save it by using /Graph Save. Also remember that a PIC (graphic) file cannot be retrieved in a 1-2-3 worksheet. You have to retrieve the worksheet file that generated the corresponding PIC file in the 1-2-3 worksheet (this file has the WK1 extension).

15-5 More on the Settings Command

When you choose Settings from the main menu, you will be given the following options:

Image   Hardware   Action   Save   Reset   Quit

Let us briefly explain these options.

15-6 Hardware Considerations

When you choose Settings Hardware, the following menu will be presented to you (see Figure 15-3):

Graphs-Directory   Fonts-Directory   Interface   Printer   Size-Paper   Quit

PrintGraph automatically searches drive A for the Graphs and Fonts directories. You can change these directories to drive B by typing B:. With hard disk systems you have to

FIGURE 15-1 *The PrintGraph Main Menu*

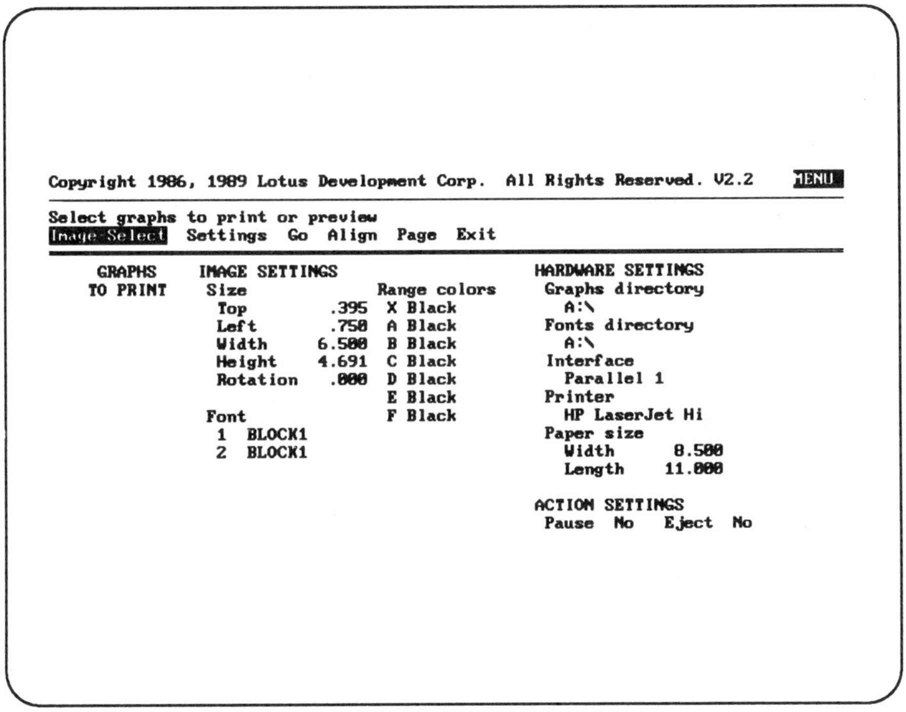

```
Copyright 1986, 1989 Lotus Development Corp.  All Rights Reserved. V2.2   [MENU]

Select graphs to print or preview
[Image-Select]  Settings  Go  Align  Page  Exit

        GRAPHS      IMAGE SETTINGS                          HARDWARE SETTINGS
        TO PRINT    Size                 Range colors       Graphs directory
                    Top          .395    X Black              A:\
                    Left         .750    A Black            Fonts directory
                    Width       6.500    B Black              A:\
                    Height      4.691    C Black            Interface
                    Rotation     .000    D Black              Parallel 1
                                         E Black            Printer
                    Font                 F Black              HP LaserJet Hi
                    1  BLOCK1                                Paper size
                    2  BLOCK1                                  Width      8.500
                                                              Length    11.000

                                                            ACTION SETTINGS
                                                            Pause  No   Eject  No
```

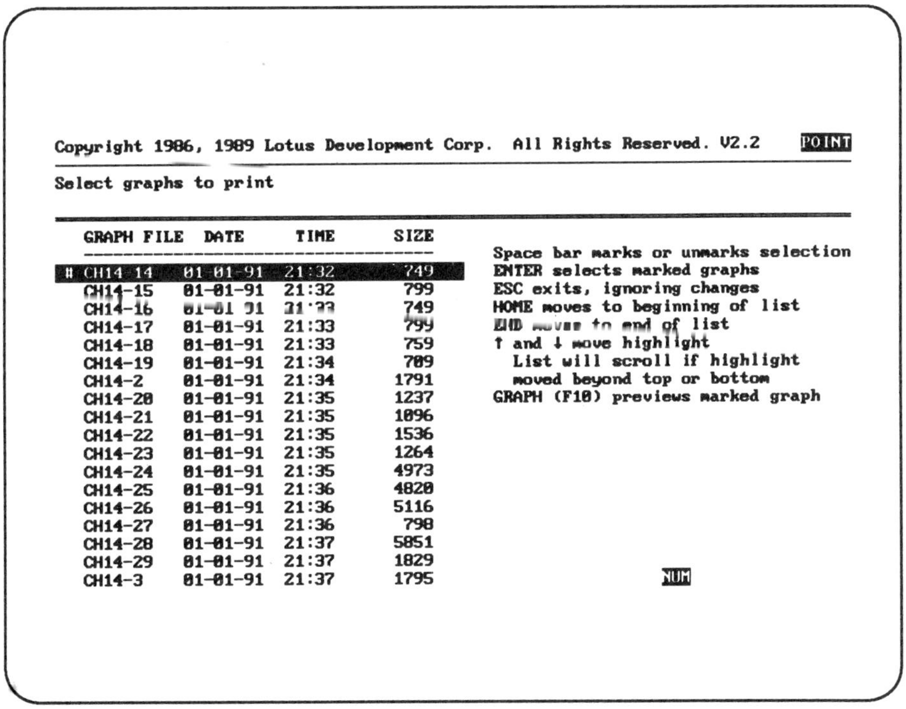

```
Copyright 1986, 1989 Lotus Development Corp.  All Rights Reserved. V2.2   [POINT]

Select graphs to print

   GRAPH FILE  DATE      TIME    SIZE
   --------------------------------------     Space bar marks or unmarks selection
 # CH14-14     01-01-91  21:32    749         ENTER selects marked graphs
   CH14-15     01-01-91  21:32    799         ESC exits, ignoring changes
   CH14-16     01-01-91  21:33    749         HOME moves to beginning of list
   CH14-17     01-01-91  21:33    799         END moves to end of list
   CH14-18     01-01-91  21:33    759         ↑ and ↓ move highlight
   CH14-19     01-01-91  21:34    789           List will scroll if highlight
   CH14-2      01-01-91  21:34   1791           moved beyond top or bottom
   CH14-20     01-01-91  21:35   1237         GRAPH (F10) previews marked graph
   CH14-21     01-01-91  21:35   1096
   CH14-22     01-01-91  21:35   1536
   CH14-23     01-01-91  21:35   1264
   CH14-24     01-01-91  21:35   4973
   CH14-25     01-01-91  21:36   4820
   CH14-26     01-01-91  21:36   5116
   CH14-27     01-01-91  21:36    798
   CH14-28     01-01-91  21:37   5851
   CH14-29     01-01-91  21:37   1829
   CH14-3      01-01-91  21:37   1795                              [NUM]
```

FIGURE 15-2 *A Sample of Graphs Directory and a Candidate for Printing*

FIGURE 15-3 The Menu for Settings Hardware

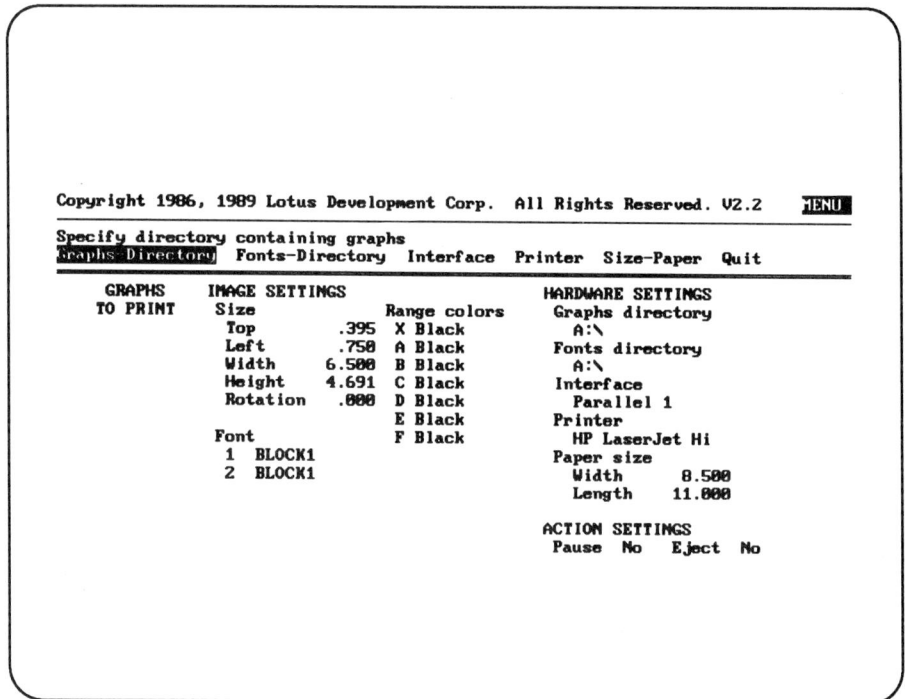

```
Copyright 1986, 1989 Lotus Development Corp.  All Rights Reserved.  V2.2   MENU

Specify directory containing graphs
Graphs Directory  Fonts-Directory  Interface  Printer  Size-Paper  Quit

  GRAPHS    IMAGE SETTINGS                            HARDWARE SETTINGS
  TO PRINT    Size               Range colors          Graphs directory
              Top        .395    X Black                 A:\
              Left       .750    A Black               Fonts directory
              Width     6.500    B Black                 A:\
              Height    4.691    C Black               Interface
              Rotation   .000    D Black                 Parallel 1
                                 E Black               Printer
              Font               F Black                 HP LaserJet Hi
              1  BLOCK1                                Paper size
              2  BLOCK1                                  Width       8.500
                                                        Length     11.000

                                                      ACTION SETTINGS
                                                        Pause  No   Eject  No
```

change the default to C drive, or the drive where you have stored your graphs. This procedure is done during the installation of your system (see Appendix C). If you look back at Figure 15-1, you will see the default settings as follows:

Graphs Directory: A:\
Fonts Directory: A:\
Interface: Parallel 1; etc.

Your interface can be either parallel or serial. If you specify a serial interface for hardware settings (e.g., Settings, Hardware, Interface), you must also specify the baud rate setting of your printer. The baud rate is the speed at which data is transferred. Choose the fastest baud rate available for your printer. The following are baud rates in order of increasing speed:

Setting	Baud Rate
1	110
2	150
3	300
4	600
5	1,200
6	2,400
7	4,800
8	9,600
9	19,200

You must configure the serial printer to the following settings:

Setting	Value
Data bits	8
Stop bits	For baud 110, 2; otherwise,1
Parity	None

Remember, these settings must be changed on your printer, not in the PrintGraph program.

The Size-Paper option in this menu will give you the following three options:

Length   Width   Quit

These options can change the default settings of PrintGraph.

15-7 The Image Option

The Image option will give the following menu:

Size   Font   Range-Colors   Quit

Choosing the Size option, you can select Full, Half, Manual, or Quit.

With the Full and Half options, PrintGraph will automatically fit your graph onto the entire page or onto half of the page and will set the height and width of the graph accordingly.

The Manual option enables you to change top and left margins manually. It also defines the width, height, and rotation of the graph, from zero to 90 degrees.

The Rotation option sets the number of degrees that the graph is turned counterclockwise. If PrintGraph sets a graph size automatically, it preserves the aspect ratio or the ratio of graph width to graph height, approximately 1.385 to 1 for X and Y axes, respectively. Therefore, remember that if you change either X or Y, the other axis must be changed proportionately. For example, if X = 4, then Y = 2.88 (X/Y = 1.385/1, 4/Y = 1.385, Y = 4/1.385 = 2.88).

When you draw a pie chart, you must always maintain the standard aspect ratio of 1.385(X-axis)/1(Y-axis) in order to preserve the circular shape, otherwise you may end up with an ellipse instead of a circle. The default settings for Top, Left, Width, Height, and Rotation are presented in the body of the main menu (see Figure 15-1).

One of the options under Settings Image is the Font option. If this option is chosen you will be given two more choices, 1 or 2. Both graph fonts 1 and 2 have 11 options (see Figure 15-4). In the Font menu, the higher the option, the darker the print; for example, SCRIPT2 is darker than SCRIPT1. You can choose Font 1 for the heading and Font 2 for the rest of the graph. If you don't choose Font 2, PrintGraph will print the entire graph in Font 1. Figure 15-4 illustrates a sample of the eleven options in Font 1. Figure 15-5 illustrates PrintGraph fonts.

When you choose Settings, Image, Range-Colors, PrintGraph displays a menu that shows the graph ranges, X and A to F. This setting depends on the type of printer that you are using; you will see different colors only with color printers. Range-Colors can be selected only if you have specified a particular printer or plotter by choosing Hardware, Printer.

Printing a colored pie chart is done in a slightly different way from the other types of graphs. The colors of the wedges are defined by the values in the B range when you save your graph using the /Graph Save command. If you recall from Chapter 14, the B range was used for generating crosshatches. Value 1 in the 1-2-3 worksheet corresponds to the

FIGURE 15-4 The Font Menu

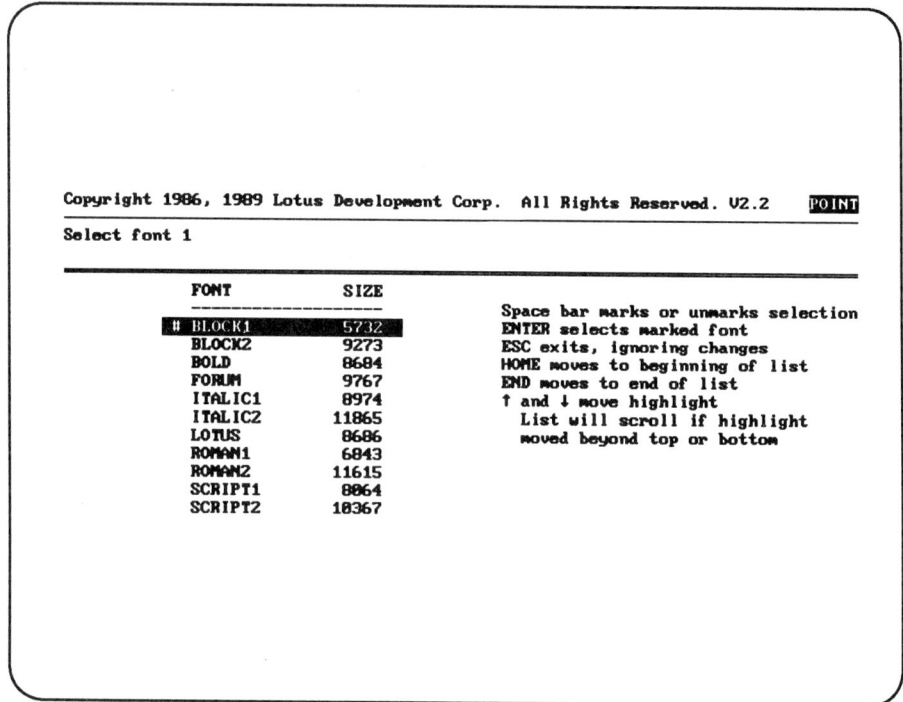

```
Copyright 1986, 1989 Lotus Development Corp.  All Rights Reserved. V2.2    POINT

Select font 1

       FONT          SIZE
       ------------------------
     # BLOCK1         5732        Space bar marks or unmarks selection
       BLOCK2         9273        ENTER selects marked font
       BOLD           8684        ESC exits, ignoring changes
       FORUM          9767        HOME moves to beginning of list
       ITALIC1        8974        END moves to end of list
       ITALIC2        11865       ↑ and ↓ move highlight
       LOTUS          8686           List will scroll if highlight
       ROMAN1         6843           moved beyond top or bottom
       ROMAN2         11615
       SCRIPT1        8864
       SCRIPT2        10367
```

X range in PrintGraph, Value 2 to A, value 3 to B and so forth up to Value 7 of the B range in the 1-2-3 worksheet to F in PrintGraph. Besides the color black, there are nine other colors: red, green, blue, orange, lime, gold, turquoise, violet, and brown.

15-8 The Action Option

One of the options under Settings is Action. If you choose Action from this menu, you will be given the following three choices:

Pause Eject Quit

The Action option monitors the operations of PrintGraph, telling you what PrintGraph does between printing. You can choose Pause or Eject. If you choose the Pause option, you will be given two choices: Yes or No.

The Yes option makes PrintGraph pause. This is useful if you would like to change some of your settings after printing a graph. If you choose the No option, PrintGraph will not pause between printing graphs. This is useful if you are not going to change any of your settings from graph to graph.

The Eject option controls whether PrintGraph automatically advances the paper or not. If you choose this option, you will be given two more choices: Yes or No. Yes will give you one graph per page. No is used if you want more than one graph per page. If PrintGraph cannot fit the second graph on the same page, it advances to the next page automatically.

FIGURE 15-5 *PrintGraph Fonts*

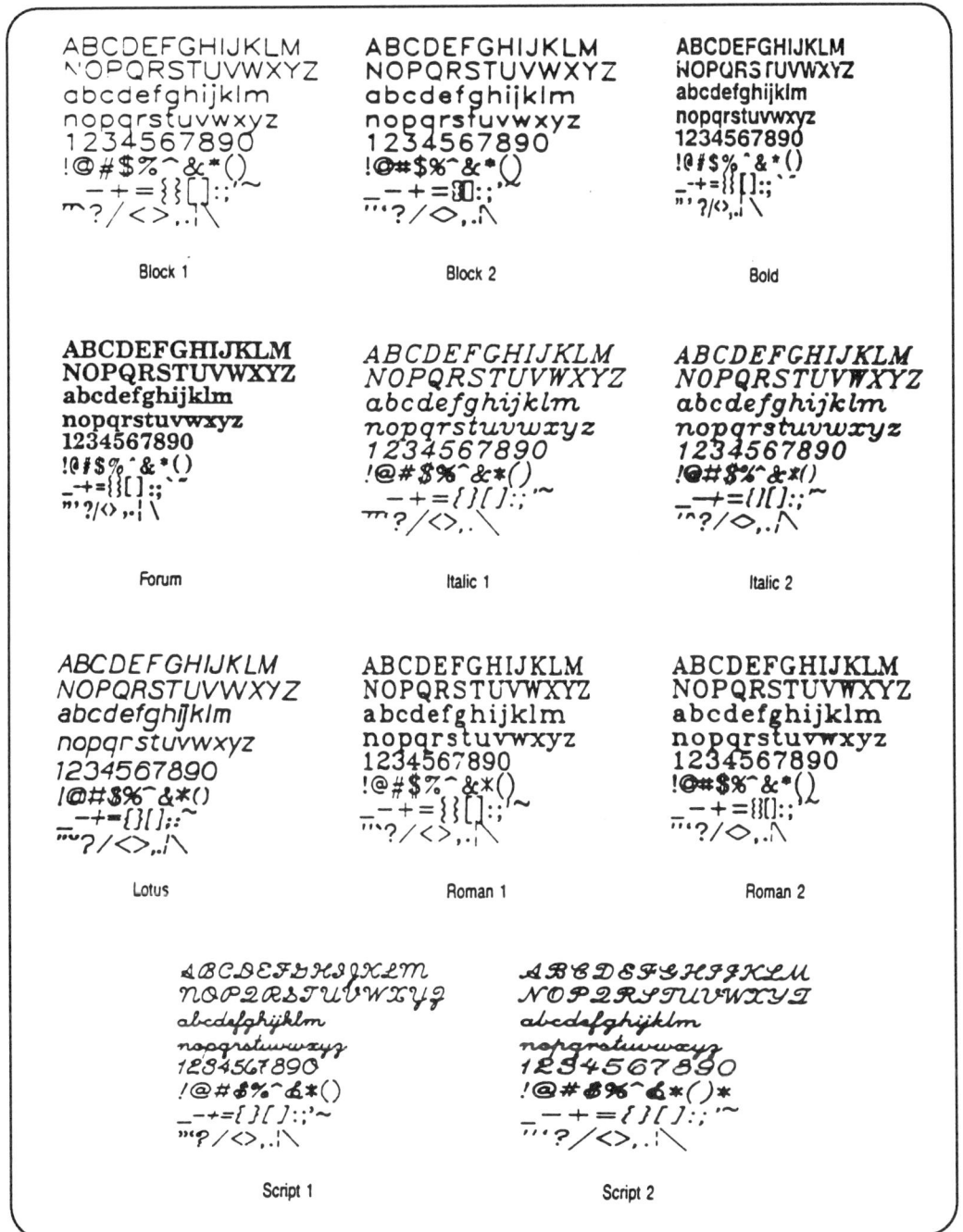

15-9 Save and Reset Options

Under the Settings menu, there are three other options: Save, Reset, and Quit.

The Save option can be used if you wish to save some of the present settings and use them in another session. If you do not choose this option, PrintGraph will not remember the most recent settings, which you may have changed during the last session. Therefore, it reads from the PGRAPH.CNF file (the default settings).

The Reset option is the opposite of Save. It replaces the current settings with those in the PGRAPH.CNF file(the default settings).

The Quit option will let you exit from this menu.

15-10 An Example of the Final Product

To wrap up this chapter, we developed an example using several of the options we have talked about. Look at Figure 15-6. First, by using Settings, Hardware, Printer, we chose the printer, in this case a HP LaserJet printer. Then we chose Image-Select (settings were the default values). Finally, we chose Go.

SUMMARY

This chapter reviewed the PrintGraph program. This is the only program not included on the main 1-2-3 System disk. PrintGraph allows you to generate hard copies of the graphs you have created on your monitor with different settings. You can specify the size of the paper, the angle, the typeface, the size of the graph. The Font option provides you with 11 typefaces for the graph. If you have access to a color printer or plotter, you can generate color graphics.

Remember that at installation time, you must specify the type of printer and /or plotter you are using. As you will see in Appendix C, you can use a wide variety of printers and plotters with Lotus. If yours is not on the list, you may want to contact the Lotus Development Corporation.

REVIEW QUESTIONS

* These questions are answered in Appendix I.
1.   How do you start PrintGraph?
2.   How do you exit from PrintGraph?
3.* When you exit from PrintGraph, do you return to DOS or to the Lotus Access System?
4.   What is the purpose of Image-Select in the main menu?
5.* Can you see your graph on the monitor using the PrintGraph program?
6.   Can a PIC file (a graphic file) be retrieved in a 1-2-3 worksheet?
7.* How do you modify a graph's parameters in the PrintGraph program?
8.   What is the purpose of the Align command in the main menu?
9.   How many choices are available under the Font options?
10. How many colors are supported by the PrintGraph program?
11. What is the aspect ratio? What is this ratio in the default setting?
12.* Does the aspect ratio have to be fixed for pie charts? If yes, why?
13. How do you change the Graph directory from A drive to B drive?
14. How many interfaces are available?
15. The baud rate is required for which type of interface?

FIGURE 15-6 An Example of a Graph Generated by Default Settings

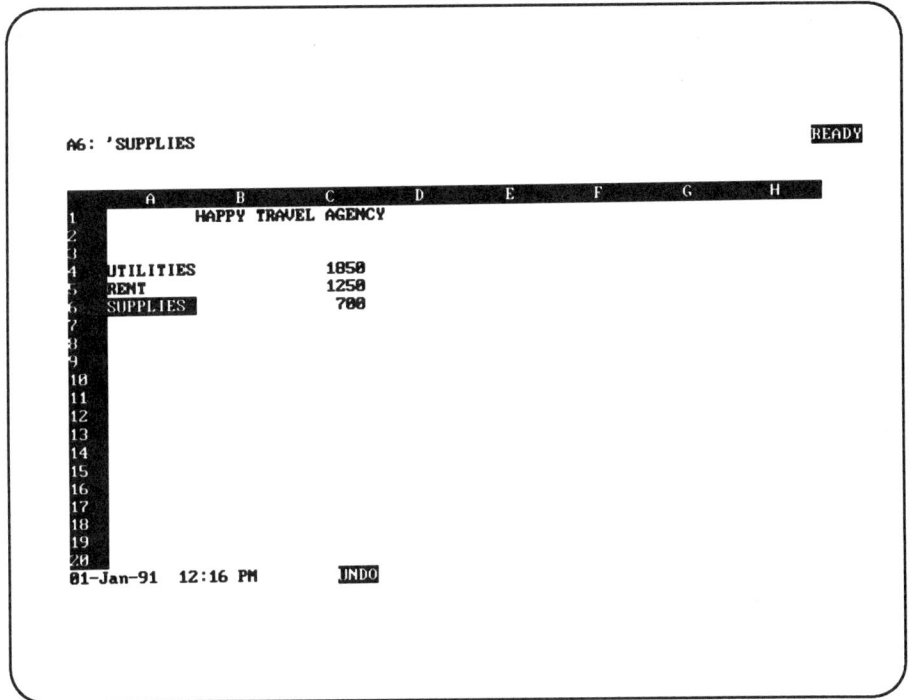

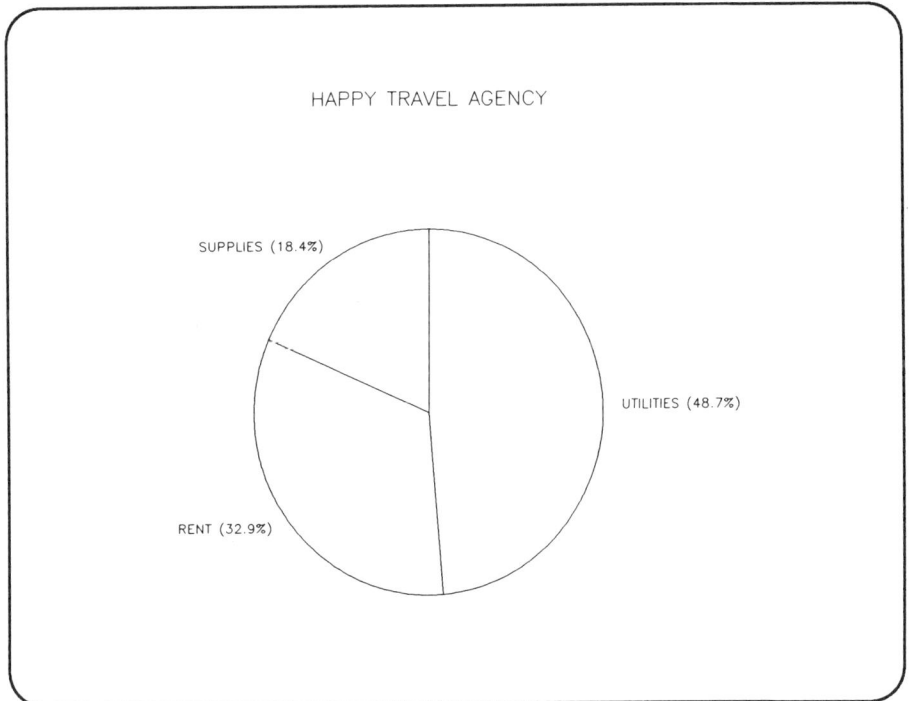

A6: 'SUPPLIES   READY

	A	B	C	D	E	F	G	H
1		HAPPY TRAVEL AGENCY						
2								
3								
4	UTILITIES		1850					
5	RENT		1250					
6	SUPPLIES		700					
7								

01-Jan-91   12:16 PM   UNDO

HAPPY TRAVEL AGENCY

SUPPLIES (18.4%)

UTILITIES (48.7%)

RENT (32.9%)

FIGURE 15-6 (Continued)

16.* What are the maximum and minimum baud rates?
17. What choices are available under Action?
18.* What does Pause do?
19. What does Eject do?
20. What is the purpose of Save and Reset in the Settings menu?

HANDS-ON PRACTICE

1. Using the PrintGraph program, print all the graphs produced from Figure 14-31.
2. The following are oil production figures for Exatec Oil Company:

1981	200,000 barrels
1982	250,000 barrels
1983	350,000 barrels
1984	400,000 barrels
1985	450,000 barrels
1986	400,000 barrels
1987	475,000 barrels

Design and print a line graph, a bar graph, and a pie chart for this data.

MISCONCEPTION AND SOLUTION

M – In a PrintGraph session, if you change some of the default settings and want to use these settings later, PrintGraph will not save these settings automatically.

S – Use the Settings Save command to save the current settings to the PGRAPH.CNF file before you exit from the PrintGraph session.

16

Database Operations/Part One: Lotus as an Electronic File Cabinet

16-1 Introduction

In this chapter we will discuss the principles of database management using Lotus, including file creation, updating, sorting, and searching. We will use examples to illustrate the major databae operations. Chapter 17 discusses advanced database operations.

16-2 What Is a Database?

In simple terms, a *database* is an organized collection of data stored in a central location. We all have used many databases, but we may not have called them that. A telephone directory is a good example of a database, one that has been organized alphabetically.

A better example of a database is the Yellow Pages. This database is also organized alphabetically; however, it is organized internally as well. If you are looking for a restaurant, you go to the *R* section, find *Restaurants*, and then search alphabetically for a particular restaurant.

In computer terminology, we call a database a collection of files, or more specifically, a collection of a series of integrated files. A *file* is a collection of records. A *record* is a collection of related fields, and a *field* is a collection of characters.

Your name, age, or occupation is an example of a field. If you put several name, age, and occupation fields together, you have constructed a record. Putting several student records together would establish a student file. At the same time, you can have a staff file, a faculty file, and so on. The collection of all these files is a database.

Most small and medium-size businesses use file cabinets to store their data. File cabinets are organized using a series of manila folders. Data in each folder is organized alphabetically, numerically, or by some other organizational scheme. Such a file cabinet and the information it contains can be called a manual database.

There are several differences between a manual and an automated database. An automated database is faster, more accurate, and occupies less space than a manual database.

16-3 Lotus as a Database

Lotus 1-2-3 offers some basic database capabilities. Using Lotus as a database management system, you can store up to 8,192 records. Each record can include up to 256 fields; each field can include up to 240 characters. However, compared to database packages such as dBASE III Plus or R-BASE 5000, Lotus offers limited database capabilities.

The size of a database depends on the size of the memory in your computer (RAM). Each character is equal to one byte of memory. So 1,000 records, each with 200 characters, is equal to 200,000 bytes, or approximately 195K. Lotus Release 2.2 requires 320K of memory. With Always you need 512K of RAM memory.

Since a database generated by Lotus resides in RAM, processing speed is extremely fast. Using Lotus as a database is also helpful when you import files from other programs to perform database operations (for information on file transfer, see Appendix D).

16-4 Basic Database Operations Using Lotus

The Lotus database is simply an expansion of the spreadsheet. This spreadsheet includes 8,192 rows (records) and 256 columns (fields). Major database operations are:

• Database creation
• Database update
• Database sort
• Database search

Database creation simply means putting labels, formulas, or figures in different cells, something we have been doing all along. If the length of a particular field is larger than nine characters (the default value), it can be modified by using /Worksheet Global Column-Widths /Worksheet Column Set-Width or /Worksheet Column Column-Range.

Database update includes changing the content of a particular field (simple editing), insertion of a new record or field (/Worksheet Insert Row or /Worksheet Insert Column, respectively), deletion of a record or field (/Worksheet Delete Row or /Worksheet Delete Column, respectively), deletion of an entire database (/Worksheet Erase Yes), or deletion of a portion of a database (/Range Erase).

You can sort your database in either ascending or descending order by using a primary key and a secondary key. A *primary key* is the first field chosen for a sort operation; for example, last name. The *secondary key* is the second field chosen for a sort operation; for example, sex. Finally, you can do any type of search using different criteria.

Other complex database operations such as the join operation (putting two databases side by side) can be performed with the /File Combine command. A merge operation (adding one database to the bottom of another one) can also be performed by using the / File Combine command. For other database operations, such as label generation or managing multiple databases, macros (discussed in Chapters 18–20) can be developed.

16-5 Your First Database

Figure 16-1 shows an example of a database. This database has 15 records, each with six fields. Each field starts with a field name. The field name must be a label; however, it can be a numeric label such as "5" or "9", etc. The field name can be more than one line in length but only the last row will be considered the field name. Field names must be unique.

Figure 16-1 has been created in the same fashion as other worksheets. Numbers and figures are right-justified and labels are left-justified.

FIGURE 16-1 *An Example of a Database*

A1: [W12]   READY

	A	B	C	D	E	F	G
1		MY FIRST DATABASE					
2							
3	FIRST NAME	LAST NAME	AGE	SEX	OCCUPATION	INCOME	
4	Randy	Alexander	36	M	Professor	$40,000	
5	Fay	Alexander	30	F	Mayor	$30,000	
6	Adam	Alexander	31	M	Engineer	$30,000	
7	Andrea	Byan	36	F	Teacher	$31,000	
8	Joe	Byan	40	M	Officer	$40,000	
9	Bob	Adam	32	M	Engineer	$72,000	
10	Anna	Adam	4	F	Unemployed	$11,000	
11	Vicki	Adam	9	F	Unemployed	$12,000	
12	Paula	Bobby	55	F	Housewife	$20,000	
13	Jack	Jones	69	M	Artist	$19,000	
14	Mary	Fishler	30	F	Interpreter	$19,000	
15	Sue	Hayword	22	F	Student	$10,000	
16	Tammy	Smith	29	F	Student	$10,000	
17	Jacky	Brown	72	F	Engineer	$52,000	
18	Lora	Jones	30	F	Nurse	$31,000	
19							
20							

01-Jan-91   04:12 PM   UNDO

16-6 Sorting Your Database

The database can be sorted by any field, in ascending or descending order. To access the Sort command, choose Data from the main menu and then select the Sort command. The Sort command has the following options (see Figure 16-2):

Data-Range   Primary-Key   Secondary-Key   Reset   Go   Quit

The data-range usually includes all data items in your database, though in reality you can include only a portion of your database. The field names must not be included in the data-range, otherwise they will be considered as a part of the database itself and will be mixed up with data items.

The primary-key is the first key for the Sort operation. Any field in your database may be selected as the primary-key. The secondary-key is another field that may be used for a Sort operation.

Reset is used when you decide to change the parameter of your database. When you choose the Reset command all current settings will go back to the default setting. For example, if your previous data range was A1..A50, after choosing the Reset command your data range will be erased. Now you have to define a new database range.

Go executes the Sort operation. And finally, Quit will let you leave the menu.

Figure 16-3 shows Figure 16-1 after having been sorted by last name. This figure was generated as follows:

/Data, Sort, Data-Range A4..F18, **Return**, Primary-Key, B4..B18, **Return**, A, **Return**, Go

FIGURE 16-2 Sort Menu

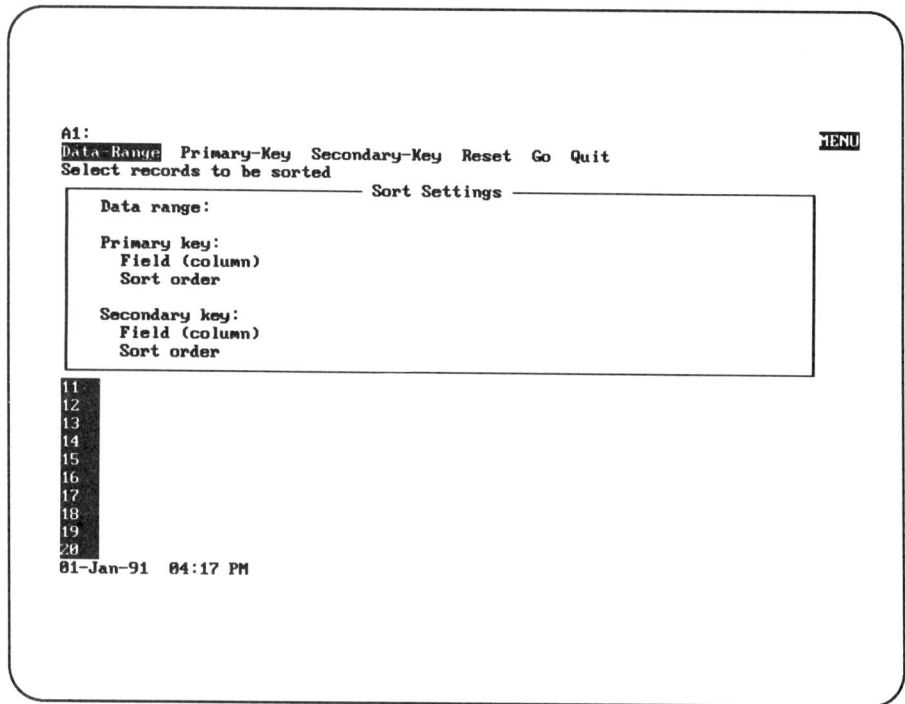

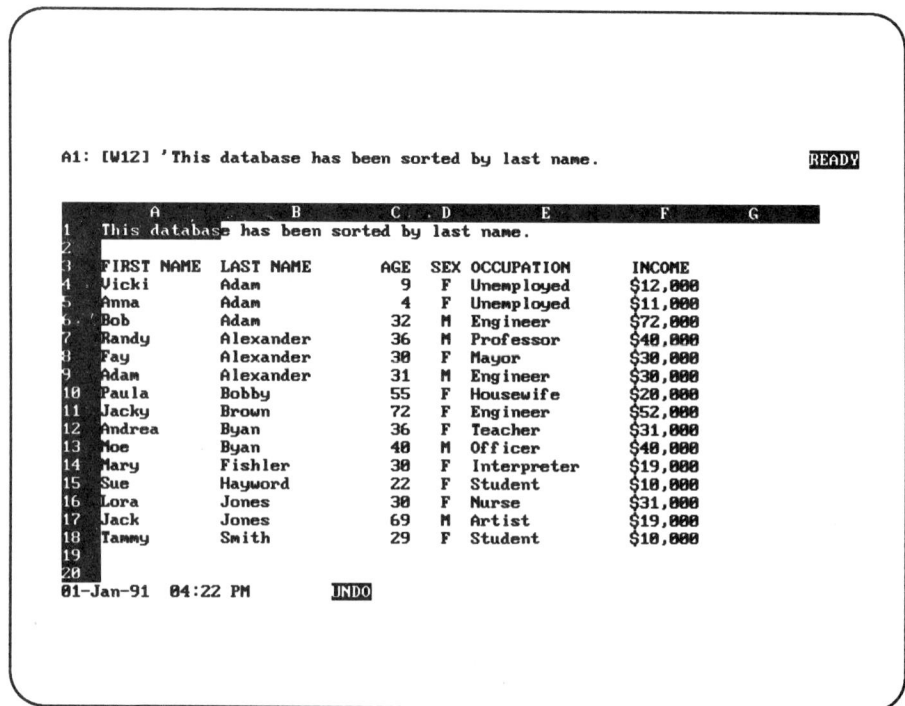

FIGURE 16-3 Figure 16-1 Sorted by Last Name

Remember, after you sort your data unsorting is not possible. You may want to make a copy of your database before sorting is done.

By default, Lotus sorts in descending order. If you do not want this default setting, type A (ascending) and press the **Return** key. Otherwise, press **Return** without typing anything; this means you are choosing the default setting. The order in which Lotus performs a sort is determined by a collating sequence. You may choose one of three collating sequences during the install operations (see Appendix C):

• Numbers last
• Numbers first
• ASCII
• Numbers last means blank cells; labels beginning with letters in alphabetical order; labels beginning with numbers in numerical order; labels beginning with other characters. The sort ignores capitalization and most accent marks.
• Numbers first means blank cells; labels beginning with numbers in numerical order; labels beginning with letters in alphabetical order; labels beginning with other characters. The sort ignores capitalization and most accent marks.
• ASCII means blank cells; all labels, using their ASCII values.

Uppercase and lowercase letters have the same value. As a general rule, nonlabel, nonnumeric, and composed characters (F1 + Alternate) fall at the end of the listing. (For ASCII codes see Appendix H.) As a general rule do not leave any empty row or column in your database.

16-7 Sorting with Two Keys

There are instances when you want to sort a database using two fields. The Yellow Pages, for example, has been sorted by business type and within each type, businesses are sorted alphabetically. In Figure 16-4, we sorted the original database (Figure 16-1) using two keys. The primary-key is sex and the secondary-key is age. Within each group, individuals are sorted by age. Figure 16-4 was generated as follows:

/Data, Sort, Data-Range A4..F18, **Return**, Primary-Key, D4..D18, **Return**, A, **Return**, Secondary-Key, C4..C18, **Return**, A, **Return**, Go

Remember, Data-Range cannot include field names.

16-8 Search Operations

In search operations we are interested in a specific record or series of records that meet certain criteria. For example, in a student grade file we might want to search for all students who have a GPA greater than 3.60, or in an employee file, employees who hold a master's degree. To conduct a search operation, access Data from the main menu and then choose Query. Under Query we have:

Input   Criterion   Output   Find   Extract   Unique   Delete   Reset   Quit

Input includes the entire database, including the field names. For example, in Figure 16-1 the Input range is A3..F18.

The criterion range is a part of the worksheet entered separately outside the database range, which includes the name of the field and the criterion we are searching for. The

FIGURE 16-4   *Figure 16-1 Sorted by Sex and Age*

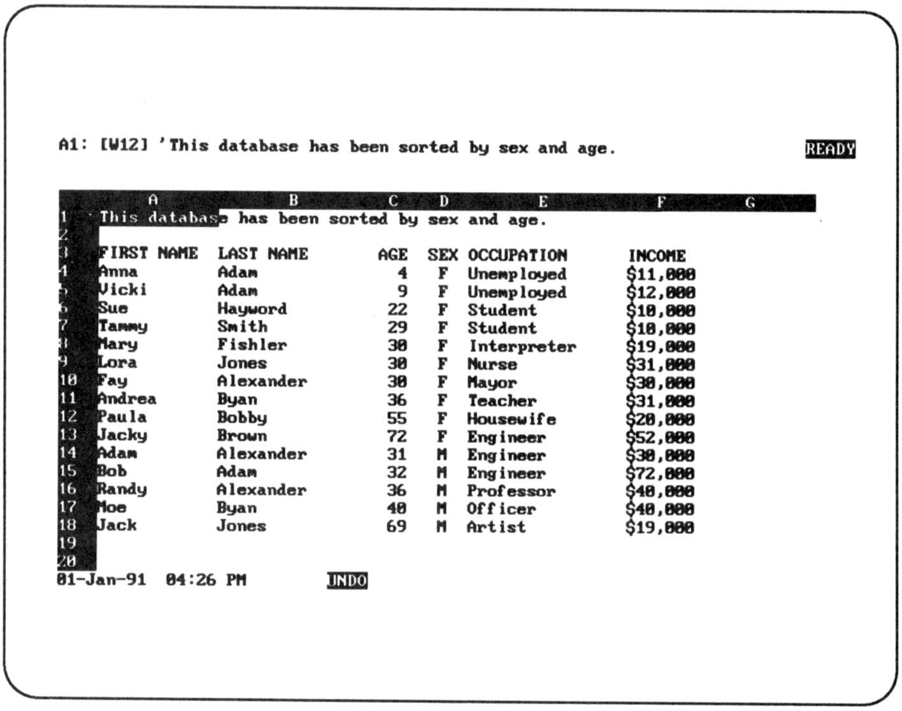

```
A1: [W12] 'This database has been sorted by sex and age.                 READY

        A              B           C    D    E            F            G
 1   'This database has been sorted by sex and age.
 2
 3   FIRST NAME   LAST NAME    AGE  SEX  OCCUPATION      INCOME
 4   Anna         Adam           4   F   Unemployed      $11,000
 5   Vicki        Adam           9   F   Unemployed      $12,000
 6   Sue          Hayword       22   F   Student         $18,000
 7   Tammy        Smith         29   F   Student         $18,000
 8   Mary         Fishler       30   F   Interpreter     $19,000
 9   Lora         Jones         30   F   Nurse           $31,000
10   Fay          Alexander     30   F   Mayor           $30,000
11   Andrea       Byan          36   F   Teacher         $31,000
12   Paula        Bobby         55   F   Housewife       $20,000
13   Jacky        Brown         72   F   Engineer        $52,000
14   Adam         Alexander     31   M   Engineer        $30,000
15   Bob          Adam          32   M   Engineer        $72,000
16   Randy        Alexander     36   M   Professor       $40,000
17   Moe          Byan          40   M   Officer         $40,000
18   Jack         Jones         69   M   Artist          $19,000
19
20
01-Jan-91  04:26 PM        UNDO
```

criterion range must have field names identical to those used in the database; therefore, the Copy command is optimal for creation of the criterion range field names. For example, in our database (Figure 16-1), the criterion range for all the engineers would be:

OCCUPATION
Engineer

Occupation is the field name in which we have a field containing Engineer. Up to 32 fields can be considered for the search in the criterion range.

The output range is a selected portion of a worksheet outside the database range used to store records based on the criterion range. It must contain the names of the fields in the database which you want to extract (uppercase or lowercase doesn't matter).

The Find option is used to choose a record or a series of records based on the criterion range (output range is not needed with the Find option). To use the Find option all you need to define is the Input range and the Criterion range, and then choose the Find option. When the option is executed, the selected records will be highlighted.

With the Extract option, a portion of a database can be copied to the output range, based on the criterion range (assuming you have already defined the output range).

The Unique option is used in order to extract only a unique portion of a database. In this case, duplicate records will not be chosen. For example, if you would like to choose one representative of each occupation, only one engineer will be selected, one professor, and so forth.

The Delete option is used to erase a portion of a database, based on the criterion range. The following section illustrates these options.

16-9 Search with Single Criterion

In Figure 16-5 we have searched the database on the left side of the figure for all engineers. First, we typed the criterion range data in Cells F6 and F7. The information in Cell F5 is only for documentation purposes and it is optional. This example was generated as follows:

/Data, Query, Input A5..D13, **Return**, Criterion F6..F7, **Return**, Find

As you see, when you choose the Find option, the cursor will point to the first record that meets a particular criterion. If you move the cursor down to the records below the first selected one, you will see it point to the next candidate (if there is any). This will continue until all the candidates are highlighted. Now, if you try to move the cursor farther down, you will hear a beep. This means there are no more candidates to be highlighted.

To demonstrate the actual output we have used the Extract option. We first copied the field names in row 16. The information in row 15 is only for documentation purposes and it is optional. Figure 16-6 was generated as follows:

/Data, Query, Input A5..D13, **Return**, Criterion F6..F7, **Return**, Output A16..D20, **Return**, Extract

Remember, the output range does not need to include the entire range for the extracted output (assuming you have enough empty space for the extracted data). If you copy only the names of the fields from the database and specify the first line of the output range, that would be adequate. The first line of the output range is always the row containing the name of the fields for the extracted output.

FIGURE 16-5 Example of Search with Single Criteria (All Engineers)

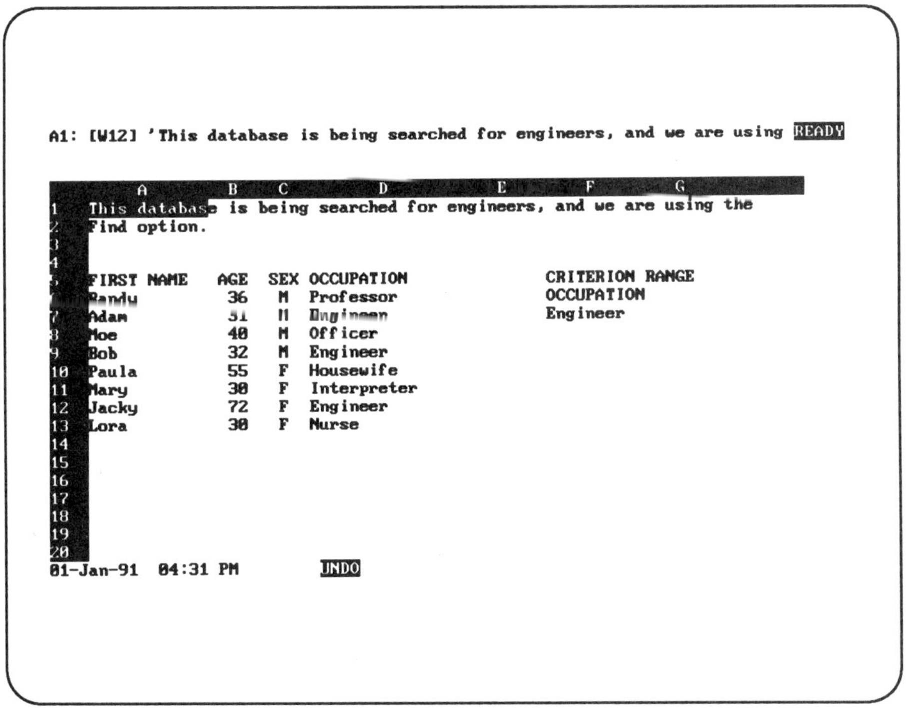

FIGURE 16-6 Example of Search with Single Criteria (All Engineers) with Output Range

```
A1: [W12] 'This database is being searched for all engineers, and we are us READY

          A        B     C       D           E        F        G
1    This database is being searched for all engineers, and we are using the
2    Extract option.
3
4
5    FIRST NAME   AGE   SEX  OCCUPATION                 CRITERION RANGE
6    Randy        36    M    Professor                  OCCUPATION
7    Adam         31    M    Engineer                   Engineer
8    Moe          40    M    Officer
9    Bob          32    M    Engineer
10   Paula        55    F    Housewife
11   Mary         30    F    Interpreter
12   Jacky        72    F    Engineer
13   Lora         30    F    Nurse
14
15   OUTPUT RANGE
16   FIRST NAME   AGE   SEX  OCCUPATION
17   Adam         31    M    Engineer
18   Bob          32    M    Engineer
19   Jacky        72    F    Engineer
20
01-Jan-91  04:35 PM           UNDO
```

16-10 Search for Either Criterion

There are numerous occasions when you are interested only in a couple of criteria; either one would be acceptable. For example, you might look for an employee with a bachelor's degree *or* 17 years of experience, or a student who is majoring in MIS *or* computer science. In computer terminology this is called an OR condition (either condition is acceptable). The opposite is the AND condition, meaning that all the conditions must be met. In an AND situation all conditions must be true for a record to qualify for selection. For example, in a student database, if you are interested in those students that are MIS majors, female, under 22, and speak French, every candidate must meet all those criteria in order to be selected. If a student is majoring in MIS, is female, and speaks French but is 24 years old, this student will not be selected because she failed to meet one of the four conditions. In an OR situation you may be interested in students who are MIS majors, or female, or under 22, or speak French. If any of these conditions is true the student will qualify for selection. The OR criteria must be in a vertical line; that is, in a column. The AND criteria must be in a horizontal line; that is, in a row. In Figure 16-7, we searched the database for individuals who are either engineers or teachers. As before, first type or copy the information needed for the criterion and ouptut ranges. This figure was generated as follows:

/Data, Query, Input A3..E11, **Return**, Criterion G4..G6, **Return**, Output A15..E20, **Return**, Extract

FIGURE 16-7 *Examples of Search with Either Criteria (Engineer or Teacher)*

```
A1: [W12] 'This database is being used to search for engineers or teachers.READY

        A       B     C        D           E         F         G
1    This database is being used to search for engineers or teachers.
2
3    FIRST NAME  AGE  SEX   OCCUPATION    INCOME            CRITERION RANGE
4    Adam        31   M     Engineer      $30,000           OCCUPATION
5    Andrea      36   F     Teacher       $31,000           Engineer
6    Moe         40   M     Officer       $40,000           Teacher
7    Bob         32   M     Engineer      $72,000
8    Paula       55   F     Housewife     $20,000
9    Mary        30   F     Interpreter   $19,000
10   Jacky       72   F     Engineer      $52,000
11   Lora        30   F     Nurse         $31,000
12
13
14   OUTPUT RANGE
15   FIRST NAME  AGE  SEX   OCCUPATION    INCOME
16   Adam        31   M     Engineer      $30,000
17   Andrea      36   F     Teacher       $31,000
18   Bob         32   M     Engineer      $72,000
19   Jacky       72   F     Engineer      $52,000
20
01-Jan-91  04:40 PM         UNDO
```

16-11 Search with Wild Cards

Lotus includes three wild card characters that can be used in the criterion range. They can be used only with labels not with the numeric data. Each has its own unique application. The three are the asterisk (*), the question mark (?), and the tilde (~). Placing an asterisk after a character means that you will retrieve that character *plus* any and all characters that follow it. For example, you would use *B* and an asterisk if you are interested in everyone who has a last name starting with B: Byan, Brown, Bandary, and so on.

The question mark will retrieve any character in one position. For example, ?anny will give you Fanny and Danny; ?ortland will give you Portland and sortland.

Finally, the tilde will retrieve all values *except* those that follow it. For example, ~engineer gives you every occupation listed except engineers. Figures 16-8, 16-9, and 16-10 show the effects of using these wild cards.

Figure 16-8 was generated as follows:

/Data, Query, Input A4..D11, **Return**, Criterion F5..F6, **Return**, Output A15..D20, **Return**, Extract

Figure 16-9 was generated as follows:

/Data, Query, Input A4..B11, **Return**, Criterion D5..D6, **Return**, Output A16..B20, **Return**, Extract

Figure 16-10 was generated as follows:

/Data, Query, Input A3..E11, **Return**, Criterion G4..G5, **Return**, Output A15..E25, **Return**, Extract

*FIGURE 16-8 An Example of Wild Card * (Asterisk)*

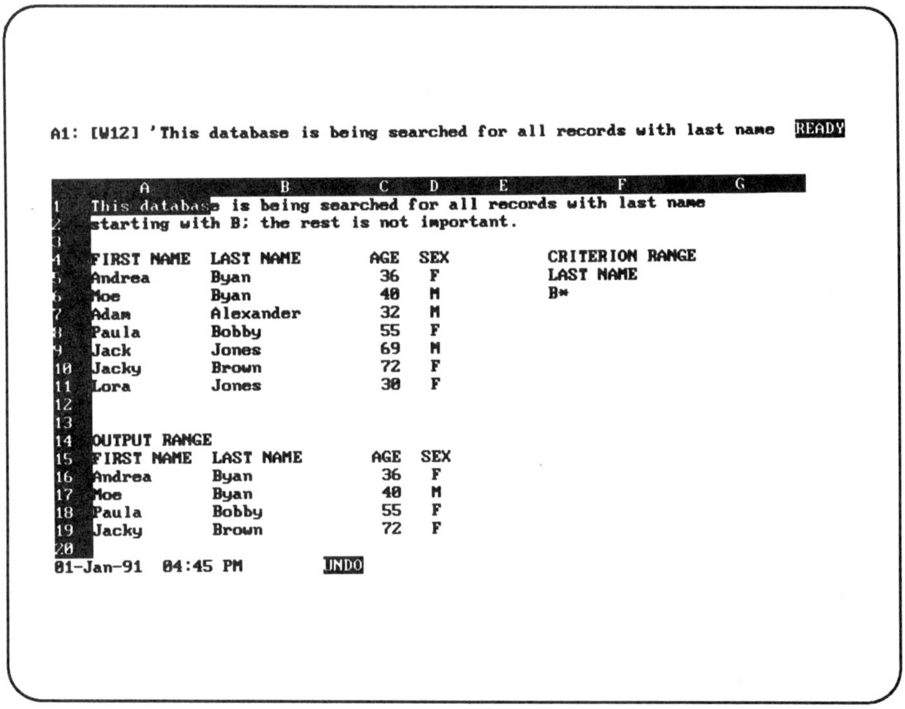

```
A1: [W12] 'This database is being searched for all records with last name   READY

          A            B           C   D      E          F             G
  1   This database is being searched for all records with last name
  2   starting with B; the rest is not important.
  3
  4   FIRST NAME   LAST NAME      AGE SEX          CRITERION RANGE
  5   Andrea       Byan           36  F           LAST NAME
  6   Moe          Byan           40  M           B*
  7   Adam         Alexander      32  M
  8   Paula        Bobby          55  F
  9   Jack         Jones          69  M
  10  Jacky        Brown          72  F
  11  Lora         Jones          30  F
  12
  13
  14  OUTPUT RANGE
  15  FIRST NAME   LAST NAME      AGE SEX
  16  Andrea       Byan           36  F
  17  Moe          Byan           40  M
  18  Paula        Bobby          55  F
  19  Jacky        Brown          72  F
  20
  01-Jan-91  04:45 PM        UNDO
```

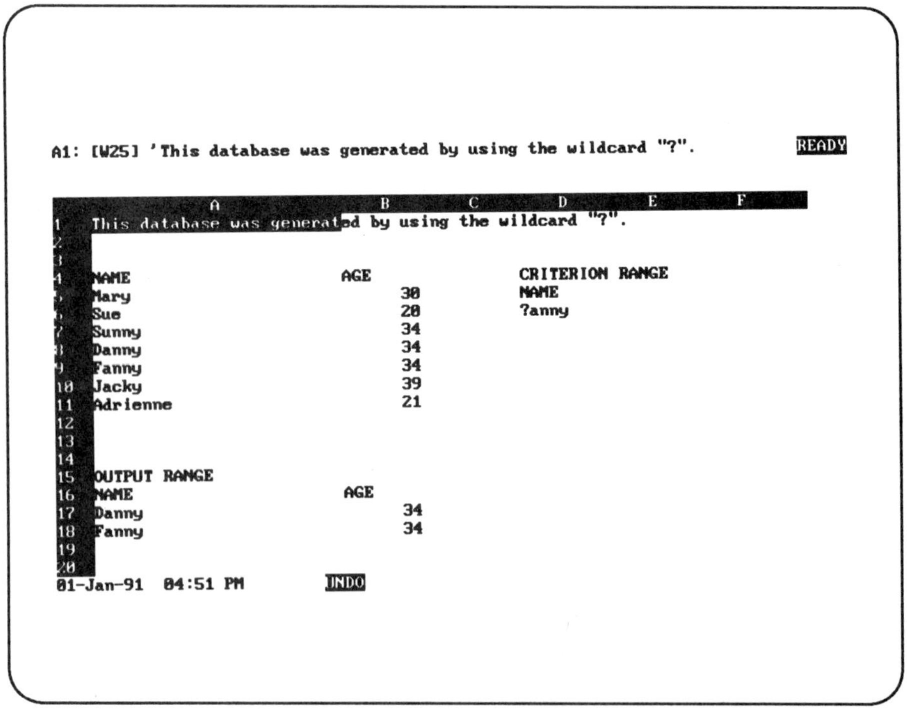

```
A1: [W25] 'This database was generated by using the wildcard "?".        READY

          A                 B         C       D          E        F
  1   This database was generated by using the wildcard "?".
  2
  3
  4   NAME              AGE                 CRITERION RANGE
  5   Mary              30                  NAME
  6   Sue               20                  ?anny
  7   Sunny             34
  8   Danny             34
  9   Fanny             34
  10  Jacky             39
  11  Adrienne          21
  12
  13
  14
  15  OUTPUT RANGE
  16  NAME              AGE
  17  Danny             34
  18  Fanny             34
  19
  20
  01-Jan-91  04:51 PM        UNDO
```

FIGURE 16-9 An Example of Wild Card ? (Question Mark)

FIGURE 16-10 An Example of Wild Card ~ (Tilde)

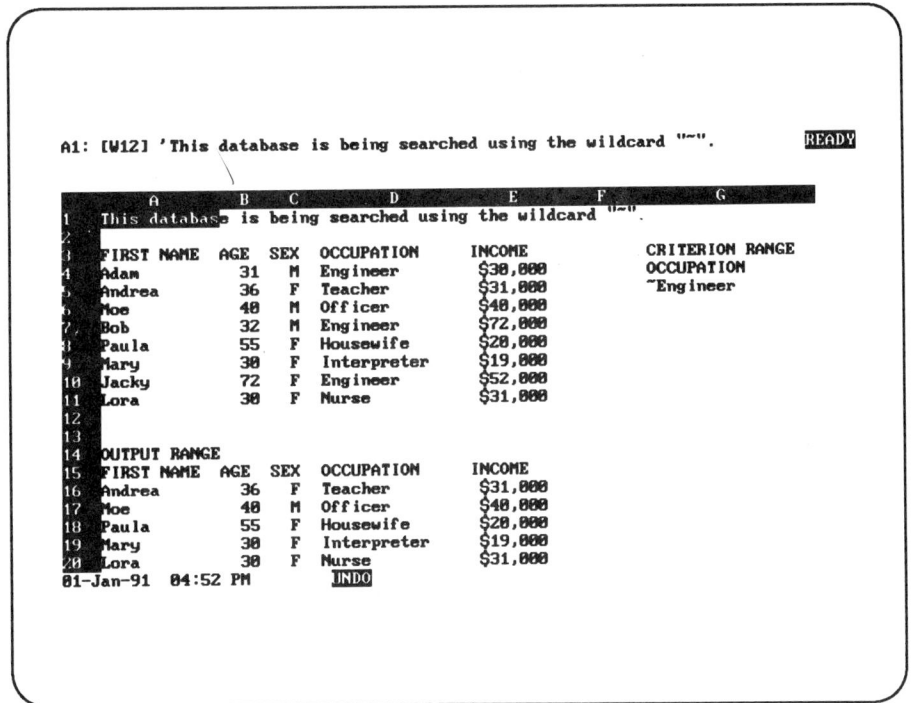

16-12 Search with Multiple Criteria

Sometimes you may be interested in searching for records meeting multiple criteria. This is called an AND condition. For example, you may want to search for all the students who have a GPA of 3.6 or better *and* are MIS majors, or all the employees who have 10 years of experience and have a bachelor's degree and speak Spanish. An employee must meet all the criteria to be selected. The AND criteria must be in a horizontal line; that is, in a row.

Figure 16-12 illustrates an AND condition: all female engineers who make more than $50,000 and are less then 60 years old. We searched the database in Figure 16-11 to find the names that met all these criteria. Figure 16-12 was generated as follows:

/Data, Query, Input A4..F19, **Return**, Criterion I5..L6, **Return**, Output G11..L30, **Return**, Extract

Remember, in cell L6 in Figure 16-12 we useed Text format in order to show the actual contents of the cell. If you do not use the Text format you see either 1 or 0. You will see 1 (true) if the first record passes all the conditions. You will see 0 (false) if the first record does not pass all the conditions.

As we mentioned earlier, you can include up to 32 fields in your criterion range. You can also combine AND and OR conditions as long as you are forming a rectangle in your Criterion range. This means all the field names are arranged in one row.

When AND/OR are combined 1-2-3 starts from the top of the database and compares each record to the criteria established in the criterion range. If there is a match that record is pulled out, otherwise the record is skipped.

FIGURE 16-11 Database Used for Multiple Criteria Search

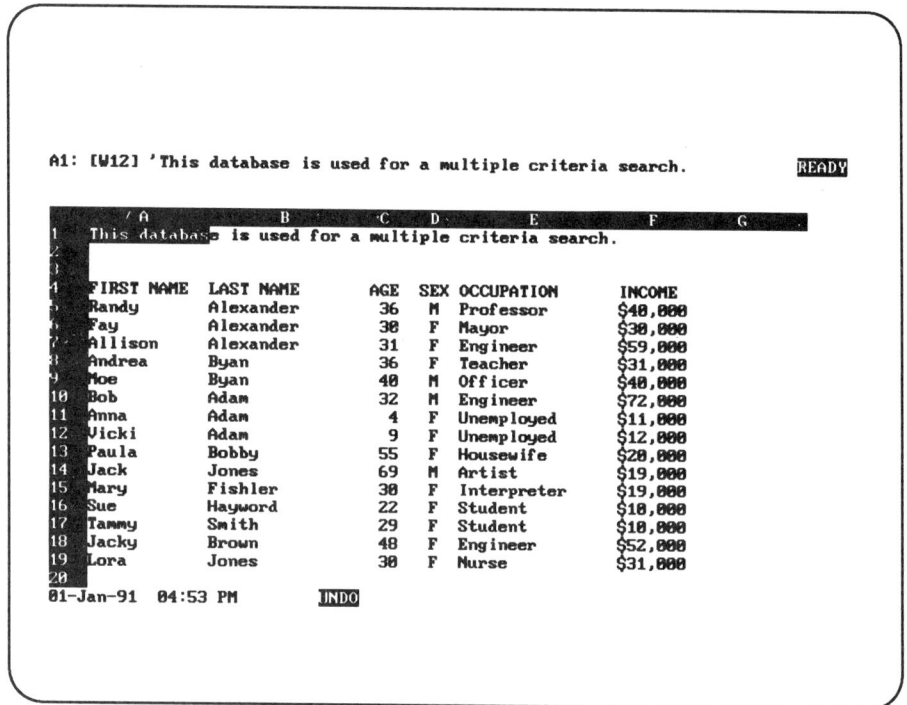

```
A1: [W12] 'This database is used for a multiple criteria search.          READY

     /  A           B           C    D      E           F          G
  1  This database is used for a multiple criteria search.
  2
  3
  4  FIRST NAME   LAST NAME    AGE  SEX  OCCUPATION       INCOME
  5  Randy        Alexander     36   M   Professor       $40,000
  6  Fay          Alexander     30   F   Mayor           $30,000
  7  Allison      Alexander     31   F   Engineer        $59,000
  8  Andrea       Byan          36   F   Teacher         $31,000
  9  Moe          Byan          40   M   Officer         $40,000
 10  Bob          Adam          32   M   Engineer        $72,000
 11  Anna         Adam           4   F   Unemployed      $11,000
 12  Vicki        Adam           9   F   Unemployed      $12,000
 13  Paula        Bobby         55   F   Housewife       $20,000
 14  Jack         Jones         69   M   Artist          $19,000
 15  Mary         Fishler       30   F   Interpreter     $19,000
 16  Sue          Hayword       22   F   Student         $10,000
 17  Tammy        Smith         29   F   Student         $10,000
 18  Jacky        Brown         48   F   Engineer        $52,000
 19  Lora         Jones         30   F   Nurse           $31,000
 20
01-Jan-91   04:53 PM          UNDO
```

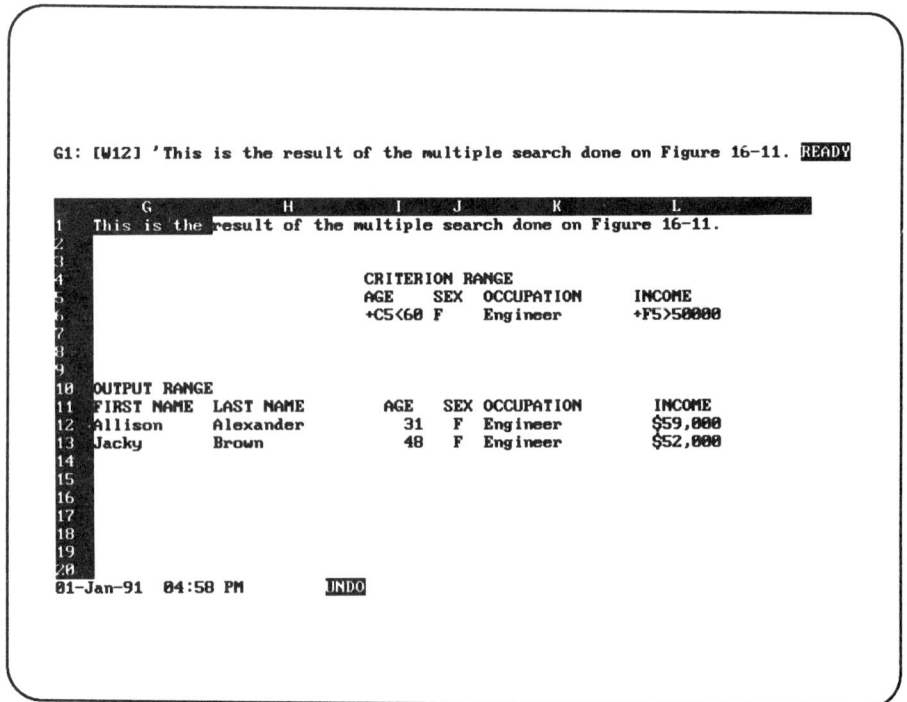

```
G1: [W12] 'This is the result of the multiple search done on Figure 16-11. READY

        G           H           I    J       K           L
  1  This is the result of the multiple search done on Figure 16-11.
  2
  3
  4                           CRITERION RANGE
  5                           AGE    SEX  OCCUPATION       INCOME
  6                           +C5<60  F   Engineer        +F5>50000
  7
  8
  9
 10  OUTPUT RANGE
 11  FIRST NAME   LAST NAME    AGE  SEX  OCCUPATION       INCOME
 12  Allison      Alexander     31   F   Engineer        $59,000
 13  Jacky        Brown         48   F   Engineer        $52,000
 14
 15
 16
 17
 18
 19
 20
01-Jan-91   04:58 PM          UNDO
```

FIGURE 16-12 An Example of Multiple Criteria (AND Option)

FIGURE 16-13 Sample Worksheet for Multiple Search

Figure 16-13 was searched to give the results in Figure 16-14. Figure 16-14 was generated as follows:

/Data, Query, Input, A4..F19, **Return**, Criterion I5..L8, **Return**, Output, G11..L30, **Return**, Extract

In the first row of the criterion range we are looking for whoever meets the following four criteria: Age < 60, Sex = F, Occupation = Engineer, Income > $50,000. As you see, there is only one candidate who meets all criteria, Allison Alexander.

In the second row of the criterion range, we are looking for candidates who meet the following criteria: Age > 90, Sex = Either (since the cell under sex is blank), Occupation = Teacher, Income = Any (since the cell under income is blank). Only one candidate meets all these criteria, Lora Jones.

In the third line of criteria we are looking for any candidate who is a student; sex, age, and income are not important.

As you see, many of these criteria can be combined with the OR and AND conditions. Remember, if you leave a criterion empty in the criterion range, any data item can fill that range (any profession, any sex, etc.).

Another interesting search would be to apply AND/OR choices to one particular field. In Figure 16-15, we searched for individuals who are between the ages of 30 and 40. The figure was generated as follows:

/Data, Query, Input, A3..B18, **Return**, Criterion, E4..E5, **Return**, Output, E9..F18, **Return**, Extract

In Figure 16-16, we searched for individuals who are younger than 10 or older than 70. The figure was generated as follows:

/Data, Query, Input, A3..B18, **Return**, Criterion, E4..E5, **Return**, Output, E9..F18, **Return**, Extract

FIGURE 16-14 An Example of a Multiple Search

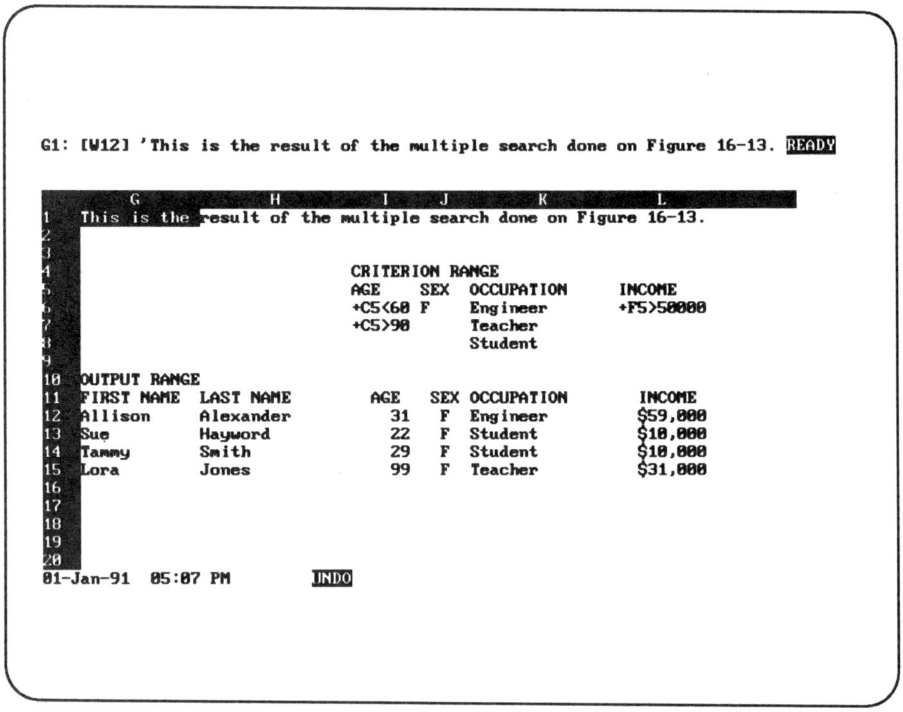

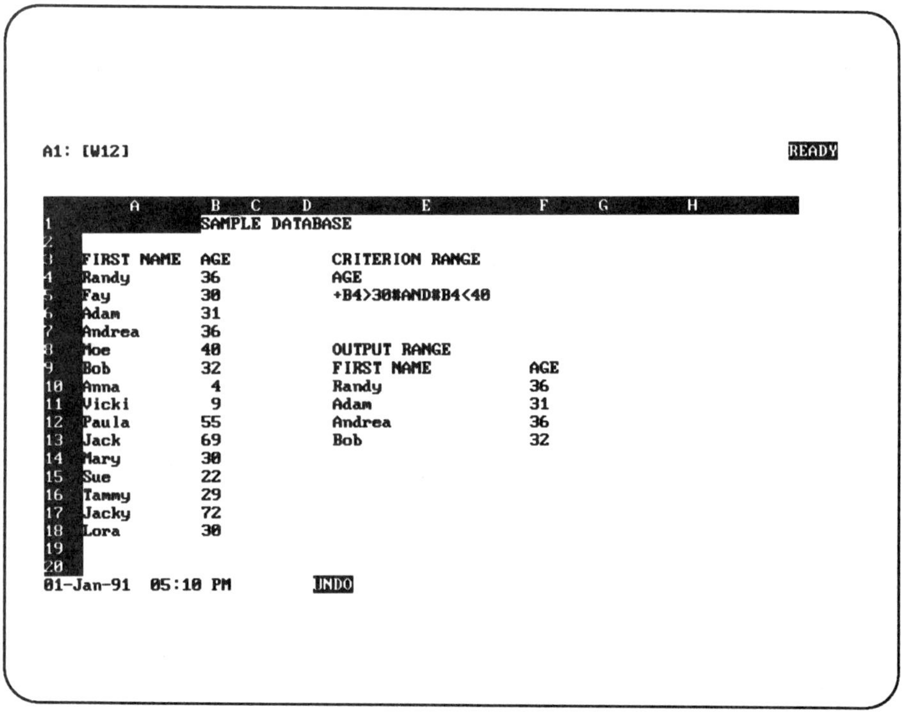

```
G1: [W12] 'This is the result of the multiple search done on Figure 16-13. READY

      G            H            I    J        K            L
1  This is the result of the multiple search done on Figure 16-13.
2
3
4                         CRITERION RANGE
5                         AGE     SEX  OCCUPATION        INCOME
6                         +C5<60  F    Engineer          +F5>50000
7                         +C5>90       Teacher
8                                      Student
9
10 OUTPUT RANGE
11 FIRST NAME  LAST NAME       AGE   SEX OCCUPATION        INCOME
12 Allison     Alexander        31   F   Engineer         $59,000
13 Sue         Hayword          22   F   Student          $10,000
14 Tammy       Smith            29   F   Student          $10,000
15 Lora        Jones            99   F   Teacher          $31,000
16
17
18
19
20
01-Jan-91  05:07 PM         UNDO
```

```
A1: [W12]                                                          READY

      A         B  C  D      E            F    G      H
1               SAMPLE DATABASE
2
3  FIRST NAME  AGE       CRITERION RANGE
4  Randy       36        AGE
5  Fay         30        +B4>30#AND#B4<40
6  Adam        31
7  Andrea      36
8  Joe         40        OUTPUT RANGE
9  Bob         32        FIRST NAME        AGE
10 Anna         4        Randy             36
11 Vicki        9        Adam              31
12 Paula       55        Andrea            36
13 Jack        69        Bob               32
14 Mary        30
15 Sue         22
16 Tammy       29
17 Jacky       72
18 Lora        30
19
20
01-Jan-91  05:10 PM         UNDO
```

FIGURE 16-15 Search with AND within One Field

FIGURE 16-16 Search with OR within One Field

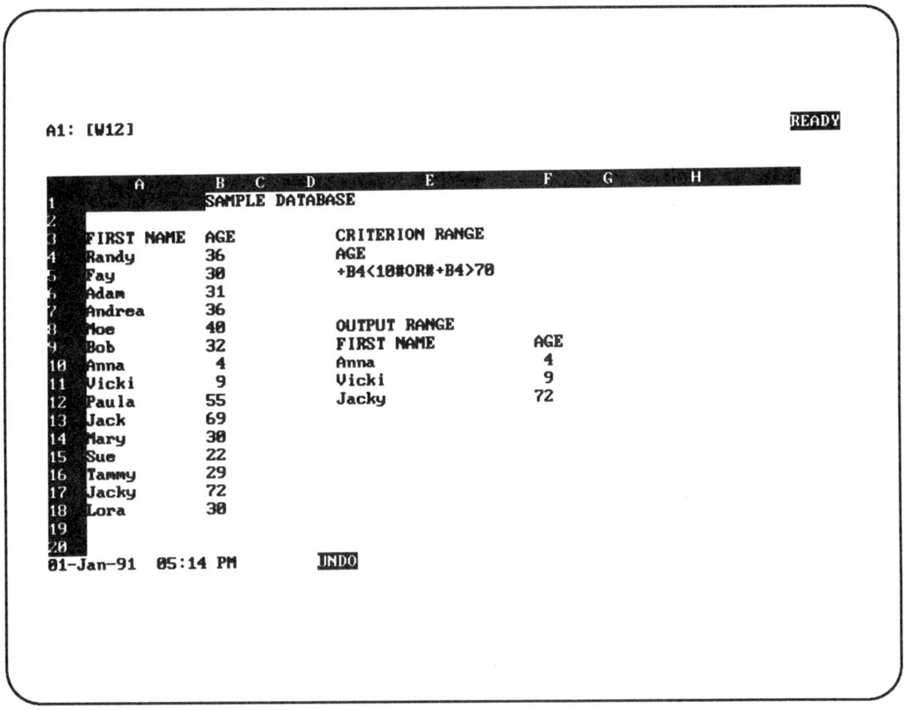

```
A1: [W12]                                                          READY

         A         B   C    D          E             F      G        H
1                     SAMPLE DATABASE
2
3        FIRST NAME  AGE          CRITERION RANGE
4        Randy       36           AGE
5        Fay         30           +B4<10#OR#+B4>70
6        Adam        31
7        Andrea      36
8        Moe         40           OUTPUT RANGE
9        Bob         32           FIRST NAME          AGE
10       Anna         4           Anna                 4
11       Vicki        9           Vicki                9
12       Paula       55           Jacky               72
13       Jack        69
14       Mary        30
15       Sue         22
16       Tammy       29
17       Jacky       72
18       Lora        30
19
20
01-Jan-91  05:14 PM          UNDO
```

16-13 Extract vs. Unique Options

Sometimes there are duplicate records in the database. Let us say you would like to generate a mailing list for a series of business organizations and you want to send a memo to each organization. As an example, you would like to send a memo to one university in each system; one memo to the Cal State system, one to the UC system, and so forth. In this case, the Extract option may not do the job if the organization is listed more than once in your database. If you use the Unique option, only one occurrence of each record will be selected.

Figure 16-17 shows a database used to compare the Extract and Unique options. Figure 16-18 compares the results of using these two options. This figure was generated as follows:

For the Extract option:

/Data, Query, Input A5..B20, **Return**, Criterion M18..N19, **Return**, Output G4..J21, **Return**, Extract

For the Unique option:

/Data, Query, Input A5..B20, **Return**, Criterion M18..N19, **Return**, Output K4..N16, **Return**, Unique

Remember, when the Unique option is used the entire record must be unique, not just one or more fields.

16-14 Delete Option

Besides using the /Worksheet and /Range commands for deleting a portion of your database, you can use the Delete option. You must be very careful with this command.

Save your worksheet first, then use this command. The deleted data is gone for good. Figure 16-20 was generated by using the database in Figure 16-19 and deleting all the engineers. Figure 16-20 was generated as follows:

/Data, Query, Input A3..F18, **Return**, Criterion B19..B20, **Return**, Delete, Delete

This command should be used carefully. You may find it useful to make a copy of the database before executing this command.

SUMMARY

This chapter covered the rudiments of database operations and creation, update, sort and search procedures. Having the Lotus database in RAM makes the processing speed extremely fast. For this reason, a Lotus database is an impressive tool for business database applications. Chapter 17 will discuss advanced database operations in detail.

REVIEW QUESTIONS

* These questions are answered in Appendix I.
1. What is a database?
2. How do you create a database using Lotus?
3. What is the difference between numeric and nonnumeric data in a database?
4.* How do you erase a record in a database?
5. How do you erase a field in a database?
6. How many fields can you have in your database?

FIGURE 16-17 *Database Used for Extract and Unique Options*

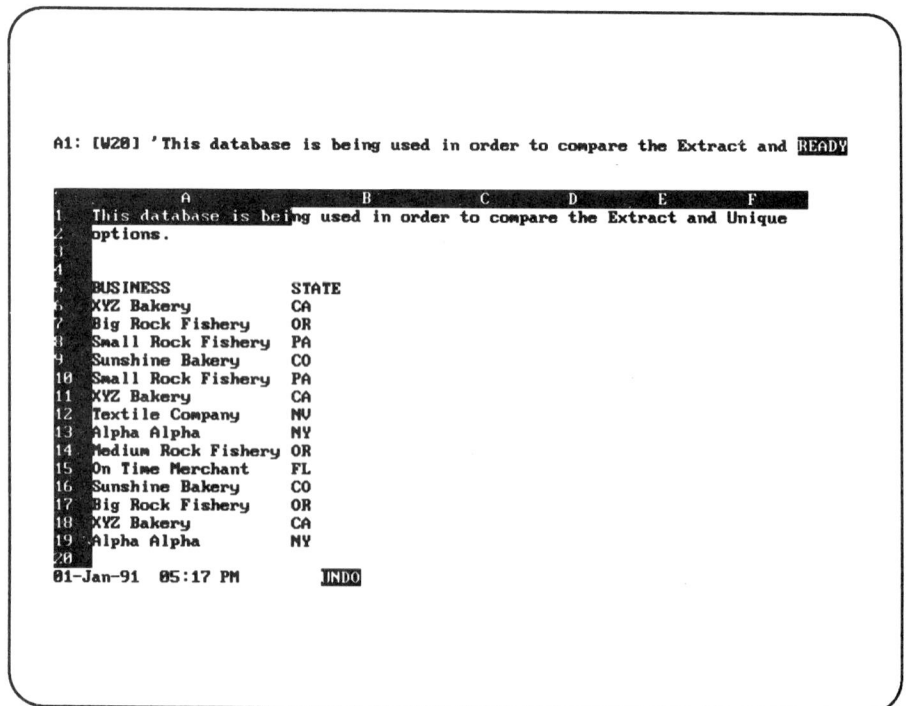

```
A1: [W20] 'This database is being used in order to compare the Extract and READY

         A                    B          C          D      E       F
1    This database is being used in order to compare the Extract and Unique
2    options.
3
4
5    BUSINESS              STATE
6    XYZ Bakery            CA
7    Big Rock Fishery      OR
8    Small Rock Fishery    PA
9    Sunshine Bakery       CO
10   Small Rock Fishery    PA
11   XYZ Bakery            CA
12   Textile Company       NV
13   Alpha Alpha           NY
14   Medium Rock Fishery   OR
15   On Time Merchant      FL
16   Sunshine Bakery       CO
17   Big Rock Fishery      OR
18   XYZ Bakery            CA
19   Alpha Alpha           NY
20
01-Jan-91  05:17 PM            UNDO
```

FIGURE 16-18 *Comparison of Extract and Unique Options*

```
G1: 'The comparison between Extract option and Unique option.          READY

        G       H        I        J        K        L        M        N
 1  The comparison between Extract option and Unique option.
 2
 3  OUTPUT RANGE FOR EXTRACT              OUTPUT RANGE FOR UNIQUE
 4  BUSINESS                   STATE      BUSINESS                   STATE
 5  XYZ Bakery                 CA         XYZ Bakery                 CA
 6  Big Rock Fishery           OR         Big Rock Fishery           OR
 7  Small Rock Fishery         PA         Small Rock Fishery         PA
 8  Sunshine Bakery            CO         Sunshine Bakery            CO
 9  Small Rock Fishery         PA         Textile Company            NV
10  XYZ Bakery                 CA         Alpha Alpha                NY
11  Textile Company            NV         Medium Rock Fishery        OR
12  Alpha Alpha                NY         On Time Merchant           FL
13  Medium Rock Fishery        OR
14  On Time Merchant           FL
15  Sunshine Bakery            CO
16  Big Rock Fishery           OR
17  XYZ Bakery                 CA                    CRITERION RANGE
18  Alpha Alpha                NY                    BUSINESS STATE
19
20
01-Jan-91  05:21 PM        UNDO
```

```
A1: [W12]                                                              READY

        A           B           C      D      E              F          G
 1              MY FIRST DATABASE
 2
 3  FIRST NAME  LAST NAME       AGE    SEX    OCCUPATION     INCOME
 4  Randy       Alexander       36     M      Professor      $40,000
 5  Fay         Alexander       30     F      Mayor          $30,000
 6  Adam        Alexander       31     M      Engineer       $30,000
 7  Andrea      Byan            36     F      Teacher        $31,000
 8  Moe         Byan            40     M      Officer        $40,000
 9  Bob         Adam            32     M      Engineer       $72,000
10  Anna        Adam             4     F      Unemployed     $11,000
11  Vicki       Adam             9     F      Unemployed     $12,000
12  Paula       Bobby           55     F      Housewife      $20,000
13  Jack        Jones           69     M      Artist         $19,000
14  Mary        Fishler         30     F      Interpreter    $19,000
15  Sue         Hayword         22     F      Student        $10,000
16  Tammy       Smith           29     F      Student        $10,000
17  Jacky       Brown           72     F      Engineer       $52,000
18  Lora        Jones           30     F      Nurse          $31,000
19              OCCUPATION
20              Engineer
01-Jan-91  05:26 PM        UNDO
```

FIGURE 16-19 *Database Used for the Delete Option*

FIGURE 16-20 An Example of the Delete Option

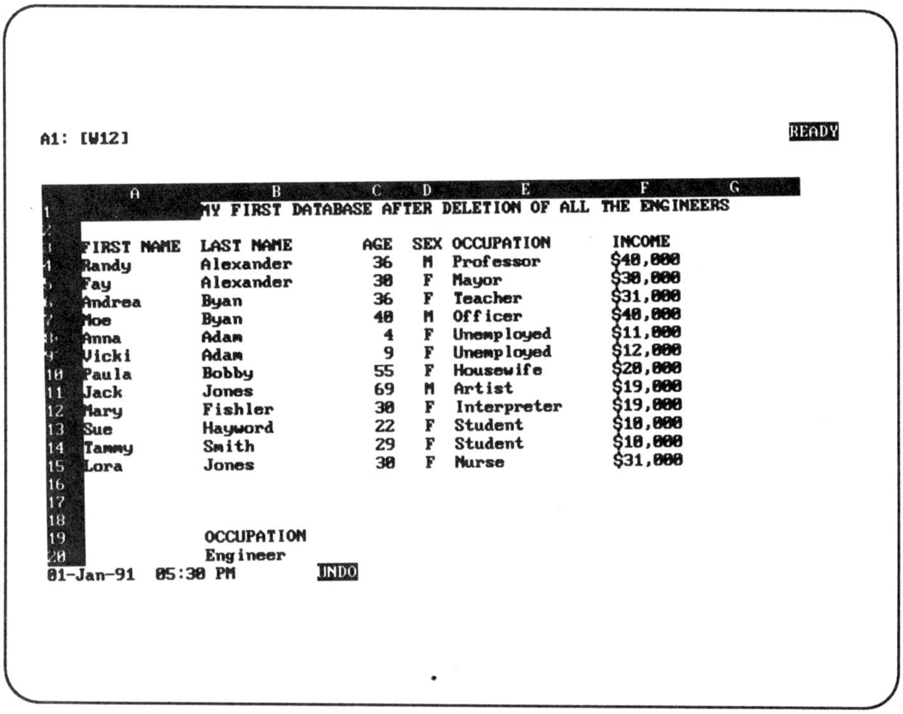

```
A1: [W12]                                                              READY

       A            B          C    D       E            F        G
1                       MY FIRST DATABASE AFTER DELETION OF ALL THE ENGINEERS
2
3    FIRST NAME   LAST NAME    AGE  SEX OCCUPATION      INCOME
4    Randy        Alexander    36    M   Professor      $40,000
5    Fay          Alexander    30    F   Mayor          $30,000
6    Andrea       Byan         36    F   Teacher        $31,000
7    Moe          Byan         40    M   Officer        $40,000
8    Anna         Adam          4    F   Unemployed     $11,000
9    Vicki        Adam          9    F   Unemployed     $12,000
10   Paula        Bobby        55    F   Housewife      $20,000
11   Jack         Jones        69    M   Artist         $19,000
12   Mary         Fishler      30    F   Interpreter    $19,000
13   Sue          Hayword      22    F   Student        $18,000
14   Tammy        Smith        29    F   Student        $18,000
15   Lora         Jones        30    F   Nurse          $31,000
16
17
18
19                OCCUPATION
20                Engineer
01-Jan-91   05:30 PM              UNDO
```

7. How many records can you have in your database?
8. How do you perform editing in your database?
9. How do you sort your database?
10.* What is the difference between the primary-key and secondary-key options?
11. How many ways can you sort your database?
12.* How many ways can you search your database?
13. What is the difference between the AND condition and the OR condition in the criterion range?
14. How many wild cards are available? What is the unique application of each wild card?
15.* What is the difference between the Extract option and the Unique option?
16.* How many fields can be included in your criterion range for an AND search?
17. What is the difference between a sort and a search range?

HANDS-ON PRACTICE

1. Generate the following database:

First Name	Last Name	Major	Age	Sex	GPA
Cora	Barnes	CS	22	F	3.20
Sue	Jones	MIS	29	F	2.80
Bobby	Trana	CS	30	F	3.70
Tammy	Smith	Marketing	22	F	3.85
John	Porsche	Management	36	M	3.60
Brian	Raban	Accounting	19	M	2.20

First Name	Last Name	Major	Age	Sex	GPA
Adam	Vigen	MIS	21	M	3.70
Clark	Standard	CS	28	M	3.00
Stanley	Jones	Personnel	24	M	2.90
Harry	Mohan	Management	26	M	2.75

   a. Add two more students to this list.
   b. Sort this list by GPA.
   c. Sort this list by age.
   d. Sort first by sex, then by age.
   e. Extract all MIS majors.
   f. Extract all MIS majors with GPA > 3.7.
   g. Extract either MIS or accounting majors.
   h. Extract students with age > 25 and GPA > 3.50 and who are female.
   i. Extract students who are between 20 and 30.
   j. Extract students who are either younger than 20 or older than 30.

2. Using the database present in Figure 16-21 do the following:
   a. Extract all the employees whose phone number starts with the digits 58.
   b. Extract all the employees who are on the fourth floor and whose phone number starts with the digits 58.
   c. Extract all the employees who are on the fourth floor, whose phone number starts with the digits 58, and who are in office 16.
   d. Extract all of R&D employees.
   e. Sort the database by phone numbers in descending order.
   f. Sort all the employees by department in descending order, then by floor in ascending order.

FIGURE 16-21 A Sample Database

COMPREHENSIVE LAB ASSIGNMENT

Retrieve CHAPT14 and perform the following:
1. Sort the existing database by age.
2. Sort the existing database by total scores of each student.
3. Sort the existing database by sex and major.
4. Extract all the MIS majors.
5. Extract all the MIS majors who are female.
6. Extract all the MIS majors who are female and are graduate students.
7. Extract all the students who have a total average score of greater than 92.
8. Extract all the students who are MIS or CS majors.
9. Using the Unique option, print one representative of each major.
10. Save this worksheet under CHAPT16.
11. Using the Delete option, delete all the students who are majoring in CS and are freshmen.

MISCONCEPTIONS AND SOLUTIONS

M – If you try to sort a worksheet, but leave out a portion of the worksheet in your data range, there is no way to return to the original database.

S – Either save the original database in a file or make sure that you have included the entire database in your sort range.

M – You have used the Extract option, but not all the appropriate data has been extracted.

S – Check that your output range is large enough.

Database Operations/Part Two: Lotus as a Sophisticated Database

17-1 Introduction

In this chapter we will study some of the sophisticated operations performed by the Lotus database functions, including statistical functions. As you will see, these functions provide a lot of flexibility compared with their statistical counterparts. We will explain table building using the /Data Fill command, what-if analysis performed by /Data Table 1 and /Data Table 2, and distribution analysis using the /Data Distribution command.

/Data Matrix and /Data Regression will be discussed at the end of this chapter. With these two commands, you can use the tremendous power of Lotus. A matrix of up to 90 rows by 90 columns can be easily inverted. This means that a 90 by 90 system of linear equations can be solved. Using /Data Regression, Lotus can handle a multiple linear regression of up to 16 variables. A dependent variable, such as income, can be predicted based on several independent variables (up to 16), such as education, number of years of experience, or field of study. /Data Matrix and /Data Regression can help you to develop fairly sophisticated forecasting models.

17-2 Database Statistical Functions

The seven statistical functions you saw in Chapter 12 can be used with database data with a minor variation. A database statistical function follows this format:

@Dfunction name(database range, offset value, criterion range)

The database range or input range is usually the entire database or a selected portion, and the offset value defines which column of the database is under investigation. This value starts from zero and goes to N-1, where N is the number of columns in a database. So if the offset value is 2, it means you are interested in column 3 of the database or field 3. If it is 10, it means you are interested in column 11. The criterion range must have a field heading. Below it you can define any criteria that you may be interested in.

There are seven database statistical functions: @DAVG, @DCOUNT, @DMAX, @DMIN, @DSTD, @DSUM, and @DVAR. These functions provide more flexibility than their statistical counterparts. By just changing the criterion range, you can perform all sorts of analyses. To make the power of these functions clearer consider a database for a state university that includes the information related to 8,000 students. Each record includes the student's first name, last name, major, age, nationality, GPA, sex, the name of the high school from which the student graduated and Social Security number. Using the database statistical functions you can be selective on this database, an option you did not have when you used the statistical function. For example, you can count the number of students who are majoring in computer science, are female, and are under 21 years of age. You can find the youngest and the oldest student in this group and so forth. You can calculate the average age of female students and compare it with the average age of male students. Figures 17-1 and 17-2 show some examples of database statistical functions.

In Figure 17-1, the database range is A3..C18; the offset value is 1, which means column 2 is under investigation; and the criterion range is H19..H20. In this example we are only interested in individuals who are older than 10 years. (In cell H20, we used the Text format in order to show the actual content of this cell.)

In Figure 17-2 we changed a couple of the criterion ranges. This demonstrates the flexibility provided by database statistical functions. You can include or exclude any portion of the database just by changing the criterion range.

17-3 Table Building Using the /Data Fill Command

You can use the /Data Fill command to build tables. All you need is to define a range, which becomes the table that you wish to build, then define the start, step, and stop values. These values will be filled in the table from top to bottom and from left to right. If you do not specify any value and press the **Return** key at the prompt, Lotus will use default values for start (0), step (1) and stop (8191).

FIGURE 17-1 *Database Statistical Functions*

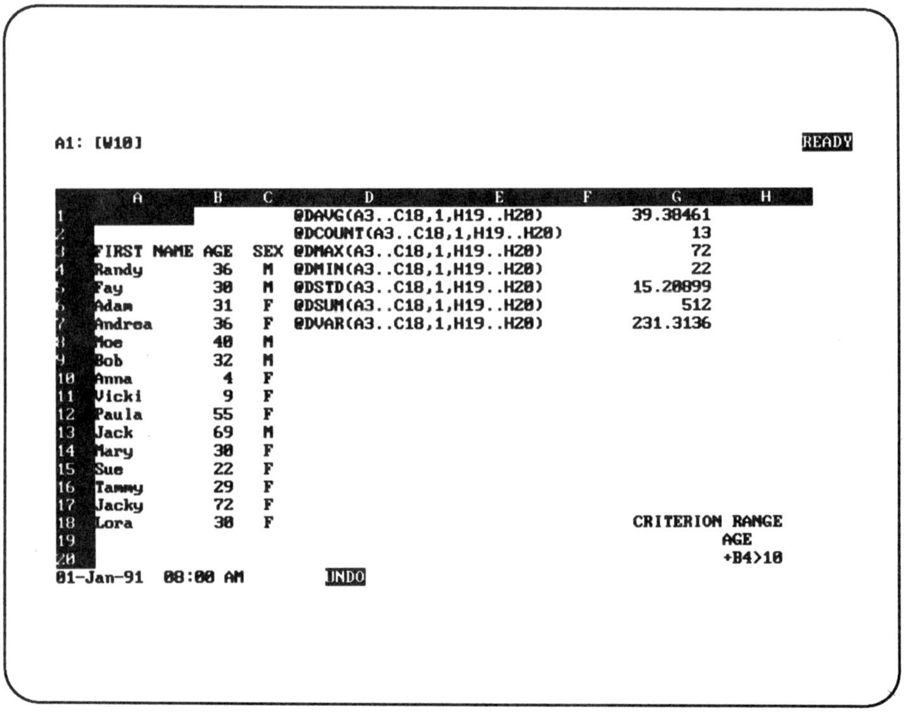

FIGURE 17-2 Database Statistical Functions with a Different Criterion Range

```
A1: [W10]                                                            READY

         A        B     C        D             E           F       G         H
1                                  @DAVG(A3..C18,1,H19..H20)        39.38461
2                                  @DCOUNT(A3..C18,1,H19..H20)            13
3    FIRST NAME  AGE   SEX  @DMAX(A3..C18,1,D18..D19)                     72
4    Randy        36    M   @DMIN(A3..C18,1,D18..D19)                     55
5    Fay          30    F   @DSTD(A3..C18,1,H19..H20)               15.28899
6    Adam         31    M   @DSUM(A3..C18,1,E18..E19)                     72
7    Andrea       36    F   @DVAR(A3..C18,1,H19..H20)               231.3136
8    Joe          40    M
9    Bob          32    M
10   Anna          4    F
11   Vicki         9    F
12   Paula        55    F
13   Jack         69    M
14   Mary         30    F
15   Sue          22    F
16   Tammy        29    F
17   Jacky        72    F                       CRITERION RANGE
18   Lora         30    F   AGE                 AGE
19                          +B4>50              +B4>70                        AGE
20                                                                            +B4>10
01-Jan-91  08:04 AM              UNDO
```

Table building will continue until either the range is filled or the stop value has been reached. Any of the three values can be a formula if the formula is defined when that it is needed by /Data Fill. In any situation where numeric values increment by a certain number you can use the /Data Fill command. For example, in an inventory situation, if the parts are numbered from 1 to 8,000 in increments of 5, the /Data Fill command can simplify the data entry task. All you need to do is to specify the range for the inventory data; the start value, which is 1; the step value, 5; and stop value, 8,000.

An excellent application of the /Data Fill command is to return a sorted database to its original unsorted form. To do this, you can either use the /Data Fill Command to number all the records in the database into an adjacent column or just number them by entering a sequence number. In this case the start value is 1, the step is 1, and the stop value is the number of records in the database. When the entire database is sorted, this column will be sorted as well. To return the database to its original form, choose this column as the primary key and sort the database again. You will see the original database. Figures 17-3 and 17-4 show some examples of the /Data Fill command.

In the upper portion of Figure 17-3, we defined a high value for stop (5,000), but the table building was stopped as soon as range A1..D1 was filled. In the lower portion of Figure 17-3, table building stopped when the stop value was reached (19,000), and the specified table was not filled.

In Figure 17-4, we created a simple database in cells A3..C8. We made a copy of the database in cells A11..C16 and this database was sorted in ascending order.

The sequence numbers are no longer ordered. To return this database to its original form, we made a copy of it in cells E11..G16 and sorted this database using the sequence number field as the primary key, returning the database back to its original form.

FIGURE 17-3 /Data Fill Command

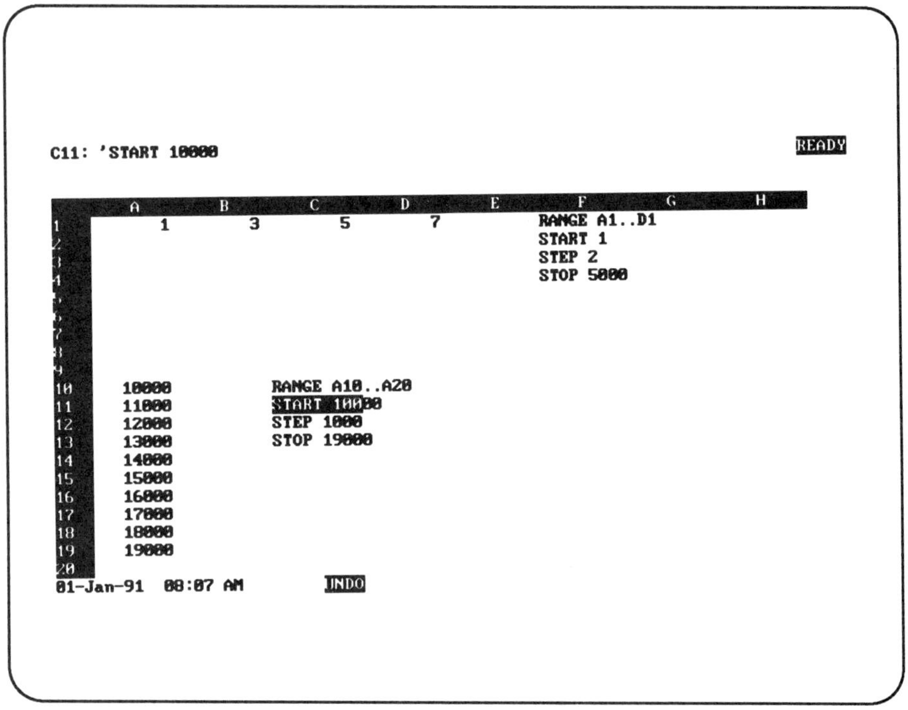

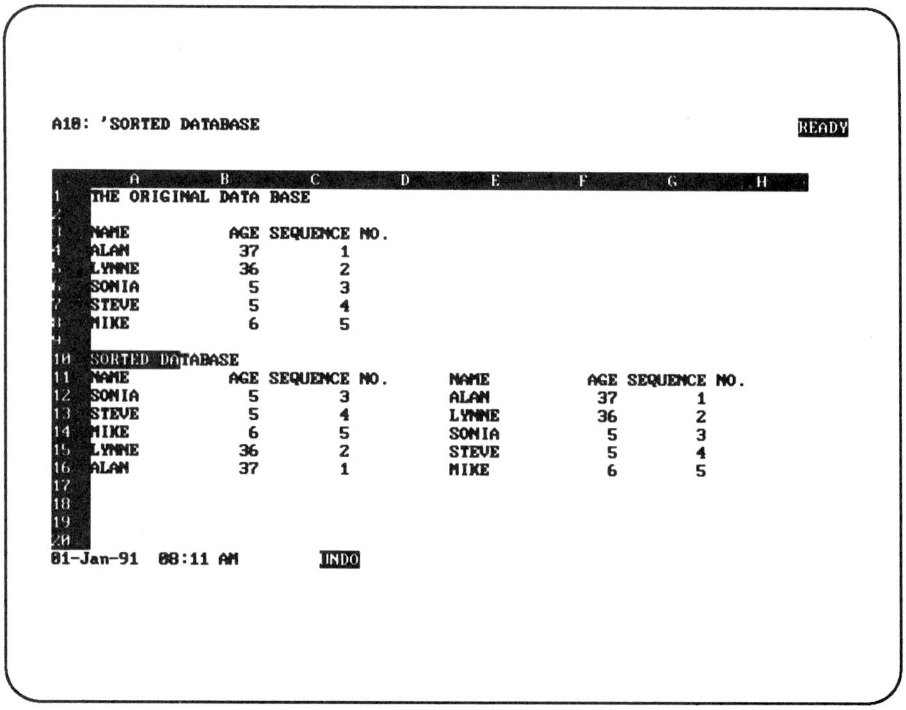

```
C11: 'START 10000                                                    READY

         A         B         C         D         E         F         G         H
 1       1         3         5         7                   RANGE A1..D1
 2                                                         START 1
 3                                                         STEP 2
 4                                                         STOP 5000
 5
 6
 7
 8
 9
10      10000                RANGE A10..A20
11      11000                START 10000
12      12000                STEP 1000
13      13000                STOP 19000
14      14000
15      15000
16      16000
17      17000
18      18000
19      19000
20
01-Jan-91  08:07 AM              UNDO
```

```
A10: 'SORTED DATABASE                                                READY

         A         B         C         D         E         F         G         H
 1    THE ORIGINAL DATA BASE
 2
 3    NAME        AGE SEQUENCE NO.
 4    ALAN        37      1
 5    LYNNE       36      2
 6    SONIA        5      3
 7    STEVE        5      4
 8    MIKE         6      5
 9
10    SORTED DATABASE
11    NAME        AGE SEQUENCE NO.      NAME        AGE SEQUENCE NO.
12    SONIA        5      3             ALAN        37      1
13    STEVE        5      4             LYNNE       36      2
14    MIKE         6      5             SONIA        5      3
15    LYNNE       36      2             STEVE        5      4
16    ALAN        37      1             MIKE         6      5
17
18
19
20
01-Jan-91  08:11 AM              UNDO
```

FIGURE 17-4 /Data Fill Command for Restoring a Sorted Database

17-4 What-If Analysis Using /Data Table 1

The /Data Table 1 command can be used to determine the effect of one variable on a formula or an entire worksheet. There are many areas where this command can be useful; for example, the effect of different interest rates on an IRA plan, the effect of different interest rates on a loan, or the effect of different commission percentages on the total commission generated by a salesperson.

To use /Data Table 1, you must first establish a table range. The table range can be anywhere in the worksheet. In Figure 17-5, C4..E15 is the table range. You must choose an empty cell outside the table range as the input cell. The address of this cell will be used to change values in a formula. This is used internally by Lotus for its calculations. Do not be worried about the contents of this cell. To you it appears as a blank cell. In our example, the input cell is A5. Now fill out the changing values in a column; in our case, cells C5..C15. Above and to the right of these values is our formula, here the future value, @FV(2000,A5,20). This is the future value of a $2,000 IRA plan for 20 years with a variable interest rate. This formula is in cell D4. The same formula was also copied to cell E4, but we have changed the number of years to 30. Remember, the intersection of these values (interest rates) and the formula is empty. This empty cell will be used by /Data Table 2. After inserting your changing values and the formulas, invoke /Data, Table, 1, C4..E5, **Return**, A5, **Return**.

As soon as the parameters are defined, the entire future value will be calculated for different interest rates and for two different years. Figure 17-5 shows one application of this command. If you change some of the input values, press F8 while in READY mode

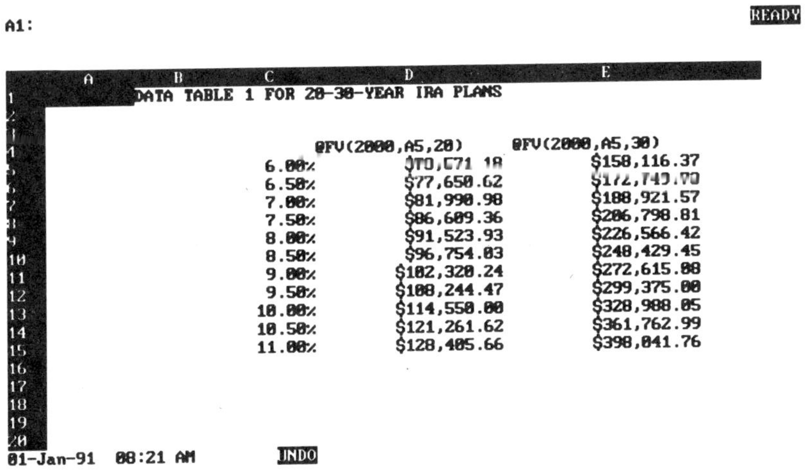

FIGURE 17-5 /Data Table 1 Showing the Effects of Different Interest Rates for Two Different IRA Plans

and the entire table will be recalculated. As you can see, this table can be a lot more complicated. You can do this calculation for several annuity periods. Simply define these periods and leave the rest of it to Lotus' amazing power and accuracy.

Figure 17-6 illustrates /Data Table 1 in a graphic format. As this figure indicates, while using /Data Table 1 you can have one or several @ functions or formulas in a row. In a column you can have one variable set. This variable can be any changing value used in the @ function(s). The intersection of the row and the column is always blank.

17-5 /Data Table 1 Using Database Data

Database statistical functions can be used as formulas with the /Data Table 1 and /Data Table 2 commands. The procedure is straightforward. In Figure 17-7, we used the

FIGURE 17-6   /Data Table 1 in Graphic Format

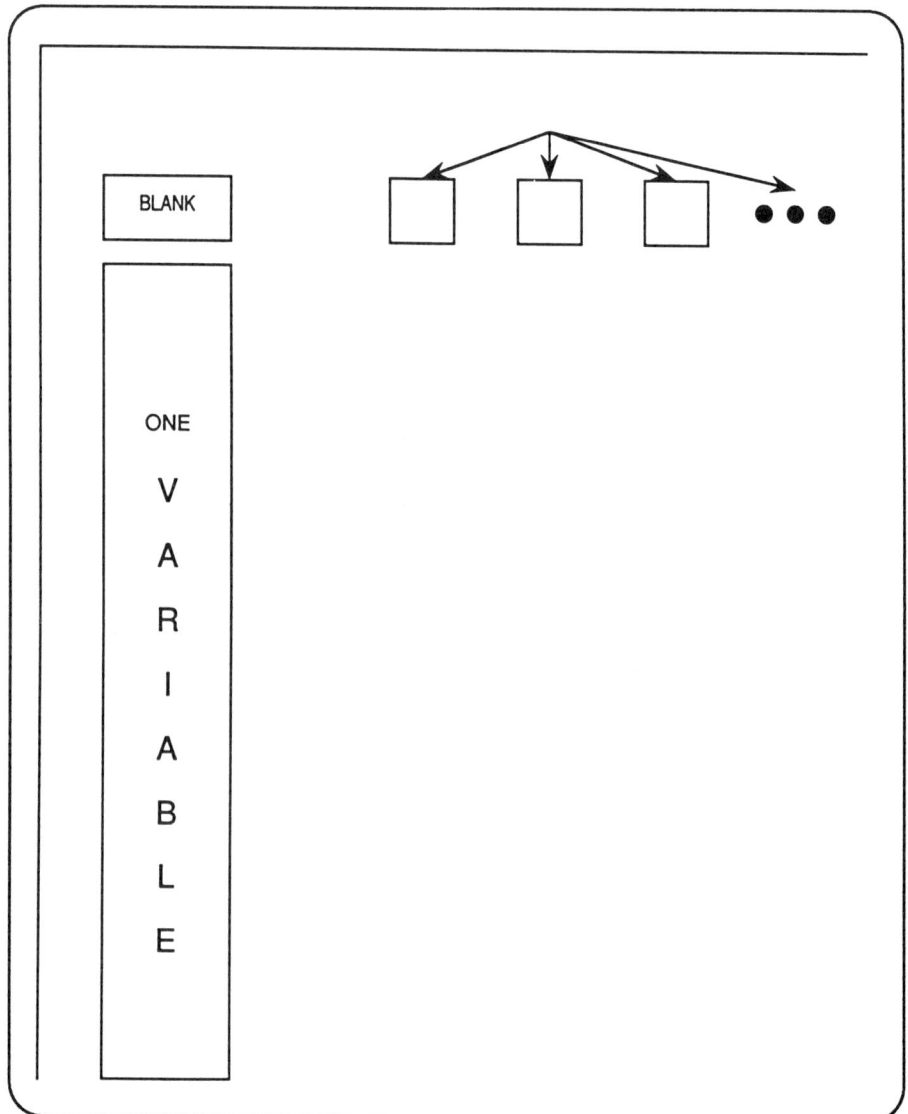

FIGURE 17-7 *Using Data Table 1 with Database Data*

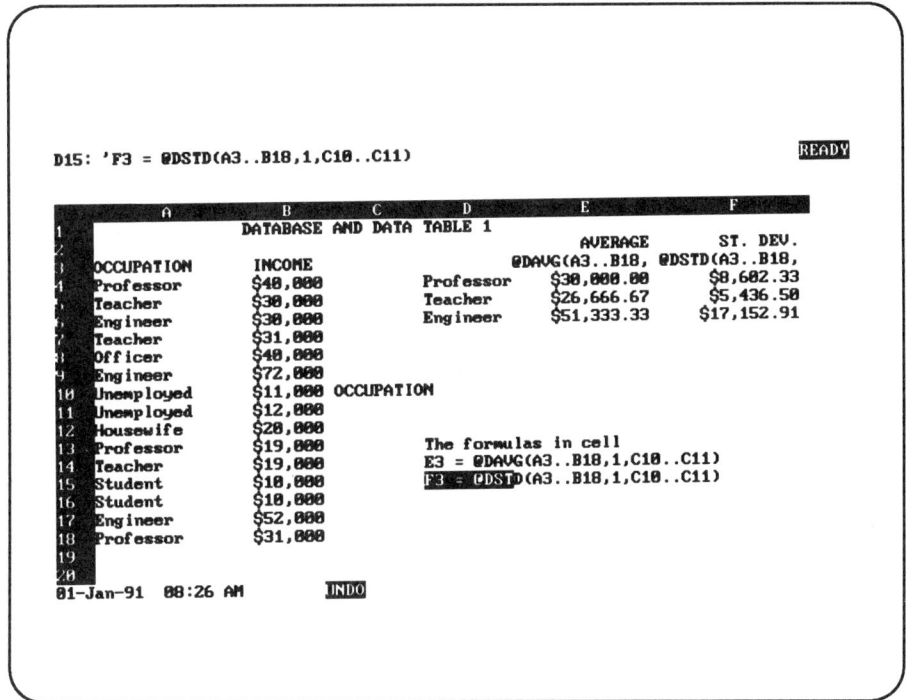

database to the left of the screen as our input range (A3..B18). The offset value is 1, meaning column 2 (income) is under investigation and the criterion range has been set up in cells C10..C11. As before, this range includes the field title and the specific criteria are below it. Since we have left cell C11 empty, this means any occupation can be entered here. Cell C11 is used also as the input cell for /Data Table 1.

In /Data Table 1, the input range is D3..F6. The entire table range includes three occupations in the column and two formulas in the row, The input cell is C11. Now Lotus matches any of these three occupations with the original database and calculates the average salary and standard deviation of these salaries. After inserting all the formulas and values invoke /Data, Table, 1, D3. .F7, **Return**, C11, **Return**.

17-6 What-If Analysis Using /Data Table 2

In /Data Table 2 the effects of two variables over the entire worksheet or a specified range can be calculated. Let us walk through an example. Sunrise Electronic Firm has designed a formula for calculating the total salary of its employees, based on the years of education (high school diploma, BS, MS, PhD) and the number of years of experience (1 to 15 years). In any case, $1,000 would be the base salary. The formula is $1000+A1*50+B1*75$, where A1 is the number of years of experience and B1 is the number of years of education. These are the input cells. For example, an employee with 5 years of experience and 12 years of education will make $1000+5*50+12*75 = \$2150$.

In Figure 17-8, we have used /Data Table 2 to calculate the entire table for the Sunrise Electronics Firm. The table range is D3..H18. Input cell 1 is A5 (years of experience), input cell 2 is B5 (years of education). Remember, the formula $1000+A5*50+B5*75$ was copied into cell D3, the intersection of row 3 (years of education) and column D (years

FIGURE 17-8 /Data Table 2 Showing the Effect of Years of Experience and Education on Salary

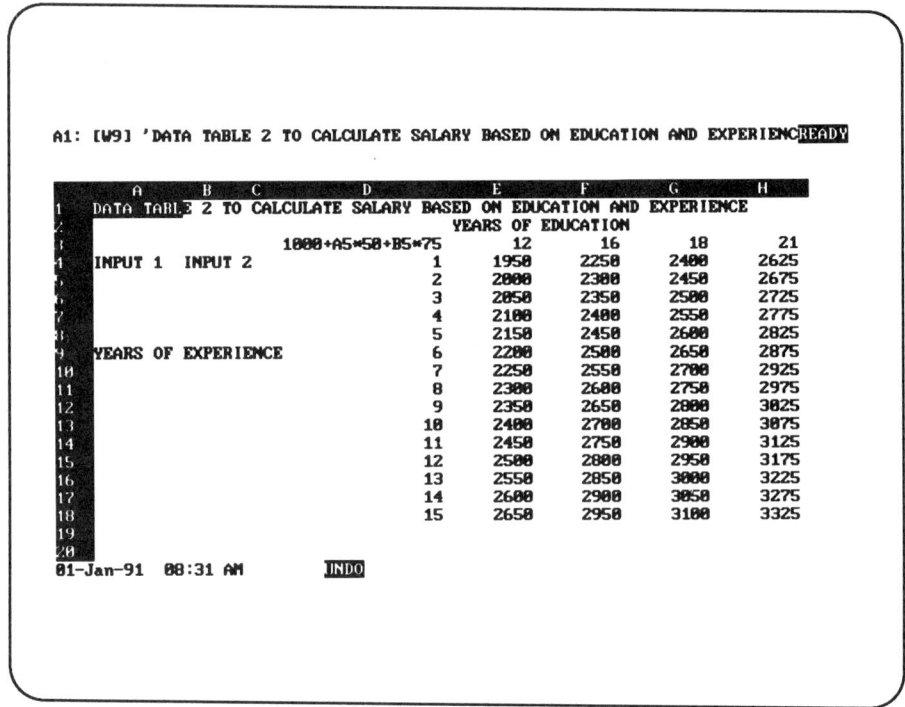

```
A1: [W9] 'DATA TABLE 2 TO CALCULATE SALARY BASED ON EDUCATION AND EXPERIENC READY

         A      B      C         D           E        F        G        H
 1   DATA TABLE 2 TO CALCULATE SALARY BASED ON EDUCATION AND EXPERIENCE
 2                                    YEARS OF EDUCATION
 3                   1000+A5*50+B5*75       12       16       18       21
 4   INPUT 1   INPUT 2          1         1950     2250     2400     2625
 5                               2         2000     2300     2450     2675
 6                               3         2050     2350     2500     2725
 7                               4         2100     2400     2550     2775
 8                               5         2150     2450     2600     2825
 9   YEARS OF EXPERIENCE         6         2200     2500     2650     2875
10                               7         2250     2550     2700     2925
11                               8         2300     2600     2750     2975
12                               9         2350     2650     2800     3025
13                              10         2400     2700     2850     3075
14                              11         2450     2750     2900     3125
15                              12         2500     2800     2950     3175
16                              13         2550     2850     3000     3225
17                              14         2600     2900     3050     3275
18                              15         2650     2950     3100     3325
19
20
01-Jan-91  08:31 AM        UNDO
```

of experience). To complete this table invoke /Data, Table, 2, D3..H18, **Return**, A5, **Return** B5, **Return**. Again, do not be worried about cells A5 and B5. Lotus uses these for internal calculations. They appear blank to you.

You can change any of these values and press F8. The entire table will be recalculated immediately.

Figure 17-9 illustrates /Data Table 2 in a graphic format. As this figure indicates, while using /Data Table 2, you can have one variable set in a column, and another variable set in a row. The intersection of the column and the row is one formula or function that uses these two variables. These variables can be any changing value used by the formula or the function in the intersection of the row and column.

17-7 /Data Table 2 Using Database Data

/Data Table 2, like /Data Table 1, can be used effectively with database statistical functions. To show this we have collected a summary of a large survey in Figure 17-10. A group of professors in different disciplines were surveyed in different states. We are interested in finding out the average salary of each type of professor in three different states.

The table range is F4..I7, which includes three types of professors (CS, ACC, MIS, the column) in three states (OR, CA, ND, the row). Input cell 1 is D6, which will be either CS (computer science), ACC (accounting), or MIS (management information systems). Input cell 2 is E6, which will be either OR (Oregon), CA (California), or ND (North Dakota). The criterion range is defined in cells D5..E6. Notice under Type and State there are empty cells which means any professor as long as he/she is in CS, ACC or MIS. Also under State there is an empty cell which means any state as long as it is OR, CA or ND. Cell F4, the

FIGURE 17-9 /Data Table 2 in Graphic Format

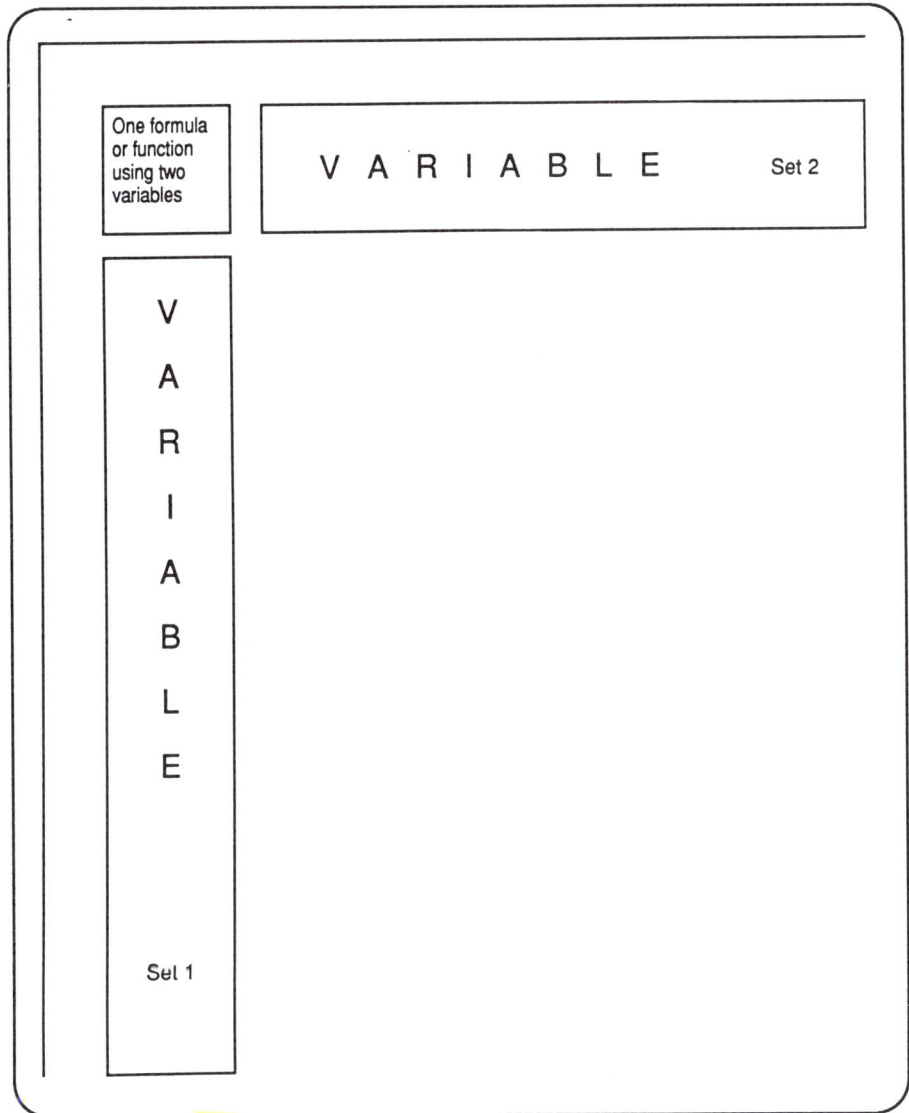

intersection of row and column, contains the formula @DAVG(A3..C18,0,D5..E6). When you enter your formulas and data invoke /Data, Table, 2, F4..I7, **Return**, D6, **Return** E6, **Return**.

Lotus searches for a CS professor in the state of Oregon (there are three of them) and calculates the average salary; ($31,000+$41,000+$39,000)/3 = $37,000. In California there is only one with a salary of $40,000; and so forth. We used Text Format in cell F4 to show you the actual formula used for our calculations.

17-8 Distribution Analysis Using the /Data Distribution Command

There are many cases where you may be interested in classifying a series of data into an orderly group, for example, classifying the salary of all the employees of Jack's

FIGURE 17-10 *Data Table 2 Using Database Data to Calculate the Average Salary of Three Different Types of Professors in Three Different States*

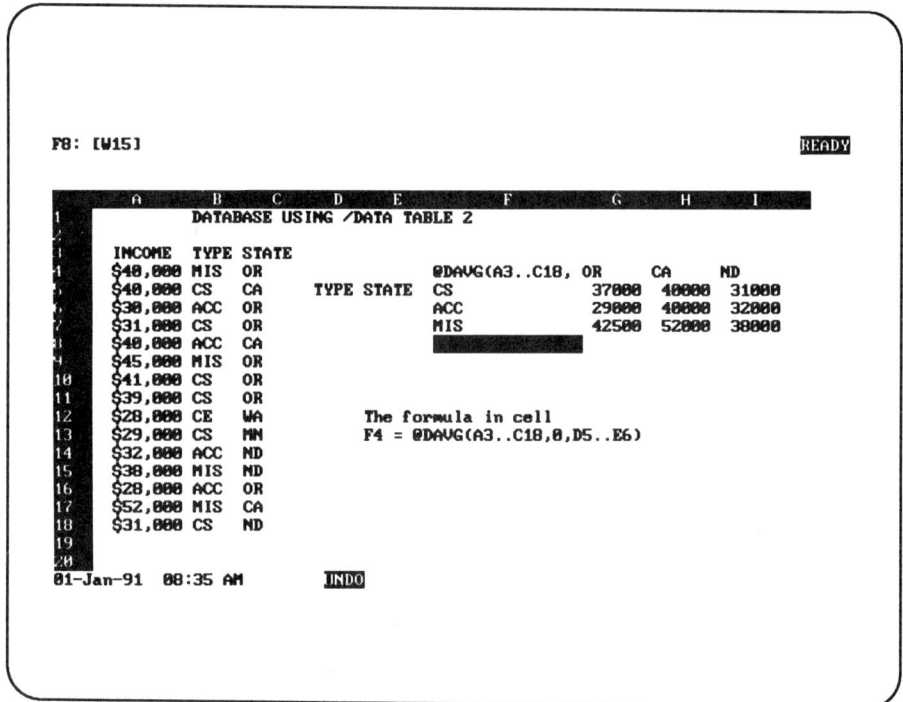

Manufacturing into ten groups, or classifying your customers in nine sales groups. The / Data Distribution command will perform these types of analysis for you.

To use this command, define the range of values you would like to classify. Then select two empty columns. The first one is used for your bin range in ascending order, for example, salaries of 10,000, 12,000, 15,000, 18,000, etc. The empty column adjacent to the bin range will be used by Lotus to provide the frequency distribution. Figure 17-11 shows an example of the /Data Distribution command.

In this figure, the value range is B4..B17 and the bin range is D4..D8 (we have organized salaries into five groups in ascending order). As you see, the first number under the frequency is 6. This means there are six individuals whose income is between $0 and $20,000. There are four individuals whose income is between $20,001 and $40,000; and so on. The last frequency value is 0. This means nobody is making more than $100,000. When you enter all your data in the worksheet invoke /Data, Distribution, B4. .B17, **Return**, D4. .D8, **Return**.

17-9 Inverting a Matrix Using the /Data Matrix Invert Command

Inverting a matrix that can be used in solving a system of linear equations is a time-consuming and complex task. Lotus provides an easy solution. The inverse of a matrix is a matrix which, if multiplied by the original matrix, will create an identity matrix. An *identity matrix* is one that has a diagonal of ones and the rest of the matrix filled by zeros. Figure 17-12 shows an original matrix, its inverse, and the result of the multiplication of the original matrix by its inverse. As you see, the result is an identity matrix. All the

FIGURE 17-11   *An Example of /Data Distribution*

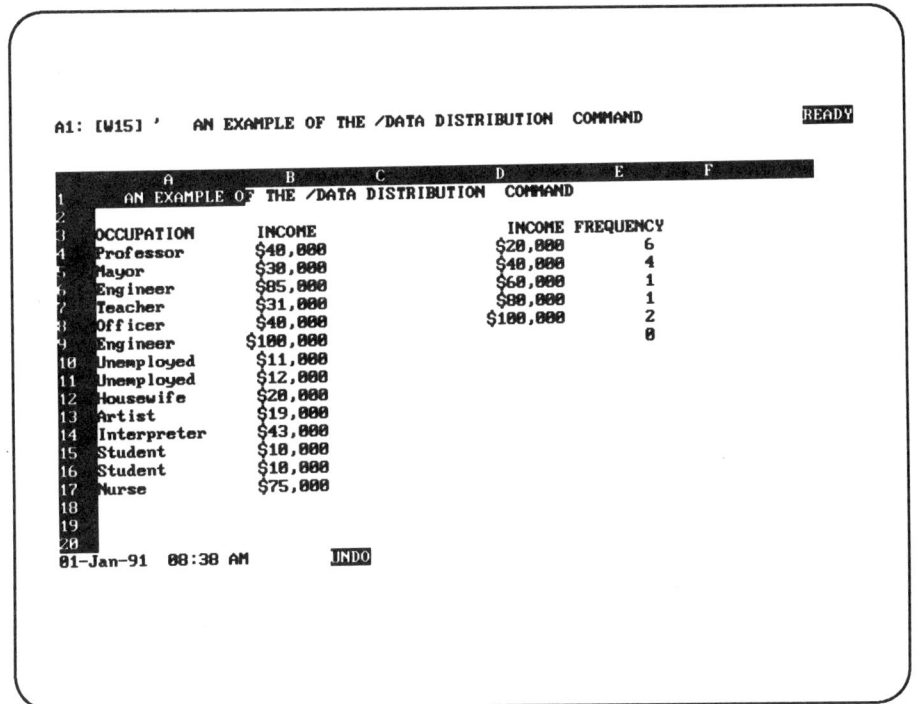

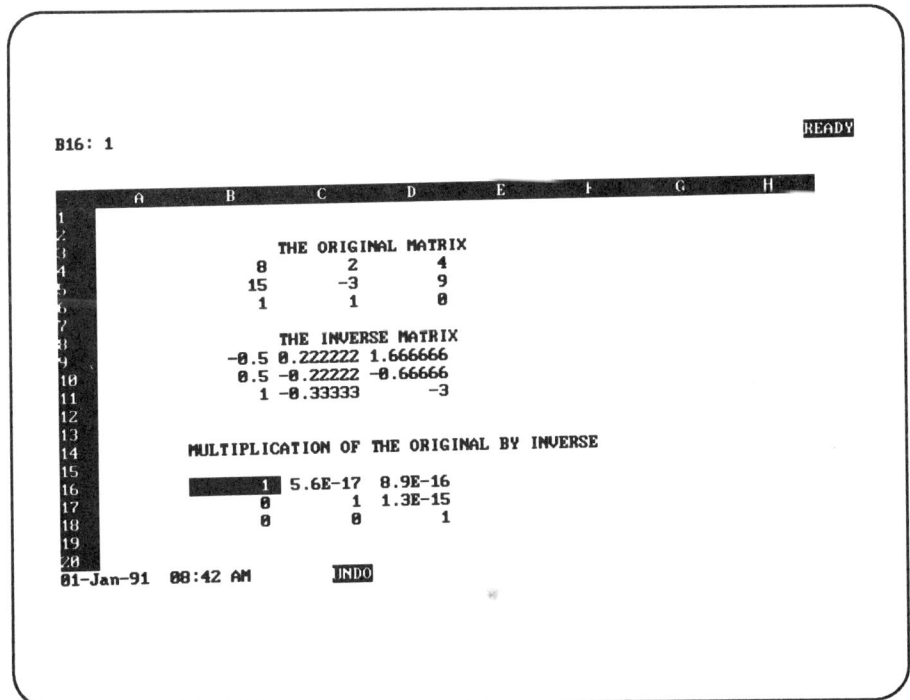

FIGURE 17-12   *Calculation of the Inverse of a Matrix*

nonzero numbers are indeed very close to zero. If you format this matrix with two decimals, you will see the zeros.

To generate this result first we enter the original matrix in range B4..D6, then invoke the /Data Matrix Invert command. The range chosen was B4..D6; the output range was B9..D11. To verify this result we multiplied the original matrix by its inverse. To do this invoke /Data, Matrix, Multiply, B4. .D6, **Return**, B9. .D11, **Return**, B16, **Return**.

17-10 Matrix Addition, Subtraction, and Multiplication

Matrix addition and subtraction can be done by using /File Combine Add and /File Combine Subtract. For matrix multiplication, Lotus provides an additional facility under /Data Matrix Multiply.

To multiply two matrices by each other, the number of the columns of the first matrix must be equal to the number of the rows of the second matrix. For example, a 5 by 5 matrix can be multiplied by a 5 by 1 matrix. Invoke /Data Matrix Multiply, then define the data range and the output range for your two matrices. Figure 17-13 shows an example of the operations. This figure was created by /Data, Matrix, Multiply, B2. .F6, **Return**, B8. .F12, **Return**, B14, **Return**.

17-11 Solving a System of Linear Equations Using the Lotus /Data Matrix Command

A combination of /Data Matrix Invert and /Data Matrix Multiply can be used to solve a system of linear equations. The solution to a system of linear equations with n variables is as follows:

$$
\begin{bmatrix} X1 \\ X2 \\ X3 \\ X4 \\ \cdot \\ \cdot \\ \cdot \\ X_n \end{bmatrix} = \begin{bmatrix} \text{inverse of matrix} \\ \text{of} \\ \text{Coefficients} \\ \end{bmatrix} * \begin{bmatrix} b1 \\ b2 \\ b3 \\ b4 \\ \cdot \\ \cdot \\ \cdot \\ b_n \end{bmatrix}
$$

where X1, X2, ... Xn are the number of unknowns and b1, b2, ... bn are the righthand side of equations 1, 2, 3, ... n. Therefore to solve a system of linear equations, the inverse of the matrix of coefficients will be multiplied by the array of the righthand side. The result of this multiplication is the solution to the system of the linear equations. Figure 17-14 shows an example using Lotus to solve a system of linear equations. The following equations were used in this example:

-10x1+18x2+	30x3	-40x4	+12x5	=	10
120x1+30x2+	100x3	-140x4	-10x5	=	100
25x1+15x2+	10x3	-20x4	-5x5	=	25
38x1+16x2+	24x3	-30x4	-8x5	=	40
20x1+10x2+	40x3	-10x4	+20x5	=	60

FIGURE 17-13 Matrix Multiplication

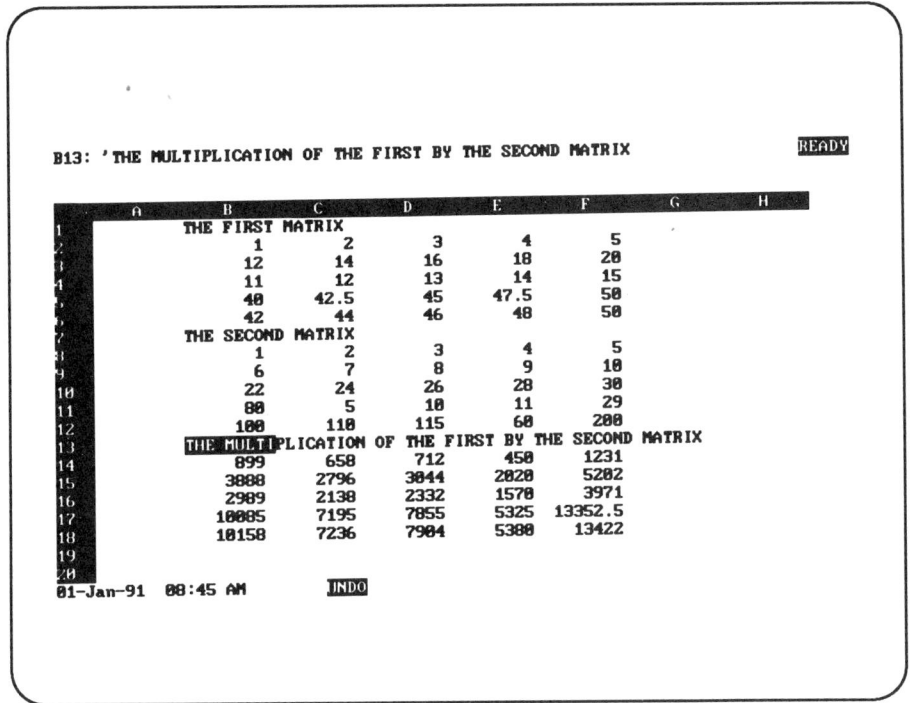

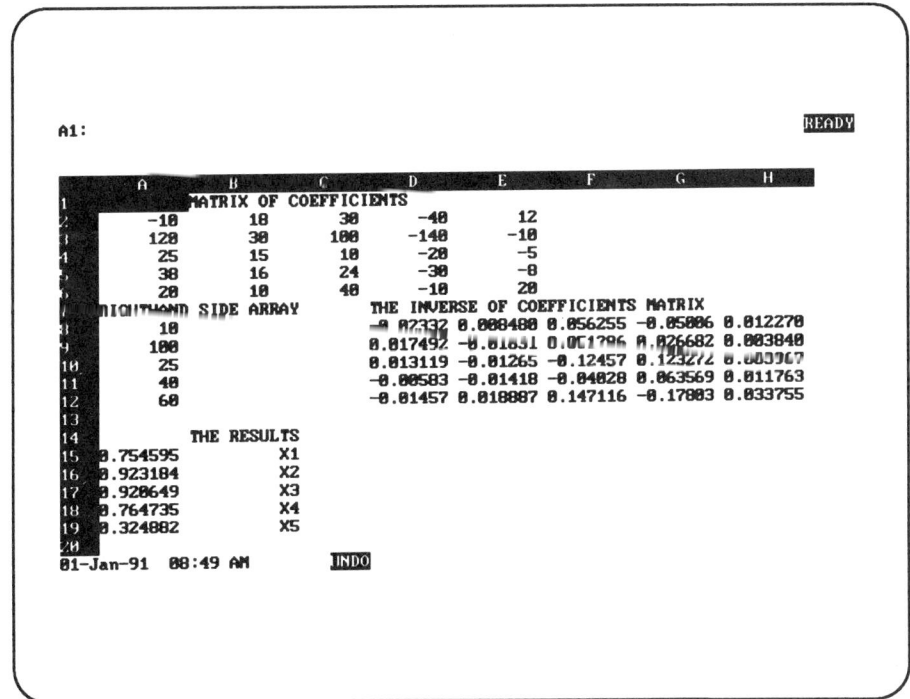

FIGURE 17-14 Solving a System of Linear Equations

The answers for x1, x2, x3, x4 and x5 are presented at the bottom of Figure 17-14. After entry the matrix of the coefficients in range A2. .E6 and the right-hand side array in range A8. .A12, we invoked /Data, Matrix, Invert, A2. .E6, **Return**, D8, **Return**. /Data, Matrix, Multiply, D8. .H12, **Return**, A15, **Return**.

17-12 Regression Analysis Using the /Data Regression Command

Simple linear regression is a tool used for either medium-range (less than two years) or long-range forecasting (two years or more). The formula for a simple linear regression is as follows:

$Y = A + BX$ (equation for a straight line)

where Y is the dependent variable, such as income, total sales, total costs; X is the independent variable, such as education, advertising budget, fixed cost; A is the intercept; and B is the slope of the line.

In order to apply this model to forecasting problems, values for A and B must be estimated. One way of estimating these values is by using the least squares method.

The least squares method estimates the values of A and B in such a way that the mean squared deviation between actual and predicted values is as small as possible. The following two formulas will be used to satisfy the requirements of the least squares method:

$$B = \frac{N\Sigma XY - \Sigma X \Sigma Y}{N\Sigma X^2 - (\Sigma X)^2}$$

$$A = \frac{\Sigma Y}{N} - \frac{B \Sigma X}{N}$$

To measure the strength of the relative association between two variables we use the *correlation coefficient*. The correlation coefficient, r, can vary from -1 to +1; r = 0 indicates no correlation, r = -1 indicates perfect negative correlation, and r = +1 indicates perfect positive correlation.

The formula for the correlation coefficient is as follows:

$$r = \frac{N\Sigma XY - \Sigma X \Sigma Y}{\sqrt{[N\Sigma X^2 - (\Sigma X)^2][N\Sigma Y^2 - (\Sigma Y)^2]}}$$

The square of the correlation coefficient is called the *coefficient of determination*. The coefficient of determination is the ratio of the sum of explained variation over the sum of total variation. The following formula indicates this:

$$r^2 = \frac{[N\Sigma XY - \Sigma X \Sigma Y]^2}{[N\Sigma X^2 - (\Sigma X)^2][N\Sigma Y^2 - (\Sigma Y)^2]}$$

This ratio shows how well a regression line can define the total variation in a series of data points. This ratio varies from 0 to 1; 0 means that the regression line does not explain any variation in the data points and 1 means that total variation is perfectly explained by the regression line.

Let us say you have an equation of $Y = 10,000 + 250X$, where Y is the total sales and X is the amount of advertising. This equation indicates that if you do not advertise at all (x=0), your estimated total sales would be $10,000. For every one dollar of advertising, your estimated total sales would increase by $250.

Figure 17-15 shows an example of simple linear regression for total sales and advertising for Pacific Rain Glass Company. This forecast is based on the past 12 years of available data. To generate this forecast, first enter your data then invoke the /Data Regression command. For the X-Range, independent variable, we have data in cells C5..C16. For the Y-Range (dependent variable) we have data in cells B5..B16. For the output range we chose E1 (only the left corner). We chose the intercept to be calculated. Then choose Go and you will see the result. As you see the final equation is:

$$Y = -247,600 + 20.04091x \text{ (do you see where these values are coming from?)}$$

Also, as R squared shows, there is a high correlation between the amount of advertising and the total sales (0.840304).

17-13 Multiple Linear Regression Using Lotus

Simple regression finds the relationship between two variables. Lotus has provided you with the ability to include up to 16 independent variables. Naturally a multiple regression can be more comprehensive and more accurate information can be revealed. In Figure 17-16 we have demonstrated an example of a multiple regression.

In this analysis, the independent variables are a salesperson's age, high school GPA, and number of years' selling experience. The dependent variable is the total sales generated by the salespeople.

In this example the /Data Regression command was invoked. For the X-Range we defined B5..D14, for the Y-Range, we defined A5..A14, and the output range starts at cell F3. You need only one empty cell. Lotus will provide you with all the calculated results.

Even though Lotus can perform all these calculations, it cannot report some very important statistical measures, such as a t-test, Durbin-Watson test, and so on. We believe these are some of the limitations of this otherwise very powerful command.

SUMMARY

In this chapter we have covered some of the advanced operations performed by a Lotus database: database statistical functions, table building using /Data Fill, sophisticated what-if analysis using /Data Table 1 and /Data Table 2, and /Data Distribution. At the end of this chapter, we spent some time on /Data Matrix and /Data Regression commands. These two sets of commands are extremely powerful since a Lotus can solve system of linear equations with up to 90 variables. Multiple linear regression in Lotus is also capable of handling up to 16 independent variables.

REVIEW QUESTIONS

* These questions are answered in Appendix I.
1. How many database statistical functions does Lotus have?

FIGURE 17-15 Simple Regression

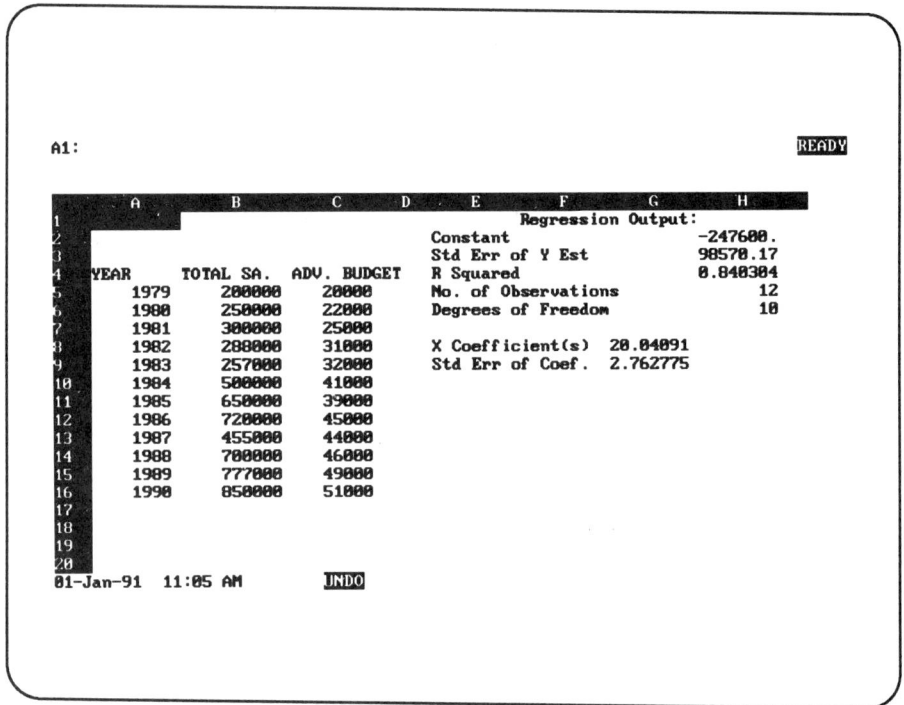

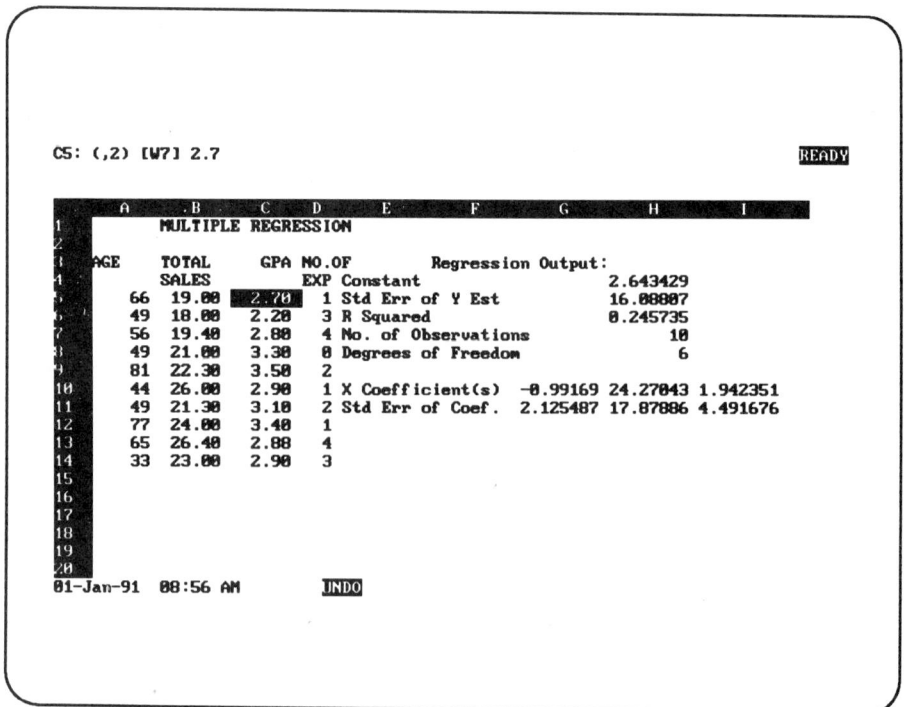

```
A1:                                                                      READY

        A          B          C       D     E        F         G         H
1                                              Regression Output:
2                                           Constant                  -247600.
3                                           Std Err of Y Est         98570.17
4    YEAR      TOTAL SA.  ADV. BUDGET        R Squared               0.840304
5        1979    200000      20000          No. of Observations           12
6        1980    250000      22000          Degrees of Freedom            10
7        1981    300000      25000
8        1982    288000      31000          X Coefficient(s)  20.04091
9        1983    257000      32000          Std Err of Coef.  2.762775
10       1984    500000      41000
11       1985    650000      39000
12       1986    720000      45000
13       1987    455000      44000
14       1988    700000      46000
15       1989    777000      49000
16       1990    850000      51000
17
18
19
20
01-Jan-91  11:05 AM            UNDO
```

```
C5: (,2) [W7] 2.7                                                        READY

        A     .B      C     D      E        F         G        H         I
1            MULTIPLE REGRESSION
2
3    AGE    TOTAL   GPA NO.OF         Regression Output:
4           SALES       EXP  Constant              2.643429
5     66    19.00   2.70   1 Std Err of Y Est      16.08007
6     49    18.00   2.20   3 R Squared             0.245735
7     56    19.40   2.80   4 No. of Observations        10
8     49    21.00   3.30   0 Degrees of Freedom          6
9     81    22.30   3.50   2
10    44    26.00   2.90   1 X Coefficient(s)  -0.99169 24.27043 1.942351
11    49    21.30   3.10   2 Std Err of Coef.  2.125487 17.87886 4.491676
12    77    24.00   3.40   1
13    65    26.40   2.88   4
14    33    23.00   2.90   3
15
16
17
18
19
20
01-Jan-91  08:56 AM            UNDO
```

FIGURE 17-16 Multiple Regression

2. What is the major difference between these database functions and their statistical counterparts?
3. What are two applications of the /Data Fill command?
4. What are the default values for the /Data Fill command?
5.* When does table building in the /Data Fill command stop?
6. Why and how can /Data Table 1 and /Data Table 2 be used as a DSS tool?
7. Give two applications of /Data Table 1 and /Data Table 2.
8.* When you use a database with /Data Table 1 or /Data Table 2, are the input cell and criterion range the same?
9. What are some of the applications of the /Data Distribution command?
10. Why must bin range in data distribution be in ascending order?
11.* What will happen in /Data Distribution if one of your data items does not fall within the bin range?
12. How do you invert a matrix?
13. Do all matrices have an inverse?
14. How do you multiply two matrices?
15.* Can you multiply any two matrices?
16. How do you solve a system of linear equations?
17.* What is the righthand side array?
18.* What are some limitations of the /Data Regression command?
19. What statistics are generated by the /Data Regression command?

HANDS-ON PRACTICE

1. Using the /Data Fill command, build a table with the following values: Start value = 10, step value = 5, and stop value = 200.
2. Using the /Data Distribution command, classify the following sales data into six groups. The interval between each group is 20,000. 100,000, 150,000, 135,000, 200,000, 164,000, 169,000, 220,000, 300,000, 250,000
3. Using /Data Table 1, calculate the payment for a $20,000 automobile in a 5-year agreement and interest rates of 8, 9, 10, 11 and 12 percent.
4. Using /Data Table 2, calculate the payment of the above automobile for 3, 4, 5 and 6 year agreements with interest rates of 8, 9, 10, 11 and 12 percent.
5. Using the worksheet presented in Figure 17-17, do the following:
   a. Sort the database by department.
   b. Using statistical database functions calculate the total sales in 1989 and 1990 by department. This means all departments that start with 10 separately, 11 separately, and 12 separately.
   c. Plot a bar graph by department for each year.
6. Using the /Data Matrix Invert command, invert the following matrix:

5	-5	15
10	-7	-3
6	-3	-3

7. Using the /Data Matrix command, solve the following system of linear equations:

   $$5x1 \quad -5x2 \quad +15x3 \quad = \quad 5$$
   $$10x1 \quad -7x2 \quad -3x3 \quad = \quad 0$$
   $$6x1 \quad -3x2 \quad -3x3 \quad = \quad 0$$

8. Following are sales data for the past seven years for Cotton Textile Firm. Using /Data Regression, generate a forecast for total sales for 1988:

FIGURE 17-17 A Sample Database

```
A1: [W4]                                                          READY

      A        B              C           D        E     F     G
 1          WEST TEXTILE PERSONNEL
 2
 3    DPT SALESPERSON        1989        1990
 4    111 Jim Evans         435,200     490,250
 5    113 Don Smith         234,525     375,255
 6    106 Fred Johnson      175,675     225,500
 7    112 Bill Jones        345,525     385,750
 8    109 Jack Parsons      672,900     825,345
 9    118 Bob Marshall      575,000     585,255
10    114 Rick Fisher       670,100     627,450
11    117 Shelly Hanson     450,000     465,275
12    124 Lisa Fuller       375,255     325,225
13    121 Marsha Grayson    401,250     398,700
14    126 Linda Flores      275,750     325,725
15    104 Pamela Murphy     297,655     310,755
16    116 Ann Taylor        372,500     375,210
17    129 Karen Young       497,500     150,000
18
19        TOTAL           5,778,835   5,865,695
20
01-Jan-91  09:02 AM         UNDO
```

1981	100,000
1982	130,000
1983	175,000
1984	155,000
1985	200,000
1986	250,000
1987	300,000

COMPREHENSIVE LAB ASSIGNMENT

Retrieve CHAPT16 and perform the following:
1. Using /Data Fill, number all students from 1 to 10 in column K.
2. Sort this new database by age.
3. Using column K as the key, return the worksheet to its original shape.
4. Using database statistical functions, generate the seven statistics for male and female students.
5. Using /Data Regression, calculate the R^2 between the total scores and the student's age. In this case, we assume age as the independent and total scores as the dependent variable. Is there any correlation between these two variables?
6. Using /Data Distribution, generate a distribution analysis for the total scores.
7. Save this final worksheet under CHAPT17.

Macros/Part One: Typing Alternatives

18-1 Introduction

In this chapter we will discuss the principles of macro design and use. We will provide guidelines for naming, debugging, and documenting macros, and we will introduce more than 50 of the most commonly used macros. We also review the automatic recording features and macro manager facilities of Lotus Release 2.2. In Chapters 19, 20 and 21 we introduce advanced features of macro operation.

18-2 What Is a Macro?

In simple terms, a *macro* is a collection of a series of keystrokes. As you have learned, everything in Lotus is a series of keystrokes, therefore everything in Lotus can be done by using a macro. Let us assume that you have to type the following statement in many different locations of your worksheet:

THE TOTAL COSTS OF PRODUCTION FOR THIS PERIOD

You have two alternatives. Either type this statement over and over, or create a macro. Whenever you are doing something repeatedly, think of using macros. They increase the speed and accuracy of operations, since they repeat the same sequence over and over.

18-3 Your First Macro

The first question asked by new macro users is, where do we put a macro? You can put a macro in any of the empty cells in your worksheet. It is a good practice to put a macro in a location that is easy to reach but where it will not get in your way. Some users put their macros in column AA. This is twenty-six columns to the right, close enough for easy access. However, you must be careful when you use the /WDR or /WIR commands. These two commands can destroy your macros. For this reason some macro users follow the diagram presented in Figure 18-1. As this diagram indicates, the macro is outside of your active worksheet. Follow one of these formats, whichever you find more comfortable.

Let us move the cursor to column AB1 (save AA1 for the macro name) and type the label:

THE TOTAL COSTS OF PRODUCTION FOR THIS PERIOD

FGURE 18-1 *Design of Macro within the Spreadsheet*

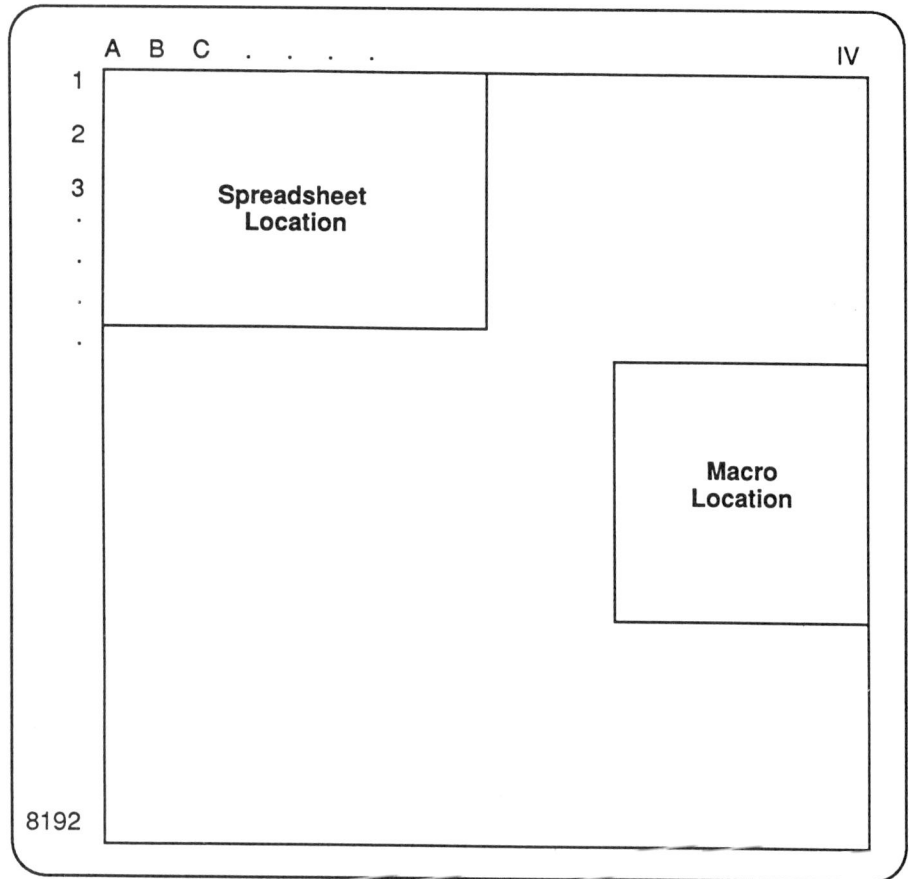

The next task is to name the macro. A macro name can be any letter of the alphabet. It does not matter if it is uppercase or lowercase. The name must start with a backslash (\). You must also enter the name as a label. This means you must use one of the label prefixes (' or " or ^). If you do not use a prefix, the letter used for the macro name will be repeated, which you do not want. Next, you should name the location in which the macro is residing. Use /Range Name Create and name your macro \A (remember no label prefix here). To name a macro, you can also use /Range Name Label Right (assuming the cursor is to the left of the macro, at the name cell). Figure 18-2 shows your first macro.

Naming a macro in Release 2.2 can be done either by using a backslash (\) and a letter of the alphabet (A–Z) and 0 (zero), or by specifying a name of up to 15 characters. As usual issue /RNC, then specify the name and the desired range.

The next question is, how do you execute this macro? It can be executed from any location in the worksheet. Move the cursor to cell A1, hold down the **Alt** key (macro key), and at the same time, type A (the name of your macro). You will see THE TOTAL COSTS OF PRODUCTION FOR THIS PERIOD appear at the top of the screen in the control panel. Just press the **Return** key in order to enter this label into cell A1.

In Release 2.2 you can invoke your macro by pressing Alt-F3 (Run) and specifying the macro name.

Can you include Return in your macro? The answer is yes. Each key on your keyboard has a representative in macro design. Table 18-1 shows all key representations and certain commands. As you can see in this table, the representative for **Return** is the tilde (~).

FIGURE 18-2 Your First Macro

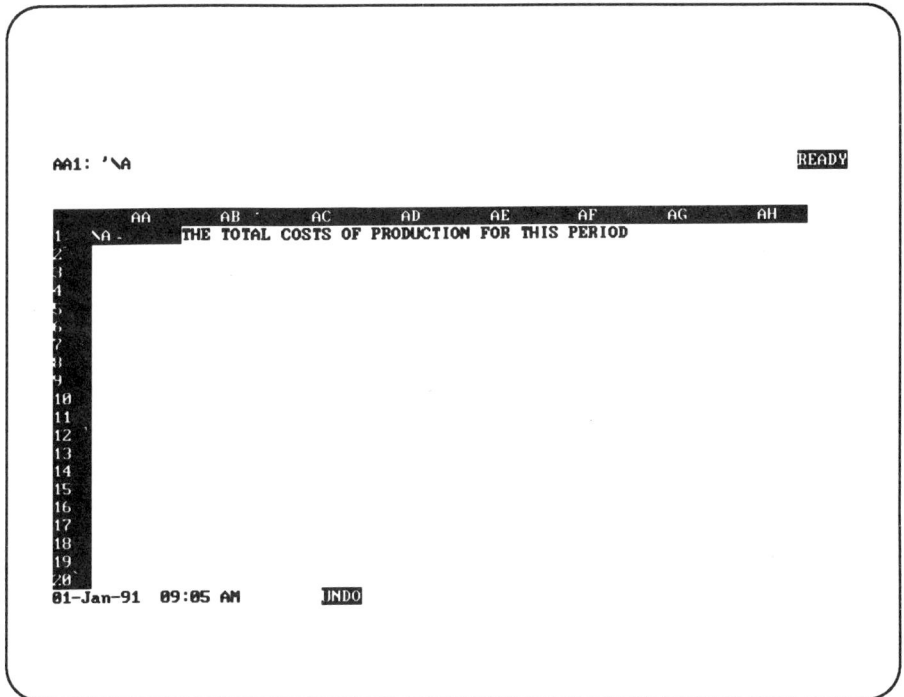

Move to cell AB1 and edit the content of this cell by pressing F2. Add a tilde to the end of the label. Now the content of cell AB1 is as follows:

THE TOTAL COSTS OF PRODUCTION FOR THIS PERIOD~

Now move the cursor to cell A2 and invoke your macro. Hold down the **Alt** key and type A. You will see that the label enters directly to cell A2.

Which cell is the address for naming your macro? All you need to do is to use the first cell as the address for the range. In this case cell AB1 is the beginning of the range. However, if you want to provide the entire range address, AB1..AF1, you may. Since this is an important step in learning macros, let us summarize these steps:

1. Move the cursor to cell AA1 and type '\A.
2. Move the cursor to cell AB1 and type

THE TOTAL COSTS OF PRODUCTION FOR THIS PERIOD~

3. Invoke /RNC, type \A, Return, AB1, Return

To invoke this macro, move the cursor to your desired cell and press and hold down Alt then type A.

18-4 Your Second Macro

Your first macro only included a label. You can use a macro to automate a command or a series of commands. In order to do this, you must first record all the steps that you follow for performing a command. Release 2.2 includes an automatic recording feature. We will talk about this later in this chapter. Let us assume you are interested in formatting 20000 with the Currency format and two decimal places. Let us record the steps involved:

- / (call the menu)
- R (invoke range)
- F (invoke format)
- C (invoke currency)
- 2 (2 decimal places)
- **Return** (to enter 2)
- **Return** (to enter the correct cell as the desired range to be formatted)

TABLE 18-1 KEYBOARD REPRESENTATIVES*

DESCRIPTION	MACRO KEY
ABS	{ABS}
BACKSPACE	{BACKSPACE} or {BS}
BIG LEFT (move to left one screen)	{BIGLEFT}
BIG RIGHT (move to right one screen)	{BIGRIGHT}
BREAK	{BREAK}
CALC	{CALC}
DELETE (you must use only in EDIT mode)	{DELETE} or {DEL}
DOWN	{DOWN} or {D}
EDIT	{EDIT}
END	{END}
ESCAPE	{ESCAPE} or {ESC}
GOTO	{GOTO}
GRAPH	{GRAPH}
HELP**	{HELP}
HOME	{HOME}
LEFT	{LEFT} or {L}
NAME	{NAME}
PAGE DOWN	{PGDN}
PAGE UP	{PGUP}
QUERY	{QUERY}
RETURN (tilde)	~
RIGHT	{RIGHT} or {R}
TABLE	{TABLE}
To have braces appear as {and}	{{}and{}}
To have tilde appear as ~	{~}
UP	{UP} or {U}
WINDOW***	{WINDOW}

* In order to specify two or more consecutive uses of the same key, you can always include a repetition factor within the braces. For example:

| {DOWN 6} | tells Lotus to move the cursor six cells down |
| {UP 2} | tells Lotus to move the cursor two cells up |

**The {HELP} command accesses 1-2-3's on-line help facility. It is similar to F1. It also enables you to capture this keystroke in a {GET} command. This feature can be used to customize help screens for a specific macro.

**The {WINDOW} command moves the cursor back and forth between the two split screens. In Release 2.2 it also turns the display of settings sheets on or off when it is applicable.

First, we set the column width to 12. Now move the cursor to cell AA3 and enter \B (as label with apostrophe). In cell AB3 enter '/RFC2~~ (as label with apostrophe). Using /Range Name Create, name cell AB3 as \B.

Now move the cursor to cell AA10, which contains number 20000, and invoke your B macro. Your number is formatted. Figure 18-3 shows this process.

18-5 An Interactive Macro

In your second macro, the number which was formatted was predefined. It is possible to include a question mark (?) within your macro in order to make it interactive. This means that when you execute your macro the process stops when it encounters the question mark until you enter a number, then the process continues. Let us start with an empty worksheet. Move the cursor to column AB1 and type the following:

```
YOU TELL ME A NUMBER~
{DOWN}
{?}~
/RFC2~~
```

Name this macro \C. Remember, only cell AB1 needs to be indicated as the range since the macro will execute all rows until an empty row is encountered. Now move the cursor to cell AA6 and invoke the macro. As you see, the label YOU TELL ME A NUMBER appears in cell AA6 and CMD is displayed at the bottom of the screen, meaning the macro is in progress. The macro waits for you to enter a number. Type 36000 and press **Return**. Your number is formatted. We have set column width to 12. So the question mark within

FIGURE 18-3 *Your Second Macro*

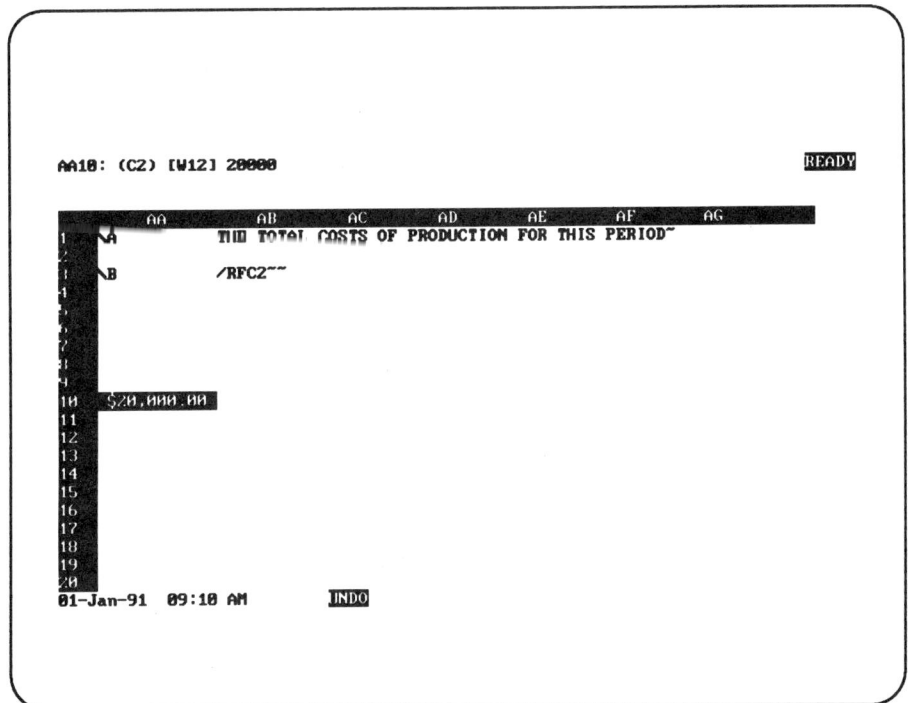

the braces in the macro makes the macro interactive. Figure 18-4 shows this process.

We can enhance the macro by including W(worksheet)C(column)S(set-width) {?} or /WCS{?}~. In this case, the column width is set by the user. We could also include a question mark in place of the number of decimal places. Figure 18-5 shows these variations of our original macro.

To stop a macro, press the **Ctrl** and **Break** keys together.

18-6 How Is a Macro Executed?

As you have seen so far, a macro is a column of keystrokes. The number of keystrokes can be as many as 240. The macro is executed from left to right and top to bottom. As soon as the macro encounters a blank cell, it halts execution. Therefore, if you are putting more than one macro in a worksheet, be sure there is at least one empty row between each macro.

It is also a good idea to document your macro. Since the name of your macro is either one letter or up to 15 characters, there is no way to remember what each macro does. So to the right of the macro, after leaving one empty cell, always indicate briefly what task a particular macro performs. In Figure 18-6 we show an example of a documented macro. In column AA1, the letter G is the name of the macro. We call this name *documentation*. In column AB1 is the macro itself. And finally, in column AD1 we have mentioned the function of the macro. We call this function *documentation* also.

18-7 Debugging Your Macro

Macros are executed extremely fast. There is always the possibility of making mistakes. Lotus provides a facility for debugging your macro. You can process your macro step by step as follows:

1. Press Alt-F2. You will see the STEP indicator displayed in the status line.
2. Invoke the macro either directly by using **Alt** and the macro name or by using the Alt-F3 command. As soon as you invoke the macro, the macro range and its contents are displayed at the left bottom corner of the screen.
3. Press any key one at a time. This will walk you through your macro one keystroke at a time. As soon as the keystrokes are completed, the STEP indicator appears again.
4. Press Alt-F2 again in order to leave the STEP mode.

As soon as you see an error in your macro, you can halt the execution by using Ctrl-Break keys and edit the macro by using the F2 key.

You can also use /WW and /WT as needed to pull data and macros close together on the screen.

18-8 Using the Automatic Recording Feature

To record your macros automatically perform the following steps:

1. Invoke /Worksheet Learn Range.
2. 1-2-3 prompts you with Enter Learn Range. Select a single cell or one column range. Remember, each cell can hold up to 40 characters. Therefore, you should make your range large enough. However, you can always adjust the range later. In our example we typed G1..G1 and pressed Enter.

FIGURE 18-4 *An Example of an Interactive Macro*

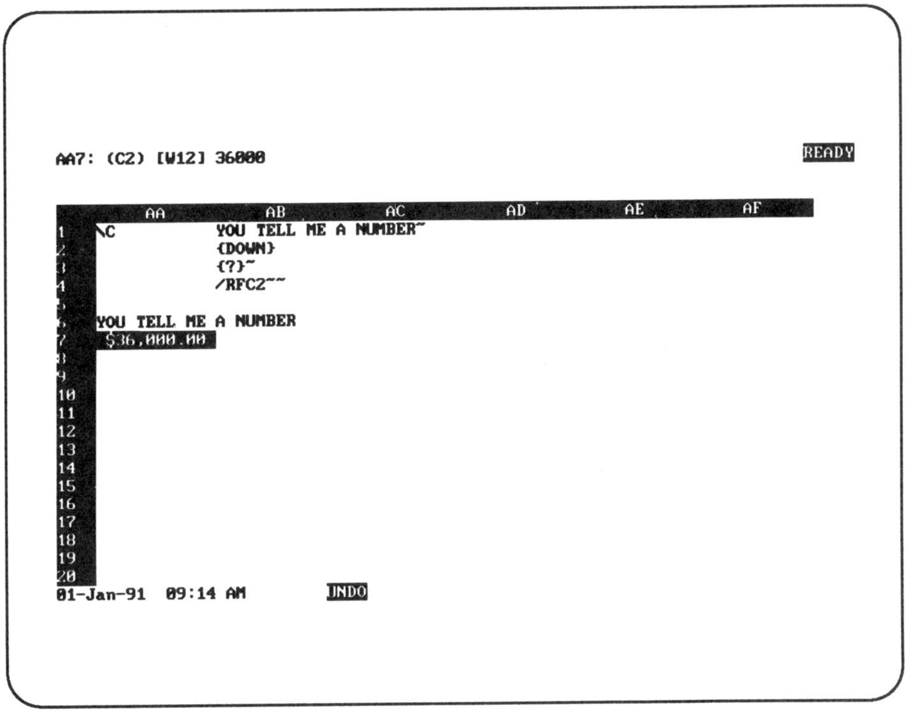

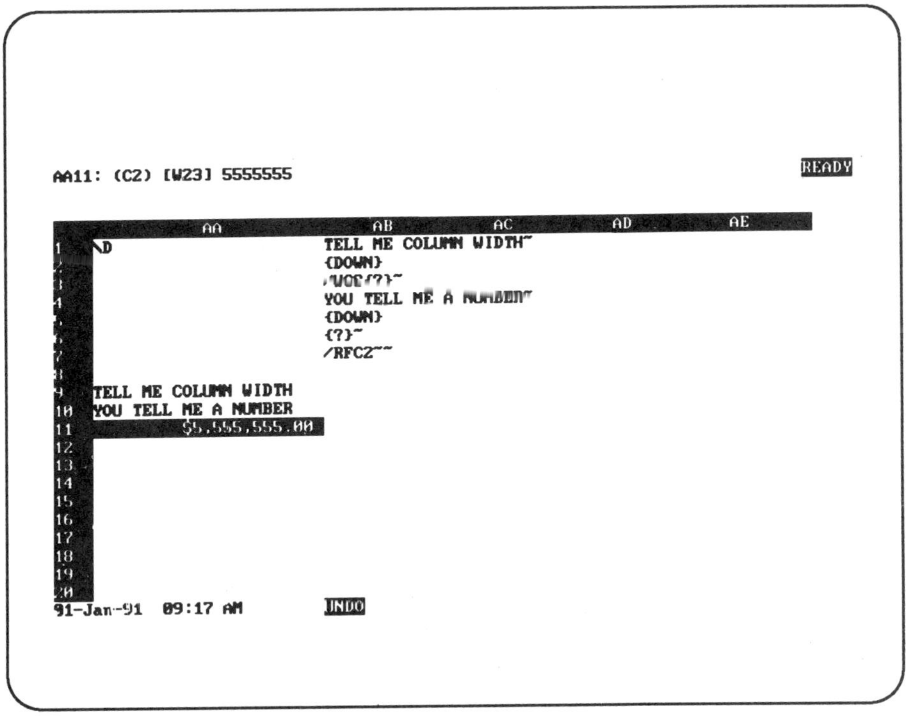

```
AA7: (C2) [W12] 36000                                              READY

          AA         AB         AC         AD        AE        AF
1   \C          YOU TELL ME A NUMBER~
2               {DOWN}
3               {?}~
4               /RFC2~~
5
6   YOU TELL ME A NUMBER
7      $36,000.00
8
9
10
11
12
13
14
15
16
17
18
19
20
01-Jan-91   09:14 AM        UNDO
```

```
AA11: (C2) [W23] 5555555                                          READY

          AA         AB         AC         AD        AE
1   \D          TELL ME COLUMN WIDTH~
2               {DOWN}
3               /WGC{?}~
4               YOU TELL ME A NUMBER~
5               {DOWN}
6               {?}~
7               /RFC2~~
8
9   TELL ME COLUMN WIDTH
10  YOU TELL ME A NUMBER
11             $5,555,555.00
12
13
14
15
16
17
18
19
20
91-Jan-91   09:17 AM        UNDO
```

FIGURE 18-5 *More Complicated Interactive Macro*

FIGURE 18-6 *An Example of a Documented Macro*

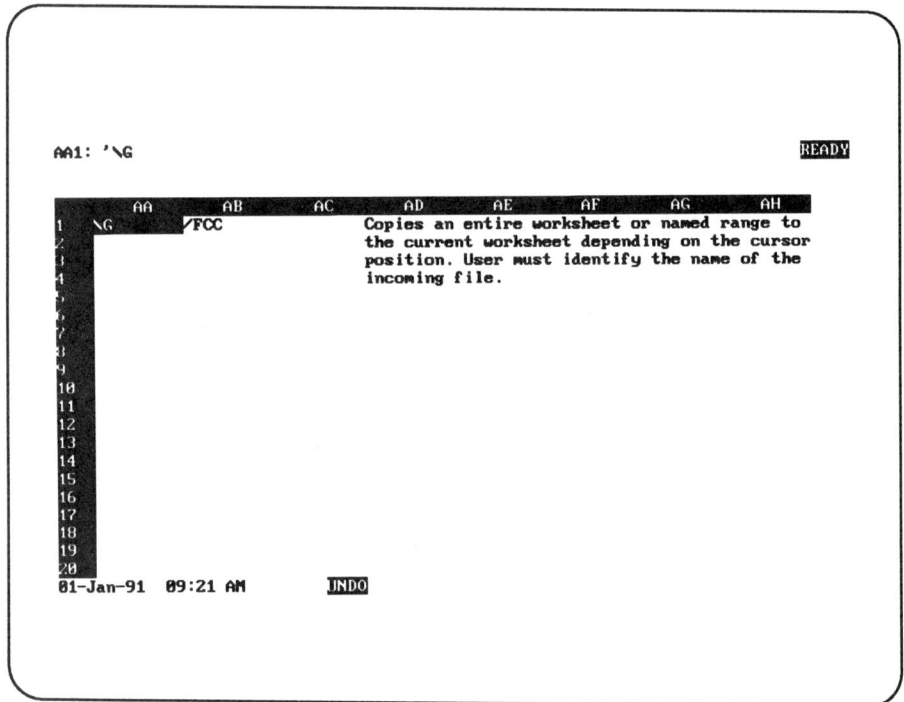

3. Press Alt-F5 to turn the recording feature on. The status indicator displays LEARN.
4. Select /RFC2~~. (You are formatting a cell with currency option with two decimals.)
5. Press Alt-F5 to turn the recording feature off.

To see your macro press /Worksheet Learn Range and you will see /RFC2~~ in cell G1.

If your macro is too large for the specified range you receive an error message, "Learn Range is Full". In such a case you have to redefine the range by /WLR. If you want to cancel the current Learn Range use /W LC (Cancel).

If you make any mistakes, you can always edit your macro as usual by using the F2 (**Edit**) key.

While you are in recording mode please remember 1-2-3 does not record any / Worksheet Learn commands. It also does not record the following keys.

Alt-F1
Alt-F3
Alt-F4
Alt-F5
Shift
Num Lock
Scroll Lock

18-9 An Automatic Macro

If you name your macro Zero (\0), it will automatically execute when the worksheet that includes it is loaded. This is very useful for designing menus. If you save the worksheet that includes the \0 macro as AUTO123.WK1, this worksheet will be automatically loaded to RAM as soon as you get the system started. A combination of AUTO123.WK1 and the \0 macro can be used for any application involving first-time computer users giving them easy access to the system. It is also handy for commonly used worksheets. Figure 18-7 shows the \0 macro.

18-10 Creating a Macro Library

When you get used to designing and using macros, you may want to use some of them from worksheet to worksheet. If you put all your macros in a remote location of your worksheet, such as column AA, and if you document them properly, you can use them over and over again. However, if you transfer your macros to a different worksheet, you must rename them. Chapter 19 will show you a macro for naming other macros. Figures 18-9 to 18-11 present some of the most commonly used macros. Figure 18-12 presents key representative macros.

18-11 Macro Library Manager

Release 2.2 offers a feature for creating and maintaining macro libraries. This feature simplifies using macros from worksheet to worksheet. To utilize this facility you first must attach the Macro Manager to your 1-2-3. To do so invoke /Add-In, Attach, MACROMGR.ADN. 1-2-3 prompts you with:

No-Key   7   8   9   10

FIGURE 18-7 *Automatic Worksheet and Automatic Macro*

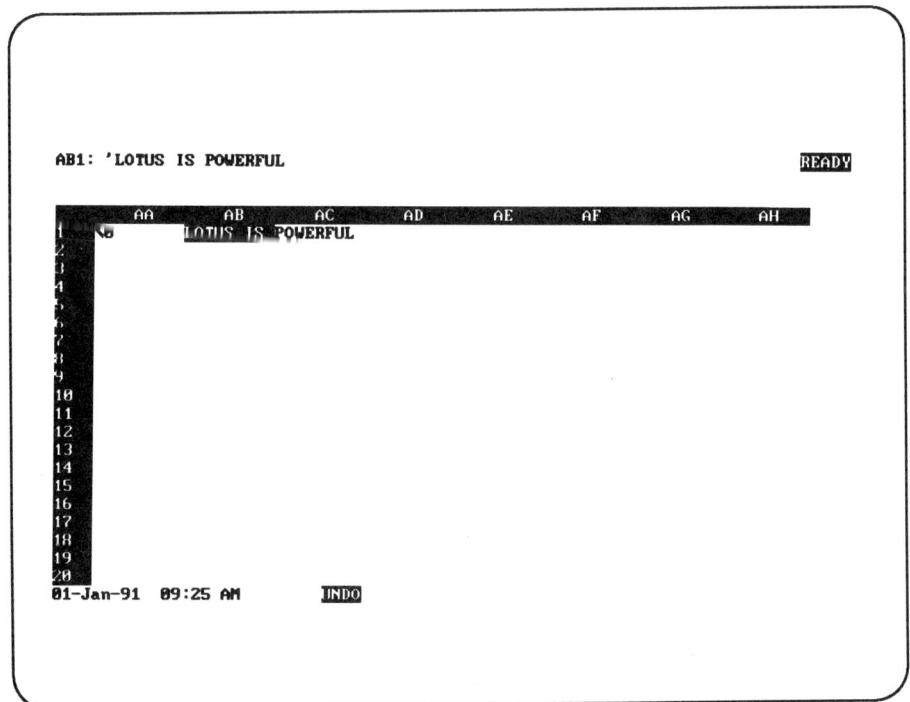

As you did with the Allways add-in program, you can select any of these options. If you select a key, later you can activate the Macro Manager by pressing **Alt**, then the function key you assigned. Remember not to use the function keys that you have already assigned to Allways or other add-in programs that you may have. If you select the No-Key option, to activate the Macro Manager you must use the Add-In Invoke command.

To detach the Macro Manager, select /Add-In, Detach, Specify MACROMGR.ADN, and then press **Return**.

When you invoke the Macro Library Manager, you will see the menu displayed in Figure 18-8. To use a macro library you must first create it and save it to the disk by using the Save command (from the menu in Figure 18-8). When you select the Save command, 1-2-3 prompts you:

Enter Name of Macro Library

Specify a name, and remember this file will be saved with the MLB extension. As soon as you specify the name, 1-2-3 prompts you:

Enter Macro Library Range

Specify the desired range and press Enter. Then 1-2-3 prompts you with the No Yes option. Using the Yes option allows you to select a password. A password protects a macro library from being edited or viewed in STEP mode, but it does not prevent someone from loading and using the library.

To use a macro library, select the LOAD option. If the macro library already exists in memory, 1-2-3 prompts you with the Write Overwrite option. You can choose either of these options.

FIGURE 18-8 *Macro Library Manager Menu*

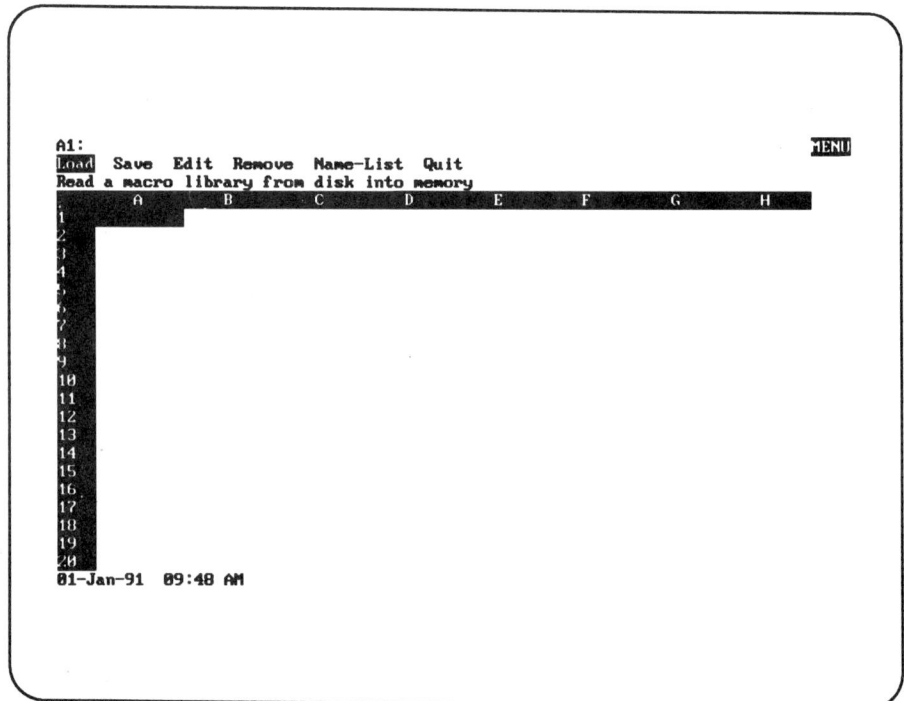

FIGURE 18-9 Commonly Used Macros Part 1

```
A1: [W4] '\a                                                            READY

      A      B          C          D          E          F          G
1   \a  /wgc12~         resets all column widths to 12
2
3   \b  /wglc          centers all labels to be entered in a worksheet
4
5   \c  /rlc           centers all labels in a given range that have
6                      already been entered in the worksheet
7
8   \d  /wgff2~         formats the entire worksheet with the fixed format
9                      option with two decimal places
10
11  \e  /wir{?}~        inserts a specified row(s) in the worksheet
12
13  \f  /wdr{?}~        deletes a specified row(s) from the worksheet
14
15  \g  /wic{?}~        inserts a specified column(s) in the worksheet
16
17  \h  /wdc{?}~        deletes a specified column(s) from the worksheet
18
19  \i  /wch{?}~        hides a specified column in the worksheet
20
01-Jan-91  09:31 AM              UNDO
```

```
A21: [W4] '\J                                                           READY

      A      B          C          D          E          F          G
21  \j  /wcd{?}~        reveals (displays) a hidden column in the worksheet
22
23  \k  /wey           erases the entire worksheet
24
25  \l  /ru            selectively unprotects a specified range of cells
26
27  \m  /rp            protects a specified range of cells from modification
28
29  \n  /wgzy           suppresses the display of cells that have a numeric
30                     value of zero
31
32  \o  /wwv            splits the screen vertically where the cursor is
33                     positioned
34
35  \p  /wwh            splits the screen horizontally where the cursor is
36                     positioned
37
38  \q  /wtb            freezes all cells to the left and above the cursor
39                     so the cells cannot move off the screen
40
01-Jan-91  09:35 AM              UNDO
```

FIGURE 18-9 (Continued)

FIGURE 18-9 (Continued)

```
A41: [W4] '\r                                                      READY

        A        B           C        D        E        F        G
41  \r    /wgrm              changes the worksheet from the standard automatic
42                           recalculation to manual recalculation
43
44  \s    /rnc{?}~{?}~       allows the user to specify a name for any range
45
46  \t    /re{?}~            erases a specified range
47
48  \u    /rfc0~{?}~         formats a specified range with the currency format
49                           option and zero decimal places
50
51  \v    @TODAY~            formats today's date with the long international date
52        /rfd4~             format
54  \w    /rfdt2{?}~         formats a specified range with the #2 time option
55
56  \x    /rf,2~{?}~         formats a specified range with the comma format
57                           option and two decimal places
58
59  \y    /rfh{?}~           hides a specified range
60
01-Jan-91  09:39 AM         UNDO
```

```
A61: [W4] '\z                                                      READY

        A        B           C        D        E        F        G
61  \z    /rft{?}~           formats a specified range with the text format option
62
63
64
65
66
67
68
69
70
71
72
73
74
75
76
77
78
79
80
01-Jan-91  09:44 AM         UNDO
```

FIGURE 18-9 (Continued)

FIGURE 18-10 *Commonly Used Macros Part 2*

```
A1: [W5] '\a                                                           READY

         A            B              C        D        E        F        G
 1  \a  /rfp2~{?}~          formats a specified range with the percent
 2                          format option and two decimal places
 3
 4  \b  /rfr{?}~            resets the format of the specified range to
 5                          the global default setting
 6
 7  \c  /fr{?}~             retrieves a specified file back to the main memory
 8                          from a data disk
 9
10  \d  /fs{?}~             saves an entire worksheet on a data disk under
11                          a specified name
12
13  \e  /fxv{?}~{?}~r~      extracts a portion of a worksheet with Values
14                          option and stores the result in a given file
15
16  \f  /fxf{?}~{?}~r~      extracts a portion of a worksheet with Formulas
17                          option and stores the result in a given file
18
19  \g  /fcce~{?}~          copies an entire file to the current worksheet
20                          depending on cursor position
01-Jan-91  09:48 AM        UNDO
```

```
A21: [W5]                                                              READY

         A            B              C        D        E        F        G
21
22  \h  /fcae{?}~          takes the values from an entire file and adds
23                         those values to the corresponding cells in the
24                         current worksheet
25
26  \i  /few{?}~y          deletes a specified worksheet file from a data
27                         disk
28
29  \j  /gtba{?}~v         sets up and views a bar graph with one data
30                         range
31
32  \k  /gtpa{?}~x{?}~otf{?}~qv    sets up and views a pie chart with
33                                 two data ranges and one title
34
35  \l  /gtla{?}~x{?}~otx{?}~ty{?}~qv    sets up and views a line graph
36                                       with two data ranges and a
37                                       title for the x- and y-axis
38
39  \m  /gotx{?}~ty{?}~qv  enters a title for the x-axis and the y-axis
40                         on a specified graph and views the graph
01-Jan-91  09:51 AM        UNDO
```

FIGURE 18-10 *(Continued)*

FIGURE 18-10 (Continued)

```
A41: [W5]                                                                 READY

       A         B             C         D          E        F        G
41
42   \n    /gosxml{?}~u{?}~qqv    overrides the automatic scale and allows
43                               the user to rescale the x-axis manually
44                               and view the changes
45
46   \o    /gnc{?}~q             names a current graph and saves all the
47                               current parameters defining that graph
48
49   \p    /gnu{?}~q             recalls a graph you have previously named and
50                               saved
51
52   \q    /gnd{?}~q             deletes a single graph name and its parameters
53                               from the worksheet
54
55   \r    /gola{?}~qq           enters a legend below the x-axis
56
57   \s    /gofgsqqv             formats all the graph lines of a graph with
58                               the symbols option and views it
59
60   \t    /dsd{?}~p{?}~g        sorts an entire database or specified data-
01-Jan-91  09:54 AM             UNDO
```

FIGURE 18-10 (Continued)

```
A61: [W5]                                                                 READY

       A         B             C         D          E        F        G
61                             range according to a primary key field
62
63   \u    /dsd{?}~p{?}~s{?}~g   sorts an entire database or specified
64                               datarange according to primary and
65                               secondary key fields
66
67   \v    /dqi{?}~c{?}~o{?}~e   searches a database and extracts a por-
68                               tion of the database to an output range
69                               based on a specified criterion range
70
71   \w    /dqi{?}~c{?}~o{?}~u   searches a database and extracts a
72                               unique portion of the database to an
73                               output range based on a specified
74                               criterion range. Duplicate records will
75                               not be chosen.
76
77   \x    /pf{?}~r{?}~gq        specifies the range of cells to be printed
78                               into a file
79
80   \y    /ppcrq                clears and resets print range
01-Jan-91  09:58 AM             UNDO
```

FIGURE 18-10 (Continued)

FIGURE 18-10 (Continued)

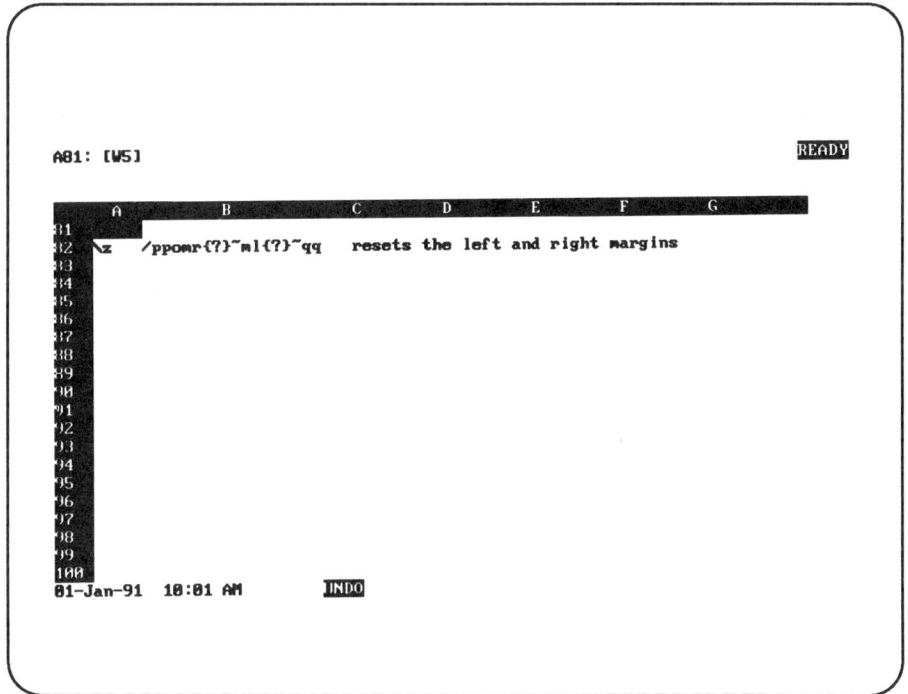

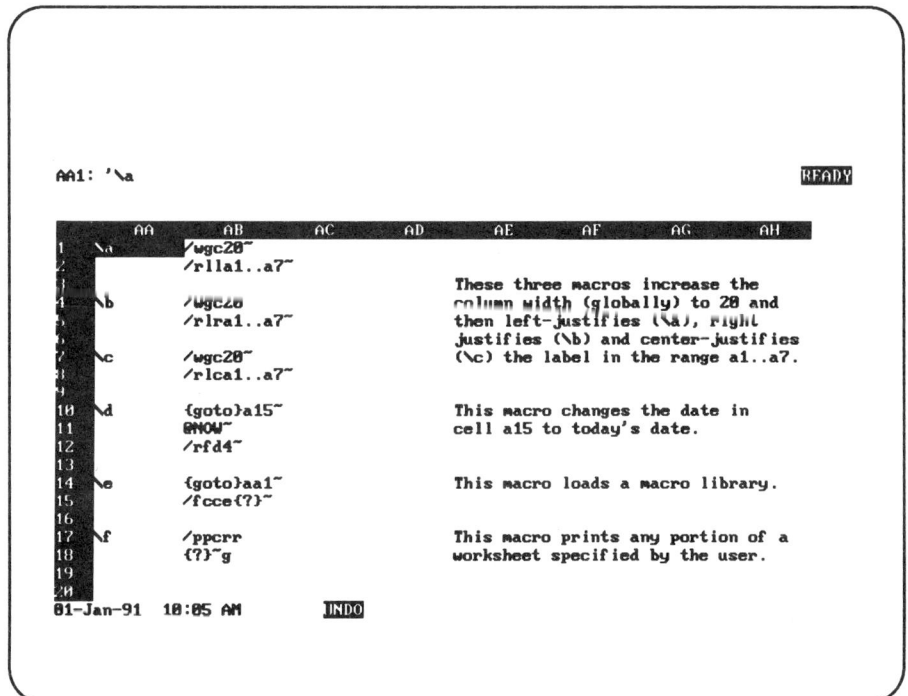

```
A01: [W5]                                                                READY

      A         B          C         D         E         F         G
01
02  \z   /ppomr{?}~ml{?}~qq    resets the left and right margins
03
04
05
06
07
08
09
10
11
12
13
14
15
16
17
18
19
100
01-Jan-91  10:01 AM        UNDO
```

```
AA1: '\a                                                                 READY

      AA        AB         AC        AD        AE        AF        AG        AH
1   \a    /wgc20~
2         /rlla1..a7~
3                                      These three macros increase the
4   \b    /wgc20                       column width (globally) to 20 and
5         /rlra1..a7~                  then left-justifies (\a), right
6                                      justifies (\b) and center-justifies
7   \c    /wgc20~                      (\c) the label in the range a1..a7.
8         /rlca1..a7~
9
10  \d    {goto}a15~                   This macro changes the date in
11        @NOW~                        cell a15 to today's date.
12        /rfd4~
13
14  \e    {goto}aa1~                   This macro loads a macro library.
15        /fcce{?}~
16
17  \f    /ppcrr                       This macro prints any portion of a
18        {?}~g                        worksheet specified by the user.
19
20
01-Jan-91  10:05 AM        UNDO
```

FIGURE 18-11 Commonly Used Macros Part 3

FIGURE 18-12 Key Representative Macros

```
AA1: '\m                                                              READY

        AA      AB        AC        AD        AE        AF      AG      AH
1    \m     {home}
2           Payment{right}Interest{right}^Term{right}Future Value~
3           {down}{end}{left}
4           100{right}.05{right}5{right}@FV(a2,b2,c2)~
5           /rfc0~a2~
6           /rfp0~b2~                             This macro uses the table
7           {goto}b4~                             building function to deter-
8           Interest~{down}                       mine the future value of
9           Rate~{right}{up}                      a specific payment based on
10          Future~{down}                         interest rates from 5% to
11          Value~{down}                          14%. The data is then
12          +d2~                                  graphed. The payment amount
13          /dfb7..b16~.05~.01~.14~               changes to $200,the
14          /rfp0~b7..b16~                        table is rebuilt and the
15          /dt1b6..c16~b2~                       graph is redrawn.
16          /wcs12~                               After execution of the
17          /rfc2~c7..c16~                        macro, the user can change
18          /gtlab7..b16~xc7..c16~vq              any of the values then
19          {goto}a2~                             press F9, the entire table
20          200~                                  will be recalculated.
01-Jan-91  10:08 AM          UNDO
```

```
AA21:                                                                 READY

        AA      AB        AC        AD        AE        AF      AG      AH
21          {table}
22          {graph}
23
24
25
26   \n     {HOME}/fcceCH16-6~                    This macro combines a file called
27          /dqia5..d13~cf6..f7~f                 CH16-6, performs a query for
28          {down}{goto}f7~                       people who are engineers,then
29          Professor~                            changes the criterion range to
30          {query}                               professor and "queries" again.
31
32
33
34
35
36
37
38
39
40
01-Jan-91  10:16 AM          UNDO
```

FIGURE 18-12 (Continued)

FIGURE 18-12 (Continued)

```
AA41: '\o                                                      READY

         AA        AB        AC      AD      AE      AF      AG      AH
 41  \o        {Home}/fcceCASHFLOW~
 42            {goto}tax~
 43            {edit}                       This macro combines the CASHFLOW
 44            {backspace 3}                file, which contains a split screen.
 45            {delete}                      The macro edits the tax rate to
 46            5~                            change it from 40% to 50% on both
 47            {window}                      sides of the window and then recal-
 48            {edit}                        culates the entire worksheet.
 49            {backspace 3}                 This macro assumes there is a file
 50            {delete}                      called CASHFLOW on the disk with
 51            5~                            split screen. It also assumes there
 52            {calc}                        is a range called tax with a value
 53                                          of .40.
 54
 55
 56
 57
 58
 59
 60
 01-Jan-91  10:20 AM            UNDO
```

```
AA61: '\p                                                      READY

         AA        AB        AC      AD      AE      AF      AG      AH
 61  \p        {home}
 62            This is home~
 63            {WAIT @now+@time(0,0,3)}
 64            {bigright}
 65            You have just moved one screen to the right~
 66            {WAIT @now+@time(0,0,3)}
 67            {pgdn}
 68            You have just moved one screen down~
 69            {WAIT @now+@time(0,0,3)}
 70            {bigleft}
 71            You have just moved one screen to the left~
 72            {WAIT @now+@time(0,0,3)}
 73            {pgup}
 74            You are back home!~
 75
 76
 77            This macro guides the user around the worksheet
 78            utilizing BIGLEFT, BIGRIGHT, PGDN, and PGUP.
 79
 80
 01-Jan-91  10:23 AM            UNDO
```

FIGURE 18-12 (Continued)

FIGURE 18-12   (Continued)

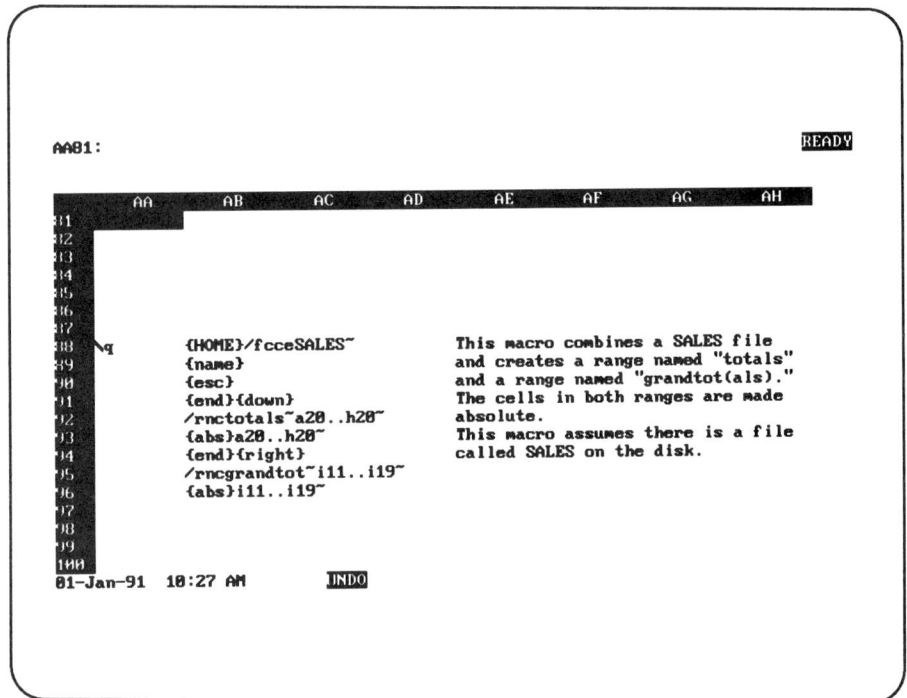

```
AA81:                                                                READY

        AA        AB        AC        AD        AE        AF        AG        AH
31
32
33
34
35
36
37
38    \q    {HOME}/fcceSALES~           This macro combines a SALES file
39          {name}                      and creates a range named "totals"
90          {esc}                       and a range named "grandtot(als)."
91          {end}{down}                 The cells in both ranges are made
92          /rnctotals~a28..h28~        absolute.
93          {abs}a28..h28~              This macro assumes there is a file
94          {end}{right}                called SALES on the disk.
95          /rncgrandtot~i11..i19~
96          {abs}i11..i19~
97
98
99
100
81-Jan-91  10:27 AM           UNDO
```

The Edit option gives you two alternatives: Ignore and Overwrite. The Ignore option does not write over conflicting range names in the worksheet. The Overwrite option writes over the conflicting range names in the worksheet.

The Name-List option allows you to list range names contained in a macro library in a worksheet.

SUMMARY

This chapter covered the principles of macro design and use, creation of a macro, documentation and invoking a macro. We also discussed debugging a macro, the automatic macro and presented a list of more than 50 commonly used macros. This should provide you with a good background for getting started with macros. The chapter also reviewed the automatic recording feature and macro manager facilities of Release 2.2. In the next chapter we will discuss macro commands.

REVIEW QUESTIONS

* These questions are answered in Appendix I.
1. What is a macro?
2. What are some of the advantages of using a macro?
3. How do you name a macro?
4.* How do you invoke a macro?
5. How do you document a macro?

6.* What is the function of a \0 macro?
7. How many macros can you have in a worksheet?
8. What is a self-booting worksheet?
9.* What are some of the applications of a self-booting worksheet?
10. How do you debug a macro?
11. What is the STEP indicator?
12. What is the automatic recording feature?
13.* What is the CMD indicator?
14. How do you get out of STEP mode?
15.* How do you halt the execution of a macro?
16.* How many keystrokes can be included in a macro?
17. How is a macro executed?

HANDS-ON PRACTICE

1. Design a macro in order to generate a pie chart using the following data:
   Sue   2,000
   Sam   18,000
   Sara   15,000
2. Design a macro to load a file from a disk to a worksheet, then erase the worksheet.
3. Design a macro to print the following message, then exit from the Lotus worksheet:
   IT WAS A PRODUCTIVE SESSION!
4. Design an interactive macro that accepts any three numbers, then calculates their average.
5. Design a macro that accepts any number up to eight digits, then format them using the comma option with three decimal places.
6. Design a macro that prints any portion of a worksheet using default settings.

COMPREHENSIVE LAB ASSIGNMENT

Retrieve CHAPT17 and perform the following:
1. Erase the current title of this worksheet.
2. Move the cursor to column AA1.
3. Generate a macro that automatically prints the old title for this worksheet.
4. Generate a macro that automatically formats all the test scores to a fixed format with two decimals.
5. Save this worksheet under CHAPT18.

MISCONCEPTION AND SOLUTION

M – Lotus handles macros and functions differently. Lotus does not adjust cell addresses when you use /Move, /Copy, /Worksheet Delete, or /Worksheet Insert. When your macro is using cell addresses after rearranging, it may no longer work.

S – To avoid this, use range names to refer to cells.

Macros/Part Two: Advanced Commands

19-1 Introduction

As we discussed in the last chapter, macros are extremely handy for automating frequently used Lotus commands, such as repeatedly typing a label in a worksheet or performing a long task requiring a series of keystrokes. In this chapter, we will teach you how to use advanced features of macro operation. We will explain the structure of an advanced macro command, then divide advanced macro commands into five groups. By using numerous examples we will highlight the real power of Lotus macros. In Chapter 20 we will demonstrate using Lotus macros as a high-level programming language.

19-2 The Structure of Advanced Macro Commands

All advanced macro commands follow a common structure:

{KEYWORD ARGUMENT1, ARGUMENT2, ...}

They must start with a left brace and end with a right brace. KEYWORD includes any valid Lotus advanced command, e.g., LET, BRANCH, INDICATE, and so on. ARGUMENT(S) are one or more of the following four groups:

1. *Address or location.* This includes the address of any of the cells within the entire worksheet. This can also include a range.
2. *Numeric value.* This includes any number, expression, or formula resulting in a specific value. The number can be in standard form (e.g., 5200) or in scientific notation (e.g., 2.002E+3).
3. *Condition.* Any valid logical operation can be used as an argument. The macro command will proceed based on the result of the logical operations.
4. *String.* Any sequence of characters up to 240 can be used as an argument for your advanced macro command.

Argument types can be either numeric or string. Some macro commands such as LET can hold either number or string. For example:

{LET R1, 2 + 3} or
{LET R1, 2 + 3: value} enters number 5 in cell R1
{LET R1, "2 + 3"} or
{LET F1, 2 + 3: String} enters string "2 + 3" in cell R1

Arguments must be separated by a comma (,) or a semicolon (;). There must be a blank space between the KEYWORD and the ARGUMENT. Arguments can be written in either uppercase or lowercase; it does not make a difference.

If you are using a label or a string and if your label contains one of the separators (, or ;), you must include the entire string within a double quotation:

{LET R28, "TYPE YOUR FIRST NAME; THEN YOUR LAST NAME"}

19-3 Valid and Invalid Macro Commands

If you do not follow the rules just mentioned, 1-2-3 will issue an error message. Following are some valid and invalid examples of LET as a macro command.

{LET Q1, 50}	Valid
{let Q2, 55}	Valid
{LET Q3, 2*G1+6*G9}	Valid
{LET Q4, 91	Invalid (second brace is missing)
{LETQ5,65}	Invalid (space is missing)
{LET Q697}	Invalid (separator is missing)
{Q7, 99}	Invalid (keyword is missing)

19-4 An Overview of Advanced Macro Commands

Macro commands have been divided into five groups based on the particular function performed by each group.

Group 1—Data Manipulation Commands are used for changing the content and/or format of data in a particular location or locations of the worksheet.

Group 2—Program Flow (branching and looping) Commands are used for controlling the flow of a macro, e.g., performing a loop (printing 200 checks), transferring the control (moving from one part of the macro to another part), and so on.

Group 3—Testing Keyboard Operations Commands allow you to perform interactive programming with Lotus. For example, a macro pauses during execution, waiting for user input.

Group 4—Screen Design and Control Commands will help you to change the appearance of the screen, both audibly and visually.

Group 5—File Operations Commands will help you to perform file operations such as data transfer between files, writing to a file, reading from a file, and so forth.

Table 19-1 illustrates the commands included in these five groups.

TABLE 19-1 SUMMARY OF ADVANCED MACRO COMMANDS

Command Name	Description
Group 1—Data Manipulation	
{BLANK address}	Erases the content of a cell or cells
{CONTENTS target-location, source-location}	Places the content of one cell into another cell as label
{LET address, data}	Stores data in an address

(continued on next page)

TABLE 19-1 (Continued)

Command Name	Description
{PUT address, column-number, row-number, number}	Stores a number in a specified address within a range
{RECALC address}	Recalculates a formula in a specified address, proceeding row by row
{RECALCCOL address}	Recalculates a formula in a specified address, proceeding column by column
Group 2—Program Flow (branching and looping)	
{BRANCH address}	Continues macro execution at a specified address
{DEFINE address1: type1, address2: type2 ...}	Specifies address and defines data type
{DISPATCH address}	Branches to a target location which is specified in address
{FOR counter, start, stop, step, starting address}	Executes a macro for a specified number of times
{FORBREAK}	Cancels execution of a FOR loop
{IF condition}	Conditionally executes a macro
{ONERROR branch-address}	Branches to branch-address if an error occurs during macro execution
{QUIT}	Terminates macro execution
{RESTART}	Cancels a subroutine
{RETURN}	Returns from a macro subroutine
{SYSTEM Command}	Executes the specified DOS command
Group 3—Testing Keyboard Operations	
{?}	Halts macro execution temporarily for user input
{BREAKOFF}	Disables the **Break** key during the macro execution
{BREAKON}	Restores thc **Break** key
{GET address}	Pauses for the user to input a single character, then stores it in address
{GETLABEL prompt-string, address}	Pauses for the user to input a string, then stores it as a string in address
{GETNUMBER prompt-string, address}	Pauses for the user to input a number, then stores it as a number in address
{LOOK address}	Checks to see if the user has typed a character

(continued on next page)

TABLE 19-1 (Continued)

Command Name	Description
{MENUBRANCH address}	Halts macro execution temporarily in order for the user to choose a menu item, then branches accordingly
{MENUCALL address}	Halts the macro execution temporarily in order for the user to choose a menu item, then executes the corresponding macro as a subroutine
{WAIT time}	Waits for a specified amount of time
Group 4—Screen Design and Control	
{BEEP number}	Causes computer's bell to sound
{BORDERSOFF}	Suppresses the display of the worksheet frame (column border letters and row border numbers)
{BORDERSON}	Displays the worksheet frame
{FRAMEOFF}	Same as {BORDERSOFF}
{FRAMEON}	Same as {BORDERSON}
{GRAPHOFF}	Removes the graph displayed by GRAPHON
{GRAPHON}	Displays the current graph and/or gets the named graph
{INDICATE string}	Changes the mode indicator to string
{PANELOFF}	Suppresses display of the control panel during the execution of the macro
{PANELON}	Restores panel display
{WINDOWSOFF}	Freezes screen display and turns off the display of the settings sheet
{WINDOWSON}	Restores normal screen display and turns on the display of the settings sheet
Group 5—File Operations	
{CLOSE}	Closes an open file (the file that was opened by {OPEN} command)
{FILESIZE address}	Determines the size of the file in bytes and puts it in address
{GETPOS address}	Determines correct position of file pointer and displays it in address

(continued on next page)

TABLE 19-1 (Continued)

Command Name	Description
{OPEN filename, access-mode}	Opens a specific file for a specific access: reading, writing, modifying, or appending
{READ bytecount, address}	Reads characters from a file into address
{READLN address}	Copies one line of data from an open file into address
{SETPOS file-position}	Sets a new position for file pointer (of an open file)
{WRITE string}	Copies string into an open file
{WRITELN string}	Copies a complete line into open file (this includes carriage-return, line-feed)

19-5 Data Manipulation Commands

These commands are used for changing the content and format of data in a worksheet. These commands include BLANK, CONTENTS, LET, PUT, RECALC, and RECALCCOL.

19-5-1 {BLANK address}

Erases the contents of a cell or cells in a worksheet. This command is equivalent to /Range Erase. For example, {BLANK G1..G5} will erase the contents of cells G1, G2, G3, G4 and G5.

19-5-2 {LET address, number, or string}

Stores a number or string in an address or location. {LET} can be used to generate a label or number entry. For example:

{LET R10, 2 + 3: value}   stores number 5
{LET R11, 2 + 3: string}   stores label 2 + 3

Figure 19-1 illustrates using the LET and BLANK commands.

19-5-3 {CONTENTS target-location, source-location}

This command is similar to LET. The only difference is that {LET} can store either a number or a string, but {CONTENTS} only stores LABEL data. A more elaborate format of this command is as follows:
{CONTENTS target-location, source-location, <width-number>, <format-number>}

The width-number and format-number are optional. If you specify format-number, you must also specify width-number. Table 19–2 contains a complete listing of the numeric format codes for the {CONTENTS} command.

One good use of this command is to use code 117 for text display of formulas for debugging. For example, if the content of H2 is 555.55, {CONTENTS H10,H2,17,36} places the 17-character label $555.550 (currency, three decimal places) in cell H10.

FIGURE 19-1 *Example of BLANK and LET Commands*

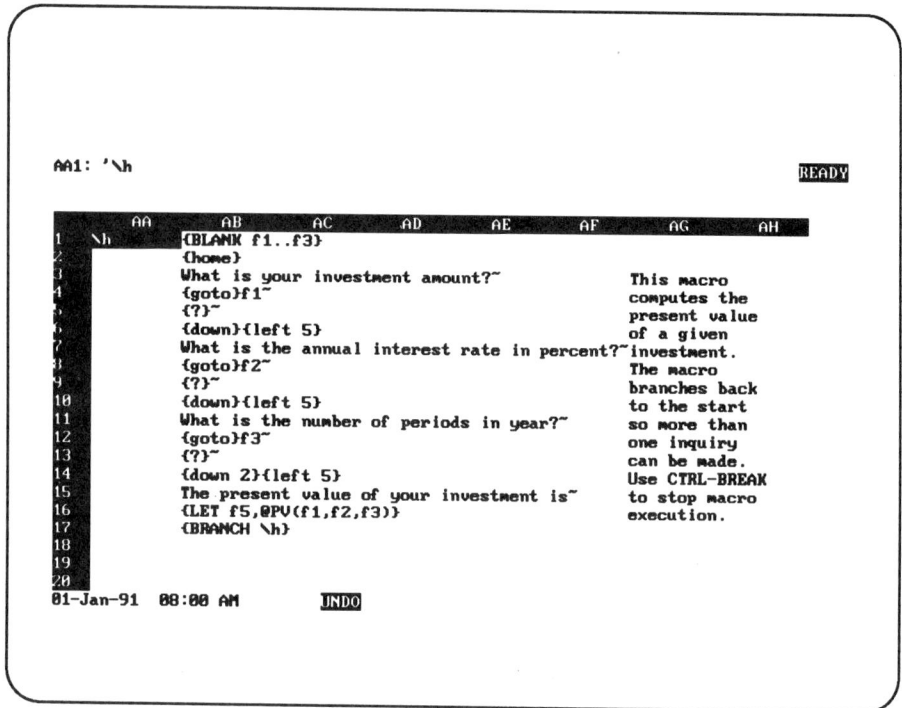

```
AA1: '\h                                                                    READY

        AA        AB         AC        AD        AE        AF       AG        AH
1   \h          {BLANK f1..f3}
2               {home}
3               What is your investment amount?~            This macro
4               {goto}f1~                                    computes the
5               {?}~                                         present value
6               {down}{left 5}                               of a given
7               What is the annual interest rate in percent?~investment.
8               {goto}f2~                                    The macro
9               {?}~                                         branches back
10              {down}{left 5}                               to the start
11              What is the number of periods in year?~      so more than
12              {goto}f3~                                     one inquiry
13              {?}~                                          can be made.
14              {down 2}{left 5}                              Use CTRL-BREAK
15              The present value of your investment is~      to stop macro
16              {LET f5,@PV(f1,f2,f3)}                        execution.
17              {BRANCH \h}
18
19
20
01-Jan-91  08:00 AM              UNDO
```

19-5-4 {PUT address, column-number, row-number, number or string}

Stores a number or a string in a specific location within a range. The difference between this command and the {LET} command is that {PUT} stores data in a particular column and row of a specified range. (Remember, column-number and row-number start from zero. {PUT A1..H20,0,5,BASIC} will put BASIC in A6 left-justified.) Figure 19-2 illustrates using the {PUT} and {CONTENTS} commands.

19-5-5 {RECALC address} and {RECALCCOL address}

RECALC recalculates a formula in a specified address, proceeding row by row. This macro command could also include condition and iteration-number as follows:
{RECALC address, <condition>, <iteration-number>}

For example, if your macro changes a value in cell C7 and you are interested in the value in cell B13, which depends on cell C7, macro {RECALC B13..C7} will do the job for you.

{RECALCCOL address, <condition>, <iteration-number>} will recalculate the formulas in a specified address, proceeding column by column. You should always remember to use {RECALC} for a formula that is located below and to the left of the cells that you are referring to. Use {RECALCCOL} if the formula is above and to the right of the cell which it refers. Use {CALC} if the formula is both above and to the left of cells whose values have changed.

If you use a condition and/or iteration number, the process of recalculation will stop regardless of which number is reached first. For example, the macro {RECALC NETPRESENT, (B5>5),12} will cause the NETPRESENT range to be calculated continuously until the value of cell B5 reaches 5 or the number of iterations equals 12. Figure 19-3 illustrates using RECALC and RECALCCOL.

FIGURE 19-2 Example of CONTENTS and PUT Commands

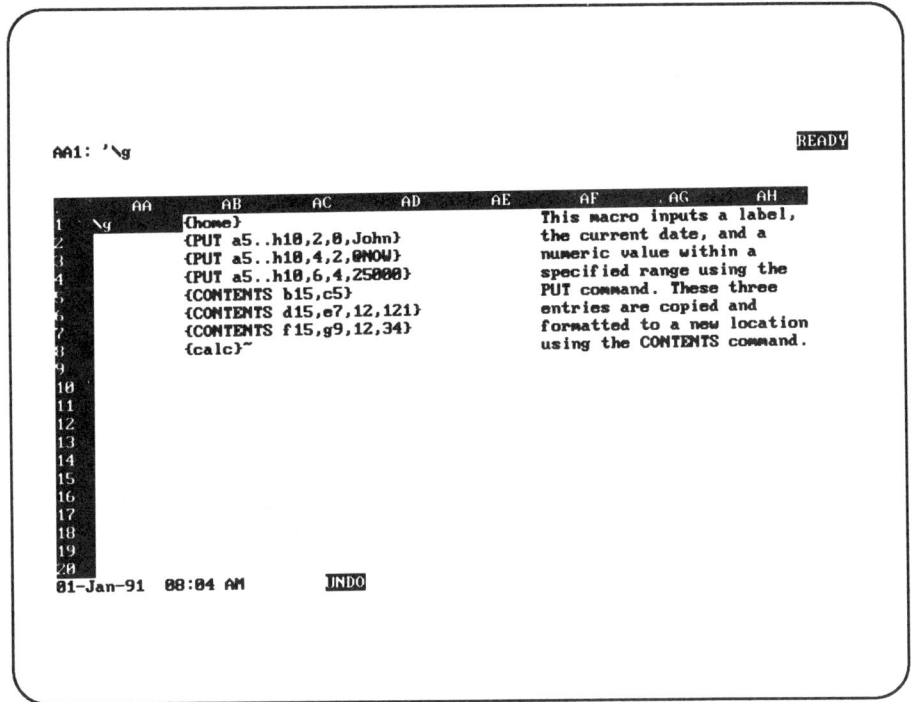

```
AA1: '\g                                                           READY

      AA      AB       AC       AD       AE       AF    , AG       AH
  1   \g    {home}                                    This macro inputs a label,
  2         {PUT a5..h10,2,0,John}                    the current date, and a
  3         {PUT a5..h10,4,2,@NOW}                    numeric value within a
  4         {PUT a5..h10,6,4,25000}                   specified range using the
  5         {CONTENTS b15,c5}                         PUT command. These three
  6         {CONTENTS d15,e7,12,121}                  entries are copied and
  7         {CONTENTS f15,g9,12,34}                   formatted to a new location
  8         {calc}~                                   using the CONTENTS command.
  9
 10
 11
 12
 13
 14
 15
 16
 17
 18
 19
 20
 01-Jan-91  08:04 AM          UNDO
```

TABLE 19-2 NUMERIC FORMAT CODES FOR THE CONTENTS COMMAND (THE OPTIONAL PART)

CODE	FORMAT EQUIVALENT
0-15	Fixed, 0 to 15 decimal places
16-32	Scientific, 0 to 15 decimal places
33-47	Currency, 0 to 15 decimal places
48-63	% (percent), 0 to 15 decimal places
64-79	, (comma), 0 to 15 decimal places
112	+/- (horizontal bar graph)
113	General
114	D1 (DD-MMM-YY)
115	D2 (DD-MMM)
116	D3 (MMM-YY)
121	D4 (Full international)
122	D5 (Partial international)
119	D6 (HH:MM:SS AM/PM)
120	D7 (HH;MMAM/PM)
123	D8 (Full international)
124	D9 (Partial international)
117	Text format
118	Hidden format
127	Default format display

FIGURE 19-3 Example of RECALC and RECALCCOL Commands

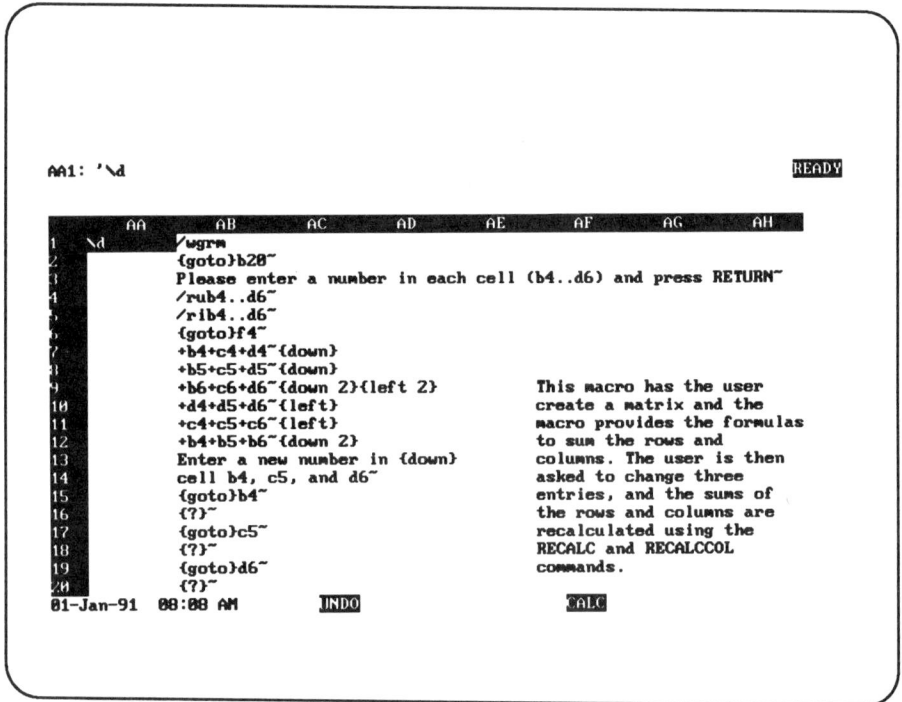

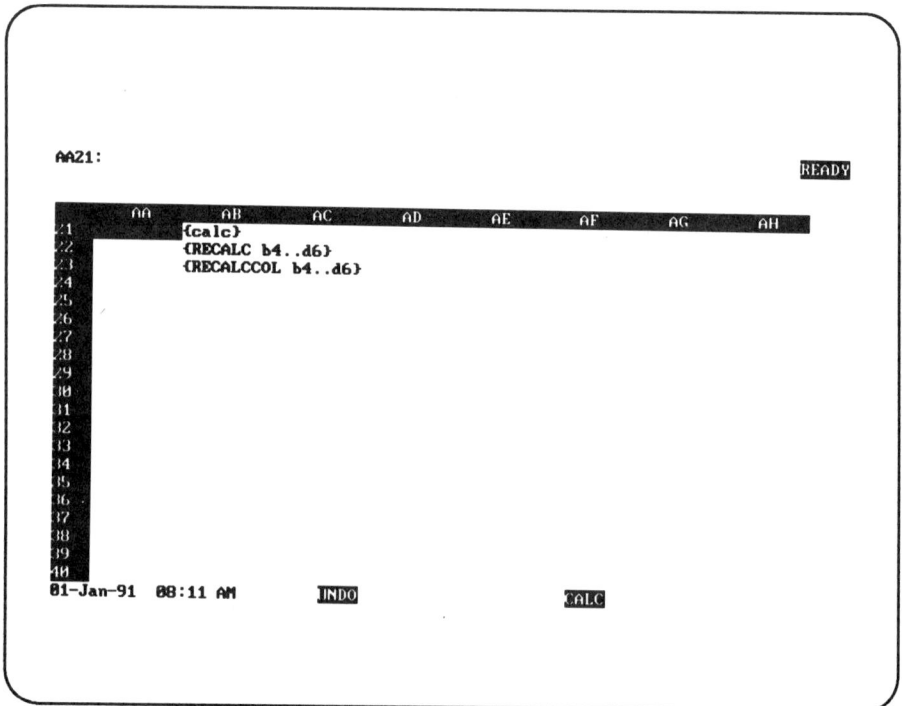

```
AA1: '\d                                                                 READY

        AA      AB        AC        AD        AE      AF       AG        AH
1   \d          /wgrm
2               {goto}b20~
3               Please enter a number in each cell (b4..d6) and press RETURN~
4               /rub4..d6~
5               /rib4..d6~
6               {goto}f4~
7               +b4+c4+d4~{down}
8               +b5+c5+d5~{down}
9               +b6+c6+d6~{down 2}{left 2}        This macro has the user
10              +d4+d5+d6~{left}                  create a matrix and the
11              +c4+c5+c6~{left}                  macro provides the formulas
12              +b4+b5+b6~{down 2}                to sum the rows and
13              Enter a new number in {down}      columns. The user is then
14              cell b4, c5, and d6~              asked to change three
15              {goto}b4~                         entries, and the sums of
16              {?}~                              the rows and columns are
17              {goto}c5~                         recalculated using the
18              {?}~                              RECALC and RECALCCOL
19              {goto}d6~                         commands.
20              {?}~
01-Jan-91  08:08 AM              UNDO                        CALC
```

```
AA21:                                                                    READY

        AA      AB        AC        AD        AE      AF       AG        AH
21              {calc}
22              {RECALC b4..d6}
23              {RECALCCOL b4..d6}
24
25
26
27
28
29
30
31
32
33
34
35
36
37
38
39
40
01-Jan-91  08:11 AM              UNDO                        CALC
```

FIGURE 19-3 (Continued)

19-6 Program Flow (Branching and Looping)

Program flow commands are used to perform loops and branches within a macro. They include BRANCH, DEFINE, DISPATCH, FOR, FORBREAK, IF, ONERROR, QUIT, RESTART and RETURN.

19-6-1 {BRANCH address}

Continues macro execution at a specified cell. The specified location or address can be either a single cell or a range. This command is the same as a GOTO command in BASIC. There is a difference between this command and the Lotus GOTO. The Lotus GOTO command moves the cell pointer. The command {BRANCH} transfers the control (or macro execution) to a specified location. Figure 19-4 illustrates an example of this command.

19-6-2 {DEFINE address1: type1, address2: type2, ...}

Specifies the location and arguments to be passed to a subroutine. This must be the first command in the subroutine. The default value for the argument is a string. There must be a match between the number of arguments in the subroutine and the DEFINE command. The following is one example of {DEFINE} and a subroutine:
SUB-GROSS-total H1, N1
DEFINE F1: value, N1: value
Figure 19-5 illustrates an example of this command.

19-6-3 {DISPATCH address}

Transfers macro execution to the location specified in the address. The difference between this command and {BRANCH} is that DISPATCH can execute instructions in several locations specified in the address. Figure 19-6 illustrates one example of this command.

19-6-4 {FOR} and {FORBREAK}

Executes a macro for a certain number of times. This is equivalent to the FOR-NEXT loop in BASIC or the DO loop in FORTRAN. Other programming languages have something similar to this command. The counter keeps track of the number of times the macro has been executed. Start is the starting value stored in the counter location. Stop marks the end of the loop. Step tells the counter how to increment the counter. The starting address is the cell address or range in which the macro starts the execution. Lotus always checks the condition of start, stop, and step before executing the macro. The FORBREAK command cancels the execution of a FOR loop. If the value of step is 0, an endless loop will be generated (a loop that never stops). If the start value exceeds the stop value, the macro will not be executed at all. Figure 19-7 is an example of the FOR command. Figure 19-8 illustrates an example of FOR and FORBREAK.

19-6-5 {IF} {QUIT}, and {ONERROR}

Executes a macro conditionally. This command is similar to the IF-THEN-ELSE command available in many programming languages. The instructions in the cell after the IF are the THEN part and those below the cell are the ELSE part. If the expression does not have a value of zero, 1-2-3 considers it true and the statement in the same cell (the cell that includes IF) will be executed, otherwise the statement in the cell below will be executed.

To protect the accurate execution of IF-THEN-ELSE clauses you may have to use

FIGURE 19-4 *An Example of the BRANCH Command*

```
AA1: '\p                                                              READY

         AA        AB        AC        AD        AE        AF        AG        AH
1   \p         {home}
2              What is your sex? Choose (M)ale or (F)emale {right 6}~
3              {GET sex}
4              {IF sex="F"}{BRANCH no_go}
5              {IF sex="M"}{BRANCH age_rtn}
6
7   age_rtn    {down 2}{LEFT 6}
8              How old are you? {right 2}~
9              {?}~
10             {IF c3<18}{BRANCH no_go}
11             {IF c3>35}{BRANCH no_go}
12             {BRANCH status}
13
14  status     {down 2}{left 2}
15             What is your marital status? Choose (M)arried or (S)ingle {righ
16             {GET marital}
17             {IF marital="M"}{BRANCH no_go}
18             {IF marital="S"}{goto}a15~
19             You qualify for overseas employment. HaHa!~
20
01-Jan-91  08:14 AM          UNDO
```

```
AA21: 'no_go                                                          READY

         AA  '     AB.       AC '      AD        AE        AF        AG        AH
21  no_go      {goto}a15~
22             Sorry, you do not qualify for overseas employment.~
23
24
25
26
27             This macro checks to see if an employee meets the
28             requirements for an overseas position by using the
29             BRANCH command to move to various subroutines.
30             The requirements for overseas employment are:
31                       1. male
32                       2. between 18 and 35 years of age
33                       3. single
34
35
36
37
38
39
40
01-Jan-91  08:18 AM          UNDO
```

FIGURE 19-4 *(Continued)*

FIGURE 19-5 An Example of the DEFINE Command

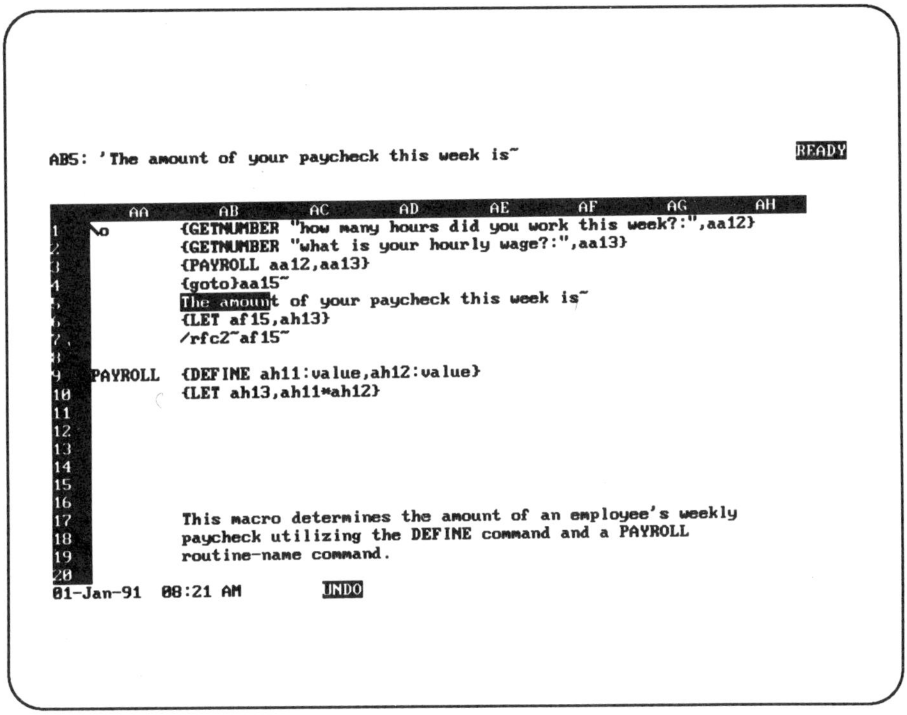

```
AB5: 'The amount of your paycheck this week is~                          READY

        AA        AB        AC        AD        AE        AF        AG        AH
 1   \o           {GETNUMBER "how many hours did you work this week?:",aa12}
 2               {GETNUMBER "what is your hourly wage?:",aa13}
 3               {PAYROLL aa12,aa13}
 4               {goto}aa15~
 5               The amount of your paycheck this week is~
 6               {LET af15,ah13}
 7               /rfc2~af15~
 8
 9   PAYROLL     {DEFINE ah11:value,ah12:value}
10               {LET ah13,ah11*ah12}
11
12
13
14
15
16
17               This macro determines the amount of an employee's weekly
18               paycheck utilizing the DEFINE command and a PAYROLL
19               routine-name command.
20
01-Jan-91  08:21 AM            UNDO
```

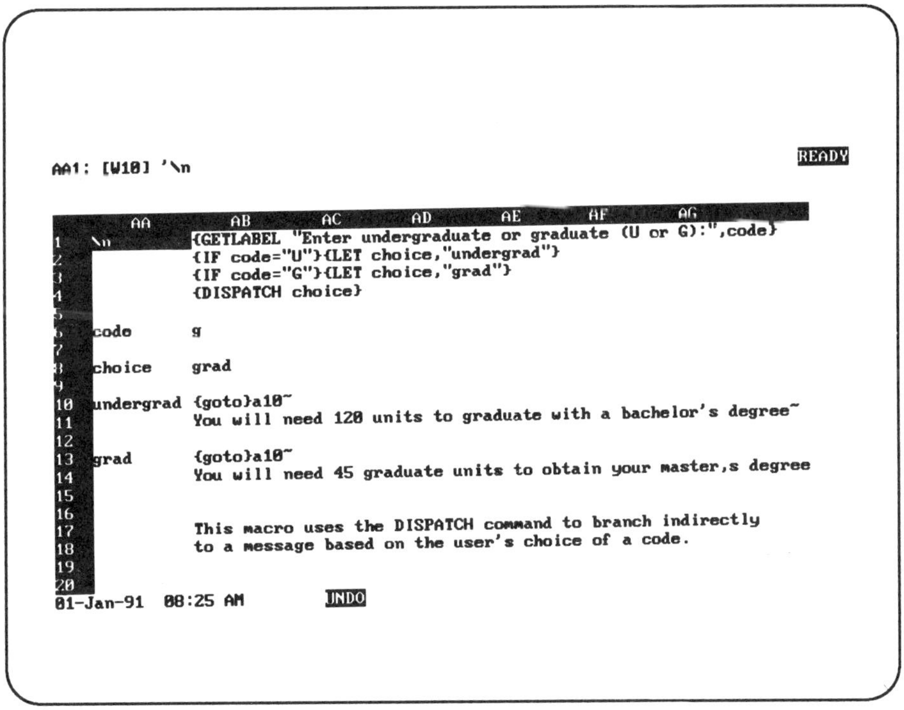

```
AA1: [W10] '\n                                                          READY

        AA        AB        AC        AD        AE        AF        AG
 1   \n           {GETLABEL "Enter undergraduate or graduate (U or G):",code}
 2               {IF code="U"}{LET choice,"undergrad"}
 3               {IF code="G"}{LET choice,"grad"}
 4               {DISPATCH choice}
 5
 6   code        g
 7
 8   choice      grad
 9
10   undergrad   {goto}a10~
11               You will need 120 units to graduate with a bachelor's degree~
12
13   grad        {goto}a10~
14               You will need 45 graduate units to obtain your master,s degree
15
16
17               This macro uses the DISPATCH command to branch indirectly
18               to a message based on the user's choice of a code.
19
20
01-Jan-91  08:25 AM            UNDO
```

FIGURE 19-6 An Example of the DISPATCH Command

FIGURE 19-7 *An Example of the FOR Command*

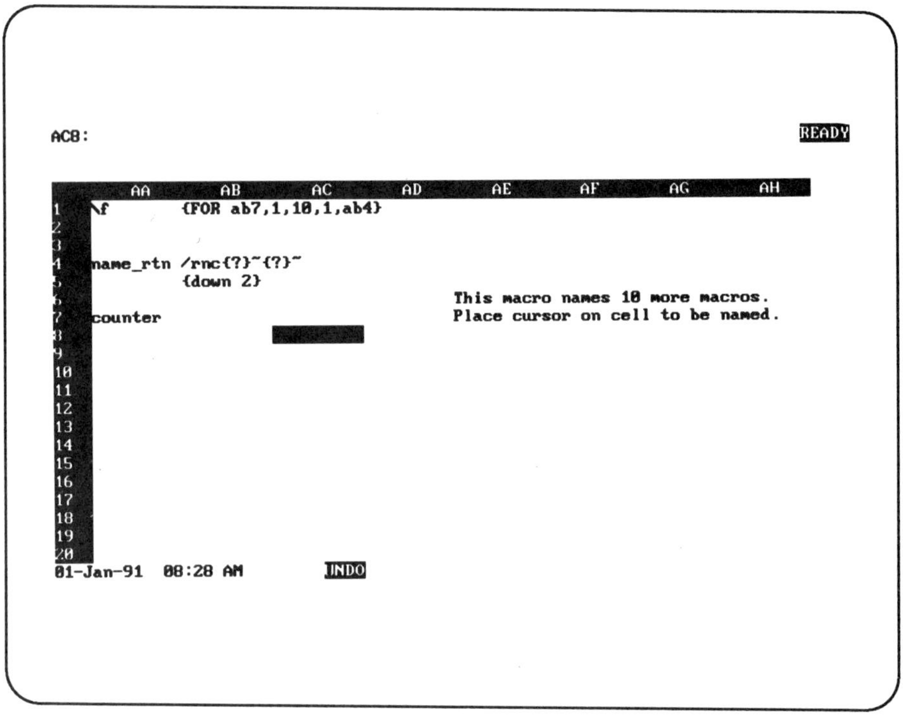

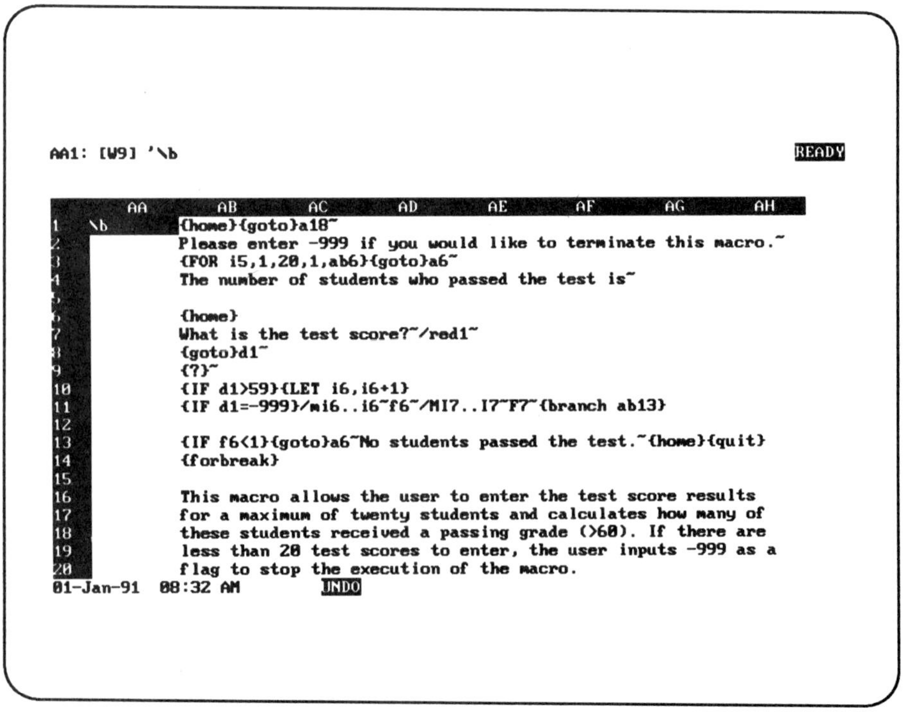

```
AC8:                                                                 READY

        AA        AB        AC        AD        AE        AF        AG        AH
1   \f        {FOR ab7,1,10,1,ab4}
2
3
4   name_rtn  /rnc{?}~{?}~
5             {down 2}
6                                                This macro names 10 more macros.
7   counter                                      Place cursor on cell to be named.
8
9
10
11
12
13
14
15
16
17
18
19
20
01-Jan-91  08:28 AM              UNDO
```

```
AA1: [W9] '\b                                                        READY

        AA        AB        AC        AD        AE        AF        AG        AH
1   \b        {home}{goto}a18~
2             Please enter -999 if you would like to terminate this macro.~
3             {FOR i5,1,20,1,ab6}{goto}a6~
4             The number of students who passed the test is~
5
6             {home}
7             What is the test score?~/red1~
8             {goto}d1~
9             {?}~
10            {IF d1>59}{LET i6,i6+1}
11            {IF d1=-999}/mi6..i6~f6~/MI7..I7~F7~{branch ab13}
12
13            {IF f6<1}{goto}a6~No students passed the test.~{home}{quit}
14            {forbreak}
15
16            This macro allows the user to enter the test score results
17            for a maximum of twenty students and calculates how many of
18            these students received a passing grade (>60). If there are
19            less than 20 test scores to enter, the user inputs -999 as a
20            flag to stop the execution of the macro.
01-Jan-91  08:32 AM              UNDO
```

FIGURE 19-8 *An Example of the FOR and FORBREAK Commands*

{QUIT} and/or {ONERROR} commands. {ONERROR branch-address} branches to a specified address. You can also include a message in this command. This is how you write the command: {ONERROR branch-address, [message-location]} {QUIT} terminates macro execution. Figure 19-9 illustrates the operation of these three commands.

19-6-6 {RESTART}

Cancels a subroutine (a series of instructions that perform a specific task) and clears the subroutine parameters. This is a useful command for canceling a series of commands if a particular condition does not exist. Figure 19-10 illustrates an application of this command.

19-6-7 {RETURN}

Returns control from a subroutine. This command is used either by a routine name or with a MENUCALL. {RETURN} instructs the macro to return to the command cell immediately after the call location. By using several subroutines you will be able to break down a large problem into several smaller units or modules (see Figure 19-11).

Macro subroutines must begin with SUBR-. The routine name is a range. The routine name cannot be one of the Lotus reserved words such as NAME (see Table 18-1 in Chapter 18 for the listing of reserved words). If duplication occurs Lotus performs the subroutine, not the keystroke (or reserved word).

19-6-8 {SYSTEM COMMAND}

Temporarily suspends the 1-2-3 session and passes a command to to operating system. When the operating system command is completed, the computer automatically resumes the 1-2-3 session and continues the macro. The command can be any operating system command, including batch files. The maximum size of such a command is 123 characters. The command must be enclosed in double quotes.

The following section of a macro suspends the 1-2-3 session, executes a batch file called Go, then returns to 1-2-3 and continues the macro operation.

    {SYSTEM "GO"}
    .
    .
    .

Please remember not to use {SYSTEM} command to load memory-resident programs. If you do so you may not be able to resume 1-2-3 because the memory-resident program may overwrite some of the memory being occupied by 1-2-3. For this reason it is advisable to save your worksheet before you execute a macro that includes this command.

19-7 Testing Keyboard Operations

These commands are used for interactive programming. During the execution of these commands, 1-2-3 will pause and ask for user input. Commands include ?, BREAKOFF, BREAKON, GET, GETLABEL, GETNUMBER, LOOK, MENUBRANCH, MENUCALL, and WAIT.

19-7-1 {?}

Halts the execution of the macro temporarily and waits for user input. The {?} command is an alternative to GET, GETLABEL, GETNUMBER, LOOK, MENUBRANCH, and MENUCALL.

19-7-2 {BREAKOFF}

Disables the BREAK key during macro execution. {BREAKON} restores the BREAK key. You must always remember that if your macro enters an endless loop and {BREAKOFF} is active you cannot stop the endless loop. The only solution is to stop the computer. The combination of these two commands is used for applications in which you want to show the execution of the entire macro without user interruption.

19-7-3 {WAIT time-serial-number}

Waits until the time-serial-number is up. You can halt a {WAIT} command by pressing the **Break** key, unless you have executed a {BREAKOFF} command. Figure 19-12 illustrates an application of BREAKOFF, BREAKON and WAIT.

19-7-4 {GET address}

Pauses for the user to input a single character, then stores it in an address. The single character can be either a standard typewriter key or a Lotus standard key (TABLE, QUERY, etc.). Figure 19-13 illustrates an example of this command.

19-7-5 {GETLABEL prompt, address} and {GETNUMBER}

Pauses for the user to type a character string, then stores it as a label in the address. {GETNUMBER} does the same thing, but stores the data as a number. Your prompt (your

FIGURE 19-9 *An Example of the IF, ONERROR and QUIT Commands*

```
AA1: '\a                                                      READY

       AA       AB       AC       AD       AE      AF      AG      AH
1   \a       {home}
2            John{down}
3            Mary{down}
4            Jack{down}
5            Sue{down}~
6            Do you want to save this file? Choose (Y)es or (N)o~
7            {GET answer}
8            {IF answer="N"}{QUIT}
9            {IF answer="Y"}{BRANCH subr_save}
10                                               This macro enters a name
11  answer    y                                  file and then asks the
12                                                user if the file is to be
13  subr_save{ONERROR full_msg}                   saved. If "no" the macro
14           /fsNAMES~                            quits. If "yes" the macro
15           {RETURN}                             goes to the save subroutine
16  full_msg {goto}a15~                           and tries to save the file.
17           Disk is full~{down}                  If the disk is full, or not
18           Replace data disk~{down}             ready  an error message is
19           Press RETURN to continue~{?}~        displayed and the user must
20           {BRANCH subr_save}                   replace the data disk
01-Jan-91  08:36 AM           UNDO
```

FIGURE 19-10 An Example of the RESTART Command

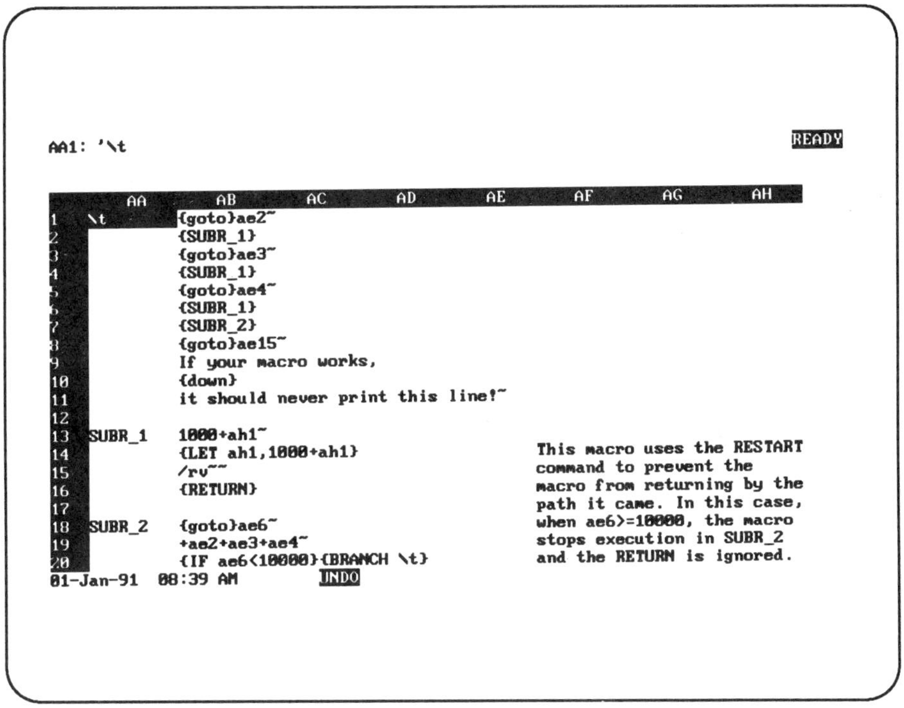

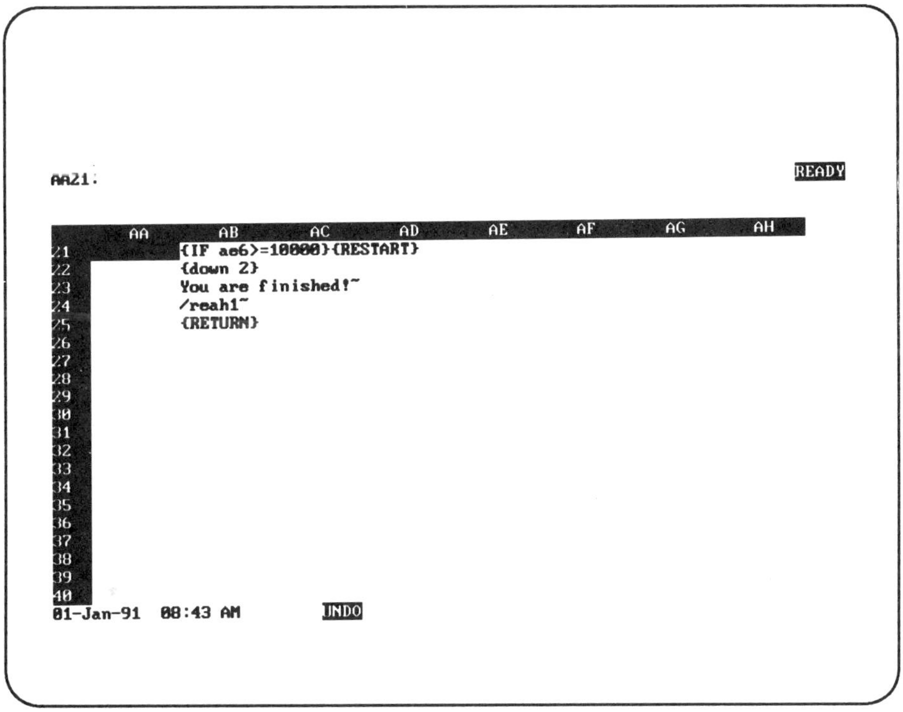

```
AA1: '\t                                                              READY

        AA          AB          AC        AD        AE      AF      AG        AH
1    \t          {goto}ae2~
2                {SUBR_1}
3                {goto}ae3~
4                {SUBR_1}
5                {goto}ae4~
6                {SUBR_1}
7                {SUBR_2}
8                {goto}ae15~
9                If your macro works,
10               {down}
11               it should never print this line!~
12
13   SUBR_1      1000+ah1~                          This macro uses the RESTART
14               {LET ah1,1000+ah1}                 command to prevent the
15               /rv~~                              macro from returning by the
16               {RETURN}                           path it came. In this case,
17                                                  when ae6>=10000, the macro
18   SUBR_2      {goto}ae6~                         stops execution in SUBR_2
19               +ae2+ae3+ae4~                      and the RETURN is ignored.
20               {IF ae6<10000}{BRANCH \t}
01-Jan-91  08:39 AM         UNDO
```

```
AA21:                                                               READY

        AA          AB          AC        AD        AE      AF      AG        AH
21               {IF ae6>=10000}{RESTART}
22               {down 2}
23               You are finished!~
24               /reah1~
25               {RETURN}
26
27
28
29
30
31
32
33
34
35
36
37
38
39
40
01-Jan-91  08:43 AM          UNDO
```

FIGURE 19-10 (Continued)

FIGURE 19-11   An Example of the RETURN Command

```
AA1: '\u                                                                    READY

        AA        AB        AC        AD        AE        AF        AG        AH
1    \u          {home}
2                What is the retail price?~
3                {goto}f1~
4                {?}~
5                /rfc2~~
6                {LET f12,f1}
7                {down 2}{left 5}
8                Is the item on sale? Choose (Y)es or (N)o~
9                {GET answer}
10               {IF answer="Y"}{subr_sale}
11               {goto}a12~
12               The final purchase price is~
13               {LET f12,f12+(f12*.06)}~
14               /rfc2~f12~
15
16   subr_sale{goto}a5~
17               Sale items are 20 percent off~
18               {LET f12,f1-(f1*.20)}
19               {down 2}
20               Does the price tag have a red star? Choose (Y)es or (N)o~
01-Jan-91  08:46 AM            UNDO
```

```
AA21:                                                                       READY

        AA        AB        AC        AD        AE        AF        AG        AH
21               {GET response}
22               {IF response="Y"}{subr_star}
23               {LET f12,f12-g9}
24               {RETURN}
25
26   subr_star{goto}a9~
27               Red star tags get an additional 10 percent off~
28               {LET g9,f1*.10}~
29               {RETURN}
30
31   answer
32
33   response
34
35
36
37               This macro is an example of a nested loop which determines
38               the final purchase price of a retail item that may have
39               one, two or no discounts and has a 6% sales tax.
40
01-Jan-91  08:50 AM            UNDO
```

FIGURE 19-11   (Continued)

FIGURE 19-12 An Example of BREAKOFF, BREAKON, and WAIT

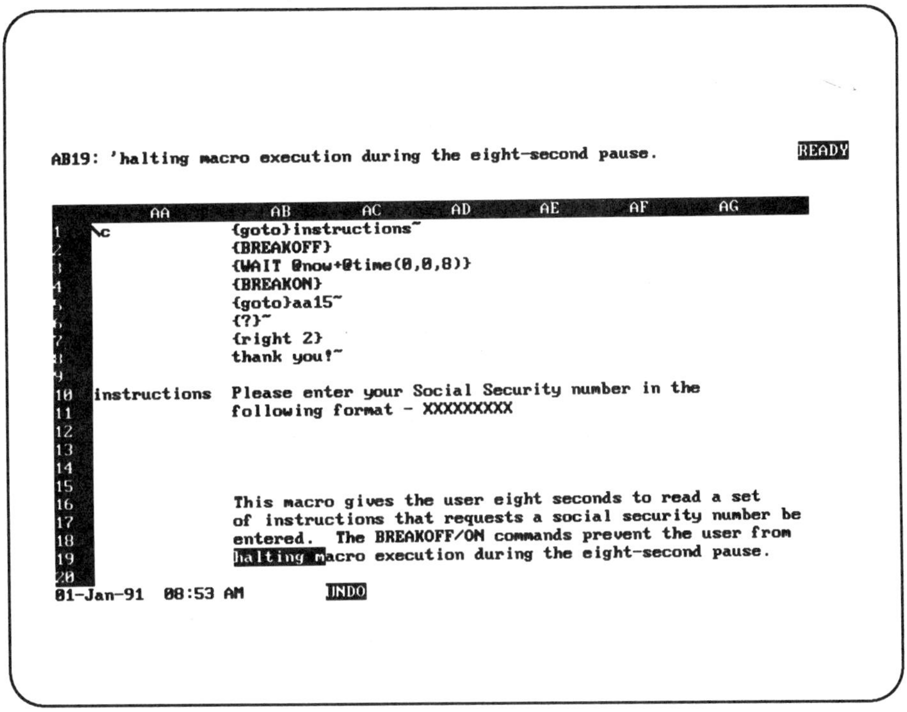

```
AB19: 'halting macro execution during the eight-second pause.          READY

        AA          AB        AC        AD        AE        AF        AG
1   \c              {goto}instructions~
2                   {BREAKOFF}
3                   {WAIT @now+@time(0,0,8)}
4                   {BREAKON}
5                   {goto}aa15~
6                   {?}~
7                   {right 2}
8                   thank you!~
9
10  instructions    Please enter your Social Security number in the
11                  following format - XXXXXXXXX
12
13
14
15
16                  This macro gives the user eight seconds to read a set
17                  of instructions that requests a social security number be
18                  entered.  The BREAKOFF/ON commands prevent the user from
19                  halting macro execution during the eight-second pause.
20
01-Jan-91  08:53 AM        UNDO
```

message or statement) must be short enough to fit into the control panel. Also, if your prompt includes separators (commas or semicolons), you must enclose the prompt in quotation marks. Figure 19-14 illustrates an application of these two commands.

19-7-6 {LOOK address}

Checks to see if the user has typed a character. LOOK is similar to GET except that LOOK does not halt the macro execution. LOOK leaves the character in the type-ahead buffer for future use by GET, GETLABEL or GETNUMBER. Figure 19-15 illustrates an example of this command.

19-7-7 {MENUBRANCH address} and {MENUCALL}

Suspends the execution of the macro temporarily in order to allow the user to choose from a menu and then continues to the macro branch. The MENUCALL address does the same thing, but it executes the corresponding macro as a subroutine. Using MENUCALL you can design your own menu consisting of any of several commands. To establish a menu, remember the following:

1. You can have up to eight commands in your menu.
2. There are three lines available to you. Line one is the name of the command (menu item). Line two is a brief description of the menu item. Line three is the command summary (macro instruction), e.g., /WIC (/Worksheet Insert Column).
3. In your menu the starting character of each menu item must be unique, otherwise 1-2-3 always chooses the first one. For example, do not use worksheet and window in the same menu.

FIGURE 19-13   An Example of the GET Command

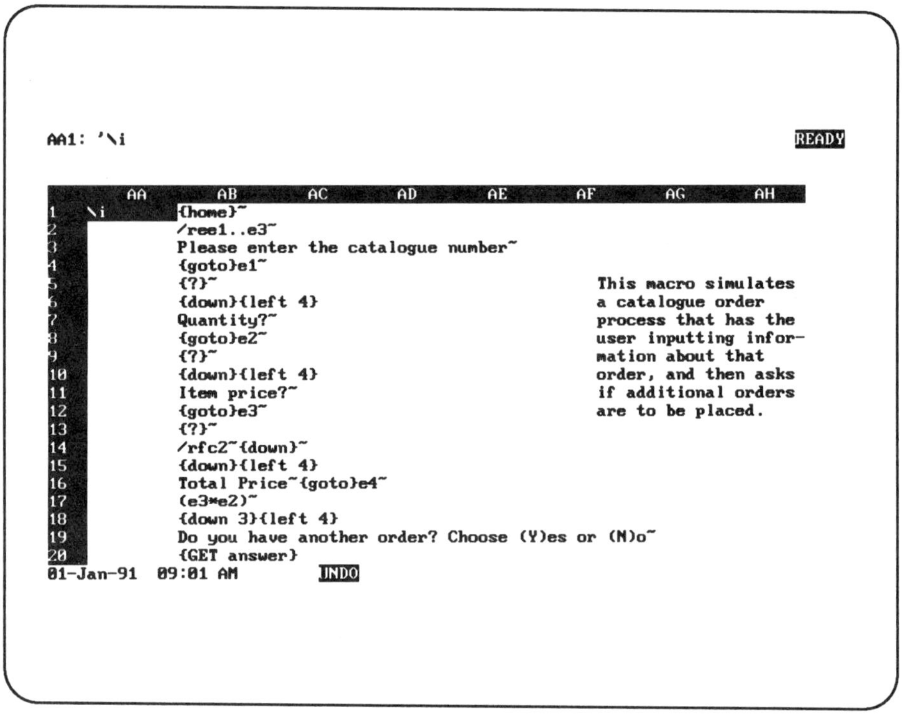

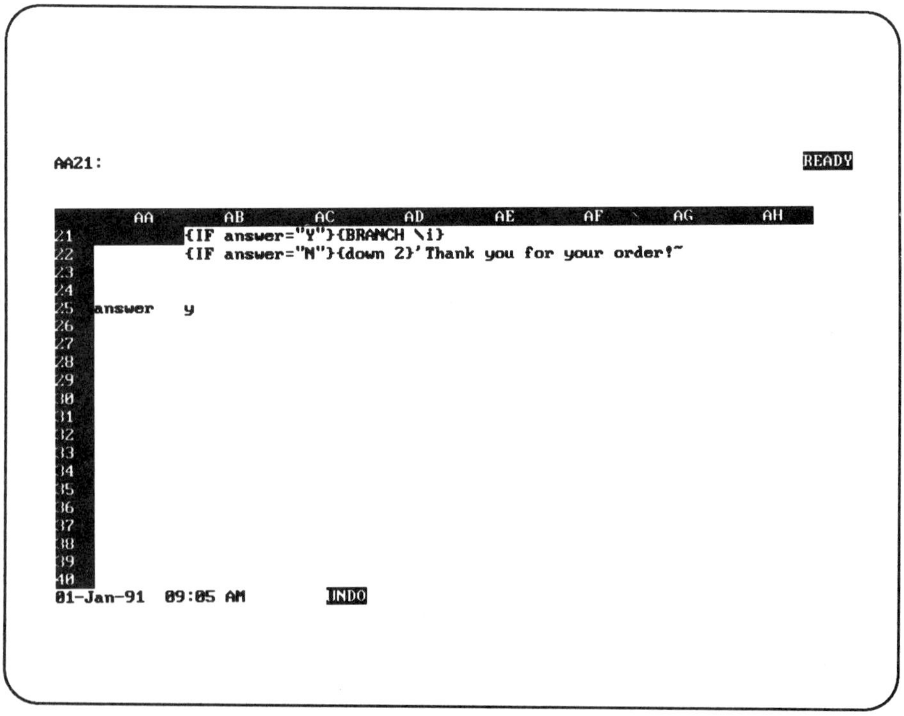

```
AA1: '\i                                                          READY

        AA      AB        AC        AD        AE      AF      AG      AH
1    \i      {home}~
2            /ree1..e3~
3            Please enter the catalogue number~
4            {goto}e1~
5            {?}~                                         This macro simulates
6            {down}{left 4}                               a catalogue order
7            Quantity?~                                   process that has the
8            {goto}e2~                                    user inputting infor-
9            {?}~                                         mation about that
10           {down}{left 4}                               order, and then asks
11           Item price?~                                 if additional orders
12           {goto}e3~                                    are to be placed.
13           {?}~
14           /rfc2~{down}~
15           {down}{left 4}
16           Total Price~{goto}e4~
17           (e3*e2)~
18           {down 3}{left 4}
19           Do you have another order? Choose (Y)es or (N)o~
20           {GET answer}
01-Jan-91  09:01 AM          UNDO
```

```
AA21:                                                            READY

        AA      AB        AC        AD        AE      AF      AG      AH
21           {IF answer="Y"}{BRANCH \i}
22           {IF answer="N"}{down 2}'Thank you for your order!~
23
24
25   answer     y
26
27
28
29
30
31
32
33
34
35
36
37
38
39
40
01-Jan-91  09:05 AM          UNDO
```

FIGURE 19-13   (Continued)

FIGURE 19-14 *An Example of GETLABEL and GETNUMBER*

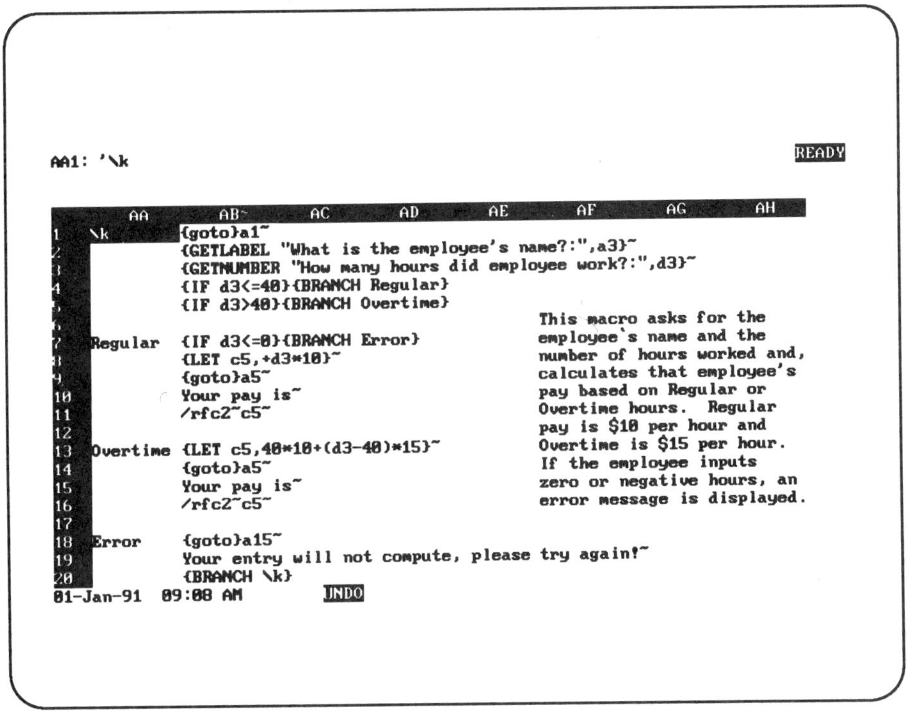

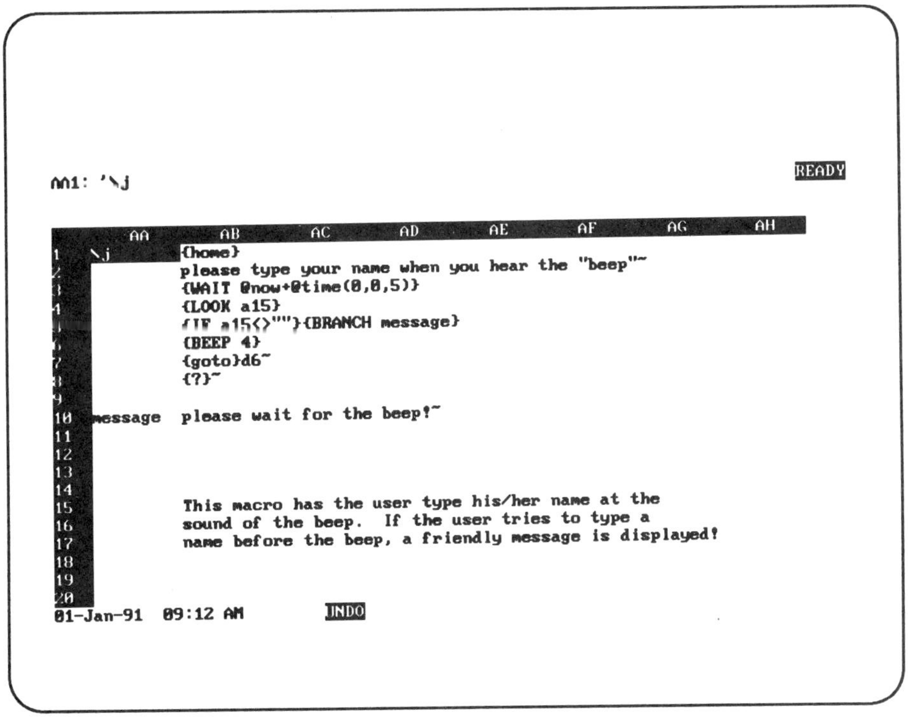

```
AA1: '\k                                                              READY

         AA      AB        AC        AD        AE        AF        AG        AH
 1  \k        {goto}a1~
 2           {GETLABEL "What is the employee's name?:",a3}~
 3           {GETNUMBER "How many hours did employee work?:",d3}~
 4           {IF d3<=40}{BRANCH Regular}
 5           {IF d3>40}{BRANCH Overtime}
 6                                                 This macro asks for the
 7  Regular  {IF d3<=0}{BRANCH Error}              employee's name and the
 8           {LET c5,+d3*10}~                      number of hours worked and,
 9           {goto}a5~                             calculates that employee's
10           Your pay is~                          pay based on Regular or
11           /rfc2~c5~                             Overtime hours.  Regular
12                                                 pay is $10 per hour and
13  Overtime {LET c5,40*10+(d3-40)*15}~            Overtime is $15 per hour.
14           {goto}a5~                             If the employee inputs
15           Your pay is~                          zero or negative hours, an
16           /rfc2~c5~                             error message is displayed.
17
18  Error    {goto}a15~
19           Your entry will not compute, please try again!~
20           {BRANCH \k}
01-Jan-91  09:08 AM         UNDO
```

```
AA1: '\j                                                              READY

         AA      AB        AC        AD        AE        AF        AG        AH
 1  \j        {home}
 2           please type your name when you hear the "beep"~
 3           {WAIT @now+@time(0,0,5)}
 4           {LOOK a15}
 5           {IF a15<>""}{BRANCH message}
 6           {BEEP 4}
 7           {goto}d6~
 8           {?}~
 9
10  message  please wait for the beep!~
11
12
13
14
15           This macro has the user type his/her name at the
16           sound of the beep.  If the user tries to type a
17           name before the beep, a friendly message is displayed!
18
19
20
01-Jan-91  09:12 AM         UNDO
```

FIGURE 19-15 *An Example of the LOOK Command*

4. You can extend the column width to any number between 1 and 240, inclusive.
5. Blank cells are not allowed between menu items.
6. The cell to the right of the final menu item must be empty.
7. Uppercase and lowercase are the same.
8. A menu item can be chosen by moving the cursor and pressing the **Return** key, or typing the first character of each command.
9. Pressing the **Escape** key will cancel a menu item.

Figure 19-16 illustrates an example of MENUCALL. Figure 19-17 illustrates an example of MENUBRANCH.

19-8 Screen Design and Control

These commands help you to design the look of the screen and the sound. They include BEEP, BORDERSOFF, FRAMEOFF, BORDERSON, FRAMEON, GRAPHON, GRAPHOFF, INDICATE, PANELOFF, PANELON, WINDOWSOFF, and WINDOWSON.

19-8-1 {BEEP <number>}

Activates the computer bell. The number argument is optional. This command is used to convey a signal to the user. The number can be either 1, 2, 3, or 4, to choose four different tones. The default value is one. Figure 19-18 illustrates an application of this command.

19-8-2 {BORDERSOFF} and {FRAMEOFF}

{BORDERSOFF} suppresses display of the worksheet frame (column letters and row numbers). When you invoke this command the worksheet frame remains hidden until 1-2-3 reaches a {BORDERSON} command or the macro is terminated. {FRAMEOFF} performs the same task as {BORDERSOFF}. These two commands are usually used to customize menus, to display help screens without having to display these features in the worksheet column or row border.

19-8-3 {BORDERSON} and {FRAMEON}

{BORDERSON} redisplays the worksheet frame (column border letters and row border numbers). This command is usually used after a {BORDERSOFF} command. {FRAMEON} is similar to the {BORDERSON} command. Consider the following example:

```
{BORDERSOFF}
{?}
{BORDERSON}
```

In this example, the macro turns off the display of the worksheet frame during a {?} command so the column letters and row numbers do not distract the user, and then redisplays the worksheet frame.

19-8-4 {GRAPHON}

The {GRAPHON} command with no arguments displays a full-screen view of the current graph while the macro is in progress.

The {GRAPHON, NAME-GRAPH, NODISPLAY} command displays the current

FIGURE 19-16 An Example of MENUCALL

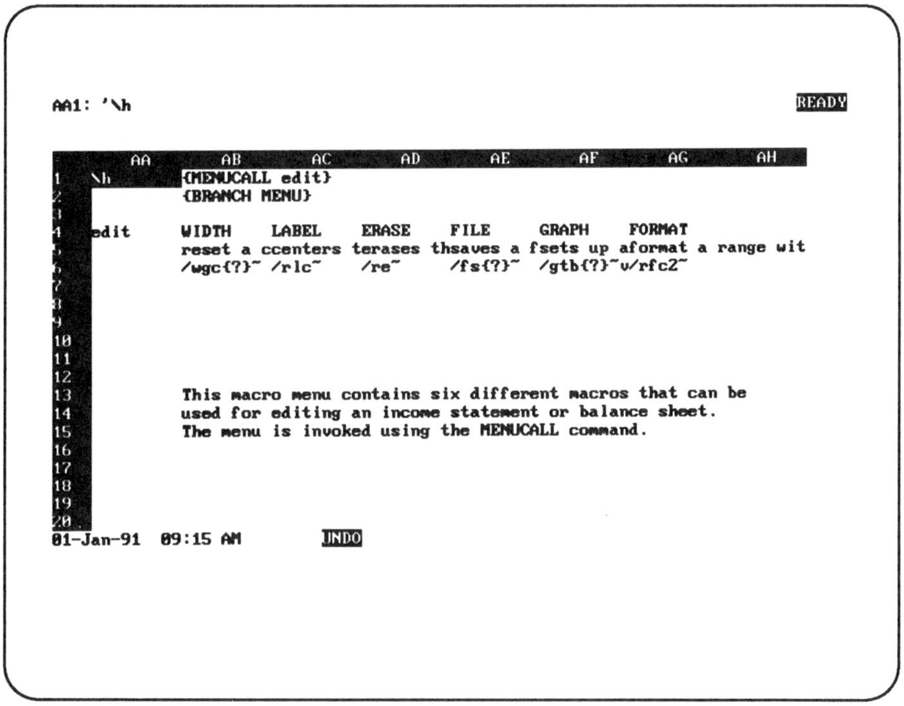

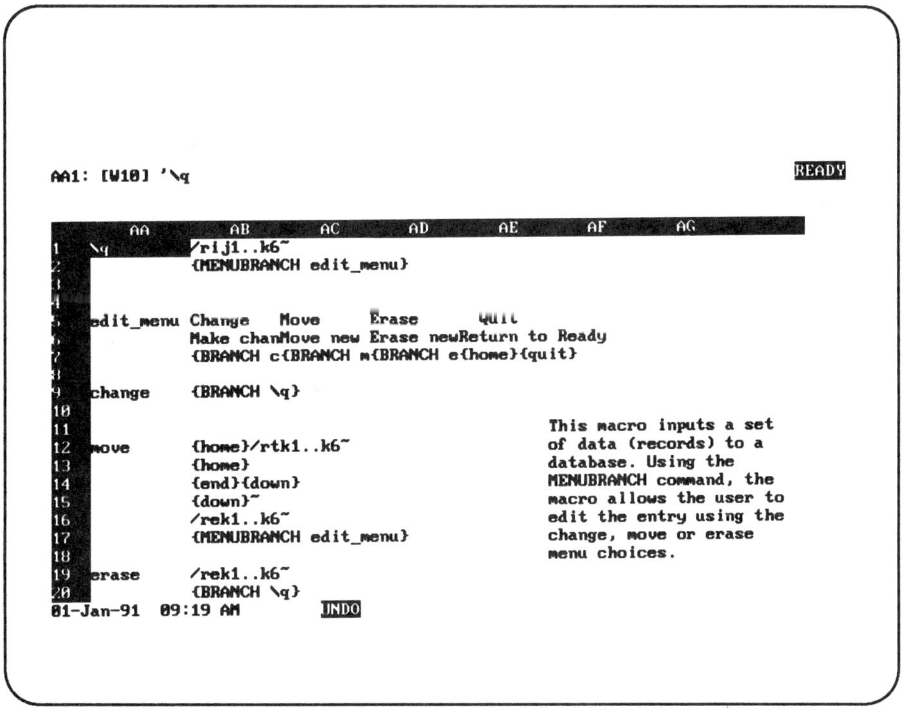

FIGURE 19-17 An Example of MENUBRANCH

FIGURE 19-18 An Example of the BEEP Command

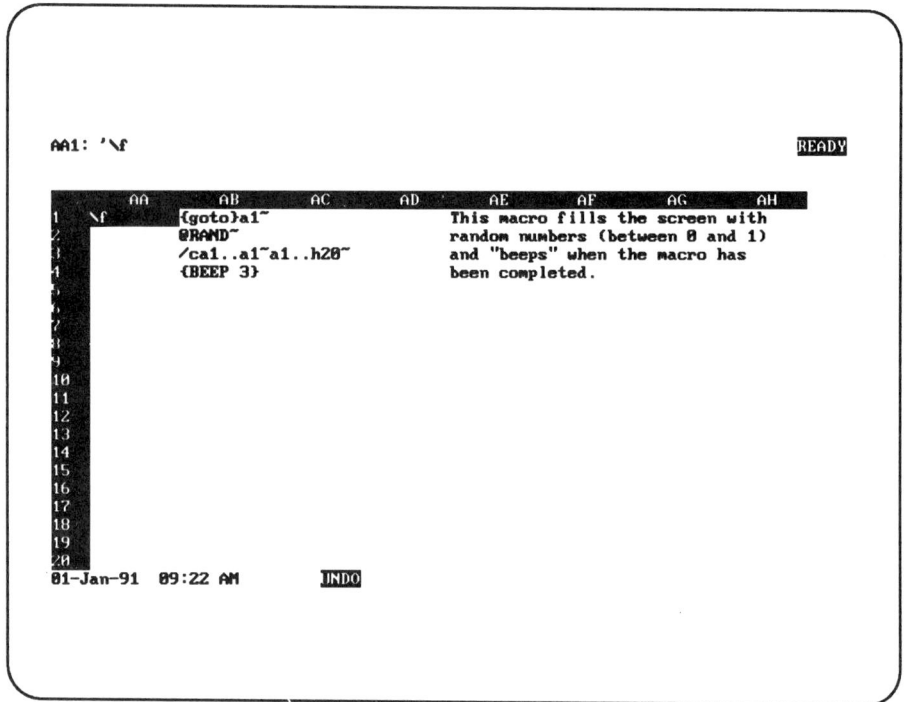

```
AA1: '\f                                                          READY

       AA        AB        AC        AD        AE       AF       AG       AH
1     \f       {goto}a1~                        This macro fills the screen with
2              @RAND~                            random numbers (between 0 and 1)
3              /ca1..a1~a1..h20~                 and "beeps" when the macro has
4              {BEEP 3}                          been completed.
5
6
7
8
9
10
11
12
13
14
15
16
17
18
19
20
01-Jan-91  09:22 AM              UNDO
```

graph or another named graph or sets the current graph without displaying it. A
{GRAPHOFF} command removes the graph from display. If you want to make a graph
your current graph but you do not want to display it, use:

    {GRAPHON, EXAMPLE, NO-DISPLAY}

(Example is our sample graph.)

19-8-5 *{GRAPHOFF}*

This command removes a graph displayed by a {GRAPHON} command and redisplays
the worksheet. Consider the following example. This macro displays four consecutive
graphs (sample1, sample2, sample3, and sample4) at 3-second intervals and then
redisplays the worksheet.

    {GRAPHON SAMPLE1}
    {WAIT @NOW+@TIME(0,0,3)}
    {GRAPHON SAMPLE2}
    {WAIT @NOW+@TIME(0,0,3)}
    {GRAPHON SAMPLE3}
    {WAIT @NOW+@TIME(0,0,3)}
    {GRAPHON SAMPLE4}
    {WAIT @NOW+@TIME(0,0,3)}

19-8-6 *{INDICATE <string>}*

Changes the mode indicator in the upper right corner of the screen. When INDICATE is
activated the only way to deactivate it is to use another INDICATE command. The default
value of string is the READY mode. To remove the mode indicator from the control panel

you can use {INDICATE " "}. Figure 19-19 illustrates an example of this command. In Release 2.2 the INDICATE command also can use a reference cell as well as a string.

19-8-7 {PANELOFF} and {PANELON}

Suppresses redrawing (display) of the control panel during the execution of the macro. {PANELON} restores the setting. {PANELOFF} is very useful when the macro is executing Lotus menu commands. Figure 19-20 illustrates an example of these commands.

19-8-8 {WINDOWSOFF} and {WINDOWSON}

Freezes the screen display (except for the control panel). {WINDOWSON} restores the normal setting. Using WINDOWSOFF will speed up the execution time of a macro since it does not do any redrawing; this is especially useful for long macros. These two commands are similar to PANELOFF and PANELON. Figure 19-21 illustrates an example of these two commands.

19-9 File Operations

The commands in this group enable you to perform file operations. These commands include CLOSE, FILESIZE, GETPOS, OPEN, READ, READLN, SETPOS, WRITE and WRITELN. These are designed only for ASCII files. (For more information on ASCII files, see Appendix D.)

19-9-1 {CLOSE}

Closes a file that was opened with the {OPEN} command.

FIGURE 19-19 An Example of the INDICATE Command

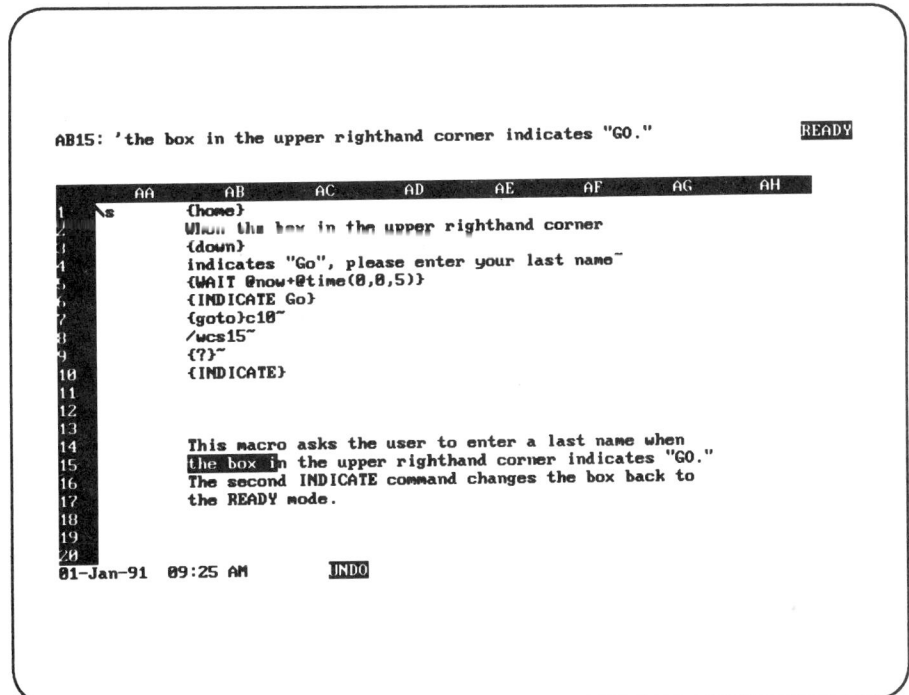

FIGURE 19-20 *An Example of PANELOFF and PANELON*

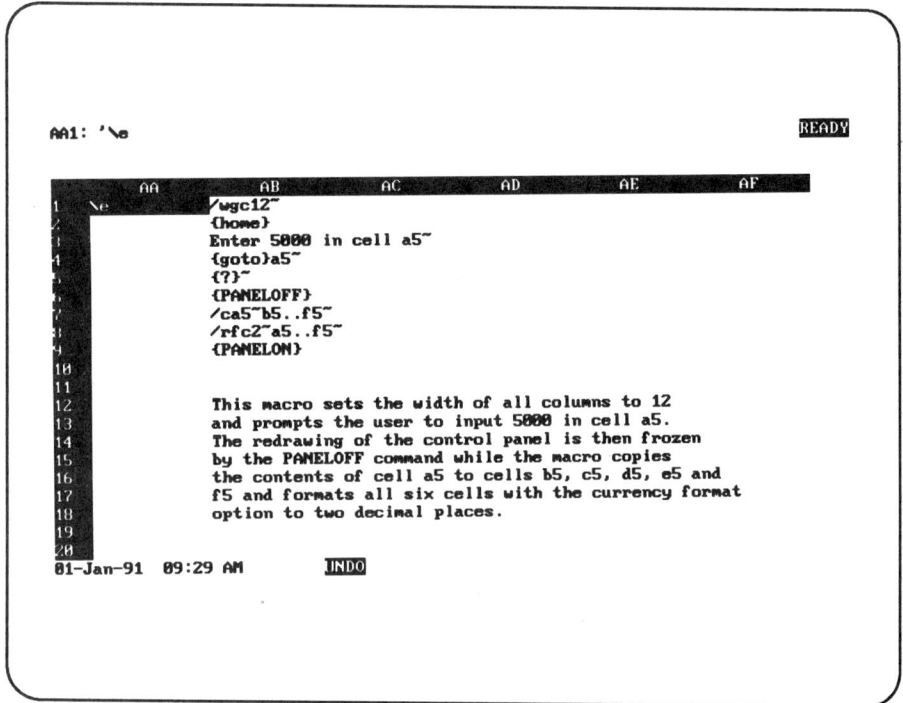

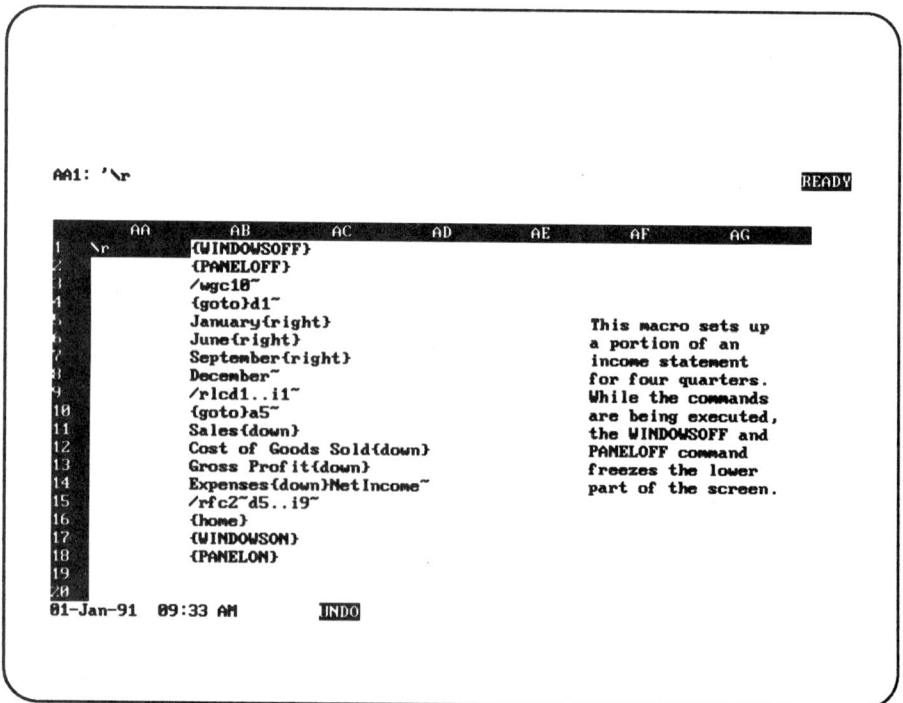

```
AA1: '\e                                                            READY

          AA        AB         AC         AD         AE         AF
 1   \e          /wgc12~
 2               {home}
 3               Enter 5000 in cell a5~
 4               {goto}a5~
 5               {?}~
 6               {PANELOFF}
 7               /ca5~b5..f5~
 8               /rfc2~a5..f5~
 9               {PANELON}
10
11
12               This macro sets the width of all columns to 12
13               and prompts the user to input 5000 in cell a5.
14               The redrawing of the control panel is then frozen
15               by the PANELOFF command while the macro copies
16               the contents of cell a5 to cells b5, c5, d5, e5 and
17               f5 and formats all six cells with the currency format
18               option to two decimal places.
19
20
01-Jan-91  09:29 AM        UNDO
```

```
AA1: '\r                                                            READY

          AA        AB         AC         AD         AE         AF         AG
 1   \r          {WINDOWSOFF}
 2               {PANELOFF}
 3               /wgc10~
 4               {goto}d1~
 5               January{right}                              This macro sets up
 6               June{right}                                 a portion of an
 7               September{right}                            income statement
 8               December~                                   for four quarters.
 9               /rlcd1..i1~                                 While the commands
10               {goto}a5~                                   are being executed,
11               Sales{down}                                 the WINDOWSOFF and
12               Cost of Goods Sold{down}                    PANELOFF command
13               Gross Profit{down}                          freezes the lower
14               Expenses{down}NetIncome~                    part of the screen.
15               /rfc2~d5..i9~
16               {home}
17               {WINDOWSON}
18               {PANELON}
19
20
01-Jan-91  09:33 AM        UNDO
```

FIGURE 19-21 *An Example of WINDOWSOFF and WINDOWSON*

19-9-2 *{FILESIZE address}*

Counts the number of bytes (characters) in an open file and then stores the result in address. The address is a cell or a range name.

19-9-3 *{GETPOS address}*

Determines the present position of the file pointer and displays the result in the address. Naturally the file must be opened first. Remember, the first position in a file is 0 (zero), not 1 (one).

19-9-4 *{OPEN filename, access-mode}*

Opens a selected file for reading, writing, modifying, or appending. The file must be in the current directory. The file name should specify a drive location and subdirectory path if needed. There are four types of access modes:

1. R (Read) allows only the read option for READ and READLN commands.
2. W (Write) allows WRITE and WRITELN commands. This option also allows READ and READLN commands. This access is for a new file.
3. M (Modify) allows READ, READLN, WRITE, and WRITELN commands. This access is for an existing file.
4. A (Append) opens an existing file for reading and writing, placing the byte pointer at the end of the file. You can use {READ}, {READLN}, {GETPOS}, {SETPOS}, {WRITE} and {WRITELN} with a file with an append access.

19-9-5 *{READ bytecount, address}*

Reads characters from an open file into an address. If the bytecount is larger than the number of characters left in the file, Lotus reads the remaining characters. The bytecount must be between 0 and 240. A negative bytecount is equivalent to the maximum positive bytecount of 240.

19-9-6 *{READLN address}*

Copies an entire line of characters from an open file into an address. This command starts reading from the present position of the file pointer and ends with a carriage return, line feed.

19-9-7 *{SETPOS file-position}*

Sets a new position for the file pointer in a specified open file. File-position is a number. The first character in the file is always at position 0, the second character at position 1, and so forth. If you specify a large number, you may pass the end of the file.

19-9-8 *{WRITE string}*

Copies a series of characters into an open file. This macro command copies from the worksheet to the current position of the file pointer in a file that has been opened with either Write or Modify.

19-9-9 *{WRITELN}*

This command does the same thing as WRITE, except that it adds a carriage-return line feed to the end of the string in the file.

Figures 19-22 through 19-25 show some simple macros to illustrate file operations.

FIGURE 19-22 *Example of OPEN, WRITELN, WRITE, and CLOSE*

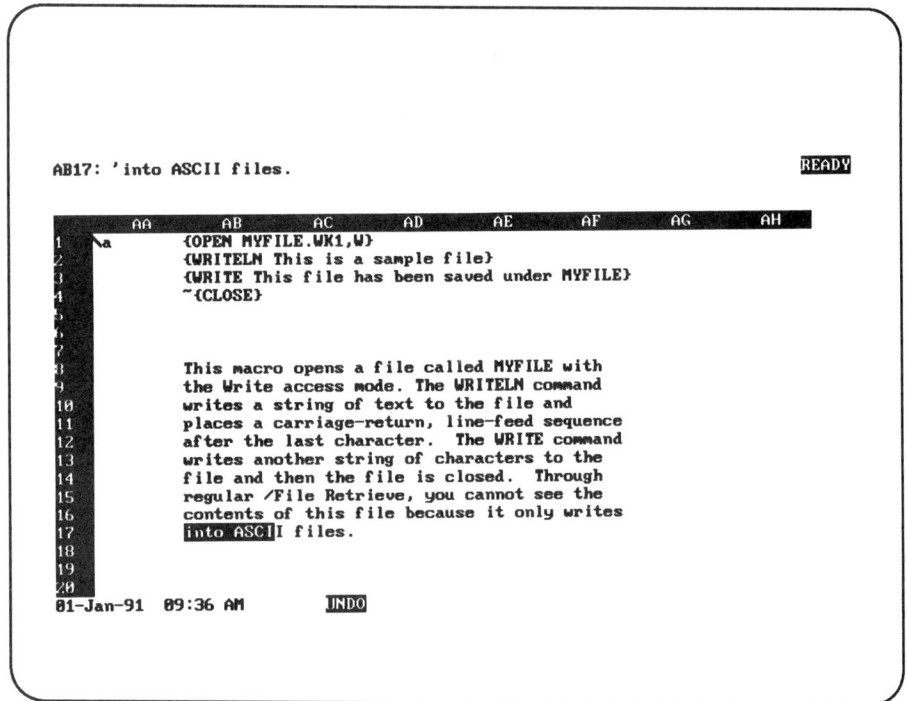

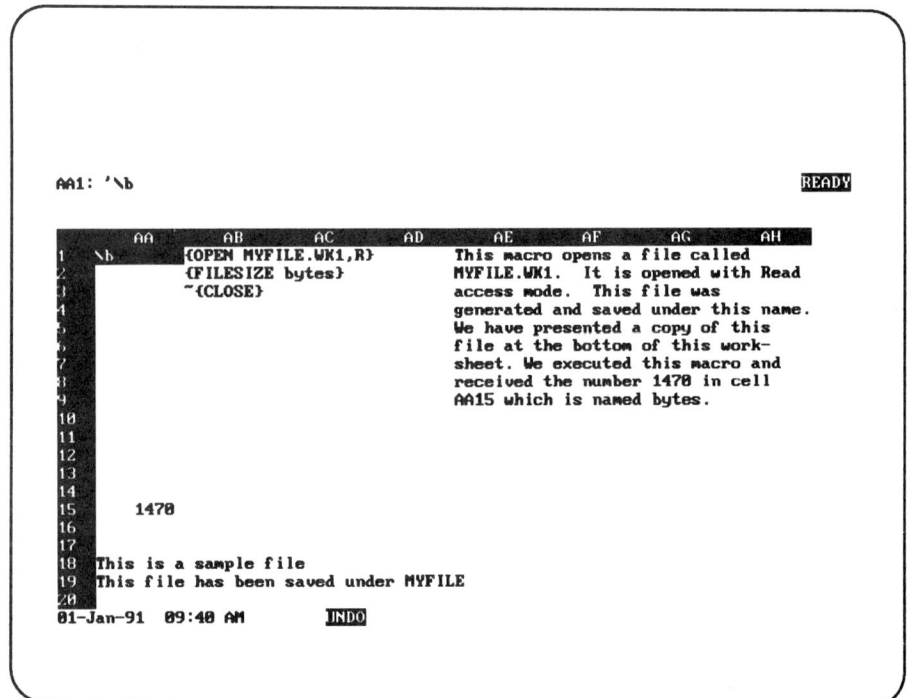

```
AB17: 'into ASCII files.                                              READY

          AA        AB        AC        AD        AE        AF        AG        AH
1    \a           {OPEN MYFILE.WK1,W}
2                 {WRITELN This is a sample file}
3                 {WRITE This file has been saved under MYFILE}
4                 ~{CLOSE}
5
6
7
8                 This macro opens a file called MYFILE with
9                 the Write access mode. The WRITELN command
10                writes a string of text to the file and
11                places a carriage-return, line-feed sequence
12                after the last character.  The WRITE command
13                writes another string of characters to the
14                file and then the file is closed.  Through
15                regular /File Retrieve, you cannot see the
16                contents of this file because it only writes
17                into ASCII files.
18
19
20
01-Jan-91  09:36 AM          UNDO
```

```
AA1: '\b                                                             READY

          AA        AB        AC        AD        AE        AF        AG        AH
1    \b           {OPEN MYFILE.WK1,R}            This macro opens a file called
2                 {FILESIZE bytes}               MYFILE.WK1.  It is opened with Read
3                 ~{CLOSE}                        access mode.  This file was
4                                                 generated and saved under this name.
5                                                 We have presented a copy of this
6                                                 file at the bottom of this work-
7                                                 sheet. We executed this macro and
8                                                 received the number 1470 in cell
9                                                 AA15 which is named bytes.
10
11
12
13
14
15        1470
16
17
18   This is a sample file
19   This file has been saved under MYFILE
20
01-Jan-91  09:40 AM          UNDO
```

FIGURE 19-23 *Example of FILESIZE*

FIGURE 19-24 Example of READ and SETPOS

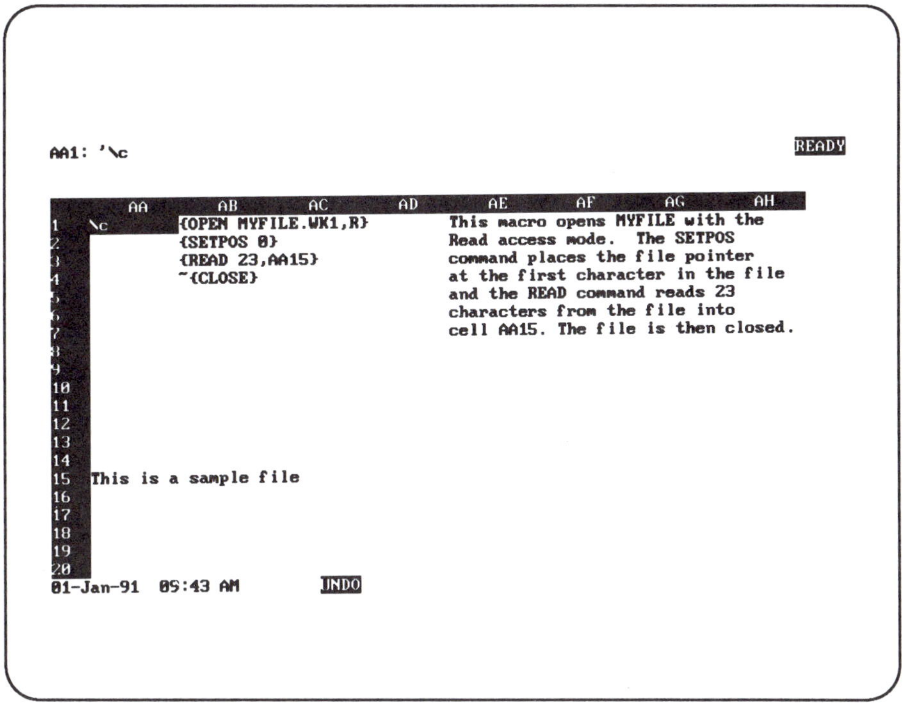

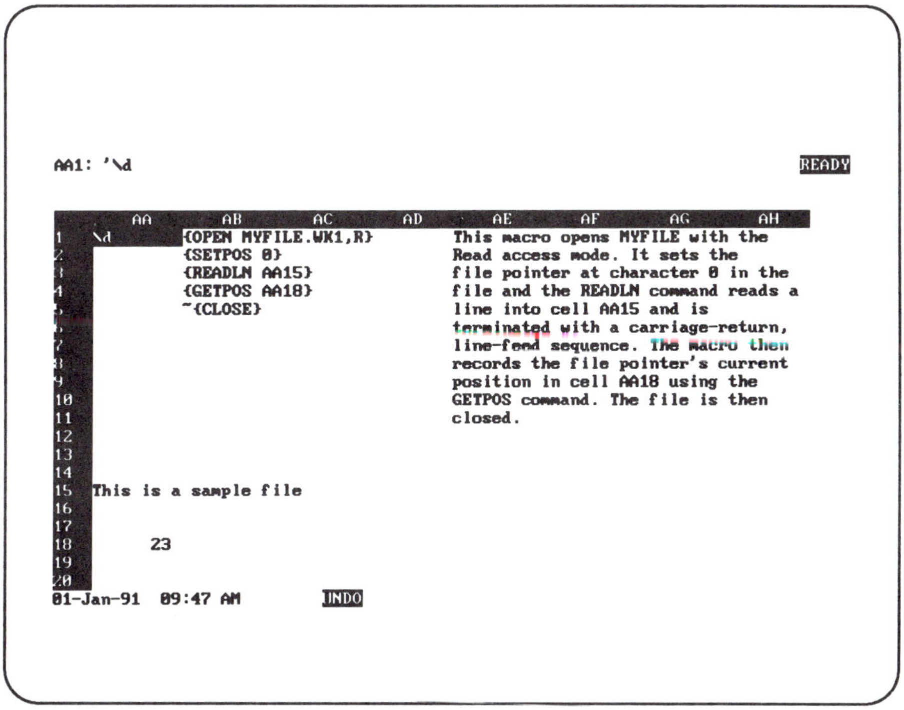

```
AA1: '\c                                                        READY
      AA        AB        AC      AD      AE      AF      AG     AH
1  \c       {OPEN MYFILE.WK1,R}          This macro opens MYFILE with the
2           {SETPOS 0}                   Read access mode.  The SETPOS
3           {READ 23,AA15}               command places the file pointer
4           ~{CLOSE}                     at the first character in the file
5                                        and the READ command reads 23
6                                        characters from the file into
7                                        cell AA15. The file is then closed.
8
9
10
11
12
13
14
15 This is a sample file
16
17
18
19
20
01-Jan-91  09:43 AM        UNDO
```

```
AA1: '\d                                                        READY
      AA        AB        AC      AD      AE      AF      AG     AH
1  \d       {OPEN MYFILE.WK1,R}          This macro opens MYFILE with the
2           {SETPOS 0}                   Read access mode. It sets the
3           {READLN AA15}                file pointer at character 0 in the
4           {GETPOS AA18}                file and the READLN command reads a
5           ~{CLOSE}                     line into cell AA15 and is
6                                        terminated with a carriage-return,
7                                        line-feed sequence. The macro then
8                                        records the file pointer's current
9                                        position in cell AA18 using the
10                                       GETPOS command. The file is then
11                                       closed.
12
13
14
15 This is a sample file
16
17
18       23
19
20
01-Jan-91  09:47 AM        UNDO
```

FIGURE 19-25 Example of GETPOS and READLN

SUMMARY

The Lotus advanced macro commands have been divided into five groups. Each group has been designed to perform a unique task: data manipulation, program flow, testing keyboard operations, screen design and control, and file operations. Lotus advanced commands also serve as a high-level programming language, closely paralleling other high-level programming languages. In Chapter 20 we will utilize these advanced commands in some simple programming assignments.

REVIEW QUESTIONS

* These questions are answered in Appendix I.
1. What is a Lotus advanced command?
2. What is the structure of an advanced command?
3.* Is an argument needed for all the advanced commands?
4.* How many different types of arguments do we have in an advanced command?
5. How many different groups of macro commands do we have?
6. Give one command as an example of each group.
7.* What is the equivalent of BLANK in a nonmacro setting (in worksheet or range commands)?
8. What is the difference between CONTENTS and LET?
9. Does LET hold numeric values, nonnumeric values, or both?
10. What is the difference between DISPATCH and BRANCH?
11.* If Start in the FOR command is larger than Stop, what will happen?
12.* Does Return need an argument?
13. What is the application of the LOOK command?
14. How do you design your own menu?
15. How many lines can you have in a menu?
16.* Why must all the commands in your menu be unique (the starting character must be unique)?
17. How many commands are included in the file operations group?
18. What is the difference between the READLN and READ commands?
19. Why must a file be opened before you invoke a command?
20.* How many different access modes do we have?

HANDS-ON PRACTICE

1. Using the FOR advanced command, design an macro that prints "LOTUS IS EASY TO LEARN" 20 times.
2. Using the MENUCALL advanced command, design a menu with four options:
   a. Extend a column length to any number between 1 and 240 characters.
   b. Center any label typed from the keyboard.
   c. Erase any range specified by the user.
   d. Format any number in Currency with two decimal places.
3. Using the INDICATE advanced command, design a macro to turn the mode indicator to "Bye."
4. Using BRANCH and other advanced commands, design a macro to select students for a dean's scholarship if they meet the following criteria:

        MIS major
        GPA > 3.70
        Age < 21
        Single

5. Using Figure 19-16, add two more options to this menu: Retrieve and Save.

6. Consolidated Company has branch offices in three different cities: Los Angeles, Chicago, and New York. Each city has its own spreadsheet that shows quarterly income, expenses, and net profit. The owners of the company want to be able to easily combine the operating results of the different cities into a consolidated spreadsheet showing total quarterly net income. The consolidation spreadsheet should be menu driven and easy to use.

    Using MENUCALL, MENUBRANCH, and other advanced macro commands, design a spreadsheet and menu-driven macro to do the following: After the spreadsheet has been called into memory, the user should press Alt-M to access the menu driven options. At this point, the user is presented with the following options:

    VIEW FOOTNOTE PRINT CONSOL SAVE QUIT.

    The VIEW option allows the user to import and view the spreadsheet data of any particular city, or of all three cities, then returns the user to the menu.

    The FOOTNOTE option allows the user to add a footnote or memo to the bottom of the consolidated spreadsheet, then returns the user to the menu.

    The PRINT option allows the user to easily print the consolidated spreadsheet, then returns the user to the menu.

    The CONSOL option allows the user to consolidate the spreadsheet data of the three different cities into a single spreadsheet, then returns the user to the menu. To do this, the computer imports the Net Profit line items out of each of the three city spreadsheets, then totals each of these amounts for a companywide Net Profit figure.

    The SAVE option allows the user to save the current spreadsheet, then returns the user to the menu.

    The QUIT option allows the user to quit the spreadsheet menu.

    Design your own spreadsheet for the three cities and insert some optional numbers.

COMPREHENSIVE LAB ASSIGNMENT

Retrieve CHAPT18 and perform the following:

1. Design a menu macro that includes three options:

    Statistics   Graph   Quit

    The Statistics option should tell us the name of the students with the highest and lowest scores. The Graph option should give a choice of a line graph of total scores or the bar graph of the total of the three test scores.

2. Design a menu macro that provides six Sort options and a Quit option on the existing worksheet:

    Name   Major   Sex   Standing   Age   Total Score   Quit

3. Save the current worksheet under CHAPT19.

4. Design an interactive macro that asks the user if he/she wants to save the worksheet under CHAPT19. If the answer is Yes, it saves the worksheet, erases the worksheet, and exits from Lotus.

MISCONCEPTIONS AND SOLUTIONS

M – A subroutine name can be any name except reserved Lotus words. If there is a duplicate, Lotus performs the subroutine, not the reserved word.

S – All Lotus reserved words are in Table 18-1. Try not to use any of these as subroutine names.

M – If macro command BREAKOFF is in effect and the macro goes into an endless loop, there is no way to get back to the 1-2-3 command mode.

S – To stop this you have to reset your computer (turn the computer off).

M – In sequential file processing, when you use the OPEN command accompanied with the access mode to open a file you may get an error message.

S – You must use the file extension with the file name.

M – In sequential file processing, Lotus does not prevent you from putting the file pointer past the end of the file.

S – You must use the FILESIZE command to determine the number of the last character in the file.

M – The BRANCH macro command and GOTO both cause branching to different locations not followed in the normal program sequence.

S – Use GOTO only if you want to move the cell pointer. Use BRANCH if you want to transfer the macro execution to a different location which is not the normal program sequence.

Macros/Part Three: Using Lotus Macros as a Super Programming Language

20-1 Introduction

In this chapter we are wrapping up our discussion of macros. We will present a quick review of the program development life cycle. Modular programming and structured programming also will be briefly discussed. We put a heavy emphasis on program documentation and the types of documentation. We will also compare Lotus macros with a typical high-level programming language.

After this brief presentation we will introduce you to several short programs using Lotus as a programming language. This chapter should provide you with a good background for further investigations into Lotus as a super programming language.

20-2 Steps in the Program Development Life Cycle

The purpose of this chapter is not to teach you how to program. In this chapter, we are trying to provide you with a quick overview of programming and the program development life cycle.

In order to use Lotus as a programming language you should follow these steps:

Step 1 Problem Definition. You should carefully define the nature and scope of the problem that you intend to use Lotus to solve. On a broader scale, you may have to perform an output analysis first. This means that you clearly define all the outputs or answers to the questions you intend to receive from your macro program. A clear definition of the problem and the output specifications may help you to achieve a solution faster.

A typical problem would be a payroll problem. Your program should be able to print accurate monthly, biweekly, and weekly paychecks for a group of employees. The paycheck is the output of the program. Naturally, some input data is needed in order to print a paycheck. In the simplest case, you need the number of hours a particular employee works, his/her pay rate, overtime rate, deductions, and so forth.

Step 2 Logic Design. In programming terminology, before you attempt to write a program, you must first define how you will reach your solution. For example, if an employee has worked more than 40 hours, what do you do? If the employee has worked less than 40 hours, what do you do? There are many tools to use in clarifying the logic of your program. The flowchart (the most commonly used tool), structure chart, or pseudocode are some of the techniques available. If you use these tools, you are safeguarding against logical errors, those that create erroneous results in your program—your program runs but the results are not correct. Other errors you may see are called syntax errors. These include using the wrong keyword or the wrong grammar. The correction of syntactical errors is usually easier than the correction of logical errors.

Using logic design tools such as a flowchart or pseudocode should assist you in minimizing or eliminating errors, especially logical errors. After you design your logic and walk through it to make sure it is working, you move to the next step.

Step 3 Coding. After designing your logic and checking it manually, you are ready to code it. Chapters 18 and 19 taught you how to use Lotus as a programming language.

The best approach for coding your program is a modular approach. This means entering the program as a series of smaller independent blocks. Test these blocks and document them; if one works, begin the next block. We will talk more about modular programming later in this chapter.

Step 4 Execution and Debugging. Usually your program will not run the first time, or it runs partially, or it may run completely but generate the wrong answers. In each case there is a bug (error) in your program. As we discussed in Chapter 18, you can debug each individual macro. To make sure that the entire program is working, you should use some simple data and run it through your program. You can then be pretty sure that your program is working correctly.

Step 5 Documentation. In order to make your program self-explanatory for other people and for your own future reference, you should document it. Documentation can be internal or external. Internal documentation may include a series of statements within your macro to explain its function.

Internal documentation can be three types. Type one is called program documentation. This may include a few lines of explanation at the beginning of the program to describe its function. Type two is called module documentation. This type describes the function of a particular module. Type three is called line documentation or segment documentation. This type of documentation explains lines or segments of a module.

External documentation may include a flowchart, pseudocode, structure chart, or program listing. Comprehensive external documentation may serve as a user's guide or user's manual for future reference. Both internal and external documentation are important and you should get in the habit of using them.

20-3 Modular Programming

Problems you may encounter in real-life situations are usually large and complex. To solve the entire problem in one shot may not be a feasible option. Modular programming methodology advocates the breakdown of a large project into several smaller ones. Solve each small module, then put them together in order to generate the answer to the entire problem. Modular programming has several unique advantages:

1. It is easier to understand.
2. It is easier to code.
3. It is easier to debug.
4. It is easier to document.
5. It is easier to modify.

In order to implement each module in Lotus, use a subroutine. In programming terminology, a subroutine is a series of instructions that performs a particular task. Any large problem can be broken down into a series of subroutines.

20-4 Structured Programming

Since the early 1970s a new methodology has become very common in a programming environment. This new methodology advocates GOTO-less programming. The intention is to eliminate the use of GOTO statements in your program. Proponents of this methodology believe GOTO statements make the program complex and difficult to debug or modify.

In structured programming, four structures are used for performing any tasks. These include sequence, selection, iteration, and CASE structures.

The sequence structure means going from step 1 to step 2 to step 3. There is no looping or branching involved here.

The selection structure is used whenever you have to choose between two options, e.g., regular routine or overtime routine, high commission or low commission.

The iteration structure indicates a loop for a specific task; for example, 100 times printing 100 different checks or 200 times calculating the commissions for a group of salespeople.

The CASE structure is used when you choose from more than two options; for example, selection of a commission formula from 15 different routines. Table 20-1 illustrates the equivalent of these structures in Lotus. The remaining part of this chapter presents some simple macro programs.

TABLE 20-1 STRUCTURED PROGRAMMING AND LOTUS

NAME OF THE STRUCTURE	PROGRAMMING EQUIVALENT	LOTUS MACRO EQUIVALENT
Sequence	LET A+10	LET, PUT, BLANK, CONTENTS, etc.
	B=25	
Selection	IF-THEN	IF, BRANCH, etc.
	IF-THEN-ELSE	DISPATCH, etc.
Iteration	FOR-NEXT	FOR, etc.
	DO-WHILE	
	DO-UNTIL	
	DO-CONTINUE	
	REPEAT-UNTIL	
CASE	CASE expression OF	BRANCH, DISPATCH, etc.

20-5 Program 1—Area and Circumference of a Circle

Our first program calculates the area and circumference of a circle. The program is in interactive mode. The user inputs the radius and the program calculates the area and the circumference of a particular circle. This is illustrated in Figure 20-1.

20-6 Program 2—Arithmetic Operations with Two Numbers

Program 2 illustrates a simple program, shown in Figure 20-2. The user inputs two numbers and then the program calculates their sum, their difference, their product, and their quotient.

FIGURE 20-1 Area and Circumference of a Circle

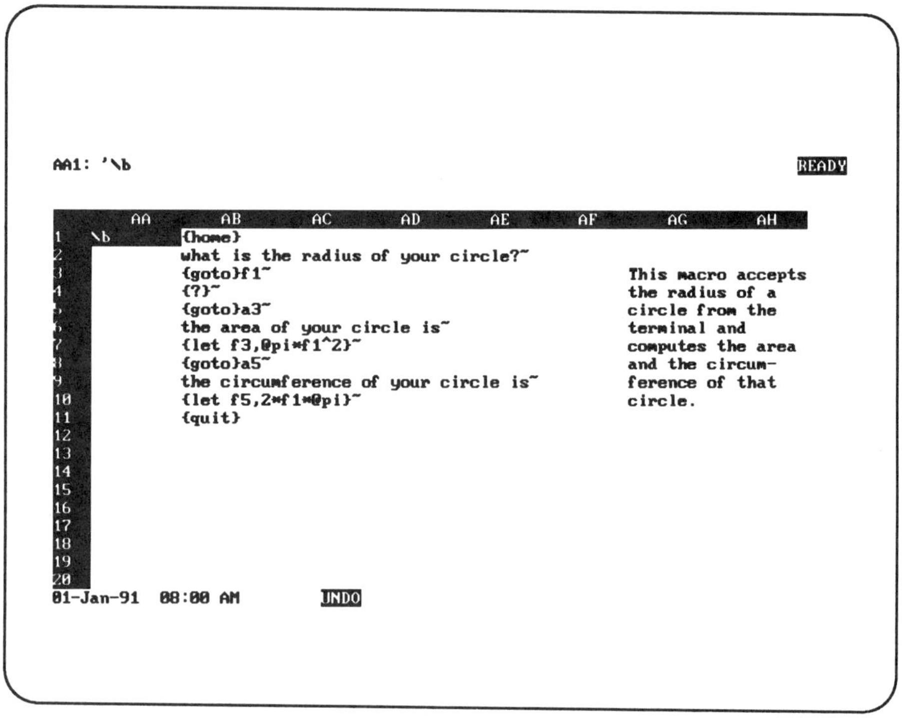

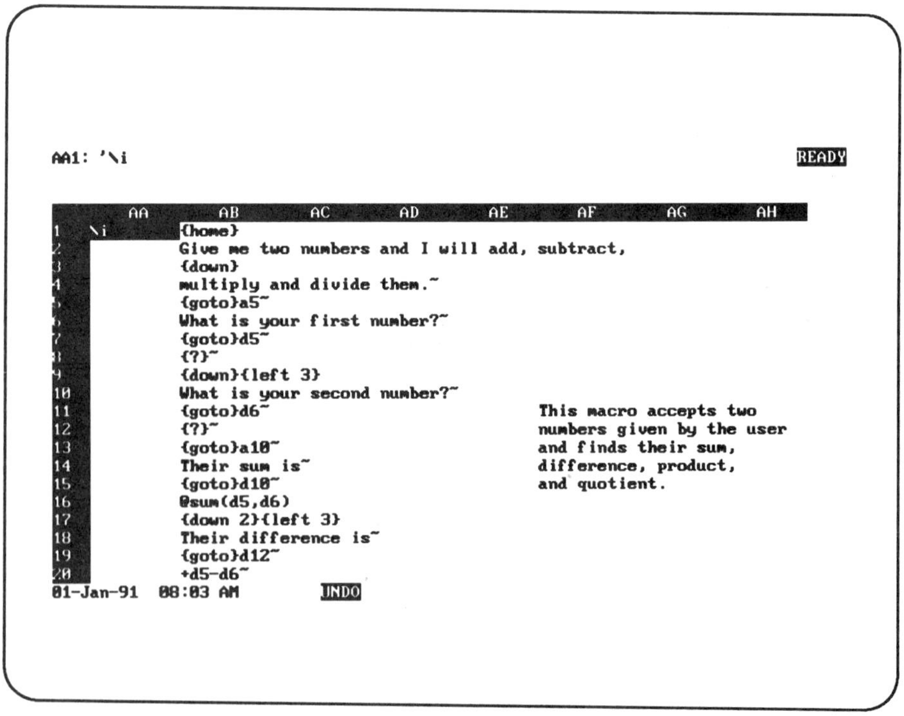

```
AA1: '\b                                                         READY

         AA        AB        AC        AD        AE        AF        AG        AH
1    \b      {home}
2            what is the radius of your circle?~
3            {goto}f1~                                      This macro accepts
4            {?}~                                           the radius of a
5            {goto}a3~                                      circle from the
6            the area of your circle is~                    terminal and
7            {let f3,@pi*f1^2}~                             computes the area
8            {goto}a5~                                      and the circum-
9            the circumference of your circle is~           ference of that
10           {let f5,2*f1*@pi}~                             circle.
11           {quit}
12
13
14
15
16
17
18
19
20
01-Jan-91  08:00 AM          UNDO
```

```
AA1: '\i                                                         READY

         AA        AB        AC        AD        AE        AF        AG        AH
1    \i      {home}
2            Give me two numbers and I will add, subtract,
3            {down}
4            multiply and divide them.~
5            {goto}a5~
6            What is your first number?~
7            {goto}d5~
8            {?}~
9            {down}{left 3}
10           What is your second number?~
11           {goto}d6~                                      This macro accepts two
12           {?}~                                           numbers given by the user
13           {goto}a10~                                     and finds their sum,
14           Their sum is~                                  difference, product,
15           {goto}d10~                                     and quotient.
16           @sum(d5,d6)
17           {down 2}{left 3}
18           Their difference is~
19           {goto}d12~
20           +d5-d6~
01-Jan-91  08:03 AM          UNDO
```

FIGURE 20-2 Arithmetic Operations with Two Numbers

FIGURE 20-2 (Continued)

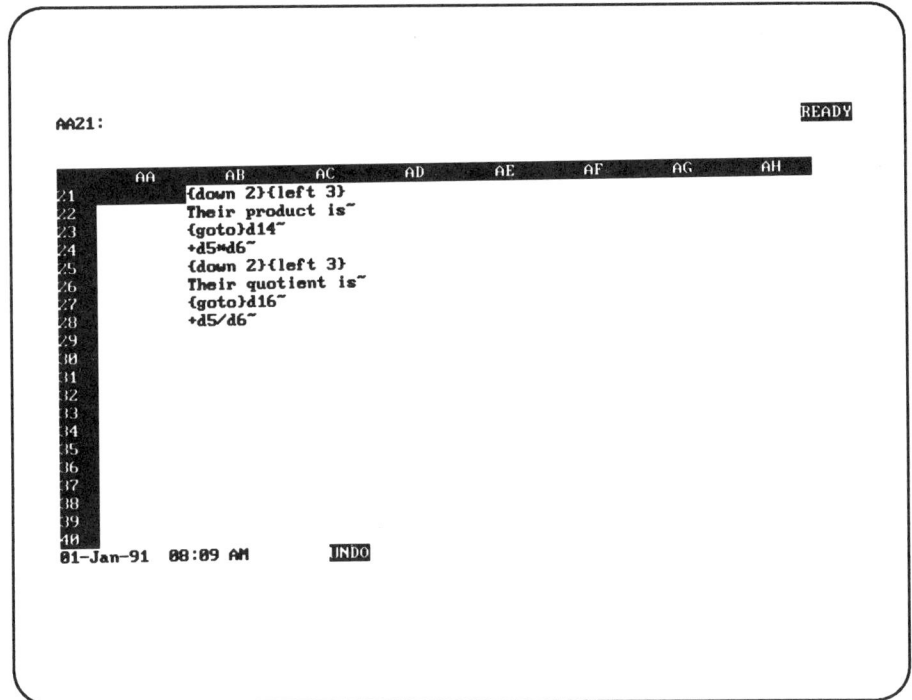

```
AA21:                                                          READY

         AA        AB        AC        AD      AE      AF      AG      AH
   21          {down 2}{left 3}
   22          Their product is~
   23          {goto}d14~
   24          +d5*d6~
   25          {down 2}{left 3}
   26          Their quotient is~
   27          {goto}d16~
   28          +d5/d6~
   29
   30
   31
   32
   33
   34
   35
   36
   37
   38
   39
   40
   01-Jan-91  08:09 AM          UNDO
```

20-7 Program 3—Average Score of Five Numbers

In Figure 20-3, if we input five different scores, the program calculates their average.

20-8 Program 4—Checking the Sign of a Number

Program 4, in Figure 20-4, inputs a number with any sign. Then the program examines the number to see if it is positive, negative, or zero. The appropriate message is printed and the program waits for six seconds, erases the previous message, and asks for a new number. To stop this program, type N (for No).

20-9 Program 5—Random Numbers Generation between Zero and One

Program 5, shown in Figure 20-5, generates as many random numbers as the user specifies. These random numbers are between zero and one.

20-10 Program 6—Random Numbers Generation between Specific Limits

In the business world random numbers have many different applications, in the production process, in acceptance or rejection of a shipment, in process control, and so forth. In many

FIGURE 20-3 Average Scores of Five Numbers

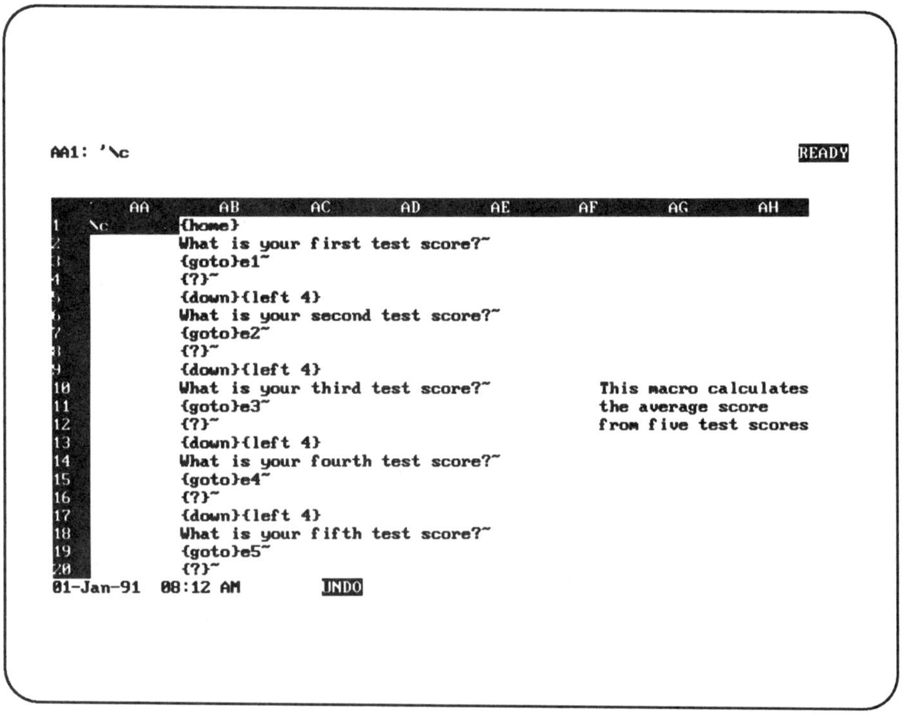

```
AA1: '\c                                                              READY

        AA        AB         AC         AD        AE        AF        AG        AH
1    \c      {home}
2            What is your first test score?~
3            {goto}e1~
4            {?}~
5            {down}{left 4}
6            What is your second test score?~
7            {goto}e2~
8            {?}~
9            {down}{left 4}
10           What is your third test score?~        This macro calculates
11           {goto}e3~                              the average score
12           {?}~                                   from five test scores
13           {down}{left 4}
14           What is your fourth test score?~
15           {goto}e4~
16           {?}~
17           {down}{left 4}
18           What is your fifth test score?~
19           {goto}e5~
20           {?}~
01-Jan-91  08:12 AM        UNDO
```

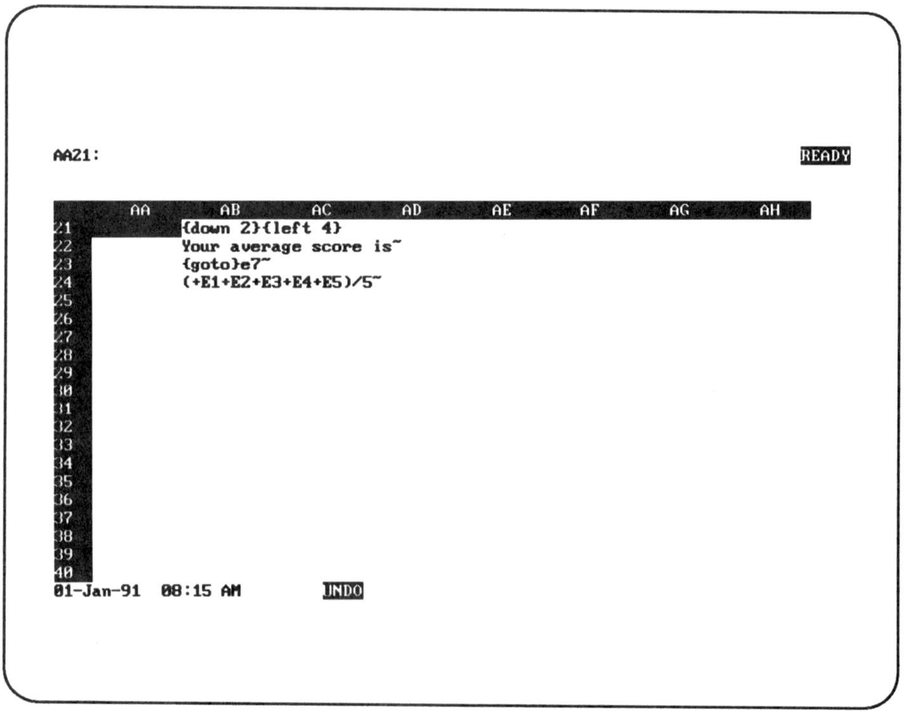

```
AA21:                                                                 READY

        AA        AB         AC         AD        AE        AF        AG        AH
21           {down 2}{left 4}
22           Your average score is~
23           {goto}e7~
24           (+E1+E2+E3+E4+E5)/5~
25
26
27
28
29
30
31
32
33
34
35
36
37
38
39
40
01-Jan-91  08:15 AM        UNDO
```

FIGURE 20-3 (Continued)

FIGURE 20-4 Checking the Sign of a Number

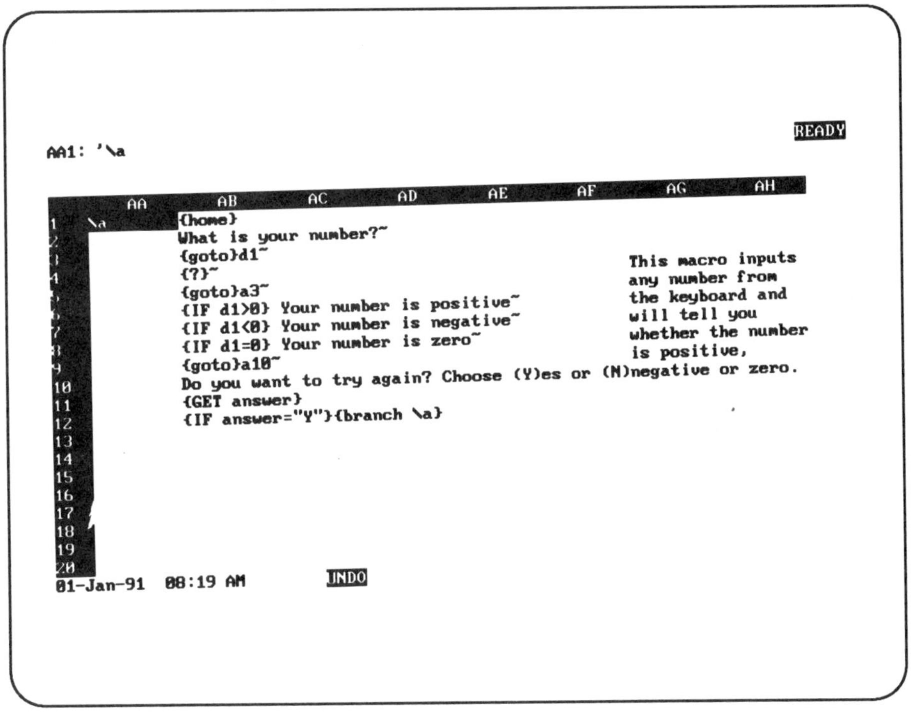

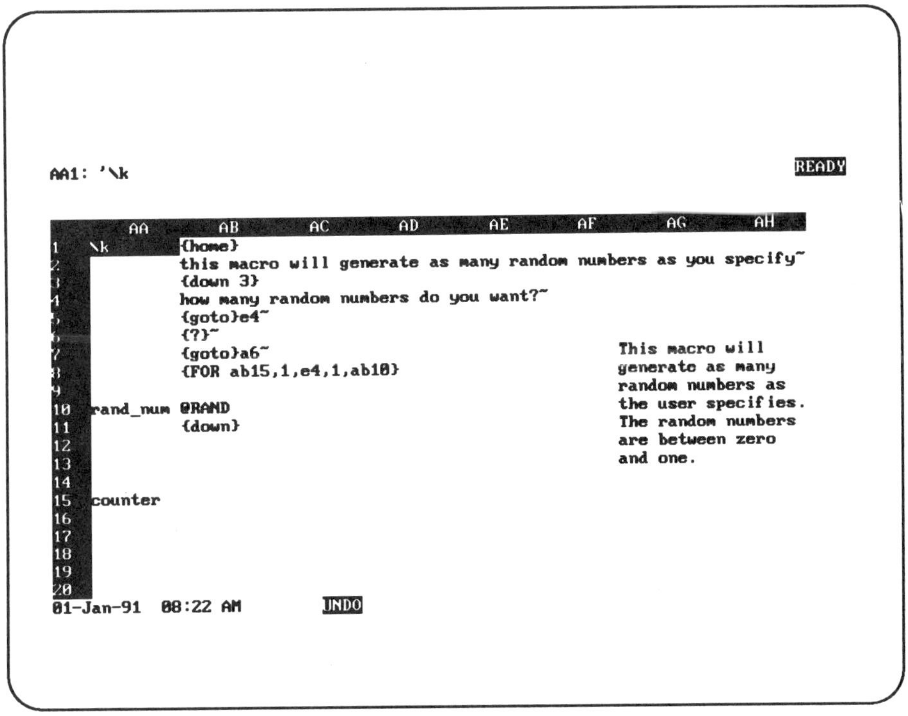

```
AA1: '\a                                                          READY

        AA        AB        AC        AD        AE        AF        AG        AH
1    \a        {home}
2              What is your number?~
3              {goto}d1~
4              {?}~                                          This macro inputs
5              {goto}a3~                                     any number from
6              {IF d1>0} Your number is positive~            the keyboard and
7              {IF d1<0} Your number is negative~            will tell you
8              {IF d1=0} Your number is zero~                whether the number
9              {goto}a10~                                    is positive,
10             Do you want to try again? Choose (Y)es or (N)negative or zero.
11             {GET answer}
12             {IF answer="Y"}{branch \a}
13
14
15
16
17
18
19
20
01-Jan-91  08:19 AM        UNDO
```

```
AA1: '\k                                                          READY

        AA        AB        AC        AD        AE        AF        AG        AH
1    \k        {home}
2              this macro will generate as many random numbers as you specify~
3              {down 3}
4              how many random numbers do you want?~
5              {goto}e4~
6              {?}~
7              {goto}a6~                                     This macro will
8              {FOR ab15,1,e4,1,ab10}                        generate as many
9                                                            random numbers as
10   rand_num  @RAND                                         the user specifies.
11             {down}                                        The random numbers
12                                                           are between zero
13                                                           and one.
14
15   counter
16
17
18
19
20
01-Jan-91  08:22 AM        UNDO
```

FIGURE 20-5 Random Number Generation between Zero and One cases the user may be interested in a random number which is within a certain limit. For example, you are interested in choosing a random number between 1 and 1,000. If this is the case, you have to do some modification with the @RAND function in order to generate a specific random number. The process is very simple.

1. Define your upper limit (in the above example, 1,000), U.
2. Define your lower limit (in the above example, 1), L.
3. Define the difference between the upper and lower limits (in the above example, 999), U-L.

The formula is (upper limit - lower limit + 1) multiply by the @RAND function, then add the lower limit. In order to generate only an integer portion of the number, you must use the @INT function. The whole formula is @INT((U-L+1)*@RAND+L). Figure 20-6 illustrates this process.

20-11 Program 7—Many Random Numbers in Any Range

Program 7, shown in Figure 20-7, is an extension of program 6. This program follows the same pattern, but the user can define as many random numbers as he/she is interested in, and in any range.

20-12 Program 8—Break-Even Analysis

There are many times when a businessperson is interested in calculating the break-even point of the operation. The break-even point is a production point at which there is no loss

FIGURE 20-6 *Random Numbers between Specific Limits*

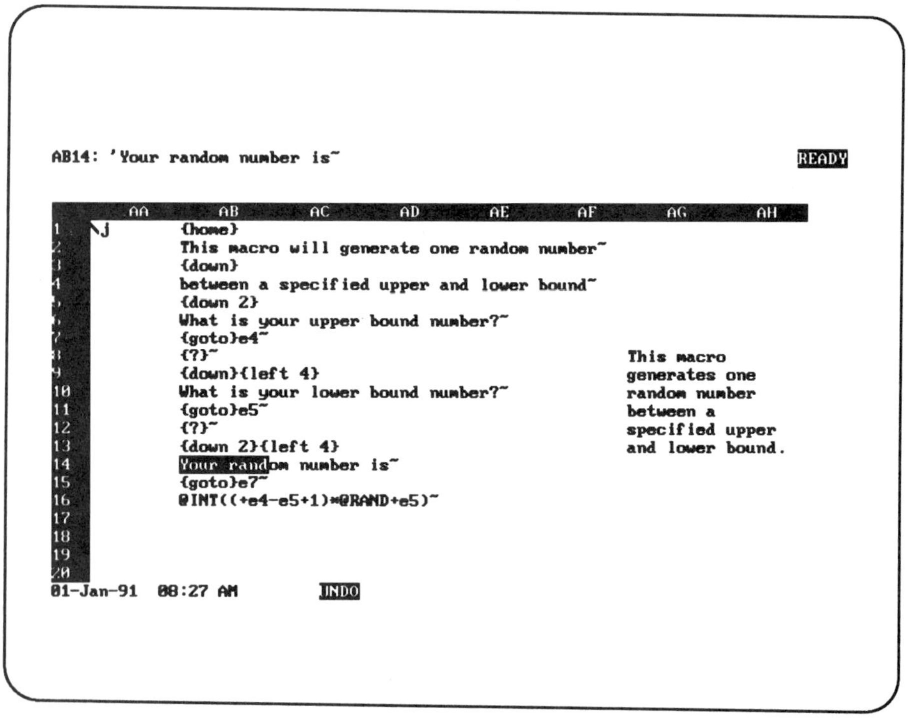

FIGURE 20-7 Many Random Numbers in Any Range

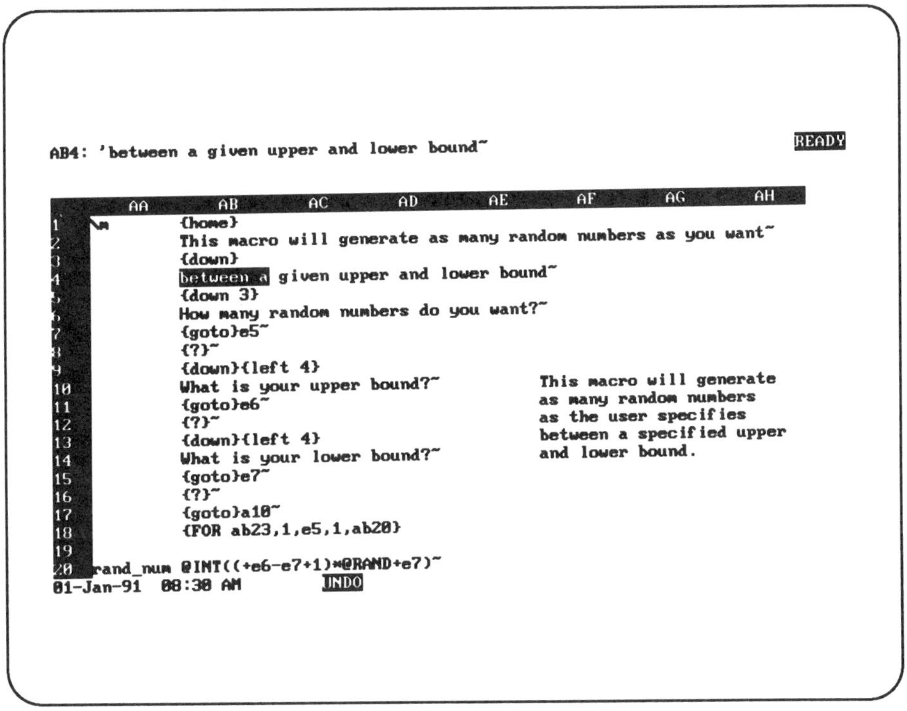

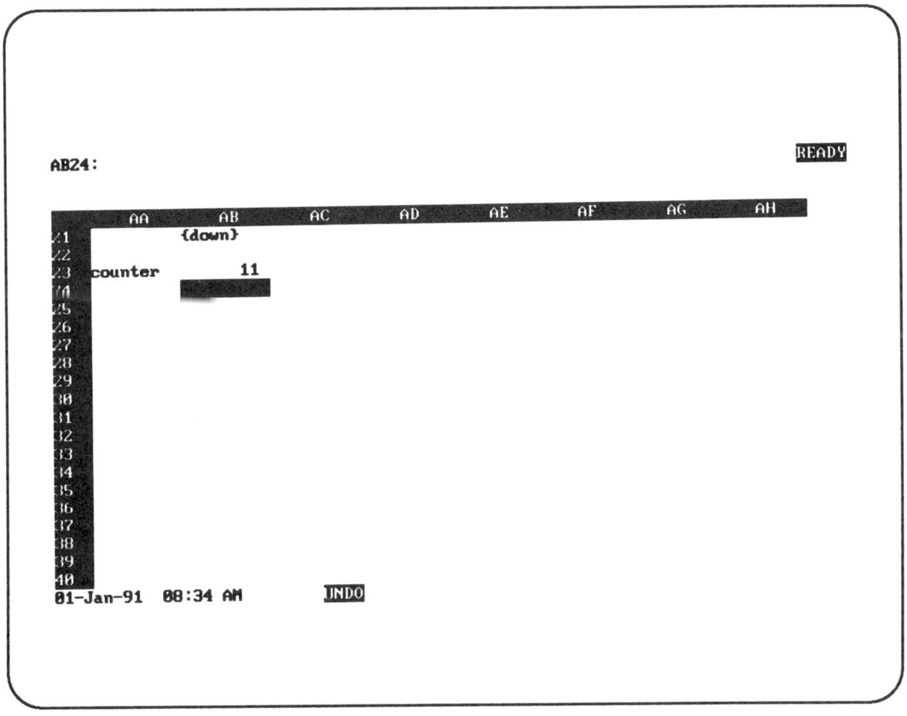

FIGURE 20-7 (Continued)

and no gain, i.e., the total revenue is equal to the total costs. To calculate the break-even point, the following items are needed:

1. FC—Total fixed costs or overhead such as rent and electricity.
2. VC—Variable costs per unit such as raw material and labor.
3. SP—Unit selling price.

The break-even point will be calculated by dividing (FC) by (SP-VC). The difference between SP and VC is called the contribution margin. For example, if FC = 500, VC = 10, SP = 15, the break-even point = 100 units. This means if you sell fewer than 100 units, you are losing money; if you sell 100 units, no loss, no gain; if you sell more than 100 units, you are making a profit.

This simple formula can be very helpful when performing what-if analysis. You may ask yourself if the variable cost increases by one dollar, what would be the effect on the break-even point? Or if you reduce the selling price by one dollar, what would be the effect? Figure 20-8 illustrates this calculation in an interactive mode.

20-13 Program 9—Economic Order Quantity

How much to order and when to order is a major concern for many businesses. Ordering large quantities may increase the cost of capital (tying up money, warehouse space, etc.). At the same time, ordering very small quantities may increase the ordering cost, cost of losing customers, and so on. A model known as the Economic Order Quantity (EOQ) has been utilized by many businesses for minimizing inventory cost. The outcome of this model is the optimum order quantity or the number of units to be ordered that will

FIGURE 20-8 Break-Even Analysis

```
AA1: '\g                                                                READY

      AA        AB          AC          AD          AE         AF          AG          AH
1   \g        {home}
2             What is the total fixed cost?~
3             {goto}f1~
4             {?}~
5             {down}{left 5}
6             What are the variable costs per unit?~
7             {goto}f2~                                        This macro
8             {?}~                                             determines the
9             {down}{left 5}                                   break-even point
10            What is the unit selling price?~                 in units for a
11            {goto}f3~                                        product based on
12            {?}~                                             the unit selling
13            {down 2}{left 5}                                 price and the
14            The unit contribution to overhead is~            known production
15            {goto}f5~                                        costs.
16            +f3-f2~
17            {down}{left 5}
18            The break-even point in units is~
19            {goto}f6~
20            +f1/f5~
01-Jan-91  08:37 AM         UNDO
```

minimize the business's total inventory costs. This model utilizes the following formula and variables:

$$EOQ = \sqrt{\frac{2*A*B}{C*P}}$$

where A = annual inventory requirements (annual sales)

B = cost of placing an order (ordering cost)

C = single unit cost (sales price)

P = percentage of inventory value allotted for carrying costs

EOQ = number of units to order that will minimize the business's total inventory cost.

This formula makes it possible for the user to compute the EOQ for many products with different selling prices and annual sales. Figure 20-9 illustrates this process in an interactive mode.

20-14 Program 10—Tabulation Analysis

Program 10 is a simple example that keeps track of entries with different code numbers. The user can enter codes 1, 2, 3 and the program keeps track of how many units of each code has been entered. If the user responds with a code that is not 1, 2, or 3, Lotus will beep. The program will also provide a percentage tabulation result. Figure 20-10 shows this example.

FIGURE 20-9 Economic Order Quantity

```
AA1: '\h                                                        READY

      AA        AB        AC        AD        AE        AF        AG        AH
1   \h        {home}
2             What is the single unit cost?~
3             {goto}g1~
4             {?}~
5             {down 2}{left 6}
6             What are the number of units sold annually?~
7             {goto}g3~
8             {?}~
9             {down 2}{left 6}
10            What is the cost of placing and handling an order?~
11            {goto}g5~
12            {?}~
13            {down 2}{left 6}
14            What is the percentage of inventory value allotted~
15            {down}
16            to carrying costs? (please answer using decimal)~
17            {goto}g8~
18            {?}~
19            {down 2}{left 6}
20            The economic order quanitity (EOQ) is~
01-Jan-91  08:41 AM        UNDO
```

FIGURE 20-9 *(Continued)*

```
AA21:                                                                    READY

        AA        AB        AC        AD        AE        AF        AG        AH
21           {LET g10,@ROUND(@SQRT(2*g3*g5/(g8*g1)),0)}~
22
23
24
25
26
27           This macro determines the economic order quantity
28           that will minimize total inventory costs.
29
30
31
32
33
34
35
36
37
38
39
40
01-Jan-91   08:44 AM              UNDO
```

```
AA1: '\j                                                                 READY

        AA        AB        AC        AD        AE        AF        AG        AH
1    \j      {home}
2            /rea6..e8~
3            This macro keeps totals for Republicans, Democrats and Others~
4            {down}
5            Republicans = 1~
6            {down}
7            Democrats = 2~
8            {down}
9            Others = 3~
10   \P      {goto}a6~
11           Please enter the code number~
12           {goto}e6~/RE~
13           {?}~
14           {IF e6=1}{BRANCH Rep_tot}
15           {IF e6=2}{BRANCH Dem_tot}
16           {IF e6=3}{BRANCH Other}
17           {down}{left 4}
18           You have not entered a proper code number, please try again~
19           {BEEP 2}
20           {WAIT @now+@time(0,0,10)}/RE~
01-Jan-91   08:48 AM              UNDO
```

FIGURE 20-10 *Tabulation Analysis*

FIGURE 20-10 (Continued)

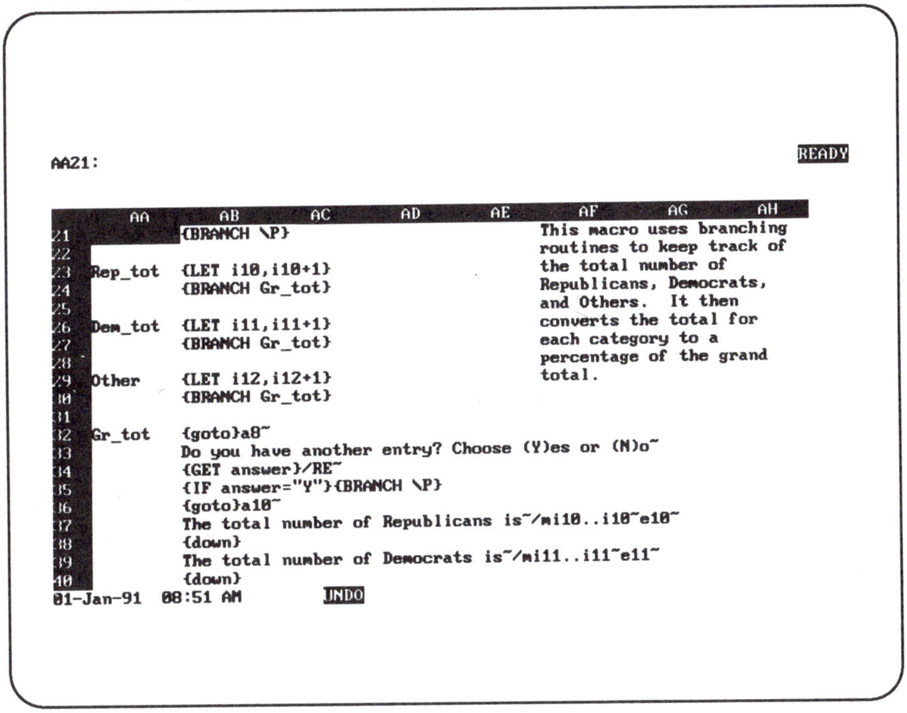

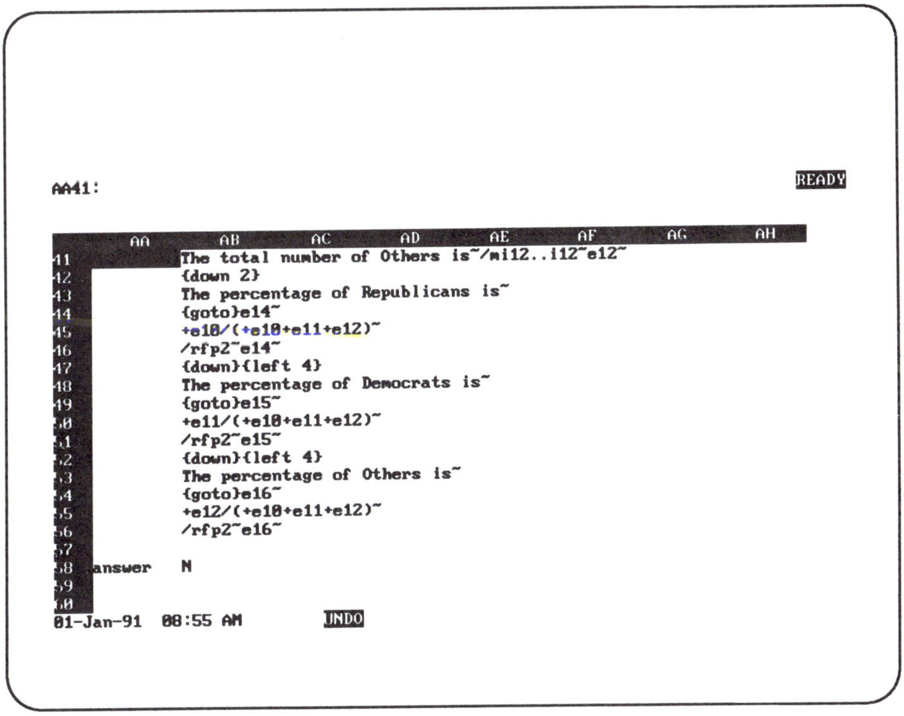

```
AA21:                                                                    READY

        AA        AB        AC        AD        AE        AF        AG        AH
21               {BRANCH \P}                                     This macro uses branching
22                                                               routines to keep track of
23  Rep_tot  {LET i10,i10+1}                                     the total number of
24           {BRANCH Gr_tot}                                     Republicans, Democrats,
25                                                               and Others.  It then
26  Dem_tot  {LET i11,i11+1}                                     converts the total for
27           {BRANCH Gr_tot}                                     each category to a
28                                                               percentage of the grand
29  Other    {LET i12,i12+1}                                     total.
30           {BRANCH Gr_tot}
31
32  Gr_tot   {goto}a8~
33           Do you have another entry? Choose (Y)es or (N)o~
34           {GET answer}/RE~
35           {IF answer="Y"}{BRANCH \P}
36           {goto}a10~
37           The total number of Republicans is~/mi10..i10~e10~
38           {down}
39           The total number of Democrats is~/mi11..i11~e11~
40           {down}
01-Jan-91  08:51 AM         UNDO
```

```
AA41:                                                                    READY

        AA        AB        AC        AD        AE        AF        AG        AH
41               The total number of Others is~/mi12..i12~e12~
42               {down 2}
43               The percentage of Republicans is~
44               {goto}e14~
45               +e10/(+e10+e11+e12)~
46               /rfp2~e14~
47               {down}{left 4}
48               The percentage of Democrats is~
49               {goto}e15~
50               +e11/(+e10+e11+e12)~
51               /rfp2~e15~
52               {down}{left 4}
53               The percentage of Others is~
54               {goto}e16~
55               +e12/(+e10+e11+e12)~
56               /rfp2~e16~
57
58  answer    N
59
60
01-Jan-91  08:55 AM         UNDO
```

FIGURE 20-10 (Continued)

20-15 Programs 11, 12, and 13—Depreciation Assessment

As you saw in Chapter 12, Lotus Release 2.2 provides functions for three depreciation calculations: straight line, sum-of-the-years' depreciation, and double-declining balance. Figures 20-11, 20-12, and 20-13 illustrate the macro version of these functions.

SUMMARY

In this chapter we have seen that Lotus macros can be used as a super programming language. Basic programming structures such as sequence, selection, iteration, and CASE can be performed by macros. We reviewed the principles of programming and the program development life cycle. Several simple examples highlighted the application of Lotus macros as a programming language.

REVIEW QUESTIONS

* These questions are answered in Appendix I.
1. What is a program development life cycle?
2. Why is problem definition so important?
3. Why is program documentation important?
4.* How many types of documentation do we have?
5. What is the difference between external and internal documentation?

FIGURE 20-11 Straight-Line Depreciation

FIGURE 20-12 Sum-of-the-Years'-Digits Depreciation

```
AB10: 'What is the economic life (in year)?~                          READY

        AA      AB      AC      AD      AE      AF      AG      AH
1   \f          {home}
2               What is the cost?~
3               {goto}f1~
4               {?}~
5               {down}{left 5}
6               What is the salvage value?~
7               {goto}f2~
8               {?}~
9               {down}{left 5}                  This macro calculates
10              What is the economic life (in year)?sum-of-the-years'digits
11              {goto}f3~                        depreciation based on the
12              {?}~                             cost, the salvage value,
13              {down 3}{left 5}                 and the economic life
14              {LET a7,Period}                  of a given asset.
15              {LET c7,SYD depreciation}
16              {goto}a9~
17              {FOR h1,1,f3,1,ab19}
18
19  calc_rtn    +h1~
20              /rv~~
01-Jan-91  09:01 AM           UNDO
```

```
AB30:                                                                READY

        AA      AB      AC      AD      AE      AF      AG      AH
21              {right 2}
22              @SYD(f1,f2,f3,h1)~
23              /rv~~
24              {down}{left 2}
25
26
27
28
29
30
31
32
33
34
35
36
37
38
39
40
01-Jan-91  09:05 AM           UNDO
```

FIGURE 20-12 (Continued)

FIGURE 20-13 Double-Declining-Balance Depreciation

```
AA1: '\e                                                                READY

        AA        AB         AC        AD        AE        AF        AG        AH
1    \e       {home}
2             What is the cost?~
3             {goto}e1~
4             {?}~
5             {down}{left 4}
6             What is the salvage value?~
7             {goto}e2~
8             {?}~                                   This macro calculates
9             {down}{left 4}                         double-declining-balance
10            What is the economic life?~            depreciation based on the
11            {goto}e3~                              cost, the salvage value,
12            {?}~                                   and the economic life
13            {down}{left 4}                         of a given asset.
14            {LET a7,Period}
15            {LET c7,DDB depreciation}
16            {goto}a9~
17            {FOR h1,1,e3,1,ab19}
18
19   calc_rtn +h1~
20            /rv~~
01-Jan-91  09:08 AM          UNDO
```

```
AA21:                                                                   READY

        AA        AB         AC        AD        AE        AF        AG        AH
21            {right 2}
22            @DDB(e1,e2,e3,h1)~
23            /rv~~
24            {down}{left 2}
25
26
27
28
29
30
31
32
33
34
35
36
37
38
39
40
01-Jan-91  09:12 AM          UNDO
```

FIGURE 20-13 (Continued)

6. What are some of the tools for external documentation?

7.* Logic design methodology is useful for eliminating and reducing one type of error. What kind of error?

8. What is modular programming?

9. What are some of the advantages of modular programming?

10. What is structured programming?

11.* Why has structured programming become so popular?

12. Can Lotus be used as a full-fledged structured programming language? If yes, why? If no, why not?

13.* Why do we use random numbers?

14. What are some of the business applications of random numbers?

15. What is the break-even point? How is it calculated?

16. What is EOQ? How is it calculated?

17.* What is a nested subroutine? What are some uses of this type of subroutine?

18.* What are some of the advantages of using macros to calculate depreciation methods?

HANDS-ON PRACTICE

1. Extend the macro presented in Figure 20-10 in order to generate a bar graph from 10 sets of data; for example, three of code 1, five of code 2, and two of code 3.

2. Design a macro that accepts grades A–F, then calculates a G.P.A. Also, your program should print the following message:

Excellent   for G.P.A. $>= 3.8$
Good   for G.P.A. $>= 3.5$
Average   for G.P.A. $>= 2.5$
In trouble   for G.P.A. $<= 2.0$

3. Design a macro to generate a mailing list. The output should include three lines as follows:

First Name   Last Name
Street Address
City, State, Zip

Your macro must accept any number of data items, then generate a mailing label.

Lotus Applications in Specific Disciplines

21-1 Introduction*

You have seen throughout this book that Lotus can handle an unlimited number of applications. Any application that can utilize row and column settings, any mathematical formula, if it is translated properly, can be solved by Lotus. The amazing speed and user-friendliness of Lotus add to the beauty of the process.

Whenever you want to use Lotus for any application, you have two options. The first option is to use the Lotus worksheet in a straightforward manner. This means putting your figures an numbers in cells and conducting manipulations. The second option is to develop a series of macros and let them do the job. The advantage of the second approach is that the user does not need to know anything about Lotus and/or the application itself. He/she only needs to answer a series of questions and the rest is done by Lotus.

Applications in this chapter are divided into two groups. First, we introduce you to a series of specific applications and provide you with some guidelines and hints for finishing and expanding them. Later on you may develop macros to perform these tasks with more flexibility. The second group consists of five macro-based applications, to give you the necessary background for developing your own macros. To execute the macros, you need a minimum knowledge of Lotus and the particular application.

The materials presented in this chapter should illustrate the tremendous power and versatility of this amazing software. Try to be creative and invent your own application!

Remember, these applications are by no means a comprehensive coverage of Lotus capabilities. These are only some of the more common applications.

21-2 Lotus for Home Use

Lotus has many applications for home use. Probably the most common is for an automated telephone directory. You can use the Lotus worksheet to keep track of your friends' addresses, telephone numbers, birthdates, and so on.

Forgetting a friend's birthday can be embarrassing. You can keep track of your friends' birthdays in an address database. Then you can ask Lotus to tell you all the birthdays in the next two weeks or so. The design is very easy. Enter the following information:

*For implementation of these applications using macros consult: Hossein Bidgoli, Advanced Lotus 1-2-3 with Applications, West Publishing Company, 1989.

Column A	First name
Column B	Last name
Column C	Street address
Column D	City
Column E	State
Column F	Zip code
Column G	Telephone number
Column H	Birthdate

Adding to or deleting from this database is no problem. There are 8,192 rows (records) and 256 columns (fields) available to you. Modification would also be an easy job. A sort can be done and nay specific values can be searched. The default settings, however, may not be adequate for this application. For example, some of the columns must be extended beyond nine characters (/WCS).

When this database is designed, you could generate mailing labels for Christmas cards or for inviting all your friends to a party.

Another home use could be a database for recipes. The rows would be for recipes, number 1 to number 8,192, and the columns could be for ingredients. Many inquiries can be answered by this database. You could list all the 1987 recipes, all the Chinese food recipes, and so on.

Lotus financial functions can be used for home financial planning, mortgage payments, planning for your children's college education, retirement planning, and so forth.

21-3 Accounting Applications

Any task in the accounting environment can be done by Lotus. (However, dedicated accounting packages may be more suitable for specific accounting and bookkeeping applications.) We have developed a series of macros that prepare a balance sheet an an income statement at the end of this chapter. Here, we will show you one very common accounting application: issuing a list of aged accounts receivable.

Let us say column A includes the purchase date, column B is the amount of purchase, column C is the payment, column D is the balance, and column E is today's date. You can perform a variety of analyses using this database. Let us say that if the balance is positive AND the difference between today's date an the purchase date is ≥ 45 days, issue a message or charge interest. Or you could say if the difference between purchase date and today's date is 30 days OR the balance is $\geq 5,000$, issue a message.

As you remember from Chapter 16, AND (horizontal search), OR (vertical search), and NOT (search with tilde) analysis can be done in a Lotus database. Also, dates in Lotus can be expressed in numbers, so that mathematical calculations can be done with them.

21-4 Tax Analysis

Lotus can be used effectively for calculating taxes. The design process is very easy. Let us say:

Column A	includes the taxpayer's wages
Column B	includes interest income
Column C	includes dividends
Column D	includes other income

Column E   includes adjustments such as moving expenses, medical bills, professional training, etc.

Column F   includes all other itemized deductions

Column G   includes number of exemptions

Column H   includes allowance per exemption

You can make this as complicated as you want. Naturally, the values included in these cells are different for different taxpayers. For example, a single person differs from a family with 18 children or a taxpayer who has a lot of business expenses.

In the above example, the taxable income for a fictitious taxpayer, assuming everything is in row 1, would be:

+A1+B1+C1+D1-E1-F1-G1*H1

The next step would be to build a tax table somewhere in the worksheet. And the final step would be to use a lookup table (horizontal or vertical). The lookup search will tell you how much the tax is, based on a particular taxable income.

You can put as much taxpayer data as you have room for in the worksheet. In theory, you can have up to 8,192 taxpayers in your worksheet.

21-5 Cross-Tabulation Analysis

Cross-tabulation analysis simply means analyzing a row by column data. One common application of this type of analysis is used for questionnaire analysis.

Let us say you have designed a questionnaire with 52 questions regarding customers' reactions to a new product. Each question has a rating scale of one to seven: one means the least satisfaction, four means average satisfaction, and seven means the most satisfaction. When you collect and store this data in your Lotus worksheet, a variety of analyses can be done to answer the following questions:

How many people answered 7?

How many people answered 1?

What is the standard deviation of each question?

What is the mean of each question?

You can use/Data Distribution in order to find out the distribution of each answer; how many ones, how many twos, etc. You can also graph the data in any fashion. When you are more comfortable with macros you may want to develop a macro-based program to analyze a questionnaire and provide important statistics.

Another kind of cross-tabulation application can be used, for example, by a police department. A portion of data collected recently is as follows:

	1988	1989	1990
Homicides	15	17	25
Robberies	22	29	32
Thefts	91	107	99
Rapes	17	13	18
Forgeries	22	25	21
Assaults	62	69	62
Burglaries	73	85	81
Other	19	28	37

You can put this data in the worksheet and answer several interesting questions:

What is the total number of crimes committed in each year?
Which crime had the greatest growth rate for the past three years?
Which crime was the smallest and which crime was the biggest in each year?
Generate a line graph for any of these crimes.
Generate the percentage of each crime to the total number using a pie chart for each year.
Generate a forecast for the year 2000 based on this data using /Data Regression.

21-6 Examination Analysis

Examination analysis is another application of cross-tabulation. Imagine a teacher preparing final grades in the final week of classes. The teacher has given five exams, seven homework assignments, two presentations, and a grade for class participation. Grading can be a time-consuming and complicated task. In this case you are dealing with a matrix of 15 columns and, let us say, 50 rows (50 students).

If this data is stored in a worksheet of 50 by 15, a variety of analyses can be done in a short period as follows:

• Total score of each student, e.b., @SUM.
• Sorted list of students by their total score in descending order.
• Distribution of grade, e.g., how many ≥90, ≥80, ≥70, ≥60.
• Maximum of total score.
• Minimum of total score.
• Mean, variance, and standard deviation of each exam.
• A line graph of total scores of all students.
• Best and worst performance in each of 15 cases of grading.
• Comparing this year's average with the last three years.

21-7 Banking Applications

Lotus has been utilized in the banking industry from the first day of its existence. Accounting and financial analyses, portfolio analysis, and future investment analysis are very common applications of Lotus in the banking industry. What-if, goal-seeking, and sensitivity analyses using different interest rates can be done easily. We would like to show you one common application: a checking account report stating how much the customer should be charged for the number of checks written.

Each bank has a different policy regarding checking accounts. Let us say Plaza Bank of Ocean City has established the following formula for its checking accounts:

Balance ≥$500 No charge for writing checks
Balance≥$300 and <$500 15 cents charge per check
Balance<$300 $5 base charge plus 12 cents per check

Your task is to calculate the charge for each customer. If you design a worksheet like the one below, you can do this calculation.:

Column A   includes the beginning balance
Column B   includes all the deposits
Column C   includes monthly total checks written
Column D   includes final balance (A + B -C)
Column E   includes number of checks

A simple comparison of Column D against the above formula will tell you to which group a particular customer belongs. Then the charge can be calculated. Of course this analysis and database can be expanded to include more sophisticated analyses, such as:

• The largest check written by a particular customer.
• His/her average amount per check.
• His/her smallest check.
• Average balance of the customer per day.
• Highest and lowest balance of a customer in a particular month.

21-8 Lotus Applications in Personnel Administration

Personnel departments of medium to large organizations often have tow application areas that Lotus can handle. One is compiling affirmative action statistics and the other is examination analysis. For the affirmative action case you are usually dealing with a typical data table, as follows:

Column A   Employee name
Column B   Sex
Column C   Age
Column D   Marital status
Column E   Education
Column F   Number of years of experience
Column G   Race
Column H   Handicap status
Column I   Veteran status
Column J   Annual salary

This data matrix can be of any size. Let us say you have 2,000 employees. Your matrix would then be 2,000 by 10. Numerous vital statistics can be generated to answer the following questions:

• Is the average salary of female employees and male employees the same?
• For the same age group, which employees make more money, male or female?
• Which ethnic group makes the highest salary?
• Which ethnic group makes the lowest salary?
• What is the mean salary for male employees?
• What is the mean salary for female employees?
• Plot a line graph of male employees' salary.
• Plot a line graph of female employees' salary.
• Data distribution of different ethnic groups.
• Pie chart of different ethnic groups.
• Pie chart for years of education of all the employees.

You can go on and on, generating more statistics and expanding this database by including other data items.

The second common application for a personnel department is entrance examination score analysis. Let us say you have a data matrix as follows:

Column A   includes prospective employee age
Column B   includes prospective employee high school GPA
Column C   includes prospective employee SAT test score

Column D   includes prospective employee aptitude test score
Column E   includes prospective employee years of experience

Using this database some very useful statistics can be generated:

- The highest and lowest of each test score.
- The youngest and oldest prospective employee.
- Is there any correlation between age and aptitude test?
- Is there any correlation between the aptitude test and the SAT test?
- Is there any correlation between the high school GPA and the aptitude test?

To do the last three analyses you can use /Data Regression and look at the correlation coefficient (also study the discussion in Chapter 17 on simple linear regression).

21-9 Microeconomic Analysis

Lotus can be used to perform cost analysis, revenue analysis, production analysis, and so forth. There is a simple example. Let us say the cost equation of Productive Manufacturing Firm is estimated as $R^3 - 18R^2 + 385$, where R is the number of units produced. Let us further assume that this firm can sell any unit produced at $800 per unit. The revenue equation would be $800R$ and the profit would be $800R - (R^3 - 18R^2 + 385)$. Lotus can help you to generate a scenario regarding total cost, total revenue and total profit as follows:

Column A   includes +800 *R1 (row10)
Column B   includes +R1^3 - 18 *R1^2 + 385 (row10)
Column C   includes + A10 - B10 (row 10)

Now you can input any value for R (number of units produced) and Lotus will calculate total cost, total revenue, and total profit.

Also, you can conduct some interesting what-if, goal-seeking, and sensitivity analyses. The production and revenue equation can be a lot more complicated than the one here. Just do the translation and leave the rest to Lotus.

21-10 Computerized Matching System

You can establish a fairly large database of all possible candidates for any selection purposes (up to 8,192). You can also include up to 256 attributes for each candidate (e.g., age, height, education, income). When the database is built, you can perform any database and/or statistical analyses. You can do complicated searches with up to 32 fields with AND, OR, and NOT combinations. You can develop your own dating service or any other search system (see Chapters 16–17).

21-11 World Population Analysis

It is a fact that the birth rate is higher than the death rate. This means that if noting unexpected happens to reduce the world population, it will eventually explode. The following formula is used for predicting world population growth:

$P = C*[1 + (X - Y)]^N$

Where:

P = Predicted level of future world population
C = Current level of world population
X = Birth rate
Y = Death rate
N = Number of years in the future

Put these values in a worksheet as follows:

Column A   includes C   (row 1)
Column B   includes X   (row 1)
Column C   includes Y   (row 1)
Column D   includes N   (row 1)
Column E   includes A1*(1+(B1-C1))^D

Putting different values in cells A1, B1, C1, D1, you will see some horrifying numbers for the year 2500 and beyond. In 1976 the world population was approximately 4 billion, the birthrate was 2.5 percent and the death rate was .9 percent. Use these numbers and put 15 for N. See what happens?

21-12 Calculation of Quadratic Roots

Quadratic equations have the general formula:

$$Y = AX^2 + BX + C$$

$$X = \frac{-B \pm (B^2 - 4AC)^{1/2}}{2A} = \frac{-B \pm (B \wedge 2 - 4*A*C)^{1/2}}{2*A}$$

Let us use Lotus to calculate different values for X, giving different values for A, B, and C. Build the following worksheet:

	A	B	C	D
(row 1)	10	12	2.70	$\frac{-B1 + (B1 \wedge 2 - 4*A1*C1)^{1/2}}{2*A1}$

We only translated the positive root, not the negative or imaginary root. If you put in any valid values for A, B, and C, Lotus will tell you how much X is.

21-13 Production Analysis*

Suppliers of perishable products and those in service businesses face a serious question: How much to supply in order to satisfy demand but not to oversupply? Spoilage or extra service is a problem. One method for minimizing the cost of oversupply and/or undersupply is known as expected opportunity loss. The following example explains the way this method works.

The manager of Always-Open Rental Car Company is faced with the question of how many rental cars to make available for customers. Oversupply and undersupply is a problem. Past experience shows that the number of rental cars demanded ranges from 15 to 21 with the following probabilities:

Demand	Probability
15	.12
16	.12
17	.10
18	.08
19	.20
20	.25
21	.13

How many cars should the Always-Open Rental Car Company make available in order to minimize the supply cost? The cost of renting a car for this company is $20 and customers pay $28 for renting a car.

The following table is known as the opportunity loss table. Whenever the supply is equal to demand there is no opportunity loss. Each unit of oversupply will cost the company $20. Each unit of undersupply will have an $8 opportunity cost (the company could have been able to make this much profit).

OPPORTUNITY LOSS TABLE FOR ALWAYS-OPEN RENTAL CAR COMPANY

NUMBER OF RENTAL CARS DEMANDED	PROBABILITY OF PAST DEMAND	NUMBER OF RENTAL CARS SUPPLIED						
		15	16	17	18	19	20	21
15	.12	0	20	40	60	80	100	120
16	.12	8	0	20	40	60	80	100
17	.10	16	8	0	20	40	60	80
18	.08	24	16	8	0	20	40	60
19	.20	32	24	16	8	0	20	40
20	.25	40	32	24	16	8	0	20
21	.13	48	40	32	24	16	8	0

The expected opportunity loss of supplying 15 cars is $27.12, as follows: 0(12)+8(.12) + 16(.10) + 24(.08) + 32(.20) + 40(.25) + 48(.13) = 27.12. The expected opportunity loss for the other units of supply is as follows:

Supply	Expected Opportunity Loss
15	27.12
16	22.48
17	21.20
18	22.72
19	26.48
20	35.84
21	52.20

As we see, supplying 17 cars has the minimum opportunity cost.

We have developed a macro-based program to calculate the opportunity loss for various levels of demand. The macro can plot a graph if your computer has graphics capability. Figure 21-1 shows the documentation, the macro-based program, and the execution of the program.

FIGURE 21-1 Documentation for Opportunity Loss Table

```
I1: [W9]                                                                  READY

          I'         J      K    L      M      N      O      P      Q      R
1                   OPPORTUNITY LOSS TABLE FOR ALWAYS-OPEN RENTAL CAR COMPANY
2
3         ENTER THE COST OF EACH UNIT OVERSUPPLIED:   $20.00
4         ENTER THE OPPORTUNITY COST FOR EACH UNIT UNDERSUPPLIED:   $8.00
5
6         RENTALS    PROB. OF           NUMBER OF RENTAL CARS SUPPLIED
7         DEMANDED  PAST DEMAND   15     16     17     18     19     20     21
8
9            15       0.1200    0.00   20.00  40.00  60.00  80.00 100.00 120.00
10           16       0.1200    8.00    0.00  20.00  40.00  60.00  80.00 100.00
11           17       0.1000   16.00    8.00   0.00  20.00  40.00  60.00  80.00
12           18       0.0800   24.00   16.00   8.00   0.00  20.00  40.00  60.00
13           19       0.2000   32.00   24.00  16.00   8.00   0.00  20.00  40.00
14           20       0.2500   40.00   32.00  24.00  16.00   8.00   0.00  20.00
15           21       0.1300   48.00   40.00  32.00  24.00  16.00   8.00   0.00
16                    -------
17        TOTAL       1.0000
18                                      NUMBER OF RENTAL CARS SUPPLIED
19        THE EXPECTED         15     16     17     18     19     20     21
20        OPPORTUNITY LOSS -- 27.12  22.48  21.20  22.72  26.40  35.84  52.20
01-Jan-91  05:49 AM            UNDO                                 CAPS
```

21-14 Financial Analysis

To measure the financial strength of a company many analysts use financial statement analysis. In order to perform this task a series of ratios are computed and compared with those of other companies in the same industry or with the past years of the company itself. However, ratio analysis for determining a company's financial strength can be misleading. These ratios can be manipulated in order not to reflect a company's actual financial situation. But if these ratios are calculated periodically in a straightforward manner, they can be a good basis for further financial investigation. Some of the most commonly used ratios are as follows:

Return on investment:

R = I/E, where:
R = return on investment
I = net income
E = owners' equity

Earnings per share:

G = I/S, where:
G = earnings per share
I = net income
S = number of shares outstanding

FIGURE 21-1 (Continued) Macro-Based Program for Opportunity Loss Analysis

```
\C    {PANELOFF}{GOTO}INAREA~{GOTO}OVER~  *--- To enter the data ---*
      {GETNUMBER "Enter the cost of oversupplied: ",OVER}
      {GOTO}UNDER~
      {GETNUMBER "Enter the Opp. cost of undersupplied: ",UNDER}
      {GOTO}LOWER~
      {GETNUMBER "Enter the minimum car demanded: ",LOWER}
      {GOTO}PROB15~/re.{down 6}~
   PROBAB/RETEMP~           *--- Entering the probability for each event ---*
      {MENUCALL WARN}
      {GETNUMBER "Enter the probability of the cars demanded: ",PROB15}
      {DOWN}{LET TEMP,TEMP+PROB15}~
      {GETNUMBER "Enter the probability of the cars demanded: ",PROB16}
      {DOWN}{LET TEMP,TEMP+PROB16}~
      {GETNUMBER "Enter the probability of the cars demanded: ",PROB17}
      {DOWN}{LET TEMP,TEMP+PROB17}~
      {GETNUMBER "Enter the probability of the cars demanded: ",PROB18}
      {DOWN}{LET TEMP,TEMP+PROB18}~
      {GETNUMBER "Enter the probability of the cars demanded: ",PROB19}
      {DOWN}{LET TEMP,TEMP+PROB19}~
      {GETNUMBER "Enter the probability of the cars demanded: ",PROB20}
      {DOWN}{LET TEMP,TEMP+PROB20}~
      {GETNUMBER "Enter the probability of the cars demanded: ",PROB21}
      {LET TEMP,TEMP+PROB21}~{GOTO}PROB15~{PANELON}
      {IF TEMP=1}{BRANCH RESULT}
      {GETLABEL "The total prob.<>1, please hit <RET> and reenter.",JUNK}
      {GOTO}PROB15~{BRANCH PROBAB}~

   JUNK2        *--- Temporary storage ---*

   JUNK  Y      *--- Temporary storage ---*
   RESULT{GOTO}OUTPUT~     *--- Arrange the result and draw the graph ---*
      /DSDDATA~PPRIMARY~A-G~{GOTO}BEST~
      {GETLABEL "Enter 'Y' or 'y' to see the graph: ",JUNK}
      {IF JUNK<>"Y"}{QUIT}~
      {IF JUNK<>"y"}{QUIT}~
      /GRGTLXXAXIS~AVALUE~
      OSYFCO~QTFTHE OPPORTUNITY LOSS GRAPH~
      TXCARS SUPPLIED~TYTHE EXPECTED OPPORTUNITY LOSS~QQ
      {GETLABEL "Hit <RET> & F10 keys to see the graph. ",JUNK2}

   WARN  Now enter the probability of each event and watch out for the total.
         Make sure it is not more than 1. Hit <Return>
              *--- Warning label for entering the probability ---*
```

Price to earnings ratio:

C $=$ P/G, where
C $=$ price to earnings ratio
P $=$ market price per share
G $=$ earnings per share

Quick ratio:

Q $=$ $A/L1$, where

FIGURE 21-1 (Continued) Execution of Macro-Based Program for Opportunity Loss Analysis

```
****************************************************************************
                              DOCUMENTATION
****************************************************************************
THE PURPOSE OF THIS PROGRAM:
     To calculate the opportunity cost of over- and undersupplying
     rental cars for a fictitious car rental company.  It will calculate
     the opportunity cost and give the result according to the lowest
     opportunity cost.  It will also draw the opportunity cost graph.

INSTRUCTIONS:
   1. The macro for this program can be activated by pressing <ALT> and C
      keys simultaneously.

   2. You will be asked to enter several inputs while running the
      program.

   3. The first input is the cost of oversupplying per car, followed by
      the opportunity cost of undersupplying per car. Then you will be
      asked to enter the minimum number of rental cars demanded, then the
      probability for each demand. For example, if the probability of a
      certain number of cars is 12%, enter the probability as 0.12.

   4. If you made any mistakes, hit <CTRL> and <BREAK> keys
      simultaneously.  Hit <ESC> keys and follow step 1 to start again.
LIMITATIONS:
   1. The range of the cars calculated is limited to the [(minimum
      demanded) + additional 6 cars].

   2. You are not allowed to make any changes to the table.
```

Q = quick ratio
A = quick Assets
L1 = current liabilities

Debt to equity ratio:

D = L2/E, where.
D = debt to equity ratio
L2 = total liabilities
E = owner's equity

We have developed a macro-based program to calculate seven of these ratios. The program is fully interactive. Figure 21-2 shows the documentation, the macro-based program, and the actual execution of the macro-based program.

21-15 Capital Budgeting Analysis

Many financial analyses are classified under the capital budgeting domain. Present value, future, value, internal rate of return, and return on investment are some of the most important techniques used in capital budgeting analysis. To show a simple example, we

FIGURE 21-1 (Continued)

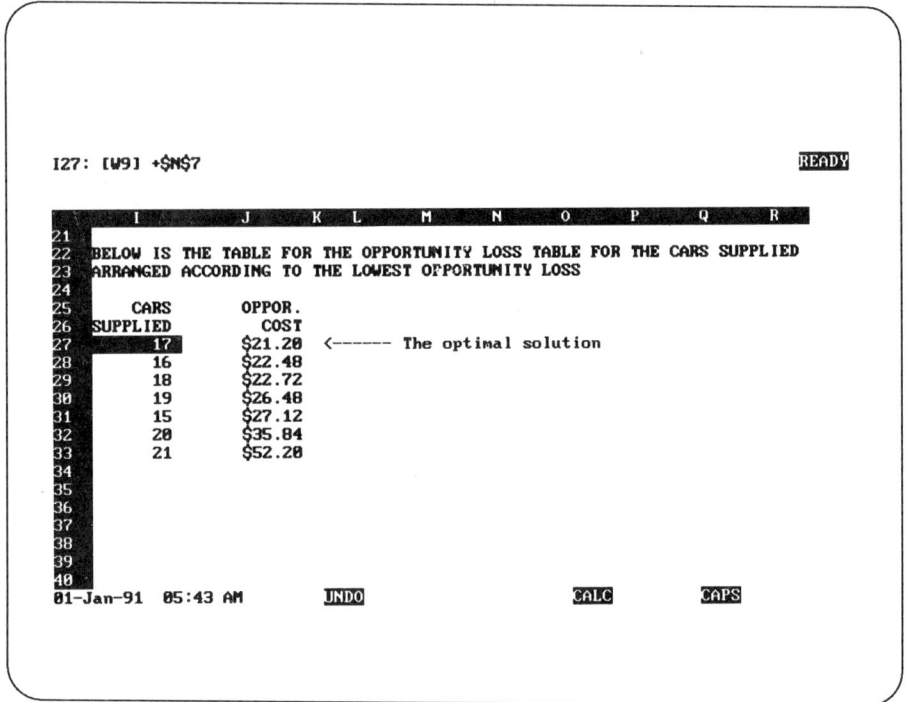

```
I27: [W9] +$N$7                                                    READY

        I          J       K     L      M       N      O      P      Q      R
21
22  BELOW IS THE TABLE FOR THE OPPORTUNITY LOSS TABLE FOR THE CARS SUPPLIED
23  ARRANGED ACCORDING TO THE LOWEST OPPORTUNITY LOSS
24
25      CARS        OPPOR.
26   SUPPLIED        COST
27        17        $21.20   <------ The optimal solution
28        16        $22.48
29        18        $22.72
30        19        $26.48
31        15        $27.12
32        20        $35.84
33        21        $52.20
34
35
36
37
38
39
40
01-Jan-91  05:43 AM          UNDO                      CALC          CAPS
```

have developed a macro-based program designed to calculate net present value (NPV), internal rate of return (IRR), and the profitability index (PI). Figure 21-3 shows the documentation, the macro-based program, and the execution of this macro-based program.

21-16 Accounting Applications: A Second Look

Preparing a balance sheet and an income statement are two of the most common tasks performed by any organization. Regardless of the size of the company, a balance sheet and an income statement are needed to determine its financial status. Balance sheets and income statements can be very long and complicated. However, they all follow the same format. We have developed a macro-based program to prepare these two important financial statements for you. This simple model should give you ideas for developing balance sheets and income statements. Figure 21-4 shows the documentation, the macro-based program, and the execution of this macro-based program.

21-17 S-Curve

Forecasting, or projecting the future of total sales, total expenses, manpower planning, etc., is a common practice in the business world. In order to predict the future of a particular variable, some previous data is needed. Depending on the nature of the data (seasonal, trend, cyclical) and the time horizon for the forecast (short range, medium range, long range), different forecasting models can be chosen. As we discussed in Chapter 17, /Data Regression provides you with a tool for long-range forecasting. There are many forecasting

FIGURE 21-2 *Documentation for Macro-Based Financial Analysis Program*

```
**********************************************************************
                            DOCUMENTATION
**********************************************************************
THE PURPOSE OF THE PROGRAM:
     This program will produce a balance sheet and an income statement
     and calculate the financial ratios for a fictitious company after
     the user has entered the values for the different variables upon
     request.

INSTRUCTIONS:
  1. The macro for this program can be activated by pressing <ALT> and
     A keys simultaneously.

  2. The user will be asked to input the values while the program is
     executing.

  3. The first section will ask the inputs for the company's assets. The
     inputs are: CASH, ACCOUNTS RECEIVABLE, INVENTORY, LONG-TERM
     INVESTMENTS, PLANT & EQUIPMENT, and ACCUMULATED DEPRECIATION.

  4. The second section will ask the inputs for the company's
     liabilities and owners' equity. The inputs are: ACCOUNTS
     PAYABLE, TAXES PAYABLE, BONDS PAYABLE, COMMON STOCK, and RETAINED
     EARNINGS.

  5. The program will check the balance of the balance sheet.  It will
     alert the user if the balance sheet is not balanced.

  6. The third section will ask the inputs for the company's income
     statement. It will calculate the company's income. The inputs
     are: SALES, COST OF GOODS SOLD, SELLING EXPENSES, ADMINISTRATIVE
     EXPENSES, INTEREST EXPENSES, and CORPORATE TAX LEVEL.

  7. The fourth section is where all the financial ratios are. They are:
     A. EARNINGS PER SHARE    = Net Income / (Common Stock / Par Value).
     B. PRICE-EARNINGS RATIO = Stock Price / Earnings Per Share.
     C. RETURN ON ASSETS      = (Net Inc.+(Int.Exp.*(1-Income Tax)))/
                                Total Assets.
     D. QUICK RATIO           = (Current Asset - Inventory)/Current
                                Liabilities.
     E. CURRENT RATIO         = Current Assets/Current Liabilities
     F. DEBT TO EQUITY RATIO = (Current Liabilities + Bonds)/Total
                                Stockholders' Equity.
     G. RETURN ON INVESTMENT = Net Income / Stockholders' Equity.

  8. When you are done entering all the inputs, a menu will appear. Use
     the cursor keys to make the selection and hit <RETURN>.

  9. If you made any mistakes while entering the inputs, hit <CTRL>
     and <BREAK> keys simultaneously followed by <ESC>.  Repeat
     step 1 to start again.

LIMITATIONS:
  1. The user may not change the format of the balance sheet and income
     statement because it is predefined.
```

FIGURE 21-2 (Continued) Macro-Based Program Performing Financial Analysis

```
\A  {GOTO}BALANCE~{GOTO}CASH~                *--- To enter the input to Balance Sheet ---*
    {GETNUMBER "Enter the cash amount: ",CASH}{DOWN}
    {GETNUMBER "Enter the amount acc. receivable: ",ACC.REC}{DOWN}
    {GETNUMBER "Enter the amount on Inventory: ",INV}{GOTO}LT.INV~
    {GETNUMBER "Enter the amount of Long Term Investment: ",LT.INV}
    {GOTO}PLANT~
    {GETNUMBER "Enter the amount of Plant & Equipment: ",PLANT}
    {GOTO}DEPRE~
    {GETNUMBER "Enter the amount of Depreciation: ",DEPRE}{GOTO}TOT.AS.~
    /reOFF~{LET OFF,OFF+TOT.AS.}~
    {GETLABEL "Hit <RETURN> key to go to the LIABILITIES section",JUNK}
    {PGDN}{GOTO}ACC.PAY~                      *--- Liabilities & Owners' Equities Section ---*
    {GETNUMBER "Enter the amount of Account Payable: ",ACC.PAY}
    {LET OFF,OFF-ACC.PAY}~
    {GOTO}TAX.PAY~
    {GETNUMBER "Enter the amount of Taxes Payable: ",TAX.PAY}
    {LET OFF,OFF-TAX.PAY}~
    {GOTO}BONDS~
    {GETNUMBER "Enter the amount of Bonds Payables: ",BONDS}
    {LET OFF,OFF-BONDS}~
    {GOTO}STOCK~
    {GETNUMBER "Enter the amount of Common Stock: ",STOCK}
    {LET OFF,OFF-STOCK}~
    {GOTO}RET.EARN~
    {GETNUMBER "Enter the amount of Retained Earnings: ",RET.EARN}
    {LET OFF,OFF-RET.EARN}~
    {GOTO}TOT.EQ~{IF (TOT.AS.-TOT.EQ)>0}{BRANCH NO}~
    {IF (TOT.EQ-TOT.AS.)>0}{BRANCH NOT}
    {GETLABEL "Hit <RET> to go to the INCOME STATEMENT. ",JUNK}
    {GOTO}R1~{GOTO}SALES~              *--- Income Statement Section ---*
    {GETNUMBER "Enter the amount Sales: ",SALES}{GOTO}COGS~
    {GETNUMBER "Enter the amount of Cost Of Goods Sold: ",COGS}
    {GOTO}SELL.EXP~
    {GETNUMBER "Enter the amount of Selling Expenses: ",SELL.EXP}
    {GOTO}AD.EXP.~
    {GETNUMBER "Enter the amount of Advertising Expenses: ",AD.EXP.}
    {GOTO}INT.EXP~
    {GETNUMBER "Enter the amount of Interest Expenses: ",INT.EXP}
    {GOTO}TAX~
    {GETNUMBER "Enter the corporate tax level (in percent): ",TAX}{GOTO}NI~
    {GETLABEL "Hit <RET> to go to the calculated RATIOS. ",JUNK}
    {GOTO}Z1~{GOTO}ST.PRICE~            *--- Financial Ratios ---*
    {GETNUMBER "Enter the price of the stock:",ST.PRICE}~
    {GETLABEL "Hit <RETURN> key to get the menu.",JUNK}
    {GETLABEL "Use the cursor keys to make your choice and hit <RETURN>.",JUNK}
O   {MENUBRANCH MENU}
MENUAssets          Liabilities       Income Statement    Financial Ratios    Quit
    View Total AsseView Total LiabilitiView Income StatemenView Financial RatioTo QUIT the program.
    {GOTO}INPUT~    {GOTO}SECOND~     {GOTO}INC~          {GOTO}z1~           {QUIT}
    {BRANCH O}      {BRANCH O}        {BRANCH O}          {BRANCH O}
                    *--- Menu for the result ---*
junk

NO  {BEEP 3}~
    {GETLABEL "TOTAL ASSETS is more than TOTAL LIABILITIES & OWNERS' EQUITIES.",JUNK}
    {BRANCH \A}~
NOT {BEEP 3}~
    {GETLABEL "TOTAL LIABILITIES & OWNERS' EQUITIES is more than TOTAL ASSETS.",JUNK}
    {BRANCH \A}~
```

tools, such as moving average, exponential smoothing, and multivariate forecast. Any of these models can be translated into Lotus in order to generate a forecast. As an example we have chosen the S-curve for such a translation.

The S-curve model is a long-range forecasting model (two years or more). An S-curve model has a slow start, a rather steep growth, and a saturation point that comes after some period of time. The introduction of a new product, an information system life cycle, or the usefulness of a new machine all follow an S-curve model. There are several mathematical presentations of the S-curve model. The following formula is one way of showing this model:

$$Y_t = e^{A+B/t}$$

FIGURE 21-2 (Continued) Execution of Macro-Based Financial Analysis Program

```
Q1: [W3]                                                              READY

        I    J     K      L      M        N        O        P      Q
  1
  2                            BALANCE SHEET
  3  ================================================================
  4                       ASSETS                              1990
  5  CURRENT ASSETS:
  6      CASH ...............................................  $4,309,000
  7      ACCOUNTS RECEIVABLE ................................   2,070,000
  8      INVENTORY .........................................     500,000
  9                                                           _____
 10          TOTAL CURRENT ASSETS ..........................   6,959,000
 11
 12  LONG-TERM INVESTMENT ..................................     500,400
 13  PLANT & EQUIPMENT ...........................  400,500
 14  LESS: ACCUMULATED DEPRECIATION ..............   58,000
 15                                               _____
 16  NET PLANT & EQUIPMENT .................................     342,500
 17                                                           _____
 18  TOTAL ASSETS .........................................  $7,859,900
 19                                                           ============
 20
01-Jan-91  08:00 AM        UNDO
```

```
Q21: [W3]                                                             READY

        I    J     K      L      M        N        O        P      Q
 21
 22              CURRENT LIABILITIES AND OWNERS' EQUITY
 23  ================================================================
 24  CURRENT LIABILITIES
 25      ACCOUNTS PAYABLE ..................................  $4,000,500
 26      TAXES PAYABLE .....................................   2,000,500
 27                                                           _____
 28          TOTAL CURRENT LIABILITIES .....................   6,001,000
 29  BONDS PAYABLE .........................................     550,000
 30
 31  STOCKHOLDERS' EQUITY
 32      COMMON STOCK,  $15.00 par value ..........  150,000
 33      RETAINED EARNINGS ........................ 1,158,900
 34                                               _____
 35          TOTAL STOCKHOLDERS' EQUITY ....................   1,308,900
 36                                                           _____
 37  TOTAL LIABILITIES & STOCKHOLDERS' EQUITY ..............  $7,859,900
 38                                                           ============
 39      This balance sheet is off by            $0
 40
01-Jan-91  09:41 AM        UNDO
```

FIGURE 21-2 (Continued)

FIGURE 21-2   (Continued)

```
R1: [W4]                                                               READY

      R    S       T        U          U            U          X       Y
  1                              INCOME STATEMENT
  2   ====================================================================
  3                                       1990
  4   SALES ............................................ $7,000,000
  5   COST OF GOODS SOLD ...............................  1,500,000
  6                                                      _____
  7   GROSS MARGIN ....................................   6,300,000
  8   OPERATING EXPENSES
  9        SELLING EXPENSES ...............    900,500
 10        ADMINISTRATIVE EXPENSES .......  1,250,000
 11                                         _____
 12        TOTAL OPERATING EXPENSES .................    2,150,500
 13                                                      _____
 14   NET OPERATING INCOME  .........................    4,149,500
 15   INTEREST EXPENSES .............................       15,000
 16                                                      _____
 17   NET INCOME BEFORE TAXES .......................    4,134,500
 18   INCOME TAXES AT   46% .........................    2,232,630
 19                                                      ========
 20   NET INCOME ....................................   $1,901,870
 01-Jan-91  08:04 AM          UNDO
```

```
Z1: \=                                                                 READY

      Z       AA       AB    AC    AD    AE    AF      AG      AH
  1   ====================================================================
  2                         FINANCIAL RATIOS
  3   ====================================================================
  4
  5        1. EARNINGS PER SHARE ........................ $190.19
  6
  7        2. PRICE-EARNINGS RATIO
  8           ASSUMING STOCK MARKET PRICE AT $29 ........   0.1525
  9
 10        3. RETURN ON ASSETS ..........................   0.2430
 11
 12        4. QUICK RATIO ...............................   1.0630
 13
 14        5. CURRENT RATIO .............................   1.1596
 15
 16        6. DEBT TO EQUITY RATIO ......................   5.0050
 17
 18        7. RETURN ON INVESTMENT ......................   1.4530
 19
 20
 01-Jan-91  09:50 AM          UNDO
```

FIGURE 21-2   (Continued)

FIGURE 21-3 *Macro Based Program Performing Capital Budgeting Analysis*

```
*********************************************************************
                          DOCUMENTATION
*********************************************************************
THE PURPOSE OF THE PROGRAM:
     To calculate the NPV, IRR, and PI of a proposed project of
     replacing an old machine with a new automated machine.  The old
     machine is currently operated by a worker. The new machine
     requires no worker to operate it.

INSTRUCTIONS:
   1. To activate the macro for this program, press <ALT> and Q keys
      simultaneously.

   2. You will be asked to enter the inputs while running the program.

   3. The first part of the program will ask the information on the old
      equipment: all the costs associated with the old equipment, the
      original price, the expected salvage value, the expected life
      (from beginning), and the current age of the equipment. The
      corporate tax level and the required rate of return are asked in
      this module.

   4. The second part will ask for the information on the new proposed
      equipment. It will ask for the costs of the machine, delivered
      and installed. It will also ask for the expected economic life
      of the machine and expected salvage value after 10 years of
      service.

   5. The third part will show the initial cash outlay for the project.

   6. The fourth part will show the calculation of the cash flow for the
      project. It will calculate all the savings deducted by the costs
      and taxes giving the annual cash flow after taxes.

   7. The last part will show the yearly cash flow, the calculated net
      present value, profitability index, and internal rate of return.
      The conclusion will be given depending on the NPV, IRR and PI.
      The formula used:
      NPV = @NPV(Com. Req. Rate of Return, CashFlow) - Initial
            Cash outflow
      PI  = NPV / ABС(Initial Cash outflow)
      IRR = @IRR (Com. Req. Rate of Return, Cash inflow +
            Initial Cash outflow)

   8. If you make a mistake, hit <CTRL> & <BREAK> keys simultaneously
      to stop the program. To start all over again, hit <ESC> and
      follow step 1.

LIMITATIONS:
   1. The tables are predefined, so you have to follow the instructions
      while running the program.

   2. The cash flow will be calculated for only 10 years.

   3. Depreciation is calculated using the straight-line method.

   4. You are not allowed to make any changes to the table.
```

FIGURE 21-3 *(Continued) Execution of the Macro-Based Capital Budgeting Program*

```
\Q  {GOTO}INPUT~{PANELOFF}              *--- The Current Situation Data ---*
    {GETLABEL "Hit <RETURN> key and enter the current situation data.",JUNK}{GOTO}CSSALARY~
    {GETNUMBER "Enter the salary of the worker (per annum): ",CSSALARY}
    {DOWN}
    {GETNUMBER "Enter the overtime pay (per annum): ",CSO/TIME}
    {DOWN}
    {GETNUMBER "Enter the fringe benefits (insur.,paid vacation, etc. per annum): ",CSBENEFIT}
    {DOWN}
    {GETNUMBER "Enter the cost of defects (per annum) caused by the machine: ",CSDEFECT}
    {DOWN}
    {GETNUMBER "Enter the original price of the machine: ",CSPRICE}
    {DOWN}
    {GETNUMBER "What's the expected life (from beginning) of the old machine: ",CSLIFE}
    {DOWN}
    {GETNUMBER "Enter the expected salvage value of the machine: ",CSSALVAGE}
    {DOWN}
    {GETNUMBER "How old is the machine: ",CSAGE}
    {DOWN 2}
    {GETNUMBER "What's the current book value of old machine: ",CSCURSALVAGE}
    {DOWN}
    {GETNUMBER "Enter the annual maintenance: ",CSMAINTAIN}
    {DOWN}
    {GETNUMBER "Enter the marginal tax rate (in percent): ",CSTAX}
    {DOWN}
    {GETNUMBER "Enter the company required rate of return (in percent): ",CSRROR}{DOWN}
    {GETLABEL "Hit <RETURN> key to go to the proposed situation section",JUNK}
    {GOTO}I21~        *--- The Proposed Situation Data ---*
    {GETLABEL "Hit <RETURN> key and enter the data for the new machine",JUNK}
    {GOTO}PSCOST~
    {GETNUMBER "Enter the cost of new machine: ",PSCOST}
    {DOWN}
    {GETNUMBER "Enter the shipping fee: ",PSFEE}
    {DOWN}
    {GETNUMBER "Enter the installation cost: ",PSINSTALL}
    {DOWN}
    {GETNUMBER "Enter the expected life of new machine: ",PSLIFE}
    {GOTO}PSSALVAGE~
    {GETNUMBER "Enter the expected salvage value of new machine: ",PSSALVAGE}
    {DOWN}
    {GETNUMBER "Enter the expected annual maintenance cost: ",PSMAINTAIN}
    {DOWN}
    {GETNUMBER "What's the exp. cost of defects caused by the new machine (per annum):",PSDEFECT}
    {GETLABEL "Hit the <RETURN> key to get the menu. ",JUNK}
O   {menubranch AX}

TEMP                    *--- Temporary Storage ---*

JUNK                    *--- Temporary Storage ---*

AX  Initial Cash Outlay  CashFlow Section  The Conclusion   QUIT
    The calculation of I The calculation o The Results (NPV, Quit the program.
    {GOTO}I41~           {GOTO}I61~         {GOTO}I81~        {PANELON}
    {BRANCH O}           {BRANCH O}         {BRANCH O}        {QUIT}

    *--- The Menu to see the RESULT ---*
```

where Yt is the S-curve estimate, e is the constant equal to 2.718, A is the equivalent of the intercept in the linear regression model, B is the equivalent of the slope in the linear regression model, and t is time.

Since the relationship between the independent variable (t) and the dependent variable (Y) is not linear, the classical least-squares method does not apply to this model. However, by taking the logarithm of both sides, we can convert this form to a linear one, as follows:

$$\text{Log} Y_t = \left(A + \frac{B}{t} \right) \text{Log } e^e \text{ (Log } e^e = 1)$$

FIGURE 21-3 (Continued)

```
P1: \x                                                              READY

      I    J      K       L       M        N       O        P
1 xxxxxxxxxxxxxxxxxxxxxxxxxxxxxxxxxxxxxxxxxxxxxxxxxxxxxxxxxxxxxxxxxxxxx
2                    INPUT SECTION
3 xxxxxxxxxxxxxxxxxxxxxxxxxxxxxxxxxxxxxxxxxxxxxxxxxxxxxxxxxxxxxxxxxxxxxx
4                      PART ONE:
5
6 Current Situation:
7     Salary one full-time worker ...................... $12,000 /per year
8     Overtime pay ..................................... $1,000 /per year
9     Fringe Benefits .................................. $2,000 /per year
10    Cost of defect ................................... $1,000 /per year
11    Original price of hand-operated machine .......... $20,000
12    Expected life .................................... 20 years
13    Salvage value .................................... $0
14    Age of the machine ............................... 5 years
15    Depreciation method .............................. Straight line
16    Current salvage value ............................ $5,000
17    Annual maintenance ............................... $1,500
18    Tax rate ......................................... 46.0%
19    Required rate of return .......................... 16.7%
20
01-Jan-91  11:16 AM        UNDO
```

```
P21:                                                               READY

      I    J      K       L       M        N       O        P
21
22
23                    PART TWO:
24
25 Proposed Situation: Automated operation
26    Cost of machine .................................. $30,000
27    Shipping fee ..................................... $500
28    Installation cost ................................ $450
29    Expected economic life ........................... 20 years
30    Depreciation method .............................. Straight line
31    Salvage value after 10 years ..................... $0
32    Annual maintenance ............................... $350
33    Cost of defect ................................... $250 /per year
34
35
36
37
38
39
40
01-Jan-91  11:20 AM        UNDO
```

FIGURE 21-3 (Continued)

FIGURE 21-3 (Continued)

```
P41: \x                                                        READY

      I     J      K      L      M      N      O      P
41 xxxxxxxxxxxxxxxxxxxxxxxxxxxxxxxxxxxxxxxxxxxxxxxxxxxxxxxxxxxxx
42            OUTPUT SECTION
43 xxxxxxxxxxxxxxxxxxxxxxxxxxxxxxxxxxxxxxxxxxxxxxxxxxxxxxxxxxxxxxxxx
44
45                    Initial Outlay
46 Outflows
47    Cost of new machine .......................... $50,000
48    Shipping fee .................................      500
49    Installation cost ............................      450
50    Increased taxes ..............................  (4,600)
51 Inflows
52    Salvage value-old machine ...................  -   5,000
53                                                      -------
54
55    Net Initial Outlay ........................... $41,350
56
57
58
59
60
01-Jan-91  11:24 AM        UNDO
```

```
P61:                                                           READY

      I     J      K      L      M      N      O      P
61
62                                               Non-cash
63 Calculation of Differential Cash Flows   flow profit  Cash Flow
64 Savings:
65    Reduced salary ................................ $12,000  $12,000
66    Reduced overtime ..............................    1,000    1,000
67    Reduced fringe benefits .......................    2,000    2,000
68    Reduced defects ...............................      750      750
69 Costs:
70    Increased maintenance expenses ................    (350)    (350)
71    Increased depreciation expenses ...............  (1,540)
72                                                     -------  -------
73 Net savings before taxes ......................... $13,853  $15,400
74 Taxes ............................................    6,372    6,372
75                                                     -------  -------
76 Net Cash Flow after taxes ........................            $9,028
77
78
79
80
01-Jan-91  11:27 AM        UNDO
```

FIGURE 21-3 (Continued)

FIGURE 21-3 (Continued)

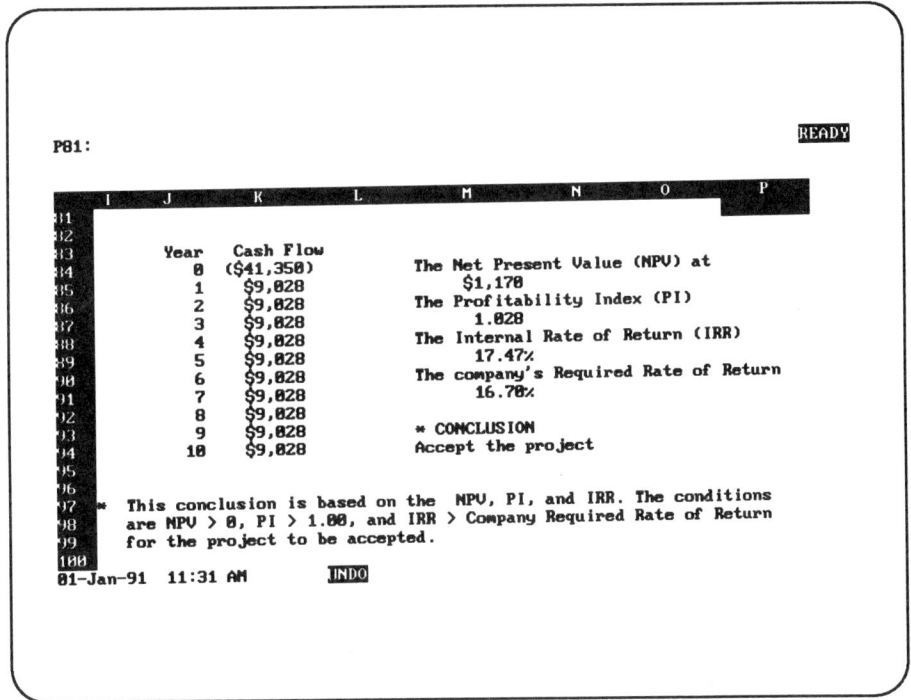

```
P81:                                                                    READY

         I      J        K        L        M        N        O        P

31
32
33      Year    Cash Flow
34        0     ($41,350)          The Net Present Value (NPU) at
35        1      $9,028                  $1,170
36        2      $9,028            The Profitability Index (PI)
37        3      $9,028                  1.028
38        4      $9,028            The Internal Rate of Return (IRR)
39        5      $9,028                  17.47%
90        6      $9,028            The company's Required Rate of Return
91        7      $9,028                  16.78%
92        8      $9,028
93        9      $9,028            * CONCLUSION
94       10      $9,028            Accept the project
95
96
97    * This conclusion is based on the  NPU, PI, and IRR. The conditions
98      are NPU > 0, PI > 1.00, and IRR > Company Required Rate of Return
99      for the project to be accepted.
100
81-Jan-91  11:31 AM          UNDO
```

and if we replace 1 by T, Log Yt by Xt we will have

$Xt = A + BT$

As we see, this has a linear form and we can apply the classical least-squares method in order to estimate the values for A and B (see the discussion of simple linear regression in Chapter 17).

We have developed a macro-based program that fits an S-curve to a series of data. Figure 21-5 shows the documentation, the macro-based program, and the execution of the program.

SUMMARY

In this chapter we discussed some of the common applications performed by Lotus. As you have seen Lotus can theoretically handle an unlimited number of applications. These applications can be solved directly using the Lotus worksheet or by developing a series of macros. The advantage of using macros is the user-friendliness of the process. The user of such a program does not need to have any previous knowledge about Lotus and/or the application area. Materials presented in this chapter should prepare you with enough background to develop much more sophisticated applications. Put your creativity into action!

HANDS-ON PRACTICE

* These questions are answered in Appendix I.

FIGURE 21-4 Documentation for Macro-Based Balance Sheet and Income Statement

```
**************************************************************************
                              DOCUMENTATION
**************************************************************************
THE PURPOSE OF THIS PROGRAM:
      This program will produce a balance sheet and an income statement
      after the user has entered the values for the different variables
      upon request.

INSTRUCTIONS:
   1. The macro for this program can be activated by pressing <ALT> & A
      keys simultaneously.

   2. The user will be asked to input the values while the program is
      executing.

   3. The first section will ask the inputs for the company's assets. The
      inputs are: CASH, ACCOUNTS RECEIVABLE, INVENTORY, LONG-TERM
      INVESTMENTS, PLANT & EQUIPMENT, and ACCUMULATED DEPRECIATION.

   4. The second section will ask for the company's liabilities and
      owners' equity. The inputs are: ACCOUNTS PAYABLE, TAXES PAYABLE,
      BONDS PAYABLE, COMMON STOCK, and RETAINED EARNINGS.

   5. The program will check the balance of the balance sheet. It
      will make sure that the TOTAL ASSETS will be equal to the TOTAL
      LIABILITIES and OWNERS' EQUITY.

   6. If the balance sheet is balanced, then it will go to the income
      statement. It will calculate the company's income. The inputs are:
      SALES, COST OF GOODS SOLD, SELLING EXPENSES, ADMINISTRATIVE
      EXPENSES, INTEREST EXPENSES, and CORPORATE TAX LEVEL.

   7. When you are done with the income statement, a menu will appear.
      Use the cursor keys to make your selection and hit <RETURN>.

   8. If you made any mistakes while entering the inputs, hit <CTRL>
      & <BREAK> simultaneously followed by <ESC>.  Repeat step
      1 to restart.

LIMITATIONS:
   1. The user may not change the format of the balance sheet and income
      statement because it is predefined.
```

FIGURE 21-4 (Continued) Macro-Based Program for Preparing a Balance Sheet and an Income Statement

```
\A  {GOTO}INPUT~{GOTO}CASH~              *--- The balance sheet input section ---*
    {GETNUMBER "Enter the cash amount: ",CASH}{DOWN}
    {GETNUMBER "Enter the amount acc. receivable:",ACC.REC}{DOWN}
    {GETNUMBER "Enter the amount on Inventory:",INV}{GOTO}LT.INV~
    {GETNUMBER "Enter the amount of Long Term Investment:",LT.INV}
    {GOTO}PLANT~
    {GETNUMBER "Enter the amount of Plant & Equipment:",PLANT}
    {GOTO}DEPRE~
    {GETNUMBER "Enter the amount of Depreciation:",DEPRE}{GOTO}TOT.AS.~
    /reOFF~
    {LET OFF,OFF+TOT.AS.)~
    {GETLABEL "Hit <RETURN> key to go to the LIABILITIES section",JUNK}{PGDN}
    {GOTO}ACC.PAY~                       *--- Liabilities & Owners' Equities Section ---*
    {GETNUMBER "Enter the amount of Account Payable:",ACC.PAY}
    {LET OFF,OFF-ACC.PAY)~
    {GOTO}TAX.PAY~
    {GETNUMBER "Enter the amount of Taxes Payable:",TAX.PAY}
    {LET OFF,OFF-TAX.PAY)~
    {GOTO}BONDS~
    {GETNUMBER "Enter the amount of Bonds Payables:",BONDS}
    {LET OFF,OFF-BONDS)~
    {GOTO}STOCK~
    {GETNUMBER "Enter the amount of Common Stock:",STOCK}
    {LET OFF,OFF-STOCK)~
    {GOTO}RET.EARN~
    {GETNUMBER "Enter the amount of Retained Earnings:",RET.EARN}
    {LET OFF,OFF-RET.EARN)~
    {IF (TOT.AS.-TOT.EQ)>0}{BRANCH NO}
    {IF (TOT.EQ-TOT.AS.)>0}{BRANCH NOT}
    {GETLABEL "Hit <RETURN> key to go to the income statement section",JUNK}
    {GOTO}INC~{GOTO}SALES~               *--- Income Statement Section ---*
    {GETNUMBER "Enter the amount Sales:",SALES}{GOTO}COGS~
    {GETNUMBER "Enter the amount of Cost Of Goods Sold:",COGS}
    {GOTO}SELL.EXP~
    {GETNUMBER "Enter the amount of Selling Expenses:",SELL.EXP}
    {GOTO}AD.EXP.~
    {GETNUMBER "Enter the amount of Advertising Expenses:",AD.EXP.}
    {GOTO}INT.EXP~
    {GETNUMBER "Enter the amount of Interest Expenses:",INT.EXP}
    {GOTO}TAXLEVEL~
    {GETNUMBER "Enter the corporate tax level (in percent): ",TAXLEVEL}
    {GOTO}NI~
    {GETLABEL "Hit <RETURN> key to get the menu.",JUNK}
    {GETLABEL "Use the cursor keys to make your choice and hit <RETURN>.",JUNK}
O   {MENUBRANCH MENU}


MENUAssets          Liabilities         Income Statement    Quit
    View Total AsseView Liabilities & OView Income StatemenQuit the program
    {GOTO}INPUT~     {GOTO}SECOND~      {GOTO}INC~          {QUIT}
    {BRANCH O}       {BRANCH O}         {BRANCH O}

junk                *--- Temporary storage ---*
NO  {BEEP 5}
    {GETLABEL "TOTAL ASSETS is more than TOTAL LIABILITIES & OWNERS' EQUITIES. ",JUNK}
    {BRANCH \A}

NOT {BEEP 5}
    {GETLABEL "TOTAL LIABILITIES & OWNERS' EQUITIES is more than TOTAL ASSETS. ",JUNK}
    {BRANCH \A}
```

FIGURE 21-4 (Continued) Execution of Macro-Based Accounting Program

```
J1: [W4]                                                        READY

     J   K    L    M    N    O    P    Q    R
1
2                      BALANCE SHEET
3    ==========================================================
4                         ASSETS                         1990
5    CURRENT ASSETS:
6         CASH ...................................... $1,600,000
7         ACCOUNTS RECEIVABLE .......................  1,500,000
8         INVENTORY .................................    900,000
9                                                     -----------
10            TOTAL CURRENT ASSETS ...................  4,000,000
11
12   LONG-TERM INVESTMENT .............................  1,000,500
13   PLANT & EQUIPMENT ........................1,500,000
14   LESS: ACCUMULATED DEPRECIATION ...............  450,000
15                                                 -----------
16   NET PLANT & EQUIPMENT ............................  1,050,000
17                                                     -----------
18   TOTAL ASSETS ..................................... $6,051,300
19                                                     ===========
20
01-Jan-91  08:08 AM          UNDO
```

```
Q21: [W12]                                                      READY

     J   K    L    M    N    O    P    Q    R
21
22                LIABILITIES & STOCKHOLDERS' EQUITY
23   ==========================================================
24   CURRENT LIABILITIES
25         ACCOUNTS PAYABLE ......................... $1,500,000
26         TAXES PAYABLE ............................    500,000
27                                                    -----------
28            TOTAL CURRENT LIABILITIES .............  2,000,000
29   BONDS PAYABLE ....................................  1,800,900
30
31   STOCKHOLDERS' EQUITY
32         COMMON STOCK,  $15.00 par value .........1,500,000
33         RETAINED EARNINGS ........................    670,400
34                                                    -----------
35            TOTAL STOCKHOLDERS' EQUITY .............  2,170,400
36                                                    -----------
37   TOTAL LIABILITIES & STOCKHOLDERS' EQUITY ........ $6,051,300
38                                                     ===========
39
40       This balance sheet is off by            $0
01-Jan-91  11:43 AM          UNDO
```

FIGURE 21-4 (Continued)

FIGURE 21-4 (Continued)

```
Z1: [W13]                                                              READY

      S   T     U         U       W         X        Y         Z
  1                        INCOME STATEMENT
  2   ======================================================================
  3                            1990
  4   SALES ..............................................  $2,000,500
  5   COST OF GOODS SOLD .................................   1,200,000
  6                                                          ---------
  7   GROSS MARGIN ......................................   1,600,500
  8   OPERATING EXPENSES
  9      SELLING EXPENSES .....................   500,000
 10      ADMINISTRATIVE EXPENSES ..............   600,000
 11                                              ---------
 12      TOTAL OPERATING EXPENSES ..........................   1,180,000
 13                                                             ---------
 14   NET OPERATING INCOME  .............................     420,500
 15   INTEREST EXPENSES .................................      12,000
 16                                                          ---------
 17   NET INCOME BEFORE TAXES ...........................     408,500
 18   INCOME TAXES AT .. 46% ............................     220,590
 19                                                          =========
 20   NET INCOME ........................................    $187,910
01-Jan-91  08:11 AM            UNDO
```

1.* If A, B, and C are 1, 10, and 1, respectively, what is the positive root in a quadratic equation?
2. If X, Y, and Z are 5, 10, and 12, respectively, what is the value of R in the following formula:
   $$R = X^3 - XYZ + (X/Z)^Y$$
3.* If the world population is 4 billion now, the birth rate 2.6 percent and the death rate .9 percent, what is the world population predicted to be in the year 2010?
4. The following are grades of students in a Lotus class. Using /Data Distribution, organize this data into five groups in ascending order.

Jack	91	Susan	75
Joe	62	Mark	81
Mary	79	Valerie	83
Harry	79	Tina	72
Sherry	81	Steve	91
Bob	98	David	69
Barbara	46	Brad	85
Luke	98	Ellen	91

5. Design a home phone directory for 50 people. Sort it by two keys. The fields include first name, last name, street address, city, state, zip, age, sex, and telephone number.
6. Choose a balance sheet and calculate 7 ratios discussed in this chapter.
7. Using the S-curve model, create a forecast for the following data items:

X	Y
1	120
2	144

FIGURE 21-5   *Documentation for the Macro-Based S-Curve Model*

```
**************************************************************************
                              DOCUMENTATION
**************************************************************************
THE PURPOSE OF THIS PROGRAM:
     To calculate the S-curve model (2 years or more) for the long-range
     forecasting model.  It will calculate the slope and intercept point
     for the S-curve and draw the S-curve graph.

INSTRUCTIONS:
  1. The macro for this program can be activated by pressing <ALT> and Z
     keys simultaneously.

  2. You will be asked to input several variables and some other inputs
     while running the macro.

  3. The first input is how many sets of data the user wants to
     consider. Then it will ask the user to input the first independent
     variable followed by the first dependent variable. This will
     continue until the user has entered all the data.

  4. The next input will be the prediction data. The user will be asked
     if he/she wants to do any predicting; then the user has to input
     the value of independent variables.

  5. Finally, this program will draw the S-curve graph based on the
     calculated values.  The user will be asked if he/she wants the
     program to draw the S-curve graph.

  6. If you made any mistakes while entering the input, hit <CTRL>
     and <BREAK> simultaneously to stop the program.  Hit <ESC>
     and repeat step 1 to start all over again.

LIMITATIONS:
  1. To draw the graph, avoid overflowing, and make it easier to use,
     you should maximize the inputs to 17 sets of data.
```

3	95
4	218
5	312

If X = 14, what is Y, based on your model?

8. Let us say that in the year 2000 you will need $58,000 for your children's college education. How much should you deposit in a bank now in order to have this amount in year 2000 (assuming the interest rate is fixed at 10 percent)?

9.* What are some Lotus applications for running a small business?

10. In what capacity can Lotus be used in the marketing department of a travel agency?

11. What are some Lotus limitations in general?

FIGURE 21-5 *(Continued) Macro-Based Program for S-Curve Model*

```
\Z        {GOTO}INAREA~{PANELOFF}
          {GOTO}START~
          {GETNUMBER "How many sets of data to consider? ",DATA}~
          {FOR K,1,DATA,1,INPUT}{BRANCH LOOP}

INPUT     /XNEnter the independent var (X): ~~
          {RIGHT}              *--- To enter the data  ---*
          /XNEnter the dependent var (Y): ~~
          {DOWN}{LEFT}

DATA      10

K         11

LOOP      /RE{RIGHT}{PGDN}~{GOTO}HEAD~/REWORKAREA~     *--- get ready for new calculation ---*
          {GOTO}TOTAL~/MTOTAL~{END}{UP}{LEFT}{DOWN}{END}{DOWN 3}{RIGHT}~{GOTO}HEAD~{DOWN}
          /C{RIGHT 3}~{DOWN}.{LEFT 2}{END}{DOWN}{RIGHT 5}~
          {GOTO}SUM(X2)~/RE~{GOTO}HEAD~{DOWN}
ONE       /RNCTEMP~~        *--- The accumulator macro for SUM(X2) ---*
          {GOTO}SUM(X2)~
          {IF TEMP>0}{LET SUM(X2),SUM(X2)+TEMP}~
          {IF TEMP>0}{ACCU}
          {IF TEMP>0}{BRANCH ONE}
          /RNDTEMP~
          {GOTO}SUM(Y2)~/RE~{GOTO}HEAD2~
          {DOWN}
DUA       /RNCTEMP~~        *--- The accumulator macro for SUM(Y2) ---*
          {GOTO}SUM(Y2)~
          {IF TEMP>0}{LET SUM(Y2),SUM(Y2)+TEMP}~
          {IF TEMP>0}{ACCU}
          {IF TEMP>0}{BRANCH DUA}
          /RNDTEMP~
          {GOTO}SUM(X2Y2)~/RE~{GOTO}HEAD3~
          {DOWN}
THREE     /RNCTEMP~~        *--- The accumulator macro for SUM(X2Y2) ---*
          {GOTO}SUM(X2Y2)~
          {IF TEMP>0}{LET SUM(X2Y2),SUM(X2Y2)+TEMP}~
          {IF TEMP>0}{ACCU}
          {IF TEMP>0}{BRANCH THREE}
          /RNDTEMP~
          {GOTO}SUM(X2^2)~/RE~{GOTO}HEAD4~
          {DOWN}
FOUR      /RNCTEMP~~        *--- The accumulator macro for SUM(X2^2) ---*
          {GOTO}SUM(X2^2)~
          {IF TEMP>0}{LET SUM(X2^2),SUM(X2^2)+TEMP}~
          {IF TEMP>0}{ACCU}
          {IF TEMP>0}{BRANCH FOUR}          *--- The Prediction Macro ---*
          /RNDTEMP~{GOTO}RESULT~{GOTO}NUM~{RECALC OUTPUT}~{PANELON}
          {GETLABEL "Do you want to do any prediction? (Y)es or (N)o: ",ANSWER}{RECALC OUTPUT}~
          {IF ANSWER<>"y"}{BRANCH DRAW}
          {IF ANSWER<>"Y"}{BRANCH DRAW}
AGAIN     {GETNUMBER "The value of Independent Var: ",NUM}{RECALC ANS}~
          {GETLABEL "Do you want to try another one (Y)es or (N)o ? ",ANSWER}
          {IF ANSWER="y"}{BRANCH AGAIN}
          {IF ANSWER="Y"}{BRANCH AGAIN}
DRAW      {GETLABEL "Do you want to draw the graph? (Yes) or (N)o: ",answer}
          {IF ANSWER<>"y"}{quit}
          {IF ANSWER<>"Y"}{quit}        *--- To draw the S-Curve graph  ---*
          {GOTO}AVAR~/GRGTLXX-A{DOWN}.{END}{DOWN}~
          OTWB OLACIVEN VARS~
          LBTHE S-CURVE~
          FASQTXDEPENDENT VARS~
          TYINDEPENDENT VARS~QQ
          {GOTO}RESULT~
          {GETLABEL "Hit the <RET> & F10 key to see the graph ",ANSWER}{PANELON}
ACCU      {GOTO}TEMP~     *--- The accumulator subroutine ---*
          /RNDTEMP~
          {DOWN}/RNCTEMP~~
          {RETURN}

ANSWER          *--- Temporary storage range ---*
```

FIGURE 21-5 (Continued) Execution of the Macro-Based S-Curve Model

```
S1: [W4]                                                              READY

      S   T     U      U      W         X       Y        Z
1                      INCOME STATEMENT
2    ========================================================================
3                           1990
4    SALES ...............................................  $2,800,500
5    COST OF GOODS SOLD ..................................   1,200,000
6                                                           ---------
7    GROSS MARGIN ........................................   1,600,500
8    OPERATING EXPENSES
9         SELLING EXPENSES ........................  580,000
10        ADMINISTRATIVE EXPENSES .................  600,000
11                                                  ---------
12        TOTAL OPERATING EXPENSES ........................   1,180,000
13                                                           ---------
14   NET OPERATING INCOME  ...............................     420,500
15   INTEREST EXPENSES ...................................      12,000
16                                                           ---------
17   NET INCOME BEFORE TAXES .............................     408,500
18   INCOME TAXES AT .. 46% ..............................     220,590
19                                                           ===========
20   NET INCOME ..........................................    $187,910
01-Jan-91  08:16 AM          UNDO
```

```
I1: [W5]                                                              READY

     I     J     K        L         M         N         O       P
1              THE INPUT SECTION:
2    X     Y          X2=1/X   Y2=LN(Y)    X2*Y2     X2^2
3    1     35         1.0000    2.3026     2.3026    1.0000
4    2     49         0.5000    3.8918     1.9459    0.2500
5    3     55         0.3333    4.0073     1.3358    0.1111
6    4     69         0.2500    4.2341     1.0585    0.0625
7    5     80         0.2000    4.3820     0.8764    0.0400
8    6     105        0.1667    4.6540     0.7757    0.0278
9    7     140        0.1429    4.9416     0.7059    0.0204
10   8     165        0.1250    5.1059     0.6382    0.0156
11   9     180        0.1111    5.1930     0.5770    0.0123
12   10    173        0.1000    5.1533     0.5153    0.0100
13
14            TOTAL   2.9290   43.8657    10.7314    1.5498
15
16
17
18
19
20
01-Jan-91  11:57 AM          UNDO                     CALC
```

FIGURE 21-5 (Continued)

FIGURE 21-5 (Continued)

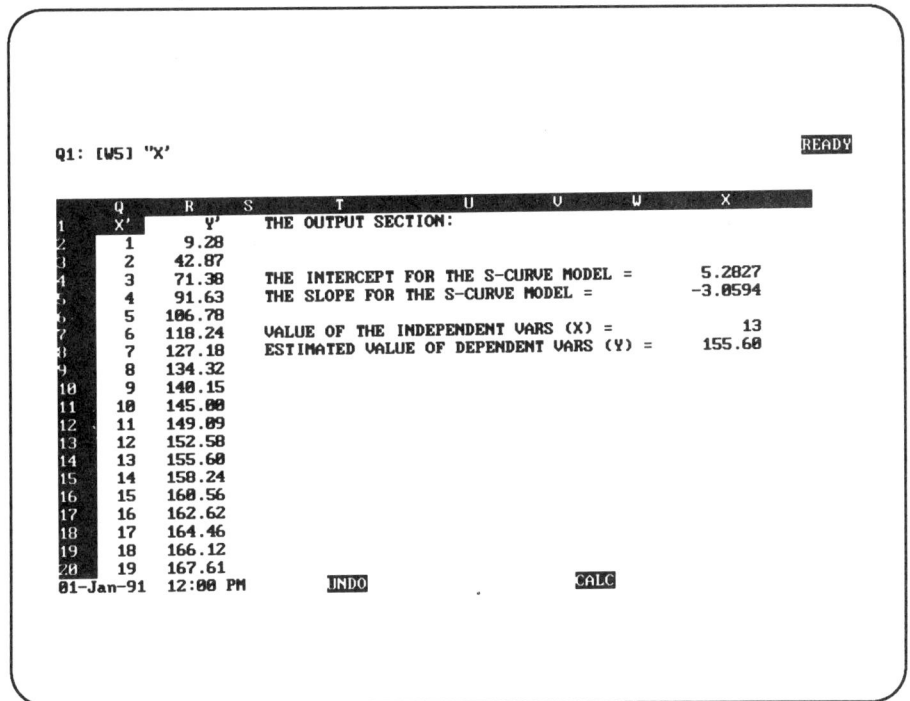

```
Q1: [W5] "X"                                                        READY

       Q     R    S        T          U        U      W       X
1      X'    Y'        THE OUTPUT SECTION:
2      1    9.28
3      2   42.87
4      3   71.38       THE INTERCEPT FOR THE S-CURVE MODEL =    5.2827
5      4   91.63       THE SLOPE FOR THE S-CURVE MODEL =       -3.0594
6      5  106.78
7      6  118.24       VALUE OF THE INDEPENDENT VARS (X) =        13
8      7  127.18       ESTIMATED VALUE OF DEPENDENT VARS (Y) =  155.60
9      8  134.32
10     9  140.15
11    10  145.00
12    11  149.09
13    12  152.58
14    13  155.60
15    14  158.24
16    15  160.56
17    16  162.62
18    17  164.46
19    18  166.12
20    19  167.61
01-Jan-91  12:00 PM      UNDO              .          CALC
```

12. The production of Generous Oil Well in Cactus City for the past six years is as follows:
1982 240,000 barrels
1983 290,000 barrels
1984 310,000 barrels
1985 285,000 barrels
1986 360,000 barrels
1987 395,000 barrels
Using simple regression, provide a forecast for the year 1997. Also generate a bar graph for the past six years.

* For more information on this technique and other business applications, see Hossein Bidgoli, *IBM BASIC with PC Literacy and DOS*, Macmillan Publishing, 1991.

Appendix A

You and Your PC:
A Friendly Interface

A-1 Introduction

In this appendix we will explain the different components of a microcomputer, discuss types of software, including system software and application software, and introduce some of the popular application software on the market. This should provide you with a better understanding of the operation of a microcomputer.

A-2 What Is a Microcomputer?

The terms personal computer, PC, or microcomputer refer to the smallest type of computer when measured by such attributes as memory size, speed, and sophistication. Although small, these computers are so powerful that sometimes the difference between a PC and minicomputer is blurred. The reason for such confusion is the ever-increasing power and capability of personal computers.

Since the beginning of the microcomputer era in roughly 1975, the capability of these computers has improved beyond imagination. Still, some experts believe this is only the beginning and there is a lot more that can be done by these computers.

A typical microcomputer consists of input, output, and memory devices. Figure A-1 illustrates a typical microcomputer system. The input device is usually a keyboard. A keyboard is very similar to a typewriter, with some additional keys. Figure A-2 illustrates an IBM PC standard keyboard. Figure A-3 illustrates an enhanced keyboard. In the future, there may be voice input devices on the market. Other input devices include a mouse, touch technology, light pens, graphics tablets, optical character readers (OCR), magnetic ink character recognition (MICR), cameras, senors, and bar codes.

The output device for a microcomputer is either a CRT (cathode-ray tube), VDT (video display terminal), or printer (impact or nonimpact). The output generated on the monitor is called soft copy and the printed output is referred to as hard copy. Other output devices include cameras and plotters.

There are two types of monitors. The majority of microcomputers utilize a monochrome-type screen. As the name indicates, this type of screen generates one color, such as green, although some are amber. Either monochrome or amber can generate graphic output if you have a graphics card or graphics adapter.

The other type of monitor is a color monitor (sometimes referred to as RGB—red-green-blue monitor). It shows data in a color format. Color monitors come in various levels of resolution. The term resolution refers to the sharpness of images on the display monitor.

FIGURE A-1 A Typical Microcomputer System

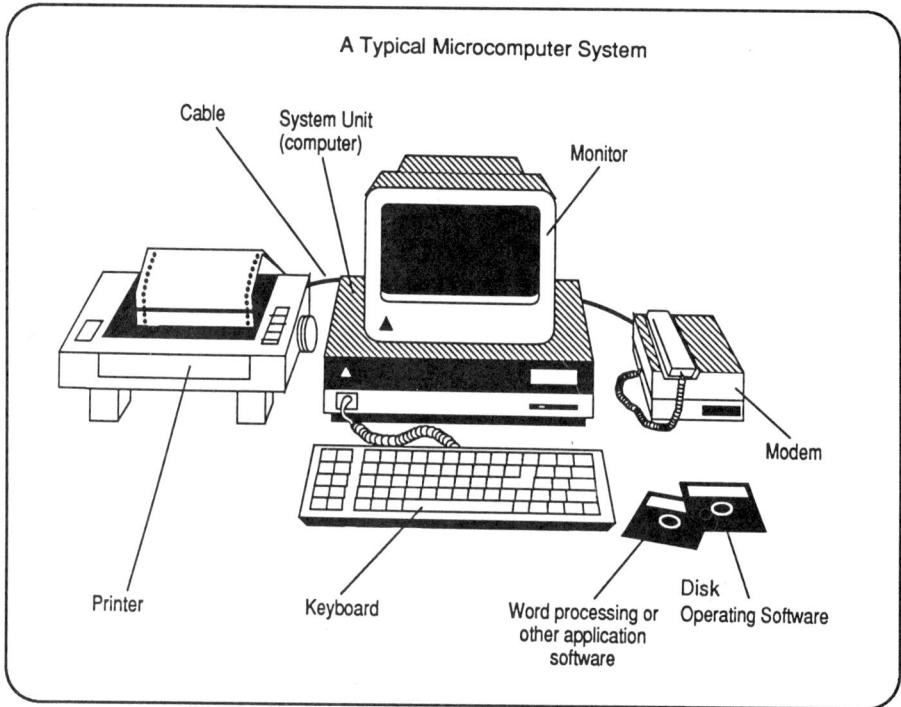

Color graphics adapters (CGA) display 320 by 200 pixels resolution in four colors. The intersection of a row and a column is called a pixel. The higher the number of pixels, the higher the resolution.

Enhanced graphics adapters (EGA) display 640 by 350 resolution in 16 colors. More advanced versions of EGA display 640 by 480 resolution in 16 colors and 320 by 200 resolution in 256 colors.

Video graphics array (VGA), the most recent graphics add-on card, displays 640 by 480 resolution in 16 colors and 320 by 200 resolution in 256 colors. This add-on card was introduced in 1987 by the IBM PS/2 series of computers.

The processing part of a microcomputer, or its CPU (central processing unit), includes three components:

The *main memory* stores data, information and instructions.

The *ALU (arithmetic-logic unit)* performs arithmetic and logic operations. Arithmetic operations include addition, subtraction, division, and multiplication. Logic operations include any types of comparisons, such as sorting (putting data into a particular order) or search (choosing a particular data item).

The *control unit* serves as the commander of the system. It tells the microcomputer what to do and how to do it.

A-3 More on the Keyboard

As you can see in Figure A-2, the typical keyboard has been divided into three sections. In the left section, there are 10 function keys. An enhanced keyboard includes 12 function keys located across the top. In most application software these keys perform special

FIGURE A-2 IBM PC Keyboard

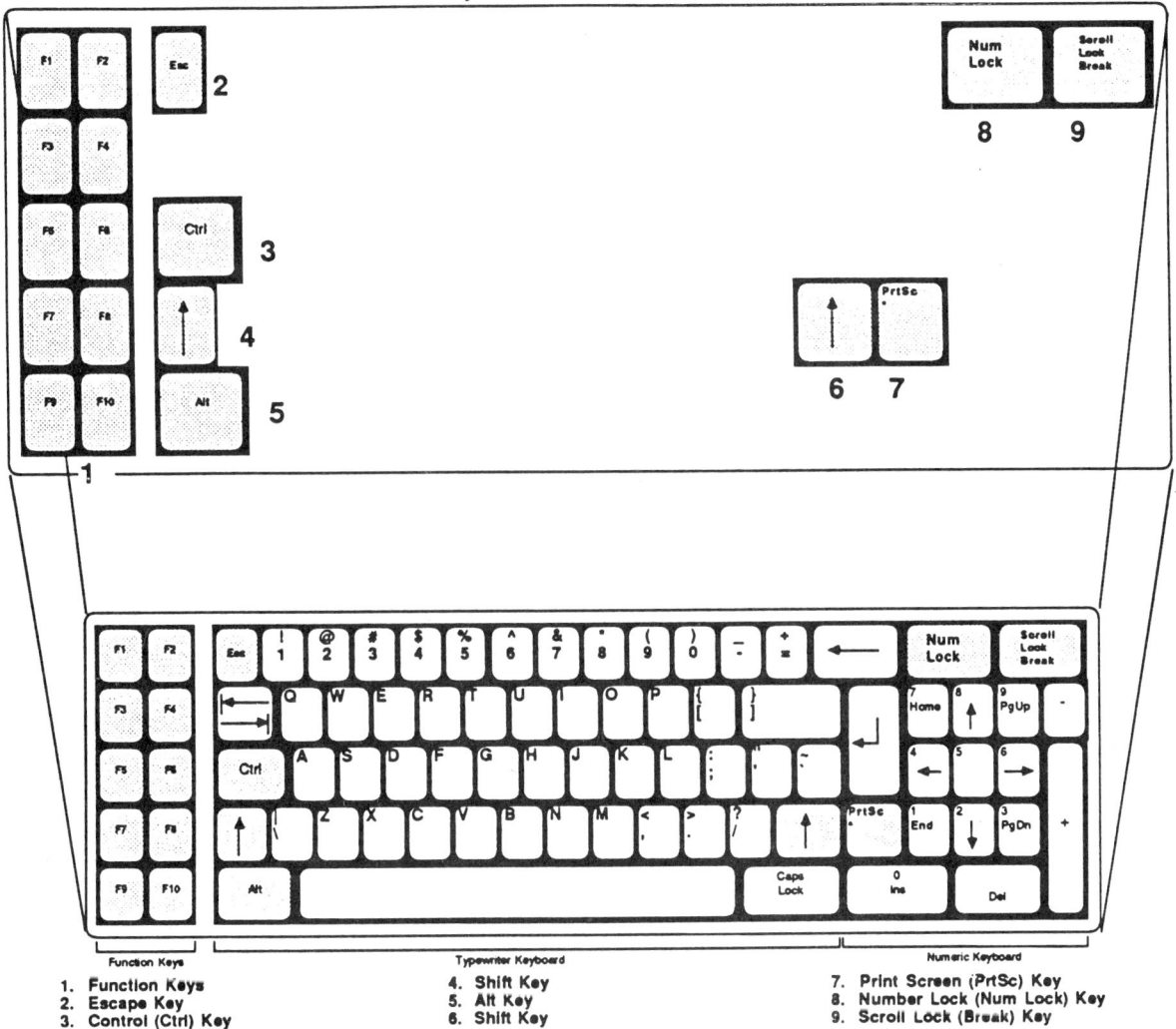

1.	Function Keys	4.	Shift Key	7.	Print Screen (PrtSc) Key
2.	Escape Key	5.	Alt Key	8.	Number Lock (Num Lock) Key
3.	Control (Ctrl) Key	6.	Shift Key	9.	Scroll Lock (Break) Key

functions. They can be programmed to perform a particular task. As we discussed in Chapter 4, Lotus effectively uses all 10 keys for performing different tasks.

The middle part of the keyboard is very similar to a typical typewriter. However, there are some special keys that a typewriter does not use, e.g., the Alt key.

The right section can serve both as a 10-key machine (when Num Lock is on) or for arrow movement.

Function keys have been designed for more convenient utilization of a software package or a program. For example, in 1-2-3 to receive on-line help, you press F1.

The **Escape (Esc)** key is used either to erase a line or exit from an operation (in Lotus). The **Control** key (**Ctrl**) is always used with another key. For example, **Ctrl** and **Break** together will halt the current operation.

Shift keys are used for generating uppercase characters or characters listed on the upper part of the keys.

Print Screen (PrtSc), if used with the **Shift** key, will print a hard copy of material on the screen. On enhanced keyboards pressing PrtSc alone will generate a hard copy of the material on the screen. **Number Lock (Num Lock)** will convert the right side of your keyboard into a 10-key machine for faster numeric data entry.

FIGURE A-3 An IBM Enhanced Keyboard

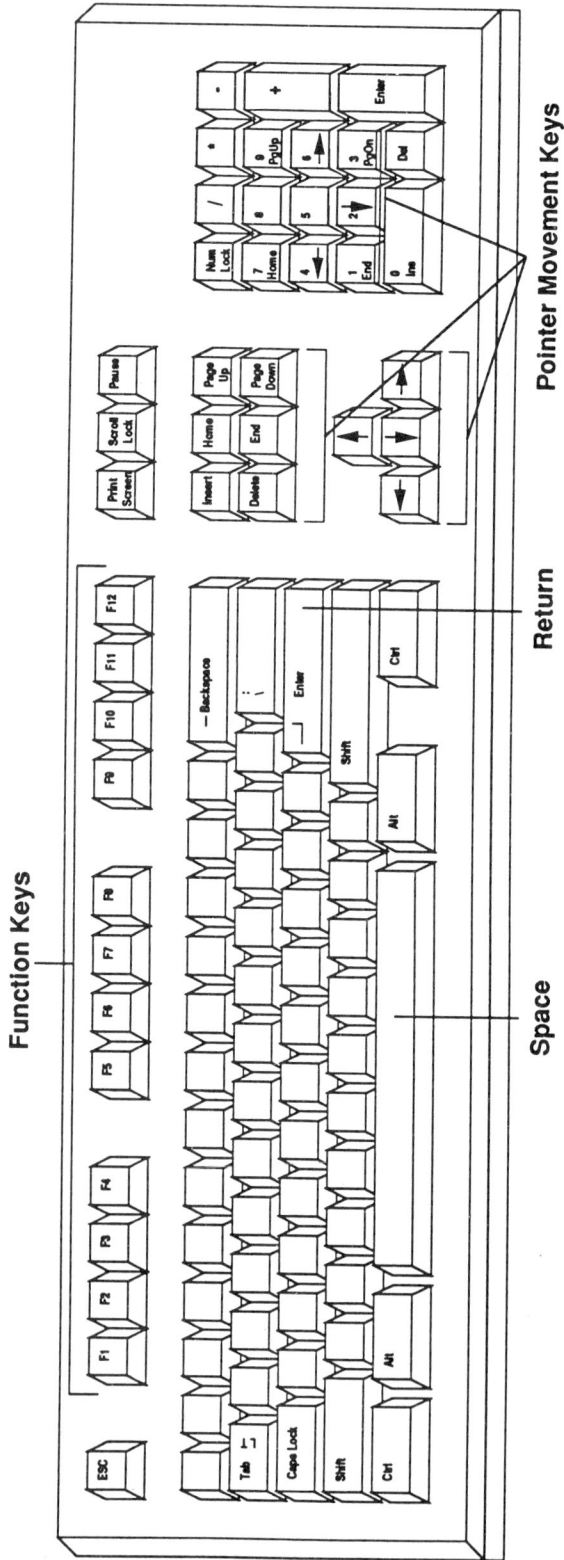

The purpose of function keys and some of the special keys may vary in different application programs. For example, F1 in BASIC gives you the listing of your program while in Lotus it will access an on-line help command. In WordPerfect, it is used as the Cancel key.

A-4 Types of Memories

There are two kind of memories: main memory and auxiliary (secondary) memory. Main memory is the heart of the microcomputer, usually referred to as RAM (random-access memory). This is a volatile memory. If you have any data in this memory and there is a power failure, all your work will be lost. To avoid this, you should always save your work on a permanent memory, such as a diskette.

Three other types of memories can be referred to as main memory, but the user cannot have direct access to them. These include:

ROM, read-only memory, a prefabricated chip supplied by vendors. This memory stores some general-purpose instructions or programs. For example, some DOS commands are stored on ROM chips.

PROM, programmable read-only memory. By using a special device the user can program this memory. However, when it is programmed, the user cannot erase it.

EPROM, erasable programmable read-only memory. This type of memory can be programmed and changed later on.

The second type of memory is called auxiliary or secondary memory. This includes diskette, mini floppy, hard disk, and Bernoulli Box. Since the main memory of a microcomputer is limited, expensive, and volatile (in case of a power shutdown, the information will be lost), we have to use secondary memory for storing permanent data. The capacity of a diskette or a hard disk depends on its technical features. There are three types of standard floppies: 3 1/2 inches, 5 1/4 inches, and 8 inches. They can be single-density, double-density, or high-density. They can also be single-sided or double-sided. A 5 1/4 inch, single-sided, double-density floppy can hold roughly 250K; a 5 1/4 double-sided, double-density floppy can hold roughly 500K; and a high-density can hold more than 500K. A 3 1/2 inch floppy stores either 720K or 1.44 megabytes of information. (A K or Kilobyte is the equivalent of 1024 characters.) The 2-inch floppy disks are already on the market and may become common in the near future.

A hard disk or Winchester disk can be either 14, 8, 5 1/4 or less than 4 inches in diameter. The capacity of these devices varies from 5 megabytes to 1 gigabyte.

A-5 Memory Capacity and Speed

The capacity of a storage device, either main or auxiliary, is measured in terms of bits of information stored on that device, as follows:

0 or 1 is equal to one bit
8 bits is equal to one byte
1,024 bytes is equal to one K
1,048,576 bytes is equal to one megabyte
1,073,741,824 bytes is equal to one gigabyte
10,995,627,776 bytes is equal to one terabyte

A byte is simply a character. For example, the word Bobby is 5 characters, or 5 bytes.

Microcomputers usually start from 512K or 640K and go up. Some vendors have already started offering 1 to 8 megabyte PCs.

For present and future planning you have to be able to do some calculations to get the memory requirements for your company's computing requirements. For example, if you have a PC with 640K of RAM, all of it may not be accessible to you. A large portion of this memory may be used by the application software. As an example, Lotus Release 2.2 (without Allways) takes up almost 320K of RAM. So in a 640K PC, you are left with only 320K of user memory (640 - 320 = 320).

Another consideration regarding memory is speed. The speed of the processor is measured in megahertz (MHz) and usually varies from 4 to 33. Soon we will see PCs with the speed of 50 MHz and maybe higher. Naturally, the higher the speed, the faster the computer. Another factor which has direct impact on speed is the word size of the processor. It varies from 8 to 32 bits for microcomputers. The bigger the word size the faster the computer would be. The speed of your microcomputer may have a direct impact on your business operation. With a faster computer you can process more information in a shorter period of time.

A-6 Hardware/Software Concepts

Any computer, regardless of its size, must include two sets of components in order to process data and information. The first component is hardware and the second component is software.

The hardware includes all the physical components of the microcomputer. Keyboard, printer, monitor, and disk drive are some examples of the hardware components of a microcomputer.

Software includes all the programs that run your microcomputer.

Before we go further, let us give a brief definition of a program. A program is simply a series of instructions for performing a particular task. For example, the following is a program in BASIC:

```
10    A   =      5
20    B   =      10
30    C   =      A+B
40    PRINT C
50    END
```

This program is telling a computer to add A and B, store the result in a place called C, then print the result.

Sometimes large programs are broken down into a series of smaller programs or modules. A subprogram or a module is usually called a subroutine. A subroutine is a series of instructions intended to perform a particular task needed in several places in a single program.

Software is divided into two groups: system software and application software. There are two types of system software: programming languages and operating systems.

Programming languages include BASIC, COBOL, FORTRAN, and so on. In order to code in any of these languages, you have to have a compiler (translator) for that language.

There are five classes of programming languages. The first class is called machine language. This language is closest to the machine and the most remote to human beings. It is simply a series of 1s and 0s. Coding in machine language is difficult and slow. Also, machine language coding is hardware dependent; this means a code written for IBM computers may not work for Honeywell computers.

The second class of programming languages is assembly languages. Coding in assembly language is simpler than in machine language. The codes are a series of mnemonics, short codes designed to perform specific tasks. They still must be translated in order to be understood by a computer. The translator for an assembly language program is called an assembler. Assembly languages are also machine dependent.

The third class is called high-level programming languages. There are more than 700 of these languages, which are more like English. Different types have been designed for different applications. For example, FORTRAN is designed for scientific applications and COBOL for business applications. Most of these languages are machine independent.

The fourth class of programming languages is called 4-GL (fourth-generation languages). These languages are very similar to English. There are many of these languages, too. IFPS (by Execucom), EXPRESS (by MDS), and AUTOFAB (by Capex) are some examples of these languages.

The fifth class, and probably the most exciting group from the user's point of view, is called natural languages. These are in the process of being developed further. Their aim is to make the user/computer interface *very* user-friendly.

As we discuss in Appendix B, the operating system, or more specifically, the disk operating system, is a program that runs the entire operation of your microcomputer.

Application software is designed to perform different applications. Some of these programs have a special purpose, for example a general ledger program. The others are general-purpose programs. In this group we can include spreadsheets, databases, word processing, communication, graphics, and so on.

A-7 More on Application Software

There are many different application software programs on the market for microcomputers. This software covers a broad range of applications.

Spreadsheet programs are of two types. The first is a dedicated spreadsheet, which only performs spreadsheet analysis. VisiCalc (by VisiCorp) is a good example of this type.

The other type of spreadsheet, such as Lotus, is integrated software, which can perform more than one task. Lotus can perform spreadsheet analysis as well as creating databases and graphics. In any case, the number of tasks performed by a spreadsheet program is unlimited. Throughout this book, you have seen many applications of Lotus as an integrated package. Other popular spreadsheet include Quattro (by Borland International) and Excel (by Microsoft Corp.).

Database programs are designed to perform database operations. This includes file creation, deletion, modification, search, sort, combine, and so on. As we discussed in Chapters 16–17, Lotus is capable of performing some basic database operations. Other popular database programs include dBASE III Plus (by Ashton-Tate), Business Filevision (by Telos Software Products), PC-File III (by Buttonware, Inc.), and FoxBase by Fox Software.

A *word processing program* or a dedicated word processor or a microcomputer used as a word processor is very similar to a typewriter with a memory. With such a facility, you can generate documents, delete, insert, cut and paste, and so forth. There are numerous word processing programs on the market. Some of the popular ones include WordStar (by MicroPro International), Officewriter (by Office Solutions), and WordPerfect (by WordPerfect Corp.).

Graphics software has been designed to convert data into graphics. As we explained in Chapter 14, Lotus provides some impressive graphics capabilities. However, there are some limitations. For example, you can plot only up to six data ranges. There are some popular dedicated graphics packages on the market. These include Freelance (by Lotus Development Corporation) and Harvard Graphics (by Software Publishing Corporation).

Communications software, using a modem, enables your microcomputer to connect you to a wealth of information available in public and private databases. Some packages such as Symphony (by Lotus Development Corp.) include a communication program within the package itself. However, there are many other communications software programs on the market. Among them are On-Line (by Micro-Systems Software), Pfs:Access (by Software Publishing Corp.), Smartcom II (by Hayes Microcomputer Products, Inc.), and Crosstalk (by Microstuf, Inc.).

There are many other application software packages, which cover such areas as education, desktop publishing, finance, general utility, and more. You can do a lot with your microcomputer. Be creative!

A-8 Guidelines for Successful Selection of a Microcomputer

There are many microcomputers on the market, which makes the selection task a difficult one. We will provide you with some general guidelines regarding the purchase and maintenance of a microcomputer. These guidelines may help you to choose a suitable computer and have an easier time maintaining it.

Before you start, you must define your requirements. Sometimes this is called the wish list approach. You should have a clear idea of buying a microcomputer and the specific applications you want it to handle.

After the needs are defined, you have to think about software. Remember, if there is software, there must be hardware to run it.

After defining the software and hardware, you must look at technical support and vendor reputation. We have summarized the important factors regarding selection and maintenance of a microcomputer:

Software Selection
Good software must:

• have a reasonable cost
• be easy to use
• be able to handle your business volume
• have good documentation
• have training available
• have updates available (free of charge or for a minimum charge)
• have local support
• come from a reputable vendor

Hardware Selection (processor and keyboard)
Good hardware must:

• have a reasonable cost
• have a comfortable keyboard
• have function keys
• have a general operating system, e.g., MS-DOS, PC-DOS, OS/S, etc.
• have 16-bit or bigger processor size
• be expandable (memory and peripheral)
• have enough channel capacity or expansion slots (for peripherals to be attached to)

Hardware Selection (CRT)
A good monitor must:

• have a separate CRT (not a built-in one)
• be easy to read (high resolution)
• hold a standard number of characters per row and column

Hardware Selection (disk drive and hard drive)
A good disk drive must:

• have a built-in, not separate, disk drive
• have reasonable storage capacity
• have a hard disk option

Hardware Selection (printer)
A good printer must:

• have a reasonable cost
• have a standard printer interface (without additional devices)
• produce quality output
• have reasonable speed
• have a reasonable amount of noise suppression
• let you change tape, ribbons, and toner easily

Vendor Selection
A good vendor must:

• have a good reputation
• have knowledgeable staff
• have training available for hardware and software
• have a hot-line available
• support newsletter and user groups
• provide a "loaner" in case of breakdown
• provide updates, e.g., trade-in options

Contract Selection
A good contract must:

• have a reasonable warranty period (3 months to 1 year)
• state a flexible time for repair
• have reasonable terms for contract renewal
• allow relocation and/or reassignment of the present contract
• observe confidentiality issues

Taking Care of Your Microcomputer
To maintain the health of your microcomputer you must consider the following factors:

• Protect your microcomputer against dirt, dust, and smoke.
• Make backups for security reasons.
• Avoid any kind of liquid spills.
• Maintain steady power. Use surge protectors for power fluctuations and use lightning arrestors in mountainous areas.
• Protect the machine from static by using humidifiers or antistatic devices.

A-9 You and Your Microcomputer

If the disk operating system (DOS) is in drive A, when you turn the computer on, your microcomputer will ask for the date. Remember, any IBM or IBM compatible comes with a DOS disk. Either type the date in the desired format or press the **Return** key. The computer then asks you for the time. Either type the time in the desired format or press the **Return** key. Now you are at the A> prompt. Figure A-4 illustrates how to get the system started. If your computer has a hard disk this procedure is slightly different. You will get the system started from the hard disk and your prompt will be C> instead of A>. In any case, from this mode or disk operating system mode you can go to any application software. For example, pull the DOS diskette out, put the Lotus System diskette in, and then type 123 and press the **Return** key. As we mention in Appendix B, from DOS you can access any other application software.

SUMMARY

In this appendix, we explained microcomputer components including hardware and software. We explained main and auxiliary memories. We briefly introduced the memory and speed capabilities of a typical microcomputer. Different types of software were introduced. The information provided in this appendix should help you to better understand the operation of your microcomputer.

REVIEW QUESTIONS

* These questions are answered in Appendix I.
1. What is a PC?
2.* Are a PC and a microcomputer the same?
3. What are some of the components of a typical PC?
4. What are the components of the CPU?
5.* What is the purpose of the function keys on the keyboard?
6. Can these function keys be programmed? If yes, how?
7. How many types of memories are there?

FIGURE A-4 Getting the System Started

```
Current date is Tue 1-01-1980
Enter new date (mm-dd-yy): 1-1-1991
Current time is 0:00:25.04
Enter new time: 8:45


The IBM Personal Computer DOS
Version 3.30 (C)Copyright IBM Corp 1981, 1982, 1983, 1984, 198?

A>
```

8.* What factors determine the speed of a PC?
9. How much is a terabyte?
10. How many different types of software do we have?
11. What is the difference between system software and application software?
12. What are some examples of application software?
13. Where does Lotus fit in software categories?
14.* When you turn on a PC, what will happen?
15. Is the A> prompt a DOS prompt or a Lotus prompt?
16.* Is DOS in ROM or RAM or neither?
17. Mention 10 factors that should be considered before choosing a microcomputer.
18. How can your microcomputer communicate with another PC?
19. What is the computer language of the future?

Appendix B

Disk Operating System

B-1 Introduction

In this appendix we provide you with a quick review of the disk operating system for the IBM PC and PC compatibles. We'll cover disk file creation and use, customizing your system, and manipulation of your directory. We also list more than 50 of the most commonly used DOS commands.

B-2 What is DOS?

In simple terms, DOS (disk operating system) is a collection of programs that enable you to interact with your computer. There are several uses for DOS:

• getting the system started
• housekeeping (e.g., creating backup disks)
• house cleaning (e.g., deleting redundant files)
• customizing your PC (changing the prompt, self-booting your system, etc.)
• helping individuals with minimum computer background with easier system access

There are several versions of DOS available. Some of them are general purpose, such as OS/2, MS-DOS, PC-DOS, and UNIX. Many software programs can be run by these operating systems. Each special-purpose DOS has been designed for a particular microprocessor chip and brand of computer, for example, Apple DOS or TRS DOS. Naturally, these operating systems run only the products for which they were designed.

Many advanced features, such as directory designing and program linkage, can be done by DOS. However, these topics are beyond the scope of this appendix.[1]

In this appendix we only discuss MS-DOS or PC-DOS. You can always assume that between you and your application program (Lotus) there is a gate called DOS. To get to your Lotus program you have to go through DOS.

B-3 Types of DOS Commands

When you get your system started have the DOS disk in drive A and turn the computer on. Usually the system will ask you for the date and time. If you respond with the date and time in the proper format, the A> prompt will appear. You can bypass the date and time

---

1   For more information, consult Hossein Bidgoli, *Introduction to MS-PC DOS With PC Literacy*, Macmillan Publishing Company, 1991.

by pressing the **Return** key twice, but it is a good practice to enter them. If you save a program, the date an time will be saved in your program. You will know which version of your program is the most recent. Figure B-1 shows this process.

The A> prompt means the disk operating system is activated in disk drive A. In other words, your default drive is A. You can change A to B or C by typing B: or C: and pressing the **Return** key. The default drive is always A unless a hard disk is used to boot DOS (the computer assumes your selected drive is A). It is possible to change the system prompt by using the DOS command PROMPT. For example, if at A> you type PROMPT Good Morning, your prompt will be changed to Good Morning. Also, if you type PROMPT PG, you will be able to see exactly in what directory or subdirectory you are at any given time. It is a very good idea to type PROMPT PG at the beginning of the session at the DOS prompt.

At this point you can access two types of DOS commands: external and internal. To execute any external command, you must have the DOS disk in one of your disk drives. An example of an external command is DISKCOPY (Disk copy - for copying a disk). All the commands and files with the extensions BAT, COM, or EXE are external. To execute an internal command the DOS disk does not need to be in any of the drives. At the A> prompt, for example, you can type CLS and press **Return** to clear the screen.

B-4 File Specifications

Any disk file will have three distinct parts:

• drive name and/or directory name

FIGURE B-1 *Getting the System Started*

```
Current date is Tue 1-01-1980
Enter new date (mm-dd-yy): 1-1-1991
Current time is 0:00:25.04
Enter new time: 8:45


The IBM Personal Computer DOS
Version 3.30 (C)Copyright IBM Corp 1981, 1982, 1983, 1984, 1987

A>
```

• file name
• file extension

A drive name can be A:, B:, C:, etc. If you do not specify a drive name, the computer assumes the default drive is selected. A directory is a specific location on a disk.

A file name can be up to eight characters long. It can include digits 0 to 9. Don't use reserved words as file names, such as DISKCOPY or CON (console).

The file extension is optional. If used, it can be up to three characters in length. Digits can be used as well.

You should always remembers which drive is the source drive and which is the target drive. The source drive is the one with the original program and the target drive is the one to which you transfer a copy. Mistaking these two drives can be dangerous.

It is a good practice to select names that have some meaning. For example, Payroll, Credit, or Check are some good names for business applications. Don't include any spaces in your file names or extensions. Uppercase and lowercase are treated the same.

B-5 Wild Card Characters

Two characters have specific meaning to DOS. One is the question mark(?) and the other is the asterisk (*). When you use the question mark it means any character in that particular position. For example, at the A> prompt if you type DIR AB?JACK you will see the following files (assuming such files are in the A drive):

ABAJACK
ABXJACK
ABBJACK
ABZJACK
ABCJACK, etc.

When you use the asterisk, it means that from that position on you can have any characters. For example, at the A> prompt DIR AB* will list all files starting with the letters AB. The rest of the name is not considered. At the A> prompt DIR *.* will give you all the files with any name and any extension. A>DIR *.WK1 will give you all the files with extension WK1. DIR *.WK? will give you a listing of all different versions of Lotus files such as WKS, WKE and WK1.

These two wild cards can be very helpful for accessing specific files. For example, COPY B:*.WK1 will copy all the worksheet files from the disk in drive B to the disk in drive A, assuming your current drive is A.

B-6 Redirection and Piping

It is possible to direct the output of a command to a different device other than the standard one, such as a monitor. For example, at the A> prompt DIR>PRN will transfer the listing of your directory to the printer. At the A> prompt DIR>Myfile will transfer the listing of your directory to a file called "Myfile."

Piping takes lace when you combine two commands. For example, A>DIR|SORT (remember SORT is an external command) will sort your current directory. DIR|SORT>Myfile will sort your current directory and write the output into a file called "Myfile." Then, at the A> prompt you can type TYPE Myfile and the computer will give you the sorted listing of your files.

B-7 Batch and Autoexec Files

Batch files are disk files designed for a specific use. A batch file can have any standard name but the extension must be always BAT. In theory, batch files can have any length. You can include any valid command or statement in your batch file. To enter a command, you must first type the command and then press the Return key after the specific command. To generate a batch file you can use EDLIN, the line editor available on DOS, or any word processing program. For simple files you can use a version of the copy command. At the A> prompt type:

```
COPY CON My file.BAT   (press Return)
Command or statement   (  "      "   )
     "            "     (  "      "   )
     "            "     (  "      "   )
```

To save a batch file press **Ctrl** and **Z** together or the F6 function key. To execute a batch file all you need to do is to type the name of the file at the A> prompt.

We have designed a simple batch file as follows:

```
COPY CON HELLO.BAT   (press Return)
DIR                  (  "      "   )
CLS                  (  "      "   )
BASICA               (  "      "   )
                     (press Ctrl -Z) (press Ctrl and Z keys together)
```

If you type HELLO at the A> prompt, you will see your directory, the screen will clear, and BASICA will be loaded to RAM (assuming BASICA is on the disk in the A drive).

The only limitation with COPY CON is that you cannot edit a file that has been created. For editing you have to redo the entire file, use EDLIN, or use some other word processing or editor-type systems. In other words, COPY CON does not provide any editing features.

To stop the execution of a batch file, press Ctrl and Break at the same time.

If you name your file AUTOEXEC.BAT, it will be executed automatically as soon as you get the system started. As a matter of fact, DOS always looks for this file first. If you have such a file all its commands will be executed. This facility can be very helpful. You can design a menu or customize your system and also help other people unfamiliar with computers. Batch files in general are very helpful if you have to do a series of repetitive operations.

B-8 Directory and Subdirectory in DOS

In order to effectively manage all the files in your secondary storage device (diskette and/or hard disk), it is advisable to establish a tree-structured directory. In this fashion, you will be able to organize groups of related files in separate directories. To access a particular file you have to define a path leading to it. Let us assume that Ocean City Manufacturing has stored all its files on a hard disk using a PC as follows:

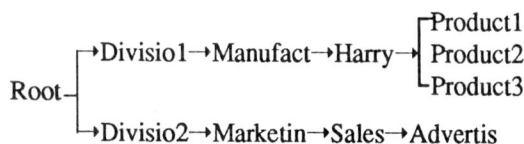

```
                                        ┌Product1
           ┌→Divisio1→Manufact→Harry→┤ Product2
Root─┤                                 └Product3
           └→Divisio2→Marketin→Sales→Advertis
```

This tree-structured directory can help you access any of these files more effectively than a simple directory. For example, to list all the files under Product1 from the root directory, you have to type:

DIR Division1\Manufacturing\Harry\Product1

The root directory always starts with a backslash (\). This directory is automatically generated when you format a diskette. The distance to reach to a particular file is called the path of that file. The above path for Product1 is one example. A root directory in a single-sided diskette can hold up to 64 files, a double-sided up to 112, and a high-density diskette can hold up to 224 files.

There is another type of directory called the subdirectory. Subdirectory names follow the same format as file names. The extension is optional.

The default directory is called the current directory. You can always change the current directory by using the CHDIR (CD) command. In the above example, to change the root directory to Sales, you will type:

CD\Divisio2\Marketin\Sales

There is no limitation on the number of subdirectories. As we discussed earlier, the subdirectories are separated by a series of backslashes (\). Remember, the length of a directory path cannot exceed 63 characters. To create a directory you use the MKDIR (MD) command. To display the directory structure, you must use the TREE command. As an example, to establish the subdirectories mentioned earlier you type:

MD	Diviso1	(press **Return**)
MD	Diviso2	(press **Return**)
CD	Diviso1	(press **Return**)
CD	Harry	(press **Return**)
MD	Product1	(press **Return**)
MD	Product2	(press **Return**)
MD	Product3	(press **Return**)

You have to do the same steps for Diviso2. To remove a directory, you first must erase all the files and consequent directories. Then by using the RD command you can remove a given directory.

B-9 Important DOS Commands

In Table B-1 we have summarized most of the commonly used commands in DOS. To become more familiar with these commands you have to practice them. All you need is a DOS disk and a blank diskette. Remember that FORMAT and DISKCOPY commands can be very dangerous!

We have divided these commands into two groups. Group 1 is used quite often. Group 2 is for advanced users and advanced applications. Following are brief descriptions of some of these commands.

The COPY command is used for copying one or a series of individual files. The source and target drives can be any drive.

The CHDSK command is used in order to find out about any free space on a particular diskette and your computer RAM memory.

CLS is used to clear the screen. This is an example of a DOS internal command.

DEL or ERASE is used for the deletion of a disk file. Remember, to delete a disk file, you must always use the file name and extension.

DIR is used for displaying the directory of your system. The drive identified can be A:, B:, C:, etc.

DISKCOPY is used for duplicating a diskette. When you use this command, the target diskette does not need to be formatted. DISKCOPY formats the target diskette while it is doing the copying.

DISKCOMP and COMP are used for comparing two diskettes and comparing two files, respectively. If two diskettes and/or two files are not identical you receive an error message.

FORMAT is used to format, or prepare, a diskette. Any brand new disk must be formatted before it can be used. If for any reason the diskette is damaged, you will receive an error message.

FORMAT/V command is used for formatting and labeling a diskette. Labeling simply means putting a name on your diskette. The label name can be any combination of characters up to 11. This is a nice feature to have for internal identification of diskettes. For example, one diskette could be for total sales, one for total cost, and so on.

The RENAME command is used for changing a file name to a different one.

The TYPE command will give you a listing of the contents of a file in DOS.

To implement the majority of DOS commands, type the command, then follow the system prompt.

TABLE B-1 IMPORTANT DOS COMMANDS

(To execute all these commands we assume the "A>" prompt is apparent.)
A stands for A drive
B stands for B drive
ext stands for file extension (any three valid characters)
Filename can be any valid file name

Group 1

COPY Filename.ext B:	Copy Filename.ext to B
COPY B:Filename.ext	Copy Filename.ext to A
COPY *.ext B:	Copy all files with the same ext from A to B
COPY B:*ext	Copy all files with the same ext from B to A
COPY *.*B:	Copy all files from A to B
COPY B:*.*	Copy all files from B to A
COPY Filename1.ext Filename2.ext	Copy a file from A to A with a different name
COPY B:Filename1.ext B:Filename2.ext	Copy a file from B to B with a different name
COPY Filename1.ext B:Filename2.ext	Copy a file from A to B with a different name
COPY B:Filename1.ext Filename2.ext	Copy a file from B to A with a different name
CHKDSK	Displays free space on diskette and RAM
CHKDSK B:	Displays free space on diskette in drive B
COMP	Compares two disk files to determine if they are the same or if they are different
CLS	Clears the screen
CTRL - ALT - DEL	System reset
DATE	To reset system date
DEL Filename.ext	To erase Filename.ext from drive A
DEL B:Filename.ext	To erase Filename.ext from drive B
DEL B:Filename.*	To erase all Filename with any extension from drive B (with the same file name)

DEL B:*.ext	To erase all files with the same extension from drive B
DIR	Directory of A
DIR B:	Directory of B
DIR/P	To display a complete directory of drive A with a pause before scrolling off the screen
DIR B:/P	Does the same as above, for drive B
DIR/W	To display a wide directory of drive A
DIR B:/W	To display a wide directory of drive B
DIR ISORT	To display a sorted directory of drive A
DISKCOPY A: B:	Copy a diskette in drive A to a diskette in drive B
DISKCOMP	Compares two diskettes track by track, sector for sector to determine if their contents are identical
ERASE Filename.ext	Erase Filename.ext on A
ERASE B:Filename.ext	Erase Filename.ext on B
ERASE *.ext	Erase all files with the same .ext on A
ERASE B:*.ext	Erase all files with the same .ext on B
FORMAT	Erases and formats a diskette
FORMAT B:	Erases and formats a diskette in drive B
FORMAT/V	To format a diskette with a volume label
FORMAT B:/V	To format a diskette with a volume label in drive B
LABEL	Creates, changes, or deletes a volume label for a disk
RENAME Filename1.ext Filename2.ext	Rename a file on A
RENAME B:Filename1.ext B:Filename2.ext	Rename a file on B
SHIFT - PrtSc key (or only PrtSc on enhanced keyboards)	To print a copy of the screen
TYPE Filename.ext	Display content of Filename.ext on A
TYPE B:Filename.ext	Display content of Filename.ext on B
TIME	To reset system time

Group 2

ASSIGN	Tells DOS to use a different disk drive from the one specified by a program or command
ATTRIB	To make a file a read-only file. If a file is read-only, it cannot be erased accidently. ATTRIB + R Filename.ext makes a file read-only. ATTRIB - R Filename.ext removes the read-only status.
BACKUP	Backs up files from a hard disk or diskette onto a diskette or another hard disk
CHDIR (CD)	Changes the current directory or displays the current directory path.
CD\	Changes the current directory of drive A to its root directory.
MKDIR (MD)	Creates a subdirectory on a disk

PATH	Instructs DOS to search a specified directory for a program that cannot be found in the current directory
PROMPT	Customizes the DOS system prompt
RECOVER	Recovers a disk or a file with defective sectors
RESTORE	To put a crashed hard disk back in order. RESTORE A: C:*.*/S copies backup files from drive A to drive C
RMDIR (RD)	Removes a subdirectory from a disk
SYS	Puts a copy of operating system files IBMDOS.COM and IBMBIO.COM on the specified diskette or hard disk
TREE	Displays the structure of the current directory
VER	Displays the DOS version number on the screen
VERIFY	Checks the data just written to a disk to be sure the data has been correctly recorded and then displays whether the data has been checked VERIFY ON › sets verify status on VERIFY OFF › sets verify status off VERIFY › shows verify status
VOL	Displays the volume label of a disk, if the label exists

SUMMARY

In this appendix we have provided a brief discussion of disk operating system, DOS, as the starting point for using any application program and Batch and AUTOEXEC files for more convenient system operations. We have also provided you with two sets of DOS commands. Group 1 consists of some of the most commonly used while group 2 commands are used for advanced applications. Knowledge of these commands should be very helpful for more effective use of your PC.

REVIEW QUESTIONS

*These questions are answered in Appendix I.
1. What is DOS?
2. How many different types of DOS do we have?
3.* Which DOS is used for the IBM PC? For its clone/compatibles?
4.* What is the difference between external and internal DOS commands?
5. How many different DOS prompts do we have?
6.* What is the purpose of the DATE and TIME commands?
7. How do you bypass these prompts?
8. Can you customize your DOS prompt? If yes, how?
9.* What is the difference between DISKCOPY and COPY *.*?
10. When you use DISKCOPY, do you need to format your diskette first or not?

11. What is a batch file?
12. What are some of the uses of a batch file?
13. How do you design a batch file?
14. What is an AUTOEXEC file?
15. What are some of the uses of an AUTOEXEC file?
16. How many different ways can you use the DIR command?
17. How do you rescue a file from a damaged disk?
18. How do you stop the execution of a batch file?

HANDS-ON PRACTICE

1. Get your system started. Format a blank disk, then copy three files from DOS disk to this blank disk.
2. Copy your DOS disk to any blank disk.
3. Using the wild card *, get a listing of all files with the BAS extension.
4. Sort your directory and direct the result to a file called Sfile. Now, using your printer, generate a printed copy of this file.
5. Generate a batch file that, when it is used, will do the following:
   Change directory B:
   Change directory back to A:
   Generate a wide directory
   Erase the screen
6. Generate a directory that includes three subdirectories as follows:
   Worksheet
   Graph
   Print
   Include three files in each subdirectory.
7. Using ATTRIB, make the COMMAND.COM in your DOS disk a read-only file.

MISCONCEPTIONS AND SOLUTIONS

M – If you want to transfer the content of one diskette to another, you can either use DISKCOPY or COPY *.*. However, DISKCOPY will first erase the content of the second diskette, then copy the first diskette to the second one.

S – Use COPY *.* if you want to keep the content of the second diskette.

M – You turn the computer on, and you may see a message which is not familiar to you, e.g., OK Prompt instead of A> prompt. Your computer has booted the BASIC from ROM.

S – You either forgot to put the DOS disk in drive A or you inserted your disk from the wrong direction. Insert the DOS disk into drive A and reboot the system.

M – You issue a DOS command and the error message says BAD COMMAND.

S – You have probably issued a DOS external command without having the DOS disk in one of the drives. Insert DOS into the right drive and issue the appropriate command again.

Appendix C

Installing Lotus

C-1 Introduction

In this appendix, we will explain how you can tailor Lotus to your particular system. This procedure is needed if you just purchased Lotus or if you made some changes in your existing equipment. You do the installation only once. Installation simply means tailoring Lotus to different hardware. If you do not install Lotus your program will still run, but you won't be able to use your printer or generate any graphs. This appendix should answer questions regarding tailoring the Lotus program to different systems.

C-2 Why Is Installation Needed?

Since Lotus has been designed to work on many different systems, you must tailor this program to your specific hardware. Installation is needed for three different components:

Monitor Which monitor are you planning to use (color, black and white, monochrome with Hercules graphics card, etc.)?

Printer Is it a standard dot matrix printer, letter quality, a printer with 132 characters, laser, or ink jet printer?

Secondary Storage (data disk) Which drive will be used for storing data and programs generated by Lotus, drive A, drive B, or drive C (hard disk)?

C-3 Getting Ready for Installation

To install Lotus 1-2-3, follow these steps:

• Initialize the system disk.
• Make a backup copy of all the disks.
• Install the 1-2-3 disks on your system.

C-4 Initializing 1-2-3

First you must transfer your name and your company name (if any) to the Lotus system disk. Follow these steps:

1. At the A> prompt insert the Lotus system disk in drive A.
2. Type INIT and press Enter.

3. Lotus asks for your name. You can type your first and last name. Together they can be up to 30 characters. After typing your name press Enter, then press Y (yes) to confirm this. If you make typing mistakes before confirmation you can correct them by using the Backspace key.

4. Type your company name (if there is any) and press the Enter key. When Lotus tells you that initialize is complete, press Enter to return to the operating system prompt.

C-5 Backing Up Your 1-2-3 Disks

Lotus 1-2-3 Release 2.2 comes in one of the following packages:

5 1/4" Disks	**3 1/2" Disks**
System Disk	System, Help, and PrintGraph Disk
Help Disk	Translate and Sample Files Disk
PrintGraph Disk	Install and Install Library Disk
Translate Disk	
Install Disk	
Install Library Disk	
Sample Files Disk	

Release 2.2 also includes the Allways disks.

The system disk includes everything you need except instructions for printing graphs. This information is stored on the PrintGraph disk. Before you do the installation, it is advisable to make a backup copy of all disks and do the installation with the copies. In case of damage to any of the backup disks, you will still have an original copy of it. To make backup copies of 1-2-3 disks, follow these steps:

1. Prepare (format) seven 5 1/4" or three 3 1/2" disks. To do so put the DOS disk in drive A, put a blank disk in drive B, type FORMAT B:, and press the Enter key. If you have a hard disk, you can insert the blank disk in drive A and issue the Format command from the C drive. Do this for all the disks. (For more information on formatting, see Appendix B.)

2. Now you have to make a copy of all the disks. At the A> prompt put one of the formatted disks in drive B, one of the original disks in drive A, then type Copy *.* B: and press the Enter key. Follow these steps for all the other disks. You now have a backup copy of all the disks.

C-6 Getting Ready for Installation: Hard Disk Systems

If you have a system with hard disks (drive C) and one floppy drive (drive A), follow these steps:

You have to copy all Lotus disks onto your hard disk.

1. If drive C is not the default drive, make it the default drive by typing C: and pressing the **Return** key.

2. Create a subdirectory to hold 1-2-3 programs. Type MD 123 and press Enter (see Appendix B for more information on subdirectories).

3. Make this subdirectory the current directory by typing CD 123 and press Enter.

4. Now copy all Lotus disks onto drive C by putting one of the disks in drive A and typing COPY *.* C:. Do this for the other disks.

Now, you are ready to go to the Install program.

C-7 Installing the Drivers

To tailor Lotus to your particular system, you have to transfer a series of drivers to Lotus disks. Drivers are simply a series of programs that monitor and run the hardware. To run the Install program, you must know the specifications of your hardware. To get the procedure started, put the DOS disk in drive A and boot the system. At the A> prompt, pull the DOS disk out, put the Install disk into drive A, and type INSTALL. This procedure is for a two-disk drive system. For hard disk systems you first have to change the current directory to the subdirectory containing the Lotus programs (CD C:\123) and at the C prompt type INSTALL. In any event, you will be given a screen describing the procedure. Press the **Return** key and the program will ask you to remove the Install disk and put the Install Library disk in drive A. Do this and press the **Return** key. Now it asks you to put the System disk in drive A and press the **Return** key. The Install menu will appear. You will be given four options:

First-Time Installation
Change Selected Equipment
Advanced Options
Exit Install Program

If you just purchased Lotus, choose First-Time Installation, Change Selected Equipment is used if you must change one of your components. Advanced Options allows you to do certain things that you can't do elsewhere in the Install program; for example, adding new drivers to the library, modifying the current drivers set, or changing the collating sequence (for sorting, the number to come first or the number to be last). The last option is used to exit the menu. The rest of the procedure basically means following a series of menus. If you follow these menus carefully, you should not have any problem installing the Lotus program for any system that Lotus supports.

Driver programs must be installed on the System disk and PrintGraph. You can do these one by one, replacing the System disk with the next disk.

C-8 Defining Default Settings for Secondary Storage and Printer

You can change and/or maintain the default settings of your secondary storage (drive A, B, or C) and the printer. The /Worksheet Global Default Printer command will tell you the default settings of your printer. This includes:

Interface Auto-LF Left Right Top Bottom Pg-Length Wait
Setup Name

Any of these settings can be changed and restored for the future by issuing /Worksheet Global Default Update.

/Worksheet Global Default Directory will tell you the current directory or the current secondary storage. These settings can be changed, and then by issuing /Worksheet Global Default Update the changes will become permanent.

If you encounter any problems, consult *Setting Up 1-2-3*. This brief manual explains these steps in detail.

SUMMARY

In this appendix, we have provided you with some guidelines regarding tailoring Lotus to your system. Since Lotus has been designed to work on several systems, customization is needed. If you don't install Lotus, your 1-2-3 program will still run but you won't be able to generate graphs or use your printer. We gave a quick review of the Install and Install Library programs. These two programs provide you with the information needed for the installation of 1-2-3 and its companion programs.

REVIEW QUESTIONS

*These questions are answered in Appendix I.
1.   Why must Lotus be installed?
2.   If you do not install Lotus, which part of the program may not work?
3.* Which disk among the disks is the most important?
4.* How do you make a backup copy of the PrintGraph disk?
5.   Why must you make copies of all the disks?
6.   How do you copy PrintGraph to a hard disk?
7.   What is a directory? A subdirectory?
8.   How do you make a directory the current directory?
9.   On which disk is the Install program?
10.* How do you get the installation procedure started?
11.   What are drivers?
12.   How many driver sets can you have?
13.   What is the default driver name for 1-2-3?

Appendix D

File Transfer between Lotus and Other Software

D-1 Introduction

In this appendix we will provide you with some guidelines for importing and exporting files to and from Lotus. This facility enables you to utilize the best features of each software package. Also, by importing other files, you should be able to save time and frustration by not duplicating the same data file. Lotus provides several facilities for data transfer. The Translate utility provided by Release 2.2 is an excellent program that makes the task of file transfer a very easy job. In this appendix, we will talk about these facilities. We will also talk about the /File Import and /Data Parse commands.

D-2 Why File Transfer?

There are several reasons for using file transfer facilities. File transfer simply means the transfer of a file generated by one applications software program to another. There are three reasons for such a task:

1. Utilizing a facility of one software package that is not available in another; for example, transferring a Lotus spreadsheet to a report generated by a word processing program. There are several benefits to this process, e.g., factual and comprehensive reports by integrating worksheet analysis into your WordStar report.

2. Utilizing the enhanced power available for the same basic tasks performed by two application software programs. For example, since the database operations performed by Lotus are much faster than dBASE III Plus, you want to bring a dBASE file into a Lotus worksheet for processing.

3. Converting data files from earlier applications software programs to more recent versions. This is a very common practice. Consider converting VisiCalc files into Lotus files. Without data transfer facilities you would have to enter all the data again, a time-consuming and tedious task.

D-3 What Is an ASCII File?

ASCII (American Standard Code for Information Interchange) is a data format generated and accepted by many applications software packages.

An ASCII file, or simply a "print image" file, is a file in standard keyboard characters. To verify whether a file is ASCII or not is very simple. At the A> prompt in DOS, enter "TYPE filename.extension". If a file is listed in standard keyboard characters, it is ASCII; otherwise it is not. For example, Lotus files generated by the /Print File command (files with the PRN extension) are ASCII files. VisiCalc generates all its files in ASCII, as do WordStar, WordPerfect, dBASE II and III, and BASICA (sequential files).

D-4 Lotus Facilities for File Transfer

Lotus Release 2.2 provides several facilities that make the job of file transfer a relatively easy task. These tools include the Lotus Translate utility program, /File Import command, /Data Parse command, /Print File Options Other Unformatted command, and Lotus macros related to sequential ASCII files.

In the next few pages we will explain techniques for accessing these facilities and provide you with several examples. The goal of this section is to help you to better understand these powerful features provided by Lotus.

D-5 Lotus Translate Utility Program

When you access the Lotus Access System, one of the options provided is Translate. When you select this option, Lotus gives you a series of options and asks you "what do you want to translate from?" See Figure D-1.

FIGURE D-1 The First Menu of the Translate Utility

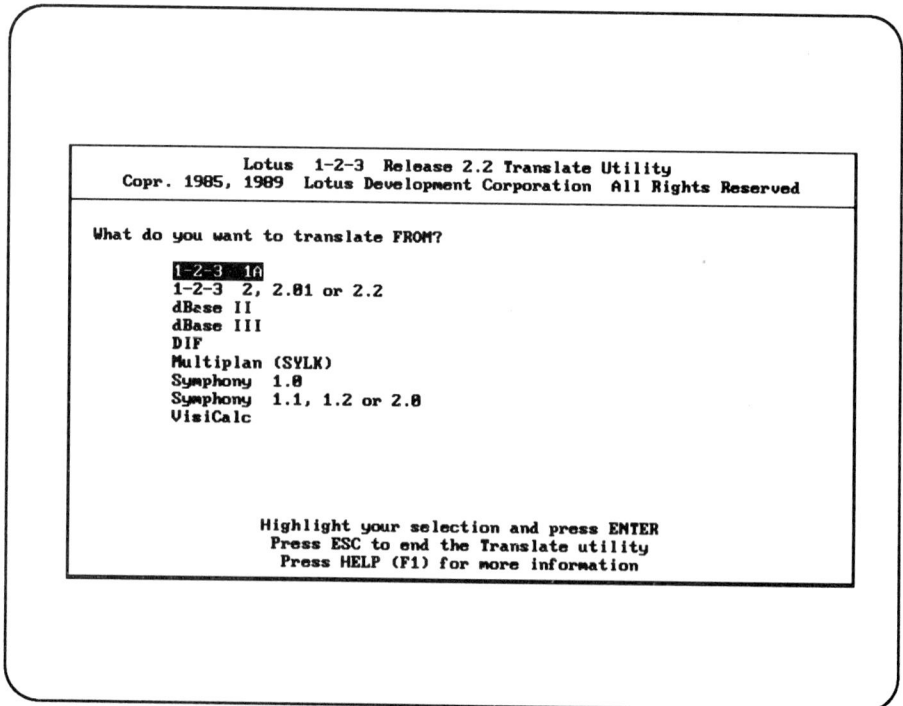

You may select any of these options and press the **Return** key. As soon as you select an option, you will see Figure D-2. To exit the Translate utility, press the **Escape** key. Should you require assistance you can press F1 for on-line help.

You can translate files from any of the above nine options to any of the seven options. If you select 1-2-3, Release 2, you will be given a series of instructions. Continue to press **Escape**. Insert the diskette that includes the desired files. Move the cursor to the file you would like to translate. We chose the file in Figure D–3 which is in our current directory. The menu will indicate that the source file with the WK1 extension will be changed to a file with the DBF extension (database file). If you correctly follow the sequence specified, the final message will be "Translation Successful". Now if you look at the directory of the diskette, you will see that the file you just translated has DBF (database file) as an extension.

Remember, if you do not follow the right sequence, you will receive an error message. You must follow the instructions provided by the Translate utility exactly.

After translation this is a dBASE file and you can perform any operation with it using all the dBASE commands.

D-6 Using the /File Import and /Data Parse Commands

To demonstrate how the /File Import and /Data Parse commands work, we will walk through an example. We used /Print File to write the worksheet in Figure D–4 to a new file (Figure D–5). This file is now an ASCII file with a PRN extension. (The /Print File command was discussed in Chapter 9).

Now we want to bring this file back to the worksheet. When you issue /File Import,

FIGURE D-2 The Second Menu of the Translate Utility

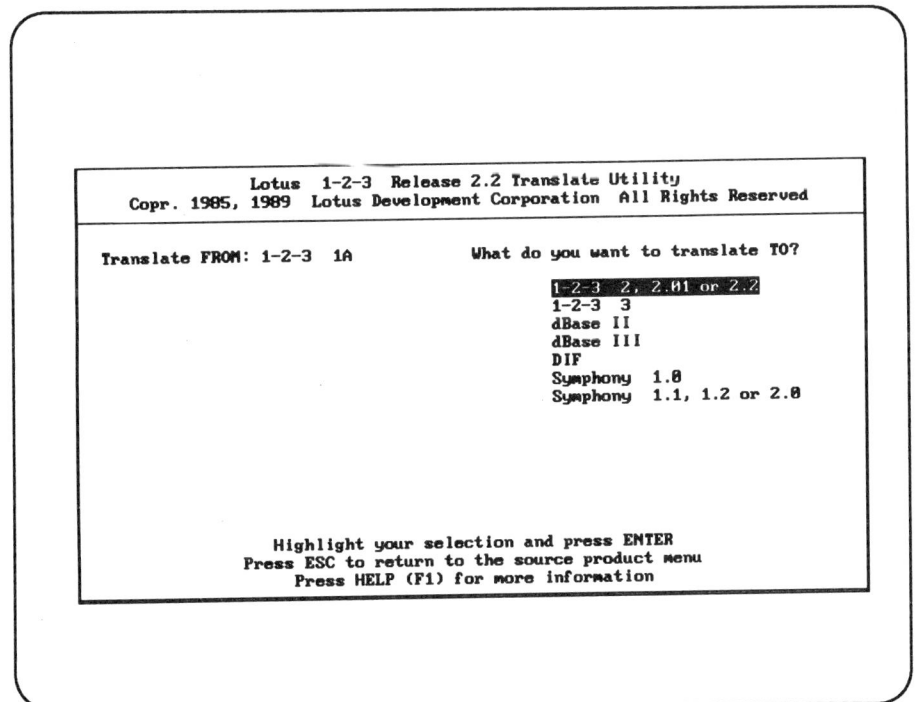

FIGURE D-3 An Example of a Lotus Worksheet File Translated into a dBASE III File

```
A1: [W12] 'FIRST NAME                                           READY

        A           B           C    D   E            F            G
1   FIRST NAME  LAST NAME     AGE  SEX OCCUPATION   INCOME
2   Randy       Alexander      36   M   Professor    $40,000
3   Fay         Alexander      30   F   Mayor        $30,000
4   Adam        Alexander      31   M   Engineer     $30,000
5   Andrea      Byan           36   F   Teacher      $31,000
6   Moe         Byan           40   M   Officer      $40,000
7   Bob         Adam           32   M   Engineer     $72,000
8   Anna        Adam            4   F   Unemployed   $11,000
9   Vicki       Adam            9   F   Unemployed   $12,000
10  Paula       Bobby          55   F   Housewife    $20,000
11  Jack        Jones          69   M   Artist       $19,000
12  Mary        Fishler        30   F   Interpreter  $19,000
13  Sue         Hayword        22   F   Student      $10,000
14  Tammy       Smith          29   F   Student      $10,000
15  Jacky       Brown          72   F   Engineer     $52,000
16  Lora        Jones          30   F   Nurse        $31,000
17
18
19
20
01-Jan-91  09:25 AM              UNDO
```

```
A2: (G) [W9] 'NAME                                              READY

        A        B       C       D        E        F       G       H
1               MY FIRST DATABASE
2   NAME       AGE      SEX     OCCUPA   INCOME
3   Randy       36       M      Professor  40000
4   Fay         30       F      Mayor      30000
5   Adam        31       M      Engineer   30000
6   Andrea      36       F      Teacher    31000
7   Moe         40       M      Officer    40000
8   Bob         32       M      Engineer   72000
9
10
11
12
13
14
15
16
17
18
19
20
01-Jan-91  08:10 AM              UNDO                           CAPS
```

FIGURE D-4 A Sample Worksheet

FIGURE D-5 Sample File Retrieved by File Import

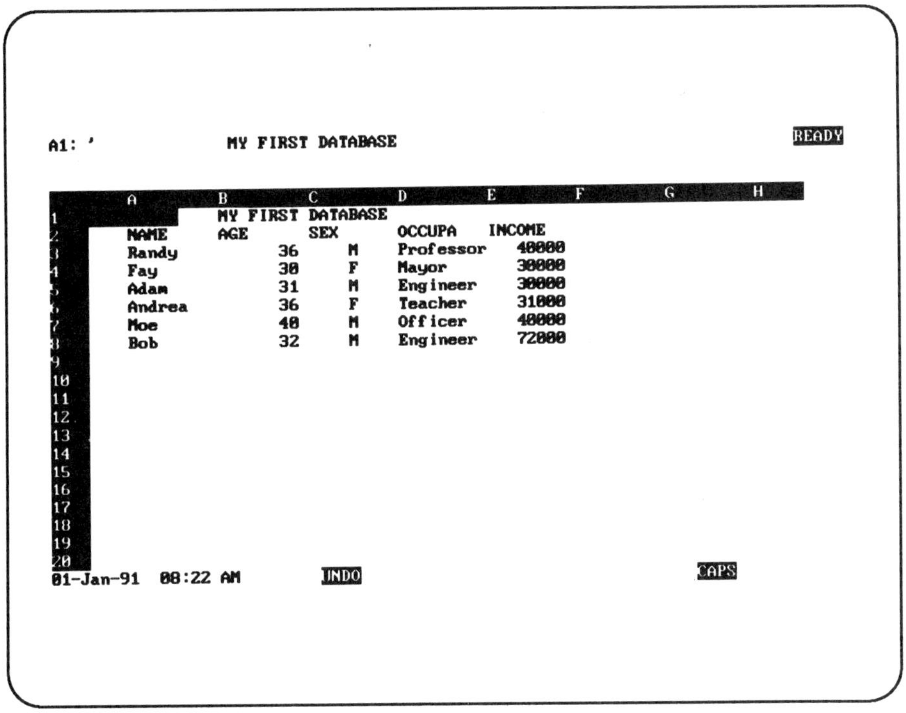

Lotus gives you two options: text or numbers. We chose the text option (if the numbers option is chosen, only numeric values will be transferred).

If you move the cursor, you will see that each line of the ASCII file has been entered into one cell. For example, Cell A2 contains FIRST NAME AGE SEX OCCUPATION INCOME. Naturally, this file cannot be manipulated by Lotus spreadsheet commands. We have to use the /Data Parse command in order to parse the data. Parsing splits the long labels into a series of data items or labels.

The procedure for using this very powerful command is straightforward. Move the cursor to cell A2, which contains the first data item. Now invoke the /Data Parse command. You will be given the following options:

Format-Line Input-Column Output-Range Reset Go Quit

The Format-Line command will provide you with a pattern or patterns for splitting up the numbers or labels. You can change it or take it as is. If you select the format-Line there are two options: Create or Edit. Choose the Create option. You will see a format line starting with four asterisks (four spaces), L (for labels), three > (greater than sign), another L and so on. As you see, all together there are five Ls which stand for five labels—name, age, sex, occupation, and income. Press Q (Quit) to exit the menu. Now move the cursor to cell A4 and select /Data, Parse, Format-Line, Create. This time you will see three Ls and two Vs (for Value or numeric data) accompanied by *, > .

Besides the L and V options, there is option D for Date, T for Time, S to Skip the corresponding characters in the input line, > to continue the field, and * for characters that are undefined but belong to the current block.

The Input-Column specifies the range to be parsed. In our example, the range is A2..A10.

Output-Range is the left corner of the block for the parsed data. We specified A12.

Reset will cancel the previous settings, and Go will execute the /Data Parse command.

Remember, in this example we have used two format lines; one for database fields FIRST NAME, AGE, SEX, OCCUPAT, and INCOME, and the other for database records. The result of this /Data Parse operation is in cells A12..E18. As you see, the currency format is lost. But all the data was split and you will be able to use this database for any Lotus operation. Figure D–6 shows the result. This is the easiest method for parsing. Remember, we used the default setting for Column widths and label justification.

Remember that there are other commands provided by Lotus to split a long label. For example, string functions (@Left, @Mid, @Right) can be used to extract substrings from whole strings. The /Range Justify command can split a long label into several shorter ones. The /Data Parse command is more flexible and easier to use than the other commands.

Lotus macros for sequential file processing can provide you with some extra features for file handling between Lotus and other standard ASCII files (see Ch. 19).

D-7 File Transfer between Lotus and Word Processing Programs

As mentioned earlier, the /Print File command generates an ASCII file with the PRN extension. This file can be exported to a variety of programs that accept ASCII files. WordStar, WordPerfect, and Volkswriter are three such programs. To make the ASCII file generated by /Print File a more suitable candidate for use in other software programs, consider the following steps:

• Word processing programs accept up to a certain number of columns as a full line

FIGURE D-6 *An Original Database and the Parsed Version*

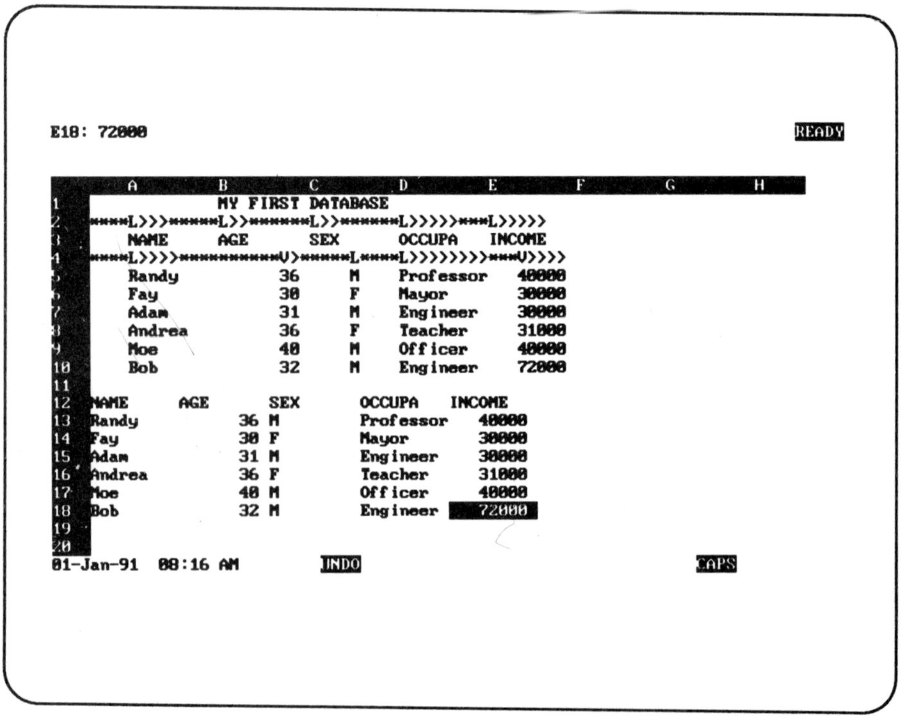

(e.g., 40, 80, etc.). Set the right margin to the maximum number accepted by your word processing program.

• Set the right margin to max and all the other margins top, bottom, left, to 0.

• By using /Print File Options Other Unformatted eliminate headers, footers, and other spacing in the files.

To bring a file from a word processor that generates ASCII files into your Lotus worksheet you must use /File Import Text. The file will be entered to the Lotus worksheet from the present position of the cursor one line per cell from top to bottom, left to right, e.g., cell A1, A2, etc.

If there are unwanted characters in the imported file, by using the F2 function key you can edit the file and change it to the desired format. If you would like to split long labels, you must use the /Data Parse command.

D-8 Lotus and BASICA Sequential Files

BASICA can generate ASCII files in several ways. The following program is one that can be used to generate a sequential ASCII file. The resulting file can easily be imported to a Lotus worksheet by using the /File Import command.

```
10   REM TO CREATE ASCII FILE CALLED STUREC
20   OPEN "STUREC" FOR OUTPUT AS #1
30   FOR I=1 TO 3
40      READ A$,B$,C
50      WRITE #1,A$,B$,C
60   NEXT I
70   CLOSE
80   DATA SUSAN SHAY, BUSINESS, 3.85
90   DATA KIM BROWN,COMPUTER, 2.60
100  DATA ED STRONG,MATH, 4.00
110  END
```

In order to see the contents of the ASCII file STUREC, follow these instructions:

```
RUN                (program will run)
SYSTEM             (change from BASICA to SYSTEM mode)
A > TYPE STUREC
"SUSAN SHAY", "BUSINESS",    3.85
"KIM BROWN", "COMPUTER",     2.60
"ED STRONG", "MATH",         4.00
```

Also, if a file is saved under SAVE"Filename.BAS",A command, this file is saved in ASCII format.

BASICA can read an ASCII file by using the LINE INPUT #1 command. For example, you can read an ASCII file line by line into a one-dimensional array in a BASICA program.

The following routine reads a Lotus ASCII file (PRN file) into array X$(100):

```
10   DIM X$(100)
20   OPEN "Myfile.PRN" FOR INPUT AS #1
30   J=1
40   WHILE NOT EOF(1)
```

```
50      LINE INPUT #1, X$(J)
60      J=J+1
70  WEND
```

The following routine prints the contents of array X$:

```
FOR I=1 TO J
PRINT "X$(I)=",X$(I)
NEXT I
```

Every line of the ASCII file in Figure D–7 has been entered into one of the X$ array's cell.

Figure D-7 is a listing of a Lotus ASCII file generated by /Print File. Figure D–8 is a BASICA program listing and the contents of Array X$.

If you would like to enter each data item to a cell instead of the entire line, the ASCII file must be comma-delimited. To make a file coma-delimited, one option is to use the @STRING function as illustrated in Figure D–9.

As discussed in Chapter 19, Lotus macros for sequential file processing enable you to read from and write to an ASCII file.

D-9 File Transfer and R:BASE 5000

R:BASE 5000, a powerful database management system, is also capable of file export and import to and from a number of popular software programs including Lotus 1-2-3. Through a utility program called the FileGateway, R:BASE 5000 can import from the following software:

FIGURE D-7 An ASCII File Example

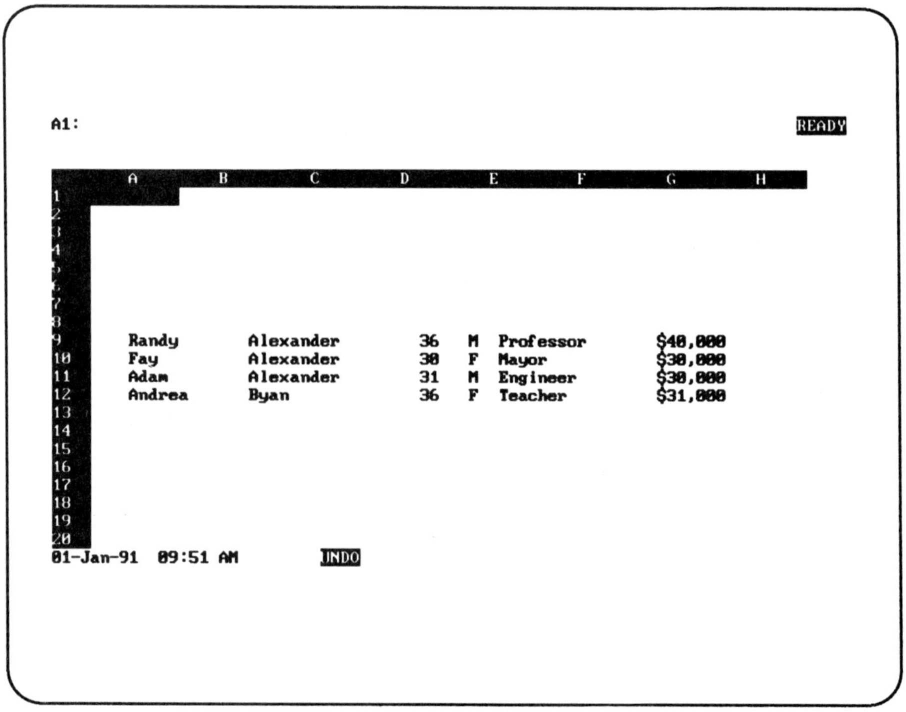

FIGURE D-8 Program Listing and Output of the BASIC Program Reading an ASCII File

```
Ok
LIST
10 DIM X$(100)
20 OPEN "MYFILE.PRN" FOR INPUT AS #1
30 J=1
40 WHILE NOT EOF(1)
50    LINE INPUT #1,X$(J)
60    J=J+1
70    PRINT X$(J)
80 WEND
90 END
Ok
RUN


      Randy      Alexander     36   M   Professor    $40,000
      Fay        Alexander     30   F   Mayor        $30,000
      Adam       Alexander     31   M   Engineer     $30,000
      Andrea     Byan          36   F   Teacher      $31,000
```

```
A7: [W12] '=================================================================READY


      A         B         C    D    E              F         G
1               MY FIRST DATABASE                            "
2                                                           ","
3  FIRST NAME  LAST NAME  AGE  SEX  OCCUPATION     INCOME   ","
4  Randy       Alexander   36   M   Professor       40000   ,"
5  Fay         Alexander   30   F   Mayor           30000

7  ===========================================================
8
9  "Randy","Alexander",36,"M","Professor",40000
10 "Fay","Alexander",30,"F","Mayor",30000
11
12
13                              A
14
15
16 THE FOLLOWING FORMULA WAS USED TO GENERATE A COMMA-DELIMITED FILE
17
18 +$G$1&A13&$G$2&B13&$G$3&@STRING(C13,0)&$G$4&D13&$G$2&E13&$G$3&@STRING(F
19
01-Jan-91  09:41 AM       UNDO
```

FIGURE D-9 Operating a Comma-Delimited File

dBASE
Lotus 1-2-3
Symphony
PFS:FILE
DIF files from VisiCalc
SYLK files from MultiPlan
ASCII files from a majority of micro and mainframe computers

For more specific information, consult the R:BASE Series 5000 user's manual, Chapter 13, "The FileGateway Contents."

SUMMARY

In this appendix, we have provided a review of Lotus facilities for file transfer between programs. The Translate utility can assist you in transferring files between versions of Lotus, dBASE, DIF, Jazz, VisiCalc, and Symphony. Also, by using the /File Import command, you should be able to import any ASCII file to your worksheet. The /Data Parse command will enable you to parse (split up) long labels into a series of labels and values. Be aware that other commands and facilities for file handling are available in Lotus. These include Lotus macros for sequential files, string functions, and /Print File for generating ASCII files. We also provided guidelines for import/export to and from other software including word processors, BASICA, and R-BASE 5000.

REVIEW QUESTIONS

*These questions are answered in Appendix I.
1. Why is file transfer needed?
2.* What are the requirements for any file transfer?
3. How do you get the Translate utility started?
4.* What application software packages can directly benefit from the Translate utility?
5.* How do you ask for help in the Translate utility?
6. How do you exit the Translate utility?
7. When a file is translated from Lotus to dBASE, what is actually changed?
8.* How do you generate an ASCII file using Lotus?
9. How do you verify if a file is an ASCII file?
10. How do you load an ASCII file into the Lotus worksheet?
11. What is the major function of the /Data Parse command?
12.* Why is parsing needed?
13. Are there other methods of data parsing besides using the /Data Parse command?
14. What are the options available under the /Data Parse command?
15.* What is the function of Reset in the /Data Parse menu?
16. How many format lines are needed for a typical database?
17. Choose one of the worksheets in any of the chapters of this book and convert this worksheet into a dBASE III file. How will you know if your translation is successful?
18. Using the /Print File command, generate an ASCII file.
19. Using /Data Parse, split a long label into four shorter labels.
20. Generate a comma-delimited file in Lotus.
21. Export a Lotus ASCII file into a BASICA program.

Misconceptions and Solutions

M – When you translate, if you generate a file with the same name as one of the existing files on your directory, this new file will overwrite the old file regardless of differences in size.

S – Check your directory first, then do the translation.

M – The translate utility is constrained by the limitations of the program. For example, if you are translating from dBASE to Lotus, your dBASE file cannot have more than 8,192 records.

S – Break the large databases into a series of smaller ones, then do the translation.

M – Translation between dBASE and Lotus may produce incorrect decimal places.

S – In the 1-2-3 worksheet, use Format options besides the General default option and specify as many decimal places as needed. When the dBASE file is generated, you will have the same number of decimal places.

M – Field names and numbers moved from 1-2-3 to dBASE may cause errors.

S – Your database in the 1-2-3 worksheet must follow the same rules that apply to field names in dBASE, e.g., 1 to 10 characters long, include only letters of the alphabet, use digits 0-9, and start with a letter of the alphabet. Also, from Release 2, 2.01 and 2.2 to dBASE III Plus you cannot have more than 128 fields.

M – If you use /File Import Numbers to import an ASCII file to your Lotus worksheet, you may generate undesired results.

S – Check the spacing in the incoming file. There must be at least one space between each field or, if your data is nonnumeric, these must be enclosed in double quotation marks and separated by commas. Usually /File Import Text is safer than /File Import Numbers.

Appendix E

Differences between Release 2.0/2.01 and Release 1A

Lotus Release 2.0/2.01 includes a series of enhanced features not available in the earlier releases of this package. These enhancements include new security features, memory management, additional worksheet and range commands, new functions, and a number of new macro commands that complement the macro commands available in Release 1A and make Lotus a full-featured programming language.

Memory management gives you complete freedom to utilize a worksheet in any style. For example, a data item in cell A1 or cell A2000 will occupy the same amount of memory. However, in Release 1A, the active area is important. In the above example the active area would be the entire rectangle of A1..A2000. This means you will run out of memory very fast.

Release 2.0/2.01 implements security features by allowing you to have a password for a file. You can also use the /Range Protect or /Worksheet Global Protection commands.

In Release 2.0/2.01 you can access DOS from the 1-2-3 spreadsheet by using the System command from the main menu. This release also enables you to export or import files between 1-2-3 Release 1A or 2, dBASE II, dBASE III, DIF, Jazz, Symphony Release 1.0 and 1.10, and VisiCalc.

For those who are still using Release 1A or who are interested in knowing some of the differences between Release 2.0/2.01 and Release 1A, we have provided Table E-1. This table should assist you in quickly discovering all the features available in Release 2.0/2.01 but not in Release 1A.

In some cases the commands are different but perform the same task; this table also highlights such cases.

TABLE E-1 RELEASE 2.0/2.01 AND RELEASE 1A COMPARISON

Feature	Release 2.0/2.01	Release 1A
	GENERAL INFORMATION	
Worksheet size	256 columns by 8,192 rows	256 by 2,048
The entire package	System disk	System disk
	Backup system disk	Backup system disk
	Utility	Utility disk
	PrintGraph	PrintGraph

TABLE E-1 (Continued)

Feature	Release 2.0/2.01	Release 1A
	GENERAL INFORMATION	
	A View of Lotus	Tutorial disk
	Install library	
Alt & F1	available	not available
	WORKSHEET COMMANDS	
/Worksheet Global Protection	available	not available
/Worksheet Global Default Other		
International	Currency available	not available
	Date available	not available
	Time available	not available
/Worksheet Global Zero	available	not available
/Worksheet Column Hide	available	not available
/Worksheet Column Display	available	not available
/Worksheet Status	available	not available
/Worksheet Page	available	not available
	RANGE COMMANDS	
/Range Unprotect or Protect	available	not available
/Range Name Table	available	not available
/Range Transpose	available	not available
/Range Value	available	not available
/Range Format Hidden	available	not available
File Extension	WK1 (worksheet)	WKS (worksheet)
	FUNCTIONS	
@ATAN2 (A,B)	available	not available
@CTERM	available	not available
@TERM	available	not available
@SLN	available	not available
@SYD	available	not available
@DDB	available	not available
@ISNUMBER	available	not available
@ISSTRING	available	not available
@CHAR	available	not available
@CODE	available	not available
@CLEAN	available	not available
@EXACT	available	not available
@FIND	available	not available
@LEFT	available	not available
@LENGTH	available	not available
@LOWER	available	not available
@MID	available	not available
@N	available	not available

TABLE E-1 (Continued)

Feature	Release 2.0/2.01	Release 1A
	FUNCTIONS	
@PROPER	available	not available
@REPEAT	available	not available
@REPLACE	available	not available
@RIGHT	available	not available
@S	available	not available
@STRING	available	not available
@TRIM	available	not available
@UPPER	available	not available
@VALUE	available	not available
@DATE	available	not available
@DATEVALUE	available	not available
@NOW	available	not available
@TIME	available	not available
@TIMEVALUE	available	not available
@HOUR	available	not available
@MINUTE	available	not available
@SECOND	available	not available
@@	available	not available
@CELL	available	not available
@HLOOKUP	available for both numeric and nonnumeric search	available for numeric search only
@INDEX	available	not available
@VLOOKUP	available for both numeric and nonnumeric search	numeric search only
@CELLPOINTER	available	not available
@COLS	available	not available
@ROWS	available	not available
	GRAPHICS	
Exploding a pie chart	available	not available
	PRINTGRAPH	
Availability of several interfaces for DOS Device		
LPT1	available	not available
LPT2	available	not available
LPT3	available	not available
LPT4	available	not available
Choosing font option	available	not available
	DATABASE	
/Data Matrix		not available
Invert	available	not available
Multiply	available	not available
/Data Regression	available	not available

TABLE E-1 (Continued)

Feature	Release 2.0/2.01	Release 1A

MACRO COMMANDS

Feature	Release 2.0/2.01	Release 1A
BIGLEFT	available	not available
BIGRIGHT	available	not available
Multiple action (e.g., DOWN 6 or UP 2)	available	not available
BLANK	available	not available
LET	available	not available
CONTENTS	available	not available
PUT	available	not available
RECALC	available	not available
RECALCCOL	available	not available
BRANCH	available	/XG
DEFINE	available	not available
DISPATCH	available	not available
FOR and FORBREAK	available	not available
IF	available	/XI
QUIT	available	/XQ
ONERROR	available	not available
RESTART	available	not available
RETURN	available	/XR
SUBR-Name	available	/XC Name
BREAKOFF	available	not available
WAIT	available	not available
GET	available	not available
GETLABEL	available	/XL
GETNUMBER	available	/XN
LOOK	available	not available
MENUBRANCH	available	/XM
BEEP	available	not available
INDICATE	available	not available
PANELOFF	available	not available
PANELON	available	not available
WINDOWSOFF	available	not available
WINDOWSON	available	not available
CLOSE	available	not available
FILESIZE	available	not available
GETPOS	available	not available
READ	available	not available
READLN	available	not available
SETPOS	available	not available
WRITE	available	not available
WRITELN	available	not available

Appendix F

Differences between Release 2.0/2.01 and Release 2.2

Release 2.2 is an upgrade of Release 2.01. It has a number of enhancements over its predecessors. Please remember that Release 2.2 by no means changes the way you have been using 1-2-3. The unique enhancements of Release 2.2 over 2.01 include:

• The ability to link cells from one worksheet to another worksheet.
• Enhanced report generation using the Allways add-in program.
• The ability to UNDO a command.
• A minimal recalculation capability that allows Release 2.2 to recalculate only those cells affected by a change in the worksheet.
• The ability to create macros automatically.
• The ability to store and access macros in an area of the memory separate from the worksheet.
• A few enhancements make Release 2.2 an easier program to use than its predecessors. For example, you can enter a data range for a group of graphs, you can adjust the widths of several columns in a range at once, and you can search and replace labels and strings in formulas.
• The ability to view all settings on a settings sheet when you select certain menus.

TABLE F-1 RELEASE 2.2 AND RELEASE 2.0/2.01 COMPARISON

Feature	Release 2.2	Section Number	Release 2.0/2.01
Worksheet			
/Worksheet Global Zero Label	Available	6-10	Not Available
/Worksheet Global Default Other Clock Filename	6-9		
/Worksheet Global Default Other Beep	"	6-9	"
/Worksheet Global Default Autoexec	"	6-9	"
/Worksheet Global Default Other Add-In Set	"	6-9	"
/Worksheet Column Column-Range	"	6-13	"

TABLE F-1 (Continued)

Feature	Release 2.2	Section Number	Release 2.0/2.01
/Worksheet Global Default Other Undo	"	6-9	"
/Worksheet Global Default Other International Negative	"	6-9	"
Alt-F3 (Run)	"	4-5	"
Alt-F4 (Undo)	"	4-5	"
Alt-F5 (Learn)	"	4-5	"
Alt-F7 (App1)	"	4-5	"
Alt-F8 (App2)	"	4-5	"
Alt-F9 (App3)	"	4-5	"
Alt-F10 (Add-in)	"	4-5	"
RO (status indicator)	"	4-4	"
UNDO (status indicator)	"	4-4	"
File and Clock Indicator (indicator)	"	4-4	"
Range			
/Range Search	"	5-15	"
File			
/File Admin Reservation	"	8-12	"
/File Save Backup	"	8-12	"
/File Admin Link-Refresh	"	8-12	"
/File List Linked	"	8-12	"
/File Admin Table	"	8-12	"
/File Extension BAK (Backup)	"	8-12	"
/File Extension ADN (Add-In)	"	8-12	"
Functions			
@ISAPP("Name")	"	13-2-3	"
@ISAAF("Name")	"	13-2-4	"
Graph			
/Graph Name Table	"	14-2-3	"
/Graph Group	"	14-13	"
/Graph Reset Ranges	"	14-2-3	"
/Graph Reset Options	"	14-2-3	"
/Graph Options Data-Labels Group	"	14-2-3	"
/Graph Options Legend Range	"	14-2-3	"
Macros			
{BORDERSOFF}, {FRAMEOFF}, {BORDERSON}, and {FRAMEON}	"	14-8-2	"
{GRAPHON} and {GRAPHOFF}	"	19-8-4	"
{SYSTEM}	"	19-6-8	"
{HELP}	"	18-3	"
/WORKSHEET LEARN	"	18-18	"

Appendix G

Highlights of Releases 3 and 3.1

Release 3 and Release 3.1 are the most recent versions of Lotus 1-2-3. We have gathered the following information from Lotus Development Corporation.

1-2-3 Release 3 has been rewritten in C to provide support for multiple hardware platforms. The product will be compatible (file and macro) with all previous releases of 1-2-3, and will read and write Release 2.X files directly.

1-2-3 Release 3 is character-based and will support DOS 2.X, 3.X, and OS/2 operating environments in the same package. The DOS version will be compatible with the Lotus/Intel/Microsoft (LIM) Expanded Memory Specifications, version 4. This will allow 1-2-3 to support up to 32 megabytes of expanded memory under LIM.

Enhancements have been made to all areas of the product, including spreadsheet, graphics, database, printing, and usability.

Spreadsheet:

• Three-dimensional worksheets.
• Multiple files in memory.
• Formulas linked with files on disk as well as in memory.
• Increased size of the working area in 1-2-3 Release 3 to 256 worksheets, each containing 256 columns by 8,192 rows.
• Spreadsheet auditing and range and formula annotation.
• Automatic cell formatting.
• Techniques to maximize calculation speed: minimum recalculation of spreadsheet cells that are dependent on what's been changed, and background recalculation to allow the user to continue working in the spreadsheet.

Graphics:

• "Hot graph" window (automatic updating of an on-screen graph when the related worksheet is changed).
• Support for new graph types including open-high-low-close, mixed line and bar, area charts, and horizontal graphs.
• Support for graphic metafiles.
• Control over colors, fonts, hatching patterns, and size of graphs.
• Support for customization options such as logarithmic scaling and two Y-axes.

Database:

• Direct access to external databases (1-2-3 database functions performed on databases without having to translate external files or leave 1-2-3).
• Sorting on multiple keys (up to 256).
• Simple resorting from database entries.

Printing:

• Graphics printed directly from the 1-2-3 menu.
• Text and graphics printed on the same page.
• Support for PostScript devices.
• Print queuing.

Usability:

• Not copy protected.
• Network capabilities, including file reservation.
• Undo command.
• Keystroke recorder for easy macro creation.

Lotus Extended Applications Facility

Release 3 will have built-in hooks to support a new application programming language, currently referred to as the Lotus Extended Applications Facility. This facility goes far beyond the capabilities of macros and will allow users to extend and customize various Lotus applications. Available separately as a tool kit, this facility will replace the current Developer Tools and provide a more powerful and easy method for creating add-ins.

Multiple Environments

Lotus also has developed and has under development several other compatible versions of 1-2-3 including 1-2-3/G, designed for OS/2 and Presentation Manager; 1-2-3 for Apple Computer's Macintosh family of machines; and 1-2-3/M, designed to run on IBM mainframes with the same familiar user interface as 1-2-3 for the PC.

1-2-3 is the only spreadsheet that will be available in a range of environments, offering the user consistent commands, an efficient way to manage and consolidate information, and standardized training, support, and custom applications development.

Lotus 1-2-3, Release 3.1, includs all the features of the Release 3 and also provides desktop publishing quality. The WYSIWYG add-in provides a good set of graph customization features. The outputs generated by this release are nicer and better-looking than the earlier outputs.

Appendix H

Lotus International Character Set

Lotus uses the Lotus International Character Set (LICS) for displaying, transmitting, printing, and storing characters. These 256 characters are represented by numbers 0 through 255. Numbers 0 through 32 represent control characters (**Ctrl** - a letter); 32 through 127 represent ASCII codes; and 128 through 255 represent international characters.

The *compose sequence* is a series of keystrokes used to enter a character that is not on the keyboard. To do this, press **Alt**, then the desired compose sequence.

For printers and monitors that cannot directly represent all LICS characters, there are fallback presentations. These are listed in Table H-1. Table H-1 has been adopted from Lotus Development Corporation, 1987 and 1990, used with permission.

LICS Code	Character	Description	Compose Sequence	Fallback Monitor Presentation	Fallback Printer Presentation
0	Control @				
1	Control A				
2	Control B				
3	Control C			*(Note: Character codes 0 through 31 are not LICS codes.)*	
4	Control D				
5	Control E				
6	Control F				
7	Control G				
8	Control H				
9	Control I				
10	Control J	Line feed			

LICS Code	Character	Description	Compose Sequence	Fallback Monitor Presentation	Fallback Printer Presentation
11	Control K				
12	Control L	Form feed			
13	Control M	Return			
14	Control N				
15	Control O				
16	Control P				
17	Control Q				
18	Control R				
19	Control S				
20	Control T				
21	Control U				
22	Control V				
23	Control W				
24	Control X				
25	Control Y				
26	Control Z				
27	[Escape]				
28	FS				
29	GS				
30	RS				
31	US				
32	(Space)				
33	!				
34	"				
35	#		+ +		
36	$				
37	%				
38	&				
39	'	Apostrophe			
40	(				
41	)				
42	*				
43	+				
44	,				
45	-				
46	.				
47	/				
48	0				
49	1				
50	2				
51	3				
52	4				
53	5				
54	6				
55	7				
56	8				
57	9				
58	:				
59	;				
60	‹				
61	=				
62	›				
63	?				
64	@		a a A A		
65	A				
66	B				
67	C				

LICS Code	Character	Description	Compose Sequence	Fallback Monitor Presentation	Fallback Printer Presentation
68	D				
69	E				
70	F				
71	G				
72	H				
73	I				
74	J				
75	K				
76	L				
77	M				
78	N				
79	O				
80	P				
81	Q				
82	R				
83	S				
84	T				
85	U				
86	V				
87	W				
88	X				
89	Y				
90	Z				
91	[		((		
92	\		/ /		
93	]		))		
94	^		v v		
95	_				
96	`				
97	a				
98	b				
99	c				
100	d				
101	e				
102	f				
103	g				
104	h				
105	i				
106	j				
107	k				
108	l				
109	m				
110	n				
111	o				
112	p				
113	q				
114	r				
115	s				
116	t				
117	u				
118	v				
119	w				
120	x				
121	y				
122	z				
123	{		(-		
124	¦		^/		

LICS Code	Character	Description	Compose Sequence	Fallback Monitor Presentation	Fallback Printer Presentation
125	}		)-		
126	˜	Tilde	--		
127	DEL				
128	`	Uppercase grave	* ` space		
129	´	Uppercase acute	* ´ space		
130	ˆ	Uppercase circumflex	* ˆ space		
131	¨	Uppercase umlaut	* " space	"	"
132	˜	Uppercase tilde	* ˜ space		
133					
134					
135					
136					
137					
138					
139					
140					
141					
142					
143					
144	`	Lowercase grave	* space `		
145	´	Lowercase acute	* space ´		
146	ˆ	Lowercase circumflex	* space ˆ		
147	¨	Lowercase umlaut	* space "	"	"
148	˜	Lowercase tilde	space ˜		
149	ı	Lowercase i without dot	i space		
150	_	Ordinal indicator	_ space		
151	▲	Begin attribute (display only)	b a		
152	▼	End attribute (display only)	e a		
153	■	Unknown character (display only)			
154	•	Hard space (display only)	space space		
155	←	Merge character (display only)	m g		
156					
157	▶	Tab character			
158					
159					
160	ƒ	Dutch Guilder	f f		f
161	¡	Inverted exclamation mark	! !		i
162	¢	Cent sign	c: C: c/ C/		c⟨BS⟩:
163	£	Pound sign	L= l= L- ⊢		L⟨BS⟩=
164	"	Low opening double quotes	* ^	"	"
165	¥	Yen sign	Y= y= Y- y-		Y⟨BS⟩=
166	Pts	Pesetas sign	* PT pt Pt		Pt
167	§	Section sign	SO so SO sO		Sc
168	¤	General currency sign	XO xo XO xO		O⟨BS⟩=
169	©	Copyright sign	CO co CO cO	c	(c)
170	ª	Feminine Ordinal	a_ A_		a⟨BS⟩_
171	«	Angle quotation mark left	< <		<<
172	Δ	Delta	d d D D		D
173	π	Pi	* PI pi Pi		pi
174	≥	Greater-than-or-equals	* > =		> =
175	÷	Divide sign	: -		/
176	°	Degree sign	^ 0		o(superscripted, if possible)
177	±	Plus/minus sign	+ -		+⟨BS⟩_
178	²	Superscript 2	^ 2		2 (superscripted, if possible)
179	³	Superscript 3	^ 3	3	3 (superscripted, if possible)
180	„	Low closing double quotes	" v	"	"
181	µ	Micro sign	* / u		u

Do not type *. It indicates that compose sequence is order-sensitive.

LICS Code	Character	Description	Compose Sequence	Fallback Monitor Presentation	Fallback Printer Presentation
182	¶	Paragraph sign	! p ! P		Pr
183	·	Middle dot	·		·(superscripted, if possible)
184	™	Trademark sign	* TM Tm tm	T	TM
185	¹	Superscript 1	^ 1	1	1 (superscripted, if possible)
186	o	Masculine ordinal	o _ O _		o⟨BS⟩ _
187	»	Angle Quotation mark right	> >		> >
188	¼	Fraction one quarter	* 1 4		1/4
189	½	Fraction one half	* 1 2		1/2
190	≤	Less-than-or-equals	* = <		= <
191	¿	Inverted question mark	? ?		?
192	À	Uppercase A with grave	A `	A	A
193	Á	Uppercase A with acute	A ´	A	A
194	Â	Uppercase A with circumflex	A ^	A	A
195	Ã	Uppercase A with tilde	A ¯	A	A
196	Ä	Uppercase A with umlaut	A "		A
197	Å	Uppercase A with ring	A *		A
198	Æ	Uppercase A with ligature	* A E		AE
199	Ç	Uppercase C with cedilla	C ,		C ⟨BS⟩ ,
200	È	Uppercase E with grave	E `	E	E
201	É	Uppercase E with acute	E ´		E
202	Ê	Uppercase E with circumflex	E ^	E	E
203	Ë	Uppercase E with umlaut	E "	E	E
204	Ì	Uppercase I with grave	I `	I	I
205	Í	Uppercase I with acute	I ´	I	I
206	Î	Uppercase I with circumflex	I ^	I	I
207	Ï	Uppercase I with umlaut	I "	I	I
208	Ð	Uppercase eth (Icelandic)	D ¯	D	D ⟨BS⟩ ¯
209	Ñ	Uppercase N with tilde	N ¯		N
210	Ò	Uppercase O with grave	O `	O	O
211	Ó	Uppercase O with acute	O ´	O	O
212	Ô	Uppercase O with circumflex	O ^	O	O
213	Õ	Uppercase O with tilde	O ¯	O	O
214	Ö	Uppercase O with umlaut	O "		O
215	Œ	Uppercase OE diphthong	* O E	O	OE
216	Ø	Uppercase O with slash	O /		O ⟨BS⟩ /
217	Ù	Uppercase U with grave	U `	U	U
218	Ú	Uppercase U with acute	U ´	U	U
219	Û	Uppercase U with circumflex	U ^	U	U
220	Ü	Uppercase u with umlaut	U "		U
221	Ÿ	Uppercase Y with umlaut	Y "	Y	Y
222	Þ	Uppercase thorn (Icelandic)	P ¯	P	P ⟨BS⟩ _
223	ß	Lowercase German sharp s	s s		ss
224	à	Lowercase a with grave	a `		a ⟨BS⟩ `
225	á	Lowercase a with acute	a ´		a ⟨BS⟩ ´
226	â	Lowercase a with circumflex	a ^		a ⟨BS⟩ ^
227	ã	Lowercase a with tilde	a ¯	a	a ⟨BS⟩ ¯
228	ä	Lowercase u with umlaut	a "		a ⟨BS⟩ "
229	å	Lowercase a with ring	a *		a
230	æ	Lowercase ae with ligature	a e		ae
231	ç	Lowercase c with cedilla	c ,		c ⟨BS⟩ ,
232	è	Lowercase e with grave	e `		e ⟨BS⟩ `
233	é	Lowercase e with acute	e ´		e ⟨BS⟩ ´
234	ê	Lowercase e with circumflex	e ^		e ⟨BS⟩ ^
235	ë	Lowercase e with umlaut	e "		e ⟨BS⟩ "
236	ì	Lowercase i with grave	i `		i ⟨BS⟩ `
237	í	Lowercase i with acute	i ´		i ⟨BS⟩ ´
238	î	Lowercase i with circumflex	i ^		i ⟨BS⟩ ^

LICS Code	Character	Description	Compose Sequence	Fallback Monitor Presentation	Fallback Printer Presentation
239	ï	Lowercase i with umlaut	i "		i ⟨BS⟩ ¨
240	ð	Lowercase eth (Icelandic)	d –	d	d ⟨BS⟩ -
241	ñ	Lowercase n with tilde	n ˜		n ⟨BS⟩ ˜
242	ò	Lowercase o with grave	o `		o ⟨BS⟩ `
243	ó	Lowercase o with acute	o ´		o ⟨BS⟩ ´
244	ô	Lowercase o with circumflex	o ^		o ⟨BS⟩ ^
245	õ	Lowercase o with tilde	o ˜	o	o ⟨BS⟩ ˜
246	ö	Lowercase o with umlaut	o "		o ⟨BS⟩ ¨
247	œ	Lowercase oe with diphthong	o e	o	oe
248	ø	Lowercase o with slash	o /	o	o ⟨BS⟩ /
249	ù	Lowercase u with grave	u `		u ⟨BS⟩ `
250	ú	Lowercase u with acute	u ´		u ⟨BS⟩ ´
251	û	Lowercase u with circumflex	u ^		u ⟨BS⟩ ^
252	ü	Lowercase u with umlaut	u "		u ⟨BS⟩ ¨
253	ÿ	Lowercase y with umlaut	y "		y ⟨BS⟩ ¨
254	þ	Lowercase thorn (Icelandic)	p –	p	p ⟨BS⟩ _
255					

Appendix I

Answers to the Selected Review Questions

Chapter 1

2. VisiCalc, SuperCalc, ProCalc, and Context MBA. (Context MBA was introduced approximately at the same time as Lotus.)
4. Release 2.2 allows the Undo feature and also lets you link worksheets together more effectively.
6. VisiCalc.
9. Seven 5 1/4" or three 3 1/2" disks. Release 2.2 also includes Allways disks.
15. Forecasting to integrate database, spreadsheet, and graphic capabilities; financial analysis to again utilize these three components.

Chapter 2

2. A> prompt means that the disk operating system is in drive A or the default drive is A. Yes, we have other prompts, like B and C for drive B and drive C and OK for the BASIC language.
4. Home will put you back to cell A1.
7. Escape either erases a line in Edit mode, or gets you out of the present operation.
10. Type a caret first (^), then type the data.
12. By putting them inside parentheses.

Chapter 3

1. Type either 123 or Lotus at the A> prompt, assuming your system disk is in Drive A.
4. It is not. However, numbers are right-justified and labels are left-justified.
6. Press the **Slash** key (e.g., /).
10. Use either **PrtSc** and the **Shift** key or use the Print command. On enhanced keyboards, pressing Prtsc alone will print the screen.
12. Insert the DOS disk in drive A, and at the A> prompt type Format, press the **Return** key, and then follow the prompt.
14. Choose Quite from the main menu.

Chapter 4

7. The READY mode.
10. Press Alt and F2 together.
12. When a macro is being executed.

Chapter 5

2. Yes. Range A1..IV8192 is equal to the entire worksheet.
8. Use the /Range Name Table command; this will give you an alphabetical list of names with their addresses.
17. Precede the range name with a dollar sign, e.g., $Income.

Chapter 6

3. Nine.
5. For a large worksheet, you choose manual in order to bypass the intermediate results. This can immensely improve the speed of calculations.
7. The command /Worksheet Global Label-Prefix must be issued first. Then enter data.
17. /Worksheet Page generates a page break. It must be in Column A.

Chapter 7

2. There are 10 options: Fixed, Scientific, Currency, Comma, General, +/-, Percent, Date, Text, and Hidden.
3. The Currency operation separates every three digits by a comma and also includes a dollar sign to the left of a number. The Comma option does the same thing but does not include the dollar sign.
6. To display the actual formulas in a cell for debugging purposes.
10. Yes.

Chapter 8

3. Five types of files: PIC, WK1, PRN, BAK and ADN.
6. Any combination of digits and letters of the alphabet, up to 15 characters.
8. /File Combine Add adds the incoming data to the worksheet. /File Combine Copy copies the incoming data to the current worksheet. You must always remembers the present position of the cursor.
10. Yes. If your worksheet contains numeric data and if the cursor is in the occupied portion of the worksheet, the incoming data will overwrite the current worksheet.
14. Type /File Erase. When Lotus asks for a file name type the name of the file or point to it. For example, type PAY*.*. Lotus will give you a listing of all the files that start with PAY. You can erase them one by one. If you want to erase them all at once, you must use DOS wild card and the Del or Erase command.

Chapter 9

2. At the A> prompt type TYPE Filename.PRN. This will give you a listing of your file on the monitor. Transfer this to the printer.
6. The at sign (@).
9. No. /Worksheet Page may not override this command if the number of lines specified by /Print, Printer, options, Pg-Length is less than the number of lines covered by /Worksheet Page.
10. To print the exact characters, formulas, date, and so forth in a worksheet or a range.
14. Out of 66 lines per page, only 56 lines are available to you.
16. First use /Worksheet Global Default Printer. Change whatever you would like to change, then use /Worksheet Global Default Update.

Chapter 10

4. WYSIWYG means your printout will be exactly like the display on your monitor.
7. Press the Esc key or select Quit from the Allways menu.
12. Graphics mode and Text mode. By using the F6 function key.
19. Two.
22. To create ASCII files.

Chapter 11

5. By using the @ command.
9. As a series of "Gs."
12. Eight. You use /Display Colors to change the colors that Allways uses.

Chapter 12

2. A Lotus function simplifies operations performed by users. For example, to add 100 different cells, you can either add them up cell by cell or just use the @SUM function.
6. An invalid argument is one that does not follow the convention regarding a function's argument. For example, @SQRT(-25) is invalid because in this function the argument must be positive.
8. The @ABS function treats any numeric value as a positive value. It always returns a positive answer. This can be used when you calculate the root of an equation and you are only interested in the positive root.
10. Yes. Add 0.50 to the argument, then use the @INT function.
13. You may raise the argument of a function to the power of one-half; e.g., +B10^1/2.
14. @FV can be used to tell you about the future value of an annuity. For example, you IRA Plan. @PV function can tell you what is the present value of a series of equal payments in the future.
16. In the @PV function the cash flows must be equal. In the @NPV function the cash flows need not be equal.

Chapter 13

2. @ISNUMBER is useful for testing the content of a cell. It tells you if the cell holds a numeric value. After this test you may want to conduct some arithmetic operation. If the cell content is not numeric, you cannot perform any arithmetic operations.
3. @CHAR returns the ASCII/LICS equivalent of the argument.
8. The @DATEVALUE function uses a single string value as its argument, while @DATE accepts any Lotus date format.
13. HLOOKUP conducts a horizontal search, VLOOKUP conducts a vertical search.
15. They can be used in any table search, for example, searching tax tables, commission tables, production tables, and so on.

Chapter 14

3. One limitation is that you can only use six data ranges. Another limitation is the variety (only five types); a third limitation is that the graphs are only two-dimensional.
4. In an XY graph there must be two sets of data, one for the X-axis and the other for the Y-axis; one of these two data ranges must be X. There is no such limitation in a line graph.
6. The X range is used for labeling the X-axis. It is also used as one of the data ranges in an XY graph and for labeling the pieces of a pie chart.
8. Yes. Your worksheet will have extension WK1; your graph will have extension PIC.
9. No.
11. There is no limit.
13. Two types: horizontal and vertical.
16. The Scale option gives you the opportunity to override the automatic scaling done by Lotus. This means you can tell Lotus how to fit your data on the X and Y axes.
18. Legends are used to make your graph more understandable. They will tell you, for example, which symbol belongs to which data.

Chapter 15

3. It depends on how you got to the PrintGraph program in the first place. If you got to it from DOS, naturally you will return to DOS. If you got to the program from Lotus Access System, you will return to the Lotus Access System when you exit.
5. Yes. Press F10.
7. You cannot. You have to go to the worksheet and retrieve the worksheet file, do all your changes there, save it by using /Graph Save, then go to PrintGraph and print the new graph.
12. Yes. Otherwise you will create an ellipse instead of a circle.
16. Minimum is 110 and maximum is 19,200.
18. Action, Pause, Yes makes PrintGraph pause between printing.

Chapter 16

4. Use /Worksheet Delete Row, then specify the row address.
10. The primary key is the first field chosen to sort and the secondary key is the second field chosen to sort. There are no other differences between these two keys.

12. You can search with single criteria, double criteria, multiple criteria, or with wild cards.

15. The Extract option extracts all the records that meet a particular criteria. The Unique option will extract only the records that have at least one field different from the others.

16. Up to 32 fields.

Chapter 17

5. It stops either when the range is filled or the stop value has been reached.

8. No.

11. This will show up at the end of Frequency. For example, 1 means there was one data item that was not included in the bin range.

15. Yes, if the number of columns of the first matrix is equal to the number of rows of the second matrix; otherwise, no.

17. The righthand side array is the right side of all the equations. For example, in

$$X1 + X2 \quad = \quad 10$$
$$X1 - X2 \quad = \quad 15$$

10 and 15 are the righthand side array.

18. This command does not provide important statistical measures such as a T-test, Durbin-Watson test, and so on.

Chapter 18

4. Press the **Alt** key and the name of the macro at the same time. In Release 2.2, you can also use the RUN command which is Alt-F3.

6. The zero macro will be executed automatically as soon as the worksheet including this macro is loaded.

9. It can be very useful for designing menus and helping non computer experts with easy system access.

13. The CMD indicator means a macro is being executed.

15. Press **Ctrl** and **Break** together.

16. Up to 240.

Chapter 19

3. No. Some advanced commands do not need arguments. For example, QUIT, RETURN, RESTART, etc.

4. There are four types of arguments. These include address or location, numeric value, condition and string.

7. /Range Erase.

11. The macro will not be executed at all.

12. No.

16. Otherwise Lotus will always choose the first item in the menu.

20. Four. Read, Write, Modify and Append.

Chapter 20

4. Two types: external and internal.
7. Logic errors.
11. Because this methodology advocates programming techniques which are easier to develop and maintain. Also, this methodology increases a programmer's productivity.
13. Random numbers are used for investigation of a random process. For example, in an inspection of a shipment, we must decide whether to accept it or reject it. We may take a random sample and based on this sample we make a decision.
17. When there is a subroutine within another subroutine, we call this a nested subroutine. There are many uses of such a subroutine. For example, a subroutine calculating the net pay may call another subroutine for tax calculation.
18. If a macro is designed for depreciation calculation, the user does not need to know detailed operations about Lotus in order to use this function.

Chapter 21

1.
$$X = \frac{(-B+(B2-4AC)^{1/2})}{2A} = \frac{(-10+(100-4X1X1)^{1/2})}{2X1} = \frac{(-10+(96)^{1/2})}{2} = -0.10$$

3. $P = C*[1+(X-Y)]^N = 4* [1+(.026-.009)]^{13} = 4.98$
9. Lotus can perform many different tasks for a small business. They may include: balance sheet, income statement, budget analysis, fixed asset, mailing list, database.

Appendix A

2. Yes.
5. To make the user's job easier. For example, in BASIC, to run your program you can either type RUN or press the F2 function key.
8. Word size, type of operating system, type of chip.
14. In the majority of IBM-type PCs, when you turn the computer on, if you do not have any diskettes in any of the drives, you will go directly to BASIC mode.
16. DOS is usually on a diskette, so it is in neither ROM nor RAM. You can always transfer DOS from a diskette to RAM.

Appendix B

3. PC DOS for the IBM PC and MS-DOS for its clones.
4. To execute DOS external commands you have to have the DOS disk in one of the drives. For internal commands, as long as the DOS prompt is apparent, you can execute the command.
6. Date and Time are used to document your file. This means if you save a file it will also save the time and date.
9. DISKCOPY erases and formats the target disk then copies the source disk to the target disk. COPY will not erase the target disk.

Appendix C

3. The System disk.
4. Put DOS in drive A, type DISKCOPY A: B: and press **Return**. Then follow the prompt.
10. At the A> prompt put the Install disk into drive A and type INSTALL. Then follow the prompt.

Appendix D

2. The file to be transferred must be compatible to the file structure of the destination system. For example, if a system accepts only an ASCII file, your file must be in ASCII before the transfer can take place.
4. dBASE II, III, and III Plus, VisiCalc, Symphony, DIF, SYLK, and Jazz.
5. Press the F1 key.
8. You have to use /Print File.
12. It is used to split long labels into a series of shorter one.
15. Reset will cancel the previous settings. This means, for example, that all your data ranges will be erased.

Index

Lotus Command Menu

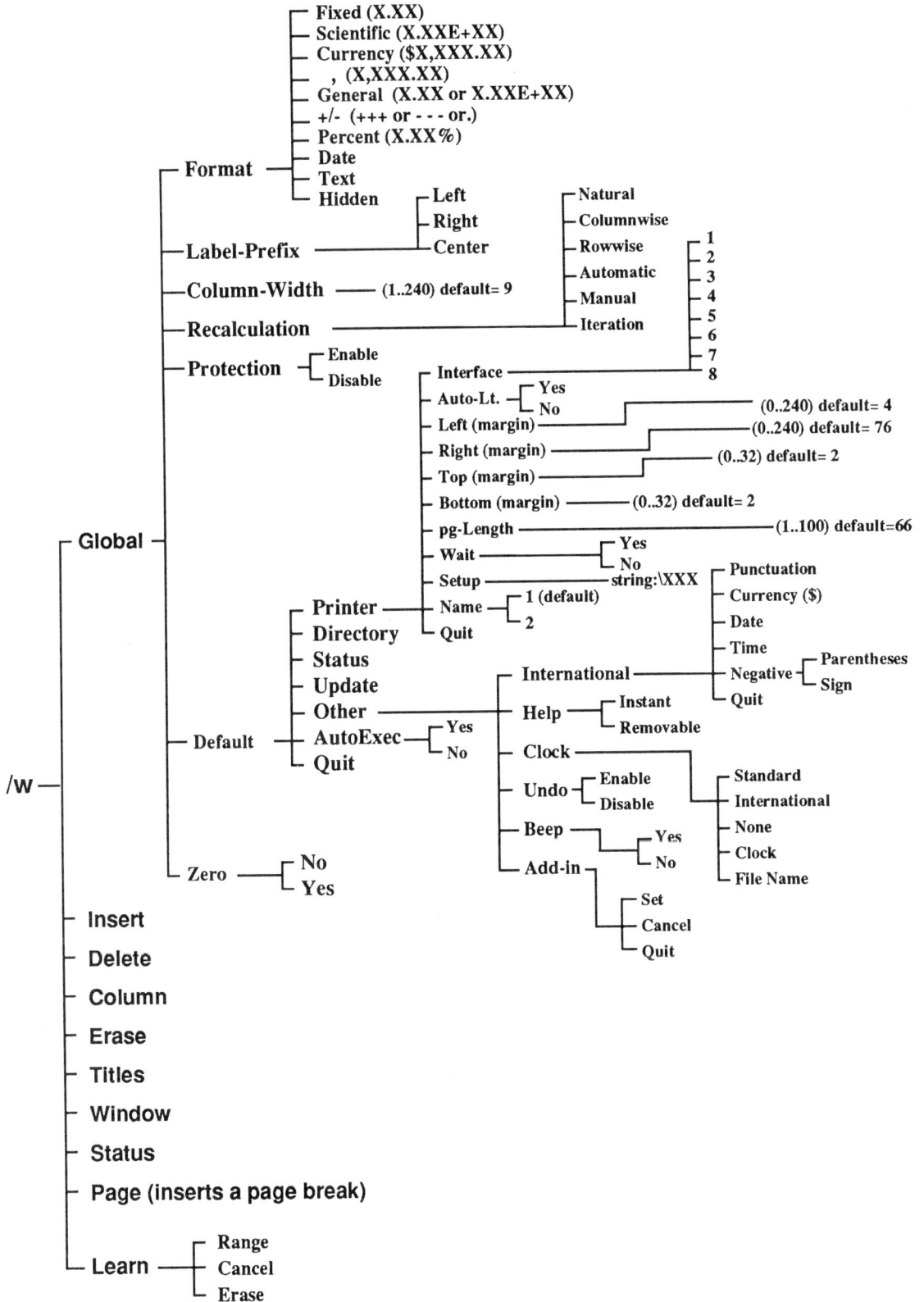

/W

- **Global**
  - **Format**
    - Fixed (X.XX)
    - Scientific (X.XXE+XX)
    - Currency ($X,XXX.XX)
    - , (X,XXX.XX)
    - General (X.XX or X.XXE+XX)
    - +/- (+++ or - - - or.)
    - Percent (X.XX%)
    - Date
    - Text
    - Hidden
  - **Label-Prefix**
    - Left
    - Right
    - Center
  - **Column-Width** — (1..240) default= 9
  - **Recalculation**
    - Natural
    - Columnwise
    - Rowwise
    - Automatic
    - Manual
    - Iteration — 1 2 3 4 5 6 7 8
  - **Protection**
    - Enable
    - Disable
  - **Default**
    - **Printer**
      - Interface — 1 2 3 4 5 6 7 8
      - Auto-Lt.
        - Yes
        - No
      - Left (margin) — (0..240) default= 4
      - Right (margin) — (0..240) default= 76
      - Top (margin) — (0..32) default= 2
      - Bottom (margin) — (0..32) default= 2
      - pg-Length — (1..100) default=66
      - Wait
        - Yes
        - No
      - Setup — string:\XXX
      - Name
        - 1 (default)
        - 2
      - Quit
    - **Directory**
    - **Status**
    - **Update**
    - **Other**
      - International
        - Punctuation
        - Currency ($)
        - Date
        - Time
        - Negative
          - Parentheses
          - Sign
        - Quit
      - Help
        - Instant
        - Removable
      - Clock
        - Standard
        - International
        - None
        - Clock
        - File Name
      - Undo
        - Enable
        - Disable
      - Beep
        - Yes
        - No
      - Add-in
        - Set
        - Cancel
        - Quit
    - **AutoExec**
      - Yes
      - No
    - **Quit**
  - **Zero**
    - No
    - Yes
- **Insert**
- **Delete**
- **Column**
- **Erase**
- **Titles**
- **Window**
- **Status**
- **Page** (inserts a page break)
- **Learn**
  - Range
  - Cancel
  - Erase

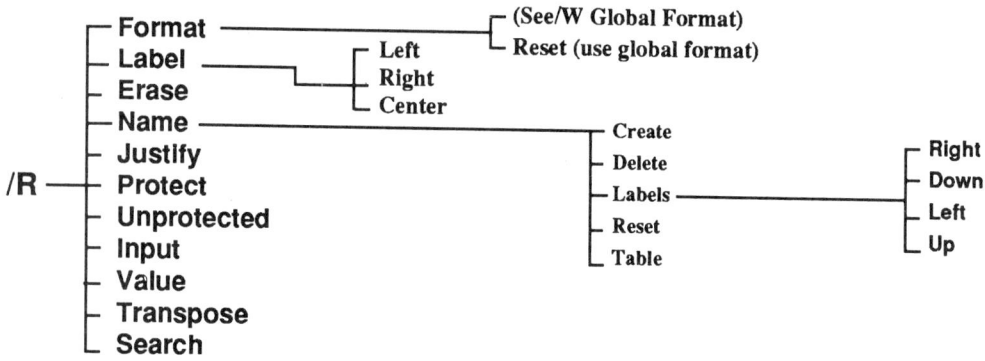

```
         ┌─ Format ──────────────────┬─ (See/W Global Format)
         ├─ Label ──────────┐        └─ Reset (use global format)
         ├─ Erase           ├─ Left
         │                  ├─ Right
         │                  └─ Center
         ├─ Name ────────────────────────┬─ Create
         ├─ Justify                       ├─ Delete                ┌─ Right
/R ──────┤  Protect                       ├─ Labels ───────────────┤  Down
         ├─ Unprotected                   ├─ Reset                 ├─ Left
         ├─ Input                         └─ Table                 └─ Up
         ├─ Value
         ├─ Transpose
         └─ Search


/C ─────────── Enter range copy FROM, Enter range to copy TO


/M ─────────── Enter range copy FROM, Enter range to copy TO


         ┌─ Retrieve
         ├─ Save
         ├─ Combine ──────────────┬─ Copy ──┐      ┌─ Entire file
         │                        ├─ Add    ├──────┤  Named/Specific-range
         ├─ Xtract ─┬─ Formulas   └─ Subtract┘
         │          └─ Values          ┌─ Worksheet          ┌─ Worksheet
         ├─ Erase ─────────────────────┤  Print              ├─ Print
/F ──────┤                             ├─ Graph              ├─ Graph
         ├─ List ──────────────┐       └─ Other              ├─ Other
         ├─ Import ─┬─ Text     │                            └─ Linked
         │          └─ Numbers  │
         ├─ Directory
         │                 ┌─ Reservation ───────┬─ Get      ┌─ Worksheet
         └─ Admin ─────────┤  Table              └─ Release  ├─ Print
                           └─ Link-Refresh                   ├─ Graph
                                                             ├─ Other
                                                             └─ Linked


                                 ┌─ Header
                                 ├─ Footer                  ┌─ Left (0..240) default = 4
                      ┌─ Range   ├─ Margins ────────────────┤  Right (0..240) default = 76
                      ├─ Line    ├─ Borders ─┬─ Columns     ├─ Top (0..32) default = 2
                      ├─ Page    ├─ Setup    └─ Rows        └─ Bottom (0..32) default = 2
          ┌─ Printer ─┤  Options ─┼─ Pg.-Length ── (1..100) default = 66
/P ───────┤           │           ├─ Other ──────────────────────────┐
          └─ File ────┤  Clear ─┐ └─ Quit (return to print menu)      │
                      ├─ Align  │                                     │  ┌─ As-Displayed
                      ├─ Go     ├─ All                                ├──┤  Cell-Formulas
                      └─ Quit   ├─ Range                              │  ├─ Formatted
                                ├─ Borders                           │  └─ Unformatted
                                └─ Format
```

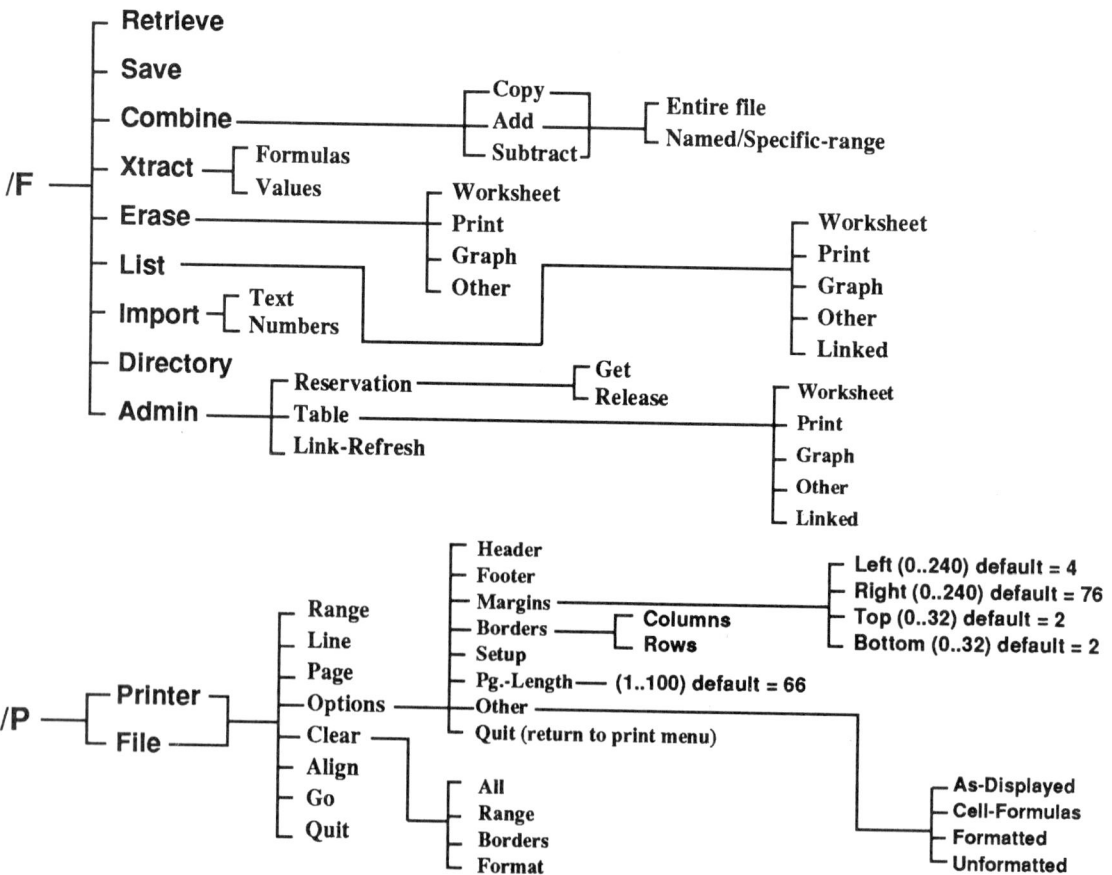

/G ── Type ─── Line
              Bar
              XY
              Stacked-Bar
              Pie
      X
      A
      B
      C
      D
      E
      F
      Reset
      View
      Save
      Options ─── Legend ─── A
                             B
                             C
                             D
                             E
                             F
                  Format
                  Titles ─── First
                             Second
                             X-Axis
                             Y-Axis
                  Grid ─── Horizontal
                           Vertical
                           Both
                           Clear
                  Scale ─── A
                            B
                            C
                            D
                            E
                            F
                            Group
                            Quit
                         ─── Y Scale
                             X Scale ─── Automatic
                                         Manual
                                         Lower
                                         Format (see/W Global Format)
                                         Indicator
                                         Quit
                             Skip (1..8192) default = 1
                  Color
                  B & W
                  Data-Labels
                  Quit

      Options ─── Graph
                  X
                  A
                  B
                  C
                  D
                  E
                  F
                  Ranges
                  Options
                  Quit

                  Graph
                  X
                  A
                  B
                  C
                  D
                  E
                  F
                  Quit ─── Lines
                           Symbols
                           Both
                           Neither

      Name ─── Use
               Create
               Delete
               Reset
      Group
      Quit

/D ── Fill
      Table ─── 1
                2
                Reset
      Sorts ─── Data-Range
                Primary-Key
                Secondary-Key
                Reset
                Go
                Quit
      Query ─── Input
                Criterion
                Output
                Find
                Extract
                Unique
                Delete ─── Cancel
                           Delete
                Reset
                Quit
      Distribution
      Matrix ─── Invert
                 Multiply
      Regression ─── X-Range
                     Y-Range
                     Output Range
                     Intercept ─── Compute
                                   Delete
                     Reset
                     Go
                     Quit
      Parse ─── Format-Line ─── Create
                                Edit
                Input Column
                Output Range
                Reset
                Go
                Quit

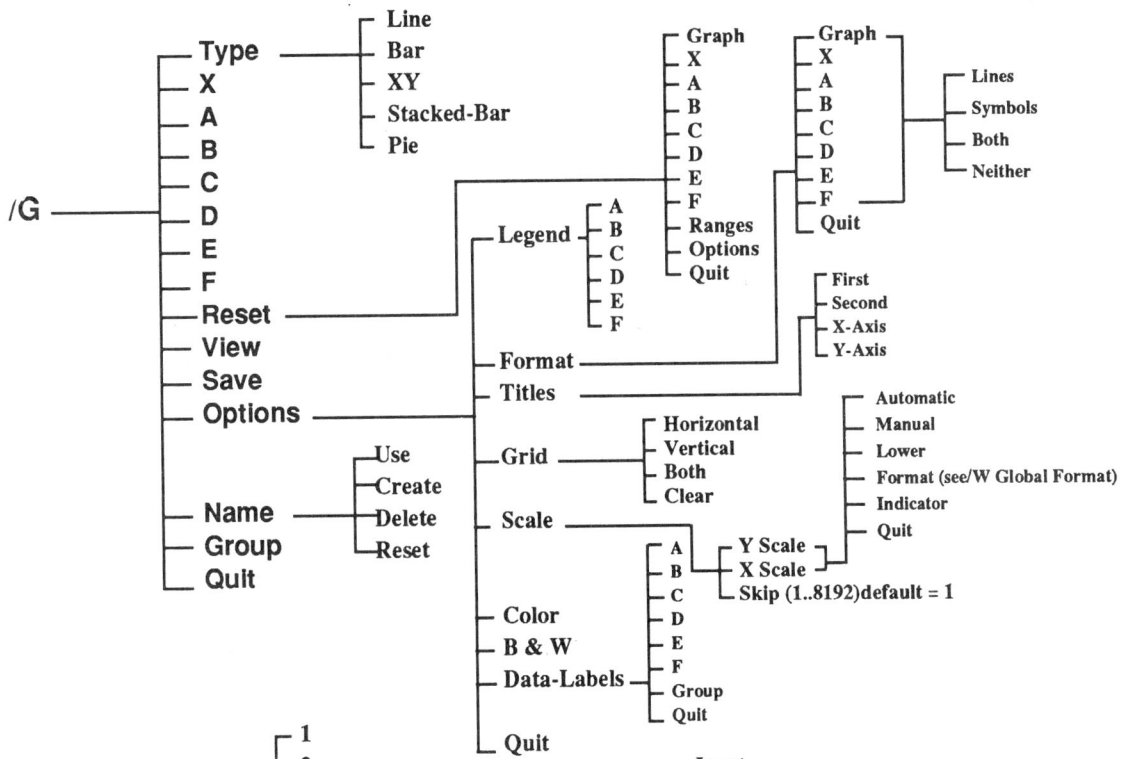

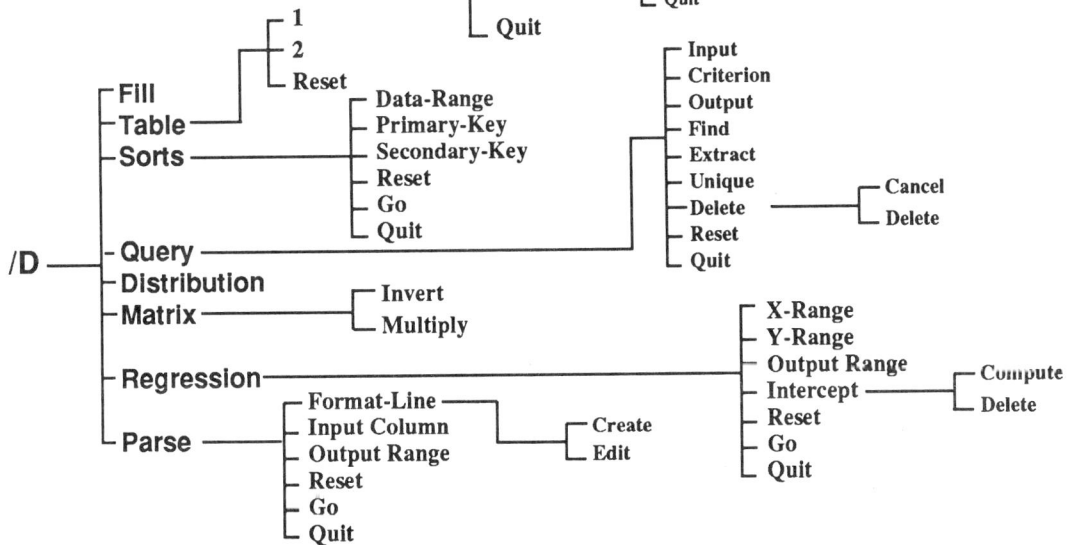

/S ─── Invoke the DOS Command

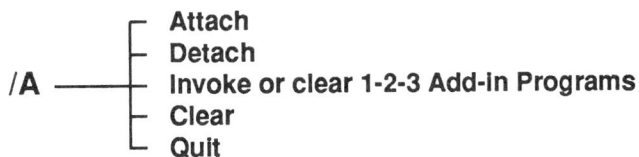

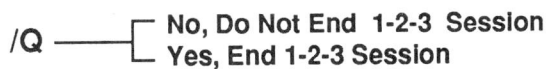

/A ─── Attach
       Detach
       Invoke or clear 1-2-3 Add-in Programs
       Clear
       Quit

/Q ─── No, Do Not End 1-2-3 Session
       Yes, End 1-2-3 Session

Allways Command Menu

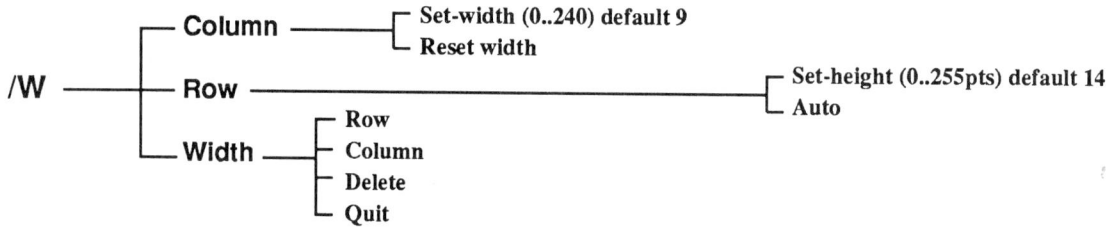

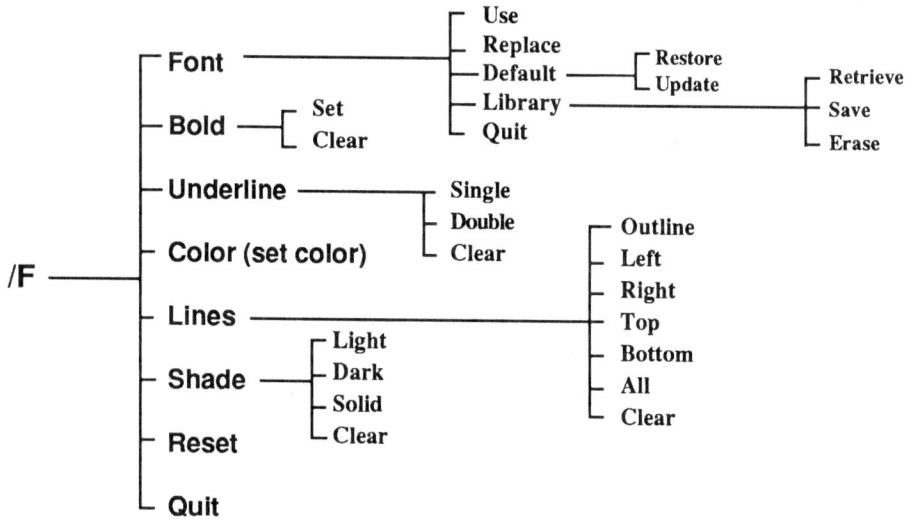

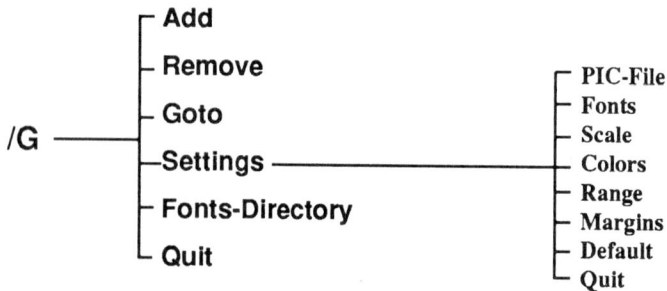

```
                              ┌─ Set-width (0..240) default 9
                     Column ──┤
                              └─ Reset width
                                                                    ┌─ Set-height (0..255pts) default 14
/W ──────────────── Row ────────────────────────────────────────── ┤
                              ┌─ Row                                 └─ Auto
                              ├─ Column
                     Width ───┤
                              ├─ Delete
                              └─ Quit
```

```
                              ┌─ Use
                              ├─ Replace
                     Font ────┤                ┌─ Restore             ┌─ Retrieve
                              ├─ Default ───────┤                     │
                              │                 └─ Update             ├─ Save
                              ├─ Library ─────────────────────────────┤
                   ┌─ Set     └─ Quit                                 └─ Erase
                     Bold ────┤
                   └─ Clear
                                          ┌─ Single
                     Underline ───────────┤
                                          ├─ Double
                     Color (set color)    └─ Clear
                                                       ┌─ Outline
/F ────────────┤                                       ├─ Left
                     Lines ─────────────────────────────┤─ Right
                              ┌─ Light                  ├─ Top
                              ├─ Dark                   ├─ Bottom
                     Shade ───┤                         ├─ All
                              ├─ Solid                  └─ Clear
                              └─ Clear
                     Reset

                     Quit
```

```
                     Add

                     Remove
                                        ┌─ PIC-File
                     Goto               ├─ Fonts
                                        ├─ Scale
/G ────────────┤     Settings ──────────┤─ Colors
                                        ├─ Range
                     Fonts-Directory    ├─ Margins
                                        ├─ Default
                     Quit               └─ Quit
```

```
                   ┌─ Page-Size (select size)              ┌─ Left (.00...99.99) default = 1.00
                   │                                        ├─ Right (.00...99.99) default = 1.00
                   ├─ Margins ──────────────────────────────┤  Top (.00...99.99) default = 1.00
                   │                      ┌─ Header         ├─ Bottom (.00...99.99) default = 1.00
                   ├─ Titles ─────────────┤  Footer         └─ Quit
                   │                      ├─ Clear                                    ┌─ Top
                   │                      └─ Quit                                     ├─ Left
                   ├─ Borders ──────────────────────────────────────────────────────┤  Bottom
       /L ─────────┤                      ┌─ Line-weight ──────┌─ Normal             ├─ Clear
                   │                      │              ┌─ Yes ├─ Light              └─ Quit
                   ├─ Options ────────────┤  Grid ───────┤  No  └─ Heavy
                   │                      └─ Quit
                   │                      ┌─ Restore
                   ├─ Default ────────────┤  Update
                   │                                         ┌─ Retrieve
                   ├─ Library ───────────────────────────────┤  Save
                   │                                         └─ Erase
                   └─ Quit
```

```
                   ┌─ Go
                   ├─ File                                   ┌─ Printer
                   │              ┌─ Set                     ├─ Interface
                   ├─ Range ──────┤  Clear                   ├─ Cartridge              ┌─ Portait
                   ├─ Configuration* ────────────────────────┤  Orientation ───────────┤  Landscape
       /P ─────────┤                                         ├─ Resolution
                   │                                         ├─ Bin
                   │                                         └─ Quit
                   │                      ┌─ Begin
                   │                      ├─ End
                   │                      ├─ First
                   ├─ Settings ───────────┤  Copies          ┌─ No
                   │                      ├─ Wait ───────────┤  Yes
                   └─ Quit                ├─ Reset
                                          └─ Quit
```

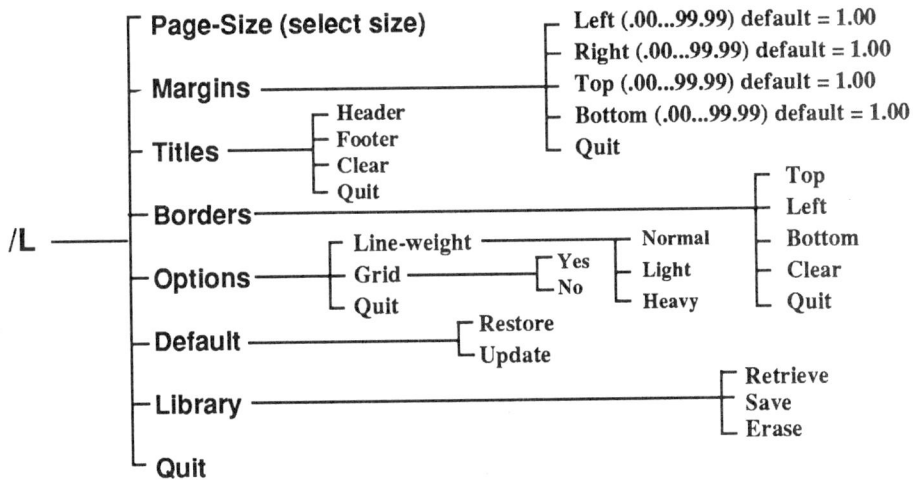

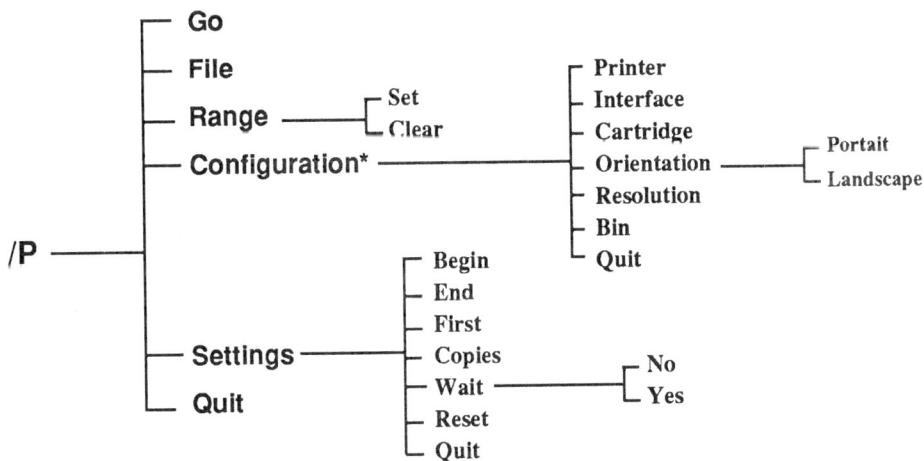

*** Options available under configuration may
vary depending on your type of printer**

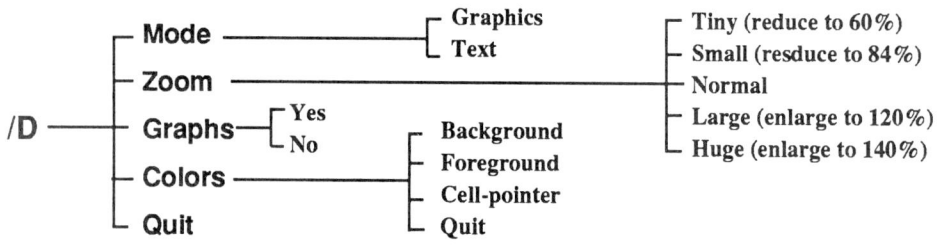

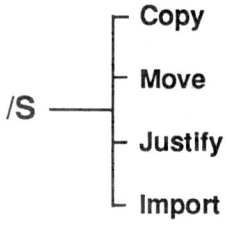

```
/D ─┬─ Mode ──────────┬─ Graphics          ┬─ Tiny (reduce to 60%)
     │                 └─ Text              ├─ Small (resduce to 84%)
     ├─ Zoom ────────────────────────────── ─ Normal
     │                ┌─ Yes                ├─ Large (enlarge to 120%)
     ├─ Graphs ───────┤                     └─ Huge (enlarge to 140%)
     │                └─ No    ┌─ Background
     ├─ Colors ────────────────┼─ Foreground
     │                         ├─ Cell-pointer
     └─ Quit                   └─ Quit


/S ─┬─ Copy
     │
     ├─ Move
     │
     ├─ Justify
     │
     └─ Import


/Q ─────── Return to 1-2-3
```